The Historical Writings

The Historical Writings

Introducing Israel's Historical Literature

Mark A. Leuchter and David T. Lamb

Fortress Press
Minneapolis

THE HISTORICAL WRITINGS

Introducing Israel's Historical Literature

Cover image: House of David/Photo©Zev Rad/Bridgeman Images
Cover design: Laurie Ingram

Library of Congress Cataloging-in-Publication Data
Print ISBN: 978-0-8006-9950-5
eBook ISBN: 978-1-5064-0785-2

The paper used in this publication meets the minimum requirements of American
National Standard for Information Sciences—Permanence of Paper for Printed
Library Materials, ANSI Z329.48-1984.
Manufactured in the U.S.A.

This book was produced using Pressbooks.com, and PDF rendering was done by
PrinceXML.

Contents

Abbreviations

AB	Anchor Bible
ANEP	*The Ancient Near East in Pictures Relating to the Old Testament*. Edited by James B. Pritchard. Princeton. 1954.
ANET	*Ancient Near Eastern Texts Relating to the Old Testament*. Edited by James B. Pritchard. 3d ed. Princeton. 1969.
B. Bat.	*Bava Batra*
BA	*Biblical Archaeologist*
BAR	*Biblical Archaeology Review*
BASOR	*Bulletin of the American Schools of Oriental Research*
Bib	*Biblica*
BWA(N)T	Beiträge zur Wissenschaft vom Alten (und Neuen) Testament
BZAW	Beihefte zur Zeitschrift für die alttestamentliche Wissenschaft
CBQMS	Catholic Biblical Quarterly Monograph Series
COS	*The Context of Scripture*. Edited by William W. Hallo. 3 vols. Leiden. 1997–.
DOTHB	*Dictionary of the Old Testament: Historical Books* (IVP Academic)
FAT	Forschungen zum Alten Testament
HSM	Harvard Semitic Monographs
IEJ	*Israel Exploration Journal*
JBL	*Journal of Biblical Literature*
JSOTSup	Journal for the Study of the Old Testament: Supplement Series
JTS	*Journal of Theological Studies*

OBO   Orbis biblicus et orientalis

SJOT   *Scandinavian Journal of the Old Testament*

VT   *Vetus Testamentum*

VTSup Supplements to Vetus Testamentum

WSS   *Corpus of West Semitic Stamp Seals.* Nahman Avigad and Benjamin Sass. Jerusalem: The Israel Academy of Sciences and Humanities. 1997.

ZAW   *Zeitschrift für die alttestamentliche Wissenschaft*

ZIBBC Zondervan Illustrated Bible Backgrounds Commentary

Figures and Maps

Sidebars

Chapter 7

Tables

Chapter 6

1

_____

Introduction

The historical books of the Bible contain some of the best known stories of Scripture. Rahab the prostitute from Jericho helped the Israelite spies, providing vital insider information on the state of the nation (Joshua 2, 6). Gideon the judge from Manasseh defeated the massive army of Midian with only three hundred men armed with trumpets, jars, and torches (Judges 7). David the shepherd from Bethlehem nailed the Philistine giant Goliath in the noggin with his slingshot and chopped off his head with the giant's own sword (1 Samuel 16). Elijah the prophet from Gilead talked trash with the prophets of Baal on Mount Carmel before his drenched altar was scorched by a flame sent by YHWH (1 Kings 18). Nehemiah the cupbearer from Susa was granted leave from King Artaxerxes of Persia to return and rebuild the wall around Jerusalem (Nehemiah 2). Manasseh the king from Judah, whose idolatry was legendary, prayed and repented from his Babylonian prison and was restored to the throne in Jerusalem (2 Chronicles 33).

However, scattered among these familiar stories are less familiar and highly disturbing ones, including the violent conquest (or genocide?) of the Canaanites by the Israelites (Joshua 6–12), the rape of the Levite's concubine by the men of Gibeah (Judges 19), and the cursing and hair-pulling of Judeans who had married foreigners by Nehemiah (Nehemiah 13). In order to understand the good, the bad, and the ugly stories of the Hebrew Bible, most readers need help. That's where this textbook comes in.

For each of the historical books (see section 5, "What are the Historical Books?," below) we'll discuss *literary concerns* such as genre and composition, as well as the overall structure of the book, and how it connects to the broader context of Scripture, first to other historical books, then the rest of the Old and New Testament. We will examine the relevant *historical issues*, the dating of the book, what light archaeology may shed on its interpretation, any chronological problems that emerge, and how the historical background of the ancient Near East helps us understand the text better. We'll also reflect upon *theological themes*, by addressing some of the following questions. How does the text depict God and God's relationship with Israel and other peoples? What did role did worship, idolatry, and the temple play in that relationship? How does the text describe God's response to obedience and sin? What models of leadership does the text seem to endorse, or condemn (prophets, priests, kings, governors, etc.)?

After engaging these literary, historical, and theological concerns, each chapter will then include a *commentary*, which will not only mention how these three concerns appear or are addressed in relevant passages, but will also discuss and explain the text in a more systematic manner, working through the book section by section. Chapters will also have numerous *sidebars* for important artifacts (The Tel Dan Stele), for intriguing questions (What Was So Bad about Jeroboam's Altars?), and for problematic issues (The Sacrifice of Jephthah's Daughter). Along the way, you will see plenty of maps, tables, and charts, as well as images of ancient artifacts, geographic features, and even biblically themed art (something visual for everyone).

Before proceeding, we need to cover four rather mundane, but necessary details about this textbook. First, since scholars use several terms to refer to the broader section of Scripture that these historical books are a part of we will also speak of the Old Testament, the Hebrew Bible, and the Hebrew Scriptures.

Second, the name of the God of the Old Testament is usually translated into English as "the Lord," and sometimes it appears as Yahweh, but we will use the term YHWH (all capitals, no vowels). In the Hebrew text, whenever the divine name *Yahweh* appears, it was written with those consonants, but the wrong vowels were intentionally included, those of the word *'adonay* ("lord"), to signify to readers that

that the name was not to be pronounced, but *'adonay* was to be spoken instead.

Third, words that you encounter in the text in bold will be defined and explained in the glossary at the back of the book.

Sidebar 1.1: The *Tanak*

The Jewish designations for this part of the Christian Bible are simply "the Bible"—Jews do not regard the Christian "New Testament" as scripture—or *Tanak,* an acronym for the Hebrew names *Torah* (the Pentateuch), *Nevi'im* (the "former" and "latter *Prophets*"), and *Kethuvim* ("Writings": everything else).

Fourth, both authors wrote this first chapter; David Lamb wrote Joshua, Judges, and Kings; and Mark Leuchter wrote Samuel, Ezra—Nehemiah, and Chronicles. While we don't typically announce this in our writings, the reader may benefit from knowing that Mark Leuchter is Jewish and David Lamb is Christian. One of the remarkable aspects of contemporary biblical scholarship is that Jews and Christians (and others!) share a great deal of common ground in the academic approach to scripture, something that sadly was not true in previous generations of scholarship. It is that commonality that we wish to present to our readers here.

1. History, Historiography, and Time

To approach any biblical text (like the Book of Samuel or Kings) as an historical work, we must first define what we mean when we use the terms "historical" or "history." To most modern audiences, history is simply the events of the past, but this is not actually as appropriate a definition as one might expect. History is the record, or memory, of the events of the past; there have always been (and will always be) events that occur without any notice, recollection, or reaction, and these events are not historical, strictly speaking. For example, a person may order a meal for dinner at his or her favorite restaurant, but few people would identify this as an historical event. Put differently, history is the awareness of past events, and takes place in the consciousness of a culture, group, or individual who holds that awareness.

Moreover, history is a somewhat particular phenomenon, because what is not historical to one group or individual might very well be of immeasurable historical significance to another. The reign of the Maharajah Ashoka in northern India in the third century BCE is of great importance to the history of India and the development of Buddhism, but would not register on the conceptual radar of a remote tribal group living in the Amazon rain forest in South America. It is only through holding a certain perspective—one informed by geography, language, economy, technology, and politics—that events can be considered historical, and this usually entails accounting for those events and interpreting their significance in a way that is meaningful to certain groups or cultures. The United States Civil War (1861–1865) is widely recognized as a meaningful event in history, but its meaning varies from place to place. A citizen of the American deep south might conceive of that historical event in a way dramatically different than a citizen living in the state of Pennsylvania. The southerner may hold an opinion that the Civil War was really a war of "northern aggression" that sought to change and place limits on southern social customs and economic institutions, while a northerner might look back upon the war as a struggle to end the legality of slavery.

The biblical authors seem to have recognized these issues and express their awareness in a number of ways. Some events are passed over without much detail but notice is still given to them (e.g., the "source citations" in the book of Kings referring the reader to royal events not depicted in the biblical text), while other events that were almost certainly widely known throughout large swaths of ancient audiences are deliberately left out of the narrative (e.g., the destruction of the Shiloh sanctuary ca. 1050 BCE, remembered in Jer. 7:12–15 and Ps. 78:60–66 but not mentioned in the book of Samuel). In other cases, multiple accounts offering different explanations of common events or the origins of specific toponyms ("place names") are both preserved (e.g., the back-stories for the toponym "Havvoth Yair" in Deut. 3:14 and Judg. 10:4; the explanation for "is Saul also among the prophets?" in 1 Sam. 10:12–13 and 19:24). In some cases, the necessary perspective for understanding historical events provides readers with insights into the true causes of those events that might run counter to the plain sense of the events themselves (e.g., the lengthy theological explanation for the fall of the northern kingdom of Israel in 2 Kgs.

17:13–23; the theological explanation for the literary framework of the book of Judges in Judg. 2:11–23). And in other cases, the historical events known and experienced in more recent days are used to qualify and make sense of more remote events that retained some place in common discourse (e.g., Samuel's denunciation of kingship in 1 Sam. 8:11–18, which knows and refers to hardships endured under the Neo-Assyrian empire in the late-eighth to early-seventh centuries BCE).

This brings us to the difference between history and historiography. If *history* is the recollection or accounting of past events, *historiography* is a genre of literature that works these recollections into narrative form and attempts to project a specific point or value from the events. Historiographic works lay claim to historical recollections, sometimes highlighting or diminishing them for various purposes. Political propaganda is one common goal for ancient historiography, and many biblical texts readily fall into this category in part or in full (e.g., in the narratives in 1 Samuel 9–11 extolling the virtues of Saul; the deeds and accomplishments of Solomon in 1 Kings 3–10, the tale of the rebuilt temple and the restoration of sacrifice and cult in Jerusalem in Ezra 1–6). But historiography also functions polemically, presenting versions of known events that undercut normative or common presuppositions or perceptions (such as the condemnation of "mixed" marriages in Ezra 9–10).

Biblical historiography is also characterized by an additional feature: wisdom. Israel's historical legacy is framed and retold in a manner meant to cultivate a sense of awareness regarding the complexity of society, the power of the divine in human affairs, and the ethical responsibilities of groups and individuals to each other. When the redactors of the Book of Kings direct the reader to the non-mentioned "other" deeds of Israelite rulers by saying "are they [the deeds in question] not written in the annals of the Kings of Israel/Kings of Judah?" the historiographic work containing these rhetorical questions alerts the reader that there is always more to the story than what is being reported. But it also raises the question why some events, and not others, are reported, as well as the issue of which sources or authorities one should consult or trust in attempting to connect with the past.

Historiography is also a vehicle for the historiographers themselves to assert their power. We find parallels in our own contemporary world: different news media outlets regularly spin their own versions of events, often for the sake of supporting a particular worldview (a comparison of Fox News coverage vs. MSNBC coverage can be quite illuminating here) and constructing a particular historical narrative that supports this worldview. One might be tempted to question the degree to which the writing of an historiographic narrative equals an expression of social or cultural power until one realizes that written texts held a very auspicious place in a primarily oral culture such as that of ancient Israel (on which, see section 2 below). To produce an historiography automatically meant that the historiographer was educated, had access to expensive materials for writing, and traveled in elite, probably priestly (or quasi-priestly) circles. To create an historiographic work, then, immediately spoke to a culture of power and prestige with sacral and even ritual overtones; even if such a work was conceived to be propagandistic and was recognized as such, its production would have commanded attention and its contents could not be easily brushed aside or otherwise ignored.

The authors of biblical historiographies also did not write brief tales akin to folklore (even if folkloristic tales served in part as their sources) but constructed extensive narratives that covered many eras or went into enormous detail regarding important individuals. The weight and impact of such literarily complex works demanded engagement or at least reaction from its audience, which propelled the historiographers themselves into important positions as shapers of cultural agenda, social ethics, and theology. In effect, the production of historiography is an attempt to take a relatively private view of the past and use it to annex and claim public perceptions of that same past in some way.

Yet in speaking of both history and historiography, we must not forget that both must be distinguished from ancient Israelite understandings of time. In ancient Israel—as with the entire ancient Near East—time was understood as both linear and cyclical. Time was linear insofar as events took place in the past and contemporaneous conditions could affect how those events resonate in the future. A king coming to power might charge his scribes to recount how his reign either broke with institutions of an earlier era or built upon them, all for the sake of ensuring the durability of that king's accomplishments. In this way, moments in time could retain their importance beyond the immediacy of their occurrence. Time was a vehicle for values and priorities to persist, change, or be challenged, and historiographic works could attempt to qualify or reinforce those values and priorities in a constructed refraction of earlier days for the benefit of the present and the future.

Figure 1.1: Statue of a scribe of the Fifth
Dynasty (third millennium BCE), from
Saqarra, Egypt. Royal scribes were some of
the most important figures in ancient
courts. Commons.wikimedia.org.

Monumental architecture, for example, often represented the builder's
desire to have a moment in time endure well beyond its temporal
occurrence; building inscriptions deposited in these spaces specified
the circumstances of the space's construction or restoration, extending
its durability across time. In biblical texts, the stone pillar known as
the *masebah* (see, for example, Jacob's *masebah* in Gen. 28:17–18) did the
same, representing a pilgrim's ongoing homage and devotion to a deity
at a sacred place even after the pilgrim departed. From these and other
factors, the linearity of time becomes clear: Israelite historiographers
situated themselves and their works on a horizontal axis of experience.

But time was also cyclical insofar as many of the events of note were
merely earthly symbols of mythic realities, realities that were always
occurring and recurring in the divine realm. The aforementioned
monumental spaces—especially temples and sanctuary sites—were
places where mythic events standing beyond the linearity of time
could be experienced again and again. Researchers who focus on the
development of Israelite religion often situate a number of prayers
and hymns in settings such as these. The eminent American scholar
Frank Moore Cross famously argued that the oldest composition in the
Bible, the **"Song of the Sea"** (Exod. 15:1–18), contained a mythological
rehearsal of YHWH's salvation of Israel from Egypt in the mythic past,
but this event was re-experienced every time the hymn was recited

at a sanctuary. But the idea of history repeating itself in cycles occurs explicitly within the narrative framework of the Book of Judges, where Israel repeatedly sins, is repeatedly punished, repeatedly repents, and is repeatedly redeemed and saved by a warrior-Judge.

Perhaps it is better, then, to envision Israelite concepts of time as a successive progression of cycles—events and ideas were observed and considered over time, but in a recurring manner. Such an understanding of time invariably affected how Israelite historiographers set about writing their works, transmuting into textual form an iteration of concepts and values that had long been preserved and experienced in both time and space. But what this means is that history could be encountered in textual form through historiographic narrative alongside the encounter with history in rituals, hymns, and social institutions. Over time, as Israel endured calamities and challenges that led to separation from long-standing social and spatial institutions (such as exile from ancestral estates and central/communal sanctuaries) historiographic narratives became a very important way for Israelites to maintain a sense of identity and a connection to a past now enshrined in written form.

2. Authors and Audiences

Who were the authors/writers that stand behind a given biblical text, and who was the intended audience for these writers? These questions are deeply interrelated, because authors are often part of the audience of a text—that is, they write for themselves (or for people just like them) as much as for other people. Literature uses language, themes, patterns, issues, and values that often reflect the experience of the authors, an experience that is certainly shared by the author's community. Authors also write for the purpose of creating literature that is *not* meant for a wide audience: legal contracts, for example, are often composed with technical language not meant for readers who are not trained in the practice or principles of law. Moreover, such documents are also meant to be private or semi-private in nature; . . . they pertain to a specific and very limited group of people (i.e., those involved in the contract arrangements) and are usually not meant to be part of a public discussion. Contrast this to, say, a children's book meant to be read widely and to be understood—on different levels—by children and adults who might read them to young audiences.

This same type of diversity in forms of literature, authorship, and intended audience applies to the study of ancient Hebrew literature preserved in the Bible. A range of authors (royal scribes, priests, administrators, sages, and prophets) stand behind the texts in our possession. It is for this reason that so many of the narratives relating historical events do so from very different perspectives. The stories about Samuel strongly emphasize the role of priesthood and prophecy within the world of the average Israelite, reflecting (to some degree) their origins in a group of authors who counted themselves among Israel's priestly-prophetic circles. The narratives about Joshua address military events and contain extensive lists of territorial boundaries, suggesting origination in an authorial circle with a knowledge of warcraft. The language in much of the story of David's reign reveals the culture of royal courts, pointing to authors who were part of a royal establishment. Later authors inherited these narrative works and added different dimensions to them reflecting their own experiences, interests, and agendas.

But when these authors set about shaping their works, did they do so for the "common" Israelite? Were their compositions meant for wide public dissemination, or for much smaller and selective audiences? Moreover, at what point does authorship itself change? A narrative could be "authored" on the oral level by a circle of prophets who were critical of priesthood or the royal administration, but the survival of such narratives in the Hebrew Scriptures means that at some point, priests and royal agents must have inherited these works, and most certainly shaped them as they were transmitted over time. The resulting texts might well have been made part of a textual collection geared for a wide audience, but this does not mean that they first were conceived for such a purpose. Texts might therefore might have been "safeguarded" by the circles of authors who wrote them for a long time before they were incorporated into a larger literary network that had a different type of audience in mind.

Ancient Israelite audiences understood the very existence of literature in different ways. Audiences with a greater degree of literacy (mostly among the elite classes) not only had greater access to the contents of a text but could understand its role among other important textual works. By contrast, audiences of more modest economic means usually possessed very limited literacy in antiquity; not only would they not possess much familiarity with other texts, they would likely not have had the opportunity to closely engage the contents of a given literary composition in the first place. Much of ancient Israel was oral in its manner of transmitting ideas, values, memory, and information and down to a certain period in history (the late-seventh century BCE). Written documents were not common fixtures in their daily lives or sources of great interest. For these social circles, historical events, and other forms of narrative were not the subjects of learned textual examination, and rural audiences given to oral transmission of narrative would have had little interest in (or exposure to) texts written by a learned scribe in the Jerusalem temple. It may well be the case that such a learned scribe was well aware of this, and wrote texts geared for other scribes and social elites rather than for a wide (and quite possibly disinterested) public.

Nevertheless, some changes in these conditions may have accompanied the passing of time. Texts would have been rare in the tenth century BCE when literacy in the rural sector was highly limited, but this changed by the seventh and sixth centuries BCE. During this era it was still the case that most audiences had very limited literacy, but written texts became more commonplace due to the influence of foreign imperialism (the Neo-Assyrian and Babylonian empires of the eighth to sixth centuries BCE). These imperial powers used monumental inscriptions to project an image of power over their subjects; even if one could not read the contents of these works, they were symbols of authority. It was also during this time that imperial or royal administrators became more integrated into rural sectors, providing literary outlets for communities of limited literacy. The average Israelite may not have been able to read or write, but he or she had greater access to people who could, or was at least aware that their day to day lives were strongly influenced by the written literature.

As early Jewish writers continued their activity into the Persian and early Hellenistic eras (the historical backdrop for the composition of Ezra—Nehemiah and Chronicles), authors and audiences went through another change: to be an author meant that one had to be part of an audience, as the literati of this era were deeply enculturated in Israelite texts from earlier eras. The literature of the Pentateuch and the Deuteronomistic History (see the next section, "Deuteronomistic Redaction") most likely formed a core of common tradition for elite Jews in this period, and Persian period Jewish authors created works that directly interacted with them, quoting them and exegetically developing their contents. Many of the Hebrew Scriptures that come from the late monarchic or post monarchic eras (that is, ca. 700–160 BCE) make references to older, well known works, sometimes even quoting them explicitly. This means that the authors of these later texts were very much part of the audiences for them, and wrote their works to highlight, promote, and sometimes to argue against ideas that these older texts contained.

The later we move into history, the more varied are these understandings of (and written responses to) earlier text traditions. For example, the author of the Book of Chronicles (from the late Persian period) shaped his work to include explicit references to earlier texts that emphasized certain ideas, but also affirmed that those earlier texts were important and should be part of the religious culture of his day. This occurs in other late biblical texts as well. The Hebrew Scriptures were shaped not only by their authors but, in a very real way, by their audiences as they were re-read and transmitted, and newer additions to that collection were regarded as consistent with the older sources to which they referred. A different attitude, however, is encountered in the ancient Jewish books that did not make their way into the canon of Hebrew Scriptures. The Book of Jubilees (composed ca. 150 BCE), for example, revisits material from Genesis and Exodus but departs from it in radical ways, offering an alternative to the Pentateuch rather than supporting or extending its teachings. So too do we find passages in the ancient Jewish apocalyptic work 1 Enoch (compiled in the late-third to second centuries BCE) that have much in common with parts of Genesis, the prophetic texts, and the Book of Daniel, but which were excluded from the canon of Hebrew Scriptures because they contained teachings that ran counter to the Pentateuch and related authoritative texts. The authors of those non-canonical Jewish works were also audiences for the older material, but the texts they produced reveal that even if audiences share common texts, their reactions to them could be quite different.

3. Deuteronomistic Redaction of the Former Prophets

Scholarly discussions about the authorship on the books of Joshua, Judges, 1—2 Samuel, and 1—2 Kings tend to focus on the redactors of the text, who brought together their various sources and edited or redacted them into the form we are familiar with. In these four books (also called the **Former Prophets**), scholars perceive terms, language, and themes that are reminiscent of the book of Deuteronomy, and that serve to unify these historical books that tell Israel's story from conquest to exile. Joshua—Kings are therefore often referred to by scholars as the **Deuteronomistic History**, and these editors are referred to as **Deuteronomistic redactors.**

What does a redactor, Deuteronomistic or otherwise, do? Scholars theorize that biblical redactors typically had sources, oral or written, that they would use to create a distinct composition. These redactors could then omit material from their sources that they didn't think was interesting, relevant, or supportive of the main points they were trying to make. They could add new material to fill in gaps, or to smooth transitions between their source material. They could emphasize and highlight certain themes that are important to them and their theological tradition. For example, most scholars think obedience was a key theme in Deuteronomistic ideology.

How does one determine that there were different authors, editors, or redactors of a text? Perhaps a simple example will help. This book has two primary authors (Mark and Dave), each of whom has a distinct writing style. While we identify the individual author for chapters 2—7, this introductory chapter is written together by the two of us. The diligent reader of this textbook, after reading chapters 2—7, may be able to come back to this first chapter and, based on the writing style, discern which of us wrote the various sections of the Introduction. This book also has an editor (Neil Elliott) whose job it is to make the writing style of each author less distinct and more consistent. Good editors make the process of distinguishing the various authors harder.

You might say, "Isn't the identification of potential authors or redactors a rather subjective process?" Yes, it is, which gives scholars a lot of issues to discuss and debate. Scholars typically disagree about how many Deuteronomistic redactors there were, when their **redaction** took place, and what sections of these four books they worked on. These disagreements regarding Deuteronomistic redaction has dominated scholarship on the Former Prophets for the past sixty years.

Let's review the story of the various Deuteronomistic redactors starting with Martin Noth. Noth, writing in Germany around the time of World War II, initially formulated the theory of a single Deuteronomistic redactor (Dtr) working during the Babylonian exile. Noth's theory has dramatically shaped scholarship on the Former Prophets and all subsequent discussions of redaction use Noth as a starting point (see Noth, *The Deuteronomistic History*).

In the United States, the "double redaction" perspective, first proposed by Frank Cross and later expanded by Richard Nelson, has been favored. Cross's theory concluded that an initial Deuteronomist (Dtr1) worked during the reign of Josiah in the late-seventh century BCE and had a favorable attitude toward the monarchy, but then a second Deuteronomist (Dtr2) reworked the materials with an anti-monarchical bias during the Babylonian exile in the sixth century.

Figure 1.2: Martin Noth (1902–1968).

In Germany, the "triple redaction" theory developed by Rudolf Smend and two of his students (Timo Veijola and Walter Dietrich) has more followers. Smend did not originally perceive three layers of redaction, but merely a primary historical layer (DtrH) whose work was added to by a nomistic redactor (*nomos* is Greek for "law") concerned with obedience to the law (DtrN). Dietrich then modified Smend's theory by adding a third redactor characterized by a prophetic concern (DtrP). Dietrich dates all three of the layers to the exilic period.

However, the so-called double and triple redaction theories each have various problems. While Cross and Nelson discuss the redaction of Kings in depth, they are often accused of ignoring Joshua, Judges, and

13

Samuel. Any comprehensive redactional theory of the DH needs to take into greater account these other books. The complexity of the theory of the Smend school undermines one of the biggest strengths of Noth's initial theory: its simplicity. How does one objectively distinguish three different levels of Deuteronomistic redaction from historical sources?

These and other problems have led to a growing lack of scholarly consensus regarding Deuteronomistic redaction, which in turn has given rise to a variety of alternative perspectives. Many scholars today speak of a Deuteronomistic school of scribes and editors that may have worked not only on the four books of the Former Prophets, but also on other books such as Jeremiah. Antony F. Campbell and Mark A. O'Brien combine aspects from the perspectives of Cross and Smend. Robert Polzin, Hans-Detlef Hoffmann, and John Van Seters approach study of the Deuteronomistic History more synchronically, perceiving the Deuteronomist as more of an author than redactor. The plethora of perspectives on issues of redaction reveals that no scholarly consensus exists regarding how these books were composed. Discussions of possible levels of Deuteronomistic redaction can appear to the non-specialist (and even sometimes to the specialist!) to be characterized by subjective reasoning and esoteric argumentation.

Specific issues related to possible Deuteronomistic redaction of the individual books will be discussed in each of the relevant chapters.

4. Ancient Versions of the Bible

One of the most complicated issues in the scholarly study of the Bible is that of text criticism, or the study of variants in different versions of the Hebrew Scriptures that existed in the ancient world. Just as we encounter different versions of the Hebrew Scriptures in various translations of the Bible today (in English, French, Spanish, etc.), so too were there different versions of the Hebrew Scriptures circulating in antiquity. The circumstances, however, were rather far afield from those characterizing different translations today. While modern translations are usually based on a very limited set of fixed manuscript traditions from the Medieval period, those Medieval manuscripts represent the tail end of a very long chain of development involving a much more fluid concept of what constituted a sacred text.

A good example of this is found in the Book of Samuel, especially in 1 Samuel 16—18. In one version of the Hebrew Scriptures (the Septuagint or "LXX"; see paragraphs just below), this stretch of narrative is much shorter than the version of the book of Samuel that is reflected in most English translations: the shorter version lacks 39 verses found in most Bibles. And yet, in the verses that this shorter version shares with the longer, there are several extra words speckled throughout. Scholars view these details and wonder if the shorter version is missing verses that were part of an original tradition or, perhaps, if the original tradition was somehow expanded and developed . . . in which case, the shorter version is "closer" to the original tradition than the longer version. This brings with it a host of other questions.

The further one looks back along a historical timeline, the more fluid the circumstances involved in the production of a text. The words of a prophetic performance may have been remembered and written down shortly after they were uttered by different scribes, each incorporating minor variants. These works, in turn, were consulted, memorized, and performed/taught by later scribes whose own re-writing of these works may have involved additional minor adjustments: the addition of formulaic phrases, the inadvertent omission of words or letters, the repetition of well-known passages to compensate for missing information in texts that did not match common memories regarding figures or events. All of these yielded a wide spectrum of literary sources in antiquity, many of which survived in different communities over many centuries. The Medieval manuscripts noted above are reproductions or copies of the "winners" of this game, insofar as they emerged as the dominant and authoritative standards for defining what constituted the Hebrew Scriptures following the rise of rabbinic Judaism (ca. 70 CE and persisting for many centuries). But they were certainly not the only versions circulating in antiquity and were by no means the most widely accepted or revered at any given time before the Medieval period. The field of study known as text criticism involves the study of ancient versions of the Hebrew Scriptures and the variations they contain.

In terms of the ancient Hebrew traditions, the text-critical study of the Bible has traditionally involved two major branches of texts: the Masoretic Text (MT) and the Old Greek version of the Hebrew Scriptures (also known as the Septuagint or the LXX). The MT—so named for the Hebrew word *masoret* ("tradition")—represents the collection of Hebrew Scriptures preserved in the Hebrew language from antiquity and used actively in Jewish faith communities from the early Medieval period down to the present. The oldest physical MT manuscripts in our possession date from the tenth century CE, but linguistic analysis of their contents confirm that they are based on very ancient traditions from the Persian period (ca. 539–332 BCE) and even earlier. The tradition of rabbinic commentary from the Roman period and later utilized the MT as their primary text tradition, regarding it as the inspired, divine word and suitable for use in synagogue service as well as for sacred study. There are reasons to accept the view that early versions of its contents were part of the official scriptural library of the Jerusalem temple before its destruction in 70 CE.

The LXX has a different story. According to an apocryphal document called the Letter of Aristeas (ca. 130 BCE), a Greek ruler in Egypt named Ptolemy Philadelphus commissioned the translation of Jewish sacred writings into Greek in the early-third century BCE. Seventy (or, on some accounts, seventy-two) Jewish scholars set about working on this translation (thus the term LXX—the Roman numeral for "seventy"), producing the LXX as it currently exists. A few different manuscripts of the LXX attest to very minor variants; in broad strokes, they show a good deal of agreement in terms of content. It is clear, however, that the Hebrew text from which the ancient Jewish scribes created the LXX was different from the Hebrew text that led to the MT. That is, two different collections of Hebrew Scriptures existed in antiquity, one transmitted and developed in the Hebrew language that became the MT and the other translated into Greek and preserved in the LXX.

Both traditions made major impressions on the development of Judaism and Christianity: while the Rabbis seem to have adopted the MT, the LXX appears to have been known to the authors of the New Testament, and was probably the more common text tradition known to Greek-speaking Jewish populations whose members contributed to the rise of Christian communities.

When we compare individual units within these different versions of the Hebrew Scriptures, we notice some significant discrepancies. The MT tradition seems to be longer in many places than the LXX; the book of Jeremiah, for example, is approximately 13 percent longer in the MT than in the LXX. In other places, the LXX contains material that is absent in the MT (the book of Daniel, for example, has material in the LXX that does not appear in the MT, as does Esther). A long debate raged among text-critical scholars as to which version was "better," or "older." Some argued that the MT—with its longer parallel units—represented expansions of a more pristine tradition preserved in the LXX. Supporting this position was the fact that the oldest manuscripts for the LXX dated from the fourth century CE, while the oldest manuscripts for the MT dated to several centuries later.

Figure 1.3: The Aleppo Codex, prepared in the early tenth century. Photograph by Ardon Bar Hama. Commons.wikimedia.org.

Other scholars took the opposite view, however: the MT often preserved better and older versions of a given tradition, and the shorter parallels in the LXX represent textual corruptions and accidental deletions of content.

The discovery of the Dead Sea Scrolls in 1947 changed the nature of this debate. The manuscripts discovered at Qumran (an ancient

Roman period site on the western coast of the Dead Sea) were centuries older than even the old LXX manuscripts. They provided a window into how the Hebrew Scriptures looked ca. 150–100 BCE. What they revealed was a variety of text traditions, some of which resembled the MT while others resembled the LXX, but none of which were strictly one or the other. This strongly suggests that in the late Second Temple period (and probably persisting down to the end of that period in 70 CE), there existed multiple versions of the Hebrew Scriptures, some of which derived from communities who preserved traditions that survived in some form in the MT. Others derived from communities whose traditions informed the Hebrew prototype of the LXX.

In some cases, the Qumran texts show that major portions of old traditions somehow fell out of use altogether as the MT and LXX developed. An oft-cited example is found in a scroll containing a version of the book of Samuel (known as 4QSam[a]). In 4QSam[a] we find a version of 1 Samuel 11 that is virtually identical to the MT version of that chapter, but 4QSam[a] contains an introductory paragraph that is missing in the MT (and, for that matter, the LXX) which introduces us to the Ammonite king Nahash. This king is a character in the rest of the chapter as well—the same material that we find in most translations of the MT and the LXX. (The NRSV translation is one exception, as it incorporates the material from Qumran into its version of the book of Samuel.) The additional material in 4QSam[a] provides greater character development and detail. This introductory paragraph reads very well in the context of the larger chapter and its linguistic character is ancient. Most scholars see it as an original part of the story that, for some reason, fell out of the transmission of both the MT and LXX text families. Yet for the community that lived in Qumran, this version of the book of Samuel (and this longer version of 1 Samuel 11) was considered sacred and authoritative, and it is likely that other text traditions now lost to us probably contained similar versions of this additional material, as well as others. The different ancient text traditions that have survived from antiquity represent the sacred literature of different communities, some of which managed to survive longer than others, ensuring that their texts survived as well.

5. What are the Historical Books?

It is difficult to define the historical books of the Hebrew Bible, and therefore lists of the historical books vary depending upon the criteria used to determine historicity (see also section 1 above, "History, Historiography and Time"). In this textbook we will focus on six books: Joshua, Judges, Samuel, Kings, Ezra—Nehemiah, and Chronicles. In most English Bibles, all of these books except Joshua and Judges are divided into two separate books (1 and 2 Samuel, 1 and 2 Kings, Ezra and Nehemiah, and 1 and 2 Chronicles). The reasons for these divisions and why we examine them together will be discussed in more depth in the individual chapters.

Just to be clear, though, the historical sections of the Old Testament are not limited to these six books. We find historical information about the formation of Israel as a nation in the Pentateuch, particularly in Genesis and Exodus. A number of psalms have historical elements as they review Israel's story in poetry (see Psalms 105, 106, 136). Portions of prophetic literature refer to historical events and appear to be identical to historical sections of the books of Kings and Chronicles (Isaiah 36—39; Jeremiah 52).

Since many books of the Old Testament include historical elements or are considered historical, why just focus on these six? While these six books include diverse genres of literature including poetry, genealogy, oracles, and laments, their primary interest is history—perhaps not understood as we would understand it, but understood as a record of Israel's story. Joshua narrates the conquest and settlement of the people into the Promised Land and then Judges recalls their cyclical struggles to hold onto the land against foreign enemies. Samuel and Kings report the rise and fall of the Israelite monarchy, as well as the construction and destruction of the temple. Ezra—Nehemiah records how the people rebuilt the temple, the wall, and the nation. Chronicles retells the macro story, beginning with Adam and ending with Cyrus' commission to rebuild. Thus, these books tell the stories of individuals, but always in the context of the broader narrative of the people of God, a story spanning many centuries, from conquest, through exile, to reconstruction.

Sidebar 1.2: What about the Books of Ruth and Esther?

It is difficult to know where to categorize Ruth and Esther in the canon of the Hebrew Bible. They are both masterfully told narratives, but their unique literary quality doesn't make the process of categorization any easier. For several reasons they are often included among the historical books. Ruth is set during the time of the judges and is located between Judges and Samuel in English Bibles. Esther is set during the post-exilic period in the Persian capital of Susa and follows Nehemiah in English Bibles.

But despite their historical settings and their proximity in our Bibles to these other historical books, they are really a different genre: not primarily historical, more narrative, each basically a short story focused on a unique individual. Additionally, Ruth and Esther were included in a very different location in the Hebrew Bible (their English Bible locations are based on the Septuagint), not adjacent to any of these six historical books but among the five scrolls (Song of Songs, Ruth, Lamentations, Ecclesiastes, and Esther) in the third and final section called the Writings. The earliest interpreters of the Hebrew Bible didn't include them among the historical books, and therefore neither will we in this textbook.

2

Joshua

1. Introduction

1.1. The Book

Conflicts in the Middle East often dominate the news cycles, many of which are related to, or centered upon the land of Israel and the nation's relationships with surrounding nations. While the story of the land and people of Israel is long and complex, contemporary conflicts are often intertwined, at least in much popular thinking, with appeals to the book of Joshua and its account of the initial conquest and settlement in the land of the Canaanites by a nomadic people, the Israelites, after their exodus from Egypt and their wanderings in the wilderness.

The book of Joshua is the sixth book of the Bible and, according to the traditional Jewish biblical divisions, the first book of the Former Prophets (Joshua, Judges, Samuel, and Kings). In the first five biblical books, the Pentateuch, Abraham's family gradually grows from just a few individuals to a nation without a homeland. Joshua tells the story of how the twelve Israelite tribes, after centuries as nomads, immigrants, slaves, and refugees, finally reach the land that YHWH, their God, had promised Abraham.

Joshua can be divided into four sections. The first section focuses on the preparation of the nation Israel for upcoming battles (Joshua 1–5). The second narrates the conquest of the land and reports of the battles (Joshua 6–12). The third records the allotment of the tribes and reports of the boundaries (Joshua 13–21). The fourth recalls the speeches of the leaders, mainly of Joshua, but also of Phinehas and the leaders of the eastern tribes (Joshua 22–24).

Joshua includes both familiar stories of Joshua's commission, Rahab the prostitute, the Israelites marching around the city of Jericho, and the battle where the sun stood still in the sky (Joshua 1, 2, 6, 10), as well as troubling stories of conquest and slaughter.

These narratives often provoke readers to ask a variety of difficult questions about the book. Are the stories of Joshua meant to be interpreted as history or fiction, or some combination of the two? How should Israel's emergence in the land be viewed: as a dramatic conquest, or a gradual settlement? And what about those slaughters of Canaanite men, women, and children—should we understand them as a holy crusade, or an unholy genocide? While finding definitive answers may prove elusive, these are the questions we'll discuss as we examine the book of Joshua.

1.2. Joshua: The Name

Whereas each of the books of the Pentateuch is called by a different name in the Hebrew Bible than it is in the English Bible (e.g., the book that is most popularly known as "Exodus" is *shemot*, "Names," in the Hebrew Bible), both traditions refer to this book merely as "Joshua." In Hebrew, the name Joshua consists of two parts: the first is basically a shortened version of "YHWH" and the second means "salvation." So Joshua literally means "YHWH is salvation" or, more simply, "YHWH saves."

1.3. Joshua: The Person

Not surprisingly, Joshua is about Joshua, but unlike the book of Samuel, which begins with the story of the prophet's birth by his previously barren mother Hannah, in Joshua the book, Joshua the character is already an adult. While the man he succeeded as leader of the nation, Moses, had a dramatic birth story included in the beginning of Exodus (2:1–10), Joshua's birth story wasn't sufficiently interesting to be recorded by the biblical authors.

However, biblical readers have already encountered the man Joshua in several settings in Exodus, Numbers, and Deuteronomy. While Moses is known as the giver of the law, Joshua is as the conqueror of the land, and it is in this role as military leader that we first meet Joshua as he leads the Israelites in battle against the Amalekites immediately after they leave Egypt (Exod. 17:9–14). A few chapters later, the text states that Joshua is Moses' assistant (Exod. 24:13), and while Moses spoke to YHWH, his assistant Joshua didn't leave the tent of meeting (Exod. 33:11).

When two men are prophesying in the Israelite camp, Joshua wants Moses to shut them down, but instead is rebuked by Moses (Num. 11:26–29). In the context of Moses sending out the twelve spies to the land of Canaan, we learn that Joshua the son of Nun came from the tribe of Ephraim and that Moses changed his name from Hoshea to Joshua. Of the twelve spies, Joshua and Caleb are the only ones who are confident that they can take the land from the Canaanites (Num. 13:25—14:10). Because of their faithful perspective, they are also the only two adults to survive the forty years in the wilderness (Num. 14:30; 26:65; 32:12).

After showing Moses the promised land, YHWH told Moses to lay his hands on Joshua and commission him to lead the nation after he's gone, which he then did (Num. 27:12–23). Later, YHWH told Moses that the priest Eleazer and Joshua would be the men who would divide up the land into tribal allotments (Num. 34:17; Josh. 14:1; 19:51).

In Moses' speech at the beginning of Deuteronomy, Moses speaks of how YHWH wanted him to encourage and empower Joshua (Deut. 1:38; 3:21, 28). In two public settings toward the end of the book, Moses first tells Joshua to be strong and courageous, and then he repeats this charge and commission (Deut. 31:3–8, 14–23). Moses and Joshua perform a duet of sorts reciting the so-called Song of Moses (Deut. 32:44). With all these events preparing him for his new role, the people were willing to follow their new leader after Moses' death because Moses laid his hands on him and he was filled with the spirit of wisdom (Deut. 34:9).

These texts from the Pentateuch would therefore suggest that Joshua was about seventy at the beginning of Joshua, perhaps much older. He dies at 110 (Josh. 24:29; Judg. 1:1; 2:8). Therefore, the span of the book is only about forty years, much shorter than the books of Judges and Kings, which cover multiple centuries, and even shorter than Samuel, which covers only about a hundred years.

Figure 2.1: *Moses and the Messengers of Canaan*, by Giovanni Lanfranco (ca. 1621–1624); The Getty Museum.

1.4. Joshua in the Canon

Scholars of previous generations often focused on connections between Joshua and the Pentateuch, and therefore some spoke of a Hexateuch (six books). The big event that the books of Genesis, Exodus, Leviticus, Numbers, and Deuteronomy anticipate is the conquest of the land, so Joshua would be a logical conclusion to this extended narrative. Additionally, as we saw in the previous section, the character Joshua establishes a narrative bridge between the books of the Pentateuch and of Joshua.

However, two main problems have led many scholars recently to reject the theory of a Hexateuch. First, the death of Moses at the end of Deuteronomy (34:5) provides a compelling ending point for the series of books where he is the dominant character. Second, Joshua has many connections to the books it follows in the Former Prophets, particularly the book of Judges. Many scholars perceive language reminiscent of the book of Deuteronomy throughout the Former Prophets, and hence often refer to these books as the Deuteronomistic History (see introduction to this chapter and also 2.3, "Deuteronomistic Redaction").

In the books that come after Judges in the Hebrew Bible, several other individuals named Joshua are mentioned, but Joshua the son of Nun only appears twice. During the period of the divided monarchy, when Hiel of Bethel rebuilds Jericho, Joshua's curse against the rebuilder's sons is recalled (Josh. 6:26; 1 Kgs. 16:34), and Joshua the son of Nun is included in a brief genealogical note (1 Chr. 7:27).

In the rest of the Hebrew Bible, the conquest of the book of Joshua is greatly overshadowed by the deliverance in the book of Exodus. While the events surrounding the exodus, the plagues, the Passover, and the parting of the Sea are referenced literally hundreds of times in the text (e.g., 1 Sam. 8:8; 2 Sam. 7:6; 1 Kgs. 3:1; Neh. 9:18; Ps. 80:8; Jer. 2:6; Ezek. 20:10), the events surrounding the conquest are only mentioned a few times again in the text. The prophet Samuel's final address to the people briefly recalls how YHWH settled the Israelites into the land (1 Sam. 12:8). A few of the historical psalms speak of how YHWH gave them the land (Pss. 78:55; 105:44) or how they didn't fully destroy the Canaanites (Ps. 106:34).

As we move to the New Testament, Israel's settlement in the promised land receives a bit more attention. Paul's speech in Pisidia mentions that seven Canaanite nations were destroyed as God gave them the land (Acts 13:19). According to the author of Hebrews, the walls of Jericho came down by faith (Heb. 11:30). The military hero Joshua is mentioned twice, once by Stephen in his speech to the council (Acts 7:45) and once in Hebrews' discussion of rest (Heb. 4:8). Perhaps a bit surprisingly, Rahab, the prostitute of Jericho (see Sidebar 2.4, "Rahab's Shocking Legacy" below) plays a more prominent role in the New Testament than Joshua as she is mentioned in three texts: in the genealogy of Jesus (Matt. 1:5), in the context of her faith (Heb. 11:30), and in the context of her works (James 2:25). However, we should also acknowledge that the name Jesus (Greek *Iēsous*) was apparently a common name in first-century Judea, being the name used in the Septuagint to translate Joshua (Hebrew *Yehošu'a*).

2. Literary Concerns

2.1. Diverse Literary Genres

Before looking at issues related to the authorship, composition, and redaction of Joshua, one needs to first observe that the book contains a wide variety of literary genres. It begins with a **call narrative** for Joshua (Joshua 1), setting him alongside other significant figures in

Israel's history who likewise receive divine commissions (e.g., Abraham, Moses, Gideon, Isaiah, and Jeremiah; see Sidebar 2.3, "Old Testament Call Narratives" below). It includes an engaging spy narrative involving a prostitute (Joshua 2) as well as more mundane etiological notices explaining how places got their names (Josh. 5:9; 7:26). While the books of the Former Prophets don't include much poetry, and Joshua includes less than the other three, one still finds two brief poems in the book: a curse on anyone who should attempt to rebuild Jericho and a request for more hours of daylight in the midst of a battle (Josh. 6:26; 10:12–13). Interspersed throughout the book are ritual and ceremonial texts recounting how the people set up memorial stones, circumcised a new generation, practiced the Passover, constructed an altar, and renewed the covenant (Josh. 4:1–9; 5:1–12; 8:30–35; 24:1–28). The book concludes with a series of rhetorical speeches given by Joshua, which are often connected by scholars to Deuteronomistic editors (see 2.3 below). The two other major genres, conquest narratives and tribal allotment notices, warrant longer discussions since they dominate much of the book of Joshua (see 2.4, 2.5).

2.2. Composition of Joshua

Like many books of the Hebrew Bible, Joshua speaks of no author. Perhaps based on the textual report that Joshua wrote down "these words in the book of the law" (Josh. 24:26), the Babylonian Talmud attributes the book to Joshua himself: however, few scholars follow this traditional attribution. The diverse variety of genres discussed in the previous section would suggest either that Joshua was composed by a variety of individuals, or that whoever put the book together in its final form had access to numerous sources.

Up until the middle of the twentieth century, many scholars thought Pentateuchal sources carried into the book of Joshua, particular the priestly (P) source and the Yahwist (J) source. But most scholars have found persuasive Martin Noth's seminal work, *The Deuteronomistic History* (in German, 1943; in English, 1981), which argued that these sources didn't continue into Joshua (see more on Deuteronomistic redaction in Joshua below).

While scholars speculate that there may have been sources behind the conquest narratives and tribal allotment notices and that Joshua's speeches show evidence of Deuteronomistic redaction (see below on these three sections), the only source the book directly mentions is the book of Jashar (Josh. 10:13). The author of Joshua speaks of the book of Jashar as if the readers should be familiar with it, which may have been true when the book was written, but it is no longer the case. The Hebrew word translated as "Jashar" (*yāšār*) could be translated as "upright," which doesn't really clarify matters much. The book of Jashar is mentioned in one other text, in the context of David's lament over the deaths of Saul and Jonathan in battle (2 Sam. 1:18). The fact that the contexts of the references in Joshua and Samuel are both poems associated with battles would suggest that Jashar was an ancient source of epic poetry.[1]

One other possible textual indication regarding the book's composition is the repetition of the phrase "to this day" (Heb. *'ad hayyôm hazzeh*), which appears sixteen times in Joshua (more often than in any other biblical book; Josh. 4:9; 5:9; 6:25; 7:26 [2]; 8:28, 29; 9:27; 13:13; 14:14; 15:63; 16:10; 22:3, 17; 23:8, 9).[2] The contexts of these expressions speak of various things that have somehow continued until "this day," i.e., the day of the book's composition. The relevant question then is, when is "this day"? Some of these phenomena have relatively short time frames. One notice reports that Rahab is still alive (Josh. 6:25), which would suggest a relatively short gap between the destruction of Jericho and the composition of the book. Four of the notices speak of stone piles being intact or city ruins still being present (Josh. 4:9; 7:26; 8:28, 29), which, depending upon factors such as weathering, erosion, and the size of the stones, could mean either a short or long duration. Other phenomena could involve a much longer time frame: place names not changing (Josh. 5:9; 7:6), or Canaanite residents remaining in certain locations (13:13; 15:63; 16:10). So, while these notices are tantalizing as we search for clues regarding the composition, we need to acknowledge that the book itself provides few definitive answers to our quest.

2.3. Deuteronomistic Redaction

Many critical scholars detect elements of Deuteronomistic influence in the book of Joshua, establishing linkages between the Former Prophets (also known as the Deuteronomistic History) and the book of Deuteronomy. While many scholars agree in principle that redaction

---

1. See Alter, 51.
2. See also Hess, 110.

by Deuteronomistic editors took place, many questions remain: how much redaction? when was it done? by whom? For an extended discussion of Deuteronomistic redaction in the Former Prophets more generally, see chapter 1. Here, we'll focus on the book of Joshua.

The book of Joshua includes a variety of terminology that echoes language from the book of Deuteronomy. We'll include a few examples here. In both books, Israel is commanded to "love YHWH" exclusively (Deut. 5:10; 6:5; Josh. 22:5; 23:11) and to "not serve other gods" (Deut. 5:7; 6:14; Josh. 23:7; 24:14). Israel is called to "walk in YHWH's ways" (Deut. 8:6; 10:12; Josh. 22:5), and YHWH promises that they will receive rest from their enemies (Deut. 3:20; 25:19; Josh. 1:13; 21:44; 22:4; 23:1). The Deuteronomistic concern for obedience is also seen as the Israelites are called to turn neither to the right nor to the left away from the law of Moses (Deut. 5:32; 17:11, 20; 28:14; Josh. 1:7; 23:6).

Deuteronomistic themes can be found connecting these two books, particularly ones focused on conquest and settlement. Both Deuteronomy and Joshua speak repeatedly of destroying the Canaanite peoples (Deut. 7:1–2; 20:16–18; Josh. 9:24; 11:12) and of distributing the land among the tribes (Deut. 31:7; Josh. 14:2, 5). Noth argued that the Deuteronomist (he only spoke of one person) focused the Deuteronomistic terminology and themes into speeches.

Many scholars perceive a concentration of Deuteronomistic ideology in the final speeches of Joshua at the end of the book in chapters 23 and 24. Similarly, there is general agreement that redaction is minimal or absent from the sections narrating the conquest narratives or the sections describing the tribal allotments. Presumably, this information came from earlier source material, which will be discussed in the following two sections.

2.4. Conquest Narratives

The key event of the book of Joshua is the conquest of the promised land by the Israelites. However, apart from two brief notices (Othniel captured Kiriath-sepher: Josh. 15:17; the tribe of Dan captured the city of Lesham: Josh. 19:47), Joshua's battles are concentrated in just six of the twenty-four chapters of the book (Joshua 6—11). The conquest narrative section of the book is concluded with a summary of the kings and nations conquered first by Moses, then by Joshua (Joshua 12).

Figure 2.2: Canaanite sites between the fifteenth and twelfth centuries BCE (before the settlement of Israel).

With the possible exception of the summary, the conquest narratives are distinct from the rest of the book, particularly the rather tedious tribal allotments that follow them. We'll discuss some of the

29

ethical problems related to these battles later (see 4.8), but if you like warfare, you'll love the conquest narratives of Joshua. There's not a lot of dialogue, but there's a lot of action, strategy, intrigue, and bloodshed.

Along the way, Joshua used a wide variety of military tactics to achieve victory. He sent spies to Jericho and Ai for reconnaissance, which worked well in the first instance, but not in the second. The Israelites practiced seven days of ritualistic marching around the city of Jericho before (in the words of the song) the "walls came a-tumbling down." After their first attack didn't work out so well against Ai, Joshua used a clever plan involving deception and an ambush (which is surprisingly similar to the strategy utilized by the Israelites against the Benjaminites in Judges 20). Joshua was the victim of a clever deception by the Gibeonites, who tricked him into making a covenant with them.

However, the text emphasizes that these strategies ultimately aren't what made the difference in their eventual success. Even when Joshua and his forces appear to be massively outnumbered, they receive divine assistance in the form of walls falling down, widespread panic among enemy forces, hail thrown down from heaven, and the sun standing still in the sky. The one exception to this pattern illustrates how vital YHWH was to their success; in their first attack against Ai, YHWH allowed them to lose because one member of their community (Achan) had taken items devoted to destruction from Jericho.

While these conquest chapters of Joshua lack obvious Deuteronomistic terminology and ideas, they are full of the language of battle. The military language in the book is concentrated in these chapters in Joshua as a brief sample of three terms illustrates. The verb "fight" (lāḥam) appears nineteen times in Joshua, thirteen times in these six chapters (Josh. 9:2, 5, 12; 10:5, 14, 25, 29, 31, 34, 36, 38, 42; 11:5) and only six times in the other eighteen chapters of the book (Josh. 19:47; 23:3, 10; 24:8, 9, 11). The verb "strike down" (nākāh) appears thirty-eight times in Joshua, thirty-one times in chapters 6–12 (e.g., Josh. 7:3, 5 [2]; 8:21, 22), seven in the rest of the book (Josh. 13:12, 21; 15:16; 19:47; 20:3, 5, 9). The noun "sword" (ḥereb) appears twenty times in Joshua, fourteen times in chapters 6–11 (Josh. 6:21; 8:24 [2]; 10:11, 28, 30, 32, 35, 37, 39; 11:10, 11, 12, 14), and six times elsewhere (Josh. 5:2, 3, 13; 13:22; 19:47; 24:12).

The conquest narratives can be divided into three sections. The first campaign in the center of the country is against Jericho where everything goes as planned, and the walls come down as scheduled, and against Ai, where it takes two attempts to finally defeat the city (Joshua 6—8). The second campaign is centered in the south as the city of Gibeon first deceives Joshua into making a covenant, and then a coalition of five southern cities (Jerusalem, Hebron, Jarmuth, Lachish, Eglon) attack Gibeon. This draws Joshua and his forces into battle where they defeat this southern coalition in overtime thanks to divine intervention in the form of hail and extra sunlight (Joshua 9—10). The third campaign takes place in the north as another coalition of both cities (Hazor, Madon, Shimron, Achshaph) and peoples (Canaanites, Amorites, Hittites, Perizzites, Jebusites, Hivites) join forces, but are still defeated by the Israelites with the help of YHWH (Joshua 11).

2.5. Tribal Allotments

After the battles are over, the process of dividing up the land remains. In contrast to the dramatic activity of the conquest narratives (Joshua 6—12), most readers of Joshua will find the reports of tribal allotments rather boring (Joshua 13—21).

Just as military terminology characterizes the conquest narratives, distinctive terminology characterizes the tribal allotment section. The noun "inheritance" (*naḥǎlāh*) appears fifty times in Joshua, only five times outside of the tribal allotments section (Josh. 11:23; 23:4; 24:28, 30, 32), and forty-five times within the section (e.g., Josh. 13:6, 7, 8, 14 [2], 23, 28, 33 [2]). The noun "territory" (*gěbûl*) appears eighty-four times in Joshua, six times outside the tribal allotment section (Josh. 1:4; 12:2, 4, 5; 22:25; 24:30), and seventy-eight times within it (e.g., Josh. 13:3, 4, 10, 11, 16, 23 [2]). The boundaries were determined by lot and the noun "lot" (*gôrāl*) appears twenty-six times in Joshua, all within this section, often at the beginning of a new territorial description (e.g., Josh. 14:2; 15:1; 16:1; 17:1, 14, 17; 18:6, 8; 19:1).

The allotment section begins by acknowledging that despite Joshua's successful military campaigns there was a lot of the land left unconquered by Israel and still controlled by the Philistines, the Canaanites, the Amorites, and the Sidonians (see 2.6 below). After this initial acknowledgment, the rest of this section alternates between notices of various types related to the allotment of the land. The text includes two summary reports of the lands conquered first on the east side and then on the west side of the Jordan (Josh. 13:8–14; 14:1–5). There are two types of boundary descriptions: long detailed ones, most notably for the tribes of Judah and Benjamin (Josh. 15:1–63; 18:11–28), and short terse ones; see for example the descriptions for Issachar and Dan (Josh. 19:17–23, 40–48). Often following the descriptions of the tribal boundaries are lists of specific cities that belong to the tribe (e.g., Josh. 15:20–63; 18:21–28; 19:1–9).

Interspersed among these various reports are other notices or brief narratives that don't fit into the pattern but are often connected to other stories either in the Pentateuch or the book of Judges. Joshua's fellow optimistic spy, Caleb, the only other Israelite to survive the wilderness wanderings (Num. 14:30), receives a special allotment, and the text records his eventual occupation of that land within that of his tribe, Judah (Josh. 14:6–15; 15:13–19). The romantic and heroic story of how Othniel won the hand of Caleb's daughter Achsah by conquering the city of Kiriath-sepher in response to his future father-in-law's challenge is recorded first in Joshua and then retold at the beginning of Judges (Josh. 15:16–19; Judg. 1:12–15). The daughters of Zelophehad were promised by Moses that, because their father had no sons, they would receive land as an inheritance, so a short notice records the fulfillment of this promise to this group of soon-to-be land-owning women (Num. 27:1–11; 36:1–12; Josh. 17:3–4). While one might expect numerous tribal squabbles as lands are being divided up (based on my many experiences of dessert portions being divided up among my family members), the allotments proceed smoothly until the two tribes from Joseph (Ephraim and Manasseh) protest about their small portion (essentially, "we've got the smallest piece!"). They are finally appeased by Joshua's wise response, which displayed confidence in them for their greatness and their ability to clear and possess their lands (Josh. 17:14–18). A brief notice in Joshua that the tribe of Dan's campaign to take their tribal allotment was unsuccessful (Josh. 19:47) is reiterated at the beginning of the book of Judges and then is the catalyst for a much longer narrative toward the end of Judges (Judg. 1:34; 18:1–31).

2.6. Partial or Complete Conquest?

As we've examined both the conquest narratives and the tribal allotment records, we find what appear to be two contradictory perspectives on the completeness of the promised land conquest. Scholars love to discuss these types of tensions, so we probably should discuss them also, and this discussion will also provide a good transition into the historical section which follows.

A strong argument can be made that the text of Joshua is claiming that the conquest was *complete* and the land was fully conquered. At the beginning of the book, YHWH declares that he will give the Israelites "all the land" (Josh. 1:4) and toward the end the text records that YHWH gave them "all the land" (Josh. 21:43). Both the spies and the Gibeonites declare that YHWH was going to give Israel "all the land" (Josh. 2:24; 9:24). And the text then reports that Joshua actually conquered "all the land" (Josh. 10:40; 11:16, 23).

A strong argument, however, can also be made from the text that the conquest was *partial* or incomplete. First, the tribal allotment section begins by unabashedly declaring that major portions of the land were left unconquered (Josh. 13:1–7). Second, scattered throughout the tribal allotments section are verses that clearly state that the Canaanite residents of the land were not driven out by the Israelites (Josh. 13:13; 15:63; 16:10; 17:12; 19:47). Third, the book of Judges begins by listing various groups of Canaanites that the Israelites had been unable to drive out from their land (Judg. 1:19, 21, 27, 28, 29, 30, 31, 33).

How does one reconcile these tensions? We will discuss the relevant historical issues related to this question in the next section, but here we'll look at the question from a literary perspective.

Some scholars argue that the literary genre of the conquest is *fiction*,[3] which in addition to solving the problem of the contradictory accounts, solves any ethical problems associated with a genocide (see 4.8 below). According to this perspective, there's therefore no need to reconcile these contradictory accounts because they are both simply stories with little historical basis. While supporters of this perspective find this solution attractive, as the problem disappears, many scholars argue that it doesn't take the text seriously. (For more on the topic of the historicity of Joshua, see 3.2, 3.3 below.)

Other scholars think that the contradictory perspectives on the conquest are evidence of *multiple authors* or editors. One author (the "glass is half-full" one) was concerned with showing how the Israelites were faithful to the commission to drive out the Canaanites. Another author (the "glass is half-empty" one) focused on how they disobeyed, which explains all of their problems with enemy nations and idolatry in the book of Judges. A problem with this perspective is that it makes the final editor seem rather incompetent and unaware of what appear to us to be glaring inconsistencies.

Yet other scholars believe that these accounts can be *harmonized*.

3. See Dever, 39–41.

They acknowledge that there are tensions, but they are by no means irreconcilable ones. They assume that the conquest was not complete and typically make three points. First, the conquest was supposed to be complete, but because of Israel's lack of faithfulness or courage they were unable to achieve total appropriation of the land. Second, the language of the conquest texts could be intentionally hyperbolic, which is typical of ancient Near Eastern conquest narratives.[4] Third, if one examines the contexts of the notices that seem to speak of a complete conquest, one sees they are focused on specific regions of the land, which explains why the comment needs to be repeated. When the text speaks of "all the land" in these contexts it essentially means "all the region." If the whole land were in view, repetition wouldn't be necessary. The nature of the conquest will be revisited at several points in the next section discussing the history of the book of Joshua.

3. Historical Issues

A variety of historical issues regarding the book of Joshua warrant discussion: the date of the conquest, possible models of how the conquest should be understood, the archaeology of the conquest specifically focusing on the key cities, and finally the ancient Near Eastern background related to these various issues.

3.1. The Date of the Conquest

We'll begin by looking at the date of the conquest. From the perspective of biblical history, the book of Joshua is framed between the deaths of two national leaders: Moses at the beginning and Joshua at the end (Josh. 1:1; 24:29). While the text records that Joshua was one hundred and ten years old when he died, we should remember that according to the biblical record he could have easily been seventy or older when the book began. He would have presumably been at least thirty when he led the nation in battle against the Amalekites (Exod. 17:8–14), and then he reportedly survived the forty years in the wilderness.

Based on these figures (which may have been rounded), we can conclude that the time range of the book was perhaps between twenty and forty years, encompassing the later years of the life of Joshua.

---

4. See Younger, 203–6.

Thus, the book of Joshua would have the shortest time frame of any of the books of the Former Prophets.

Where in Israel's history should one situate the twenty- to forty-year window of time in which the conquest occurred? Among scholars who assume some sort of conquest (or settlement) took place as described in Joshua, there are two primary views, an early date (late-fifteenth century BCE) and a late date (late-thirteenth century BCE).

The early date is based on a literal interpretation of 1 Kgs. 6:1, which states that Solomon's temple was completed 480 years after the conquest. Solomon's completion of the temple is often dated to about 960 BCE, which would put the exodus at about 1440 BCE and, after forty years in the wilderness, the conquest at about 1400 BCE. The main problem with this date is that the land of Canaan was under Egyptian control during the fourteenth and thirteenth centuries, but the books of Joshua and Judges make no reference to this situation, despite speaking of numerous battles with Canaanite people.

Scholars who hold to the later conquest date interpret 1 Kgs. 6:1 more figuratively and base their date on, among other things, the reference to the construction of the storage city Ramesses (Exod. 1:11), presumably named after the Pharaoh Ramesses II (1279–1213 BCE). This would fit well into the mid-thirteenth century for the exodus, and then a late mid-thirteenth century date for the conquest (about 1200 BCE). Egypt was less of a factor in Canaan during this period, which would explain why they weren't engaged militarily in the books of Joshua and Judges.

3.2. Models for the Emergence of Israel

The textual tension between a partial and complete conquest has led to a wide varieties of models for how to understand the historical nature of the emergence of Israel. While much has been written on this topic, I will include only two representative scholars (see also bibliography) for each of these perspectives.[5]

Conquest (Albright and Bright). This traditional perspective takes the biblical record seriously and more literally than any of the other models. It basically interprets the archaeological evidence as supporting the historicity of the conquest in three stages (central, southern, and northern) as described in the book of Joshua. Critics of

---

5. For summaries of the various views see Younger 178–91; Dever 71–74.

this view make two points. First, of the many locations that the book of Joshua describes as being conquered by Israel, only two archaeological sites show evidence of destruction in the thirteenth century. Second, the literal interpretation of the biblical text is simplistic and doesn't take the diversity of style and genre seriously.

Figure 2.3: The Merneptah stele, at the Cairo Museum. Photo: Webscribe, Commons.wikimedia.org.

Rejection (Thompson and Davies). In stark contrast to the traditional conquest model, a group of scholars (sometimes referred to as "the Minimalists") reject the idea of a conquest, basically arguing that the conquest of Joshua is fiction and that Israel as a nation didn't emerge until much later in history, perhaps as late as the Persian period. While this perspective has a group of loyal adherents, many scholars reject the rejection model, arguing that there are better options for understanding the conquest than the two extremes of the fictional rejection perspective or a strictly literal interpretation of Joshua.

Settlement (Alt and Noth). In this perspective (also called the "Peaceful Infiltration Model"), the people that became the Israelites were originally pastoral nomads who gradually settled in the unoccupied hill country. Conflicts were not a factor in this model and so the conquest as described in Joshua didn't happen. Tensions arose naturally between the farmers who were in the land already and the newly immigrated nomads. The Israelite people eventually formed a loose confederation of twelve tribes, sometimes called an amphictyony (a term borrowed from classical Greece). Both the idea of an amphictyony in ancient Israel and this model's skepticism both toward the biblical and archaeological records have been criticized widely in scholarly circles.

Revolt (Mendenhall and Gottwald). Rather than immigrating groups of nomads as in the Settlement model, this theory proposes that the conflicts and turmoil in Canaan during this period in history was due to widespread revolts by peasants and slaves already in the land against the existing Canaanite power structures and nobility. The revolt may have been triggered by a group of escaped slaves from Egypt. Were these the Israelites? Mendenhall equates the oppressed people the *'apiru* with the Hebrews. (On the **'apiru,** see below at 3.5.) Gottwald in particular views this revolt along Marxist lines, as a sort of rebellion of the peasantry against their oppressive rulers. Critics of this perspective argue that there is no reason to assume that nomads would prefer an egalitarian political system over a hierarchical system and that the *'apiru* shouldn't be equated to the Hebrews as the term is used to refer to a wide variety of other groups of people.

Other **Indigenous Models** (Dever and Finkelstein). Several other recent models also describe scenarios where Israel emerges from within the land of Canaan, not from outside it. The perspective of Dever is similar to the revolt model, but he speaks of a collapse among the Canaanite coastal cities, which coincided with a move into the hill country by "proto-Israelites" who had originated from the fringes of Canaanite society. They had advanced agricultural technology (terraced farming, hewn water cisterns, stone silos, and iron implements). Most interestingly, their sites lacked pig bones, which would support the theory that these dwellings were Israelite. Looking at the same data as Dever, Finkelstein sees cycles of nomadic people who moved in and permanently settled in the highlands.

While some of these perspectives overlap, others directly contradict each other. However, each of these perspectives receives some biblical or archaeological support and will therefore continue to be adhered to by at least a segment of the scholarly community. It is unlikely that a definitive model of the emergence of ancient Israel will emerge from the diversity of voices on this subject. To conclude, we'll make two recommendations based on the advice Younger includes after his extensive discussion of the various models. First, we need to acknowledge the complexity of the biblical portrayal of Israel's emergence in Joshua. Younger argues that instead of a strict literal approach to the conquest narratives, in light of both Joshua's genre and ancient Near Eastern parallels, one needs to interpret these texts more figuratively, with an awareness of hyperbole and ideology. Second, we need to acknowledge the complexity of the archaeological record relative to Israel's emergence. Just as biblical texts are open to multiple interpretations, so are archaeological records. This leads us into the next section.

3.3. Archaeology

For scholars who hold to the theory of a historical conquest of the land of Canaan by the Israelites as described in Joshua, there are a variety of problems when one examines the archaeological evidence. The series of destructions that one would expect from a military conquest are lacking thus far in the archaeological record.[6]

While some scholars argue that the archaeological evidence proves that the conquest never happened, other scholars point out that the biblical evidence only describes three cities being destroyed in Joshua's military campaign: Jericho, Ai, and Hazor (Josh. 6:24; 8:28; 11:13). The text makes it clear that for the northern campaign, Hazor was the only city that was destroyed. So a lack of widespread urban destructions doesn't necessary undermine Joshua's historicity.

Discussions that attempt to harmonize the biblical and the archaeological records therefore focus on these three cities that Joshua describes as being burned and destroyed. While we've touched on archaeological issues in the discussions above on the conquest (2.6; 3.2), an examination of these three cities in particular is still necessary.

Jericho (Josh. 6:24). Archaeologists found evidence of a major destruction of Jericho, but for scholars looking for support for Jericho's walls coming down according to Joshua 6, the destruction date is far too early (about 1550 BCE). And the city appears to have been unoccupied for the next three centuries, which is problematic whether you favor the early or late date for the conquest. Some scholars respond to these problems by making the following points.[7] First,

---

6. See a summary of the evidence in Dever, 41–50.
7. See Hess, 137–38.

Jericho isn't described as a major city in Joshua, in contrast to Gibeon and Hazor (Josh. 10:1; 11:10), so one should be hesitant to make definitive conclusions based on the lack of evidence either of occupation or destruction. Second, the fact that Jericho's ruler is called a "king" (Josh. 2:2) doesn't necessarily mean it was a major city, since the term can often seem to suggest no more than a tribal chieftain, or in modern parlance, a mayor. Third, some of the archaeological layers appear to have suffered erosion, and so cannot give precise evidence regarding the destruction of the city.

Ai (Josh. 8:28). Similar to Jericho, there is archaeological evidence for the destruction of Ai, but it's even earlier (about 2200 BCE), and the city also appears to be unoccupied from 1550 to 1200 BCE. Scholars attempting to harmonize the biblical and archaeological record typically make several points.[8] First, the site that archaeologists have identified as biblical Ai (et-Tell) might be another city such as Bethel, or perhaps a more complete excavation will result in evidence that supports the account in Joshua. Second, the Hebrew name for Ai (*hāʿay*) literally means "the ruin," which could suggest that the city was already a ruin at the time of Joshua, so one shouldn't expect evidence of other ruins at this site dated to Joshua's conquest.

Hazor (Josh. 11:13). For the scholars who advocate for a historical conquest, Hazor is the one bright spot.[9] The book of Joshua describes Hazor as the primary city in the region (Josh. 11:10) and this description is supported by the fact that the tell associated with the ancient site of Hazor (Tell el-Qedah) is one of the largest Bronze Age tells in Palestine. Archaeologically, Hazor also appeared to be well-fortified and underwent a major destruction in the thirteenth century BCE, which supports the perspective of a later conquest (see 3.1 above), but undermines the theory of an earlier conquest.

3.4. Merneptah Stele

The Merneptah Stele contains the oldest reference to Israel in any ancient source and the only one in Egyptian sources, making it one of the most important finds for the history of ancient Israel. It was discovered at Thebes by Sir Flinders Petrie in 1896 and is usually dated to about 1210 BCE, during the reign of Pharaoh Merneptah (1213–1203 BCE), the son of Ramesses the Great. Merneptah commissioned the stele

8. See Hess, 157–59.
9. See Hess, 212–14.

to commemorate his victory over Libya, but in the final lines he concludes by referring to his Canaanite campaign:

"Libya is captured, while Hatti is pacified.
Canaan is plundered, Ashkelon is carried off, and Gezer is captured.
Yenoam is made into non-existence; Israel is wasted, its seed is not."
(COS 2:41)

Figure 2.4: Letter by Aziru, leader of Amurru, one of the Amarna Letters written in cuneiform on a clay tablet. EA 161. Commons.wikimedia.org.

While the archaeological evidence for dramatic conquest as described in the book of Joshua is problematic, the Merneptah Stele clearly speaks of Israel as an established people living in the land of Canaan by the end of the thirteenth century BCE.[10] The claim that Israel was wiped out is clearly hyperbolic, a characteristic typical of conquest and victory narratives.[11] (Curiously, the books of Joshua and Judges never refer to a conflict with Egypt that the Merneptah Stele describes.)

10. See Dever, 201–6.
11. See Younger, 197–98, 203.

The book of Joshua mentions several of the people and places over which Merneptah claims victory. *Hatti* refers to the land of the Hittites, who appear throughout Joshua (1:4; 3:10; 9:1; 11:3; 12:8; 24:11). *Canaan* obviously refers to the Canaanite residents of the land who feature prominently in the book (Josh. 5:12; 14:1; 21:2; 22:9, 10, 11, 32; 24:3). The Canaanite city of *Gezer* was included in both the Merneptah Stele as an Egyptian conquest and in Joshua as one of Israel's conquests (Josh. 10:33; 12:12; 16:3, 10; 21:21). The Philistine city of *Ashkelon* is included in the Merneptah Stele among the Egyptian conquests, but in Joshua, the city is in the list of unconquered lands at the beginning of this section (Josh. 13:3). The city-state *Yenoam* (also spelled Yanoam) is also thought to be Canaanite, but it doesn't appear by this name in the Hebrew Bible.

For scholars who argue that there was no ancient Israel (the "minimalists" described above), the Merneptah Stele is problematic for three reasons. First, according to the inscription, Israel was significant enough to be mentioned by the Egyptians. Second, Israel was a people, probably even a political entity,[12] surrounded by Canaanites which, at least in this respect, is consistent with the portrayal of Israel found in Joshua and Judges. Third, the people of Israel were sufficiently established in the land (probably the central highlands) at some point in time before the date of the inscription, about 1210 BCE.

3.5. The Amarna Letters

While not as significant for Israel's history as the Merneptah Stele, the Amarna Letters provide useful background for understanding the ancient context shortly before Israel may have arrived in the land of Canaan. Most of the letters were discovered at Tel el-Amarna (initially in 1887) along the Nile in Egypt, and many of them are addressed to the Pharaoh (both Amenhotep III and Akhenaten) from petty rulers in Canaan requesting help from various threats. Most of the letters are dated from the mid-fourteenth century BCE, so if one assumes the later date for the conquest, before Israel appeared in Canaan.

Two features of these letters are relevant to study of the Hebrew Bible, or Joshua in particular. First, the Amarna Letters repeatedly refer to Canaanite cities mentioned in the book of Joshua. Table 2.1 lists eleven cities mentioned in both sources.

12. See Dever, 206.

41

Table 2.1: Cities Mentioned both in the Amarna Letters
and Joshua

City	Amarna Letter #	Joshua Reference
Ashkelon	EA[13] 287, 320	Josh. 13:3
Bethlehem	EA 290?	Josh. 19:15
Gath	EA 289, 290	Josh. 11:22; 13:3
Gaza	EA 289	Josh. 10:41; 11:22; 13:3; 15:47
Gezer	EA 254, 287, 290, 292, 298	Josh. 10:33; 12:12; 16:3, 10; 21:21
Hazor	EA 227	Josh. 11:1, 10–13; 12:19; 15:23, 25; 19:36
Jerusalem	EA 287, 289	Josh. 10:1, 3, 5, 23; 12:10; 15:8, 63; 18:28
Keilah	EA 280, 290	Josh. 15:44
Lachish	EA 287, 288	Josh. 10:3, 5, 23, 31–35; 12:11; 15:39
Megiddo	EA 244, 245	Josh. 12:21; 17:11
Shechem	EA 289	Josh. 17:2, 7; 20:7; 21:21; 24:1, 25, 32

While one must not overstate the case, the fact that many of the locations that Joshua speaks of are also mentioned in these ancient Amarna documents, dated to the fourteenth century BCE, argues for taking the record of Joshua seriously as a historical source.

Second, some scholars also perceive that the repeated references in the Amarna texts to a group of people, the 'apiru (also spelled Ḫabiru), should be associated with the Israelites because of etymological similarities between 'apiru and Hebrew. While they are far more frequently called *Israelites* in the Old Testament, they are occasionally referred to as *Hebrews* (e.g., Exod. 1:15; Jon. 1:9), often by foreigners, with negative connotations (e.g., Gen. 39:14; Exod. 1:22; 1 Sam. 4:6; 29:3). This connection is only an option for scholars who situate the exodus and conquest to the fifteenth century BCE, since the Amarna Letters are dated to the fourteenth century.

The 'apiru are mentioned in other ancient Near Eastern sources beyond the Amarna Letters. The context is usually derogatory, as they are generally described as marginalized people, social outcasts, acting against the power structures (against Egyptian interests particularly in the Amarna Letters).

While some of these characteristics seem to fit the Israelites, few

13. EA stands for El-Amarna tablets. See Moran 1992.

scholars still associate the *'apiru* with the Hebrews for a variety of reasons. First, many scholars question whether the two terms should be linked etymologically.[14] Second, the term doesn't appear to describe a specific ethnic group (as the Israelites are presented in the Hebrew Bible), but a lower class or disenfranchised people more generally. The English term *outcast* is sometimes used as a rough equivalent.

Figure 2.5: Top, Achan is stoned by Israelite soldiers; bottom, the Israelites then successfully attack Ai.
Illustrations by William Brailes, thirteenth century; Walters manuscript 106; Walters Art Museum, Baltimore. Commons.wikimedia.org.

4. Theological Themes

4.1. The Voice

The book of Joshua is the only one of the Former Prophets to lack any references to a prophet (see for example, Judg. 6:8; 1 Sam. 10:18; 1 Kgs. 11:31). However, the book begins with the voice of YHWH speaking directly to Joshua, commissioning him to lead the people into the promised land (Josh. 1:1–9) and YHWH continues speaking to Joshua throughout the book.

YHWH speaks to Joshua both before and after the crossing of the Jordan, instructing him how to traverse the river (Josh. 3:7; 4:15). Once

14. See Howard, 49.

the people have crossed over (but the ark-bearing priests are still mid-river), YHWH tells Joshua to set up memorial stones (Josh. 4:1), and shortly afterwards he commands Joshua to circumcise the nation (Josh. 5:2). YHWH gives Joshua directions about the conquest of Jericho (Josh. 6:2–5) and then rebukes the nation over the sin of Achan (Josh. 7:10–15). During the conquest, YHWH reiterates the themes he first mentioned in Joshua's commission, to not be afraid and that he would give them the land (Josh. 1:9; 8:1, 18; 10:8; 11:6). Post-conquest, YHWH gives guidance to Joshua about how to divide the land (Josh. 13:1) and about how to set up the cities of refuge (Josh. 20:1). While the book lacks a prophet, at the end during the covenant renewal ceremony Joshua speaks to the people using the standard prophetic messenger formula, "Thus says YHWH . . ." (Josh. 24:2). YHWH's speech in the book of Joshua therefore focuses on many of the primary theological themes of the book. The rest of this section will discuss these themes: the land, rest, covenant, obedience, leadership, and YHWH as a warrior.

4.2. The Land

Taking possession of the land is one of the most important theological themes of the Pentateuch and arguably the most significant theme of the book of Joshua. While Genesis describes how God initially gave the first humans land in the form of a garden, their choice to eat the forbidden fruit led to their exile from the land of Eden (Gen. 2:8; 3:23). YHWH next promised the land to Abraham upon his arrival in Canaan (Gen. 12:7), and then reiterated this promise to him (Gen. 13:15; 15:7, 18–21; 17:8) as well as to his son Isaac (Gen. 26:3–4) and his grandson Jacob (Gen. 28:4, 13; 35:12). Each of the subsequent books of the Torah then repeat the idea that at some point in the future, the Patriarchs' descendants would eventually take possession of the land (Exod. 12:25; 13:5; Lev. 20:24; 25:2; Num. 14:8; 34:13; Deut. 1:8; 6:10).

As modern readers, we encounter the extended descriptions of the tribal allotments (Joshua 13—21), which seem tedious, even boring, and ask, "Why spend so much time describing territorial boundaries?" But within the ancient context, the author clearly felt like the readers would be interested to finally discover how the story ends. The conquest and subsequent division of the territory is the final resolution—the climax—to a narrative that has lasted centuries. The people, who had been homeless, finally have a home. And the detailed descriptions are necessary not only to bring closure to the story, but also to provide tangible evidence to the people that, even though they had to wait a long time, God came through on his promises.

In contexts of dividing up the land, the word "inheritance" (*naḥălâ*) is used, appearing fifty times in the book (e.g., Josh. 11:23; 13:6, 7, 8, 14, 23), which begs the question, "Who are they inheriting the land *from*?" From the perspective of the text, the Canaanite residents are not the owners (see 4.8 below, "Holy War or Genocide?"). YHWH is.

The book of Joshua describes how YHWH gives the land (Josh. 1:6; 5:6; 8:7; 9:24; 21:43), and fights for the land throughout the conquest (see 4.7 below). The fact that he wants the Israelites to divide the land into their respective tribal territories by the use of the lot (Num. 26:55–56; Josh. 14:2; 15:1; 16:1; 17:1) communicates that he wanted to be involved in the whole process, even deciding who gets what land.

Thus, the four books of the Former Prophets are basically the story of the Israelites in the land, first under the leadership of Joshua, then under judges, and then under kings. In the beginning, YHWH gives them the land just as he did to the first humans in Eden. In the end, YHWH takes away the land because of disobedience, sending them into exile (2 Kgs. 17; 25), just as he did to the first humans in Eden.

4.3. The Rest

Along with the land, rest is another major theme of both the Pentateuch and the book of Joshua. After creating for six days, God rested on the seventh (Gen. 2:2–3), then after delivering them from Egyptian enslavement God commanded his people to follow his example in creation by taking a Sabbath rest (Exod. 20:8–11; 31:12–17; Deut. 5:12–15). Moses spoke of a future period when YHWH would give the Israelites a land to inherit and rest from their enemies (Deut. 12:10; 25:19).

The book of Joshua frequently revisits the topic of rest. Early in the book, Joshua reminds the tribes east of the Jordan (Reuben, Gad, and half of Manasseh) that God had promised all of them a place of rest (Josh. 1:13, 15). Toward the end of the book, Joshua then recalls his previous words and notes that YHWH had in fact given them the promised rest (Josh. 22:4), and the narrator makes similar remarks about God's fulfillment of this rest promise (Josh. 21:44; 23:1).

The promised rest is not just for the people of Israel, but it is also for the land of Israel. As the conquest battles wind down, the text repeats the phrase "the land had rest" (Josh. 11:23; 14:15). When the people experience rest, forms of the verb *nûaḥ* are used, but when the land experiences rest, forms of the verb *šāqāṭ* are used. For the land, rest primarily involves a cessation of warfare.

Unfortunately, throughout the Former Prophets, permanent rest eludes Israel, as they were constantly battling with the surrounding nations. In the book of Judges, after YHWH hands them over to their enemies, they become oppressed, until YHWH sends a deliverer, which leads to temporary cyclical periods of rest in the land (Judg. 3:11, 30; 5:31; 8:28). Similarly, under the reign of David, YHWH gives him rest from his enemies before he received a promise of an eternal dynasty (2 Sam. 7:1). The New Testament book of Hebrews speaks of Joshua as being unable to bring the disobedient generation who died in the wilderness into the place of rest (Heb. 4:8). While this assessment may seem a bit unfair (he and Caleb tried to convince the people to go into the land; see Numbers 13—14), the author of Hebrews seems to be using Joshua as a foil for Jesus, who, according to the author, was able to successfully bring people into a place of rest (Heb. 4:1–14).

4.4. The Covenant

YHWH and his people have a long history of making covenants prior to the book of Joshua. The ancestors of the Israelites who took possession of the land in Joshua were already partners to three covenants in the Pentateuch (see Sidebar 2.1, "Old Testament Covenants"), so it shouldn't surprise readers of Joshua to see the theme feature prominently in the book.

The word "covenant" (*běrît*) appears twenty-two times in Joshua in three distinct contexts. First, it appears five times as the Gibeonites deceive the Israelites into making a covenant with them (Josh. 9:6, 7, 11, 15, 16) in violation of YHWH's prohibition against covenanting with the Canaanite residents (Exod. 23:32). Second, it appears thirteen times as part of the expression "the ark of the covenant" (Josh. 3:3, 6 [2], 8, 11, 14, 17; 4:7, 9, 18; 6:6, 8; 8:33). Third, it appears four times in describing Israel's covenant with YHWH (Josh. 7:11, 15; 23:16; 24:25). While the final of these contexts is clearly focused on Israel's covenantal relationship with their God, the second of these has a similar focus. The fact that the ark, the physical manifestation of the divine presence (Exod. 25:22), is explicitly connected by name to the covenant emphasizes the importance of this theme for the nation of Israel.

The Israelites engage in two separate covenant renewal ceremonies in the book. First, after they successfully conquer the city of Ai on their second attempt, Joshua leads them in a ceremony at Mount Ebal involving the construction of an altar, the offering of a sacrifice, and the copying and reading of the law of Moses (Josh. 8:30–35).

Second, at the end of the book, Joshua gathers all the tribes at Shechem, where he reviews their history, exhorts them to put away their idols, questions their commitment, but eventually still makes a covenant with them, and records it in a book and establishes a stone as a witness of the event (Josh. 24:1–27). In every covenant there are obligations, and just as YHWH would need to fulfill his promise to give them the land, so Israel would need to fulfill their commitment to obey the law. While both of these ceremonies in Joshua involve a type of recommitment to the covenant, the second one is more detailed, more elaborate, and the only one where the text actually describes what Joshua and the people do as making a covenant (Josh. 24:25).

Sidebar 2.1: Old Testament Covenants

YHWH makes a lot of covenants with his people. Table 2.2 lists six Old Testament covenants, including the primary and secondary partners, the nature of the covenant, the signs, and the biblical references. The covenants with Abraham and Moses each have multiple references, since they appear to be revealed in stages. Of the passages listed below, all of them except two (Gen. 12:1–7; 2 Sam. 7:1–17) use the word "covenant" to describe the agreement taking place between YHWH and his people.

Table 2.2: Old Testament Covenants

Primary Partner	Secondary Partners	Nature of the Covenant	Signs	Reference
Noah	All people, animals, plants, the earth	God won't destroy by flood again	Rainbow	Gen. 9:8–17
Abraham	His descendants, all families of the earth	Blessing, land, and descendants	Circumcision, Stars, Sand, Dust	Gen. 12:1–7; 15:1–21; 17:1–22

Moses	The people of Israel	Obedience to the Ten Commandments	Worship on Mt. Sinai; Two tablets	Exod. 19:5; 24:3–8
Joshua	The people of Israel	Recommitment to Mosaic covenant	Witness stone	Josh. 24:1–28
David	David's house	Eternal royal dynasty	The temple?	2 Sam. 7:1–17
Jeremiah	The house of Israel	Law written on Israel's hearts	Israel will know YHWH	Jer. 31:31–34

Thus, the covenant that Joshua and the Israelites make at the end of Joshua continues a tradition of covenants going back to pre-Patriarchal times and going forward to exilic times. Each of these covenants has a primary individual partner, as well as secondary corporate partners. While the covenants began broadly—Noah's covenant includes all people, all life, plants, animals, even the earth—they gradually narrow. Abraham's covenant focuses on his descendants who are prophesied to be as numerous as the stars, the sand, and the dust, but it also includes all the families of the earth (but not animals and plants like Noah's). Moses' covenant is primarily concerned with the people of Israel, although some of the Mosaic laws concern foreigners (e.g., Exod. 22:21). The secondary partners of Joshua's covenant continue to be the people of Israel, but moving forward, David's covenant (which technically never uses the word "covenant"; *běrît*) involves the narrowest partnership, specifically David's ruling descendants. For Jeremiah's covenant, the focus widens to include "the house of Israel." The nature of the covenant also varies, as three seem to be granted merely as rewards for earlier obedience (Noah's, Abraham's, and David's), while others explicitly are conditioned on continual obedience (Moses' and Joshua's).

4.5. Obedience

In the covenant of Moses, and the renewed covenant of Joshua, the key component of the agreement for Israel is obedience to the law of Moses. This theme of obedience to the law is mentioned in Joshua's call (Josh. 1:6–9), in the covenant renewal after the conquest of Ai (8:31–34), in Joshua's words to the eastern tribes as they return to their own territory (22:5), and in his final speeches to the nation (23:6; 24:24).

Within Joshua's speeches, the form of disobedience primarily targeted is idolatry, which establishes a connection to the book of Judges. While in Judges Israel's disobedience primarily involved idolatry, in Joshua the worship of other gods as a topic is essentially limited to the final two chapters (Josh. 23:7, 16; 24:2, 14, 15, 16, 20, 23).

God first commands Joshua to obey the law of Moses (Josh. 1:7). Then in turn, Joshua commands the people to obey Moses in the beginning, the middle, and the end of the book (Josh. 1:13; 8:31–35; 22:5; 23:6). In his final speech, Joshua uses a variety of tactics to compel the people to be more obedient. He reviews what YHWH has done for them (Josh. 24:1–13); he gives them a direct command to serve YHWH (24:14); he tells them to make a choice (24:15a), he speaks of his own family's example (24:15b); he uses reverse psychology ("You cannot serve YHWH"; 24:19); and finally he sets up a witness stone that will somehow testify against them if they don't obey (24:26–27). In response to Joshua's exhortations to obey the law of Moses, the people of Israel agree initially (Josh. 1:16–18), they listen willingly (8:34), and they commit enthusiastically (24:24).

A variety of incentives are provided to motivate the people to obey. Obedience will be rewarded with prosperity and success (Josh. 1:7, 8), and disobedience will result in YHWH being angry at them (Josh. 22:18; 23:16), YHWH no longer driving out the Canaanites (23:13), and YHWH consuming them (Josh. 23:16; 24:20). The text of Joshua speaks of two major examples of disobedience and consequences. First, Joshua reminds the people that their ancestors did not listen to the voice of YHWH so they were punished with forty years of wilderness wanderings (Josh. 5:5–6). Second, Achan kept some of the things from Jericho that were devoted to destruction (Joshua 7). The story of Achan's sin in the context of the failed attack on Ai makes the point that disobedience has severe consequences, both for the individual and for the community.

While the dramatic examples of Israel's disobedience may receive more attention, the text of Joshua also includes many examples of obedience. The priests stopped at the edge of the Jordan before the water of the river is cut off (Josh. 3:8, 15). Twelve men set up twelve memorial stones in the Jordan (Josh. 4:1–9), which served as a stark contrast to the twelve spies who brought back an unfavorable report (Num. 13:25–33). The people marched around the city of Jericho in an elaborate ritual before the wall came tumbling down (Joshua 6). They destroyed Canaanites as Moses commanded (Josh. 10:40; 11:12;

see 4.8 "Holy War or Genocide" below). They divided up the land by lot as YHWH commanded Moses (Josh. 14:2, 5). The Levites were given cities as Moses had commanded (Josh. 21:8). Joshua concluded that the people have kept all that Moses commanded (Josh. 22:2).

Map 2.6: Cities of the Amarna letters. Cf. CARTA p. 29 (Canaanite Kings in the Amarna age).

4.6. Leadership

While YHWH is the primary figure of the book of Joshua, mentioned 224 times (e.g., Josh. 1:1; 1:9, 11, 13, 15), much of the book focuses on how YHWH works through the leaders he has called. There is a clear chain of command beginning with YHWH, then Moses, Joshua, other leaders, and finally the people (e.g., Josh. 8:32–35; 11:15; 23:2).

Despite his dying before the book even begins, Moses' legacy as Israel's pre-eminent leader still looms large in Joshua as he is mentioned fifty-eight times in the book (e.g., Josh. 1:2, 3, 5, 7, 13, 14, 15, 17; 3:7). In the Pentateuch, Moses is described variously as a shepherd (Exod. 3:1), a lawgiver (Exodus 19–24), and a prophet (Deut. 18:15, 18). Moses' role as giver of the law continues to be mentioned in Joshua (1:7; 8:31, 32; 22:5; 23:6), but the book emphasizes his distinctive position as "the servant of YHWH," repeating the title fourteen times (Josh. 1:1, 13, 15; 8:31, 33; 11:12; 12:6 [2]; 13:8; 14:7; 18:7; 22:2, 4, 5; 24:29), whereas the title only appears four times elsewhere in the Hebrew Bible (Deut. 34:5; 2 Kgs. 18:12; 2 Chr. 1:3; 24:6).

Joshua, the book's eponymous leader, is mentioned 168 times, more than Moses, but not as often as YHWH. It is difficult to categorize Joshua as a leader because he played so many different roles. Joshua was Moses' successor (Deut. 31:23; 32:44; 34:9; Josh. 1:1–5; 4:14). And he, like Moses, was clearly the leader of the entire nation in a time before judges and kings. However, in at least two aspects, Joshua was different from his predecessor. First, even though he valued the law of Moses, he wasn't described as a lawgiver. Second, he did not appoint his own successor. One could argue that this oversight contributed to the nation's problems during the period of the judges, since no leadership succession plan was established during Israel's early days in the land.

Joshua also served in a variety of other leadership roles. His primary role was that of military leader (Josh. 8:3–29; 10:7–11; 11:16–23; 12:7–24). Even though the book never called him a priest or a prophet, he served in each of these capacities as he built an altar and offered sacrifices (Josh. 8:30), and he delivered divine messages to the people (Josh. 3:9; 14:6; 20:1; 24:2).

The book of Joshua includes other official leadership roles, most of which are mentioned in a section of Deuteronomy (16:18–18:22) that serves as a form of a national constitution as it explains how various leaders (judges, officers, priests, Levites, kings, and prophets) should be chosen and what they should do. This legal section of Deuteronomy codifies leadership roles for some future point in time from the perspective of Deuteronomy, a time when the Israelites are in the land (i.e., during the period of Joshua) and, eventually, establish a king (i.e., during the period of Samuel). It will therefore be instructive to see how the leaders of the book of Joshua compare to what they are supposed to do in the law of Moses.

Table 2.3 lists the types of leaders mentioned in the book of Joshua, beginning with the roles mentioned in the leadership code of Deuteronomy (16:18—18:22). Even though the leadership positions are given in singular form in the table below ("judge," "officer," "priest"), for many of these positions the text of Joshua speaks of a group of individuals who served in the role ("judges," "officers," "priests").

Table 2.3: Leadership Roles in Deuteronomy and Joshua

Position	Deuteronomy 16:18—18:22	Joshua	Unique function in Joshua
judge (*šōpēṭ*)	16:18(2); 17:9, 12	**3 times:** 8:33; 23:2; 24:1	Unclear since only mentioned along with other leaders
officer (*šōṭēr*)	16:18	**5:** 1:10; 3:2; 8:33; 23:2; 24:1	Relaying Joshua's messages to the people
priest (*kōhēn*)	17:9, 12, 18; 18:1, 3	**37:** 3:3, 6, 8; 4:3, 9; 6:4, 6; 8:33 . . .	Carrying the ark, blowing trumpets, receiving towns
Levite (*lēbî*)	17:9, 18; 18:1(2), 6, 7	**17:** 3:3; 8:33; 13:33; 14:3, 4; 18:7 . . .	Similar to priests
king (*melek*)	17:14, 15(2)	**112:** 2:2; 6:2; 8:1; 9:10; 10:1 . . .	Only foreign rulers, none over Israel yet
prophet (*nābî'*)	18:15, 18, 20(2), 22(2)		Joshua speaks for YHWH, but isn't called a prophet
elder (*zāqēn*)		**8:** 7:6; 8:10, 33; 9:11; 20:4; 23:2; 24:1, 31	Mourning over sin, mustering people, gathering people
head (*rōš*)		**9:** 14:1; 19:51; 21:1(2); 22:14, 21, 30; 23:2; 24:1	Clan leaders involved in division of the land
leader (*nāśî'*)		**9:** 9:15, 18(2), 19; 13:21; 17:4; 22:14(3), 30, 32	Leaders of the congregation, leaders of foreign lands

In Deuteronomy, ***judges*** primarily render judicial decisions; in the book of Judges, they are primarily military deliverers; in Joshua, it is difficult to say what unique function judges serve since they are only mentioned three times, and are always listed alongside other leaders.

In Deuteronomy, **officers** are only mentioned once alongside judges. In Joshua, they don't seem to play any judicial role, but merely relay messages to the people. Curiously, in two texts "officers" appear at the end of lists of Israel's leaders (Josh. 23:2; 24:1)

In Deuteronomy, **priests** assist judges and work alongside the Levites offering sacrifices. In Joshua, among other things (they are mentioned 37 times in the book), they carry the ark across the Jordan, blow trumpets outside Jericho, and receive their allotted towns. The role of **Levites** is similar to that of priests in both this section of Deuteronomy and Joshua.

In Deuteronomy, **kings** are limited in their acquisition of horses, wives, and gold; they must not be a foreigner; and they are meant to read and study the law. There are many kings mentioned in Joshua, but they are all rulers of foreign cities and peoples (e.g., Josh. 2:2; 6:2; 8:1; 9:10; 10:1). Saul, Israel's first king, is still centuries in the future from the perspective of Joshua (1 Sam. 9).

According to Deuteronomy, **prophets** are to play a significant role in delivering messages from YHWH to the people, and prophets did perform this key function both during the period of the monarchy and later. While no individual is called a prophet in the book of Joshua, the leader Joshua serves as YHWH's spokesperson throughout the book, as was noted above.

The final three types of leaders mentioned in Joshua are not included in Deuteronomy's leadership section. **"Elders"** are mentioned eight times in Joshua and they serve by mourning over sin (putting dust on their heads), by mustering the people before war and gathering with the people before Joshua's final speeches. **"Heads"** of families and clans are mentioned nine times in Joshua (the text also speaks of other "heads" not referring to leaders, but actual heads), usually in the context of dividing the land into tribal allotments. **"Leaders"** of congregations and leaders of foreign lands and peoples are also mentioned nine times in Joshua, but it isn't clear what role these generic leaders play.

4.7. YHWH as a Warrior

At a critical juncture in the narrative of Joshua, the transition between the preparation of the nation (chapters 1–5) and the conquest of the land (chapters 6–12), a mysterious military figure appears to Joshua with drawn sword in hand, identifying himself as the commander of the army of YHWH (Josh. 5:13-15). We'll discuss this perplexing encounter in more detail below (see 5.1), but at this point we'll merely note three reasons that this character is meant to be none other than YHWH himself. First, Joshua worshipped the character and the character didn't rebuke him for doing so, suggesting that he was divine. Second, while not necessarily the case, it is still reasonable to assume that the commander of YHWH's army would be YHWH himself. Third, Joshua is told to remove his sandals because the ground is holy, presumably because of the divine presence. The incident also closely parallels the call of Moses, as YHWH uses almost identical language to prompt Joshua's predecessor to remove his sandals because of the holy ground (Exod. 3:5). While it is difficult to be definitive due to the confusing nature of this passage, it appears that YHWH, as commander of the army, wants to hold a strategic meeting before the fighting begins with Joshua, his first officer.

The image of YHWH as a warrior, fighting for his people, is a major theme of the Old Testament. In the Song of the Sea, Moses and the people sing "YHWH is a warrior" (Exod. 15:3). With only three hundred warriors, YHWH leads Gideon to defeat the Midianites (Judg. 7). When the Assyrians are besieging the city of Jerusalem, YHWH slaughters 185,000 of Sennacherib's soldiers (2 Kgs. 19:35). We'll discuss some of the problematic aspects of this side of God's character in 4.8, but here will merely examine how YHWH fights for Israel in the book of Joshua.

While YHWH's loyalties aren't clear in the encounter between Joshua and the mysterious commander, throughout the rest of the book (with the exception of Joshua 7) YHWH is clearly on the side of Israel. Confidence and psychological preparation are crucial to military success and YHWH encourages his forces, promising victory beforehand against Jericho (Josh. 6:2), against Ai (8:1), against the southern coalition (Josh. 10:8, 17, 25), and against the northern coalition (Josh. 11:6). The text repeats that the Canaanite residents of the land were melting in fear, including the people of Jericho (Josh. 2:9-11), the Amorite kings (5:1), the Gibeonites (9:24), and the king of Jerusalem (10:1-2). In turn, YHWH repeatedly tells Joshua and the Israelite forces to not be afraid (Josh. 8:1; 10:8; 11:6).

Both in the middle of the conquest narratives and at the end of the book the text states that YHWH was fighting for Israel (Josh. 10:14; 42; 23:3; 24:8, 11). He put Israel's enemies in a panic (Josh. 10:10). He used his power over to nature to help fight battles for his people, sending hail (Josh. 10:11) and even stopping the sun (Josh. 10:12-14). In one of

Joshua's final speeches he reminds the people that one man was able to cause a thousand men to flee expressly because YHWH was fighting for them (Josh. 23:10).

4.8. Holy War or Genocide?

How should one view the brutal battles and devastating destruction of the book of Joshua? Some scholars call it genocide; others simply describe it as holy war. Before looking at possible ways to understand the violence, let's begin by summarizing the problem.

As has already been observed, the book of Joshua includes numerous examples of battles and warfare, all of which are problematic, but what is particularly troubling is the abundance of bloodshed, and the gruesome nature of it, even against non-combatants, specifically woman and children. Joshua and his army completely destroyed the cities of Jericho, including all its inhabitants (Josh. 6:21), and Ai (8:24, 26; 10:1). In case it wasn't clear, the text explicitly states that women and children were victims of this violence (Josh. 6:21; 8:25). God's people crushed the armies of five southern cities (Jerusalem, Hebron, Jarmuth, Lachish, Eglon; Josh. 10:20), killed their kings (10:26), then completely slaughtered the residents of these cities plus a few others in the region: Makkedah (10:28), Libnah (10:30), Lachish (10:32), Gezer (10:33), Eglon (10:35), Hebron (10:37), Debir (10:39). After this southern devastation, Israel defeated and utterly destroyed the northern cities who were allied against them (Josh. 11:12, 14), before completely wiping out the Anakim as well (11:21). While the Bible includes many troubling tales of bloodshed, these stories of brutal conquest and utter annihilation of the Canaanite residents of the land are perhaps the most disturbing of all.

In recent years, there has been a spate of books and articles addressing the problem of the Canaanite genocide.[15] Among the two options for understanding this brutal bloodshed mentioned above, holy war or genocide, both are problematic. While the term "holy war" has been used frequently by scholars to describe YHWH's militaristic efforts in the Hebrew Bible, Scripture never uses the term "holy war" (see Sidebar 2.2, "Holy War and the *Herem*").[16]

---

15. See Copan 2011; Copan and Flannagan 2014; Lamb 2011a, 2011b, 2013; Siebert 2009, 2012; and Wright 2008.
16. Ibid.

Sidebar 2.2: Holy War and the *Herem*

In the conquest narratives of Joshua, either the Hebrew noun *herem* or forms of the related verb *haram* are used to describe things that are to be banned or devoted to destruction (e.g., Josh. 2:10; 6:17, 18, 21; 7:1, 11, 12, 13, 15; 8:26; 10:1, 28, 35, 37). Items to fall under the *herem* (or the ban) to be totally destroyed include valuables, animals, and most problematically, humans. Because YHWH himself commands his people to devote these thing to destruction and he is the one that presumably gives the Israelites victory in these military contexts, the term "holy war" has been used to describe these narratives. However, the phrase "holy war" does not translate any Hebrew phrase in Scripture, and in most of the Hebrew Bible, warfare is not associated with *herem*. Scholars are therefore increasingly avoiding use of the phrase "holy war" even in discussions of Joshua. I argue elsewhere that motivations other than holiness need to be considered for divine warfare in Scripture, specifically those of wrath against oppression and compassion for the oppressed.[17]

More troubling, however, than usage of the term "holy war" is the book of Joshua's portrayal of behavior that could be considered genocide. There are several troubling aspects to this issue. The brutal act itself is disturbing: Israelites killing Canaanite men, women, and children. But since history is full of genocides and genocidal rulers (just in the last century, Hitler, Stalin, and Pol Pot were each responsible for the death of millions), what is even more disturbing for people of faith is that God commanded the genocide, as the text makes clear (Josh. 8:2; 10:40; 11:10–15; see also Deut. 20:16–18). Ironically, the people who were later the victims of Hitler's "final solution" are the spiritual descendants of the people in Joshua who are the perpetrators of the crime, goaded on by none other than God himself.

While no solution can do justice to this issue, or "solve" the problem to make it go away, here are six arguments used to address these disturbing questions: Why does God appear to command his own people to kill apparently innocent women and children? How are people of faith supposed to respond when God behaves badly? For the sake of simplicity, I'm using my own titles for these arguments.[18]

---

17. See Lamb 2013.
18. See Lamb 2011a, 2011b.

For each argument, I will state its essential point, a strength, and a weakness.

The fictional argument. There are two variations of this argument. One states that the Canaanite conquest as described in the book of Joshua is fiction; it didn't happen. The other acknowledges that even if the conquest did happen, God didn't command it. Both view an aspect of the text as fictional, either the account of the bloodshed, or the divine mandate for the bloodshed. The strength of this argument is that the problem conveniently disappears. The weakness is that it establishes a precedent that many readers may not be comfortable with, labeling as fiction sections of Scripture that don't seem to make sense, a rule which could potentially apply to many other sections of the Bible.

The whirlwind argument. In the biblical book of Job, God speaks to Job from the whirlwind with a barrage of questions, essentially putting him in his place for questioning God (Job 38—41). This argument states that we, like Job, shouldn't question God since our puny minds could never comprehend divine mysteries like why he commanded that all the Canaanites be killed. While this argument is perhaps a realistic assessment of human limitations when it comes to understanding divine behavior, it goes against much of what we find in Scripture as people often question God and cry out to him about their tragic situation (e.g., Abraham, Moses, the authors of the psalms of lament).

The context argument. In the ancient Near East, victorious nations often would completely slaughter defeated foes, so within Israel's context, the type of bloodshed we encounter in Joshua wasn't unusual.[19] Several ancient rulers (e.g., Ashurnasirpal of Assyria and Mesha of Moab) even bragged in their inscriptions about wiping out cities and killing women and children. This argument takes seriously the many differences between the world of the Bible and that of our own, including, for example, the distinction of combatants and noncombatants, which are often ignored or under-appreciated in simplistic readings of the Bible. However, to many readers of Scripture it might sound like the sort of thing a teen would say to their parent, "All the other nations are committing genocide. Why can't I (Israel) do it, too?"

The hyperbole argument. The descriptions of the violence targeting the Canaanites are hyperbolic, since we know from the books of Joshua

19. See Hess, 42–43.

and Judges that many Canaanites were still living in the land (Josh. 13:1, 13: 15:63; 17:12; Judg. 1). While the texts describing the slaughter get our attention, the text more frequently speaks of the residents of the land being "driven out" (Exod. 23:28–31; 34:11; Num. 32:21; 33:52–55; Deut. 4:38; 7:1; 9:3–6; 11:23; 18:12; 33:27; Josh. 3:10; 14:12; 17:18; 23:5). While this argument has many strengths as it takes the all the various texts on both sides of the issue seriously, it might appear to be a compromise that pleases neither the folks who favor the fictional argument or the ones who are suspicious of anything less than a literal interpretation of these events.

The punishment argument. The Canaanites were being punished for wicked behavior. This argument lacks support in Joshua but finds extensive support in the Pentateuch (e.g., Exod. 23:32–33; Deut. 12:29–31; 18:9–14). Similar to the previous argument, the strength of this one is that it takes the biblical text seriously and acknowledges that the Canaanites were guilty of many crimes, including attacking the Israelites when they were weak as they were fleeing from an oppressive situation (Exod. 17:8–13; Num. 21:1, 21–26, 33–35). However, many people troubled by this issue may wonder, "Isn't it harsh and even ironic to violently wipe out an entire nation for being too violent?"

The remnant argument. From among the Canaanites, a righteous remnant was saved as every person who showed hospitality to Israel was delivered: Rahab and her entire family (Josh. 6:22, 25); the Gibeonites (Joshua 9); a man from Bethel (Judg. 1:24–25); the Kenites (1 Sam. 15:6). The most compelling aspect of this argument is that it focuses on the mercy shown by Israel and YHWH to the various groups of Canaanites who survived the conquest. Rahab, the Canaanite prostitute, is even viewed quite positively from the perspective of the New Testament (see Sidebar 2.4, "Rahab's Shocking Legacy" below). The biggest problem with this argument is that God's voice appears to be absent as an initiator of these rescues, although he never condemns them.

All of these arguments have problems and none of them are going to fully satisfy both the skeptics and the faithful when it comes to the bloodshed of Joshua. Readers of the book will therefore need to decide for themselves which arguments are helpful in making sense of one of the most problematic aspects of Scripture.

5. Commentary

5.1. The Preparation of the Nation (Joshua 1—5)

While the heart of the book of Joshua centers on battling for and dividing up the land, the beginning and end of the book focus on speeches (chapters 1, 23, and 24). The first chapter includes four of these: 1) YHWH to Joshua (1:1–9); 2) Joshua to the Israelite leaders (1:10–11); 3) Joshua to the Transjordan tribes (1:12–15); 4) the Transjordan tribes to Joshua (1:16–18). (The Transjordan tribes were the two-and-a-half tribes—Reuben, Gad, and half of Manasseh—who were already given land on the east side of the Jordan; Numbers 32; Deut. 3:12–20.)

5.1.1. YHWH Commissions Joshua (Joshua 1)

The first speech of the first chapter consists of the call of Joshua (see Sidebar 2.1, "Old Testament Call Narratives"), as YHWH first reminds Joshua of the death of Moses (recorded in Deut. 34:5), then commissions him to take over where his successor left off. Moses crossed the Red Sea to bring the Israelites out of the land of Egypt and Joshua will cross the Jordan to bring them into the land of Canaan. While Moses on his exit needed to defeat the army of Egypt, Joshua in his entrance will need to defeat the numerous armies of Canaan. The borders that YHWH describes here for the land are enormous, "huge and fabled,"[20] which to Joshua could seem overwhelming. Not surprisingly, therefore, much of Joshua's call focuses on divine empowerment before he begins the battles for conquest. According to Deuteronomy, toward the end of his life, Moses charged his successor to "be strong and bold" (Deut. 31:23) and this theme is reiterated in YHWH's commission with the triple repetition of the exhortation to "be strong and courageous" (Josh. 1:5, 7, 9). At another critical point in Israel's history, the prophet Haggai recalls a similar tone by thrice repeating the exhortation "be strong" in his words to Joshua (son of the high priest), to Zerubbabel (governor of Judah), and to the returning exiles as they rebuild the second temple (Hag. 2:4). In his call to the conqueror of the promised land, YHWH promises that Joshua will be successful if he's obedient to the law of Moses.

---

20. According to Hubbard, 78.

After his divine call, Joshua prepares the people for the Jordan crossing. In his speech to the men of the Transjordan tribes, he reminds them of their commitment to cross over and fight with their fellow Israelites while their families remain east of the Jordan (Josh. 1:12–15). Their response, "as we obeyed Moses in all things, so we will obey you," should have made Joshua nervous since the Israelites often disobeyed his predecessor. They complained, worshipped the golden calf, and refused to enter the land (Exod. 14:11–12; 15:24; 16:2; 17:3; 32:6; Num. 14:1–4). This perhaps naïve assessment of their own proclivity toward obedience in the beginning of the book is echoed by a similar sentiment at the end in response to Joshua's call to serve YHWH exclusively, "Far by it from us to worship other gods" (Josh. 24:16). The Transjordan tribes' response to Joshua also echoes two key components of YHWH's call to Joshua, a request for YHWH's ongoing presence and an exhortation to be "strong and courageous" (Josh. 1:18).

Sidebar 2.3: Old Testament Call Narratives

A common feature of Old Testament literature is the call narrative, appearing in the Pentateuch, the historical books, and the prophets. Table 2.4 lists eleven leaders, the reference to their call, and the divinely mandated task to which they were commissioned.

Table 2.4: Old Testament Call Narratives

Leader	Reference	Divinely Mandated Task
Noah	Gen. 6:13–22	Build an ark, bring animals on board.
Abraham	Gen. 12:1–3	Leave your family, go to Canaan.
Moses	Exod. 3:1—4:17	Bring the Israelites out of Egypt.
Joshua	Josh. 1:1–9	Take the Israelites into the land. Be strong.
Gideon	Judg. 6:11–25	Deliver Israel from Midian.
Samuel	1 Sam. 3:2–14	Pronounce judgment on the house of Eli.
Isaiah	Isa. 6:1–13	Tell Israel, "Listen, but don't comprehend . . ."
Jeremiah	Jer. 1:4–10	Be a prophet to the nations.
Ezekiel	Ezek. 2:1—3:11	Eat the scroll, speak to Israel (be rejected).

Amos   Amos 7:14–15   Prophesy to the people of Israel.

Jonah   Jon. 1:1–2; 3:1–2   Cry out against the wickedness of Nineveh.

In his classic discussion of the forms of call narratives, Norman Habel lists six general components.[21] Habel only focuses on the calls of Gideon, Moses, Jeremiah, Isaiah, and Ezekiel. While most of these narratives do not include all of the elements, and Joshua's only includes a few, it will be helpful to go over the general pattern.

1. *The divine confrontation.* While the leader is busy doing his job (for Moses, watching sheep; for Gideon, beating out wheat), YHWH or his angel appears and somehow gets his attention (for Moses, with a burning bush; for Isaiah, with a dramatic vision). The call thus interrupts the normal life of the leader.

2. *The introductory word.* Before delivering the commission there's an introduction of sorts, explaining the context of what is about to come. For Moses, YHWH tells him to remove his sandals. For Joshua, YHWH reminds him of the death of Moses. In several instances, YHWH calls the leader by name (e.g., Moses, Samuel).

3. *The commission.* This is the heart of the call narrative, the critical task that YHWH is commissioning his leader to perform. Most of the early tasks primarily involve deliverance (Noah, Moses, Joshua, and Gideon), while the later ones involve prophets delivering divine messages (Samuel, Isaiah, Jeremiah, Ezekiel, Amos, and Jonah).

4. *The objection.* After hearing the commission the human typically objects, usually basing their argument on their own perceived insufficiency. Moses includes a series of five objections (Who am I? Who are you? The Israelites won't listen to me. I can't speak well. Please pick someone else.) Joshua appears to offer no objection. Gideon is reluctant because his clan is the weakest and he is the least in his family. Isaiah is a man of unclean lips. Jonah doesn't say anything, but he just heads in the opposite direction of Nineveh.

21. See Habel 1965.

5. **The reassurance.** In response to the objection, YHWH merely reassures the leader that it doesn't matter. Typically, YHWH doesn't correct the leader's self-assessment ("No, Gideon, you're not weak"), but shifts their focus from themselves to himself. The reassurance often involves a promise of divine presence. In their call narratives, YHWH says to Moses, Joshua, Gideon, and Jeremiah, "I will be with you." The theme of YHWH being with Joshua and his people reappears elsewhere in the book (Josh. 1:17; 3:7; 7:12).

6. **The sign.** The sign often accompanies the commission to confirm and empower the leader to perform their appointed task. Moses' sign was to worship YHWH on Mount Sinai. In response to Gideon's request for a sign, the angel torches his sacrifice. The sign that Samuel's prophecy will come true is given in a parallel, earlier prophecy, that Eli's sons Hophni and Phinehas will die on the same day (1 Sam. 2:34). For prophets, not surprisingly the signs often involve their mouths. YHWH touches the mouth of Jeremiah, has a seraph touch Isaiah's mouth with a coal, and gives Ezekiel a scroll to eat.

5.1.2. The Spies Visit Rahab (Joshua 2)

Joshua next sends out two spies to check out the land, particularly Jericho. Forty years earlier, Moses had sent out twelve spies to see the land, but only two (Joshua and Caleb) gave a hopeful report (Num. 13:30; 14:6–9), so perhaps Joshua thinks two is a better number than twelve for "covert ops." These two end up at the home of Rahab, a prostitute of Jericho.[22] Some readers may be shocked at the idea, but many scholars, because of the numerous hints of sexuality in the text,[23] speculate that these two young men, in addition to performing their clandestine service to the nation, have come to pay her a professional visit (a bit like the womanizing James Bond?). The men "lie down"

22. For a discussion of Rahab and prostitution in the Old Testament, see Lamb 2015, 87–112.
23. See Nelson, 43–44.

(*šākab*) at her house (Josh. 2:1), a verb that can imply sex (Gen. 19:32; 1 Sam. 13:11), and they "come (in) to" (*bo'*) her twice (Josh. 2:3, 4), an expression which often has sexual connotations when a woman is the object (e.g., Gen. 6:4; Judg. 16:1). While it would be naïve to conclude that nothing sexual could have gone on at Rahab's (as if no Israelite man would ever sleep with a prostitute . . . except Judah, Samson, Hosea, and perhaps a few others!), we need to be careful not to make things up when the text isn't explicit.

Soon after they arrive at Rahab's home, the king of Jericho somehow finds out and sends men to capture the spies, but Rahab cleverly deceives them (Josh. 2:2-7). She has hidden the spies on her roof, but she sends the king's men off quickly in "pursuit" of them. After the king's men depart, she gives the two spies what they are looking for, the lowdown on how the people of the land feel about them. The residents of Jericho and Canaan melt in fear of the Israelites and their God. She then utters a dramatic monotheistic declaration, that their God is "indeed God in heaven above and on earth below" (Josh. 2:11).

Rahab and the two spies then make a deal. She won't report them to the king. They will rescue her and her entire family when they come back and destroy Jericho. She gives them guidance about how to avoid getting caught (climb out her window, scale down the wall, head to the hills, hide for three days, then go return to your camp). To signify her home, she is supposed to hang a scarlet cord (see Table 2.5, below) from her window. The two spies follow her directions, return to Joshua, and report favorably to him that YHWH has given the land into their hands (Josh. 2:22-24). For more on her story, see Sidebar 2.4, "Rahab's Shocking Legacy."

Sidebar 2.4: Rahab's Shocking Legacy

While the text repeatedly calls Rahab a prostitute (Josh. 2:1; 6:17, 25), the fact that she was established in this particular ancient profession didn't prevent the biblical authors from describing her in highly favorable terms. She is clearly the heroine of the story of Jericho. The spies are not named, but the prostitute is (forty years earlier, the text provides names for all twelve spies; Num. 13:4-16). She risks her life by committing treason against her own people to save her own family. She gives the spies all the information they were looking for. She is

---

more confident because of second-hand testimony about the power of YHWH from his deeds in Egypt than ten of the initial spies were after witnessing the events first-hand.

Her New Testament legacy is also shockingly favorable. Rahab is the second woman mentioned in the New Testament, appearing in the genealogy of Jesus right after Tamar, who was also associated with prostitution (Genesis 38; Matt. 1:3–5). Joshua, the conqueror of Canaan, is omitted from the "Hall of Faith" in the book of Hebrews, but Rahab, the Canaanite prostitute, is given her own verse, alongside the other heroes of faith: Abraham, Moses, Samuel, and David (Heb. 11:31), her great, great, grandson (according to Matt. 1:5–6). Rahab is one of only three Old Testament figures mentioned in the book of James: Abraham, Elijah, and Rahab (James 2:21, 25; 5:17), a patriarch, a prophet, and a prostitute.

5.1.3. Israel Crosses the Jordan (Joshua 3—4)

While some scholars see the account of Israel's crossing of the Jordan River as convoluted,[24] others think the text as it stands makes sense.[25] You'll have to decide for yourself. The forty-one verse narrative can be divided into three parts: the preparation (Josh. 3:1–13), the crossing (3:14–17), and then the memorial (4:1–24).

After hearing the report about Jericho from the two spies, Joshua mobilizes the camp and prepares the people to approach the Jordan River (Josh. 3:1–6). YHWH gives instructions for the crossing to Joshua, who relays them to the priests and the people, who in turn proceed to follow Joshua's direction. The priests carry the ark toward the river and as their feet touch the water, the flow gets cut off, allowing the people to cross over on dry ground.

The text includes many parallels between the events that began the exodus, the Passover and crossing of the Red Sea (Exodus 12, 14), and the crossing of the Jordan, which begins their entry into the promised land. The Passover lamb was selected on the tenth day of the first month (Nisan), and the Israelites crossed the Jordan on the tenth day of the first month (Exod. 12:3; Josh. 4:19). The most dramatic parallel

---

24. E.g., Nelson, 55.
25. E.g., Hubbard, 149.

is also the most obvious—a supernatural crossing of a body of water, and in case we missed it, the text makes the connection explicit (Josh. 4:23). In each instance the Israelites cross over on dry ground (although different Hebrew words are used for the "dry ground"; Exod. 14:9; Josh. 3:17). In both cases the waters rise in a "heap," *ned* (Exod. 15:8; Josh. 3:13, 16). Both events are memorialized, with a song after the sea crossing (Exodus 15) or a pile of stones after the river crossing (Josh. 4). (For more on the memorial stone pile, see Sidebar 2.5, "Symbolic Objects in Joshua.") The stone stack is supposed to provoke future Israelite children to ask what they mean, which will then lead to opportunities to retell the story of the river crossing (Josh. 4:6–7, 21–24). As a result of the Jordan crossing, the people of Israel stood in awe of Joshua as they did Moses (Josh. 4:14), which will come in handy as he soon will be calling them into battle.

Sidebar 2.5: Symbolic Objects in Joshua

Within the book of Joshua symbolic objects play a crucial role in the narrative, serving as tangible reminders of things that should not be forgotten. They memorialize what YHWH has done; they remind Israel what they need to do; they testify to covenants and agreements. Table 2.5 lists five of these objects, their references, and their significance.

Table 2.5: Symbolic Objects in Joshua

Object	Joshua References	Significance
Scarlet cord	2:18, 21	The cord signifies the location of Rahab's house (don't destroy the people who live here!).
Ark of the Covenant	3:3–17; 4:5–18; 6:4–13; 7:6; 8:33	The ark symbolizes the presence of YHWH.
Twelve stones	4:1–9	The stones memorialize YHWH cutting off the Jordan for the Israelites to cross.
Witness altar	22:10, 26–34	The altar testifies that both the tribes on the east and west of the Jordan worship the same God, YHWH.
Witness stone	24:26–27	The stone witnesses the Israelites covenant to obey.

The two spies instruct Rahab to tie a scarlet cord outside her window to signify her location to the Israelites, which should prevent them from killing anyone inside her home. The cord is curiously not mentioned again later when the Israelites destroy Jericho, but apparently it served its purpose, since Rahab's entire family was rescued (Josh. 6:25).

The most significant of these objects is the Ark of the Covenant (see Exod. 25:10–22; 37:1–9) which is referenced thirty times in Joshua (sometimes just called "the ark"; Josh. 3:15; 4:10). The ark signifies the presence of YHWH with his people, and serves as a reminder of their covenant with their God. The ark was carried by the priests and played a central role in the crossing of the Jordan (Josh. 3:6–17; 4:9–18), and the marching around Jericho (6:4–13).

After crossing the Jordan, twelve stones were set up as a permanent memorial of the event. Since each tribe selected a stone, this rock pile is reminiscent of the twelve stones on the priestly breastplate, each bearing the name of one of the tribes (Exod. 28:21; 39:14).

The final two objects serve as non-human witnesses to important events. The witness altar testifies to future generations that the tribes both on the east and on the west side of the Jordan River worship the same God, YHWH. The final object, a witness stone, was to testify as a reminder to the Israelites of the covenant they made with YHWH at the end of the book.

Three other piles of stones are mentioned in Joshua. These serve to memorialize certain events, but they aren't in the same category as these other objects since they lack a significant symbolic meaning. Heaps of stones mark the graves of Achan and the king of Ai, and a pile of ruins marks the destroyed site of the city of Ai. The text states that all three of these rock piles have somehow remained "to this day" (Josh. 7:26; 8:28, 29).

5.1.4. Circumcision, Passover, and Visitation (Joshua 5)

As Israel's conquest of the land is about to commence, the final preparations involve religious rituals of circumcision and Passover. But first the text reports that as word of the dried up Jordan spread, the hearts of the Canaanites reportedly melted (Josh. 5:1). The melted heart phenomenon was seen earlier in Jericho (2:9, 11, 24), and later among the Israelites after their defeat by Ai (7:5).

Circumcision was a sign of the covenant between Israel and YHWH beginning with Abraham (Genesis 17), and it was a requirement for participation in the Passover (Exod. 12:48). But none of the Israelite males born during the forty years in the wilderness were circumcised, so YHWH told Joshua to circumcise the new generation (Josh. 5:2). After the circumcision ritual was over, the nation rested to recover (Josh. 5:8). (During recovery from circumcision, even battle-hardened soldiers will be vulnerable. Moses' ancestor Levi and his brother Simeon took advantage of the Shechemites immediately after their circumcisions to slaughter them during their recovery to pay them back for Shechem's rape of their sister Dinah; see Genesis 34.)

The location of the circumcision ceremony was Gibeath-haaraloth, literally "Hill of the Foreskins" (perhaps not the ideal spot for a picnic). The ceremony apparently took place between the tenth of the month, when they crossed the Jordan (Josh. 4:19), and the fourteenth of the month, when they celebrated the Passover (Josh. 5:10) as the law required (Exod. 12:6, 18). The Passover celebration is yet another parallel from this section of Joshua that hearkens back to Israel's exodus from Egypt. Presumably, a three-day recovery from circumcision was sufficient for the celebration of the Passover, but would not have been sufficient for them to be ready to go against Jericho (Joshua 6). While several sections of the Pentateuch gave guidance regarding the Passover (Exod. 34:25; Lev. 23:5; Num. 9:2–14; 28:16; Deut. 16:1–6), the text records few actual observances of the festival during Israel's time in the wilderness (Num. 9:5; 33:3).

After the Passover, the text records that the divinely provided mystery food, the manna, finally stopped appearing (Josh. 5:12). Immediately after leaving Egypt, the Israelites complained to YHWH that they were starving, so he began to send manna (literally, "what is it?"; Exod. 16:31–35; Num. 11:6–9). So after forty years of eating the same meal, they finally get some variety in their diet as they begin to eat the produce of the land (Josh. 5:12), which should have been tasty, a welcome change in a land flowing with "milk and honey" (Exod. 3:8; Deut. 6:3; Josh. 5:6).

After the circumcisions and celebrations, Joshua receives a visitation from a mysterious figure with a drawn sword in hand, an image that could inspire fear even in a warrior like Joshua. Angels with a drawn sword appear to Balaam (initially only to his donkey) to warn him not to curse Israel (Num. 22:23, 31) and to David in the midst of a plague as punishment for taking a census (1 Chr. 21:16). When Joshua asks him whose side he's on, he gives the cryptic answer, "Neither," and merely identifies that he's come as commander of YHWH's army (we argue above that the commander is meant to be YHWH himself; see 4.8). His ambiguous answer to Joshua's question is consistent with what happens in the following two chapters. He first fights for Israel and against Jericho, and then against Israel and for Ai, before helping his people defeat Ai on their second engagement (Joshua 6—7).

5.2. The Conquest of the Land (Joshua 6—12)

5.2.1. Jericho (Joshua 6)

The city of Jericho lies about four miles west of the Jordan River (at approximately 850 feet below sea level!) and was a crucial stop on an important east-west route. After spying out Jericho, hearing a report on its condition, and camping out on the plains near it during their various celebrations, the time has finally arrived to conquer the city, which has been shut for a siege, with no one coming in or out (Josh. 6:1). YHWH passes on directions to Joshua, who relays them to the priests and to the people. YHWH first instills confidence by promising victory, and then he gives them detailed instructions centered around the number seven, repeated in the text eleven times in twelve verses (Josh. 6:4–15). The Israelites are to walk around the wall for six days, with seven priests carrying seven trumpets, and on the seventh day, they are to circle the city seven times. The elaborate six days plus one day ritual follows a creation pattern (Gen. 2:2–3), but because of the eventual destruction, Robert Alter calls it an "anti-creation" story.[26]

The procession included an initial armed guard, the trumpet-blowing priests, the ark-bearing priests, and a rear guard (Josh. 6:6–9). While the trumpets are blaring over the course of the initial six days, the people are to be silent. On the seventh day, after the seventh lap, Joshua gives one final instructive speech, reminding them to devote everything to destruction except Rahab, her family, and all the gold, silver, bronze, and iron, which are earmarked for the treasury (the metals, not the people). The references to the treasury (Josh. 6:19, 24) appear anachronistic since there is no other reference to a treasury in Joshua, and the only other time the Hebrew word for "treasury" ('ôṣār) appears in the Former Prophets is much later in the context of Solomon's treasury (e.g., 1 Kgs. 7:51; 14:26; 15:18). After six days of

---

26. Alter, 30.

silence (except for the blasting of trumpets), the people shout, which knocks down the walls of the city (Josh. 6:20). The Israelites appear to obey Joshua's directions (we'll find out later that Achan didn't) by killing all the residents, burning all the city, saving the all valuables, and rescuing all Rahab's family. Appropriately, the two spies she hosted are the ones who locate and bring Rahab and her family out of the destruction (Josh. 6:21–24). The narrative ends with Joshua's poetic, prophetic curse against the rebuilder of Jericho, a prophecy that was fulfilled over three centuries later when Hiel of Bethel lost his oldest and youngest sons as he rebuilt the city down by the river (1 Kgs. 16:34).

5.2.2. Ai (Joshua 7—8)

While it may have appeared that all the Israelites obeyed Joshua, one man did not. Achan kept something from Jericho that he shouldn't have (the text doesn't reveal yet what it was), which angered YHWH (Josh. 7:1). Curiously, as the text identifies Achan it names not just his father, which is typical, but his grandfather, great-grandfather, and tribe. The text never explicitly states what YHWH's anger caused him to do, but the clear implication is that it resulted in an initial defeat against Ai, a city situated about ten miles west of Jericho (see Figure 2.6).

In stark contrast to the narrative thus far, YHWH gives no guidance to Joshua before the campaign against Ai. But Joshua, the former spy (Num. 13:16), decides to send spies, since that strategy worked well with Jericho. The spies report the town is small, so only a few thousand are necessary for an attack. Joshua follows their advice, not thinking he needs any divine direction (YHWH is apparently still angry, but silent). The small Israelite contingent is routed, which prompts Joshua to mourn, lament, and question their commission to conquer the land (Josh. 7:4–9).

Joshua's complaint is reminiscent of Israel's grumbling in the wilderness (Exod. 14:10; 16:2, 7; 17:3; Num. 14:2), so it is not surprising that YHWH shows him no sympathy at this point ("Stand up!" Josh. 7:10). YHWH explains that they were defeated by Ai because they sinned; not a single individual, but the whole nation sinned. He then provides specific guidance how to determine the culprit, which was presumably done with the use of the Urim and Thummim (Exod. 28:30;

Lev. 8:8; Num. 27:21; Deut. 33:8), objects which would respond to binary questions with either a "yes" or a "no" (1 Sam. 14:41).

Figure 2.7: *The Seven Trumpets of Jericho*, by James Tissot (ca. 1896–1902); gouache on board.

As Joshua begins the sinner discernment process we discover why Achan's detailed genealogy was supplied earlier. The tribe of Achan (Judah) is first chosen, then the clan of his great-grandfather (Zerah), then the family of his grandfather (Zabdi), and finally Achan son of Carmi is chosen. Joshua gives Achan the chance to confess, which he does. We finally find out exactly what he took: a mantle, some silver, and some gold (Josh. 7:21). Despite Joshua's words that the guilty party would be burned, one might hope that forgiveness would be shown to Achan because of his confession. But no, the community stones him to death, burns him with fire, and buries him with stones. Why was no forgiveness shown to Achan after his confession? Perhaps to set an example for the nation since, according to the text, his sin resulted in the deaths of thirty-six of his countrymen.

Round two against Ai begins when YHWH gives detailed advice to Joshua, as he did with Jericho, specifically mentioning how he would hand over the residents of Ai (Josh. 8:1). In contrast to the advice given to Gideon (reduce your force from over 30,000 down to 300 men; Judg. 7:1–8), YHWH tells Joshua to take all his fighting men and set up an ambush, a plan which bears striking similarities to a tactic used by the combined tribes against the tribe of Benjamin toward the end of the book of Judges (chapter 20). Israel lures the main contingent of Ai's army away from the city, pretending to flee as they did with the first engagement against the city (Josh. 7:4–5; 8:15–16). The rest of the men in the city join the pursuit, which allows the Israelites who had hidden in ambush to enter the unguarded city, which they then burn. The army of Ai looks back, see the city burning, and are disheartened. Joshua then turns his army around and routs the men of Ai. The city is destroyed and left as a ruin (Josh. 8:28), a tragic yet perhaps appropriate ending for a city whose name literally means "the ruin" (hā'ay).

To bring closure to the incident of the sin of Achan and the initial devastating loss to Ai, Joshua then leads the people in a covenant renewal ceremony (8:30–35; see also 4.4 above). The book of Joshua records four ceremonies: circumcision (Josh. 5:2–9), Passover (5:10–12), this covenant renewal, and a final covenant renewal (24:1–28). Joshua builds an altar on Mount Ebal, which is curious since the location was not adjacent to either Ai or Jericho but would have involved a twenty- to thirty-mile hike to the north. It appears that Joshua is attempting to be faithful to Moses' words that after the people enter into the land they were to supposed to set up a blessing on Mount Gerizim and a curse on Mount Ebal (Deut. 11:26–32). Moses had also commanded them to write the laws on stones (Deut. 27:2–3), so part of Joshua's covenant renewal involved copying the law of Moses on stones (presumably big ones). The ceremony was then concluded with a public reading of the law to all the gathered assembly of Israel (Josh. 8:34–35).

5.2.3. Gibeon (Joshua 9)

After word continues to spread among the various Canaanite peoples of the defeats of Jericho and Ai, we see two different responses. Two groups of cities form coalitions against Israel, one in the south (Joshua 10), and one in the north (Joshua 11). Another collection of cities, the Gibeonites, take a completely different approach and form an alliance with Israel. Somehow knowing that Israel was planning to annihilate only the Canaanite residents of the land, they put on an elaborate show involving moldy food, worn-out clothes, and patched sandals as they pretend to be from a distant land (Josh. 9:3–5). In reality, the Gibeonite cities were located between five and ten miles northwest of Jerusalem and a few miles west of Ai. They ask to make a treaty, but the Israelites are initially skeptical (Josh. 9:6–8). So the Gibeonites relate how they came from their very distant, but curiously unnamed, country because they heard what YHWH had done in Egypt and how he had helped Israel defeat the Amorite kings, Sihon and Og (according to Rahab, the residents of Jericho had heard similar divine exploits; Josh. 2:10). The Gibeonites graciously offer to share their moldy food and the Israelites, perhaps not wanting to offend their generous hosts, freely partake in their nasty provisions (Josh. 9:12–13). Joshua then makes a covenant with them but, as the text adds, without seeking direction from YHWH (Josh. 9:14–15), and unknowingly going against the clear mandate not to form alliances with the indigenous Canaanite people (Exod. 34:11–12; Deut. 20:16–18).

The Israelites arrive a few days later at the Gibeonite cities (Gibeon, Chephirah, Beeroth, and Kiriath-jearim, towns later mentioned in the tribal allotments for Benjamin in Josh. 18:25–28) and realize they had been deceived, but they can't attack the Gibeonites because of their agreement. The Israelite people become upset at their leaders. The text uses the same word, "to grumble" (lûn), to describe the people's response here that was previously used for the complaining in the wilderness (e.g., Exod. 15:24; 16:2, 7; 17:3; Num. 14:2, 27), although in this context their complaint seems warranted because of their leaders' hasty decision to form an alliance with a people they were supposed to destroy (Deut. 20:17). The Gibeonites, happy to survive because of their clever deception, are willing to become menial servants for the Israelites as "hewers of wood" and "drawers of water" (see Deut. 29:9–10).

5.2.4. The Southern Alliance (Joshua 10)

Previously in Joshua, word of Israel's exploits spread rapidly throughout Canaan (Josh. 2:10; 5:1; 9:1, 3), and now Adoni-zedek, the king of Jerusalem hears about Jericho, Ai, and the treaty between Gibeon and Israel (10:1). Gibeon was a major city with a reputation for a strong military; it was therefore highly troubling to Jerusalem's ruler that Gibeon felt like they couldn't withstand Israel. In response to the looming threat, he contacts the kings of Hebron, Jarmuth, Lachish, and Eglon (cities to the southwest of Jerusalem) to form a southern Canaan anti-Israel alliance. Their first cooperative effort is to attack Gibeon (Josh. 10:2–5).

Because of their freshly minted treaty, Israel is bound to help the Gibeonites against these five cities. But Israel's assistance to Gibeon was, according to the text, primarily of a divine nature as YHWH once again fought for them. YHWH first encourages Joshua not to fear this southern coalition (Josh. 10:8), as he had done before the defeat of Ai (8:1), and as he would do before the battle against the northern coalition (11:6). YHWH then throws the armies of these five cities into panic (Josh. 10:10). While they are fleeing he rains massive hailstones, which apparently were large enough to kill more soldiers than the Israelite swords (Josh. 10:11). In response to Joshua's poetic prayer, the final act of divine assistance is to stop the sun in the sky, which presumably provides the sufficient extra time that Joshua and his men forces need to complete their victory (Josh. 10:12–15). In an interesting astronomical parallel to Joshua's sun standing still, Thutmose III describes how his deity Amun-Re caused a "star" (presumably a meteor) to shoot toward his enemies, which resulted in a panic and eventual victory for the Egyptian ruler (COS 2:17). David Howard discusses five options for how to understand Joshua's sun standing still phenomena.[27]

While victory in the south has been achieved, there is still work to be done and the remainder of the chapter narrates the final destruction. After killing the kings of these five cities who had been hiding in a cave (Josh. 10:16–27), Joshua embarks on a campaign of utter destruction against seven cities, all of which generally fall into what will become the tribal allotment of Judah. Of the seven cities, four were not part of the southern alliance (Makkedah, Libnah, Gezer, and Debir), and three were part of the alliance (Lachish, Eglon, and Hebron). The other two cities of the alliance, Jarmuth and Jerusalem, aren't mentioned in the mop-up activities, but during the period of the monarchy we learn that Jerusalem was controlled by the Jebusites until the time of David (2 Sam. 5:6–9). The textual descriptions of these destructions are rather formulaic: see Richard Hess's table of phrases used to describe these southern conquests (Table 2.6).[28] Joshua and Israel attack each city, YHWH gives them into their hands, they put the residents to the sword, they totally destroy the city, and they leave no survivors (Josh. 11:28–38). The narrative concludes with a summary of Joshua's southern victories, and a notice of how they had obeyed YHWH's

27. See Howard 1998, 241–49.
28. See Hess 1996, 203.

command to wipe out the Canaanite residents (see 4.8, "Holy War or Genocide?").

Table 2.6: Phrases Repeated in Joshua 10:28–39 Conquests[29]

Phrases	Makkedah	Libnah	Lachish	Gezer	Eglon	Hebron	Debir
he took it							
he took up positions	X		X		X	X	X
he attacked it			X		X		
the LORD gave that city		X	X				
its king	X	X				X	X
its villages						X	X
he put it to the sword	X	X	X		X	X	X
he totally destroyed it	X				X		X
everyone in it	X	X	X		X	X	X
he left no survivors	X	X				X	X
he did to Y as he had done to Z	X	X	X		X	X	X

5.2.5. The Northern Alliance (Joshua 11)

Joshua 11 begins in a similar manner to Joshua 10 as a certain king, this time Jabin of Hazor, hears about Israel's conquests, so he contacts his neighboring kings to form an alliance against Israel (Josh. 11:1). Like Jerusalem in the south, Hazor was perhaps the most important city in the north, located in what would become the tribal allotment of Naphtali (Josh. 19:36). Jabin's northern allies are the cities of Madon, Shimron, Achshaph, as well as other unnamed cities associated with six peoples (Canaanites, Amorites, Hittites, Perizzites, Jebusites, and Hivites; Josh. 11:3). This northern alliance appears to be broader and more expansive than the southern one, and the text describes their forces as numerous as the "sand of the sea" (Josh. 11:4), a phrase used elsewhere in the Hebrew Bible to describe both the population of the nation of Israel (Gen. 32:12; 2 Sam. 17:11; 1 Kgs. 4:20, 29; Isa. 10:22; Jer. 33:22; Hos. 1:10) and that of their opponents in battle (Judg. 7:12; 1 Sam. 13:5).

29. Ibid., based on NIV.

Before the battle against this northern coalition, YHWH gives his typical pep talk to Joshua ("Don't fear . . . I'll give them into your hands"), but this time he gives them a few more details about what they are supposed to do to their opponents (hamstring their horses and burn their chariots), which is exactly what Joshua and the Israelites eventually do. Joshua's forces proceeded to capture Hazor, kill their king, and destroy all their inhabitants, but they preserved the livestock. The text emphasizes three times that Joshua and the Israelites were completely faithful to Moses' command to totally wipe out the Canaanite residents of the land (Josh. 11:12, 14, 15).

Before the summaries of conquered kings in Joshua 12, the next section of Joshua 11 summarizes geographically the conquered lands, speaking generally of Joshua killing kings, making war, wiping out peoples, and establishing peace with none except the Gibeonites (Josh. 11:16-19). In the midst of these summaries, the extermination of the Anakim is curiously tacked on (Josh. 11:21-22). In language reminiscent of the plagues in Egypt (e.g., Exod. 4:14; 7:3; 8:15; 9:12; 10:1; 14:8), the text informs us that YHWH hardened the hearts of the Canaanites so that they attacked Israel in battle because he wanted them to be wiped out (Josh. 11:20). A final concluding notice records that Joshua took the land, that he gave it to Israel as an inheritance (to be divided up in the next section), and that the land finally had rest from war (Josh. 11:23).

5.2.6. Summary of Conquered Kings (Joshua 12)

Before detailing the unconquered lands in Joshua 13, a terse list of conquered kings is recorded in Joshua 12. The list can be divided into two sections: the kings conquered by Moses first (Josh. 12:1-6), and the kings conquered by Joshua second (12:7-24). While one might expect these lists to be similar, they are quite different.

The first list includes the conquests on the east side of the Jordan recorded in the Pentateuch (Num. 21:21-35; Deut. 2:26—3:11) while Moses was still alive, and the second list includes conquests on the west side of the Jordan recorded in the book of Joshua (chapters 6—11). Moses' list includes only two rulers, while Joshua's includes thirty-one. Moses' list mentions the two rulers by name (Sihon and Og), but Joshua's list only mentions the cities that were ruled over.

Figure 2.8: Ruins of a Canaanite temple at Hazor. Photograph by user Mboesch at Commons.wikimedia.org.

Both lists provide geographic details, but in the second list this information is given before the rulers are mentioned. After the geographic details, Joshua's conquests record is highly formulaic, stating merely "the king of" then mentioning each city, then including a tally, even though the number in each instance is always "one." Joshua's list at the end informs readers that there were thirty-one rulers conquered (Josh. 12:24). Joshua's list appears to be in the same order as the conquests took place in the book, beginning with Jericho and Ai, moving to the southern cities (e.g., Jerusalem, Hebron), then concluding with the Northern cities (e.g., Hazor).

5.3. The Allotment of the Tribes (Joshua 13—21)

5.3.1. Unconquered Lands (Josh. 13:1–7)

The tone of the book of Joshua makes an abrupt shift in chapter 13, moving from narratives reporting espionage, supernatural assistance, religious ceremonies, and conquest battles, to lists of cities, tribal allotments, and geographic borders (see also 2.5, 2.6 above). For readers bothered by bloody battles of total annihilation, the shift may be perceived positively, but for readers bored by detailed descriptions of towns and territories, this next section probably won't hold their attention. However, for Israelites this section would have been the vital climax to a long story of their final settlement into their land. YHWH plays a less active role in this section, no longer fighting for Israel and speaking rarely to Joshua, only at the very beginning (Josh. 13:1–7), and toward the end before the designation of the cities of refuge (20:1). While YHWH seems silent, the reader may presume he was understood to be divinely directing the tribal allotment process.

The extended tribal allotment section begins with a speech from YHWH to Joshua listing the areas of the land that Joshua had been unable to conquer (see 2.6 above). Before describing these unconquered locations, YHWH informs Joshua that he is "old and advanced in years" (Josh. 13:1), an assessment that is repeated by Joshua himself at the beginning of one of his final speeches near the end of the book (23:1), which could suggest that little time transpired between these two notices, or that he was remarkably well-preserved when he gave his final speeches, or that the long section from Joshua 13—23 is not meant to be viewed in chronological order. In any case, the fact that Joshua is old means he won't be leading any more military engagements, and that these unconquered lands may not be taken any time soon.

Among the unconquered regions are various peoples and locations in the southern, middle, and northern regions of Canaan, but perhaps the most interesting group mentioned are the Philistines (Josh. 13:2, 3). While it's difficult to be certain, the Philistines (sometimes called "the Sea Peoples") are thought to have arrived in Canaan from the region of the Aegean Sea around 1200 BCE, which makes this reference problematic, depending upon when one dates the conquest. The Philistines are also mentioned in the Pentateuch (which is even more problematic; Gen. 10:14; 21:32, 34; 26:1–18; Exod. 13:17; 23:31), but these references are their first ones in Joshua. They were a union of five cities (a "pentapolis") consisting of Gaza, Ashdod, Askelon, Gath, and Ekron. They would continue to be Israel's rivals during the judgeships of Shamgar, Samson, and Samuel (Judg. 3:31; 13—16; 1 Samuel 4—7) and during the reigns of Saul and David (1 Samuel 13—2 Samuel 23).

YHWH informs Joshua that he himself will drive out these other peoples (since they couldn't) and that Joshua should divide up the conquered land on the west side of the Jordan for the nine-and-a-half tribes (all except the Transjordan tribes: see the next section).

5.3.2. Overview of the Tribes East of the Jordan (Josh. 13:8–14)

While Joseph was certainly one of Jacob's most famous sons (he was the first son of Jacob's favorite wife Rachel), one rarely hears of the "tribe of Joseph" since it is only mentioned a few places in Scripture (Num. 13:11; 36:5; Josh. 17:14, 16; 18:11). Joseph's "tribe" is divided between his two sons, his older son, Manasseh, and his younger son, Ephraim (Gen. 41:51–52). To make matters more complicated, Manasseh, which is technically a half-tribe already, is divided again into two halves, one half that settles on the west side of the Jordan, and one half that settles on the east side. At this point, Manasseh's eastern half-tribe (it could be called a quarter-tribe—isn't that what we usually call a half of a half?—but this designation probably wouldn't catch on) receive their tribal allotment, along with their fellow Transjordan tribes, Reuben and Gad. These Transjordan allotments have already been mentioned twice previously in the Pentateuch (Num. 32; Deut. 2:26—3:17), and they are described twice in this chapter, first in brief overview (Josh. 13:8–13), then in a more detailed recording by tribe, from south to north: Reuben (Josh. 13:15–23), Gad (13:24–28), Eastern Manasseh (13:29–31).

Sidebar 2.6: The Tribes of Israel

Jacob was the grandson of Abraham, and son of Isaac, and was given the new name "Israel" after a divine wrestling encounter (Gen. 32:28). Jacob had twelve sons, six by his wife Leah (Reuben, Simeon, Levi, Judah, Issachar, and Zebulun), two by his wife Rachel (Joseph and Benjamin), two by Rachel's concubine Bilhah (Dan and Naphtali), and two by Leah's concubine Zilpah (Gad and Asher). During Israel's time in Egypt, the descendants of Jacob's twelve sons grew into twelve tribes. In the Historical books, when the text mentions the name of one of Jacob's sons, it usually refers to the tribe, and not their eponymous ancestor.

5.3.3. Reuben (Josh. 13:15–23)

The description of the tribal allotment for Reuben is the first for the twelve tribes in this section.[30] Why begin with Reuben? Both the geographical descriptions for the eastern Transjordan tribes in Joshua

13 and the descriptions for the western tribes in the following chapters begin in the south and generally move north. It therefore makes sense that the text begins with Reuben, the southernmost tribe on the eastern side of the Jordan. But Reuben was also Jacob's oldest son, so one wonders if primogeniture was also a factor (although birth order doesn't appear to play a role elsewhere in these lists). Jacob had twelve sons by four women, two wives, Leah and Rachel, and two concubines, Bilhah and Zilpah (Gen. 29:31—30:24; 35:16–18).

The description of the allotment for Reuben begins with the southern border, the river Arnon, and then moves north through territory which at later points in Israel's history will belong either to Moab or Ammon, including the cities Aroer, Dibon, Medeba, and Heshbon. To the north will lie the allotment of Gad, and to the west will lie the Jordan River and, although it's not mentioned, the Dead Sea (Josh. 13:15–23).

5.3.4. Gad (Josh. 13:24-28)

The allotment to Gad (Gad was Jacob's first son by the concubine Zilpah) is bordered on the south by Reuben, and includes territory later occupied by the Ammonites and the expansive land of Gilead, including the cities of Jazer and Succoth. Both the allotments of Gad and Reuben include area previously ruled by Sihon, king of the Amorites (Josh. 13:21, 27; Num. 21:21–31). Gad has a long western border along the Jordan River. The northern border of Gad goes east from the southern tip of the Sea of Chinnereth (the Sea of Galilee), which will also be the southern border of eastern Manasseh.

5.3.5. Eastern Manasseh (Josh. 13:29-33)

The allotment of eastern Manasseh included land that had belonged to Og, king of Bashan (Num. 21:33–35), and later would belong to Syria (also called Aram). This region, which, in addition to Bashan, included the northern portion of Gilead, extended east of the Sea of Chinnereth. After this third allotment the text includes a brief notice stating these are inheritances that Moses had previously allotted in the plains of Moab (Num. 32:33).

Bookending these detailed territorial boundaries of the Transjordan tribes are two comments informing readers that the tribe of Levi

---

30. For a helpful table graphically representing all the tribal allotments, see Howard 1998, 316.

(Leah's third son) would receive no tribal inheritance from Moses (Josh. 13:14, 33), despite the fact that it was Moses' own tribe (Exod. 2:1–10). However, the text will later record the cities allotted to the Levites (Joshua 21). To compensate them for this lack, they are to inherit fire offerings (Josh. 13:14) and YHWH himself (Josh. 13:14, 33; Num. 18:20; Deut. 18:2).

5.3.6. Overview of the Tribes West of the Jordan (Josh. 14:1–5)

The section describing the tribal allotments for the nine-and-a-half tribes on the west side of the Jordan begins with an overview that both looks back to what has already occurred and looks forward to what will soon happen (Josh. 14:1–5). As was described in the previous chapter, Moses had already given the Transjordan tribes their allotment. As will be described in the following chapters, the territories will be determined by lot, Joseph's descendants will receive two separate tribal allotments (Manasseh and Ephraim), and the Levites will not receive an inheritance but towns instead (see Joshua 21).

5.3.7. Judah (Josh. 14:6—15:63)

The eastern allotments begin with the tribe of Judah, who was the fourth son of Leah. This territory is also on the southern end of Israel's border. But before describing the territory for the entire tribe, Judah's oldest remaining member, Caleb, is singled out, presumably since he was one of two spies who, along with Joshua, were confident that the people could conquer the land forty years before (Num. 13:30—14:9). Caleb, now eighty-five years old and apparently as strong as ever, doesn't need to remind Joshua of what happened—but he does anyway (Josh. 14:7–12). Moses had promised to reward Caleb for his faithful report by Moses. Joshua then blesses his old espionage partner and gives him the important southern city of Hebron (Josh. 14:13–14), which was wiped out at the end of the battle against the southern coalition (10:36–37).

The allotment for the rest of Judah is next described (Josh. 15:1–12). Their southern border will be Edom and the wilderness of Zin. Their eastern border will be the Dead Sea (called the Salt Sea in the text). Their northern border cuts west from the northern tip of the Dead Sea past Jerusalem, which will be the southern borders of Benjamin and Dan. Their western border will be the Mediterranean Sea (called the

Great Sea), although much of this coastal territory will be controlled by the Philistines (Josh. 13:3–4).

Before recording Judah's cities, a short description of Caleb's occupation of his allotment is included (Josh. 15:13–19), which includes the tale of how Caleb's nephew Othniel won the hand of Caleb's daughter Achsah for capturing the fortified city of Kirath-sepher (a story repeated in Judg. 1:11–15).

While many of the tribal descriptions include lists of cities, none approach the length of Judah's city list, with forty-three verses recording over a hundred locations (Josh. 15:20–62). Notable cities from this list include Beer-sheba, Jarmuth, Libnah, Keilah, En-gedi, and three Philistine cities (Ekron, Ashdod, and Gaza). Jerusalem is noticeably missing from this list, because Judah couldn't drive out the Jebusite residents of that city (Josh. 15:63). Similar statements are made later about Canaanites not being driven out by Ephraim (Josh. 16:10) or by Manasseh (Josh. 16:12). Later we'll discover that the allotment for Simeon is situated within Judah's tribal territory (Josh. 19:1–9).

5.3.8. Ephraim (Joshua 16)

In a brief overview before describing the next two tribal allotments, the text includes a short notice that the land along the west bank of the Jordan was given to the descendants of Joseph (Josh. 16:1–4). The tribal allotment of Ephraim, Joseph's younger son, was smaller than Judah's (Josh. 16:5–10). Ephraim's territory was fully surrounded by other Israelite tribes (as were the allotments for Simeon, Benjamin, Zebulun, and Issachar). Ephraim was bordered to the east by the Jordan River (with Gad across the river). Dan was to their west, wrapping around to the south, and the rest of their southern border was Benjamin. To the north was the western section of Manasseh. The text doesn't include a city list for Ephraim. Toward the end of the monarchy, after the first deportation by Tiglath-pileser III of Assyria (733 BCE; 2 Kgs. 16:29; see also Table 5.6 in chapter 5), all that remained of the northern kingdom was essentially the tribal allotment of Ephraim.

5.3.9. Western Manasseh (Joshua 17)

Before describing Manasseh's allotment, the text needs to bring closure to the dilemma of one of Manasseh's descendants, Zelophehad, who had five daughters (Mahlah, Noah, Hoglah, Milcah, and Tirzah), but no sons (Josh. 17:3). Since the family inheritance was normally passed down through sons, the daughters of Zelophehad had requested that they receive their father's inheritance, so his name would not be wiped out, and Moses, with divine approval, had agreed (Num. 27:17). These daughters now remind Joshua and the leaders of this agreement, and they are granted an inheritance (Josh. 17:4).

The text then describes Manasseh's border. To the south was Ephraim (along the river Kanah), to the west the Mediterranean Sea, to the north the tribes of Asher, Zebulun, and Issachar, and to the east the River Jordan.

Manasseh's section ends with a minor dispute, as "the tribe of Joseph" (a combination of Ephraim and Manasseh) complains that their allotment is too small since they are a numerous people, and their territory includes hills, forests, and Canaanites with iron chariots (Josh. 17:14–16). Joshua responds by affirming them for their greatness, and displaying confidence in their ability to clear the forests and drive out the Canaanites (Josh. 17:17–18). His affirmation appears to resolve their complaint satisfactorily since they no longer press the issue.

5.3.10. The Seven Remaining Allotments (Josh. 18:1–10)

The five more significant tribes now have their allotments (Reuben, Gad, all of Manasseh, Judah, and Ephraim). After rebuking the people for being slackers when it comes to taking possession of the rest of the land, Joshua comes up with a plan for dividing up the tribal allotments between the remaining seven tribes (Benjamin, Simeon, Zebulun, Issachar, Asher, Naphtali, and Dan). Joshua sends out three scouts from each of these seven tribes into the rest of the land and together they will divide it into seven comparable portions, which will then be apportioned by lot before their God (Josh. 18:1–10). The textual descriptions for these final seven allotments will be briefer and more uniform than those of the previous five.

5.3.11. Benjamin (Josh. 18:11–28)

The tribe of Benjamin, who was Rachel's second son, was chosen first. Their territory was to lie between the Jordan River to the east, the tribe of Dan to the west, the tribe of Judah to the south and the tribe of Joseph (specifically, Ephraim) to the north. With short borders on the east and west, and long borders to the north and south, Benjamin appears to be mainly surrounded, almost "protected," by the tribes of Joseph and Judah, which curiously echoes the situation of their ancestors in Egypt as Judah and Joseph protected their youngest brother Benjamin (Gen. 43:34–44:34). Notable cities in Benjamin include Jericho, Gibeon, and Jebus (also called Jerusalem, which won't be captured for a while; 2 Sam. 5:6–9). The description of Benjamin's tribal allotment is much longer than the remaining six.

5.3.12. Simeon (Josh. 19:1–9)

Simeon, the second son of Leah, was chosen second by lot, and since Judah's territory was apparently too large, Simon's tribal allotment would fall with the tribal allotment of Judah (see also Joshua 15). Notable cities in Simeon included Beer-sheba, Hormah, and Ziklag.

5.3.13. Zebulun (Josh. 19:10–16)

Zebulun, the sixth son of Leah, was the third lot chosen, and the tribe's allotment would be surrounded by several of the other minor tribes in the north. It was bordered to the south-west by Manasseh, the south-east by Issachar, the north-east by Naphtali, and the north-west by Asher. None of Zebulun's cities are particularly remarkable. The Bethlehem mentioned is not the one most people are familiar with as the birthplace of David and Jesus. This Bethlehem's only claim to fame is that it would become the death-place of the minor judge Ibzan (Judg. 12:8–10).

5.3.14. Issachar (Josh. 19:17–23)

Issachar, the fifth son of Leah, was chosen fourth by lot. The tribe's inheritance was bordered by Manasseh to the south, the Jordan River (and Gad) to the east, Naphtali to the north, and Zebulun to the northwest. Perhaps the most notable city among their list is Jezreel, in the Jezreel valley. Jezreel was the location of one of Ahab's palaces, Naboth's vineyard, Jehu's bloody coup, and Jezebel's gruesome execution (1 Kgs. 18:45–46; 21:1, 23; 2 Kgs. 9:15–10:11; Hos. 1:4–5, 11).

5.3.15. Asher (Josh. 19:24–31)

Asher, the second son of the concubine Zilpah, was chosen fifth. Asher's inheritance is a long, narrow coastal territory along the Mediterranean Sea to the far north, bordered by Manasseh to the south, Zebulun to the south-east, and Naphtali to the east. During most of the monarchical period, this territory would be controlled by the Phoenicians. Notable cities in Asher include Tyre and "Greater Sidon," as well as Mount Carmel, the scene of Elijah's famous encounter with the prophets of Baal (1 Kgs. 18:19–20).

5.3.16. Naphtali (Josh. 19:32–39)

Naphtali, the second son of the concubine Bilhah, was chosen sixth. Naphtali's territory was long and thin, stretching north-south, with long borders to the west with Asher and to the east the Jordan River (and Manasseh), and eventually Dan to the north-east. To the south-west of Naphtali lies Zebulun, to the south, Issachar, and to the south-east, the Sea of Chinnereth (Galilee). Notable cities in Naphtali include Chinnereth, Hazor (burned in Josh. 11:11), and Kedesh. Kedesh was a city of refuge (Josh. 20:7), and a city of the Levites (Josh. 21:32). Much of Naphtali, including Kedesh and Hazor, was captured by Tiglath-pileser III of Assyria in 733 BCE (2 Kgs. 15:29).

5.3.17. Dan (Josh. 19:40–48)

Dan, the first son of Bilhah, was chosen last. The tribe of Dan was unable to hold on to their original allotment, which was to the north of Judah, west of Benjamin and Ephraim, south of Manasseh, with a western border of the Mediterranean Sea. While other tribes were unable to drive out the Canaanites in their territories (Josh. 15:63; 16:10; 17:12), the Danites were unique in that they moved to a completely new area, to the far north (between Naphtali and eastern Manasseh), and captured Leshem, which they renamed Dan, after their eponymous ancestor (this conquest is also re-told in Judg. 18:1, 27–29). The first ruler of the divided northern kingdom, Jeroboam I, erected two golden calves, one at Bethel in the far south and one at Dan in the far north (1 Kgs. 12:28–30) and these alternative worship locations were severely condemned throughout the book of Kings (e.g., 1 Kgs. 15:26, 34; 16:26).

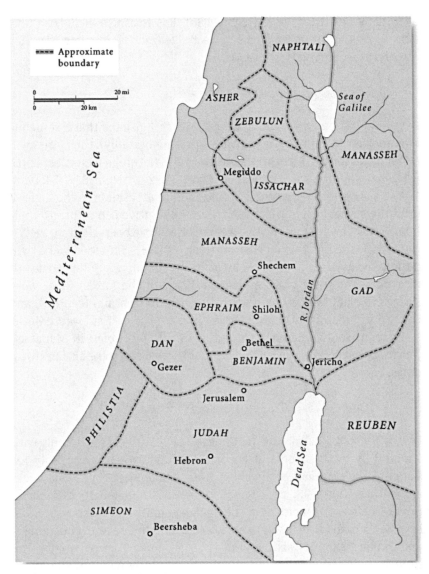

Figure 2.9: Twelve Tribes of Israel.

5.3.18. Joshua (Josh. 19:1–51)

Just as the territorial allotments west of the Jordan began with Caleb (Josh. 14:6–15), the faithful spy, so they end with **Joshua,** the faithful spy, who received an inheritance, the city of Timnath-serah in the hill country of his own tribe, Ephraim (Josh. 19:49–50). Joshua would eventually be buried there (Josh. 24:30). The text also includes a final notice that Joshua and the priest Eleazar were now finished distributing the land (Josh. 19:51).

5.3.19. Cities of Refuge (Joshua 20)

In several passages in the Pentateuch, Moses legislated that if someone kills another person accidentally (not pre-meditatedly), then cities will be set aside for the killer to flee to and receive refuge from the people who may want to exact vengeance (Exod. 21:12–14; Num. 35:9–34; Deut. 19:1–13). These cities of refuge would then grant asylum to the fugitive until the current high priest dies; then the fugitive can return to their home city. Now that all the tribal territories have been allotted, YHWH reminds Joshua of this legislation (Josh. 20:1–6). Six cities were then designated as cities of refugee, listed in the text in a counter-clockwise direction. The three cities on the west side of the Jordan River were Kedesh in Naphtali (in the north), Shechem in Ephraim (central), and Hebron in Judah (south). The three cities on the east side were Bezer in Reuben (south), Ramoth in Gad (central), and Golan in Manasseh (north; see also Deut. 4:41–43). All six of these cities were also Levitical cities.

5.3.20. Cities of Levi (Joshua 21)

Levi was Leah's third son. In Genesis, Levi was cursed (along with Simeon) by Jacob to be scattered throughout Israel, presumably for slaughtering the men of Shechem (Gen. 34:25–31; 49:5–7). One could argue that their lack of a tribal allotment is linked to this curse. However, after the incident of the golden calf, it was Moses' own tribe, Levi, who rushed to his side and meted out the severe punishment upon their fellow Israelites, and thus ordained themselves for the service of YHWH (Exod. 32:26–29). As the priestly tribe for the entire nation, it makes sense that they are spread out throughout the land. Forty-eight cities are given to the tribe of Levi, basically four per tribe (Naphtali only contributes three, but Judah and Simeon together contribute nine). The cities were divided among Levi's three sons: Kohath, Gershon, and Merari (Gen. 46:11). There are four sets of cities, since two sets go to the descendants of Kohath, one for the priestly side of the family associated with Aaron, and one for the non-priestly side of the family. As has often been the case thus far in Joshua, an overview is first given (Josh. 21:4–8), before a detailed description is provided (Josh. 21:9–40), then a brief notice is included which summarizes that these forty-eight cities and their pasture lands were allotted to the Levites (Josh. 21:41–42). An additionally summary is then tacked on which brings closure to the tribal allotment, stating that YHWH had given them rest, and (hyperbolically) that none of their enemies were able to withstand them.

Sidebar 2.7: A Brief History of the Land of Israel

In 1948, by UN mandate, Israel became an autonomous nation for the first time in over two millennia. As we trace the history of Israel back over the past two thousand years, the land has been ruled by Western Europeans, Ottomans, Mamluks, Crusaders, Arabs, and Romans. But the fascinating story of the land of Israel is also a major theme of the Hebrew Bible. (Biblically, the proper noun "Israel" has many referents: a person, an ethnic people, a nation, the united monarchy, or the divided northern kingdom.) One can summarize the biblical account of the land of Israel, paraphrasing from the book of Job, as "God gives and God takes away" (Job 1:21).

According to Genesis, God gave the land to Abraham and his family (Gen. 15:18), but then God sent the descendants of Abraham, Isaac, and Jacob (who was renamed Israel) to Egypt (Gen. 45:8; 50:20). God brought the descendants of Israel out of Egypt and sent them toward the land of Canaan (Exod. 3:8). But God delayed their arrival in the promised land by forty years (Num. 14:33–34). During the period when Israel was ruled by judges and kings, when they were unfaithful or idolatrous God gave them into the hands of their enemies, but when they cried out for help, he delivered them (Judg. 2:11–23). Because Israel's kings and people were disobedient and rebellious, God allowed Assyria to conquer and deport the northern kingdom of Israel in 733 and 722 BCE (2 Kgs. 15:29; 17:5–6) and allowed Babylon to conquer and deport the southern kingdom of Judah in 597, 587, and 582 BCE (2 Kgs. 24–25; Jer. 52; see also Table 5.6). According to Chronicles, God prompted Cyrus of Persia to allow the Israelite exiles to return to their land and rebuild their temple in 538 BCE (2 Chr. 36:22–23). During what is sometimes called the Second Temple period (or the intertestamental period), the people of Judea were ruled by a series of empires—the Persians, the Greeks, and finally the Romans—with only about a century of Jewish independence (the Hasmonean dynasty, 166–63 BCE).

5.4. The Speeches of the Leaders (Joshua 22—24)

5.4.1. Eastern Tribes' Return and the Witness Altar (Joshua 22)

After preparing for battle, conquering the land, and dividing up the land, the final three chapters of the book are dominated by speeches. Joshua 22 includes five speeches, three long and two short. In the *first* speech (Josh. 22:2–5), Joshua addresses the Transjordan tribes (Reuben, Gad, and eastern Manasseh). He praises them for their faithful service to fight alongside their fellow countrymen on the western side of the Jordan. He releases them from their obligation so they can return to their family across the Jordan. Using classic Deuteronomistic language (see 2.3 above), he exhorts them to observe the law of Moses, to love YHWH, and to walk in his ways.

The *second* speech of the chapter is another from Joshua, as he gives the departing Transjordan tribes a short farewell blessing. They then set up an altar near the Jordan, on the western bank, which will soon provoke a serious crisis between the eastern and western tribes (Josh. 22:6–10; see Sidebar 2.5, "Symbolic Objects in Joshua" above).

The *third* speech of the chapter is a response from the western tribes after hearing about the eastern tribes' altar. First they prepared to attack, but they also sent Phinehas and ten chiefs (one from each tribe, including western Manasseh) who delivered a long speech of rebuke and warning to the eastern tribes (Josh. 22:16–20). The law forbade the Israelites from offering sacrifices at locations other than the tabernacle (Lev. 17:8–9). Because of their altar, the western tribes accuse the eastern tribes of turning away from YHWH, following in the sinful traditions of Peor and Achan. (As Numbers told the story, at Peor, the Israelites fell into serious idolatry, worshipping Baal until a plague ensured, which was only stopped by the dramatic actions of Phinehas [Num. 25:1–18], who is present in this narrative. The sin of Achan took place more recently, when he kept some of the devoted things for himself leading to their initial loss at Ai [Josh. 7].)

The *fourth* speech, the longest of the chapter, is the eastern tribes' response to the western tribes' rebuke (Josh. 22:22–29). They inform the western leaders that they weren't acting in rebellion or idolatry. The altar wouldn't be used for offerings or sacrifices but was supposed to serve as a witness to future generations, specifically to Israelites on the western side of the Jordan, that the Israelites on the eastern side worship the same God as they do, YHWH.

The *fifth* speech brings closure to the crisis as the priest Phinehas delivers a short address to the eastern tribes, affirming them for their response (Josh. 22:31). The western leadership delegation then returns home and gives a report to the rest of their people that conflict has been avoided. The narrative concludes with a brief note that the eastern tribes named the altar "Witness." (While most English translations include it twice, the word "witness," *'ēd*, is only present once in the second half of the verse; Josh. 22:34.)

5.4.2 Joshua's Exhortation (Joshua 23)

The final two chapters of Joshua the book focus on the final two speeches of Joshua the leader. He speaks in both addresses to all Israel and the text includes identical lists of leaders who were present: elders, heads, judges, and officers (see 4.6, "Leadership"). Both of the speeches include Deuteronomistic elements and can be characterized as hortatory, as Joshua exhorts the people to serve YHWH faithfully. Joshua's valedictory addresses are similar in style and tone to those of Israel's other significant leaders: Moses, Samuel, and David (Deut. 31:1–6; 32–33; 1 Sam. 12:1–25; 2 Sam. 23:1–7).

The text reports that Joshua, the military leader, has finally become an old man, and he begins and ends his penultimate speech by informing the people of this fact (Josh. 23:2, 14). Joshua's speech reviews recent events, and describes possible future scenarios, both good and bad. He repeats several important themes, motivating his audience with both a "carrot" and a "stick." YHWH has fought for them in the past and will continue to do so in the future if they remain faithful to YHWH and serve him (Josh. 23:3, 5, 9, 10). However, if they associate with the Canaanite people of the land by marrying them and worshipping their gods, then YHWH will not drive them out and he will judge his own people until they perish in the land (Josh. 23:7, 12–13, 16). Unlike Joshua's next speech, the people make no response this time.

5.4.3. The Covenant Renewal (Joshua 24)

In Joshua's final address to the people and leaders of Israel, he begins dramatically with the extended prophetic messenger formula, "Thus says YHWH, the God of Israel . . ." (Josh. 24:2), which only appears in one other context in Joshua, and there it is spoken by YHWH himself

(Josh. 7:13). Typically prophets began their oracles with this preamble (e.g., Judg. 6:8; 2 Sam. 12:7; Isa. 37:21; Jer. 11:3; 13:12), or a shorter version, "Thus says YHWH . . ." (e.g., 2 Sam. 7:5; 1 Kgs. 11:31; Isa. 7:7). Perhaps most relevant for Joshua, Moses used it the first time he spoke with Pharaoh (Exod. 5:1); thus the phrase bookends the exodus and the conquest narratives. While Joshua spoke in the first-person voice in the previous speech (Joshua 23), in this second speech of Joshua the first-person voice is that of YHWH initially.

YHWH (speaking through Joshua) immediately launches into a review not just of events from the book of Joshua as he did in his previous speech, but of events from the Pentateuch, beginning with Terah, Abraham, and Nahor. The reference to Abraham's brother Nahor is curious since he is only mentioned in one other context outside of Genesis (1 Chr. 1:26), but, as we keep reading this speech, YHWH appears to be making a point about brothers. He mentions Jacob and his brother Esau, as well as Moses and his brother Aaron. He describes how YHWH sent their ancestors to Egypt, but doesn't mention any of Jacob's sons by name or, specifically, Joseph. Perhaps YHWH is trying to emphasize how "brothers" should get along, since he never mentions any of the fraternal conflicts that dominate the book of Genesis. YHWH speaks of the plagues, the Red Sea, and their long time in the wilderness, but nothing about why they spent so much time there. YHWH recalls Balaam and Balak (Numbers 22–24), and then briefly recites the nations they defeated after crossing the Jordan.

As the speech shifts from review to exhortation, Joshua begins to speak in first-person language, and YHWH is spoken about in the third person: "Now therefore fear YHWH" (Josh. 24:14). Joshua uses a variety of approaches to compel his audience to serve YHWH. He *reviews* their story (Josh. 24:2-13). He gives a direct *command* to obey (Josh. 24:14). He presents them with a *choice* whom to serve (24:15a). He cites his own *example* (Josh. 24:15b). He uses *reverse psychology* ("You can't serve YHWH") when the people make what appears to be a superficial response to his first command ("Far be it from us that we should forsake YHWH . . ."; Josh. 24:16–19). After the people make a more sober commitment ("No, we will serve YHWH"), he tells them to put away their idols, then sets up a witness stone which will permanently testify to the covenant they made with their God (Josh. 24:21–27).

The book of Joshua concludes with several notices that bring closure to the story of the conquest (Josh. 24:29–33). It briefly reports the deaths of Joshua and Eleazer, the son of Aaron, and their burials in their respective inheritances. It records that Joseph's bones were also buried (at Shechem), as he had requested centuries earlier (Gen. 50:25–26). The text notes optimistically (perhaps overly so) that Israel faithfully served YHWH during Joshua's life, but this rosy perspective on Israel's behavior will soon darken as one begins to read the book of Judges, which narrates the struggles that the Israelites faced attempting to hold onto the land that they had conquered in Joshua.

Bibliography

Albright, William F. 1939. "The Israelite Conquest of Canaan in Light of Archaeology." *Bulletin of the American Schools of Oriental Research* 74: 11–23.

Alt, Albrecht. 1966. *Essays on Old Testament History and Religions*. Oxford: Blackwell.

Alter, Robert. 2013. *Ancient Israel: The Former Prophets: Joshua, Judges, Samuel, and Kings: A Translation with Commentary*. New York: Norton & Company.

Bright, John. 1981. *A History of Israel*. Philadelphia, Westminster.

Copan, Paul. 2011. *Is God a Moral Monster: Making Sense of the Old Testament God*. Grand Rapids: Baker.

Copan, Paul and Matt Flannagan. 2014. *Did God Really Command Genocide? Coming to Terms with the Justice of God*. Grand Rapids: Baker.

Davies, Philip R. 1992. *In Search of Ancient Israel*. Sheffield: Sheffield Academic Press.

Dever, William G. 2003. *Who Were the Early Israelites and Where Did They Come From?* Grand Rapids: Eerdmans.

Gottwald, Norman. 1979. *The Tribes of Israel: A Sociology of the Religion of Liberated Israel, 1250-1050 BCE*. Maryknoll, NY: Orbis.

Habel, Norman. 1965. "The Form and Significance of Call Narratives." *ZAW* 77: 297–323.

Hess, Richard. 1996. *Joshua: An Introduction and Commentary*. Downers Grove: InterVarsity Press.

Howard, David. 1998. *Joshua*. Nashville: Broadman & Holman.

Hubbard, David Allan. 1989. *Joel & Amos*. Downers Grove: InterVarsity.

Lamb, David T. 2011a. *God Behaving Badly: Is the God of the Old Testament Angry, Sexist and Racist?* Downers Grove: InterVarsity Press.

_____. 2011b. "How Do We Reconcile a Loving God with a God Who Commits Genocide?" *Relevant* 53 (September–October): 108–11.

_____. 2013. "Compassion and Wrath as Motivations for Divine

Warfare." In *Holy War in the Bible: Christian Morality and an Old Testament Problem*, edited by Heath Thomas, Jeremy Evans, and Paul Copan, 133–41. Downers Grove: InterVarsity Press.

_____. 2015. *Prostitutes and Polygamists: A Look at Love, Old Testament Style.* Grand Rapids: Zondervan.

Mendenhall, George E. 1962. "The Hebrew Conquest of Palestine." *BA* 25: 66–87.

Moran, William L. 1992. *The Amarna Letters.* Baltimore: Johns Hopkins University Press.

Nelson, Richard. 1997. *Joshua: A Commentary.* Louisville: Westminster John Knox.

Noth, Martin. 1943. Translated in 1981 by Jane Doull et al. *The Deuteronomistic History.* Sheffield: Sheffield Academic Press.

_____. 1960. Translated by Peter R. Ackroyd. *The History of Israel.* New York: Harper & Row.

Seibert, Eric. 2009. *Disturbing Divine Behavior: Troubling Old Testament Images of God.* Minneapolis: Fortress Press.

_____. 2012. *The Violence of Scripture: Overcoming the Old Testament's Troubling Legacy.* Minneapolis: Fortress Press.

Thompson, Thomas L. 1992. *Early History of the Israelite People from the Written and Archaeological Sources.* Leiden: Brill.

Wright, Christopher J. H. 2008. *The God I Don't Understand: Reflections on Tough Questions of Faith.* Grand Rapids: Zondervan.

Younger, K. Lawson. 1999. "Early Israel in Recent Biblical Scholarship." In *The Face of Old Testament Studies: A Survey of Contemporary Approaches*, 176–206. Grand Rapids: Baker.

3

Judges

1. Introduction

1.1. The Book of Heroes

The book of Judges could more accurately be called "The Book of Heroes," because it is more of a book of military exploits than one of judicial decisions. It records heroic deeds during the "Wild West" period of Israel's history, as the people continued to settle into the Promised Land, but there was yet no king to bring order from the chaos. These charismatic deliverers repeatedly rescued Israel from the surrounding nations that dominated them (Aram, Moab, Philistia, Canaan, Midian, and Ammon).

Judges records stories of underdogs overcoming obstacles to gain dramatic victories over oppressive foes. Left-handed Ehud killed obese Eglon of Moab, losing his blade in the king's rolls of fat and freeing his people in the process (Judg. 3:12–30). Jael, the tent-dwelling wife of Heber, lured Sisera of Canaan to sleep, then hammered a tent peg into his temple to kill the general, thus fulfilling Deborah's prophecy that a woman would get the glory for the victory (Judg. 4:17–22). Blind Samson pulled down the pillars of the temple of Dagon, not only destroying the building, but also killing thousands of Philistines in a kamikaze-esque suicide maneuver (Judg. 16:23–31).

Along the way, many of the book's heroic deliverers use unorthodox weapons to accomplish their feats. Shamgar used an oxgoad to kill six hundred Philistines (Judg. 3:31). Gideon used trumpets and jars to scatter the Midianites (Judg. 7:16–23). With the help of his big hair, Samson used the jawbone of a donkey to kill a thousand Philistines, as well as flaming foxes to torch their fields, groves, and vineyards (Judg. 15:5, 15–16; 16:17).

While some of these stories of unorthodox underdogs and wild weapon wielders have a comical tone to them, others are disturbingly dark, giving the book of Judges a more troubling tone, perhaps more so than any other book of the Bible. Abimelech, the son of Gideon, slaughters seventy of his own brothers in an attempt to rule over the nation (Judg. 9:5). Jephthah, the son of a prostitute, makes a foolish vow before battle which leads him to fulfill his vow by sacrificing his own daughter (Judg. 11:30–39). One of the final stories of the book illustrates the utter depravity of the nation as an unnamed Levite hands over his concubine to the wicked men of Gibeah who proceed to gang rape the abandoned woman to death (Judg. 19:22–30). Readers are left to ponder: how did a book like this make it into sacred Scripture?

1.2. The Name of the Book

While the two books surrounding it in the Hebrew canon (Joshua and Samuel) are each named after a dominant character, the book of Judges, like the book Kings, is named after the type of leaders who rule the people of Israel over the duration of the book. As one traces the evolution of the book's name, one finds little variation through the various versions. The English title "Judges" is based on the Latin Vulgate's *Iudices* (which means "judges"), which came from the Greek *kritai* (also, "judges"), which came from the Hebrew šōpĕṭim (you guessed it, "judges"). But, as we will soon see, the eponymous leaders of the book do more than just judge.

1.3. Role of the Judges

What does "judging" involve for the judges of Judges? While the charismatic leaders of the book of Judges are collectively referred to as "judges" (Judg. 2:16, 17, 18), no specific individual is called a "judge" (šōpĕṭ), except YHWH, whom Jephthah refers to as a "judge" in his message to the king of Ammon (Judg. 11:27). However, the title

"Judges" is still appropriate for the book since for nine judges the text describes their leadership over the nation using the verb "to judge" (šāpaṭ; Othniel, Deborah, Tola, Jair, Jephthah, Ibzan, Elon, Abdon, Samson; Judg. 3:10; 4:4; 10:2, 3; 12:7, 8, 11, 13; 15:20).

Figure 3.1: A page of the Book of Judges from the Aleppo Codex, copied in the tenth century by Aron ben Moses ben Asher.

While the book's title may not have varied, the judges themselves serve in a variety of roles. Not surprisingly for its pure entertainment value, the text focuses on the military exploits of these individuals over the surrounding oppressive nations. Thus the term *judge,* as it is described in the book, appears to refer primarily to a divinely appointed military deliverer (Judg. 2:16, 18). And yet, if we notice when each of these individuals is actually described as "judging," other aspects of their "judgeship" emerge beyond that of merely a charismatic hero. Deborah is unique as the only one who serves in the capacity that we might classically understand as "judge": she holds court under the palm tree named after her while the nation comes to her for judgment (Judg. 4:5). Whereas many judges appear to be like "guerilla commanders,"[1] Othniel is described like a military general going out to war, similar to how kings are described during the period of the monarchy (Judg. 3:10; 1 Sam. 8:20). Judges also serve in a prophetic role as spiritual leader and divine spokesperson for YHWH (Judg. 2:17; 4:4). While the text doesn't provide details, many judges serve as political leaders over the nation for extensive reigns involving many years (Judg. 10:2, 3; 12:7, 8, 11). Finally, for at least two of these individuals, part of what it means to be judge appears to involve being donkey-riding clan leaders (Judg. 10:4; 12:14). Thus, they were more than just judges.

1.4. Judges in the Canon

In the Hebrew canon, Judges is the second book of the **Former Prophets**, after Joshua and before the books of Samuel and Kings. Ruth, which follows Judges in English Bibles, is not included among the Prophetic books in the Hebrew Bible, but among the Writings. Within the Greek Septuagint, Ruth is positioned immediately after Judges, presumably because it is set in the time of the judges and it sets up the dynasty of David (Ruth 1:1; 4:18–21). Despite its location in the Former Prophets, within Judges only two individuals are called a "prophet" (*nābî'* or *nĕbî'â*), the judge Deborah and the anonymous individual who speaks to the nation before the call of Gideon (Judg. 4:4; 6:8). The prophetic voice of Judges is thus much quieter than it is in the latter books of the Former Prophets, particularly the book of Kings, where for long sections prophets dominate the narrative, most notably, Elijah and Elisha.

The scholarly designation for the four books making up the Former

---

1. Alter, 105.

Prophets is the **Deuteronomistic History**. More will be said about issues of redaction under composition below, but at this point we can say that the editorial work of the Deuteronomist redactors(s) appears to be more substantial in the books of Judges and Kings than it was in the books of Joshua and Samuel. In Judges, the Deuteronomist is thought to have shaped the book, giving it the cyclical framework characterized by theological explanations for the cycles of oppression and deliverance.

Just as Samuel and Kings are often linked as a history of the Israelite monarchy, **Joshua and Judges** are often linked as a history of Israel's early days in the Promised Land. The first verse of the book of Joshua informs readers that Moses is dead, and the first verse of Judges similarly declares that now Joshua is dead (Josh. 1:1; Judg. 1:1). Judges then proceeds to review key events from Joshua's life (e.g., his dismissal of the people to their inheritances, his lifetime of service), before recording another notice of Joshua's death that appears to be cut and pasted from the end of the book of Joshua (Josh. 24:29; Judg. 1:1; 2:6, 7, 8, 21, 23). While Moses also delivered the nation from oppression in Egypt, his primary biblical legacy is that of a law-giver. His successor Joshua, however, was known primarily as a military leader, and thus was more of a forerunner for the role of military deliverer played by the judges. Joshua and Judges also address the issue of how Israel became a nation in the land of Canaan. Joshua is often perceived as a sequence of successful conquests over the Canaanite inhabitants, while Judges is typically viewed as narrating a more gradual settlement into the land as Israel's neighbors are defeated over an extended period.

Unlike Samuel-Kings, which includes numerous individuals bridging the gap between books (e.g., David, Bathsheba, Joab, Solomon), there is no record of characters surviving from Judges into the book of Samuel, but four individuals in Samuel judge the nation before the monarchy is established, and other events from the book of Judges are recalled later, in the monarchical period. The priest Eli judged Israel for forty years; the prophet Samuel judged the nation "all the days of his life" (1 Sam. 4:18; 7:6, 15–17). Ironically, Samuel's act of establishing his corrupt sons Joel and Abijah as judges over Israel served as the catalyst for the establishment of a royal monarchy (1 Sam. 8:1–5). In Samuel's final address to the nation, he mentions not only Israel's defeated enemies mentioned in the book of Judges (the rulers of Canaan, Hazor, Philistia, and Moab), but also three of Israel's leaders during that period (Jerubbaal-Gideon, Bedan-Barak, and Jephthah: 1 Sam. 12:9–11). In the prophet Nathan's oracle to David promising an eternal royal dynasty, YHWH twice recalls the days of the judges (2 Sam. 7:7, 11). In his message from the front, Joab reminds David of the dangers of sieges by recalling that Gideon's son Abimelech was killed by a millstone thrown by a woman (Judg. 9:53; 2 Sam. 11:21). Toward the end of 2 Kings, the text includes a note that until Josiah's performance of the Passover, the feast hadn't been celebrated since the "days of the judges who judged Israel" (2 Kgs. 23:22).

Moving beyond the Former Prophets, the list of Israel's foreign oppressors in Psalm 83 recalls the book of Judges (Moab, Ammon, Philistia, Midian), and the psalm mentions several foreign defeated leaders by name: Sisera, Jabin, Oreb, Zeeb, Zebah, and Zalmunna (Ps. 83:9, 11). The gang rape of the Levite's concubine in Gibeah appears to be alluded to twice in the book of Hosea (9:9; 10:9). And finally, moving to the epistles of the New Testament, the book of Hebrews mentions four of the judges in its list of the heroes of faith: Gideon, Barak, Samson, and Jephthah (Heb. 11:32).

2. Literary Concerns

2.1. Structure of Judges

Before discussing the book's structure, we must acknowledge that breaking a piece of literature that lacks obvious divisions (verse and chapter numbers were added much later) into sections will always involve an element of subjectivity. However, most scholars believe the book of Judges can be divided easily into three sections. Here I include the standard titles (Introduction, Main Body, Appendix) along with my own slightly more creative subtitles.

1. **Introduction**: Conquest Reports of Success and Failure (1:1—3:6);
2. **Main Body**: Judge Stories of Apostasy and Deliverance (3:7—16:31);
3. **Appendix**: Stories of Idolatry, Rape, and Civil War in Kingless Israel (17:1—21:25).

While the standard titles "Main Body" and "Appendix" seem appropriate for their respective sections, the title "Introduction" for the first section may be misleading. By focusing on Joshua's death, the tribal allotments, and the Canaanite people of the land, the first chapter of Judges makes it clear that its primary concern is looking back to the book of Joshua, rather than setting up the book of Judges. The initial military reports state that the Israelites had not finished the conquest of the land, but except for one brief mention of the Philistines (Judg. 3:3), these reports completely ignore most of the oppressors who feature prominently in the remainder of book (Aram, Moab, Midian, and Ammon). One has to wait until the end of the second chapter to find material that serves an introductory purpose (Judg. 2:11–23). This cyclical overview fittingly introduces the Main Body of the book since it describes the cycles of apostasy and deliverance that characterize this long middle section: idolatry, oppression, petition, and salvation. The cyclical formulaic terminology that dominates the long middle of the book (see 2.4 below) is concentrated in this thirteen-verse overview (20%) but is absent from the remaining fifty-two verses (80%) of the Introduction.

The appendix does appear to be merely appended to the end of the book, and therefore *appendix* may be a more appropriate title than some of the others typically given to these final five chapters of the book (e.g., the Conclusion, Climax, Epilogue, or Finale). But the most fitting title for this final section should inform readers that these narratives merely describe a chaotic time of idolatry, rape, and civil war in Israel when there was no king. Not that the Introduction and the Appendix don't serve their ancient purposes well to open and bring closure, but if modern readers expect these sections to perform the roles that they've come to expect to introduce a book at the beginning and to conclude it at the end, they may be disappointed or confused.

Unlike the other historical books, Judges has no obvious overarching storyline unifying the three major sections of the book. While key individuals dominate the narrative of the books of Joshua (Joshua) and Samuel (Samuel, Saul, and David), the book of Judges is more like Kings. These two books respectively include extended narratives on major judges (e.g., Ehud, Gideon, and Samson) and major kings (e.g., Solomon, Jehu, and Josiah), interspersed with shorter notices on minor judges (e.g., Tola, Jair, and Ibzan) and minor kings (e.g., Abijam, Nadad, and Omri). In Judges, the cyclical narratives of the major judges therefore divide the long Main Body of the book into seven sections (Othniel, Ehud, Deborah, Gideon, Abimelech, Jephthah, and Samson).

2.2. Composition of Judges

The book of Judges, like most books of the Hebrew Bible, is written anonymously, and while the book includes phrases and language that yield clues about its possible setting, it is impossible to make definitive conclusions about its composition. The Babylonian Talmud attributes authorship of Judges to the prophet Samuel (B. Bat. 14b), but most scholars do not follow this rabbinical tradition which also attributes the book of Samuel to the prophet Samuel, despite his death in 1 Samuel 25.

Whereas the book of Joshua only covers a time period lasting half of the life of its eponymous military leader (40–50 years?), if one adds up the years chronologically, the book of Judges appears to cover a period of over four centuries. That suggests that whoever put the book together in its final form would have needed to have access to sources from a much earlier period. While we need not necessary assume the book is laid out in a strictly chronological manner, it's still reasonable to assume that the stories appearing later in the book would be set much closer in time to the setting of the book's composition than earlier ones.

What were these sources used to compose the book? It is difficult to say. Judges is the only one of Former Prophets with no references to other books that may have been used as a source (compare Josh. 10:13; 2 Sam. 1:18; 1 Kgs. 11:41; 14:19, 29). Most scholars assume that the Judge cycles were based on stories that were told in an oral fashion, as they include many elements which contribute to an entertaining tale: humor, irony, stories about underdogs, and graphic details.

One of the sources may have been the poetic Song of Deborah (Judg. 5:1–31), which, because of its style and archaic language, is thought to be one of the oldest texts in the Bible, perhaps written shortly after the event it describes (Robert Alter dates it to about 1100 BCE). The other examples of poetry in Judges (the parable of Jotham, and the riddle and song of Samson; Judg. 9:8–15; 14:14; 15:16) are much shorter, and are embedded into the surrounding story, while Deborah's song could be removed from the book without negatively affecting the narrative flow. Within the Former Prophets more broadly, poetry is not absent, but it is still unusual. The book of Joshua includes no longer poems, only the curse on Jericho (Josh. 6:26), and Kings includes just one long poetic oracle that is repeated in Isaiah (2 Kgs. 19:21–28; Isa. 37:22–29). Among these four books, Samuel includes the most poetry, numerous short poems and four long poems (1 Sam. 2:1–10; 15:22–23, 33; 18:7; 21:11; 29:5; 2 Sam. 1:19–27; 3:33–34; 22:2–51; 23:1–7).

Temporal parenthetical notices are scattered throughout Judges which suggest that the book was written much later than the original settings of the narratives. Two phrases in particular explicitly call to the reader's attention the time differential. The phrase "to this day" (*'ad hayôm hazeh*) appears seven times in the book (Judg. 1:21, 26; 6:24; 10:4; 15:19; 18:12; 19:30). The similar phrase "in those days" (*bayāmîm hāhem*) also appears seven times in the book, all of which are concentrated in the Appendix at the end (Judg. 17:6; 18:1 [2]; 19:1; 20:27, 28; 21:25). These two phrases, along with other language, are used to help the author's audience understand differences and similarities between the stories' context and the current one. Many of the changes involve new place names and within the book, six cities have new names and two regions are given names that have survived "to this day." Table 3.1 lists these renamed locations.

Table 3.1: Renamed Locations in Judges

Judges Reference	Former name	Later name
1:10	Kiriath-arba	Hebron
1:11	Kiriath-sepher	Debir
1:21; 19:10	Jebus	Jerusalem
1:23, 26 see Gen. 28:19	Luz or Bethel?	Luz or Bethel?
10:4	a region in Gilead*	Havvoth-jair
15:19	hollow place at Lehi*	Enkakkore
18:12	Kiriath-jearim	Mahaneh-dan
18:29	Laish	Dan

Similarly, if one were to read older texts recording the history of Asia Minor that mentioned Constantinople or Byzantium, an explanatory note may be included by a modern editor that those were the ancient names of modern Istanbul (which is really "nobody's business but the Turks").

Four references toward the end of the book inform the reader that during the period of the narrative there "was no king in Israel" (Judg. 17:6; 18:1; 19:1; 21:25). If one were to read Charles Dickens's *A Tale*

101

of Two Cities, a footnote stating "there was a king in France" during the book's initial historical setting (pre-Revolution) could be helpful (if one were woefully ignorant of European history). Other references in Judges provide general background which presumably would not have been known to a typical reader who was apparently far removed chronologically from some of the events described (Judg. 6:24; 18:1; 19:30).

In the repeated parenthetical phrase "to this day," the day is presumably meant to refer to the author's own context. So, what day is it? Again, it is impossible to be definitive, but the text does provide a few clues. Obviously, the author's context is sufficiently remote chronologically for these numerous parenthetical notices to be necessary. In terms of allusions to actual specific events, three comments can be made about the text.

First, when Jerusalem is mentioned in Judges, it is referred to both as Jerusalem (Judg. 1:7, 8, 21; 19:10) and Jebus (Judg. 19:10, 11), the later being the presumably older Canaanite name. The text states that the Jebusite residents have remained in the city "to this day" (Judg. 1:21), which could suggest that the day of the writing would come before David's conquest of the city when he made it his capital, approximately 1000 BCE (2 Sam. 5:6–9).

Second, the comment "in those days there was no king is Israel" (Judg. 17:6; 18:1; 19:1; 21:25) could suggest that the author was writing during the period of the Israelite monarchy, which survived from the anointing of Saul as first ruler over the nation about 1020 BCE (1 Sam. 10:1) until the destruction of Jerusalem in 587 BCE (2 Kings 25). However, if the writing took place during the exile (587–538 BCE), the author might still expect that readers would assume a king since they knew the monarchy had been in existence for many centuries of Israel's recent history.

Third, the descendants of a certain Jonathan remained as priests to the tribe of Dan until "the land went into captivity" (Judg. 18:30). The author would therefore need to be writing after this captivity took place. The five significant exiles in the history of Israel and Judah are listed in a table in chapter 5 (Table 5.6). The first of these five exiles (734) is probably the one being referred to, since Tiglath-pileser III's conquest included most of the territory of the northern kingdom, and the city of Dan was on the far northern end of Israel (2 Kgs. 15:29). Thus, we are left with clues about when the writing was meant to take place, but at this point in time the mystery of when Judges was actually written remains unsolved.

2.3. Deuteronomistic Redaction

Since a longer discussion of Deuteronomistic redaction was included in the introduction, here I will focus on issues specifically relevant to the book of Judges. Most scholars interested in Deuteronomistic redaction focus on the book of Kings because of its ultimate location in the Deuteronomistic History. However, one could argue that since the book of Judges shares many similarities to Kings—a longer time covered than Joshua and Samuel, a relatively consistent leadership model involving major and minor rulers (judges, kings), and a formulaic framework repeated throughout the book (judge cycles, regnal formulas)—it should warrant as much attention as Kings in scholarly discussions of redaction.

How did the Deuteronomist compose, edit, or shape Judges? We don't know, although it would appear that many scholars think otherwise. Scholars typically think a Deuteronomist (or perhaps a Deuteronomistic school) took the deliverer stories of the major judges, brought them together, composed material (perhaps the overview in Judg. 2:11–23), inserted other material concerning the minor judges, and added the cyclical framework with distinctive language and terminology (not necessarily in that order). It may have happened like that, but since the scholarly consensus on redaction has continued to evolve from one Deuteronomist (Noth), to two (Cross, Nelson) or three (Smend, Dietrich, Veijola), to a school of Deuteronomists, it is safe to assume that the evolution of consensus concerning the redaction of the book of Judges will continue.

One of the issues that scholars working on Judges typically address concerns the refrain, "in those days there was no king in Israel, everyone did what was right in his own eyes" (Judg. 17:6; 21:25). It is often assumed that this phrase supports the idea of a pro-monarchy Deuteronomist (perhaps writing during the time of righteous King Josiah; 2 Kings 22—23) since it seems to suggest that a king is the solution to the chaos of the time of the judges.

Three comments need to be made which undermine this theory. First, the phrase may be merely stating two independent ideas—just as there was spiritual and moral chaos during the monarchy, there was chaos during this pre-monarchic period of time—with no connotations of causality. Second, not even during the reform of righteous Josiah could one make a compelling argument that the monarchy was a good thing for Israel, morally or spiritually, since the text of Kings records that most of the kings of Israel and Judah were evil, including Josiah's father (Amon), and particularly his grandfather (Manasseh). Righteous rulers were the exception, not the rule. Third, elsewhere in Judges, kings are not viewed positively. Foreign kings oppress Israel (Eglon of Moab, Jabin of Canaan), and Israel's lone experiment with monarchy was a reign of terror as Gideon's son Abimelech slaughtered seventy of his brothers on his way to power.

While many scholars argue for their specific view of the Deuteronomistic redaction of the book of Judges, a recent commentary by Susan Niditch speaks helpfully about how the process may have taken place.[2] Niditch discerns three distinct voices in the book.

The *Epic-Bardic* voice was a story-teller, recounting heroic exploits of charismatic deliverers who, with the aid of YHWH, repeatedly defeated Israel's oppressive enemies. Niditch perceives the Bard's voice most clearly in the Song of Deborah, and in the stories involving Samson.

The voice of the *Theologian* would sound more like what scholars typically call the Deuteronomist(s) with a concern for covenant loyalty to YHWH, although it is difficult to distinguish between the possible various Deuteronomistic contributors to this layer. The Theologian wrote the overview of chapter 2 and framed the Main Body of the book to make it clear that faithfulness on Israel's part will lead to peace and military success and that apostasy will lead to oppression.

The voice of the *Humanist* told tales with little or no commentary or assessment about the behavior of the characters, as we see most clearly in the first chapter and in the final five chapters of the book. The Humanist wanted the stories to speak for themselves. The main characters in these stories were not heroic, unlike the major judges, to whom we turn next.

2.4. Major Judge Cycles

While Joshua and Samuel lack a distinguishing feature which is consistently repeated throughout the book, Judges and Kings each have characteristic pattern. In Kings, regnal formulas are repeated for

2. See Niditch 2008.

each ruler, and likewise in Judges, the cycles are repeated for each of the major judges, although the cyclical pattern in Judges is not nearly as consistent as the pattern of regnal formulas in Kings.

Scholarly representations of the judge cycles include varying numbers of elements, but in this representation we will speak of ten stages which are repeated throughout the book of Judges, although none of the judge cycles includes all ten. Table 3.2 lists the stages with references for each one. For easy reference, we've given each of the stages a one-word title based on a key word (in bold) from the cyclical terminology. In general, the pattern is thus: the Israelites do evil; YHWH becomes angry; he sells them into the hands of their enemy; they are oppressed for many years; they cry out to YHWH for help; he raises up a deliverer, to whom he gives his Spirit; the enemy is subdued; the land has rest; and the judge rules for many years. The cyclical nature of the pattern is seen first as it is laid out in the Overview (Judg. 2:11–23), then as it repeats for each of the six major judges (Othniel, Ehud, Deborah, Gideon, Jepthath, and Samson). However, there is great variety in the pattern, as will be seen in the next table.

Table 3.2: Ten Stages of a Major Judge Cycle

# Title	Stage	References in Judges
1. Evil	The sons of Israel did **evil** in the sight of YHWH	2:11; 3:7, 12; 4:1; 6:1; 10:6; 13:1
2. Anger	The **anger** of YHWH was kindled against Israel	2:14, 20; 3:8; 10:7
3. People sold	He **sold**/gave them into the hand of [their enemy]	2:14; 3:8; 4:2; 6:1, 13; 10:7; 13:1
4. Years	**Years** of oppression (Israel served, was given into hands of, or was oppressed by enemy)	3:8, 14; 4:3; 6:1; 10:8; 13:1
5. Crying out	The sons of Israel **cried** to YHWH	3:9, 15; 4:3; 6:6, 7; 10:10
6. Raising up	YHWH **raised** up a deliver for the sons of Israel	2:16, 18; 3:9, 15
7. Spirit	The **spirit** of YHWH [comes upon the deliver]	3:10; 6:34; 11:29; 13:25; 14:6, 19; 15:14
8. Enemy subdued	[The enemy] was **subdued**	3:30; 4:23; 8:28; 11:33
9. Rest	Then the land had **rest** for forty years.	3:11, 30; 5:31; 8:28
10. Judging	He **judged** Israel for [X] **years** (not used for Deborah)	3:10; 9:22; 10:2, 3; 12:7, 9, 11, 13; 16:31

We see the theological concern of these judge cycles as we examine the primary subject (underlined in the table) for each of the ten stages. We may not be surprised to discover that only one stage focuses on the land (9. Rest), but, curiously, only one stage focuses primarily on the judge (10. Judging). The judge doesn't even appear until the sixth stage and, for two of the judges (Gideon and Jephthah), long descriptions of the nation's apostasy and oppression precede the introduction of the actual judge (Judg. 6:1–10; 10:6–16). The title "Judge Cycles" is perhaps a misnomer since according to the pattern of the cyclical framework, the judge plays only a minor role.

Two stages focus on the people of Israel (1. Evil and 5. Cried) and two stages focus on Israel's oppressive neighbors (4. Years and 8. Subdued). But the primary character of the judge cycles is YHWH, as four of the stages focus on his role (2. Anger, 3. Sold, 6. Raised up, and 7. Spirit). These cycles are emphasizing that it's not the land of Israel, the people of Israel, the enemies of Israel, or the judge of Israel, but the God of Israel who controls the destiny of the characters in the narrative. Niditch's label of the Theologian for the voice behind the cyclical framework thus seems justified.

Now that we've looked at the ten stages, we can examine the cyclical pattern in the narratives of the six major judges, as laid out in Table 3.3 (please see the end of the present chapter for Table 3.3).

While there are almost forty regnal formulas in Kings with a very consistent formulaic pattern, we see less consistency in the judge cycles, as more stages are missing from the cycle for each of the judges. None of the judge cycles includes all ten stages, and the average number of stages for each judge cycle is between six and seven (see the bottom row of Table 3.3). However, all of the judge cycles include at least five of the ten stages, and two of the stages, Evil (1.) and People sold (3.), are present in all of the judge cycles.

Four general observations can be made about Table 3.3. *First*, the judge cycle with the most stages (8.) belongs to Othniel (and Jephthah) and his cycle appears to serve as an ideal or prototype. It comes first, it includes no additional narrative, and all eight of his stages are concentrated in only five verses. *Second*, the narratives of the first two judges are much shorter in terms of verses (5 and 19) than those of the final four judges (55, 100, 60, and 91), which may simply be due to the fact that they are older and came from a less complete source. *Third*, the years of rest for the land (9.) are given in multiples of forty, which scholars often assume are round numbers (we'll discuss this issue under "Chronology"). Forty is an important number in the Old Testament, most significantly as the nation was required to delay for forty years in the wilderness as they came out of Egypt as punishment for their refusal to enter the land (Num. 14:33). *Fourth*, the stage that appears the least often, Judging (10.), which only appears in the cycles of Jephthah and Samson, is also repeated in the much shorter narratives of five of the minor judges as well as in Abimelech's narrative. While Abimelech's narrative is longer than several of the major judges, since it includes none of the ten stages, he is not typically included in lists of the major judges.

As one examines the tribes of these six judges, one finds an interesting pattern of a gradual shift to the north. Othniel is probably from the tribe of Judah in the south. Ehud is from the tribe of Benjamin, just north of Judah. Deborah is from Ephraim, which borders Benjamin on the north. Gideon and Jephthah are both from Manasseh, which is north of Ephraim. Samson is from Dan, which was situated in two places, east of Ephraim and in the far north. However, Samson was not from the remote northern section of his tribe, but from Zorah, which was just north of Judah and east of Benjamin.

Figure 3.2: *Deborah the Prophetess Urges Barak to Raise an Army and Give Battle to the Army of Jabin*, by Marc Chagall (1956); etching on paper. Musée National Message Biblique Marc Chagall, Nice; Wikiart.org.

Before looking at the minor judges, it is necessary to make a comment about the cycle that includes the judge Deborah and the military leader Barak who served under her leadership. Some scholars refer to Judges 4—5 as the Barak cycle, or the Deborah-Barak cycle, presumably because Deborah does not summon the army to battle before Israel defeated the Canaanites, but it is more reasonable to refer to these chapters simply as the Deborah cycle. Not only does the text call her a prophet, but twice it describes her as judging the nation of Israel (Judg. 4:4, 5), and throughout the story she is clearly the one in charge. Barak, however is not called a judge, and he is clearly subordinate to Deborah since on two occasions she tells him what to do and he obeys (Judg. 4:6, 14). He is unwilling to fight without Deborah, and, just as Deborah prophesied, a woman (Jael, the wife of Heber the Kenite) is the one who kills Sisera, the Canaanite general.

2.5. Minor Judge Pattern

While the reports of the six minor judges are much shorter than the narratives of the six major judges, a formulaic pattern can still be seen, represented in Table 3.4, which lists the judge's name, the biblical reference, whom the judge succeeded, how long he judged Israel, where he was from, where he was buried, and other details from his narrative.

Table 3.4: Minor Judges Pattern

Judge	Shamgar son of Anath	Tola son of Puah	Jair the Gileadite	Ibzan of Bethlehem	Elon the Zebulunite	Abdon son of Hillel
Biblical Reference	3:31; 5:6	10:1–2	10:3–5	12:8–10	12:11–12	12:13–15
Came after	Ehud	Abimelech	Tola	Jephthah	Ibzan	Elon
Judged Israel for X years		23	22	7	10	8
From		Shamir in Ephraim	Gilead in Manasseh	Bethlehem in Zebulun?	Zebulun	Pirathon in Ephraim
Buried		at Shamir	at Kamon	at Bethlehem	at Aijalon	at Pirathon
Other details	Delivered Israel Killed 600 Philistines	Delivered Israel	30 sons with 30 donkeys & 30 towns	30 sons & 30 daughters		40 sons & 30 grandsons on 70 donkeys

The major judge cycles were characterized by variety, but the reports of minor judges follow a more consistent pattern. All six of the minor judge reports are only two or three verses, and they all begin by noting which leader came before him. Five of the six reports state where the judge came from and five also state the judge judged Israel for a specific number of years. The range in years for judgeship varies from seven (Ibzan) to twenty-three years (Tola), so there is no appearance of round numbers. Only one of the minor judges (Elon) includes no additional narrative details. These details mention that two of the judges delivered Israel (Shamgar and Tola) and that three of the judges had numerous descendants (Jair, Ibzan, and Abdon). Apparently for judges, children and grandchildren come in batches of thirty or forty, which sound like rounded numbers, and curiously, the only biographical detail we learn about two of these sets of descendants is that they ride donkeys.

Among the locations, two of the minor judges, Tola and Abdon, came from the territorial regions of Ephraim, although Tola was originally from the tribe of Issachar. Ibzan's home of Bethlehem could have been the home of David in Judah, but it is more likely to have been the less familiar one in Zebulun in the north (Josh. 19:15), which would mean that two of the minor judges would have come from Zebulun (Ibzan and Elon). Jair is from Gilead, from the tribe of Manasseh, on the east bank of the Jordan.

While Shamgar perhaps should not be considered a minor judge since the text never says he judged Israel, there are good arguments both for and against his inclusion in this list, so we've kept him in the table. On the one hand, one could argue that Shamgar shouldn't be included since his report is separate from the other five minor judges, which are grouped in two sections (Tola-Jair and Ibzan-Elon-Abdon). The text also doesn't mention his location, or where he was buried. On the other hand, one could argue that he was a minor judge since the text states that he came after the previous judge Ehud, implying that he served in a similar capacity. His succession notice is also similar to all the other minor judges. Like Tola and many of the major judges (Judg. 2:16, 18; 8:22; 9:17; 10:12), Shamgar delivered Israel. Anyone who kills six hundred Philistines with an oxgoad certainly qualifies as heroic, and this particular feat is comparable to the major judge Samson who killed a thousand Philistines with a jawbone of a donkey (ideally, one would like to think, from the carcass of one that had been ridden by a grandson of Abdon).

3. Historical Issues

3.1. Recording Actual Events?

While some scholars view the book of Judges as a purely fictional account of Israel's early history, many scholars still assume that the book can be viewed as a record of actual events, granted that it has its own perspective on how these events are narrated. Just as any good story-teller makes decisions about what to include and to exclude and how to frame a narrative in order to make a point, so the author of

Judges does the same with the source material. And while there is chronological information included in the book, the primary interest of the book is not historical, but theological, which will be the focus of the next major section of this chapter. Historical precision regarding the chronology of Judges will remain elusive, but this section will still set out tentative dates and time ranges for some of the events of the book.

If one assumes that the book of Joshua is laid out chronologically, the death of Joshua (Judg. 1:1; 2:8) provides a clear starting point for the book. The ending point, however, is more vague as the final verse simply informs readers that Israel had yet to establish a monarchy (Judg. 21:25). Since the monarchy under Saul the first king wasn't established until after the judgeships of Eli and Samuel (1 Sam. 10:1), the final events in the Appendix of Judges could take place during the lives of Samson, Eli, or perhaps even Samuel (Judg. 16:31; 1 Sam. 4:18; 7:6). While it may seem strange to modern readers to imagine events from Judges spilling over into the book of Samuel, an overlap is already established by the fact that Eli and Samuel are both called judges. The book of Ruth also claims to overlap with the book of Judges since it is set in the time of the judges (Ruth 1:1).

The book of Judges is thus broadly bookended by the Exodus and wilderness wanderings at the beginning and the establishment of the monarchy at the end. Among those scholars who perceive some form of the Exodus to be historical, some place it in the fifteenth century BCE, and others place it in the thirteenth century BCE. (A discussion of the various models of Israel's origin in the land was discussed in the chapter on Joshua.) Typically, Saul's ascension to the throne is set in the late-eleventh century BCE (1020?).

If one assumes a mid-thirteenth-century BCE date for the Exodus (1260?), then after accounting for Israel's wilderness wandering and the events of the book of Joshua, one could situate the beginning of Judges in the late-thirteenth century BCE (1220?). If one assumes no overlap with the book of Samuel, then after accounting for the judgeships of Eli and Samuel, one could situate the end of Judges in the mid-eleventh century BCE (1050?). In terms of ancient Near Eastern archaeological periods, Judges would then begin at the very end of the Late Bronze Age and endure for most of Iron Age I. As Judges begins, iron was a major factor in warfare as Israel's opponents had chariots of iron, which made them impervious to attack (Judg. 1:19; 4:3, 13). While these dates for Judges (1220–1050 BCE) need to be considered approximate, Webb, a scholar who favors a fifteenth-century date for the Exodus, comes up with a rather precise range, from 1326–1092 BCE for the book of Judges.[3]

3.2. Eighteen Chronological Notices

As has been noted already, the books of Joshua and Samuel cover much shorter periods of time than their neighbors in the Former Prophets, the books of Judges and Kings. The longer time frame of Judges and Kings allows for far more references to chronology.

Table 3.5: Chronological Notices in Judges

#	Judge	Oppression (years)	Peace (years)	Rule (years)	Judges References
1.	Othniel	8	40		3:8, 11
2.	Ehud	18	80		3:14, 30
3.	Deborah	20	40		4:3; 5:31
4.	Gideon	7	40		6:1; 8:28
5.	Abimelech			3	9:22
6.	Tola			23	10:2
7.	Jair			22	10:3
8.	Jephthah	18		6	10:8; 12:6
9.	Ibzan			7	12:9
10.	Elon			10	12:11
11.	Abdon			8	12:14
12.	Samson	40		20	13:1; 16:31
	Totals	**111**	**200**	**99**	**410 years**

The book of Judges in particular includes eighteen chronological notices, which can be categorized into three distinct types: 1) years of foreign oppression, 2) years of peace in the land, 3) years of rule by a judge. Table 3.5 lists these notices sorted into their three types (one per column), alongside the judge associated with the notice in the order listed in the book. The years of oppression occur before the judge is raised up; the years of peace in the land come after the judge's

3. Webb 2012, 12.

deliverance; and the years of rule are synonymous with the judge's reign. Abimelech is not called a judge, but a king (Judg. 9:6), but he's still included in the table since the text states that he ruled for three years.

Several observations can now be made about Table 3.5. Perhaps the most striking thing to note is that Israel was ruled over by twelve leaders in the book of Judges: six major judges, five minor judges, and one king (Abimelech). Twelve is a significant number in the history of Israel as Jacob's twelve sons became Israel's twelve tribes, which may explain why the book doesn't include a notice of how long Shamgar judged Israel since that would bring the total number of rulers to thirteen.

As we examine the differences between the types of judges, we see that for all of the major judges two numbers are given: years of oppression as well as either years of peace, or years of rule (but not both). But for Abimelech and all of the minor judges, only one number is given, the years of rule.

Of the eighteen numbers in the table, eight of them are a multiple of ten (in a pattern that might interest the mathematically oriented, 10 once, 20 twice, 40 four times, 80 once), when one would expect a much lower number, approximately between one and three (since 1.8 is one tenth of eighteen). We'll come back to this observation in the next section, but the high concentration of these multiples of ten suggests that some of these numbers are rounded. This apparent number rounding pattern can also been seen when one notices that fourteen of the eighteen numbers are even (only four are odd), when one would expect roughly half of the eighteen to be odd (between eight and ten).

Two other observations can be made on this subject regarding the distribution of these rounded numbers. First, all the years of peace are not just multiples of ten, but multiples of forty (forty or eighty). Second, both sets of numbers associated with the two judges Deborah and Samson are multiples of twenty (twenty and forty; forty and twenty), and curiously both sets add up to sixty. It is difficult to know what to do with these observations, except to speculate that the sources used for the years of peace in the land, or for the judgeships of Deborah and Samson, may have lacked precise numbers. It would not be surprising for the older sources for the first four judges to be more approximate since they were more distant from the time of the book's composition, but it is unexpected for the Samson source since his judgeship would have been more contemporary to the time of composition.

3.3. The Chronological Problem

At the bottom of Table 3.5, the total number of years are included for each column: 1) 111 years of oppression, 2) two hundred years of peace, and 3) ninety-nine years of rule, which gives an overall total of 410 years, if one merely adds up the three subtotals and assumes there was no overlap.

Whether one situates some form of Exodus in either the fifteenth or thirteenth centuries BCE (see Joshua chapter), it is difficult, if not impossible, to squeeze a four-century interval after the events of the book of Joshua and before the events of the book of Samuel sufficient to accommodate these eighteen chronological notices of Judges and the 410 years that they seem to suggest. In short, the numbers of Judges do not fit easily into the appropriate chronological gap.

While we will point readers with a mathematical or chronological orientation to some of the academic commentaries (i.e., Soggin, Boling, and Block) to follow the details of how this problem has been addressed, here we will merely sketch out a few of the options.

One possible way to address the chronological problem of Judges involves *rounded numbers*. The clever biblical student might point out that number rounding doesn't solve the problem, since normally about half of the numbers would be rounded up, and about half rounded down, so a cumulative total comprising rounded numbers shouldn't be significantly different from one with more precise numbers. But as one examines the rounded numbers one observes that they are by far the largest ones comprising 290 of the 410 years: $(80 \times 1) + (40 \times 4) + (20 \times 2) + (10 \times 1) = 290$. All eight are either multiples of, or fractions of, forty, which is often associated with a generation (Num. 14:33). If these numbers were rounded up consistently to describe a symbolic generation reminiscent of the Exodus wandering, then the overall total of 410 years could be lowered dramatically.

Another way to address the chronological problem of Judges is to assume that some of the twelve Israelite rulers *overlapped*, or were even contemporaneous. This solution is similar to the idea of co-regencies in the book of Kings. Textual clues suggest that reigns of some of the judges may have been localized or limited to a specific number of tribal regions. Thus, the years of oppression in one part of Israel might coincide with the years of peace in other part of Israel. Or the periods of oppression by the Ammonites and the Philistines could have overlapped (Judg. 10:8; 13:1), and the latter could have carried into the book of Samuel (1 Sam. 4:1; 7:7). Neither rounding numbers nor overlapping reigns will lead to a definitive chronology for the period of the judges, but these two theories can help diminish the problematic nature of this period in Israel's history.

3.4. The Merneptah Stele and the Amarna Letters

In order to understand the contextual background for any period of Israel's history, scholars examine both biblical references to rulers, nations, and cities outside of Israel which we know about from ancient Near Eastern sources, as well as extra-biblical references to individuals and places mentioned within the biblical narrative. For the book of Kings, historians are blessed with both extra-biblical references to biblical people and places, and biblical references to foreign rulers, nations, and cities. However, only a few of these types of connections exist between the book of Judges and other sources.

None of the regional empires that dominate sections of the book of Kings (Egypt, Assyria, and Babylon) appear in an active role in the book of Judges. Babylon and Assyria aren't mentioned in Judges, which is not surprising since their period of imperial expansion into the region coincided with Israel's divided monarchy period (see the chapter on Kings). Egypt is mentioned seven times in Judges, but always as Israel's previous location before YHWH brought them out of slavery (Judg. 2:1, 12; 6:8, 13; 11:13, 16; 19:30).

While several characters from the books of Samuel and Kings are mentioned in ancient Near Eastern sources (e.g., David, Jehu, Hezekiah), no one from Judges is mentioned in any extra-biblical texts. However, two ancient sources, both found in Egypt, mention terms and locations relevant to Judges.

One of the most significant inscriptions for students of the Hebrew Bible is the Egyptian **Merneptah Stele** (see chapter two, section 3.4), which includes the earliest reference to Israel outside of biblical sources. The stele is currently located in the Egyptian Museum in Cairo. The inscription is usually dated to 1208 BCE, which would situate it early in the period of the judges. The relevant line reads,

"Israel is laid waste, his seed is not."

Merneptah (1213–1203 BCE) was the son of Ramesses the Great, the pharaoh who is often associated with Moses (Exod. 1:11), and this inscription primarily focuses on his victories in Libya, but it concludes by describing his conquests over the Canaanite cities of Ashkelon (Judg. 1:18; 14:19), Gezer (Judg. 1:29), and Yanoam, before finally mentioning Israel. As Merneptah's stele celebrates a military victory over Canaanite enemies, it can be compared to the song of Deborah (Judges 5), which also exults over Canaanite defeat. Flinders Petrie, the man who discovered the stele in 1896, after translating the word "Israel," reportedly told his colleague, "Won't the reverends be pleased?"

While Egypt isn't mentioned as an active nation in the book of Judges, as his stele suggests, Merneptah and other Pharaohs were likely still involved in the region during the period of the judges. Although Egyptian power was on the decline during his reign, Ramesses III (1186–1155 BCE) likely campaigned in, or traveled through, the land of Canaan in his battles against the Hittites and the Sea Peoples.

Figure 3.3: Detail of the inscription on the Merneptah Stele, ca. 1208 BCE. Commons.wikimedia.org.

The **Amarna Letters** provide another ancient Near Eastern point of connection to the book of Judges (see chapter 2, section 3.5). The clay tablets on which the letters are written are scattered today among several locations; most of them are found in the Pergamum Museum in Berlin, the Egyptian Museum in Cairo, and the British Museum in London. These letters from administrators in Syria-Palestine to two fourteenth-century Egyptian pharaohs (Amenhotep III and Akhenaten) are written using the writing system of Mesopotamia (Akkadian cuneiform) as opposed to the hieroglyphic system of Egypt. They name several important locations mentioned in Judges, including Gezer (Judg. 1:29), Megiddo (Judg. 1:27; 5:19), Shechem (Judg. 8:31; 9:1, 2, 3), and perhaps most significantly Jerusalem (Judg. 1:7, 8, 21; 19:10). Several of the letters came from the ruler of Jerusalem, a certain Abdi-Heba. While previously some scholars argued that the people referred to in the letters as *'apiru* (also spelled *Ḥabiru*) should be connected with the Hebrew people (see Gen. 39:14; Exod. 2:6; 1 Sam. 4:6), more recently scholars think the connection is unlikely since the term doesn't appear to refer to a specific people like the Israelites are portrayed in the Hebrew Bible, but a class of marginalized people more generally.

3.5. Israel's Enemies

While none of the imperial powers actually oppress Israel in the book of Judges, many of their neighbors do for extended periods of Israel's history, as seen in the cyclical judge pattern. Seven neighboring peoples attack or oppress the Israelites in Judges (the Amalekites, Ammonites, Arameans, Canaanites, Midianites, Moabites, and Philistines). Most of the Judges references to these groups are as peoples (e.g., "the Philistines," "the Amalekites," and "the Midianites") and not as nations *per se* ("Philistia," "Amalek," and "Midian"). The Philistines may have been one of the Sea Peoples who gradually moved from the region around the Aegean Sea into this coastal region southwest of Israel during the twelfth and eleventh centuries BCE, primarily in five cities (Gaza, Ashkelon, Ashdod, Gath, and Ekron). In the subsequent books of the Former Prophets, many of these groups gradually become nations with more established territories and borders, but at this point in their history their status was primarily as tribal peoples, similar to that of the Israelites during the time of the judges.

Table 3.6 lists these seven enemy peoples (their locations in parenthesis), references where they appear in Judges (total number in parenthesis), any kings or leaders mentioned in Judges, their allies, and the Israelite judges who fought against them.

Three observations can be made about this table of Israelite enemies. *First*, in Judges the people of Israel were surrounded by enemies who took turns oppressing and attacking the Israelites. Moving clockwise, to the north-east of Israel is Aram; to the east, Ammon; to the south-east, Midian and Moab; to the south, Amalek; to the south-west, Philistia; and to the west, Canaan. We need to acknowledge that the locations of these seven peoples shifted as some of them were nomadic, and battles for territory were won and lost.

Table 3.6: Seven Enemy Peoples in Judges

People	Judges References	Kings, Leaders	Allies	Judge
Amalekites (S of Judah)	3:13; 5:14; 6:3, 33; 7:12; 10:12 (**6 total**)		Moab, Midian, Ammon	
Ammonites (E of Gilead)	3:13; 10:6–18; 11:4–36; 12:1–3 (**27 total**)	The king of Ammon	Moab, Amalek	Jephthah
Arameans (NE of N tribes)	3:8, 10; 10:6 (**3 total**)	Cushan-rishathaim		Othniel
Canaanites (W of Ephraim)	1:1–33; 3:1–5; 4:2, 23, 24; 5:19; 21:12 (**23 total**)	Adoni-bezek, Jabin, Sisera		Deborah, Barak
Midianites (S of Moab)	6:1–33; 7:1–25; 8:1–28; 9:17 (**31 total**)	Zebah, Zalmunna Oreb, Zeeb	Amalek	Gideon
Moabites (SE of Judah)	3:12–30; 10:6; 11:15–25 (**16 times**)	Eglon	Ammon, Amalek	Ehud
Philistines (W of Judah)	3:3, 31; 10:6–11; 13:1, 5; 14:1–4; 15:3–20; 16:5–31 (**34 total**)			Jephthah, Samson

Second, the book of Judges is dominated by warfare between Israel and these seven nations. The vast majority of the material in the Main Body of the book involves military stories, and every chapter in this middle section includes multiple references to these foreign peoples. Not only are several foreign kings mentioned, but three foreign military leaders are also mentioned by name (Sisera, Oreb, and Zeeb). According to the chronological notices discussed earlier, Israel was oppressed by these enemy peoples for a significant part of their history during the time of the judges (111 years if you merely add up the numbers).

Third, four of Israel's enemies in Judges formed alliances with other enemy peoples. To use a playground analogy, the foreign bullies often ganged up on Israel. The four nations who allied together were to the south and east of Israel (Amalekites, Ammonites, Midianites, and Moabites). The Amalekites are not mentioned as often in Judges as their three allies and they are the only people who are allied with all three of the others, as if they were always willing to help someone attack or oppress the Israelites. Another group, "the people of the east," are mentioned four times as allies of the Midianites and the Amalekites in the Gideon narrative (Judg. 6:3, 33; 7:12; 8:10), but it is difficult to be certain who they represent.

These seven people groups are enemies for much of Israel's history, occasionally before the period of the judges, but more often afterwards. Joshua just barely managed to repulse the **Amalekites** as the Israelites fled Egypt, but YHWH had promised that Amalek would be wiped out (Exod. 17:8–16), and when King Saul later defeated the Amalekites, he was punished for not fulfilling the command to destroy them completely (1 Sam. 15:2–33). The *Ammonites* don't appear nearly as often in Joshua, Samuel, and Kings as they do in Judges, but they are mentioned at both ends of the monarchic period, since Saul's first deed as ruler was to defeat the Ammonites in battle (1 Sam. 11:11), and in the final years of Judah, Ammonite bands raided the land (2 Kgs. 24:2). *Aram* plays a minor role in Israel's history in the books of Judges and Samuel, but in Kings, they are the primary enemy of Israel as Rezon raided during the reign of Solomon (1 Kgs. 11:23–25), Ben-hadad repeatedly attacked Ahab (1 Kings 20), Hazael captured territory from Jehu (2 Kgs. 10:32–33), and Rezin threatened Ahaz (2 Kgs. 15:37; Isa. 7:1–9). Military struggles against the *Canaanite* residents of the land dominate the book of Joshua (e.g., Josh. 3:10; 5:1; 9:1–2; 11:1–5), but after the first few chapters of Judges, they essentially disappear from the narrative and only appear a few times in the rest of the Former Prophets (2 Sam. 24:7; 1 Kgs. 9:16).

Other than when they joined with Moab to hire the mercenary prophet Balaam to curse Israel as they came out of Egypt (Num. 22:4, 7), *Midian* doesn't appear as a military opponent outside of Judges in the Former Prophets. While the Midian-Moab alliance against the wandering Israelites, just mentioned, led to no actual military engagement, during the period of the monarchy Israel fought against *Moab* under Saul (1 Sam. 14:47), under David (2 Sam. 8:2), and under Jehoram (2 Kgs. 3:4–27). The *Philistines* are Israel's primary foe during the Samson cycle and this adversarial relationship continues into the book of Samuel as the Philistines capture the ark (1 Sam. 4:1–11), they are routed under Samuel's judgeship (1 Sam. 7:10–11), they prompt Saul to offer a premature sacrifice (1 Sam. 13:2–15), and they are defeated numerous times by David, perhaps most famously after his battle with the Philistine giant, Goliath (1 Sam. 17:1–54; 18:27; 2 Sam. 5:17–25).

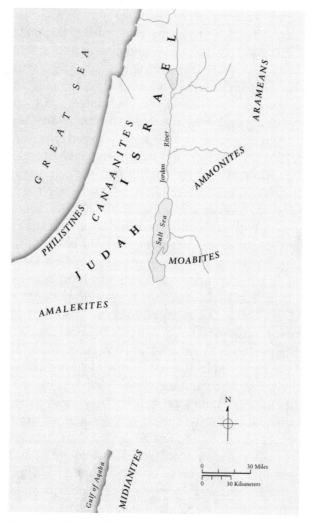

Map 3.4: Israel's Hostile Neighbors

3.6. Tribes in Tension

According to the biblical narrative, the families of the twelve sons of Jacob (Reuben, Simeon, Levi, Judah, Dan, Naphtali, Gad, Asher, Issachar, Zebulun, Joseph, and Benjamin) moved to Egypt, became a numerous people, were enslaved by Pharaoh, were delivered by YHWH, spent forty years in the wilderness, partially conquered the land of Canaan, and were divided into twelve tribal regions. While the tribe of Levi was not given a tribal region (they were dedicated to the service of YHWH), the two sons of Joseph, Manasseh and Ephraim, were given separate tribal allotments bringing the total of regions back to twelve.

An earlier generation of scholars theorized that during the period of the Judges the twelve tribes of Israel were unified in a confederation, comparable to the Greek model of an amphictyony, with a loose form of central government and centralized worship. Some type of unity among the tribes during period of the judges does appear to be present as the text frequently speaks of "all Israel," "the people of Israel," or "all the people of Israel" (Judg. 1:1; 2:4, 6; 3:2; 4:1; 8:27; 10:8; 20:1, 26).

However, Judges contains little evidence of any type of centralized government, nor any type of central shrine or worship location. While the ark of the covenant played a major role in Joshua during the conquest, and later in the books of Samuel and 1 Kings, the ark is only mentioned once, briefly, in Judges (20:27), so it is difficult to imagine that it was a significant unifying factor for the twelve tribes during the time of the judges. The theory of an Israelite amphictyony no longer has many scholarly advocates.

The book of Judges also includes well over a hundred references to the individual tribes of Israel. Table 3.7 lists the tribes (thirteen here with Levi, Manasseh, and Ephraim), their references in Judges, and notable individuals (in bold) or events associated with each tribe.

While the tribe of Gad is never mentioned in Judges, all the others are referenced multiple times, and three tribes in particular play major roles in the book (Judah, Benjamin, and Ephraim). These numerous tribal references reveal how important tribal identity was during the period of the judges, apparently more so than their Israelite national identity. Some of the references describe how certain tribes helped the various judges during a military campaign, which could appear to support the idea of a unified Israel, but the fact that the alliance needed to be mentioned may also mean that it was unusual. The narratives of many of the deliverance campaigns only mention a few of the twelve tribes, which adds further support to the idea that Israel was not functioning as a unified entity yet.

Table 3.7: Tribal References in Judges

Tribe	Judges References	Notable individuals or events in Judges
Reuben	5:15, 16 (**2 total**)	Didn't join Barak's forces against Canaanites.
Simeon	1:3, 17 (**2 total**)	Joined Judah against Canaanites.
Levi	17:7–13; 18:3–15; 19:1, 20:4 (**10 total**)	A Levite's concubine was murderously gang raped.
Judah	1:2–19; 10:9; 15:9–11; 17:7–9; 18:12; 19:1–18; 20:18 (**25 total**)	Chosen to attack first both for Canaanites and Benjaminites.
Dan	1:34; 5:17; 18:2–30; 20:1 (**12 total**)	Didn't join Barak's forces against Canaanites, conquered Laish.
Naphtali	1:33; 4:6–10; 5:18; 6:35; 7:23 (**7 total**)	Didn't drive out all Canaanites; helped Barak and Gideon.
Gad	(**0 total**)	Not mentioned in Judges, but Gilead is part of the tribal region.
Asher	1:31; 5:17; 6:35; 7:23 (**4 total**)	Didn't drive out all Canaanites, or help Barak; helped Gideon.
Issachar	5:15; 10:1 (**2 total**)	Helped Barak against Canaanites; **Tola** the minor judge.
Zebulun	1:30; 4:6, 10; 5:14, 18; 6:35; 12:12 (**7 total**)	Didn't drive out all Canaanites; helped Barak, Gideon; **Elon** the minor judge.
Benjamin	1:21; 5:14; 10:9; 19:14; 20:3–48; 21:1–23 (**45 total**)	Didn't drive out all Canaanites; helped Barak; didn't give up Gibeah, lost civil war.
Manasseh	1:27; 6:15, 35; 7:23: 11:29; 12:4 (**7 total**)	Didn't drive out all Canaanites; **Gideon** the major judge; helped Gideon.
Ephraim	1:29; 2:9; 3:27; 4:5; 5:14; 7:24; 8:1, 2; 10:1, 9; 12:1–15; 17:1, 8; 18:2, 13; 19:1–18 (**27 total**)	Didn't drive out all Canaanites; helped Barak; angry at Gideon, but still helped; angry at Jephthah, was defeated; **Micah** the idolater.

Many of the tribal references describe miscommunications, tensions, rivalries, and even warfare among the Israel tribes. Conflict in the book of Judges did not merely involve external enemies. Table 3.8 lists five incidents of conflict between Israelites. In each case there is a proponent portrayed in a generally positive light and an opponent portrayed in a negative light. The cause and result of the conflict are also included.

In the first conflict, several tribes (Reuben, Dan, and Asher; the region of Gilead probably encompassing much of the tribe of Gad) were unwilling to join other Israelites to free the people from their Canaanite oppressors and their shameful behavior is memorialized in the song of Deborah. The second and third conflicts involve Gideon, as he successfully defused the tension with the Ephraimites who were offended for not being invited to the battle (Judg. 8:1–3), but in his pursuit of the remnant of the Midianite army, the cities of Succoth and Penuel (both in the tribal region of Gad) haughtily refuse to provide food for his army so he later returned and taught them a lesson.

Table 3.8: Tribal Tensions in Judges

Judges Text	Proponent	Opponent	Cause	Result
5:15–17	Israel under Deborah	Tribes of Reuben, Dan, Asher, Gilead	Unwilling to fight Canaanites	Shame, song taunt
8:1–3	Israel under Gideon	Ephraimites	Insult over no invitation to fight	Gideon affirms Ephraim, their anger subsided
8:4–17	Israel under Gideon	Cities of Succoth, Penuel (in Gad)	Unwilling to feed Gideon's army	Trampling, destruction, death
12:1–6	Gilead under Jephthah	Ephraimites	Unwilling to fight Ammon, insulted	42,000 killed for not saying "Shibboleth" properly
20:1–48	All Israel	Benjaminites	Unwilling to hand over Gibeah rapists	25,000 Benjaminites and 40,000 Israelites killed

The fourth conflict, which starts out like the second, ensued after a dispute about whether or not the Ephraimites were willing to join Jephthah against the Ammonites, and resulted in disaster for Ephraim as forty-two thousand were killed when they couldn't pronounce "Shibboleth" properly. The final conflict involved a civil war after the Benjaminites were unwilling to hand over the men of Gibeah who committed a murderous gang rape of the Levite's concubine.

The conflicts dramatically escalate in significance and violence as they began with shame, shift to destruction of cities, then culminate in tribal destruction and civil war. Causes of these tensions among the Israelites included unclear communication, not establishing precedents for military provision, and not setting up protocols for tribal extradition to ensure justice; all of these culminated in a devastating civil war.

4. Theological Themes

4.1. Introduction

The main character in Judges, as is the case in many books of the Hebrew Bible, is YHWH. His name appears 175 times in the book, beginning with the opening verse when the Israelites ask him who should be the first tribe to attack the Canaanites. As was observed above, the judge cycle formula emphasizes YHWH's primary role in Israel's story at this point in their history by making him the active figure in four of the ten stages: 1) he gets angry over their idolatry; 2) he sells Israel to be oppressed by their enemies; 3) he raises up deliverers to lead the nation; 4) he empowers the deliverers with his spirit. These four stages of the judge cycle focusing on divine involvement conveniently provide the four breakdowns for this section discussing the theology of the book of Judges (Idolatry, Oppression, Leadership, and Divine Empowerment).

4.2. Idolatry

The book of Exodus recounts how YHWH established his covenant with his people after delivering them from Egyptian enslavement. YHWH's expectation that the Israelites should worship him exclusively was mandated in the Ten Commandments, specifically in the commands to have no other gods and to not make idols (Exod. 20:3–4), which they as a people committed to obey while being sprinkled with ox blood (Exod. 24:3–8). In Deuteronomy, Israel is commanded to completely wipe out the Canaanite residents of the land, because if they didn't Israel would end up following their gods which would then provoke YHWH to anger (Deut. 7:1–6).

The warning of Deuteronomy proves particularly prescient in Judges as Israel doesn't fully drive out the Canaanites; they repeatedly fall into idolatry; and YHWH is forced to punish them in his anger. Because the affinities in ideological perspective between Deuteronomy and these sections of Judges, the most severe condemnations of idolatry found in Judges (2:11–19; 10:6–16) are often considered to come from the hand of a Deuteronomistic editor.

The book of Judges uses a variety of terminology to refer to idolatry. The word often translated as "gods" is *ĕlōhîm*, which can also be translated as "God," another name for YHWH in the Hebrew Bible, but fortunately the context usually makes it obvious whether *ĕlōhîm* is meant to signify YHWH, Israel's "God" (e.g., Judg. 1:7; 2:12; 3:7), or foreign "gods" (e.g., 2:3; 3:6; 5:8). The actual term "idol" (*pesel*) appears ten times in the book (Judg. 3:19, 26; 17:3, 4; 18:14, 17, 18, 20, 30, 31). The term "ephod" (*'epôd*), mentioned six times in Judges (8:27; 17:5; 18:14, 17, 18, 20), appears to refer to an object used in idolatrous worship practices in the days of Gideon and Micah. Both Gideon's ephod and Micah's idol appear to be associated not with the worship of a foreign god such as Baal, but with the worship of YHWH (Judg. 8:23–27; 17:3–13).

Figure 3.5: Bronze figurine of the god Baal, from Ras Shamra (ancient Ugarit), ca. 14th–12th centuries; now in the Louvre. Commons.wikimedia.org.

Several generic references to the gods of the surrounding peoples appear, including the gods of the Amorites (Judg. 6:10), the Ammonites, the Philistines (Judg. 10:6), and the gods of Aram, Sidon, and Moab (Judg. 10:6). Specific gods are also mentioned by name including Baal (Judg. 2:11, 13; 3:7; 6:25, 28, 30, 31, 32; 8:33; 10:6, 10), Asherah (Judg. 6:25, 26, 28, 30), Astarte (or Ashtaroth; Judg. 2:13; 10:6), Chemosh (Judg.

11:24), and Dagon (Judg. 16:23). Another obscure deity, who seems to be called both Baal-berith (literally, "lord of the covenant") and El-berith (literally, "god of the covenant"), is also worshiped by the Israelites during this period (Judg. 8:33; 9:4, 46).

The story of the theft of the Ephraimite Micah's idols and ephod by the Danites is curiously narrated with no obvious Deuteronomistic condemnation of idolatry. Similarly, Gideon's destruction of his father's Baal shrine receives no Deuteronomistic commendation, perhaps because he was afraid to do it openly during the daytime, but resorted to a clandestine nocturnal desecration.

4.3. Oppression

In Deuteronomistic ideology, idolatry naturally leads to oppression. In the book of Deuteronomy, YHWH states that if his people follow the gods of the people around them, then he will be angry and destroy them from the face of the earth (Deut. 6:14–15). In Judges, YHWH hands the idolatrous Israelites into the hands of the Arameans, the Moabites, the Canaanites, the Midianites, the Ammonites, and the Philistines. If one merely adds up the numbers from the judge cycles, Israel was oppressed by these peoples for over a century during the time of the judges.

The perspective of Judges on these oppressions is that they were primarily initiated by YHWH, not by the foreign peoples. The ancient world believed in theomachy, a battle among the gods which decided the fate of humans. Human battles are merely a reflection of what is taking place on a supernatural level. An expression of this principle is clearly seen in Jephthah's diplomatic exchange with the Ammonite king: "Should you not possess what your god Chemosh gives you to possess? And should we not be the ones to possess everything that the LORD our God has conquered for our benefit?" (Judg. 11:24). Chemosh and YHWH will determine what the Ammonites and the Israelites possess. Similarly, after capturing the bald Samson, the Philistines declare that their god has given their enemy into their hands (Judg. 16:23–24). In Judges, the primary textual explanation for their oppression was that YHWH decided to give his people over to their enemies to be oppressed in order to punish them.

What did the oppression of the Israelites involve? In addition to recording that they were actually oppressed by their enemies (Judg. 2:18; 4:3; 6:9; 10:8, 12), the text states that the Israelites served foreign rulers (Judg. 3:8, 14), they were plundered (Judg. 2:14, 16), they lost in battle (Judg. 2:14–15; 3:13), their cities were captured (Judg. 3:13), and their crops and livestock were destroyed (Judg. 6:3–5).

The resulting devastation from the oppression eventually lead the Israelites to cry out to their God for help, as seen in the fifth stage of the judge cycle (Judg. 3:9, 15; 4:3; 6:6, 7; 10:10, 12). The pattern of a cry for help to YHWH in desperate situation is a common motif in the Hebrew Bible. The Israelites' cry in slavery was the catalyst for the Exodus, and as they were caught between Pharaoh's army and the Red Sea they again cried to YHWH before the dramatic deliverance and the sea dried up (Exod. 2:23; 14:10). The judge Samuel cried to YHWH before defeating the Philistines (1 Sam. 7:9), and Jonah cried out of his distress in the belly of the fish and YHWH heard him (Jon. 2:2). In Judges, YHWH was thus prompted each time by their petitions, as well as his own compassion (Judg. 2:18; 10:16), to show mercy on his people to end the oppression by sending them a deliverer to lead them.

4.4. Leadership

As has been already been stated, the leadership style of the judges appeared to be, despite their title, not primarily administrative or judicial. It's possible that the judges spent significant time and energy making difficult legal decisions but this information wasn't recorded since, unlike heroic battles, legal cases do not generally make a compelling story (except perhaps for Solomon's decision to chop the prostitute's infant in half: 1 Kgs. 3:25). At least as the book of Judges tells the story, the judges were primarily military leaders. But as military leaders go, most of the judges, as well as others who were involved in the deliverance process, were a motley crew, not exactly the type you would expect to lead a nation into battle.

Warriors with serious disabilities performed some of the most heroic deeds in the book. The text describes the assassin Ehud as "left-handed" but the Hebrew literally means "impotent (in) his right hand" (Judg. 3:15), which is tragically ironic for him in particular since he came from the tribe "Benjamin," which literally means "son of my right hand" (see Gen. 35:18). The Hebrew thus emphasizes Ehud's disability, which is exactly what will allow him to dexterously pull out a short sword hidden on his right thigh to kill the Moabite king, Eglon. Gideon tells the angel that he was the weakest member of his family, and his clan is the weakest in Manasseh, and his doubts and his multiple requests for signs support his own self-assessment. While Samson performed many dramatic exploits, perhaps the most spectacular was performed while he was blind and needed someone to guide him to the pillars of the temple of Dagon, which he then pulled down on himself and on all the Philistine nobility (Judg. 16:23–31). While some modern readers might be encouraged at the apparent progressiveness of the book of Judges as the disabled are held up as role models, the point the text is making in these stories and throughout the rest of the book is that YHWH wants it to be obvious that he was the one who ultimately brought the deliverance. Just so, YHWH intentionally weakened his already "weakest" judge Gideon by paring down his forces from thirty-two thousand to three hundred before fighting the Midianites (Judg. 7:2). In Judges, YHWH uses the weakness and disabilities of his leaders to guarantee that the credit goes exclusively to him.

In the ancient world women were typically neither political leaders nor military heroes, but in the book of Judges they unexpectedly play both roles. As a prophet, Deborah was the spiritual leader of the nation, and as a judge she was the political leader (Judg. 4:4–5). The text doesn't provide many details concerning her role in the military deliverance over the Canaanites, except to note that Barak was unwilling to go to battle without her physical presence (reminiscent of Moses' words to YHWH in Exod. 33:12–17), and that when the crucial moment came for the forces to be joined in battle, Deborah delivers the final speech exhorting Barak to get up since YHWH had given Sisera "into his hand" (Judg. 6:14). But beyond merely being a political, spiritual, and military leader, she also served as worship leader, singing a song commemorating the event which she may have also composed (Judg. 5:1–31). Most English translations make it appear that Deborah and Barak were equal partners, almost like they were singing a duet, but the Hebrew verb for "sang" (šîr) is a feminine singular form here making it clear that her role was primary, and his, secondary, even in the singing.[4] The other hero, or we should say heroine, of this successful Canaanite campaign is also a female. As Sisera flees Barak's forces, he arrives at the tent of Jael, who agrees to take him in, then plays a maternal role by giving him milk (he asked for water), a place to sleep, and a blanket to keep him warm (but apparently no bedtime

---

4. See Alter, 131.

story), before she hammers a tent peg through his temple while he sleeps (which isn't particularly maternal: Judg. 4:17–22).

Two other unnamed women play more peripheral but still significant roles in the narrative of Judges. Jephthah's daughter (see Sidebar 3.1, "The Sacrifice of Jephthah's Daughter") could be viewed as the sacrifice necessary to achieve her father's victory over the Ammonites, and she shockingly appeared willingly to help her father fulfill his vow to YHWH (Judg. 11:29–40). Not only did Samson's mother give birth to Israel's jawbone-wielding deliverer from the Philistines, but after the angel appeared to her a second time she encouraged her terrified husband Manoah, who was sure that they both were going to die (Judg. 13:1–23).

Three of Israel's judges have spiritual and moral character flaws which would make them unlikely leaders for God's people. While Gideon is cleaning up the Midianite forces, an insult from the cities of Succoth and Penuel elicits an overly violent response, destruction of the cities, which surely was a punishment not commensurate to the crime (Judg. 8:16–17). At the end of the Gideon narrative he constructs an ephod which somehow contributed to a national idolatry, as the nation prostituted themselves to it. Jephthah, the son of a prostitute, ironically acts too nobly as he fulfills a foolish vow to sacrifice the first thing he sees upon his return. In contrast, Abimelech, the son of Gideon, acts dishonorably by slaughtering his brothers in his attempt to make himself king. Samson's lust repeatedly gets him into trouble as he first marries a Philistine woman against his parent's wishes, then divulges his riddle's solution to her, which she then passes on to her fellow countrymen (Judges 14). When he is thwarted from going into his "wife's room" because she's been given to another man, he uses various parts of foxes and a donkey to enact his revenge on the Philistines (Judges 15). He "goes into" a prostitute and escapes from the Philistines who have encircled her home only because he snuck out in the middle of the night (Judg. 16:1–3). Finally, he tells the secret of his strength to Delilah after she persists in nagging him about it, which leads to his capture and blinding by the Philistines.

Before moving past the topic of leadership, a few comments need to be made about kings in Judges. Some scholars believe the comment "in those days there was no king" necessarily implies that the author (or redactor) is arguing that the monarchy would be a spiritual improvement for Israel, since in two of the four repetitions of the phrase it is joined with the comment that everyone "did what was right in their own eyes" (Judg. 17:6; 18:1; 19:1; 21:25). However, this line of reasoning is not ultimately convincing, as there is no necessary connection between these two phenomena—correlation does not imply causation. Elsewhere in Judges, monarchy is not portrayed positively (see also 4.3 above).

During the period of the divided monarchy we see two models of leadership, charismatic in Israel as several of their early rulers were divinely elected (Jeroboam I, Baasha, and Jehu), and dynastic in Judah as all of their rulers came from the house of David. In Kings, neither model worked well to produce good leaders. The same was true in Judges. The charismatic judges have serious spiritual and moral character flaws and the only dynastic ruler, Abimelech, son of Gideon, was arguably Israel's worst leader during the period of the judges.

4.5. Supernatural Empowerment

To compensate for flaws and weaknesses in leaders, YHWH empowers them in a variety of ways to help them overcome obstacles in order to deliver his people. While in the books of Samuel and Kings, YHWH frequently speaks through prophets to empower leaders, in Judges prophets are rare (Judg. 4:4; 6:8), so YHWH raises up leaders in other ways including sending his own spirit as well as angelic messengers.

The fourth stage of the judge cycle narrates that in response to the cries of his people YHWH raises up a deliverer. Only two judges (Othniel and Ehud) are described as being raised up by YHWH (Judg. 3:9, 15), but the initial overview twice mentions that YHWH raised up deliverers (Judg. 2:16, 18), implying that all deliverers were thought to be divinely appointed. The text doesn't clarify exactly what it meant for a deliverer to be raised up, but it appears comparable to a king being divinely elected, since many of Israel's early rulers are described similarly (1 Sam. 9:16; 16:12; 1 Kgs. 11:31; 14:14).

For two of the judges the raising up process involved YHWH sending an angelic messenger. The term "angel of the LORD" (*mal'ak yhwh*) appears fifteen times in the book of Judges, far more frequently than any other book of the Hebrew Bible. (While the Hebrew word *mal'ak* can mean "messenger" or "angel," in Judges the being is associated with YHWH and performs supernatural deeds, so the translation of "angel" seems warranted.) These fifteen repetitions are scattered among the five angelic appearances in the book of Judges. Table 3.9 lists these references, as well as the audience, and the angel's message.

Table 3.9: Angelic Appearances in Judges

Judges Reference	Audience	Angelic Message
2:1–4	All the Israelites	God delivered them from Egypt, but they disobeyed, so the Canaanites will be adversaries, they'll be ensnared by foreign gods.
5:23	City of Meroz	A curse on the city of Meroz for not helping YHWH, Barak, and Deborah against the Canaanites.
6:11–22	Gideon	YHWH is with Gideon, he should go and deliver Israel from the Midianites. He will not die.
13:3–7	Manoah's wife	She will give birth to a son (Samson). He will be a Nazirite, so no wine, no razors. He will deliver Israel from the Philistines.
13:9–21	Manoah and his wife	Like he said before, no wine, no unclean food for Samson. "Why do you ask my name? It is too wonderful."

In the first two appearances, the angel rebukes the audience: in the initial case, the Israelites for not driving out the Canaanites, and in the second case, the city of Meroz for not helping Barak against the Canaanites. Gideon's extended interaction with the angel of YHWH encompasses his commission: an initial greeting, a minor debate with questions from both sides, an objection to the call, a promise of divine presence, then finally a dramatic sign to inspire the judge. Prior to Samson's birth, his mother, Manoah's wife, experiences two angelic visitations (her husband was present for the second), where the angel promises that she who was barren will conceive, and he will deliver Israel from the Philistines. Since her son is to be a Nazirite (see Num. 6:1–21) she will need to not drink wine or eat unclean foods, and he will need to continue to do so as well. He also is never supposed to cut his hair, although the correlation between his hirsuteness and his strength is not stated explicitly during this interaction.

Another way YHWH empowers deliverers in Judges is by sending his spirit to come upon them (the seventh stage of a judge cycle). The expression "spirit of YHWH" (*rûaḥ yhwh*) appears seven times in the book of Judges (3:10; 6:34; 11:29; 13:25; 14:6, 19; 15:14), more so than any other book of the Hebrew Bible; it appears only seven other times total in the Former Prophets. Four of the major judges are described as receiving YHWH's spirit (Othniel, Gideon, Jephthah, and Samson). For Samson the spirit comes upon him on four separate occasions (Judg. 13:25; 14:6, 19; 15:14). God also sent an "evil spirit" between Abimelech

131

and the lords of Shechem (Judg. 9:23). While the first four occurrences are not as dramatic, for the final three occurrences of this expression, the spirit "rushed upon" (ṣālaḥ) Samson, prompting him to tear a lion with his bare hands, to kill thirty Philistines to pay a debt, and to kill an additional one thousand Philistines with the jawbone of a donkey.

Leaders who have been given unique abilities, or who have been divinely empowered, are often categorized as charismatic, from the Greek word for gift, *charisma*. With more references to YHWH's spirit and YHWH's angels than any other book of the Hebrew Bible, Judges has a strong charismatic tone. Five of the major judges (all except Deborah) are described with at least one of these divine empowerments (being raised up, receiving an angelic visitation, receiving a spiritual manifestation), and therefore could be considered charismatic leaders on some level. However, three of them (Othniel, Gideon, and Samson) are described with multiple types of divine empowerment, and thus appear to be uniquely gifted to fulfill their roles as charismatic deliverers for their people.

5. Commentary

5.1. Introduction (1:1–3:6)

The book of Judges begins with the death of Joshua. In an attempt to determine who should fill the void left by one of Israel's greatest military leaders, the Israelites ask YHWH who should attack first as they begin their campaign to obey YHWH's mandate to drive the Canaanites from the land. YHWH's answer, "Judah," is clearly a reference to the whole tribe, but the language here makes it appear like "Judah" is just one man speaking in a single voice, perhaps to recall the manner that Israel was led previously by the one man Joshua.

The first chapter starts on a positive note with various successful campaigns to remove the Canaanite residents, but as the chapter progresses, the tone of the narrative "goes south" as success is replaced with failure. The combined forces of Judah and Simeon defeat the Canaanites and the Perizzites, amputating the thumbs and big toes of King Adoni-bezek, an appropriate introduction to one of the most violent books of the Bible as daggers are lost in obese kings' stomachs, tent pegs are driven through temples, cities are trampled, towers are destroyed, siblings are slaughtered, rulers are crushed by millstone-heaving ladies, women are gang raped and dismembered. Adoni-bezek's mutilation is the *hors d'oeuvre*, whetting our appetite for the brutal main course soon to come.

The Israelites next capture Jerusalem and several other cities (Judg. 1:8–10). To provide an additional incentive, Caleb offers his daughter Achsah as prize to whoever captures Kiriath-sepher (Judg. 1:11–15; repeated from Josh. 15:13–19), a move similar to Saul's subsequent offer of Michal, which David earned at the cost of one hundred Philistines foreskins (not a particularly romantic wedding gift: 1 Sam. 18:23–27). Achsah, however was not content to merely be a prize for the conqueror, but she also skillfully negotiated a dramatically improved dowry from her father. The Israelites achieve a few more victories over the Canaanites, and the text twice records that YHWH was with his people (Judg. 1:19, 22). A story that bears striking similarities to that of Jericho from the book of Joshua (chapters 2 and 6) involves spies sent from Ephraim and Manasseh to spy out Bethel; they meet a resident of the city who helps them (like Rahab) in exchange for a promise of safety for the resident's entire family (Judg. 1:22–26).

After a strong initial military campaign, the text begins to note some failed missions. Nine times in the remainder of the first chapter of Judges the text records that Israel did not drive out the Canaanites (1:19, 21, 27, 28–33). The iron chariots of the residents of the hill country prevent Judah from driving them out (Judg. 1:19). As a result of their failed campaigns, Canaanites live alongside the people of Manasseh, Ephraim, Zebulun, Asher, and Naphtali (Judg. 1:27–33). The chapter ends by noting that the Amorites forced the Danites back into the hill country (Judg. 1:34–36). The initial successes are now overshadowed by these later failures, and the divine mandate to fully conquer the land is left unfulfilled.

In a dramatic shift from the military reports of the first chapter, an angelic messenger of YHWH suddenly appears to give his assessment of their failure to obey the mandate to conquer, first reminding them of what God had done to bring them out of Egypt, then rebuking them for disobedience, and finally informing them that YHWH will no longer help them in this endeavor (Judg. 2:1–5). The angel's prophetic word that the Canaanites would become their adversaries and that their gods will ensnare them accurately describes their fate for the Main Body of the book, which involves cycles of idolatry, oppression, and deliverance. An etiological notice informs readers that since the Israelites respond to the angel's grim message with weeping, the site of the visitation was called Bochim (literally, "weepers"). Readers are next informed of Joshua's death a second time (Judg. 2:6–10), with more details regarding his burial which appear to be slightly modified from Josh. 24:28–31.

Then a proleptic overview of the Main Body of the book is given where the stages of the judge cycles are laid out (generally: idolatry, oppression, and deliverance). The dominant theme of this section is the rampant idolatry of the Israelites, as the text uses a variety of language to describe their idolatrous practices: they worshipped Baal and Astarte (Judg. 2:11, 13), they followed other gods (2:12, 19), they bowed down to them (2:12), and they lusted after other gods (2:17). Their abandonment of their God leads to his abandonment of his people, so they are plundered by plunderers, oppressed by oppressors, before they are delivered by deliverers. Whereas later in the book, the cycle for a major judge will include only one round of idolatry, oppression, and deliverance, in this overview we see the pattern repeated several times. There are three cycles of idolatry (2:11–13, 17, 19), two cycles of oppression (2:14–15, 20–21), and two cycles of deliverance (2:16, 18). The text also repeats the expression "whenever" (*běkōl ʾăšer*) three times (2:15, 18, 19) emphasizing the cyclical nature of the pattern. The overview ends when YHWH declares that he would no long drive out any of the remaining nations (Judg. 2:21).

Before the Main Body begins, the text states that the nations left in the land (the Philistines, the Canaanites, the Sidonians, the Hivites, the Hittites, the Amorites, the Perizzites, and the Jebusites) are essentially (with the addition of the Philistines and the Sidonians) the same nations that YHWH had commanded them to drive out of the land earlier (Exod. 3:8, 17; Deut. 7:1; 20:17). The text adds an ominous note about how Israel disobeyed two other commands from Deuteronomy by taking foreign wives and by worshipping foreign gods (Judg. 3:6; Deut. 6:14; 7:3–4).

5.2. The Main Body of Judges (3:7—16:31)

5.2.1. Othniel (Judg. 3:7–11)

Unlike the narratives of all the other major judges, the Othniel "narrative" ironically includes no narrative material or details about military exploits or victories. It includes more of the cyclical stages than all the other judges except Jephthah (eight for each), but it is by far the shortest judge narrative (only five verses long). Presumably, the sources available to the author included only the bare bones story.

With its primary location, abridged tone, and dense cyclical stage notices, Othniel's narrative serves as a model for the other judge cycles. And Othniel himself is viewed as a paradigm of the ideal judge, with none of the flaws (e.g., brutality, idolatry, lust) that characterize some of the later ones. Othniel's oppressive opponent has one of the longer names of the Hebrew Bible, Cushan-rishathaim (the second part of his name means "double-evil"). If you named your son after him, he'd be the only one in his kindergarten class. This Aramean king was defeated by Othniel after YHWH's spirit came upon the judge, and the land had rest for forty years.

5.2.2. Ehud (Judg. 3:12–30)

While Othniel's narrative lacked military details, for some readers Ehud's narrative may have too many, particularly if you have a sensitive stomach. The tale has all the classic elements of a great story—an oppressive ruler, an underdog hero, a secret plan, and scatological humor (a great story for junior high boys). The opponent this time is Eglon, king of Moab, whose physique makes Jabba the Hutt look athletic. The hero Ehud comes from the tribe of Benjamin ("the son of my right hand") but ironically he is impaired in his right-hand—he's left-handed. His plan involves establishing trust with the fat king by offering a tribute, then convincing him that they need privacy for a secret message, which takes the form of a dagger delivered into the royal belly. Eglon made no verbal response, but the message had a deep impact on him, as his guts spilled out onto the floor. The assassin left plenty of clues so Eglon's servants could quickly solve the murder—Colonel Ehud did it, with the dagger, in the roof chamber.

But Ehud had already escaped through another door. In the ensuing chaos following the royal assassination, Ehud was able to rally the Israelites, and achieve a victory over Moab, killing ten thousand Moabites in the process, which led to eighty years of peace, the longest hiatus from oppression mentioned in Judges. While his heroic tale of a dramatic deliverance would certainly have entertained Jewish audiences throughout their history, particularly during times when they were being oppressed, Ehud is not mentioned elsewhere in the Bible (the Ehud of 1 Chr. 7:10; 8:6 does not appear to be this judge).

5.2.3. Shamgar (Judg. 3:31)

Despite only brief references in two separate verses (Judg. 3:31; 5:6), Shamgar is one of the most intriguing characters of the book. The text calls him a "son of Anath," but instead of referring to his father, this title could indicate that he was dedicated to the service of Anath (also spelled Anat), a Canaanite warrior goddess. His act of deliverance was unusually resourceful, slaughtering six hundred Philistines with only an oxgoad, a feat comparable to Samson's donkey jawbone massacre (Judg. 15:15), even involving the same enemy. His second notice (in the song of Deborah) informs readers simply that the highways were dangerous during his days (Judg. 5:6).

5.2.4. Deborah, Barak, and Jael (Judg. 4:1—5:31)

After Ehud's death, the Israelites returned to their evil ways, although the text provides no details about what their evilness involved, but merely states the standard formulaic theological explanation for the subsequent oppression, this time by King Jabin of Canaan who ruled in Hazor. Hazor was located about ten miles north of the Sea of Galilee, and during the time of the Judges it was an important city in the region. The Jabin mentioned here was probably not the same Jabin who ruled Hazor thirty or forty years earlier in Joshua (11:1–15). Jabin was more likely a throne name associated with the ruler of Hazor, comparable to the royal names "Pharaoh" for Egypt (Gen. 12:15; 39:1; Exod. 1:11) and "Ben-hadad" for Aram (1 Kgs. 15:18; 20:1; 2 Kgs. 13:3). The commander of Jabin's army, Sisera, had an impressive fleet of nine hundred iron chariots, a number which some scholars think must have been an exaggeration.[5]

Perhaps no other woman in Scripture has as much spiritual or political authority as Deborah. The text calls her not just a "prophetess," but literally a "prophetess-woman" ('ishâ nebî'â), twice emphasizing her gender (Judg. 4:4). She is not called a judge (neither are any of her male judge counterparts, except generically in Judg. 2:18, 19), but she was judging Israel and the nation came to her for judgment (Judges 4, 5). As YHWH's spokesperson, she gives commands to Barak, Israel's military leader, both to get the deliverance campaign initially

---

5. See Alter, 126.

started at Mount Tabor (south-east of the Sea of Galilee), and then on the day of battle to rally the troops into battle (Judg. 4:6–7, 14).

Barak clearly looked to Deborah as a legitimate authority figure. He viewed Deborah's presence as a necessary prerequisite to victory, presumably because he wanted a prophetic voice guiding them on the field of battle, comparable to Moses not wanting to depart from Sinai without the presence of YHWH (Exod. 33:12–17). Barak's hesitancy to go without her thus doesn't need to be viewed as a sign of weakness as it often is,[6] but as healthy dependence upon spiritual leadership.[7] Barak promptly obeys her commission and calls the tribes (only Zebulun and Nephtali are mentioned at this point in the narrative).

Figure 3.6: *Jael, Deborah, and Barak,* by Solomon de Bray (1630). Museo de Arte de Ponce, Puerto Rico. Commons.wikimedia.org.

After YHWH threw Sisera's force into a panic, Barak successfully routed them. The biblical text never condemns Barak for cowardice or reluctance, but praises him for his exploits in both poetic and narrative contexts (Judg. 5:12, 15; 1 Sam. 12:11; compare Heb. 11:32).

As the battle unfolds, Deborah's prophetic words are fulfilled in

6. E.g., Block, 35.
7. Niditch, 65.

each of their aspects. Not only were Sisera's forces defeated, but just as Deborah predicted, a woman, Jael, the tent-peg wielding assassin, drove home the final blow by killing Sisera in her tent during his milk-induced slumber. The battle narrative ends with Jael proudly showing off her handiwork to Barak and a comment about how King Jabin was eventually destroyed (Judg. 4:22–24).

The Song of Deborah (Judg. 5:1–31), considered one of the oldest biblical texts (see Alter, 131), retells the events of the defeat of the Canaanites from Judges 4 in poetic form. Before observing the differences, several similarities between these two accounts can be pointed out. Both the prose and the poetic versions credit YHWH with the military victory (Judg. 4:6, 23; 5:2–5, 11), and emphasize Deborah's role as the primary spiritual leader of the nation (see 4.4 Leadership above). Both accounts mention all of the primary characters: Deborah (Judg. 4:4–5; 9–10, 14; 5:1, 7, 12, 15), Barak (Judg. 4:6, 8–10, 12, 14–16, 22; 5:1, 12, 15), Jael (4:17–22; 5:6, 24), and Sisera (Judg. 4:2, 7, 9, 12–18, 22; 5:20, 26, 28, 30). (King Jabin is absent from Judges 5, however.) In terms of battle details, there is greater discrepancy between chapter four and chapter five, but both include an extended account of Jael's assassination of Sisera. The poetic version includes a repetitive refrain about Sisera that would have been better to sing after wine:

> "He sank, he fell,
>> he lay still at her feet;
> at her feet he sank, he fell,
>> where he sank, there he fell dead" (Judg. 5:27).

While the prose version of Judges 4 includes dialogue and descriptive details, the poetic version of chapter 5 includes flowery, figurative language typical of an epic poem. The narrative account is full of commands (Judg. 4:6, 10, 13, 14, 18, 19, 20), while the song is full of questions, many of which are rhetorical (Judg. 5:8, 16, 17, 28, 30). Chapter four briefly mentions only two tribes involved in the Canaanite campaign (Naphtali, Zebulun), while chapter five goes into depth detailing all five tribes who helped, the two mentioned in chapter four plus three more (Ephraim, Benjamin, and Issachar). Deborah's song also specifically shames three tribes for their unwillingness to join in battle (Reuben, Dan, and Asher). Perhaps the most significant difference between the prose and the poetic versions is that only the latter includes a hypothetical account of how Sisera's mother first wondered about her son's delay (Judg. 5:28). She and her ladies speculated that Sisera's delay must have been due to time it would take to divide the enormous plunder (including "a girl, or two" for each of the men—wink, wink, nudge, nudge), which of course would also include some special selections of fine dyed and embroidered materials for his mother (Judg. 5:29-30). Ironically, the fate they envision for the Israelites is likely the one to befall them as the oppressors finally become the vanquished.

5.2.5. Gideon (Judg. 6:1—8:35)

The judge cycles of both Gideon and Jephthah have a long introduction in which the main character of the subsequent narrative is not mentioned (Judg. 6:1-10; 10:6-16). Since these introductions appear to be expansions of the first five stages, they are typically included in the respective judge's narrative. Part of the cyclical terminology in this introduction comes from the mouth of an anonymous prophet, who, apart from Deborah, is the only prophetic individual mentioned in the book (Judg. 6:7-10, a passage that is curiously excluded from a Dead Sea Scrolls manuscript: 4QJudg^a).

The Gideon narrative can be divided into two sections, based on who is in control, YHWH or Gideon. The first half of the narrative (Judg. 6:1—7:22) focuses on YHWH and his authority over Israel and Gideon. He first hands them over to the Midianites and then delivers them through Gideon. Throughout this section, YHWH is primary as he sends messengers, gives orders, and displays power to Gideon. Gideon is secondary as he fearfully responds to YHWH's direction or asks YHWH for more signs in order to quell his fear.

The primary distinguishing feature of this first half of the Gideon narrative is a dialogue or interaction between Gideon and YHWH, involving divine initiation, and human response. In the pattern, which is repeated seven times, YHWH takes the initiative with a dramatic sign, which not only gets Gideon's attention but also communicates a message to the judge, who responds by taking a step with increasing levels of risk. While only once in the narrative is the word "sign" ('ôt) used, in each instance the divine act clearly signifies something important to Gideon, so the use of the term seems warranted. Table 3.10 lists these seven signs, their significance, and Gideon's response.

The angel initially appears to Gideon with an ironic greeting ("mighty warrior") for a man hiding in fear, telling him that despite the oppression YHWH is present, and, after three rounds of debate with the angel, Gideon responds by sacrificing a goat. The angel torches Gideon's goat, which instills the fear of God in him, and after the angel's words of comfort he builds an altar named "YHWH is Peace." (See also Sidebar 2.3, "Old Testament Call Narratives," and Table 2.4 in chapter two.)

Table 3.10: The Signs of Gideon

Supernatural Sign	Reference	Significance	Gideon's response
Angelic Visit	6:11–16	YHWH is with Gideon despite oppression	Sacrifices a goat
Angelic Fire	6:17–24	Gideon has found favor with YHWH's angel	Builds YHWH altar
Divine Commission	6:25–32	Baal isn't a god since he didn't oppose Gideon (Jerubbaal)	Tears down Baal altar
Spirit Possession	6:33–35	YHWH's spirit is with Gideon	Troops are called
Wet Fleece	6:36–38	To let Gideon know YHWH would save Israel by his hand	Asks for another sign
Dry Fleece	6:39—7:8	To let Gideon know YHWH would save Israel by his hand	Cuts troops from 32,000 to 300
Midianite Dream	7:9–22	To calm Gideon's fear that YHWH won't give him victory	Defeats Midian with trumpets and jars

Immediately after constructing the new altar, YHWH appears to Gideon directly and commissions him to destroy his father's Baal altar, which Gideon does, but at night, out of fear (Judg. 6:25–32). His fear was apparently warranted, because the next day, the townspeople plot to kill him for the desecration and perhaps for constructing a rival altar for YHWH, but his father defends him, and declares that if Baal is really a god, he can contend for himself. Both of Gideon's names are connected to this incident since his name means "hacker," which is essentially what he does to the Baal altar,[8] and the text explains that he was called Jerubbaal ("Let Baal contend") because of his father's challenge.

The spirit of YHWH then takes possession of Gideon, which prompts him to sound the trumpet and call Israel to arms (Judg. 6:33–35). Gideon then asks for two more signs in the form of a dry fleece with wet

---

8. Alter, 14.

ground first, then a wet fleece with dry ground second, which was sufficiently fear reducing to allow Gideon to reduce his military force by ninety-nine percent, from 32,000 to 300 (Judg. 6:36—7:8). Apparently, the massive military drawdown caused Gideon's fear to return, so YHWH performed one more sign, allowing him to overhear a dream in the Midianite camp as one soldier declares to his comrade that the destructive rolling barley cake in his dream surely represents Gideon and therefore signifies an Israelite victory over Midian (Judg. 7:9–14). Inspired by the barley cake dream, Gideon proceeds to rout the Midianites with trumpets, jars, and torches (Judg. 7:15–22).

In the second half of the narrative (Judg. 7:23—8:35), Gideon takes over and YHWH disappears as an active force in the narrative, with tragic consequences. YHWH's name only appears four times in these verses, after thirty-six occurrences in Judges 6:1—7:22. In a stark contrast to the first half, YHWH and Gideon do not interact in this section, nor are there any supernatural signs. Gideon appears to have overcome his fear and no longer wants direction, guidance, or signs. Ironically, it is at this point in the narrative where Gideon expresses most clearly the ideal that YHWH should be the only one in charge, "The LORD will rule over you" (Judg. 8:22).

Figure 3.7: *Gideon's Victory against the Midianites*, by Nicolas Poussin (ca. 1625). Pinacoteca Vaticana, Rome; Commons.wikimedia.org.

According to the text, the results of Gideon's rule are disastrous. He overreacts violently to the cities of Succoth and Penuel after they refuse to provision his soldiers. He leads Israel astray by the construction of an ephod. He takes on the trappings of a king, and possibility contributes to the rise of his son Abimelech's brutal reign. Gideon claims he doesn't want to rule, yet the text speaks about him in monarchical and dynastic language, with allusions to later kings (Saul, Ahab). Thus, the text contrasts the deliverance that resulted from YHWH's theocratic rule (Judg. 7:22) in the first half with the idolatry that results from Gideon's monarchical rule in the second half (Judg. 8:27).

5.2.6. Abimelech (Judg. 9:1–57)

The end of the Gideon narrative records how Israel returned to idolatry (Judg. 8:29–35), but instead of the expected cyclical cry for help from Israel prompting YHWH to send a deliverer, one of the sons of Gideon, Abimelech, whose name means "my father is king," establishes a monarchy. To eliminate any potential rivals, he slaughtered seventy of his brothers, a feat comparable to King Jehu's slaughter of seventy of Ahab's sons, whose heads were delivered to the usurper in decorative baskets (2 Kgs. 10:6–8). Initially Abimelech's reign was probably localized, centered in Shechem, a city in the hill country of Ephraim (Josh. 20:7). Later the text states that he "ruled" over Israel for three years, but the verb used there (*śārar*) isn't typically associated with the rule of kings. The cognate noun (*śar*) is typically used merely for military commanders (Judg. 4:2, 7; 7:25; 8:3). The narrative thus appears reluctant to grant him the status of a legitimate monarch.

Jotham, the only surviving son of Jerubbaal (the text stops calling him "Gideon" in Josh. 8:35, and refers to him as "Jerubbaal" eight times in chapter 9), goes to the top of nearby Mount Gerizim (see Deut. 11:29) to deliver what has been called "the finest example in Scripture of a fable."[9] His poetic protest to the lords of Shechem involves a counsel of trees who, in their search for a ruler, invite the olive, the fig, the vine, and the bramble to reign over them (Judg. 9:7–15). The first three are all too busy producing oil, fruit, and wine, but the bramble has sufficient time in his schedule to rule the forest, assuming the other trees are acting in good faith. Jotham proceeds to explain the fable, sarcastically inquiring if the Shechemites acted in good faith with his father who delivered them from the Midianites when they slaughtered all his brothers (Judg. 9:16–21). The clear implication is that they did

---

9. Block, 316.

not act in good faith, and therefore the bramble's curse of fire should devour the city and their ruler.

In an apparent fulfillment of Jotham's curse, the text notes that an evil spirit from God came between Shechem and Abimelech (Judg. 9:23), comparable to the evil spirit from YHWH that came upon King Saul (1 Sam. 16:14–16). The Shechemites turned against Abimelech, installing a rival ruler, Gaal, in his place, which prompted Abimelech to retaliate by destroying the city, slaughtering its inhabitants, and razing its tower. Despite his success in Shechem, he met his demise in his attack on the city of Thebez. As he drew near to burn the tower gate with fire, a woman of the city dropped a millstone on his head, crushing his skull (Judg. 9:50–57), recalling the prophetic word from Jotham that fire would ultimately devour him.

5.2.7. Tola, Jair, Ibzan, Elon, and Abdon (Judg. 10:1–5; 12:8–15)

Since each of the reports regarding the minor judges are very short, only two or three verses with no extensive narrative details, I will refer back to section 2.5, which discusses the characteristics the minor judges and their pattern to avoid repeating observations already made above.

5.2.8. Jephthah (Judg. 10:6—12:7)

As a preamble to the Jephthah narrative, the text again recounts the idolatry of the Israelites, going into detail listing their seven objects of worship (Baal, Astarte, the gods of Aram, Sidon, Moab, Ammon, and Philistia). The consequences are described in typical cyclical terminology. YHWH was angry, so he gave them into the hands of their enemies, this time the Ammonites, for eighteen years. Israel repents of their idolatry and cries to YHWH for help (Judg. 10:10).

But at this point two aspects of the divine response don't fit the judges' pattern. First, according to the text, the response is given directly from YHWH to the people (Judg. 10:11). Elsewhere in Judges, divine messages were delivered by angels (Judg. 2:1–4; 5:23; 6:11–23; 13:3–21), or a prophet (Judg. 6:8). Second, instead of sending a deliverer to rescue Israel, YHWH rebukes them, reminds them of all the times he has delivered them in the past, and tells them to cry out to the gods they have been worshipping and let them provide the necessary deliverance. The seven divine deliverances (from the Egyptians, the

Amorites, the Ammonites, the Philistines, the Sidonians, the Amalekites, and the Maonites) parallel their seven objects of idolatry (see Alter, 163). After they persist in their groveling, YHWH is moved to compassion, but no specific divine intervention is mentioned. The text then narrates that the Ammonite and Israelite forces are gathered to fight in Gilead, but the Israelites lack a leader, which sets the stage for the next judge.

Jephthah the Gileadite is one of the most interesting and tragic characters in Scripture. He is introduced in a rather inauspicious manner, and yet he shares unique characteristics with two highly familiar biblical characters. Jephthah was the son of a prostitute (Judg. 11:1), but according to his genealogy in Matthew's gospel, so was Jesus, as his ancestors included Rahab the prostitute, and Tamar who pretended to be a prostitute to trick Judah into providing an heir for his dead son Er (Genesis 38; Joshua 2; Matt. 1:3, 5). Jephthah was also an outcast who attracted outlaws (Judg. 11:3), but so was David as he was being hunted by his royal predecessor, Saul (1 Sam. 22:2; 30:22).

Jephthah's reputation as a military leader prompts the Gileadite elders, who previously treated him as an outcast, to request that he lead them in battle against the Ammonites. When Jephthah appears reluctant, they persist and Jephthah agrees, with a condition, foreshadowing his later vow, that if they bring him home, and YHWH gives him victory, he will be their leader.

Despite his rough reputation, Jephthah begins diplomatically by sending messengers to the Ammonite king where, a bit like the Middle East today, each side tells a very different version of the story of how the conflict between Israel and Ammon arose. In his historical review, Jephthah appears to confuse the Moabites, the Amorites, and the Ammonites (see Numbers 20–21; Deuteronomy 2), and calls the Ammonite god Chemosh instead of Milcom.[10] The gist of his argument is that Israel tried to pass through the land of the Moabites and Amorites, but was not granted safe passage and was attacked. He's basically saying, "You started this fight, not us." Jephthah concludes by telling his potential foes that Israel's God gave Israel the land they have, and that the Ammonite god (Chemosh) gave them the land they have, so they should be content with the land their god gives them. As is the case with too many diplomatic missions, this one also failed,

10. See Block, 359–63.

and the Ammonite king didn't heed the Israelite judge's words. Conflict appeared inevitable.

Before going into battle, the spirit of YHWH descends upon Jephthah (as it does to Othniel, Gideon, and Samson), and he makes a vow to offer as a burnt offering whatever comes out of his house to meet him after his victory. While the diplomatic interaction between Ammon and Israel is narrated in depth in seventeen verses, the military encounter between the two nations is narrative briefly in only two. The text records that YHWH gave Jephthah victory over Ammon.

As he returns home, his only child, a daughter, rushes out to greet him. Jephthah tears his clothes as he realizes what he will need to do to fulfill the vow he made before the battle. Jephthah granted his daughter a two-month delay to allow her to grieve "her virginity" which apparently turned into a four-day ritual of lament for Israelite daughters (Judg. 11:39-40). (See Sidebar 3.1, "The Sacrifice of Jephthah's Daughter.")

Sidebar 3.1: The Sacrifice of Jephthah's Daughter

How are we supposed to interpret Jephthah's vow and sacrifice of his daughter? In many places in Old Testament narratives, the text is silent about the behavior of key characters that seems repulsive (e.g., Lot's suggestion that the men of Sodom rape his virgin daughters in Genesis 19). This incident involving Jephthah's daughter fits into this highly disturbing pattern. Here are some questions to ponder and possible responses.

What did Jephthah expect would meet him after his victory?

Probably an animal of some kind. The law codes mandated sacrifices of bulls, rams, sheep, and goats, and explicitly forbade child sacrifice (Lev. 18:21; 20:1-5; Deut. 18:10). Jephthah's agonized response to her appearance clearly signifies she was not what he was expecting.

Did Jephthah actually sacrifice his daughter?

Jephthah, his daughter and the text all speak euphemistically about the sacrifice, as if they were all too uncomfortable to utter what he would do to her. This ambiguity leads a few commentators to believe that he didn't actually kill his daughter: however, the text states he did what he vowed and most scholars conclude the sacrifice took place.

Figure 3.8: *The Return of Jephthah*, by Giovanni Antonio Pellegrini; ca. 1700. Denis Mahon Collection, London. Commons.wikimedia.org.

Should Jephthah have sacrificed his daughter?

Both daughter and father perceive they had no option, which seems outrageous to us. While we can't fully fathom how important vows were in Jephthah's culture, Israelite laws forbidding child sacrifice and killing (Exod. 20:13), which from the perspective of the canon come before the book of Judges, should have taken priority over Jephthah's sacred vow, making it clear that his foolish vow should have been broken.

Was Jephthah's vow necessary to defeat the Ammonites?

Jephthah's historical review makes it clear that he knows that YHWH gives military victory to his people. While we don't know that Jephthah was aware of it, the text stated that YHWH had compassion on his people (Judg. 10:16). YHWH's spirit came upon him, which was a sign that his actions already had divine blessing, just as Othniel's and Gideon's did when they achieved victory. Jephthah's vow was foolish, unnecessary, and tragic.[11]

After the battle, in an incident that bears striking similarities to one that occurred after Gideon's victory over the Midianites (Judg. 8:1), the Ephraimites rebuke Jephthah for not inviting them "to the party." Jephthah reminds them that they were invited to fight, but delayed and he couldn't wait. Unlike Gideon, who was able to successfully appease the Ephraimites earlier, Jephthah cannot calm his fellow Israelites and an intertribal battle ensues. Jephthah's Gileadite forces control the fords of the Jordan, and whenever someone wanted to cross the river, the Gileadites would ask them to say "Shibboleth" ("stream" in Hebrew; Judg. 12:6). The Ephraimites couldn't pronounce the word properly, however, so they would say "Sibboleth" and their tribal identity was revealed to the Gileadites. Thus, the word "shibboleth" is now used in English as a phrase to distinguish members of a certain group from outsiders. Jephthah's narrative ends with a brief notice that he reigned for six years, and was buried in Gilead.

5.2.9. Samson (Judg. 13:1—16:31)

Samson's narrative essentially consists of three separate stories: his birth narrative (Judges 13), his marriage to a Philistine woman, and his ongoing feud with the Philistines (Judges 14–15), and his relationships with two more women and how these led him to twice wreak havoc on Philistine public property (Judges 16).

The Samson narrative begins in the typical formulaic manner, with a note that Israel did evil, and YHWH gave them into the hands of their enemies, this time the Philistines, for forty years. And while unusual birth stories aren't unique in Scripture (e.g., Isaac, Moses, Samuel, John the Baptist, Jesus), Samson's is unique in Judges.

An angel appears to an unnamed woman, the wife of Manoah, of the tribe of Dan. He announces that she will no longer be barren, but that she'll give birth to a son, who will be a Nazirite, so no razor will touch his head, and no alcohol or unclean food will touch his lips (for background on Nazirites, see Num. 6:1-21). She then informs her husband Manoah of the angelic visitation and the text has her repeating the message (Judg. 13:6-7), but omitting the line about no haircuts, which is curious, since hair length plays such a critical role later in Samson's narrative.

Manoah apparently felt left out, so he petitioned YHWH to make

---

11. See also Phyllis Trible's discussion of Jephthah's daughter (Trible, 93–116).

an angelic curtain call. The angel reappears, but only to Manoah's wife again, as if his role didn't matter, but she was willing to share her angelic encounter with her husband, so she quickly ran to get him. Manoah asks about their son's lifestyle, and the angel almost seems perturbed, essentially saying, "I already told your wife" (Judg. 13:13). However, the angel goes on to repeat the dietary restrictions, but again leaves out the hair cutting restrictions. Manoah makes two more requests, a meal together and a revelation of the messenger's name, but both are denied by the angel. The angel grants them an opportunity to sacrifice a goat, which they do in a manner that resembles Gideon's earlier sacrifice in the presence of the angel (Judg. 6:19–24; 13:15–23).[12] After the angel's dramatic disappearance, Manoah panics and declares they are going to die, but his wife calmly reassures him that if God were going to kill them he wouldn't have accepted their sacrifice or told them they would be parents of a divine deliverer. As they disappear from the text, we need to observe that the husband is consistently insignificant and obtuse, while the wife is consistently sensible and clever. The chapter finally concludes with the birth of the judge, Samson, and with a notice that the boy was divinely blessed and divinely empowered with the spirit of YHWH (Judg. 13:24–25).

Once Samson has grown up, he sees a Philistine woman from the city of Timnah, to whom he is attracted, so he tells his parents, "Get her for me as my wife" (Judg. 14:2). As is often the case in biblical narrative, an individual's initial words define their character, and Samson's story revolves around the women to whom he is tragically attracted. When his parents are reluctant to arrange a marriage with a Philistine girl, he persists, and they relent. This union represents Samson's first move away from his sacred commission to deliver Israel, since he was supposed to defeat the Philistines, not marry them. Additionally, Israelites were not to marry non-Israelites (Deut. 7:3), which would be even more problematic for Samson since he had taken special Nazirite vows of holiness.

Samson goes to visit her, and YHWH sends his spirit on Samson as a lion attacked him, which apparently gave the judge superhuman strength so that he could tear the creature apart with his bare hands. On his next visit to his girlfriend, he notices a swarm of bees have made their home in the lion's carcass, which proves too great a temptation, so he scoops out some honey, thus breaking his Nazirite vow not to

---

12. See also Block, 411.

eat unclean food or to touch a corpse (Num. 6:6). His tasty snack thus constituted his second unholy act.

Samson next attends what is basically a pre-wedding stag party that involved thirty Philistines and lasted seven days (Judg. 14:10–11). While we don't know what he ate or drank, it is hard to imagine that this party did not include alcohol or non-kosher foods.[13] Inspired by the festivities, he issues a challenge to his companions: if they solve his riddle, he'll give them each a set of clothes (thirty sets total), but if they can't, they must give him thirty sets of clothes. His riddle recalls his recent conquest of the lion and consumption of the honey.

> Out of the eater came something to eat.
> Out of the strong came something sweet (Judg. 14:14).

The Philistines are unable to solve it so they threaten his new bride to get her to manipulate Samson into divulging the answer, which foreshadows Delilah's strategy later in the narrative. He eventually tells her, she tells them, and they then in turn tell Samson.

He accuses them of sleeping with his wife, to whom he refers as a "heifer," to obtain the solution, and then as YHWH's spirit rushes upon him, he slaughters thirty Philistines from the city of Ashkelon and gives their clothes to the men who solved the riddle. While the previous judges of the book achieve victory over Israel's enemies in clashes of armies, Samson's victories follow the pattern of this initial incident, involving heroic exploits of one Israelite defeating numerous Philistines.

After publicly calling her a heifer, Samson still thinks he can be reconciled to his wife (perhaps things were different back then?). He apparently has sex in mind as he comes to visit, but his father-in-law informs him that she was given to his best man, which prompts him to plan an elaborate revenge. He somehow captures three hundred foxes alive and ties them together in pairs by their tails, and inserts a torch in the tail knot (Samson could not have said, "No animals were harmed in this scheme"). He then let the fox pairs and their torches go running through the Philistine crops, vineyards, and orchards, destroying their harvests. The logistics of his scheme would surely have been daunting, but he was a heroic judge so it didn't seem to be a problem for Samson. It would have been funny to watch (stupid pet tricks?) if it weren't so destructive to the poor foxes.

13. See Block, 431.

The Philistines retaliate by burning Samson's estranged wife and her father as they had threatened earlier, which prompted Samson to offer a counter threat that he would continue his campaign of terror, and then he proceeded to deliver a vicious attack against the Philistines, although the details are lacking (Judg. 15:7–8).

While Samson hides in a cave, the Philistines come looking for the Israelite who keeps wreaking havoc against them, telling the men of Judah that they simply want to do to Samson what he did to them, essentially *lex talionis*, an eye for an eye (see Exod. 21:24; Lev. 24:20). The Judeans, instead of defending their fellow countryman, hunt down Samson and accuse him of behaving badly and angering their Philistines rulers. Apparently, only Samson is willing to take on the oppressive overlords. In his response to the Judeans, he also invokes the spirit of *lex talionis*—that he only did what they did to him—essentially saying, "they started it" (Judg. 15:11). While the Philistines were Israel's rulers (Judg. 13:1), apart from a brief notice about a raid on Lehi (Judg. 15:9), the text records no other oppressive behavior against Israelites. They threatened and killed his Philistine wife and father-in-law, but his retaliations included two slaughters of groups of Philistines, and a massive devastation of their crops. As the text is laid out, Samson's actions went way beyond "an eye for an eye."

As long as they don't attack him, Samson agrees to be tied up by the Judean men, yet another foreshadowing of what takes place while he is with Delilah later. The Judeans hand him over to the Philistines, YHWH's spirit comes upon him a fourth and final time (Judg. 13:25; 14:6, 19; 15:14), and he snaps through the new ropes. Displaying MacGyveresque resourcefulness, he uses the jawbone of a donkey as a weapon to slaughter a thousand Philistines, and then with Davidesque versatility, he composes a song (Judg. 15:16). Unlike the later king's praise of his God, this judges' narcissistic refrain merely celebrates his own wonderfulness, more like Lamech, the first polygamist (Gen. 4:23–24). The textual note that the bone was fresh (Judg. 15:15) would suggest that Samson again broke his Nazirite vows by handling what would have been considered part of a corpse.

After his dramatic victory, Samson cries out to YHWH in thirst and expresses his thanks for the victory perhaps as an afterthought. God then splits open a rock to provide water, reminiscent of two of Moses' rock-water miracles (Exod. 17:6; Num. 20:11). The text concludes this incident with a comment that Samson judged for twenty years (Judg.

15:20), which is curious, because a similar comment is included at the end of his narrative (Judg. 16:31).

Samson's out-of-control libido almost gets him killed on two more occasions. He is first trapped in the home of a prostitute from the Philistine city of Gaza by the men of the city, but he escapes and somehow manages to carry the city's gate almost forty miles to Hebron (Judg. 16:3). Surprisingly, no mention is made of the spirit of YHWH, or of any divine empowerment. Without its gates, the city of Gaza would have been defenseless.

After a series of unnamed females in the Samson narrative (his mother, his wife, his prostitute), the text finally informs us of the name of one, Delilah, his third and final love interest. It is difficult to be certain, but her behavior suggests that she is Philistine.

Many of the themes that we've already seen in Samson's narrative reappear in this final story. His lover persuades him to divulge a secret, this time about his strength, and after three rounds he eventually tells her the truth, he has never cut his hair. She is rewarded generously by the Philistines. When he was previously bound (once by the Judeans, and thrice earlier with Delilah), he had broken free easily. However, his Nazirite vows, compromised already with associations with unclean food, carcasses, and relationships with foreign women, are broken yet again as a razor shaves his head. While each of the previous infractions were intentional actions taken by Samson, this time he is merely passive as he is shorn in his sleep.

As he has experienced time and time again, violations of his vows don't seem to affect his strength, so he assumes that will be the case this time. But YHWH's spirit doesn't rush down—YHWH has left him (Judg. 16:20). He is seized and shackled, bound and blinded (see also the blinding of Zedekiah in 2 Kgs. 25:7).

At some point later, after his hair had begun to grow, Samson is present in the temple of Dagon during a special festival where among other things, they taunt the Israelite judge. He manages to be led to the two central pillars, and in his second recorded prayer (Judg. 15:18; 16:28), he requests a restoration of his supernatural strength, which enables him to pull down the building. His suicidal act of retribution and destruction killed more Philistines than all his other acts combined (Judg. 16:30). Thus ends the cyclical stories of the Israelite judge-deliverers.

Figure 3.9: *Samson and Delilah*, Rembrandt
(1629–1630). Gemäldegalerie, Berlin.
Commons.wikimedia.org.

5.3. Appendices (17:1—21:25)

The so-called Appendices of the book of Judges lack references to
judges or any of the typical cyclical material that dominated the major
central section of the book, but instead they include two extended
narratives. The first is about Micah, his young Levite priest, and the
Danites, and the second is about another Levite, his concubine, her
rape, and the civil war that ensued.

5.3.1. Micah and the Levite (Judg. 17:1–13)

Micah is an Ephraimite who stole from his mother eleven hundred
pieces of silver, curiously the same amount that was paid to Delilah
for betraying Samson (Judg. 16:5; 17:2). Worried about her curse, he
confesses to her, and she decides to dedicate the money to YHWH,
which might sound good to a pious reader, until one discovers that it
was used to construct an idol, a shrine, and other cult objects (Judg.
17:4–5), idolatrous practices which were forbidden in numerous legal
texts, most famously in the Ten Commandments (Exod. 20:4–5). While

no explicit connection is made to Micah's family's behavior, the text next includes the first of four comments about Israel's evil behavior during this period when there was no king (Judg. 17:6; 18:1; 19:1; 21:25). Micah then successfully convinces a young unnamed Levite to be his personal priest for his new shrine (Judg. 17:7–13).

5.3.2. The Migration, Theft, and Idolatry of the Danites (Judg. 18:1–31)

The scene shifts from Micah's family to the tribe of Dan who were still attempting to establish themselves in a tribal territory after unsuccessfully driving out the Canaanites (Judg. 1:34). In their quest for a homeland, they send out five spies to find an ideal location. On their journey, they meet Micah and his Levite, who tells them that YHWH will be looking out for them (Judg. 18:6). They continue their trip and discover that the city of Laish in the far north appears ripe and unprotected. After returning, they report to the rest of the Danites the results of their reconnaissance. As the whole tribe travels north, they again pass by the house of Micah and this time decide to steal his idol, his cultic objects, and his Levite, promising him a promotion from being a priest of a family to a priest of an entire tribe. Not being a particularly pious priest, he agrees and says nothing about the theft (Judg. 18:19–20). When Micah and his neighbors catch up to them and cry out to them, the Danites turn back and say indignantly, "What's the matter with you?" Micah's crew respond in shock over their hypocrisy, but the six hundred armed Danites warn them to calm down, otherwise they might be slaughtered by some of their hot-tempered companions. Micah simply returns home. The Danites continue north, eventually wiping out the citizens of Laish, setting up a new shrine there, and renaming the city after their tribal ancestor, Dan. The tribe of Dan thus epitomizes the downward spiral of the entire nation of Israel as they are shown to be idolaters, thieves, and brigands.

Before concluding this first section of the Appendices, we need to make three comments about how this story connects with the broader narrative of the Hebrew Bible. First, the text finally divulges the name of the anonymous priest who was so easily corrupted—it was Jonathan, the son of Gershom, the son of none other than Moses (Judg. 18:30; Exod. 2:22). Second, this early instance of blatant idolatry foreshadows a much later one where Jeroboam, the first king of divided Israel, set up two golden calves, one in the south at the city of Bethel, and another in the far north, at this same location, at the city of Dan (1 Kgs. 12:28–30). Third, the text concludes the story by referring to the exile of the land (Judg. 18:30), which was probably the first exile of the northern kingdom of Israel by Assyria in 734 BCE (2 Kgs. 15:29; see also 2.2 above).

5.3.3. The Levite and His Concubine (Judg. 19:1–30)

The text of Judges next narrates perhaps the most troubling story in all of Scripture, involving the betrayal by a husband and the gang rape by a city. And what begins as a domestic dispute serves as a catalyst for a series of events that culminate in a civil war, which nearly leads to the extinction of one of the Israelite tribes.

The story begins with an unnamed Levite, who seems to have no connection to the unnamed Levite of the previous chapter (who we later discover was named Jonathan). He has a concubine (also unnamed), which is curious, because typically a man with secondary wife like a concubine already has a wife, but no mention is made of a primary wife (Judg. 19:2). After some type of marital problem (it's hard to know who was to blame; see the various commentaries), she leaves and returns to her home. While they clearly don't have an ideal union, it would be hard to anticipate the problems that will later be exposed in their relationship. In a romantic move that is difficult to reconcile with his later behavior, he decides to pursue her and win her back (Judg. 19:3). He is received favorably by her and her family, particularly by her father whose outrageous hospitality doesn't allow the Levite to leave after a delay of several days. The concubine is overlooked and ignored as the Levite and his father-in-law enjoy each other's company with food and drink. Finally, the Levite decides he needs to leave with his servant and his concubine to return to his home in the Ephraimite hill country, but because of the concubine's father's persistent hospitality, they get a late start, a bad omen for their trip (Judg. 19:8–10).

The servant suggests stopping at Jebus (which later will be called Jerusalem), but the Levite rejects the idea because he doesn't want to stay with foreigners. They should have stayed with foreigners; it would not have been possible to have been treated any worse than they were at their ultimate Israelite destination. They finally arrive at Gibeah, in the tribe of Benjamin, and after waiting for local hospitality, an old man who is not a Benjaminite, but an Ephraimite, finally offers them a place to stay (Judg. 19:16–21).

At this point the parallels between this story and that of Lot hosting the two angels in the city of Sodom come fast and furious (Gen. 19:1–8). The language is similar in the two texts and one can read commentaries[14] for more extensive lists of the similarities, but here are a few. In both stories, travelers arrive at the city (Sodom, Gibeah) looking for housing, they are brought in to a resident's home, the residents of the city surround the house and demand to "know" them, essentially to commit homosexual gang rape of the guests, and a substitute female(s) is offered instead.

After these numerous parallels, the story in Judges 19 deviates dramatically from that of Genesis 19 regarding the fate of the females. In Genesis, Lot's daughters are spared when the angels blind the men of the city. In Judges, however, her Levite husband seizes her and tosses her outside to the "wolves," and the concubine is brutally ravished to death by the men of Gibeah (Judg. 19:25). The Gibeahites are worse than the Sodomites, and the Levite is worse than Lot.

The Levite discovers her body the next morning when she doesn't respond to his saying, "Get up." A tragic story grows even darker after he returns home to chop up her body into twelve pieces and send them out to the tribes of Israel, attempting to provoke a response from his countrymen. (See Sidebar 3.2, "The Gang Rape of the Levite's Concubine.")

Sidebar 3.2: The Gang Rape of the Levite's Concubine

Most readers of Scripture prefer to ignore or skip over the story of the gang rape of the Levite's concubine. It's hard not to wonder what the biblical authors were thinking when they decided to include such a gruesome story among their holy texts. Personally, I hate the story because it is so brutally disturbing.

While we might be tempted to bury our heads in the sand like the proverbial ostrich when we become aware of wickedly disturbing behavior like that of the Gibeahites in Judges 19, the authors of Scripture took a different approach. They decided to record the abandonment by an Israelite host, the betrayal by an Israelite husband, and the gang rape by an Israelite city.

---

14. E.g., Block, 520, 533–34.

> The text offers few answers to the questions racing through our curious minds. Why was the story included? What point is it trying to make? How should the story be interpreted?
>
> While I don't like the story, I think it's good that it was included in the Hebrew Bible, because tragically, rape happens, and catastrophically, violent gang rape also happens. By not ignoring this unnamed concubine's shocking story, we can lament her death as she was sacrificed by her husband, just as the daughters of Israel lamented the daughter of Jephthah sacrificed by her father (Judg. 11:40).[15]

5.3.4. Civil War (Judges 20)

The provocative action of the Levite elicited a dramatic response: four hundred thousand soldiers from the rest of Israel.[16] The Levite informs them what happened to his concubine but omits the detail that he tossed her out to the ravaging mob to protect himself (Judg. 20:4–7).

The extended battle narrative begins with an attempted negotiation in which the other Israelite tribes ask the Benjaminites to hand over their fellow tribesmen, the Gibeahites, but the Benjaminites refuse (Judg. 20:12–13). The Benjaminites only have twenty-six thousand soldiers, but their military skills including stone slingers (like the shepherd boy David against the Philistine giant; 1 Sam. 17:49) who could hit a hair with their projectiles. Despite being outnumbered, the Benjaminites inflict heavy casualties on the Israelites over the first two days of battle (Judg. 20:19–25). On the third day, the Israelites change strategy, similar to one used earlier against the Canaanite city of Ai (Joshua 8), and lured the Benjaminites away from the city of Gibeah into an ambush while the city of Gibeah was destroyed (Judg. 20:26–46). Only six hundred Benjaminites remained, hiding in the nearby hills. In the judgment against the Gibeahites, we see a form of *lex talionis*, an eye for an eye. Just as the Gibeahites used superior numbers to do violence against a weaker opponent, so the Israelites used superior numbers to do the same against the Gibeahites.

---

15. See also the relevant discussions of this story in Lamb 2015, 123–27; and Trible 1984, 65–91.
16. Many scholars think this number is hyperbolic; see Alter, 209.

5.3.5. The Benjaminite Solution (Judges 21)

Shortly after their victory, the Israelites realize that because of their vow to not give their daughters in marriage to the Benjaminites, one of the twelve tribes will quickly become extinct, that of the youngest "brother" Benjamin. Ironically, in sympathy for Benjamin, they decide to slaughter the men, women, and children of Jabesh-gilead—everyone except the young virgins—because that town didn't come to fight against Benjamin, and so they didn't take the vow to not intermarry with the disgraced tribe. This first stage of the final Benjaminite solution yields only four hundred virgins for the six hundred surviving men of Benjamin, so they need another plan to provide more spouses. Whereas the first plan involved a municipal slaughter, this one seems to involve rape. During the upcoming festival, the Benjaminite men hid and while the young women of Shiloh were dancing, they snatched them away to make them their wives and thus were able to rebuild their tribe. While Robert Alter views the snatching of the dancing women positively as merely an elaborate mating ritual,[17] most scholars perceive it essentially as rape, which would be ironic in light of the initial crime that precipitated the civil war. Now it's not just Gibeahites performing the rape; it's the Benjaminites, aided and abetted by the Israelites, who came up with the scheme.

After the Benjaminites manage to snatch a sufficient number of brides, the book ends with a final notice that there is still no king in Israel (Judg. 21:25), which looks forward to the next book in the Hebrew Bible, Samuel, where presumably one of the sons of these unions became the first king. There Saul is introduced, shockingly, in light of the events of Judges 19–21, as a Benjaminite (1 Sam. 9:1). The final notice of Judges also repeats that all the people did what was right in their own eyes. If one is uncertain how to interpret this expression, one merely needs to recall what it meant to do right in one's own eyes throughout the book of Judges and the actions that were committed by Israel's own judge-deliverers. Gideon and many others commit idolatry. Abimelech commits massive fratricide. Jephthah commits child sacrifice. Samson commits sexual immorality. The Danites commit theft and slaughter. Most of the tribes, but particularly Ephraim and Benjamin, are involved with tribal rivalry which eventually culminates in a civil war. The book that begins with

17. Alter 2013, 218.

the amputated digits of a king ends with the dismembered body of a concubine because first a city, and then a tribe with the help of a nation, commit rape. Their actions were right in their own eyes, but not in the eyes of their God.

Bibliography

Ackerman, Susan. 1998. *Warrior, Dancer, Seductress, Queen: Women in Judges and Biblical Israel.* New York: Doubleday.

Alter, Robert. 2013. *Ancient Israel: The Former Prophets: Joshua, Judges, Samuel, and Kings: A Translation with Commentary.* New York: Norton & Company.

Boling, Robert G. 1975. *Judges: A New Translation with Introduction and Commentary.* Garden City: Doubleday.

Block, Daniel I. 1999. *Judges, Ruth: An Exegetical and Theological Exposition of Holy Scripture.* Nashville: B & H Publishing.

Klein, Lillian R. 1988. *The Triumph of Irony in the Book of Judges.* Sheffield: Sheffield Press.

Lamb, David T. 2011. *God Behaving Badly: Is the God of the Old Testament Angry, Sexist and Racist?* Downers Grove: InterVarsity Press.

____. 2013. "Compassion and Wrath as Motivations for Divine Warfare." In *Holy War in the Bible: Christian Morality and an Old Testament Problem*, edited by Heath Thomas, Jeremy Evans, and Paul Copan, 133–41. Downers Grove: InterVarsity Press.

____. 2015 *Prostitutes and Polygamists: A Look at Love, Old Testament Style.* Grand Rapids: Zondervan.

Niditch, Susan. 2008. *Judges.* Louisville: Westminster John Knox.

Schneider, Tammi J. 2000. *Judges.* Collegeville: Liturgical Press.

Soggin, J. Alberto. 1981. *Judges: A Commentary.* Philadelphia: Westminster.

Trible, Phyllis. 1984. *Texts of Terror: Literary-Feminist Readings of Biblical Narratives.* Philadelphia: Fortress.

Webb, Barry G. 1987. *The Book of Judges: An Integrated Reading.* Sheffield: JSOT Press.

____. 2012. *The Book of Judges.* Grand Rapids: Eerdmans.

Younger, K. Lawson. 2002. *Judges, Ruth.* Grand Rapids: Zondervan.

Table 3.3: Major Judges Cyclical Pattern

Stage	Overview	Othniel	Ehud
Tribe		Judah?	Benjamin
Text	2:11–23	3:7–11	3:12–30
# of verses	13	5	19
Enemy		Aram	Moab
1. Evil	X	X	X
2. Anger	X	X	
3. People sold	X	X	X
4. Years		8	18
5. Crying out	X	X	X
6. Raising up	X	X	X
7. Spirit		X	
8. Enemy subdued			X
9. Rest		40	80
10. Judging			
# of stages	5	8	7

Deborah	Gideon	Jephthah	Samson	#
Ephraim	Manasseh	Manasseh	Dan	
4:1—5:31	6:1—8:35	10:6—12:7	13:1—16:31	
55	100	60	91	
Canaan	Midian	Ammon	Philistines	
X	X	X	X	7
		X		3
X	X	X	X	7
20	7	18	40	6
X	X	X		6
				3
	X	X	X	4
X	X	X		4
40	40			4
		6	20	2
6	7	8	5	

4

The Book of Samuel (1—2 Samuel)

1. Introduction

The struggle for power—and the violence that accompanies it—has always accompanied the formation of civilizations and their hierarchies. Who has the right to rule? What qualities and characteristics legitimize claims to authority? How do populations respond to their leaders, and at what point does the will of the leader misalign with the needs of the people? Perhaps most importantly, how are efforts to answer those questions remembered and preserved for future generations to consult to avoid similar conflicts and problems? The book of Samuel is the Bible's great testament to those questions, detailing how Israel transitioned from a turbulent tribal league into a monarchy, but one plagued by competition, duplicity, brutality, and uncertainty. The events in the book build upon the repercussions of that which precedes it until a single ruler—David—assumes the role of king and custodian of Israel's welfare. But a careful reading reveals a complex tale that offers a potent commentary on the dangers of power, the cost of corruption, the need for redemption, and the demands of justice both human and divine.

1.1. How to Approach the Study of the Book of Samuel

The book of Samuel holds together very well as a single storyline; it purports to tell the story of the rise of kingship in Israel and the major figures of the era who stood behind this change in Israelite political society, and it does this with great literary economy. But as we will see, this carefully wrought story is woven together from an assortment of shorter stories (and other sources) that were originally conceived for different purposes. The creation of the book from these different sources tells us that what we currently read is the end result of much revision, expansion, editing and orchestration at the hands of many authors. These authors—all of whom were trained and skilled ancient scribes—represented diverse social agendas and came from vastly different corners of Israelite society. For example, we will see below that some chapters dealing with the character of Samuel derive from a group of priests who saw Samuel as their great leader/founder and who sought to emphasize his importance to wider audiences at a time when various priestly traditions were in conflict. It is only a later scribal author/editor who took these chapters and worked them into a story about the royal conflict between Saul and David, Israel's first kings, and it is later still that the Deuteronomists reshaped all of this material with an eye to national history.

While one cannot deny that the end result of all of this scribal activity is a literary masterpiece, we will study this masterpiece by looking at how its component parts interact, as well as how they originated. It is important to see the sources behind the book of Samuel in their own light, which illuminates much about the complicated religious and social networks in ancient Israel as well as how the scribes remembered them. A source that was composed to bolster Saul's claims to power or criticize David's policies not only provides information about Saul and David but about how the author of the source understood or remembered each figure. What is more, it reveals what the author felt would be felt most strongly by the audience of his work: their values, fears, needs, and hopes regarding their leaders and the future of their communities. The story told in the book of Samuel is therefore the story of many factions and parties in Israel's society over many generations, at least as seen from the vantage point of the authors of its contents. Their compositions (and combination of earlier compositions) tell many stories at once, and we will approach these texts with an eye to how they navigate difficult and elusive memories in a way that their early audiences found meaningful.

1.2. The Name of the Book

A clue to the scope and nature of the book's vision may be found in the fact that in the Hebrew tradition, it is ultimately not named after David but after Samuel (*sefer shemu'el*), a priestly-prophetic figure who is credited with shepherding Israel into the monarchic era. It is Samuel who galvanizes the nation and reaffirms its covenantal character (1 Samuel 7), and it is he who establishes the book's ideological genotype as its narrative moves to other figures of national significance (1 Samuel 8, 12, 15). Samuel is thus emblematic of the pre-monarchic institutions that the book of Samuel places in a different category than the institutions and ideologies of kingship. The narrative within the book of Samuel shows a people unified by the rise of a monarchy but also torn apart by it. Had the book primarily functioned as royal propaganda (though its sources may have functioned this way), such tensions would never have survived into its pages. Saul, David and other figures who claim power over Israel all stand in the shadow of the priestly-prophetic figure Samuel, and the book implicitly aligns itself with Samuel's own sacral authority as it engages in its critique of these other characters and their actions. The later canonizers of the Hebrew Scriptures recognized this and titled the book after the character whose own ambivalence toward kingship resonates throughout the rest of the story. Yet the Septuagint preserves a different name—*Basileiōn*, or "[1–2] Reigns"—indicating the awareness that the work's place in the canon was intimately bound to the concept of kingship, both human and divine.[1]

The book of Samuel, then, provides a valuable window into how ancient Israelite scribes conceived of the past. The shapers of the book of Samuel neither attempted to idealize the era that saw the rise of kingship nor did they attempted to vilify it—even if the sources they inherited were conceived for such purposes (see section 2.2 below). Rather, the book of Samuel is a testament to difference and debate about the nature of leadership and power, pluriform in its presentation of ancient Israel's traditions from a variety of perspectives with a wide spectrum of responses and conclusions. No one perspective is left

---

1. The Septuagint tradition categorizes 1–2 Samuel with 1–2 Kings as a single work, all of which are termed "Reigns"; 1–2 Samuel is termed 1–2 Reigns, and 1–2 Kings is termed 3–4 Reigns.

without some form of counter-argument witnessed within the text; just as the reader encounters the closure of any given episode, the problems it engenders surface and pull the reader deeper into the conflict facing the characters therein. If the book of Samuel looks back upon the birth of monarchic Israel, it values both the infancy of that society as well as the birth pangs that accompanied its arrival onto the stage of history.

Figure 4.1: The prophet Samuel anoints David in the company of his brothers; fresco from the third-century synagogue at Dura Europos.

2. Literary Considerations

2.1. The Style of the Narrative

Some of the Hebrew Scriptures contain intricate, difficult language that requires a good deal of effort to "unpack," but the book of Samuel generally does not. There are passages and words that demand careful attention and carry more than one dimension of meaning, but the literary style of the book is both fairly unencumbered and quite consistent. Most of the work utilizes an "oral" form of storytelling—that is, its style reflects a culture where narratives (even extensive and intricate ones) were performed and heard in oral contexts, with very lean, simple and direct types of sentence structures. The scribes responsible for this were very likely capable of constructing much more complicated sorts of texts, but this style is very well suited for a tale of the rise of kingship at a time before literacy became a more frequent fixture in common Israelite culture.[2] It also serves a clear rhetorical purpose, since many tales and traditions of the turbulent early monarchic era must have developed and led to contradictory memories and vies about Israel's earliest kings and their deeds. A lean and direct type of narrative clarifies matters, establishing an "official" version of events but also providing an ostensibly clearer understanding of how and why various traditions and perceptions may have emerged.

Sidebar 4.1: Literary Style and Biblical Narrative

A diversity of literary styles is evident when we examine biblical narratives in some detail. The "simple" style has a sentence structure that is clear, concise, and similar to the way oral performances would convey narrative content. By contrast, other biblical narratives are written in a "dense" style—with complicated clauses and extended strings of nouns and adjectives characterizing the communication of information. While some scholars view this distinction in literary style as an indication of date, others prefer to see it as an indication of the author's or audience's social context. A "simple" style might be used in a narrative meant to appeal to rural audiences steeped in oral culture, whereas a "dense" style might be used to highlight the learned, elite character of the text's contents or authorship.

We should note, however, that these otherwise lean and clear narratives are punctuated with various poetic works at different points (1 Sam. 2:1–10; 2 Samuel 1; 2 Samuel 22, etc.). Poetry is a very different literary genre than narrative prose; scholars often understand it as drawn from other contexts such as public ceremonies or ritual settings and deposited in a narrative framework for different reasons. We see this elsewhere in the Hebrew Scriptures (most notably in Exodus 15 and Judges 5), where not only is the poem given a new meaning by virtue of its new literary function but the narrative surrounding it is infused with greater meaning as well, especially if the poem carried important symbolic attributes before its inclusion into the narrative. The various authors of the book of Samuel engage in this same process,

---

2. For a full discussion on the "lean" style vs. a more complicated "dense" style of narrative, see Polak 2003. Polak concludes that these linguistic characteristics are useful for dating these texts, but many scholars are hesitant to accept this as oral cultures persisted in Ancient Israel down to, and beyond, the monarchic era.

working old poems into the extensive narrative to both suggest the social authenticity of the narrative and to co-opt the way in which those poems were to function or be perceived by subsequent audiences. The simple, lean style of the narrative thus masks a very sophisticated strategy of ideas operating within its verses.

2.2. Sources and Redaction

There can be little doubt that the book of Samuel is indeed a compendium of vastly different sources stemming from disparate social and religious groups. Most scholars see its primary form as deriving from the hands of the Deuteronomistic scribes of the late-seventh to mid-sixth centuries BCE; in some cases their redaction incursions are quite obvious. But there is evidence of substantial narrative units that derive from authors living well before the Deuteronomists began their project. These discrete earlier sources hold the most fascination for many researchers, and may be identified here:

1. a "Samuel source" regarding his origins and rise to national prominence (1 Sam. 1—3; 7:2–17)
2. an independent narrative regarding the capture and return of the Ark (1 Sam. 4:1—7:1)
3. a propagandistic narrative regarding Saul's battlefield prowess (1 Samuel 11)
4. a folkloristic tale regarding Saul's selection by Samuel (1 Sam. 9:1—10:16)
5. a brief counter narrative somewhat critical of Saul (1 Sam. 10:17–27)
6. a lengthy narrative regarding David's rise to power (1 Samuel 16—2 Samuel 5)
7. an account of David's transferring of the Ark to Jerusalem (2 Samuel 6)
8. a divine promise for an enduring royal dynasty to David (2 Samuel 7)
9. a catalog of David's royal accomplishments (2 Samuel 8)

10. the Bathsheba-Uriah episode (2 Samuel 11–12)
11. the "Succession Narrative" (2 Samuel 13–20)
12. an appendix of ancient archival material (2 Samuel 21–24)

As we can see, the diversity of these sources is vast, and even within these sources one may sense stages of development. A famous example is again to be found in 1 Samuel 16–17, where varying accounts of David's introduction to Saul are attested, pointing to a compiler's attempt to give voice to various tales about their initial encounter. The tale of David's anointing (1 Sam. 16:1-13) is positioned as an introduction to an older tale where Saul is plagued by an evil spirit and David is brought into the royal court to sooth the troubled king with his skills as a musician and singer (1 Sam. 16:14-23). In this same complex of material we also encounter the well-known tale of David's slaying of Goliath (1 Samuel 17)—a folktale about David probably adapted from a tale about one of David's soldiers (2 Sam. 21:19). Yet in 1 Samuel 17, Saul seems never to have met David before the Goliath confrontation (v. 58), despite the tale (1 Sam. 16:14-23) that David becomes part of Saul's royal court. This suggests that the authors of 1 Samuel 17 created their story independently of 1 Samuel 16; the two were only later redacted together.

Sidebar 4.2: Who Killed Goliath?

We are informed in 2 Sam. 21:19 that it was not David but one of his soldiers, Elhanan son of Ya'arei-Oregim of Bethlehem, who slayed Goliath. This brief notice is included in a collection of "deeds and doings" of David's heroic soldiers, and is related in an unencumbered and basic manner—there is no real ideological slant or bias other than the fact that it affirms that David's soldiers could boast different military accomplishments. Because of this, many scholars see the more familiar David-Goliath episode of 1 Samuel 17 as a piece of royal propaganda based on the tale of Elhanan; that is, an author assigns to David (in much greater detail!) the accomplishment of killing Goliath. While this is an example of good mythmaking regarding David's rise to public prominence, it may not be completely disconnected from how Elhanan's act was perceived. In more modern eras, generals are credited with winning battles fought by their soldiers, and so too would ancient warlords reap the rewards of having capable soldiers working beneath them as they claimed power. It may not have been too distant

---

a leap for the author of 1 Samuel 17 to weave a compelling tale from the source in 2 Sam. 21:19 if the deeds of David's soldiers were already credited in part to his own ambition and willfulness.

When would such stories have originated? There are many scholars who prefer to see them as arising during or only shortly after the lives of the characters they depict, but there are other possibilities. We must bear in mind that literature regarding figures such as David and Saul could also serve the interests of the lineages they sired and ongoing struggle between them. Indeed, 2 Samuel 3:1 reveals that this exact situation developed, where the "house of David" and the "house of Saul" were locked in conflict, and the tale of David's deeds following the death of Saul gives notable attention to the surviving Saulides who continued to vie for monarchic power (2 Samuel 4, 9). The rivalry between Saul and David may thus be symbols, in part, for rivalry between circles of descendants who sought to displace each other over many generations. The Saulide house remained an important institution or memory in Israelite and early Jewish political culture down to the Persian period; the narrative notices regarding Davidic/Saulide struggle could conceivably date from any time during the monarchic era when tensions mounted between Davidic/Judahite culture and non-Davidic Israel monarchies in the north.

Several periods emerge, then, for the origination of the sources that comprise the book of Samuel. For example, the narrative in 1 Samuel 11 recounting Saul's battlefield prowess is especially indicative of an early period of origination. The narrative makes virtually no reference to Samuel (who appears only in v. 14, generally regarded as a secondary addition), and the tale that emulates the typology of the warrior-savior found in the Book of Judges, a typology that was no longer viable past the tenth century BCE, when royal norms replaced earlier forms of leadership. First Samuel 11 was composed at a time when an appeal to this mode of national, charismatic leadership could serve as an effective basis for accruing power and commanding allegiance.[3]

3. Hutton 2009, 313–21.

Figure 4.2: *David and Goliath,* by Caravaggio (ca. 1600);
Prado Museum. Commons.wikimedia.org.

Moreover, the narrative appears to know specifics of the old legends regarding the warrior-saviors in Judges. Saul is especially comparable to the figure of Gideon (Judges 6–8); the latter conducted a troubled battle over a lengthy narrative, culminating in the relentless pursuit of two enemy fugitives. By contrast, the account of Saul's battle is related in one concise verse, and "no two of them escaped" (1 Sam. 11:11). The author of 1 Samuel 11 is attempting to argue that Saul is a more capable warrior than the Gideon of memory, which suggests that the narrative was meant to "sell" Saul's royal viability to populations in the central highlands familiar with the Gideon tale. Such a specific appeal fits an early background when regional populations in the central highlands sustained their own distinct sense of social identity and cohesion. First Samuel 11 clearly remembers a time before the rise of kingship and thus reveals its position as an early propagandistic effort to establish Saul's kingship as conventional and traditional in nature.[4]

It is also common for scholars to date 2 Samuel—especially the **Succession Narrative** (2 Samuel 9–20)—to a relatively early period. The narrative is not likely to have emerged from a rural context, where

4. Leuchter, 2015.

the agrarian population was hardly supportive of Solomon's right to rule (see the discussion of Solomon in the chapter on the book of Kings in this volume), but it knows the rural world intimately and presupposes it as the normative cultural setting for royal events. This, one could argue, could be a feature of any royally-sponsored text if the scribe in question knew the ways of the countryside and its population. However, it is beyond doubt that the Succession Narrative was written for the purpose of explaining how and why David's kingdom rightfully passed to Solomon in the opening chapters of the book of Kings (see section 5 below), and it is likely that this royal composition originated at a time when Solomon's right to rule was still contested. A tenth- to ninth-century setting for its origination provides the best background for its compositional origins.

Sidebar 4.3: Moses and Shiloh

The Shiloh sanctuary was one of the most important sanctuary sites in pre-monarchic Israel; Jerusalem's own legitimacy is viewed in different biblical sources as the direct inheritor of Shiloh's sacred role. Part of the site's importance rests in the perception of the priesthood that dominated therein—the Elides, who were members of the Mushite priestly clan and believed to be descendants of Moses. The Mushites appear to have spread quickly in the twelfth century BCE throughout the Israelite highlands, occupying important sanctuary sites as ruling priests and cultivating traditions about their ancestor Moses in a way that would eventually lead to Moses' dominant position in the Hebrew Scriptures (Deut. 34:10–12; Ps. 90:1, etc.).

A valuable piece of evidence is the notice regarding the Dan sanctuary in Judg. 18:30–31, where we learn that Dan was home to another priestly line, that of Jonathan son of Gershom son of "Manasseh." In various manuscripts, the Hebrew word for Manasseh possesses a "suspended" letter, reading MNSH; with the N removed, the name reads as MSH, i.e., "Moses." The Danite priesthood was thus another Mushite faction, and v. 31 informs us that the Dan sanctuary was comparable to that of Shiloh. This further implies that the Shiloh priesthood saw itself as deriving from the line of Moses, and explains why Samuel's own Moses-like characteristics are highlighted during his training at the Shiloh sanctuary.

In addition, the "Samuel source" (1 Sam. 1—3; 7:2-17) should be viewed as obtaining in a relatively early period, though it is more difficult to determine a date for these narratives than for the Succession Narrative discussed above. There can be little doubt that the destruction of the Shiloh sanctuary was perceived as a result of its priesthood's shortcomings. The emphasis on Samuel's direct prophetic encounter with YHWH in 1 Samuel 1—3 provides an alternative to Elide leadership: the author of the narrative makes the case that the covenant relationship between YHWH and Israel is preserved not by priests bound to a fallen sanctuary but by a figure who was also prophetic conduit for divine will and presence. This figure—Samuel—may not have been a descendant of Moses like the Elides (1 Sam. 2:27-28), but he was in a way a "new" Moses by virtue of his unmitigated experience of the divine (1 Samuel 3).[5] Indeed, Samuel's efficacy as a priestly-prophetic leader is demonstrated in the events of 1 Sam. 7:2-17, where a Deuteronomistic introduction (vv. 3-4) prefaces a tale where Samuel, like Moses, calls upon YHWH, who answers the call by revealing his thunderous presence (cf. Ps. 99:6; Exod. 19:16-19), scattering Israel's enemies and securing their borders.

It is difficult to imagine this collection of narratives originating at a time well after the major sanctuaries of the northern and southern monarchic states had affixed themselves in national religion and a more stable priestly hierarchy had formed. The Samuel source functions most effectively in a setting when cultic infrastructure was in flux and debates regarding authoritative priestly jurisdiction were fresh. The tenth century BCE, after David had taken Jerusalem and appointed Abiathar (a descendant of Eli) as one of his chief priests, fits this description. The rehabilitation of the Elides in this manner could create problems for a circle of Samuel's disciples, yielding a situation where they would have been subservient to a higher ranking priest from the family that Samuel had earlier rivaled or displaced. The Samuel source (probably conceived and circulated orally well before it was committed to textual form) could provide a testament to the accomplishments of their master a generation earlier, reinforcing the need to maintain a place of influence for those who claimed to preserve Samuel's traditions and teachings.

Another source that likely possesses early origins is the Ark Narrative (1 Sam. 4:1b—7:1). This independent narrative has long

---

5. Leuchter 2013, 22—40.

aroused the attention of researchers due to its fairly pedestrian location within the book of Samuel (interrupting the Samuel source) and its unique content regarding the Ark's foray into enemy hands and its return to Israelite territory. The Hebrew Bible pays significant attention to the Ark of the Covenant in different literary contexts—in some, it is the repository of divine law while in others it is YHWH's war palladium, but in all it is a symbol of the indomitable status and majesty of Israel's deity. The Ark Narrative is the one place in which the question of YHWH's indomitability is addressed with respect to the Ark, describing as it does the fallout of a major battle between Israel and the Philistines, the Israelite defeat, and the Philistine capture of this sacred icon. The battle in question is usually identified with the battle of Aphek (ca. 1050 BCE), during which time the Shiloh sanctuary was destroyed, as archaeological studies have shown.

Sidebar 4.4: The Myth of the Divine Warrior

Ancient Near Eastern cultures possessed a concept of the divine where combat and conflict was a prelude to a deity's dominance as king. In Babylonian literature, Marduk does battle with the sea demon Tiamat before defeating her and ruling the universe. In Canaanite tradition, the divine warrior Baal does battle with Yamm ("the Sea") before claiming the pre-eminent position among the gods. The Ugaritic texts found at Ras Shamra (on the Mediterranean coast of northern Syria) preserve this mythology in great detail, and the Ugaritic materials have many points of contact with ancient Israelite traditions in the Hebrew Scriptures regarding YHWH. For Israel, YHWH was a warrior deity (Exod. 15:3) who marched forth against enemies and claimed the sacred landscape for himself and for his people. The forces of nature quaked at his might (Psalms 29, 114) and order was obtained through the execution of his will, just as in the other ancient myths of Canaan and Babylon.

This is a fitting background for a narrative regarding the primarily cultic icon of that sanctuary, though the narrative is itself hardly an historically transparent work. Rather, the tale of the Ark's presence wreaking havoc within the Philistine camp serves a theological purpose: YHWH's role as the divine warrior remained potent even in the wake of Shiloh's destruction and the Elides' fall from power.

The Ark narrative follows a common mythic pattern in ancient near eastern literature regarding the actions of the divine warrior against his cosmic foes leading to his triumphant return to the heavenly homestead and declaration of divine kingship. So too does the Ark travel throughout the camp of the enemy, demonstrating YHWH's indomitability before its return to Israelite hands and its resting place at Kiriath Yearim (1 Sam. 7:1), an inter-clan sacred site in Judah.

That the Ark comes to rest in Judah is indeed the key to identifying the compositional origins (perhaps on the oral level) of the narrative, for the next time we encounter the Ark is during the account of David's transfer of it to Jerusalem (2 Samuel 6). Given the importance of the Ark in northern religious tradition, it is politically significant that David, a Judahite, makes this icon the central feature of the Jerusalem cult, as it helped secure the allegiance of northern populations as he attempted to unite the Israelite tribes under his throne.

Figure 4.3: Ba'al, god of the thunderstorm; gilded bronze idol from the port of ancient Ugarit. The Louvre; Erich Lessing/ArtResource, N.Y.

During the procession of the Ark to Jerusalem, David is reported to have engaged in a ritualized dance—most likely a dramatization of the myth of the divine warrior's domination of various cosmic enemies.

All of these texts lend themselves well to early oral origination before the book of Samuel received substantial shaping. As noted above, the date of the first major redactional orchestration of the book remains a matter of contention, and a tenth-century orchestration of basic propagandistic traditions about both David and Saul remains a popular option. But much evidence points to the late-eighth century BCE as a time when another such enterprise would have occurred. Episodes such as Samuel's refutation of kingship (1 Samuel 8), Samuel's valedictory address (1 Samuel 12), the confrontations between Samuel and Saul (1 Samuel 13, 15), and Samuel's selection of David (1 Sam. 16:1–13) all emphasize prophetic perspectives regarding the subordinate role of kings to prophets, and it is in the late-eighth century that prophetic voices take on a much more prominent public role. Moreover, prophetic critiques of Israelite political figures would have received much attention between ca. 730–700, a time when the royal leadership of both the northern and southern kingdoms had opened the door either to Assyrian suzerainty or full-out conquest and exile.[6]

Sidebar 4.5: Prophecy and the Assyrian Crisis in the Eighth Century BCE

Israel's prophetic legacy can be traced back to the pre-monarchic period, as prophetic experiences of different types had characterized ancient Near Eastern culture since long before Israel emerged as a distinct culture or community. However, it is during the mid- to late-eighth century BCE that a major change took place in the prophetic tradition, with figures such as Amos, Hosea, Isaiah, and Micah emerging into the public sphere and communicating a body of oracles that were preserved and transmitted in written form. Part of the reason for this change was internal to Israel: social abuses had become more common among the elite classes leading to the exploitation of the peasantry, which occasioned complaint and comment from these prophets. But in addition, the rise of Assyria over the small Semitic nations surrounding

---

6. Some scholars refer to the redaction of such narratives as part of a "Prophetic Record," a precursor to the Deuteronomistic History. See Hutton 2009, 152–56.

Israel presented a great threat to Israel's survival and autonomy. From the mid-ninth century BCE onward, Assyrian rulers had begun intervening in local affairs, and the prophets of the eighth century BCE saw this as a sign that Israel had transgressed against divine will. With the increasing presence and danger posed by Assyria, the eighth-century prophets ramped up their rhetoric, warning their audiences that they would be destroyed by this foreign nation if they continued to disregard YHWH's demands for social justice and proper cultic behavior.

Yet a compelling argument can also be made for situation the redaction of the book of Samuel not with a prophetic circle but a royal one in the late-eighth century BCE. A particular period during Hezekiah's reign (the years 705–701) is often cited as the basis for the production of much literature.[7] It was during this time that Hezekiah rebelled against Assyrian domination, and the major social and political difficulties conducted in preparation for the Assyrian response would require justification. The production of a definitive book detailing how Hezekiah's ancestor David also rose to power and secured national independence during uncertain times would provide a venerable precedent for Hezekiah's royal policies.[8] Moreover, a work justifying David's rule over the northern tribes would speak to the diversity of Hezekiah's own subjects, many of whom were refugees from the fallen northern kingdom.

One text in particular, 2 Samuel 8, recommends itself. As Baruch Halpern has argued convincingly, this chapter is probably based upon a monumental royal inscription that commemorated (and, no doubt, exaggerated) David's conquests.[9] This inscription was transcribed into the book of Samuel, providing a window into David's reign that reified the prestige of the Davidic line, thereby justifying the initiatives of his descendant Hezekiah, and it is possible that some of the details in the chapter were drawn from other archival sources as well (such as the list of David's cabinet members). Authors with access to these materials would certainly have been the scribal officers of the royal

7. Halpern 1991.
8. See the chapter on the Book of Kings in this volume for more on Hezekiah's reign.
9. Halpern 2001:141.

court; working these details into a narrative context served the rhetorical goal of foregrounding Hezekiah's own royal initiatives within a tale that emphasized the grandeur of his great ancestor, suggesting that Hezekiah's policies should be legitimized as an extension of David's own glorious deeds.

In either case—prophetic or royal—the eighth century BCE appears to be the turning point in the orchestration of sources, yielding a work that would ultimately factor significantly in the subsequent Deuteronomistic History and, obviously, the expanse of historical narratives running throughout the Hebrew Bible.

2.3. Working (Backward) through the Composition History of the Book of Samuel

Since very few works in the Hebrew Bible have as many points of contact with other works in the biblical canon as the book of Samuel, we shall consider the layers of composition and redaction that saw the shaping of its contents over an extended period of time. We will work in reverse, considering the latest layers of substantial shaping first, working back to the earliest compositional layers.

2.3.1. The Persian Period

In its current form, most scholars see the book of Samuel as directed to a Jewish audience of the Persian period (538–332 BCE) since it is situated within the **Primary History** (Genesis—Kings), a product of that era. This edition of the book may be credited to members of the Jerusalem temple faculty, and in all probability, to **Levite scribes** situated therein. It was the Levites who shaped the materials that would become part of the Second Temple sacral curriculum taught by the Aaronide priests who governed the temple in Jerusalem. The contents of the book of Samuel fits nicely into this schema: it argues that Jerusalem was founded on royal initiative, but that the king who founded it as the basis for national faith was still accountable to a divine authority brokered by sacral agency. Within the book, this agency is primarily prophetic, but for audiences in the Persian period—especially in the fifth and fourth centuries—this sacral authority fell upon the priesthood almost exclusively, working in the wake of the prophetic movement's decline.[10]

178

2.3.2. The Neo-Babylonian Period

Babylon's domination over Judah took place well before the conquest of Jerusalem and the Babylonian exile beginning in 587 BCE. The book of Kings contains a brief episode where King Hezekiah gives a tour of the Jerusalem temple precincts to a group of Babylonian diplomats, which suggests some sort of deference to the Mesopotamian power already in the late-eighth century. It was in the late-seventh century, however, that Babylon arose as a serious threat to the Judahite monarchy. The **battle of Carchemish** (605 BCE) saw the defeat of Egyptian forces by those of Babylon under the leadership of King Nebuchadnezzar, who would later go on to take control of the Judahite royal court and eventually bring about the destruction of the city and the captivity of its population. The fall of the Davidic line at this time is intimately intertwined with the dominance and fortunes of Babylon as a world power; those Jews living under the aegis of Babylonian authority were thus constantly countenanced by the fallen fortunes of the Davidic line even after the exile had taken place and the population was separated from the fixtures of its pre-exilic life.

As most scholars agree, it was under these circumstances that the Deuteronomistic History was composed/redacted—including the book of Samuel. The Deuteronomistic History ends with the notice of the rehabilitation of the Davidic descendant **Jehoiachin** ca. 562 BCE (2 Kgs. 25:27–30), a piece of information to which the Egyptian Jewish community would only have been privy long after the fact. This leads most scholars to posit a redaction of the Deuteronomistic History among the Babylonian exiles (though many other pieces of evidence point in this direction as well), where the king resided and for whom the fate of the last scion of the Davidic house was a daily reality for much of the period of captivity. The scribes of Jerusalem taken into exile with this king as well as those who were joined to this community following the final destruction of the city in 587 BCE were the most qualified to reshape the book of Samuel at this time, and were certainly among the parties most interested in doing so. Davidic hope survived throughout the period of exile among both the lay audiences and those associated with the royal house, a sentiment that would not have gone unaddressed by the exilic redactors of the book.

---

10. On the shift from prophets to scribes in the Persian period, see Schniedewind 1995.

Sidebar 4.6: The "Ration" Tablets of Jehoiachin

In the early-twentieth century, British excavators at the site of Babylon discovered tablets containing the name of the Judahite king Jehoiachin, deposed in 597 BCE and carried away captive to Babylon in that same year according to various biblical sources. The tablets, dated to 592 BCE, mention the amount of rations that this king and his entourage were to receive. This indicates that even while being held captive in Babylon, Jehoiachin was still regarded as a figure of some political importance.

Figure 4.4: The ration list for Jehoiachin, exiled king of Judah; from ancient Babylon. Vorderasiatisches Museum, Berlin; ArtResource, N.Y.

Yet the redactors of the book balanced this sense of Davidic hope with a sober realism regarding the potential for restoration—if passages such as Samuel's salvation of the nation in 1 Sam. 7:2–17 reflect an exilic redaction of earlier sources (a position advocated by many commentators), then the exilic redactors advocate the view that stability was due to sacral, not royal leadership (a view that, as we have seen, was promoted by the Persian period literati as well). And indeed, other texts from the exilic period reveal that the argument for sacral over royal leadership was a going concern among audiences living in Babylon. Any additions to the book of Samuel during this period were likely quite minor, but this idea or ethic would most certainly have characterized the redactional reworking of earlier versions of the book.

2.3.3. The Late Monarchic Period (Ca. 720–587 BCE)

There is good reason for seeing the book of Samuel as having received significant shaping during the late monarchic period, especially in the late-seventh century BCE. It is in the late-seventh century BCE that many scholars see the production of a Samuel–Kings corpus, at which point the book of Samuel, as it existed, was worked into a considerably larger narrative reflecting (at least in part), upon the cultic reforms of King Josiah and the abrupt death of that king in the year 609 at **Megiddo**.

Sidebar 4.7: The Samuel–Kings "Corpus"

The Septuagint tradition refers to Samuel–Kings as "1–4 Reigns," which suggests that the ancient translators of the Hebrew material into Greek understood the contents of the Books of Samuel and Kings to constitute a single storyline. But there is evidence for this even before the period in which the Septuagint translation would have taken place, namely, in the Book of Chronicles. The author of Chronicles lived in the mid-fourth century BCE and utilized Samuel and Kings as a primary source for his own composition; the manner in which he treats both books suggests that he viewed them as a single, unified work regarding the era of the monarchy. It is telling that the Chronicler essentially skips over the preceding units in the Deuteronomistic History (Joshua and Judges), which may reveal that while Joshua, Judges, Samuel and Kings were all subject to Deuteronomistic redaction, at least some ancient scribes saw a special relationship between Samuel and Kings that they did not extend to Joshua and Judges.

With the integrity of the throne called into question, the redactors of Samuel–Kings created an historiography that separated David from the era of the kings who followed. It was likely during this time that the appendix of archival material in 2 Samuel 21–24 was added to the book (though almost certainly drawing from much older sources), literally separating the powerful David of the book of Samuel from the old and feeble David in the Book of Kings.[11] The more powerful character of David was thereby rendered a mythological figure of sorts, distinct from the type of monarchs encountered in the book of kings and thus made into a paragon fit for theological speculation against which subsequent kings could be judged.[12]

Sidebar 4.8: The City of Megiddo

The tradition of a final battle between good and evil—known in popular religious culture(s) as "Armageddon"—derives from the importance of the ancient city of Megiddo. Megiddo was a major Canaanite urban center in the Late Bronze Age, and later became an important city during Israel's monarchic period as well. Archaeological excavations have revealed that it served as a place for horse trading, a station for military garrisons, and an administrative center for the rulers of the northern kingdom of Israel. It is also the locale of many an important battle, including the site where King Josiah—one of the central figures in the Deuteronomistic History—was killed by an Egyptian Pharaoh named Neco in 609 BCE (2 Kgs. 23:29). This effectively brought to an end a brief period of autonomy for the kingdom of Judah and initiated its ultimate downfall in 587 BCE.

Figure 4.5: An Egyptian soldier leads Semitic captives before his king in this ivory panel from Megiddo. Israel Museum, Jerusalem; Erich Lessing/ArtResource, N.Y.

---

11. Leuchter 2010.
12. Joseph 2015.

The authors responsible for this maneuver should be sought amongst the same circle of Deuteronomists who redacted the book in the exilic period—namely, the **Shaphanide** scribal family (and affiliated confederates) with connections to both the Jerusalem temple and the royal court. It is important to note, though, that these scribes were not "royal scribes," strictly speaking. They were neither members of the Jerusalem priesthood who were subordinates to the Davidic kings nor were they royal sages on the royal payroll, but rather descendants of northern Levites who migrated to Judah following the fall of the northern kingdom in 721 BCE.[13] These scribes possessed an elite status that was no doubt based on their venerable heritage as northern Levites who had survived the calamity of an earlier era and who had been incorporated into the echelons of power in Judah. But possessing northern origins and Levite heritage enabled them to stand in between the royal and priestly institutions of Judah by the late-seventh century BCE, maintaining an historical perspective and socio-religious purview that interfaced with the Davidic myth but which was not subordinated to it.

2.3.4. The Early Monarchy (Ca. 950–850 BCE)

We have seen that there are solid grounds upon which to see a substantial amount of tradition in the book of Samuel originating in the time of the early monarchy. Most scholars who adopt this view date the relevant material to the tenth to ninth centuries BCE, though some allow for limited (probably oral) sources to date back a little earlier, namely, to the reigns of Saul and David in the late-eleventh century. At this early point, however, one can hardly speak of a "Book of Samuel." At best, one can posit disparate piecemeal tales, propagandistic or polemical in nature, emerging as the respective royal Davidic and Saulide houses competed for political dominance.

The authors of these tales are difficult to pinpoint with confidence in every case. Some tales appear to be folkloristic (e.g., 1 Sam. 9:1–10:16), lending the impression that they arose in a populist context rather than from royal propagandistic design. This, however, may not be the case, for a royal "spin-doctor" could easily craft and promote a tale that drew from a common folkloristic tradition for rhetorical purposes. In other cases, though, the authorship may be identified with a bit more

---

13. Leuchter 2008, 243n37.

certainty: the early form of Samuel's origin story is deeply indebted to Levitical ideology and most likely arose at the hands of priestly-prophetic disciples of Samuel, while the History of David's Rise (much of 1 Samuel 16—2 Samuel 8), a carefully plotted and ornate work, is taken by most commentators to be the result of a trained and highly skilled scribe retained by the royal court in Jerusalem.

3. Historical Setting

The events depicted within the book of Samuel appear to take place over a period spanning roughly a century, i.e., from approximately 1070–970 BCE. This approximate start date is based on the fact that the Shiloh sanctuary (the setting for 1 Samuel 1—3) was destroyed ca. 1050 (remembered, perhaps, in the events of 1 Samuel 4). If there is a genuine historical experience attested within these chapters, then Samuel's dedication to service at that sanctuary must be placed several years earlier than the time of its destruction. The closing date, 970, corresponds generally to the time that most scholars would estimate a near-end to David's reign in Jerusalem. Though it is only in the book of Kings where David finally meets his end, the book of Samuel draws to an end with the picture of an older, grizzled David surviving a series of exhausting personal and political crises.

Sidebar 4.9: Tenth-Century BCE Settlements in Judah

The region of Judah was quite sparsely populated at the end of the eleventh century BCE; during David's climb to power in the early years of the tenth century, few new settlements were formed, and it remained a sort of "wild west" in comparison to the more developed and densely populated northern tribal territories. Nevertheless, some important archaeological discoveries in recent years have demonstrated that some settlements in Judah at this time possess traits that could have supported the rise of a rudimentary monarchic establishment under David. The Tel Qeyeifah site, for example, has produced a small number of inscription dating from the early-tenth century. It strains the available evidence to identify this site as a royal outpost or administrative center, but the inscriptions demonstrate that some scribal figures resided there, and such figures could have been recruited to serve in an early administrative infrastructure. This does not mean

---

that the author(s) of these inscriptions were servants of David, only that their existence points to conditions more broadly throughout Judah that may have contributed to the rise of kingship in the area, later to be exploited by Solomon and his successors in the mid-tenth century and beyond.

The events depicted in the book of Samuel fit loosely into the following timeline:

Approximate Year	Episodes in the book of Samuel
1070 BCE	1 Samuel 1–3
1050 BCE	1 Samuel 4–6
1020 BCE	1 Samuel 9–15
1005 BCE	2 Samuel 5–6
1000–980 BCE	2 Samuel 7–12
980–970 BCE	2 Samuel 13–21

The book presents these episodes in linear sequence, but the likelihood is that some of these traditions developed alongside each other simultaneously, and the events in their current order may have once been set in a somewhat different chronology. For example, the "Promise to David" in 2 Samuel 7 is presented in the narrative as following immediately upon David's taking of Jerusalem in 2 Samuel 5–6, and is thus set in roughly 1000 BCE.

Figure 4.6: Iron Age ruins of Tel Qeiyafa. Photo by Ricardo Tulio Gandelman; Commons.wikimedia.org.

However, it is likely that this divine promise (or the ideology behind it) dates from much later in his reign, probably to counter the religious implications of a plague, see 2 Samuel 24 (see section 5);[14] its place in the current narrative is a matter of good storytelling rather than a desire to recount history accurately.

Nevertheless, the characterization of the lives of the major figures in the book of Samuel mirrors the turbulence of the era more generally. Following the collapse of Late Bronze Age empires in the late-thirteenth to early-twelfth centuries BCE, several new west Semitic ethnic societies began to form in the regions previous under the imperial administration of the Egyptian and Hittite empires. Many of these societies are attested within the biblical record itself (e.g., Arameans, Midianites, Edomites, Ammonites, etc.); by the late-eleventh and early-tenth centuries, they began to form more cohesive social structures and develop greater needs for resources, land, and security. Conflict between Israel and these neighboring peoples is suggested in the tales in the Book of Judges, and it certainly continued down into the earliest days of the monarchy as recounted in the book of Samuel. Indeed, the opening chapters of the book are suggestive of literary continuity between these works, and this mirrors social circumstances as well.

Israel in the late-eleventh to early-tenth centuries BCE would have invariably still been reeling from the stresses of constant struggle with outsider social groups, and fractious relationships within the Israelite tribal network would have similarly been agitated by these pressures. The historical setting of the book of Samuel is thus the last century of the Iron I period, the tail end of an era that saw the emergence of ancient Israel in Canaan in competition with various adversaries. The process of this emergence remains a matter of debate, but the archaeological evidence shows the settlement of the Canaanite highlands ca. 1200 BCE, and it is around this same time that the famous Merneptah Stele (1209 BCE) makes mention of an Israelite people in the same region. The book of Samuel introduces us to an Israelite culture that has been on the ground for roughly 150–200 years, with relatively well-formed institutions, religious praxes and social hierarchies characterizing daily life in between periods of conflict.

14. Meyers 1987, 357–476.

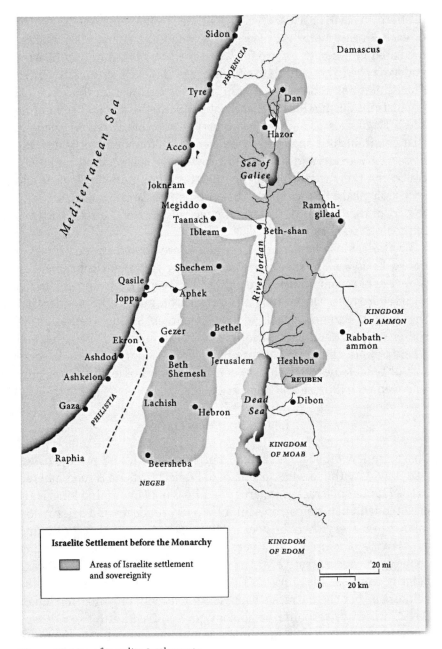

Figure 4.7: Map of Israelite Settlements.

The nature of Israelite social organization during this period is similar to that which is remembered in the Book of Judges: organized primarily by clan or tribal division, with local chieftains standing at top of each kinship network.[15] Priests stationed at the major sanctuaries mediated between these groups when matters of dispute would arise, and governed the cult that bound these different groups together. Thus chieftains and priests shared much power over local or regional populations during this time, and not surprisingly, the lines separating these typologies are somewhat blurry. The biblical record suggests that chieftainships and priesthood were both founded on the concept of sacred warfare and battlefield prowess, which secured numinous status for the successful warrior. Furthermore, anthropological and archaeological evidence shows that chieftains assumed cultic authority as part of their social status, standing at the apex of the religious lives of the lineages they ruled.[16]

By the same token, priestly groups were rooted in local kinship networks as well, so they too carried strong ties to adjacent lineages. A degree of tension must have existed between priests and chieftains with regard to social and religious jurisdiction, and it is no wonder that the book of Samuel reveals tensions between Samuel (representing the priesthood) and Saul (who is part of a family that likely helmed a Benjaminite chiefdom). According to the authors of the book, some sort of tenable negotiation between these forms of leadership is only achieved with the rise and reign of David.

3.1. How Real Was David?

There are few biblical characters more important, and more elusive, than David. Within a wide spectrum of biblical texts he is remembered as the founder of Israel's monarchy, yet he is not Israel's first king. He is credited with being a patron saint of prayer, yet death and destruction follows him everywhere he goes in the book of Samuel. He is presented as YHWH's anointed king, yet his position is consistently being challenged. The narrative of the book of Samuel goes to significant lengths to relate his story—his origins, his fidelity, his honesty, his penitence—but the narrative is presenting us with only one version of David, a literary response or apology for the David of history. Wisps of that David may be sensed in the David we encounter in the book of Samuel when the texts presenting him are carefully and cautiously examined. But this same caution and care must be brought to the

15. Van der Toorn 1996, 272.
16. Miller 2005, 8–13.

entire book of Samuel, since everything in the book, even the traditions that precede David's introduction into the narrative, have been shaped to anticipate his presence and impact. However we evaluate David within the book of Samuel, one thing is clear: his role in the book cannot be underestimated, and he receives the attention he does because within the world of the Hebrew Scriptures, his impact upon Israel's fate is inestimable.

Though the book of Samuel makes David its primary figure, and while this persists throughout much of the biblical tradition (David is rivaled only by Moses as the major character in Hebrew Scripture), many scholars have questioned over the years just how much we can say about the historical David himself or, for that matter, the major characters surrounding him in the book of Samuel. Two basic positions have emerged over the last several decades of research, the first being that the narrative in the book of Samuel pertains to real people and real events, even if those people and events are presented in stylized terms or dramatically amplified for theological reasons. There are, of course, different nuances given to this perspective, but all within this particular camp agree that the book of Samuel, masterful narrative that it may be, is a valuable resource for understanding the affairs of Israelite national life in the late-eleventh and early-tenth centuries BCE. From this view, the traditions enshrined within the book are regarded as deriving from flesh-and-blood individuals who shaped the destiny of monarchic Israel.

Within this paradigm, the David of the text is a reflection of the David of history. He is certainly idealized, promoted, and defended in the narratives that depict his deeds and doings, but this emerges from conventions of ancient literature (the **"royal apology"**) that legitimizes the steps a ruler takes to come to power.[17] The David of the text is heroic, beloved by many, a champion of traditional values and the common Israelite, and a defender of the people against foreign threat. This image may have been a response to charges to the contrary, i.e., that David was a violent warlord whose quest for power was ill-regarded by those who suffered in his wake. But even if this is the case, this means that there *was* a David who lived and ruled in Israel in one way or another; texts and traditions are not formed in a vacuum but arise from genuine generating circumstances.

By contrast, the other position is that the book of Samuel does not

17. McCarter 1980a, 489–504.

offer any reliable historical information regarding the characters and events it depicts.[18] For some, this is due to the propagandistic nature of the narrative, which obscures any objective recollection of Israelite life in this early period, let alone the words and deeds of the named individuals such as Samuel, Saul, David, Bathsheba, Absalom, etc.

Figure 4.8: Contemporary excavations, including this one, of a part of David's city beneath a parking lot in Jerusalem, continue to bring the circumstances of the early monarchy to light.

Indeed, for scholars who adopt this view, very little can be said about these figures, who are regarded as primarily legendary, including David. Recent archaeological work has literally brought the debate down to ground level, for Jerusalem itself appears to have been little more than a small walled town in the early- to mid-tenth century—hardly the metropolis that the biblical narrative paints.[19]

If Jerusalem was such a minor town in this era, the historical accuracy of events and communities surrounding it in the book of Samuel are called into question. As such, some scholars maintain that even a rudimentary state could not have emerged under David (without sufficient urban infrastructures), and the narratives regarding him as the powerful founder of an enduring dynasty would constitute little more than a fanciful projection of heroic idealism onto a socially transitional period as remembered by later writers. In this case, David was little more than a symbol of leadership held up as

18. See e.g., several of the essays in Pfoh and Whitelam 2013.
19. Pioske 2015, 84–86.

a standard to evaluate the history of the monarchy, through which later audiences could envision a model of leadership for an anticipated Messianic restoration.

However, several problems accompany the aforementioned conclusions. First, scholars who see David as an entirely fictive character do not adequately account for an important inscription discovered in 1993, which overtly refers to the kingdom of Judah as *byt dwd*, "the house of David." This text, known as the **Tel Dan inscription**, derives from an Aramean scribe of the mid- to late-ninth century BCE, who not only knows of a real David but who also regarded him as the founder of the Judahite royal dynasty. It strains credulity that the David referred to at this time would be anybody but the individual upon whom the character in the book of Samuel is based. Second, many scholars see the archaeological evidence of building projects in Israel as initiated by Solomon (even if these projects were later augmented and developed further by later kings).[20] This in turn supports the view that he inherited from David some type of monarchic system upon which he was able to capitalize.

In addition, while Jerusalem was certainly a small town or walled village in the early-tenth century, this does not preclude it from being a center for royal *administration*. Parallels have been drawn to the Jerusalem of the Late Bronze Age, when the city served an important administrative purpose within the Egyptian empire during this time despite the fact that it was a rather small enclave.[21] Likewise, parallels are drawn to the Jerusalem of the Persian period many centuries later, which also served as the administrative center of Jewish life despite its very small size. Jerusalem in the early-tenth century BCE functioned not as a major urban center but as an "agrarian stronghold," fit for the ruler of a largely **agrarian** population, and resonant with the values of that population and consistent with the image of the city as presented in the book of Samuel.[22] This is not something that writers of the late pre-exilic period or later would simply invent, and speaks to the substance of the book as carrying important information pertinent to historical reconstruction of Israel's early monarchic culture.

20. Lehmann 2003, 118–62.
21. Na'aman 1996, 17–27.
22. Pioske 2015, 85.

Figure 4.9: The Tel Dan inscription, ca. 870–750 BCE; The Israel Museum, Jerusalem. Commons.wikimedia.org.

The cumulative impact of these considerations leads to the conclusion that the book of Samuel is indeed rooted in history, preserving features of Israelite society that correspond well to what is known of the Israel of the late-eleventh to early-tenth centuries BCE. This does not mean that the book of Samuel provides us with an objective account of what transpired during this time period, and it does not mean that the narratives were ever geared to serve purposes other than apologetic, polemical or propagandistic. But the work responds to some generating circumstance and is predicated upon it, regardless of its agendas or biases.[23] The literary renditions of Samuel, Saul, David, and others in the book of Samuel tell us what the authors and audiences thought about these people, but this must relate in a meaningful way to their accomplishments and actions in history.

23. See further Kallai 1999, 345.

4. Major Themes and Motifs

4.1. New Replacing Old

Taken as a whole, the book promotes the Davidic house in the face of various obstacles and challengers, a literary reflection of the rocky politics involved in the rise not only of the Davidic royal line but indeed of the emergence of Judah—a relatively underdeveloped region until the mid-tenth century BCE—to the position of a major social entity over against the older tribal league to the north that benefitted from a greater population and richer resources. Indeed, the book of Samuel begins with an emphasis on the central-northern highlands, only to shift gears and emphasize the importance of Judah in the redemption of a northern religious and social system in dire need of adjustment and assistance. In fact, attention is drawn deeper and deeper into Judahite life as the book progresses, revealing features and textures of a geographic region that grew in population density and political significance in the first century of the monarchic period. The fate of the northern tribes of Israel is slowly but surely drawn into Judahite politics; by the end of the book, north and south are inseparable, with the latter poised to dominate the former.

Sidebar 4.10: A "Pan-Israelite" Identity

The biblical tradition paints a picture of a "United Monarchy" made up of a fully formed league of tribes sharing a uniform sense of kinship, but a closer look at the evidence reveals that this was unlikely. The tribal networks of the north and the Transjordan may have developed such relations with each other since they are among the earliest locales to see Israelite settlements in the twelfth to eleventh centuries BCE, but the situation with Judah was quite different. As noted above, Judah was a sparsely populated territory, more of a wilderness punctuated by small-scale clan networks in substantial isolation from each other. It would only be during the course of the tenth to ninth centuries that greater population networks would settle and expand in Judah, and even then the population was small in comparison to the north. Moreover, ancient poetic traditions such as the Song of Deborah (Judges 5) indicate that the northern tribes did not regard Judah as especially "Israelite," as the poem makes no mention of Judah within its discourse on Israelite

---

tribal networks. Some connection between the Israelite clans in the north and families in Judah may be sensed on a small scale (the devotion to the Shilonite Ark of the Covenant at the Judahite town of Kiriath Yearim is suggestive of some interaction), but a "pan-Israelite" tribal identity inclusive of Judah would have only emerged after the fall of the northern kingdom. It was only at this time that northern refugees fled to the south for asylum and an ideology of inclusion was required to assimilate these newcomers into the area.

The rise of Judah over Israel, then, is an essential factor determining the structure of the book, and one that is felt not only on the macro level but on smaller levels as well. The concept of a younger entity rising over an older one characterizes most of the major events as they unfold within the narrative, encountered first within the chapters concerning Samuel's origins. The Elide priesthood, long established at Shiloh and tracing their origins back to no less than Moses, are depicted from the outset as compromised and in need to correction or replacement . . . the latter option is what the authors of the narrative opt for, introducing the young Samuel as the inheritor of the Elides' authority once the latter fall from power. Samuel's outsider status—his parents are depicted as commoners—proves to be no impediment to his rise over Eli and his sons once he is devoted to sacral service at Shiloh. Indeed, his commoner status is not a detriment but an advantage, for it characterizes his roots as consistent with the agrarian ideals of the peasantry that the priesthood was meant to serve. Thus an important message within 1 Samuel 1—7 is that priestly authority is determined not by venerable and ancient lineage roots but by merit and proper ideological alignment. A newcomer embodying these qualities can outshine, and eventually outrank, priestly figures relying on lineage hierarchies as their basis for power.

The theme of turning from the old to the new permeates into the era of monarchy. It is true, of course, that Israel's first king, Saul, represents the dawn of the monarchic office as a replacement for priestly political leadership. But while Saul may be the first holder of a new Israelite monarchic office, the narrative sets him up for an eventual fall as a "newer" challenger will rise up to turn the nation away from Saul's leadership—and this challenger, obviously, is found in David. David, too, eventually finds himself in dire straits in the thematic equation of "new-replacing-old." The Succession Narrative beginning in 2 Samuel 13 sets in motion events that rock the sturdy foundations of the Davidic family, including David's own position not only as monarch but as paterfamilias of his household. Yet when all is said and done, when the smoke of the revolt clears, David defeats Absalom, returns to Jerusalem, and reclaims his position as sovereign. But since the book of Samuel is part of the Deuteronomistic History, even this return to power looks ahead to his eclipse by Adonijah and eventually Solomon in the early chapters of the book of Kings.

Sidebar 4.11: Priest-Saint "Origin" Stories

Anthropological studies have shown that priestly lines in agrarian societies usually derive authority from claims of descent from a "saintly" ancestor. This ancestor—sometimes genuine, sometimes invented—is generally credited with having a sort of revelatory or mystical experience that puts him or her in contact with the divine. As a result, the ancestor is regarded as a saint, a figure who can mediate between heaven and earth and whose power allows for the securing of blessing and protection from evil or danger. In the Hebrew Scriptures, this saintly status is frequently associated with success in battle: the Mushites, for example, promoted a tradition involving their ancestor Moses fighting Egyptian taskmasters and ruffians in Midian (Exodus 2), and Phineas the grandson of Aaron is given special priestly status for his assault against transgressor outside of the Tabernacle in the wilderness (Numbers 25); such violent actions resonate with the concept of YHWH as a divine warrior, suggesting that the deity directly empowered these figures to act. But saintly origin stories can also incorporate other types of divine encounters—the Samuel origin story crests with the direct revelation to Samuel in the Shiloh sanctuary (1 Samuel 3), and such a story could effectively challenge the power of the Elides who claimed descent from a saintly figure but who did not have direct contact with the deity themselves.

4.2. Prophetic Authority

David's fate is secured —and later sealed—by two prophetic proclamations, both voiced by the prophet Nathan. The first is the famous "Promise to David" in 2 Samuel 7, a work that has been overwritten and expanded in its current form to relate to Solomon's reign and, quite possibly, later Davidic kings as well. Yet the Promise is itself most likely based on an oracle deriving from David's own reign, as it was conventional in the ancient world for ruling kings to be granted divine sponsorship via prophetic pronouncement. Wisps of the original oracle can be detected in the current Promise, and this oracle must have secured for David assurance of a long and prosperous reign. Indeed, the very fact that the Tel Dan inscription refers to Judah as the "house of David" roughly a century after David lived is good evidence for the fact that David did indeed enjoy such a reign, though the biblical evidence reveals that it was marred by conflict.

Figure 4.10: An excavated gate at Tel Dan.

What this indicates is that the earliest traditions associated with David—even those pre-dating any semblance of a "Book of Samuel"—embedded David's tenure as monarch within a paradigm of prophetic authority. This paradigm seems to have survived to inform the remainder of the story of David, for the Succession Narrative is itself predicated upon the second prophetic pronouncement from Nathan (2 Samuel 12). This second prophecy specifies that David will survive the calamity that will be brought upon his family (v. 13), rendering it consistent with the tenor of the Promise in 2 Samuel 7. Yet both prophecies together make clear that David's kingship is not that of a complete sovereign. He remains accountable to the will of YHWH as communicated by prophets.

Prophetic authority works in a different direction in the Saulide folk tale in 1 Sam. 9:1—10:16. In this narrative, Saul's fitness to rule is rooted in different prophetic functions and experiences. First, it is through a prophet that Saul's royal fate is proclaimed: a "man of God" resides in a nearby town who might help Saul find his father's lost donkeys, and this same man of God—who turns out to be none other than Samuel—instead informs Saul that he is to rule over Israel. The scenario in which this unfolds is highly symbolic of a changing of the guard in terms of national leadership, as Saul is invited into Samuel's actual home and given a place at the table fit for the head of the household (1 Sam. 9:22–24), and the implication is that Saul is to take over as head of the "house" of Israel. In and of itself, this symbolic act may be understood as a prophetic proclamation, since prophets throughout the Hebrew Scriptures engage in symbolic sign-acts as part of their prophetic oracles. And indeed, Samuel goes on to tell Saul Saul in no uncertain terms that YHWH intends for him to be Israel's king (1 Sam. 10:1–9).

Sidebar 4.12: Prophetic Sign-Acts

Israel's prophets were known to engage in behavior of highly dramatized or symbolic dimensions in order to express a message to their audiences about YHWH's will. Isaiah ventures around Jerusalem naked (Isa. 20:2–3), Jeremiah wears a single loincloth that he is to bury and let rot (Jer. 13:1–11), Ezekiel eats a scroll (Ezek. 2:9—3:1, among other acts), and Hosea marries a woman who has children by other men (Hosea 1). All of these acts are meant to jar the audiences out of complacency, disrupting otherwise normal daily events and showing that the audience's expectations of safety and normalcy can be easily shaken and dashed by the course of history.

Even in this piece of pro-Saul propaganda, then, prophetic authority is the basis for political action, but this same narrative then goes on to challenge who may rightfully lay claim to this authority. As the narrative continues, Saul himself undergoes a prophetic experience: upon encountering a band of **ecstatic prophets**, the "spirit of God" comes upon him and he joins their ranks (1 Sam. 10:10–12), entering into a state of prophetic ecstasy that was understood in antiquity as the result of direct contact with the divine. The author of the narrative informs us that not only does this event become widely known throughout the populace, but people begin asking the question, "who is their [the prophets'] father?" (1 Sam. 10:12). The term "their father" (Hebrew *abihem*) refers here to a leader or president who oversees prophetic groups—one would imagine that Samuel would qualify, but the question implies that possibility that Saul might take on this role now that he has joined their ranks. In the end, this was not to be the case, and the incorporation of this narrative into a larger Deuteronomistic context shows that it is Samuel who retains prophetic control during Saul's reign. Nevertheless, even in this early folkloristic narrative, the concept of authority resting in prophetic experience and legitimation is powerfully attested.

Sidebar 4.13: Prophetic Ecstasy and Other Prophetic Experiences

Israelite prophets were characterized by different experiences. A common form of prophecy involved entering a trance state and engaging in ecstatic behavior—that is, having the divine spirit "possess" them and moving them to behave in a manner inconsistent with conscious decision-making. This could be understood as the manifestation of the divine presence, but it could also be criticized as an inability to function effectively in certain social settings and be viewed negatively (see 1 Sam. 19:19–24). Other prophets appear to have had visions and dreams (Zech. 1–8; Num. 12:6–8); others still are presented as able to intuit future events (1 Kgs. 22). But the Hebrew Scriptures ultimately give priority to forms of prophecy that result in oracles or teachings imparting divine will to the people, in which case the various visions/dreams/trance-states are rendered significant only if they lead to a durable message.

4.3. Fathers and Sons

The question "who is their father?" in 1 Sam. 10:12 resonates with a larger theme running through the book of Samuel regarding fathers and sons. The very first thing the reader of the book encounters is the genealogical list detailing the ancestry of Samuel's father Elkanah (1 Sam. 1:1). From the outset of the work, the relationship between parents and offspring are held up to critical scrutiny as the reader is invited to ponder the significance of this genealogical list and what this implies regarding Elkanah. Elkanah himself returns the reader to this question when he tells his childless wife Hannah "am I not better to you than ten sons?" (1 Sam. 1:8). The answer to this question goes unspoken, but the narrative strongly implies that it is "no," revealing that Elkanah does not understand how important it is for Hannah to have a son. When she finally does conceive and bear Samuel, he is given over to a different father figure, Eli, and the remainder of the Samuel origin tale pits Samuel between his biological father (and, implicitly, his household) and his adoptive father Eli. Even later in the Samuel source, Samuel's role as a priest is offset by his allegiance to his biological family connections: 1 Sam. 7:17 tells us that in his juridical down-time, Samuel returned to his family estate in Ramah.

The narrative's positioning of Eli as a father figure to Samuel is juxtaposed against the relationship between Eli and his biological sons Hophni and Phineas, who are presented in highly critical terms (1 Sam. 2:11–25). The narrative pulls no punches in depicting their abuses of priestly power, which include affronts to both the public making pilgrimages to Shiloh and to the deity worshipped there. For priests charged with safeguarding the cultic and theological nexus between Israel and YHWH, the abuses of Eli's sons constitute massive corruption with wide-ranging repercussions. As such, the narrative is clear about the problems inherent to the Elide family structure, as the egregious transgressions of Eli's sons go largely uncorrected by their father. At best, Eli gently chides his sons for their wrongdoings—hardly the role of a responsible father whose family holds so much at stake, and one is left to wonder whether this permissive father figure is to blame, in some way, for his sons' behavior. In the end, Eli and his sons are duly punished: Hophni and Phineas die on the battlefield as the Ark is captured by the Philistines, and Eli himself dies as the news of the battle reaches him (1 Sam. 4:17-18).

In a way, then, the sins of the father affect the entire family. On the other hand, Eli's responsible rearing of his other "son," Samuel, leads to Samuel's success as a priestly-prophetic figure, suggesting some degree of redemption for Eli beyond the strictures of biological parenthood. One can be an effective father by raising up different types of "sons." This notion is carried forward with Samuel himself, whose own biological sons are reported to be corrupt as well (1 Sam 8:4), yet Samuel does what Eli does not—he removes his sons from positions of power and admits to the limitations of both the line he has sired and the office he holds (though reluctantly, to be sure). In so doing, Samuel serves as a better father than Eli, placing the overall welfare of his "household" (the nation itself) above his personal family interests. And in place of his biological sons, Samuel raises up figures to succeed him that are more qualified to lead this national household, namely, Saul and David.

The father/son motif among the clergy in these early chapters of the book only foreshadows an even deeper engagement of the motif once the drama turns toward the issue of Saul's and David's respective reigns. Saul's fitness as a royal *paterfamilias* is called into question alongside tensions between him and his own son Jonathan as well as with his other children. As the authors of 1 Samuel 18—20 make clear, Jonathan feels stronger allegiance to David than to his own father, and takes measures to ensure David's survival even to the detriment of his own royal future. This, perhaps, may be the payoff to an earlier fatherly error on Saul's part in 1 Samuel 14, where Saul orders Jonathan's death due to the latter's unwitting violation of a royal edict of questionable value. It is only through the petition of the public that Saul reverses the order for his own son's death, but this signals a major problem with Saul as a father: the safety and integrity of his own lineage is of secondary importance to him than his role as a political sovereign. The man who would willingly sacrifice his own child for the sake of a self-proclaimed royal decree may be less suitable to lead the nation than one who makes the life of his offspring his highest priority. Jonathan may sense this and recognize that national fortunes are better entrusted with David.

Sidebar 4.14: Patrimonialism in Israel's Royal Culture

Canaanite royal culture in the Late Bronze Age was characterized by organizing society into a "patrimonial" structure. That is, a king was viewed as a sort of father figure, his kingdom was viewed as his household, and its citizens were seen as the king's children. Politics thereby created a sense of kinship that mimicked genuine lineage organization on the level of the family/clan. Ancient Israel preserved this ideology in its own early social organization: chieftains ruled over extended family networks and sat at the apex of power, and clans were organized by the leadership of elders who held pre-eminent social positions over the younger members/generations in the inter-related families. There is some evidence that Israel's early kings adopted this model in forming their kingdoms: 1 Sam. 9:1 emphasizes Saul's familial background, suggesting that generational organization has a role to play in the kingdom that Saul will go on to found. In a different way, Solomon organizes his kingdom on patrimonial principles, aligning his administrative districts with tribal populations to suggest that he now sits atop the tribal organizations in a patrimonial manner (1 Kings 4).

Finally, David himself becomes a focal point for the theme of fathers and sons. As with both Samuel and Saul, we are first introduced to David through his father, Jesse, and the selection of David as a replacement king for Saul occurs only after all of Jesse's other sons are paraded before Samuel (1 Sam. 16:1–13). Saul repeatedly refers to David as "the son of Jesse" (see, e.g., 1 Sam. 22:7) but also views David as his own son, both as the husband of his daughter Michal and as a member of his court. And indeed, even as Saul pursues David as a threat to his throne, the narrative goes to great lengths to present David as a loyal son to the king, foregoing various opportunities to do harm to his pursuer and maintaining bonds of fraternal piety to Saul's biological son Jonathan. That David becomes a paragon of filial devotion defends him against potential charges of usurpation by supporters of Saul, and it also cultivates a sense that a David operates in the interests of a society rooted in family-clan kinship structures and allegiances. But it also sets qualifying precedents for David to receive YHWH's patronage: as 2 Sam. 7:14 reveals, David's descendant, the one who will build a temple for YHWH, will become the deity's "son," and the deity will become that king's "father" (see also Ps. 2:7). David's filial piety secures his family's place within the structure of YHWH's own divine household.

4.4. Women and Wisdom

The role of **wisdom** and its connection to women are particularly important in the unfurling of events within the book of Samuel. From the outset, fitness to lead is bound to the ability to discern, interpret, and understand. Eli, the chief priest of Shiloh, lacks the sense to recognize Hannah's silent prayer as the expression of a desperate woman pleading for divine favor, and later lacks the sense to function both as a righteous priest and firm father when his sons abuse their religious authority. The consequence for this lack of insight and understanding is the fall of the Elide family and the loss of the Ark (1 Samuel 4).

Sidebar 4.15: Wisdom and Women in the Book of Samuel

Israel possessed different types of wisdom traditions—political, ritual, social, etc.—much of which is preserved in texts like the Book of Proverbs and a number of poems in the Book of Psalms. But wisdom is an important motif in the book of Samuel as well, and it is telling that most of the important female characters are presented as exemplifying this sapiential tradition. The wisdom of the agrarian communities in the pre-monarchic and monarchic eras may have rested in large part with particular women who were regarded as especially insightful and capable of resolving conflicts, brokering relationships and managing social networks. Even in the later wisdom texts like the Book of Proverbs that was written by male scribes and credited to a male patron saint (King Solomon), the female dimensions of wisdom are highlighted. Wisdom itself is a mythic female force or impulse, partnering with YHWH in structuring the cosmos, and the reader of Proverbs is instructed to seek out female partners who are capable and wise (Prov. 31:11-31). A strong memory of the role of women in preserving and transmitting earlier wisdom traditions is woven into Proverbs, complementing the social presuppositions regarding wise women in the book of Samuel and elsewhere.

In stark contrast to this, Samuel is presented as a capable leader not only due to his prophetic gifts but also his authority as a dispenser of justice (1 Samuel 7), a role that required sage wisdom in antiquity. Samuel also shows far greater wisdom that Eli when removing his own unfit sons from power; clearly, he learns from the errors of the past, one of the fundamental hallmarks of the wisdom tradition and its practical purpose. Samuel's wisdom is also vindicated on the macro-literary level. Knowing all too well what might happen with a questionable king in power, Samuel warns the people that difficult times lay ahead if they persist with their demands for monarchic leadership. By the end of the book, the terms of the warning have already begun to take shape, with both David's royal house and society at large severely injured by the duplicity and violence of kings and royal aspirants.

The wisdom motif extends to the royal sphere as well, beginning with a qualified critique of Saul. The pro-Saul traditions emphasize his charismatic, prophetic, and warrior qualities, but not his ability to govern wisely or deliberate with cautious and mature insight. Saul's initial actions as king are called into question from the very beginning with his reluctance to boldly accept the results of Samuel's lot-casting ritual—though his critics are lambasted as scoundrels (1 Sam. 10:27), the fact remains that the narrative gives voice to critics of the king-elect's ability to make sound decisions. Later, Saul takes more brazen initiatives, but these too are fraught with questionable judgment (1 Samuel 13–14). The worst judgment call of all, however, comes with Saul's inability to carry out the destruction of the Amalekites (1 Samuel 15); this is portrayed not simply as a breach of divine instruction but, in the larger sense of Israelite ethno-mythology, a step backward in the securing of Israelite socio-religious identity. Saul's folly, in short, not only impugns his right to rule, but also endangers Israel's national existence.

David serves as a foil to Saul in this regard. Though he, too, makes terrible errors in judgment, his reign is one that regularly tips its hat to the importance of wisdom in the conduct of daily business and the success of monarchy as a social enterprise. David's rise to power shows signs of a crafty, ambitious would-be-ruler who manipulates circumstances to his advantage. Some decisions show great social wisdom, such as the establishment of a national capital in neutral territory (Jerusalem) and the promotion of various priestly leaders to cabinet positions. The narrative appears to exonerate him from certain events that are morally and ethically questionable such as the death of various rivals and threats, but if David was behind these darker events, they too represent wise choices within the parameters of a royal aspirant. In this case, wisdom and morality are not necessarily the same thing, though in the context of an early Israelite culture characterized by incessant violence and conflict, the notion of "might makes right" may well have been an acceptable expression of political wisdom.

Most notable is the role of women in the expression and execution of wise counsel. From the beginning of the book of Samuel, women are regularly presented as more insightful, cautious, and aware than the men surrounding them. Hannah's devotion at Shiloh is cast in contradistinction to the shortcomings of both the Elides and her own husband Elkanah (who fails to grasp how badly his wife wishes to become a mother). Later, potential threats to rural order between David and the local chieftain Nabal are defused by Nabal's wife Abigail, who uses careful rhetoric and diplomacy to convince David not to retaliate with great violence against Nabal's insulting demeanor. During the tensions between David and Absalom, it is the Wise Woman of Tekoa who, through the use of a wisdom parable, negotiates a reunion between father and son. Though this reunion breaks down in time and gives way to Absalom's revolt, the narrative nonetheless reveals that David's reign was marked by a respect for the tradition of wisdom cultivated by women of the hinterland.

The ultimate wise woman in the book of Samuel, though, is Bathsheba. Though the circumstances under which she and David begin their affair suggest that she had little choice but to submit to the will of the king, every subsequent utterance from Bathsheba, few though they are, moves the narrative forward in such a way as to improve her position. If 1 Kings 1—2 are counted as part of an earlier version of the Succession Narrative, then this is amplified even further, for her actions in those chapters transform her son into the king and her into the venerable **Queen Mother** (an enduring office of sorts within the Judahite monarchy).[24] Commentaries on the book of Samuel draw special attention to Bathsheba, noting that she is among the most important characters in the book yet remains in the shadows; she is at the center of the most dramatic events in the Succession Narrative but remains mysterious. But this may be the result of deliberate dramatic and thematic design. If the character of Bathsheba is quietly affecting the unwinding of the plot to her advantage, this too constitutes a form of women's wisdom, one that shows how a woman must navigate a male dominated monarchic society in order to secure her rights and interests therein. Wisdom may not be kind or always ethical, but it is a necessity for survival. The foolish, by contrast, perish.

5. Commentary

5.1. 1 Samuel 1—7

The first block of material in the book of Samuel introduces us to a world before the rise of kingship, often identified as the era of the Judges. Read in sequence with the book of Judges, it would appear

---

24. Ackerman 1993, 385–401.

indeed as if this was the case, and subsequent passages suggest that the major religious leaders of the day should be counter among those Judges. However, read on its own, this opening unit depicts agrarian life in the **Ephraimite highlands**, and in particular, the drama taking place within the family of one man. That man is Elkanah, whose lengthy patronym points to his deep ancestral entrenchment in this region (1 Sam. 1:1). That he has two wives (Penina and Hannah) indicates his relative wealth. Elkanah, we will learn, will be Samuel's father—the author of the account begins his tale by emphasizing that Samuel's family is prominent and holds a prestigious place in the highland culture of early Israel. The tale thus commands the attention of ancient readers by making the main players emblematic of what may be at stake for such families in the face of problematic leadership . . . a major theme that will recur throughout the book of Samuel as a whole.

As the chapter continues, Elkanah's wife Hannah visits the Shiloh sanctuary to pray quietly to YHWH for a child; in her prayer, she promises to devote the child to sacerdotal service. While praying, she is spotted by the chief priest of the sanctuary, Eli, and scolded for possible drunkenness. This encounter is intriguing for a few reasons. First, it identifies the importance of Shiloh, which was the primary pre-monarchic sanctuary and provides some indication of the sort of attendance and patronage it commanded from the local population. Second, it reveals that quiet, private prayer was rare—Eli does not even consider it as a reason for why Hannah is alone and whispering in the sanctuary. Third, Eli's immediate conclusion that Hannah is drunk is suggestive of a **harvest/wine festival** as the setting for the episode, and scholars have increasingly identified such festivals as the backdrop to the development of Israel's narrative and liturgical traditions.

Sidebar 4.16: Wine/Harvest Festivals

Much of Israel's religion was bound to the land and the seasons; springtime religious festivals revolved around the tilling of the soil and the planting of seeds and the cultic ceremonies conducted at that time were connected to the creation of new life and thus a sort of mythic rebirth of the communities living on the land given to them by their deity. Likewise, the autumn was the time to reap the harvest and collect grapes from the vine to celebrate the deity's affirmation of the fruitful relationship he shared with the people. The setting of 1 Samuel 1 may be seen against this latter festival; this was a time of pilgrimage that explains Elkanah's and Hannah's trek to Shiloh, and Eli's assumption that Hannah was intoxicated may be explained by the drinking of wine at the harvest festival at the Shiloh sanctuary.

Figure 4.11: A vineyard in contemporary Israel. Photo: Udi Steinwell. Commons.wikimedia.org.

But two additional factors command our attention. Hannah's promise to devote the child to sacerdotal service is suggestive of how the priesthood in ancient Israel grew over time; new adepts and initiates could be dedicated to service, and over time establish their own priestly credentials and flock of devotees. Equally significant, the encounter calls into question Eli's capability as a priestly leader. The aggregate evidence within the biblical record (supported by comparative social-scientific evidence) points to the priesthood as the primary leadership institution that held together early Israel's diverse kinship units. For a priest such as Eli to helm a major sanctuary but also to so quickly conclude that Hannah is drunk foreshadows what will emerge about the Elide priestly family more broadly, i.e., that it is unfit to lead Israel. Hannah's promise to dedicate her child to sacerdotal service suddenly emerges as a mechanism whereby problems with extant priesthoods could be addressed by the provision of new priestly figures from beyond their ranks (which is precisely what will occur as Samuel grows into adulthood).

Upon hearing Hannah's reasons for praying, Eli offers her a blessing and assures her that her prayer will be answered. It is: she conceives and bears a son, naming him "Samuel," or *shemu'el* in Hebrew (1 Sam. 1:20). The narrative explains that the name relates to YHWH hearing Hannah's prayer; *shema* means "hear" and *el* usually means "deity" in Hebrew narrative. Another possible explanation is she-me'el, "[one who is] from the deity"—similarly identifying Samuel's birth as the answer to a prayer. Still another reading of the name is "his name is El," as some commentators have suggested based on linguistic considerations.[25] However, the author of the narrative provides his explanation because the theme of YHWH hearing prayers will be a particularly important motif in the ensuing chapters. The chapter ends with the report of Samuel being given to Eli as a priestly adept; 1 Samuel 2 then opens with an ancient poem ("Hannah's prayer" in 1 Sam. 2:1–10) to commemorate and celebrate the turn of events.

The ensuing material in 1 Sam. 2:11–3:21 form an essentially continuous narrative (Hannah's prayer works well as a pivot between this material and the episode before it). This unit amplifies the implications of the introductory tableau by revealing the depth of the problems with the Elide family: the sons are abusive of their power and their father Eli is too lax in disciplining them. All the while, we are informed that Samuel grows up untainted by these problems, waiting at the sidelines (2:18, 21b). The central passage in this unit is certainly the oracle spoken by a prophet, an anonymous **Man of God** (1 Sam. 2:27–36). This character is certainly a creation of the narrator, and makes clear that YHWH intends for a change in priestly regime—in the context of the larger Deuteronomistic History, the oracle anticipates later events, as indicated overtly in 1 Kgs. 2:26–27 (when Abiathar is dismissed from priestly service in Jerusalem). But its original purpose certainly sets up Samuel's emergence as the replacement to Eli and his corrupt sons.

---

25. The archaic form of the name (that is, the original pronunciation well before the current text was composed) is reconstructed by P. Kyle McCarter as *šimuhu-el*, "his name is El" (McCarter 1980b, 62).

Sidebar 4.17: The Deuteronomists' "Anonymous" Prophets

The Deuteronomists were deeply interested in prophecy and fashioned their narratives to emphasize the efficacy of the prophetic word. Many of their sources involved well known prophetic figures such as Deborah, Samuel, Elijah, Elisha, and Micaiah, but periodically the Deuteronomists would find a place in their redactional work to insert a prophetic message that they intuited from their sources and the traditions associated with them. At these times, the Deuteronomists used anonymous prophetic characters to express the insight or lesson they wished to impart in telling their narratives; in the case of 1 Sam. 2:27–36, an old tradition against the Elide line is placed is given literary shape by the anonymous "man of God," akin to the similar figure who declares an oracle against the Bethel altar in 1 Kgs. 13:1–10.

The payoff occurs in 1 Samuel 3. The chapter opens with the notice that "the word of YHWH was rare in those days; no prophetic vision [ever] emerged" (1 Sam. 3:1), obviously suggesting that what follows will bring a change to that circumstance. However, the notice also implicates the Elides, under whose priestly leadership prophetic visions and experience with the divine word had dwindled. Prophecy was a subset of priesthood in early Israel, and a dearth of prophetic experience is evidence of an ineffective priestly establishment. As the narrative goes on, we see that Samuel is asleep in the sacred crypt, which most scholars view as an attempt to "incubate" a **dream theophany**: Eli places the young adept before the symbol of the deity (the Ark), in the hopes that the deity will come to the child in a dream.

What happens next, however, moves in a very different direction. Samuel does indeed have an encounter with YHWH, who reveals to him a message regarding the fall of the Elide line similar to the words of the anonymous Man of God in the previous chapter (1 Sam. 3:11–15). However, this revelation does not occur as a dream. A careful reading of the chapter reveals that YHWH appears to Samuel while he is awake, standing directly before him.[26] In this way, Samuel's revelatory experience attains the same level of unmitigated holiness as the traditions regarding Moses, to whom YHWH also appeared face to face and not in a dream (Num. 12:6-8). The chapter closes with the notice

---

26. Leuchter 2013, 35–37.

that Samuel's prophetic power became well known and that once again, the divine word was active at Shiloh because of Samuel. It will thus be under his priestly leadership, not the Elides, that Israel will find its secure future.

What immediately follows is confirmation that YHWH's favor had fallen away from the Elides. First Samuel 4:1–7:1 is commonly known as the "Ark Narrative," which shows signs of late reworking, but which most likely derives from a fairly early source regarding a military catastrophe in the mid-eleventh century BCE. During this catastrophe, the Philistine armies defeated Israel's forces and probably destroyed the Shiloh sanctuary. The narrative does not speak explicitly of the fall of Shiloh, which points to its antiquity—the trauma of the event must have been so great that the narrative could only allude to the event by depicting the Philistine capture of its primary icon (the Ark of YHWH) and the death of Eli and his sons (4:11, 18). Only later texts such as Psalm 78 (Ps. 78:60–66) or Jeremiah's **Temple Sermon** (Jer. 7:12) could directly address the event.[27]

But the fall of the sanctuary is perhaps discussed in symbolic form by the brief tale about the birth of Eli's grandson Ichabod. Ichabod's mother, the wife of one of Eli's sons, goes into painful premature labor and dies during childbirth at the news of the capture of the Ark and death of her husband, his brother, and their father. The name "Ichabod" in Hebrew means "there is no [divine] glory," a reference to the departure of the divine from within Israel. The demolition of the sanctuary where YHWH's presence was affirmed in just the last chapter suggests that the child's name relates not only to the Ark's capture and the death of Eli and his sons but also to the fall of Shiloh.

Nevertheless, the fall of Shiloh and death of the leading Elides does not signify YHWH's loss of power but, rather, part of YHWH's plan for Israel's eventual success against the Philistines. The Ark Narrative relates that the Ark wrought great destruction against the Philistines in the form of a plague (1 Sam. 5:6–6:9), and that attempts to place it in a subordinate position in the temple to the Philistine deity Dagon met with failure—Dagon's statue is found broken and prostrated before the Ark (1 Sam. 5:1–5). The Philistines eventually realize that YHWH, represented by the Ark, has brought a curse upon them, and they deliver the Ark back to Israel. The Ark is given to the men of **Kiriath Yearim** in Judah, which was probably an ancient sanctuary site

---

27. Most scholars date Psalm 78 to the tenth to eighth centuries BCE; Jer. 7:12 is part of his famous speech delivered in the temple in 609 BCE (as affirmed in Jer. 26:1–3).

governed by a local priesthood deemed fit to serve as the trustees of this icon. But this also anticipates important moments later in the book of Samuel, namely, the rise of a Judahite king over Israel and his right to claim the Ark as a symbol of his own royal authority under the auspices of YHWH (2 Samuel 6). Like Samuel, who waits at the sidelines in 1 Samuel 2 until he is called by YHWH, the role of Judah in Israel's political future is represented by the Ark waiting at the sidelines as the narrative returns us to events taking place among the tribes to the north under the leadership of Samuel.

Sidebar 4.18: Kiriath Yearim

The town of Kiriath Yearim is mentioned in 1 Sam. 6:21—7:1 as the resting place of the Ark following the fall of the Shiloh sanctuary and before David brings it into Jerusalem. That this important cult icon is brought to this town indicates that Kiriath Yeairm was understood to be a cult site of some sort. A survey of texts from within the biblical record suggests that it was an inter-clan religious cite, with different cult icons stationed therein and different priests set in charge of them. Such sites are attested elsewhere in the Hebrew Scriptures: Shechem is an inter-tribal meeting point and likely was the site of a cultic establishment in the early pre-monarchic period, and the phrase *bet eloheyhem* in Amos 2:8 indicates that Bethel possessed a space where family religious icons were kept (the phrase *eloheyhem* can mean "their deity," but can also mean "their deified ancestors," i.e., small figurines used for ancestral veneration rites). While these pieces of textual evidence are indirect, they shed some light on why Kiriath Yearim was deemed fit to house the Ark: it was already a place where various religious icons were housed.

The final chapter in the unit returns us to Samuel, to whom Israel now comes as the encroaching Philistine army approaches (1 Sam. 7:2). Samuel is a man alone—a priestly-prophetic figure without a supporting priesthood, without an icon of the divine (i.e., the Ark), and without a sanctuary at which the divine presence could manifest and be consulted. He cannot fall back on the familiar bastions of Israel's sacral traditions for reinforcement, which might compromise his standing or power. However, we have already seen in 1 Samuel 3 that YHWH appears directly to Samuel just as he appeared directly to Moses; this equation of Moses and Samuel becomes highly significant here in 1 Samuel 7, for Moses led Israel at a time before Israel's cultic features (the Tabernacle, the Ark, the priesthood) had formed. The conditions under which Samuel is now called to lead mirror those that Moses faced, and thus it is fitting that Samuel demands that his people adhere to the laws taught by Moses in Deuteronomy: to put away their idols and devote themselves to him exclusively (1 Sam. 7:3–4). Samuel's words here closely match those found in the introduction to the book of Judges, which explains why Israel repeatedly faced foreign threats (Judg. 2:16–19). We thus find here the hands of the Deuteronomists, adjusting the Samuel material to work as part of a systematized view of history.

The event clearly establishes Samuel not only as the great priestly-prophetic leader of the day but also as the great political leader. Following the battle, Samuel "judges Israel all the days of his life," administering justice and making rounds throughout the major religious sites of the central highlands. First Samuel 1–7, then, establishes a paradigm of leadership that informs how the reader is to understand the role of kings in subsequent chapters. Israel's savior-figure, Samuel, emerges from a family deeply connected to the hinterland culture, and his religious authority is predicated not on inheriting priestly status or duties from an existing institution but through his direct encounter with YHWH, a sign of the deity's selection of Samuel to replace older, questionable leadership. Finally, Samuel's power as a leader is unmitigated—he requires no priesthood or sanctuary to invoke YHWH's presence and save Israel from threat. Rather, his power comes from his personal connection to the deity. It is figures like Samuel who herald YHWH to Israel and to the nations surrounding it; the canonical shape of the book of Samuel establishes these principles first in order to convey the lesson that Israel's future kings would do well to remember that their own powers are subject to higher levels of sacral and social authority.

5.2. 1 Samuel 8–15

Just as quickly as Samuel's political authority is established, it is challenged—not because he exhibits shortcomings, but because his sons do (1 Sam. 8:1–4). The opening verses of 1 Samuel 8 recall the problems involving Eli's sons several chapters earlier; the problem, it seems, is the institution of the priesthood, which is ill-equipped to deal with the increasing complexity of Israel's inter-tribal social world. This leads the elders of Israel to come to Samuel and tell him that the time has come for a great change: it is time for Israel to have a king. The entirety of 1 Samuel 8 is quite Deuteronomistic in its current form, drawing from the language of Deuteronomy in several places and invoking imagery and experiences at home in a culture emerging from **Neo-Assyrian imperialism**. Nevertheless, the chapter recalls an authentic cultural confrontation that obtained in the era where monarchy first emerged, i.e., the clash between priesthood and kingship. With the rise of kingship, Israel's priestly leaders (represented here by Samuel) would have lost significant political/administrative power; Samuel's harsh response to the request for kingship (vv. 11–18) may be a late composition but it accurately reflects the way a priestly leader at this time would have felt regarding the move to royal rule.

Sidebar 4.19: Samuel's Denunciation of Kingship as a Deuteronomistic Text

It is very likely that the shift to monarchy would have led priestly figures like Samuel to feel defensive and speak out against kingship; royal power would compromise the influence of the priesthood. The tradition in 1 Samuel 8 is thus probably quite old and authentic in broad strokes, but its current form shows much Deuteronomistic reworking. In addition to points of contact between the chapter's language and the book of Deuteronomy, Samuel's denunciation of kingship goes into specific details regarding how a king would behave that match very closely records from the Neo-Assyrian kings who conquered Israel and controlled Judah in the late-eighth century BCE. The authors of 1 Samuel 8 thus put into Samuel's mouth terms that audiences living shortly after the Neo-Assyrian period would recognize and react to with greater immediacy, looking back on the request for kingship in Samuel's day as the first of many steps that led to the Assyrian crisis centuries later.

The ensuing material in 1 Samuel 9—11 is almost entirely different than what we encounter in 1 Samuel 8, insofar as it shows very little late-Deuteronomistic reworking. In these chapters, we encounter Israel's first king, Saul, and we are introduced to him in a manner that closely resembles how we are introduced to Samuel, i.e., through his father (1 Sam. 9:1; cf. 1 Sam. 1:1). Just as Samuel's father Elkanah is presented as coming from a well-entrenched family, so too is Saul's father Kish. The character of 1 Samuel 9–11 is decidedly pro-Saul in its orientation, and probably originated at a time when claims of legitimacy were rooted in one's family standing. The introductory narrative of 1 Sam. 9:1–10:16 has the quality of a fable rooted in hinterland culture: the dutiful son Saul seeks his father's lost donkeys, and roams throughout the countryside to find them, delineating the core territory of what will eventually be his kingdom.

It is in this fable that Saul encounters Samuel, a "seer" and a "man of God" (1 Sam. 9:6-7, 11) whom he seeks out to help him with his quest. The original version of this fable probably refrained from actually naming this prophetic figure, and was later redacted to identify him with Samuel for propagandistic purposes.[28] That is, it may be that the narrative as it now stands (or in a penultimate form) was redacted to convince its audience that priest-prophets like Samuel were not against kingship (as is the case in 1 Samuel 8) but actually promoted that form of leadership.

Especially poignant here is the encounter between Saul and the band of traveling prophets following the former's departure from Samuel's home (1 Sam. 10:10-13). In this brief episode, the "spirit of God" descends upon Saul and he begins "to prophesy" with these prophets. From both the meaning of the Hebrew term "to prophesy" (wayyitnabbeh) and insights gleaned from anthropological data, scholars generally read this as Saul entering into a trance state and engaging in ecstatic behavior, a common feature of prophets throughout antiquity.[29] The implication of the episode is that Saul is somehow connected to the divine, but in a way that is consistent with familiar features of old-fashioned Israelite religion. The rhetorical question/popular slogan that ends the episode ("is Saul also among the prophets?") suggests that there actually existed an early slogan regarding Saul's prophetic qualities as part of his claim to royal authority, and that this episode provides a folkloristic etiology explaining the origins of this tradition.

The next turn in the Saul narratives, however, takes on a somewhat different tone. Whereas 1 Sam. 9:1–10:16 makes Saul the central and proactive character, 1 Sam. 10:17-27 amplifies the role of Samuel once more. Samuel convenes Israel and engages in a casting of sacred lots (the ancient equivalent of drawing straws) to determine who will rule

28. Hutton 2009, 331–36.
29. Wilson 1980.

Israel as king. Each lot reveals a more specific detail: first the tribe of Benjamin, then the clan of Matri, and finally the individual—Saul himself. But Saul does not proudly come forward at this final lot casting; rather, he is found "hiding" among the baggage in the rear of the convocation (1 Sam. 10:22).

Many scholars have viewed this episode as carrying an anti-monarchic tone, a view certainly justified by the combination of Saul's actions and Samuel's opening anti-monarchic admonition in vv. 18-19. If Samuel's opening admonition is a Deuteronomistic insertion (perhaps applied to lend consistency between 1 Samuel 8 and the present episode) and is abstracted from the narrative, then Saul's behavior is not cast in so negative a light. Rather than boldly seizing upon the moment, Saul exhibits a degree of humbleness, an honorable characteristic according to other biblical sources. In any case, the episode does introduce certain questions as to what sort of king Saul will be, as the final verse reveals that members of the populace are less than confident that Saul will be able to lead the nation (v. 27).

What transpires in 1 Samuel 11 puts to rest any such doubts. This chapter recalls many of the narratives in the book of Judges, where a foreign threat emerges and an Israelite warrior-savior, moved by the spirit of the divine, rises up to eliminate the threat. In 1 Samuel 11, the threat is the Ammonites led by the brutal and vicious Nahash (whose name in Hebrew, fittingly, means "snake").

Sidebar 4.20: 1 Samuel 11 at Qumran

One of the important discoveries made during the study of the Dead Sea Scrolls from Qumran is that there once existed a fuller version of 1 Samuel 11. The version that was discovered at Qumran—known as 1QSam A—has an introductory paragraph that tells more of the story than what has been transmitted in the biblical tradition. Following the introductory paragraph, the Qumran version of the chapter continues in a manner very similar to what we encounter in the biblical narrative, but the introductory paragraph lacking in the Bible is preserved in the Qumran scroll and reveals a more textured and more compelling storyline. The italicized portion in the excerpt below is the additional unit in 1QSam A, with the rest of the chapter carrying on thereafter:

Now Nahash king of the Ammonites oppressed the Gadites and Reubenites

---

severely. He gouged out all their right eyes and struck terror and dread in Israel. Not a man remained among the Israelites beyond the Jordan whose right eye was not gouged out by Nahash king of the Ammonites, except that seven thousand men fled from the Ammonites and entered Jabesh Gilead. About a month later . . .

Then Nahash the Ammonite came up, and encamped against Jabesh Gilead; and all the men of Jabesh said to Nahash: "Make a covenant with us, and we will serve you." And Nahash the Ammonite said to them: "On this condition will I make it with you, that all your right eyes be put out; and I will lay it for a reproach upon all Israel." And the elders of Jabesh said to him: "give us seven days' respite, that we may send messengers to all the borders of Israel; and then, if there be none to deliver us, we will come out to thee."

Upon hearing of the threat, the "spirit of God" descends upon Saul, who rallies an Israelite militia and engages in a battle against the Ammonites that meets with unprecedented success. As a result, he is affirmed as king over Israel; the episode is crafted in such a way as to suggest that kingship is the natural and ultimate fulfillment of earlier types of Israelite military leadership, and that Saul and his office represent the great hope for security and survival that Israel had always yearned for but never attained under previous warrior-saviors. It is likely that the tradition undergirding 1 Samuel 11 is the earliest of the pro-Saul narratives, and may well have stood on its own as propagandistic justification for his rise to power.

The organization of these different narratives regarding Saul probably took place at a fairly early stage in the development of the book of Samuel; 1 Samuel 9–11 cohere well and possess a literary logic that establishes a sort of foundation myth for Saul's reign. However, these events do not lead directly to Saul taking the throne. Rather, they lead to Samuel's **valedictory speech** in 1 Samuel 12. In this chapter, the priest-prophet stands before Israel and reaffirms the terms by which they may have a king: it is because YHWH allows for it, and thus it is subject to the same terms and rules that Samuel had established before the shift to monarchy. Indeed, Samuel's speech here develops the earlier moment in 1 Samuel 10 where the "constitution of the monarchy" was written and deposited in the Mizpah sanctuary (1 Sam. 10:25)—the speech in 1 Samuel 12 clarifies what that earlier document may have contained. The language of 1 Samuel 12 is quite Deuteronomistic, though the chapter itself, like 1 Samuel 8, probably points to the memory of ideologies that accompanied the tense transition from priestly leadership to monarchic leadership.

Sidebar 4.21: Samuel's Valedictory Speech

Many parallels between Samuel and Moses surface within the first several chapters of the book of Samuel, and thus Samuel's valedictory/ farewell speech in 1 Samuel 12 should be viewed with an eye to the traditions regarding Moses as well. In its current form, 1 Samuel 12 is highly Deuteronomistic, emulating ideas found in Deuteronomy and adopting the hortatory style of that book's discourses as well. And like Deuteronomy—presented as Moses' valedictory speech to Israel before they enter the promised land—Samuel's valedictory address is positioned as the pivot between one era and the next (the premonarchic and monarchic periods). Thus, like that of Moses, Samuel's speech lays out the terms by which the monarchy might thrive, but also how it might fail and the consequence of such a failure. The Deuteronomists, recognizing the existing parallels between Samuel and Moses in their sources, have conformed Samuel's speech to match that of Moses in Deuteronomy—part of a Deuteronomistic strategy to characterize Israel's history as guided by prophetic voices following in the footsteps of Moses.

Most telling, however, is the final notice in the chapter. If Israel and its king do not abide by the terms of YHWH's law, they will be "swept away" (v. 25). In 1 Samuel 12, Samuel serves as the mouthpiece for the Deuteronomists, who saw the law as the basis for national survival. Kingship was a supportive social institution and could not rival or subvert it. As Deuteronomy spells out, the king is as accountable to the law (and its priestly teachers) as any other Israelite (Deut. 17:14–20). By framing the pro-Saul material with the criticism of monarchy in 1 Samuel 8 and the qualification of it in 1 Samuel 12, the book of Samuel casts a pall over Saul's prospects for success, foreshadowing the limits of his kingship and dynasty.

This shadow is cast on the closing chapters of this unit: Saul's reign begins with external tensions, as the Philistines threaten his borders, but also with internal tensions as he and Samuel countenance each other. The famous episode in 1 Samuel 13 pits the two against each other: a sacrificial rite meant to sanctify battle against the Philistines awaits and Samuel (who must conduct it) is nowhere to be seen. Saul himself eventually takes on the responsibility of conducting the sacrifice, and immediately, Samuel appears to chastise him. One senses that some dirty work is afoot, and Samuel deliberately waited in order to force Saul to transgress boundaries and engage in behavior reserved for Samuel as a priest-prophet. But even if this is the case, the narrative leaves Saul, technically, at fault. As the conflict with the Philistines continues, Saul's wisdom as a leader is further called into question. Not only does he proclaim the counter-productive fast upon his men (who, in the throes of battle, would have desperately needed sustenance) but he is all too willing to penalize his own son, Jonathan, for unwitting breaking this royal restriction (1 Samuel 14). Despite the fact that Jonathan is reported to have encountered great success on the battlefield, Saul condemns him to death, and he is only saved by the zealous protest of the Israelite soldiers.

Several rifts thus emerge. One is between Saul and Samuel, another between Saul and his son (whose loyalties will later shift away from him) and another still between Saul and his own soldiers. A final rift, however, proves to be the final straw. In 1 Samuel 15, Samuel conveys to Saul YHWH's command to engage the Amalekites in battle and to slay all of them—men, women, children and even animals. This ban, known by the Hebrew term *herem*, is associated with Amalek in other biblical sources as well and speaks to strict boundaries between them and Israel, probably serving as an ethnic hallmark separating the two people. It is highly debatable whether the *herem* was truly applied to the Amalekites at any time, but the author of 1 Samuel 15 uses the motif to spin his narrative.

Sidebar 4.22: The Anti-Amalekite Tradition

The Pentateuch preserves calls for the eradication of the nation of Amalek, identified as an enemy of Israel from their earliest days of wilderness wandering. Echoes of this anti-Amalekite tradition inform 1 Samuel 15 and the call for Saul to engage in the herem against the Amalekites. The historical origins of this anti-Amalekite attitude are difficult to recover, but scholars often look to shifts in tribal alliances in the Iron Ia period as the background for this tension. Israel had formed alliances with various eastern groups in its early days that probably included the Amalekites, and some biblical texts indicate close relations between Israel and the Amalekites (Gen. 36:16; Judg. 12:15). At some point, however, interests changed, and a rift developed between these groups. Whatever circumstances led to this rift were remembered by the biblical writers, who used the Amalekites as a symbol of adversity and threat that Israel was charged to eradicate from its midst.

As the chapter unfolds, it is clear that while Saul is successful in battle, he fails to carry out YHWH's instructions: Saul's soldiers return to Israel with Amalekite animals taken as spoils of war, and Saul leads them with the Amalekite king, Agag, as a military prisoner. Samuel immediately declares that because Saul has ignored YHWH's command to fully apply the *herem* against the Amalekites, Saul's kingdom will be taken from him. Despite Saul's cries of remorse, Samuel literally turns his back on him, and the chapter ends with the notice that YHWH himself regretted his decision to make Saul Israel's king (v. 35). The stage is thus set for the entrance of David into the story, suggesting that 1 Samuel 15 was shaped by the Deuteronomists to account for both the cultural memory of David and their sources regarding his rise to power.

5.3. 1 Samuel 16—31

The book of Samuel gives us no less than three versions of how David became a figure of national significance. The first can be found in 1 Sam. 16:1-13, which depicts Saul's mission to Bethlehem to find and anoint one of Jesse's sons as per YHWH's instructions. Many scholars view this episode as drawn from prophetic sources: it presupposes that David is to be Israel's king, but it depicts this designation as under the auspices of Samuel's prophetic authority.[30] It is Samuel who is the pro-active figure in this episode, and David's kingship is presented as entirely a matter of prophetic legitimation. The episode also highlights a mythic dimension to the lore surrounding David's origins: he is a Judahite, and thus originates in a region that was less developed than

---

30. See above, section 2.2.

the central hill country whence Saul came. This connects David's family to the motif of the **wilderness**, a place where Israel conceived of its own origins in the mythic past. In David's day, Judah was still very much a wilderness—thus, just as YHWH comes out of the wilderness to fight for his people Israel, so too does David within the contours of the larger narrative in the book of Samuel.[31]

Figure 4.12: *David Plays the Harp before Saul*, by Rembrandt (between 1629 and 1631); oil on oak panel. Städelsches Kunstinstitut, Frankfurt am Main.

The second "introduction" to David in 1 Sam. 16:14–23 is one that returns the reader to Saul's court and forms a nice continuation of the story in 1 Samuel 15. YHWH has plagued Saul with an evil spirit—the narrative is ambiguous about what this exactly means, but it is clear that Saul is experiencing some sort of torment that is only alleviated through a bard's playing of the harp and singing of songs. That bard is none other than David, and the story provides a convenient way in which David becomes part of the royal establishment. It is important, also, that David is characterized as a bard: bards in antiquity were not

---

31. On the increase of settlements in Judah only during and after Solomon's day, see Lehmann 2003.

simply entertainers but trustees of the sacred music of a culture and the epic traditions enshrined in those pieces of music. The narrative suggests that David is not only a skilled musician but indeed well-versed in Israel's cultural legacy and capable of reciting/performing it in an effective manner.

Sidebar 4.23: Evil Spirits in the Hebrew Scriptures

Ancient Israel's conceptual world was not strictly a matter of faith in a single deity (YHWH) but a belief in a number of mythic/supernatural sources. Local spirits, demons, monsters, divine messengers and such were believed to dot the landscape, and the landscape itself was understood as animistically conscious. Within this numinous canvas, Israelite believed that various spirits could take over physical regions, households, families, and individuals, afflicting them in various ways. The authors of Samuel envisioned one such "evil spirit" directed by YHWH to afflict Saul; it may be that such a literary maneuver was meant to invoke the idea of an evil spirit afflicting more than just Saul but his entire household (and given the fate of the Saulide house in 1–2 Samuel, this may be the case), with implications for the well-being of his entire kingdom.

It is possible that this characterization was conceived to counter charges that a "country boy" from the wilderness of Judah could not effectively lead the entire people of Israel as their king; the narrative makes the argument that David was entirely fit for the job and intimately familiar with the values and traditions of Israelite life as preserved and represented by its musical tradition. But the narrative also makes clear that David was brought into Saul's court at Saul's bequest—he and his family in Bethlehem are good subjects of the king, and thus members in good standing of the realm. If there really was a charge that David was somehow not suitable for a leading role in Israelite politics, 1 Sam. 16:14–23 makes a case to the contrary.

But the most well-known of the introductions to David is certainly that preserved in 1 Samuel 17, the confrontation between David and Goliath. The tale, familiar to most readers of the Bible, pits the small David against the mighty Philistine warrior and presents David's victory as a sign not only of his courage but of YHWH's favor. How else, the narrative implies, could so might a warrior have been defeated by a young shepherd boy? The episode is a brilliant example of narrative art, but also of political propaganda. David is presented as the underdog until he manages to achieve victory, but scholars who have examined this episode in light of the conventions of ancient warfare note that if the confrontation happened as it is related in 1 Samuel 17, David actually had the upper hand. Goliath's challenge to Israel's army is to produce a warrior prepared for heavily armed combat, replete with heavy weapons and full armor. Such combat was not characterized by swift movement or dexterity—they were testing grounds for a warrior's strength and determination rather than speed and dexterity.[32]

The real takeaway from this episode is that David—unencumbered by heavy armor or weapons—does not feel the need to conform to conventional rules of engagement. He is liberated from these strictures and, working outside of expectations, is easily able to defeat the slow and therefore vulnerable Goliath. As noted above, the confrontation of 1 Samuel 17 is probably not genuinely historical, but it preserves an important memory and insight regarding David, and that is that he rose to power by standing beyond conventional behavior and exploiting the weakness of those who abided by it.

The ensuing chapters (1 Samuel 18–22) present the reader with a succession of highly-charged moments revolving around Saul's growing fear and suspicion of David. It begins with the apparent adoration of the public for David over Saul (1 Sam. 18:7) and growing tensions leading several turns where David flees Saul's court for his own protection (1 Sam. 19–21). David's survival in these chapters is facilitated by those rather familiar to Saul—Saul's children Jonathan and Michal (David's friend and wife, respectively) manage to help David escape peril. This not only amplifies the earlier depiction of Saul as tormented by a troubling spirit, it also starts to suggest that it is not only Saul who suffers here, but Saul's entire house/lineage. Son and daughter turn against their father for the benefit of an outsider in 1 Samuel 19, an idea that was alien to the kinship values characterizing Israelite society, where lineage roots trumped all other institutions and social needs.

This idea is more fully explored in 1 Samuel 20, where David and Jonathan's "ruse" to test Saul's state of mind revolves around issues of family integrity as well. At a royal festival, Saul is informed that

---

32. Halpern 2001, 10–13.

David cannot attend because of his own family-based religious festival occurring at the same time.[33] The presumption is that if Saul is of sound mind and character, he will respect David's family obligations. Saul's reaction to this is not only to declare that David should die, but even to attempt to kill his own son Jonathan for collusion with the enemy. Saul's true intentions are finally brought into the open, so the ruse is effective. Moreover, Saul's attempt to hurt his own child seriously calls into question his viability as king—for if he wished death upon his own son, how could he be trusted with the fate of an entire nation?

But the chapter is also very subtle in its meta-message regarding the complexity of the situation. We know from the planning of the ruse that Jonathan has indeed thrown in with David, and such a decision on Jonathan's part does immeasurable damage to the viability of the entire House of Saul to maintain its place as a royal dynasty. More importantly—and what is often missed—is that David and Jonathan's ruse shows that David is not above lying. David has *not* gone off to his family's religious festival; he remains hidden just beyond the palace to receive word of Saul's conduct. David exploits family religious traditions in order to gain a political upper-hand. The episode indicts Saul and his family, but it also further reveals David's ability to be duplicitous and to exploit conventional social and religious practices for his own benefit.

In the end, the narrative shows the weakness of the Saulide line, but it does not ultimately serve as a vindication of David. It shows how royal politics does not always operate in the best interests of the common Israelite as neither David nor Saul seem to sufficiently value common religious institutions.

The chapters that follow see David on the run, Saul in pursuit, and both characters showing alternately the dark underside of kingship. For Saul, this takes place in 1 Samuel 22, where Saul happens upon the priests of **Nob** and orders his forces to massacre them for their assistance to the fleeing David. Though Saul's paranoia and menacing presence has been on the rise since the introduction to David, this episode displays a new level of barbarity. The manhunt for David had, until this point, been essentially a royal vendetta against one person that Saul viewed as treacherous. But the slaughter of the priests at Nob expands this vendetta into a far more corrosive project.

The slaughter of the priests cannot be underestimated in terms of

---

33. On family-rooted religious festivals as distinct from state religion, see van der Toorn 1996, 316–38.

the narrative's characterization of Saul. The early priesthood in ancient Israel constituted a force that maintained tribal cohesion. As such, priests were beyond common reach; YHWH could chastise and punish the priests if he saw fit (as we have already seen re: the Elides at Shiloh), but no Israelite could take such liberties. This is the case even in later periods—when Solomon comes to power, he dispatches all who stood against him, but relents when it comes to dealing with the priest Abiathar (1 Kgs. 2:26). The biblical law collections remember this special status afforded the priesthood by repeatedly proclaiming that unlike the other Israelite tribes, the priestly tribe of Levi was "YHWH's portion"—they were kindred to the deity himself.

This makes Saul's massacre all the more horrific. By killing the priests at Nob, Saul transgresses against one of the cornerstones of Israelite identity and theology. Within the world of the text, his act constitutes a declaration that the monarchic system he represents supersedes the bedrock institutions of pre-monarchic Israel. In one fell swoop, Saul transgresses against traditional socio-religious values and the very terms of kingship approved by Samuel on behalf of YHWH himself (1 Sam. 10:25). It is debatable as to how historically accurate this episode may be. There is a running theme of conflict between Saul and various priestly factions leading up to 1 Samuel 22, so it is conceivable that he may well have engaged in some violence against priests during his reign. In any case, the episode contributes greatly to the negative image of Saul. Beyond simply losing divine favor as king, he shows himself here to be a sort of enemy of the state, even though the state in question is his own.

After 1 Samuel 22, there is little chance that the reader can view Saul as a viable king, and between this chapter and the report of his death in 1 Samuel 31, Saul's position and power deteriorates dramatically. This leaves David as the only real option as ruler, but David is hardly idealized in the chapters that follow. A key passage revealing the complexity—and troubling potential—of David as the nation's soon-to-be king is the mini-unit of 1 Samuel 24–26. A **doublet** relating a confrontation between David and Saul is preserved in chapters 24 and 26, which present David as compassionate and unwilling to kill a vulnerable Saul even when doing so would have ended his status as a fugitive and secured the kingdom in his own hand. These chapters derive from a tradition of Davidic apology—that is, they come from tales created to legitimize and defend David's ascent to Saul's throne, probably in the face of challenges or criticisms to how David actually managed to claim this position. In their own way, each chapter projects an image of David that is lawful, restrained, cautious, deliberate, and gracious.

Yet the voice of criticism against which chapters 24 and 26 were composed is hinted at by 1 Samuel 25, which stands at the heart of the unit. In this chapter, we encounter a different David: a ruffian, a thug, a mafia-style warlord who runs an extortion racket to which a wealthy landowner named Nabal refuses to cower or support. Rather, Nabal insults David, his lineage, and the entire culture that David represents. The word *nabal* in Hebrew, means "fool"—a fact that his wife, Abigail, makes clear as she begs David to spare his life—and indeed the episode emphasizes the foolishness of refusing a brute in such a manner. But even while pointing this out, the episode holds a critical light up to David and reveals him to be ruthless, possessive, and all too willing to engage in bloodshed to get what he wants. The episode tells us that Abigail is successful and David relents. Yet somehow, Nabal still winds up dead, Abigail winds up as David's wife, and the text leaves open the distinct (and likely) possibility that David indeed stands behind this turn of events.

The sequence of these chapters as they currently stand is revealing. First Samuel 24 and 26 flank 1 Samuel 25 and thus the "outer" David of chapters 24 and 26 essentially flank the "inner" David of chapter 25. This carries symbolic meaning, for it shows that the David presented in the book of Samuel is a complicated literary construct: the virtuous, loyal, and compassionate David (the "outer" David) is a façade masking a more dangerous, volatile, bloodthirsty David (the "inner" David). The result is a conflicted character—driven by ambition and greed on one hand but more lofty and venerable aspirations on the other. First Samuel 24—26 constructs an account that does not deny that some of the rumors about him were rooted in truth, but admits that different occasions warranted different reactions from this complex person during a turbulent and dangerous time in Israel's early monarchic period. While the larger book of Samuel rejects Saul in favor of David, this is not a ringing endorsement of the latter but a reckoning with the realities of monarchy as an institution.

The closing few chapters of the unit (1 Samuel 27—31) continue the "checkerboarding" of episodes involving David and Saul. These chapters show something that has puzzled scholars for a very long time, and that is that David has apparently thrown in with the Philistines—the enemies of Israel. In these chapters, David is portrayed as a lieutenant of Achish, a Philistine warlord, who routinely sends David out to claim resources from the subjugated Israelite population. But according to these chapters, David does not do this—he attacks others but not the Israelites, and the spoils he returns with are thus not derived from his own people. Why would such an account be included in the narrative? Why would the author(s) choose even possibly to call David's loyalty to Israel into question?

The answer must be that the historical David had *some* sort of connection to the Philistines. Indeed, the same may have been the case with Saul at some earlier point in his career, since archaeological evidence suggests that the Philistines held a controlling interest in local politics and economics.[34] However, Saul must have broken with the Philistines as he moved into a royal Israelite role, whereas David's mercenary allegiance with the Philistines must have endured for quite a while even as he sought the Israelite throne. These chapters address the rumors about David that may have spread regarding this interaction: they admit that David had Philistine connections, but they argue strenuously that he never turned on his own people. One wonders just how much of this statement could have been accepted by a reasonable audience in antiquity; the question is indeed left quite open, despite the text's surface affirmations.

By contrast, and for the first time in a long time, Saul is painted in relatively sympathetic colors. The narrative portrays him as a desperate man grasping at straws but failing as he realizes that for him, the end is near. First Samuel 28 shows this in a famous episode: Saul recruits a **necromancer** to conjure the ghost of Samuel (who has long since died) in the hopes of divining the will of YHWH. The ghost of Samuel appears and spells out certain doom for Saul: he will die, as will his son, and the Philistines will vanquish his armies. From this point on Saul knows that the end is nigh—he consigns himself to his fate, and meets his end in 1 Samuel 31 during a battle with the Philistines. Saul's death wavers between tragic and noble; mortally wounded, he takes his own life rather than be taken captive and humiliated by the Philistines.

34. Kreutzer 2006, 39–58.

Figure 4.13: *The Shade of Samuel Invoked by Saul*, by Nikiforovich Dmitry Martynov (1857). Commons.wikimedia.org.

It is debatable whether Saul truly died in this way—some scholars consider the possibility that David somehow managed to have Saul killed during the battle in order the clear the way to his throne—but the text portrays him as the agent of his own demise. Many readers see here a dramatic and painful end to a tortured ruler's life, but one must also bear in mind that in antiquity, such an act of self-sacrifice may have been viewed as a gestured geared to restore honor to Saul's family.

Social-scientific studies of biblical texts suggest that ancient Israel's culture was an **honor/shame culture**, similar to that found among contemporary tribal societies. Family honor could easily be lost and, unless reclaimed, the family would be marginalized from standard social discourse. As such, Saul's death may be presented as one last attempt to empower his line and allow for one of his sons to retain the throne, drawing from the ancient convention of the "honorable death" on the battlefield.

Yet, if this was an attempt at reclaiming family honor, it also constituted a final violation of YHWH's will, communicated several times via Samuel (including the post-mortem encounter in 1 Samuel 28) that Saul's kingdom was to pass to David. The author of 1 Samuel 31 may be characterizing Saul in noble terms on one hand but subtly continuing the book's long-running anti-Saul critique on the other, and simultaneously suggesting that notions of honor cannot subvert divine will.

5.4. 2 Samuel 1–8

The second half of the book of Samuel opens with an extended drama showing not just the rise of David but the rise of his entire "house"—that is, the brood of people supporting him on political and military levels. The opening chapter begins, fittingly, with David offering up a lament for the fallen Saul after learning that he has died. The lament (2 Sam. 1:19-27) stands as one of the classic examples of eloquent Hebrew poetry, and possesses an archaic linguistic style. Whether David wrote this lament or it was assigned by him to a scribe/ poet to compose, it certainly reflects an attempt to convey David's realization of the gravity of the death of Saul, his son Jonathan, and no doubt other important figures associated with the Saulide house.

Sidebar 4.24: Ancient Poetry in the Book of Samuel

Various poems are included in the book of Samuel of different length; most are viewed as quite ancient (the Song of Hannah, for example, in 1 Sam. 2:1-10; David's lament over Absalom in 2 Samuel 22; 2 Sam. 23:1-7). The working of ancient poetry into the narratives regarding David reinforce the traditions that present David as a singer and, ultimately, as the patron saint of the liturgical poems in the Book of Psalms (Ps. 72:20). They also align a narrative of a new political institution with the older tradition of poetic performance that pre-dated the rise of the monarchy, suggesting continuity between these epochs. Finally, if Israel's ancient poetry had liturgical characteristics and meaning, the working of some of these poems into the book of Samuel makes a political narrative into a liturgical work in its own right, full of theological and mythological significance and worthy of study and recitation beyond elite scribal contexts.

Yet it is also telling that the person who brings David the news of Saul's passing claims that Saul did *not* take his own life: rather, he himself killed Saul and straightaway brought the news to David. And straightaway after telling David this news, David has the man killed. Thus 2 Samuel 1 presents an alternative account to what we encounter in 1 Samuel 31 regarding Saul's death, and leaves open the question as to whether or not David really was responsible for it—in which case, killing the messenger may constitute David's covering his tracks.

Regardless of whether David was involved in Saul's death, the ensuing chapters show the domino effect of his passing. It is not long before Saul's son **Ishbosheth** is also killed, followed by the death of Abner son of Ner, the "chief of staff" of the Saulide house. In all of these deaths, the narrative attempts to clear David of any involvement or wrongdoing, but it is suspicious that every single potential threat to David's monarchic ambition mysteriously manages to die. Is the author of this narrative clearing David while "winking" to his audience and thus actually implicating David? It is difficult to say for certain, but the overall unfurling of events sees every major player in the house of Saul ultimately meet an untimely end for the benefit of David. The narrative summarizes the overall effect nicely: "now there was long war between the house of Saul and the house of David; and David waxed stronger and stronger, but the house of Saul waxed weaker and weaker" (2 Sam. 3:1).

Sidebar 4.25: Ishbosheth and Ishbaal

The Hebrew name of Saul's son, "Ishbosheth," means "[a] shameful man" and is certainly not the name given to him at birth. The book of Chronicles—despite its redaction in the Persian period—preserves an older tradition where he is known by a different name, "Ishbaal." While this might literally translate into "[a] man of Baal," it can also be read as "lordly man," "master," or other translations that are far more complimentary in tone. A recent inscription found in the early-tenth-century Tel Qeyeifah site contains the name "Ishbaal," evidencing its use in precisely the era when the Saul and David stories are set. The name "Ishbosheth" was probably introduced into the storyline by a pro-David author who sought to discredit or insult the Saulide line.

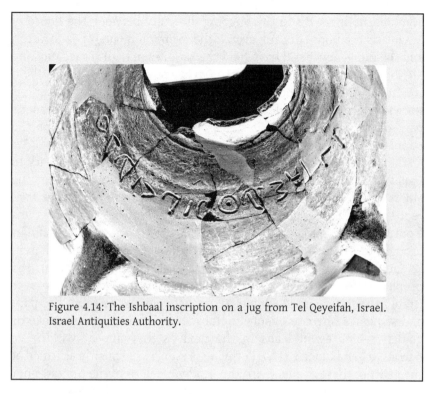

Figure 4.14: The Ishbaal inscription on a jug from Tel Qeyeifah, Israel. Israel Antiquities Authority.

A fascinating example of the complexity involved in relating these events is the relationship between David and **Mephibosheth**, the last surviving descendant of Saul and the son of David's friend Jonathan. The narrative tells us that Mephibosheth was disabled (2 Sam. 4:4), and we are later informed that David claims that he will care for him and that Mephibosheth will always have a place at his table (2 Sam. 9:10). On the surface, this would seem to be the act of a benevolent king who wishes to care for the last remaining member of a family he respected and in a way that would ensure his safety and support. Another way to interpret this, however, would be to see this as David's attempt to keep tabs on Mephibosheth as a potential threat. Perhaps the historical reality rests somewhere between these two points or combines elements of both.

If David was indeed behind the deaths of other Saulides, he could have very easily seen to the dispatching of Mephibosheth. The sparing of Mephibosheth may reflect a real hesitance on David's part to dishonor whatever genuine friendship he actually shared with Jonathan, Mephibosheth's father. Yet David's desire to keep an eye on

Mephibosheth speaks to the ongoing difficulty between the house of David and the house of Saul; even if the former did outshine the latter, and the public must still have held the Saulides in high regard, making Mephibosheth a potential threat to David's power. The narrator's bold statement that "the house of Saul waxed weaker and weaker" is therefore an example of political propaganda, shaping the reader's perception of a past that, at least among some quarters of the population, might have been told rather differently.

The narrative continues with a sense that the Saulide threats to David's rule have finally been removed, and the pace increases: the elders of the northern tribes accept David's kingship, and, in fact, request that he rule over them; David moves his base of operations from Hebron to Jerusalem (2 Samuel 5); the Ark of the Covenant is brought to Jerusalem and David's priestly faculty is established therein (2 Samuel 6); finally, David receives an oracle through Nathan the prophet that YHWH will grant him an eternal royal line to rule over Israel from Jerusalem (2 Samuel 7; see just below). The rapid-fire pace and sequence of these events contain an air of divine providence or guidance—one event leads to the next as they appear within the narrative—and indeed YHWH's divine presence is explicitly affirmed at the heart of these events (with the deadly incident in the first attempt to transfer the Ark to Jerusalem and the subsequent blessing of its interim trustee in 2 Sam. 6:8–11).

The historical accuracy of these events is, however, another story. Scholars generally agree that each episode contains a report based on actual events, but that the reports have been both ideologically amplified and arranged to create a theological impression. For example, while David most certainly "took" Jerusalem as reported in 2 Samuel 5, it is debatable as to when he would have imported the Ark of the Covenant into the city, as well as when the "Promise to David" oracle would have been proclaimed. Even if these events did take place during David's reign, they have been presented here as occurring at the outset of his time in Jerusalem as part of a theological basis for understanding the role Jerusalem was to play in the theology and identity of the Davidic monarchy. The book of Samuel is arranged thematically, not chronologically (see section 3, above); the sequence of 2 Samuel 5—7 is a linear narrative that interprets and reframes events that may not have occurred in exactly the same sequence.

A few events in this spread of material demand some closer attention, beginning with David's taking of Jerusalem. It has long been recognized that David's selection of this fortified city as his base of operations was motivated in part by tribal politics. In become sovereign over both the northern Israelite tribes and the clan populations in Judah, Jerusalem was a fitting selection insofar as it was neither and Israelite nor Judahite city. Rather, until David's storming and conquest of the city, Jerusalem was Canaanite (**Jebusite**), and was in fact a relic of the much older Late Bronze Age city-state system in Canaan that supported Egyptian governance of the area.

Sidebar 4.26: Amarna-Age Jerusalem

Though David is credited with transforming Jerusalem into an Israelite city within the book of Samuel, the city itself had a long history of regional importance well before David's day and in fact long before Israel emerged on the world stage. Letters from the fourteenth century BCE known as the Amarna Letters reveal that Jerusalem was a small but important administrative center for Egypt in the Late Bronze Age, with a king who served as a regent of Egyptian interests. It is in the Amarna Letters, too, that we get a sense of the difficult social conditions of the era, as some of the letters detail raids and assaults by groups known as the Habiru. One should not draw immediate parallels between the Habiru and the "Hebrews" of the biblical tradition, but the Amarna Letters do shed light on how and why early Israel could have emerged in the hills shortly after a social crisis in and around urban centers like Jerusalem.

Making Jerusalem the capital of his kingdom was thus a safe move in some respects as it did not privilege northern or southern culture in establishing David's throne. Furthermore, David's later importing of priests representing both northern and southern lineages (2 Sam. 8:17) reified this dimension of Jerusalem as a pan-tribal site. But it is also significant that Jerusalem was, and indeed continued to be, a well-fortified and highly defendable city. If David had to engage in campaigns or raids against populations that rejected or resisted his policies of governance (and the critical perspectives toward David preserved in the book of Samuel attest to such populations), Jerusalem was an effective base of operations from which such actions could be carried out.[35]

---

35. Pioske 2015, 85.

The author of the Jerusalem-based narrative was well aware of how Jerusalem might be viewed as a military stronghold rather than as an inclusive "neutral" capital city; the account of the transfer of the Ark to Jerusalem in 2 Samuel 6 is especially important in how the narrative combats potentially negative evaluations of David's choice to take the city and make it his home base. The tale of the Ark's transfer brings together three important views of its social and religious role: first, the Ark was a northern religious icon (having once resided at the Shiloh sanctuary) and thus represented old northern religious tradition; second, it had been held in trust in rural Judah for many years (see 1 Sam. 6:21—7:1) and therefore affirmed compatibility between northern Israelite and southern Judahite cultures; and third, David's celebratory dance during the Ark's procession into Jerusalem marks the act as a ritual rehearsal of YHWH as the divine warrior marching to his heavenly sanctuary—a powerful mythic idea that had long characterized Israelite religion (and ancient near eastern religion more generally).[36] The narrative thereby infuses a sense of mythic power into the event, affirming the importance of both northern and southern social identity as the basis for Israel's new monarchic social universe, and fusing the two together through the power of mythic prototypes. The selection of Jerusalem is thus not simply a political or military venture on David's part, but a fulfillment of Israel's destiny as intended by YHWH and as played out on the stage of history.

This leads to the **"Promise to David"** oracle we encounter in 2 Samuel 7, wherein YHWH promises David a lineage that will forever rule over Israel and symbolize the fulfillment of the divine covenant between the nation and their deity. Few passages in the Hebrew Scriptures have had more significance on subsequent Jewish and Christian intellectual and theological history, for herein lies the basis for all **Messianic ideology** that would emerge in later biblical and post-biblical tradition, and the fact that it is presented as a divine oracle conveyed through a prophet identifies it as historically transcendent and perennially binding. The oracle has been the subject of exhaustive critical scrutiny revolving around the question of when it originated and how it developed into its current form, for the current form of the oracle seems to address events that transpired long after David's reign and indeed well beyond the days of a stable and viable Israelite monarchy.

---

36. Seow 1989.

Sidebar 4.27: The "Promise to David"

. . . as spoken by Nathan the prophet in 2 Samuel 7:

. . . That same night the word of the Lord came to Nathan, "Go and tell my servant David, 'Thus says YHWH: Would you build me a house to dwell in? I have not lived in a house since the day I brought up the people of Israel from Egypt to this day, but I have been moving about in a tent for my dwelling. In all places where I have moved with all the people of Israel, did I speak a word with any of the judges of Israel, whom I commanded to shepherd my people Israel, saying, "Why have you not built me a house of cedar?"' Now, therefore, thus you shall say to my servant David, 'Thus says YHWH of hosts, I took you from the pasture, from following the sheep, that you should be prince over my people Israel. And I have been with you wherever you went and have cut off all your enemies from before you. And I will make for you a great name, like the name of the great ones of the earth. And I will appoint a place for my people Israel and will plant them, so that they may dwell in their own place and be disturbed no more. And violent men shall afflict them no more, as formerly, from the time that I appointed judges over my people Israel. And I will give you rest from all your enemies. Moreover, YHWH declares to you that YHWH will make you a house. When your days are fulfilled and you lie down with your fathers, I will raise up your offspring after you, who shall come from your body, and I will establish his kingdom. He shall build a house for my name, and I will establish the throne of his kingdom forever. I will be to him a father, and he shall be to me a son. When he commits iniquity, I will discipline him with the rod of men, with the stripes of the sons of men, but my steadfast love will not depart from him, as I took it from Saul, whom I put away from before you. And your house and your kingdom shall be made sure forever before me. Your throne shall be established forever.'"

The current form should be viewed as part of a late redaction of the book of Samuel, possibly deriving from a Deuteronomistic hand in the late pre-exilic or exilic era (or, possibly, even later). Both linguistic and thematic elements within the text point to this late level of literary development, and suggest an awareness of a long and troubled monarchic history.[37] However, a substantial part of the oracle would appear to derive from considerably earlier, focusing as it does on the importance of the construction of a temple. In the oracle, the promise made to David will be fulfilled only when one of his descendants constructs a temple in Jerusalem.

Such specific terms suggest the origination of this text from the time

---

37. For a full study of the textual growth of the Promise to David, see Schniedewind 1999.

of Solomon's reign onward, when a temple structure actually stood in Jerusalem, and one that much of the population did not feel inclined to venerate. Indeed, we later learn in the Book of Kings that the cost of the temple's construction was quite high and the entire project was rather controversial and contested (1 Kgs. 5—8; 12:16). If this was the case, then a form of the Promise to David was probably composed to justify the building of the temple and the initiatives of the king who built it (Solomon). It may date from a time after Solomon, but it relates to the events of his reign and attempts to harmonize them with the accomplishments of David in 2 Samuel 5—6.

Even if this is the case, a Solomonic or post-Solomonic oracle must be based on a tradition that originated during David's reign. The totality of David's conduct in building his kingdom involved the sidelining of all competing royal lines for the sake of establishing his own; it would be logical to conclude that some royal-cultic ideology was forged during his reign, according to which YHWH had chosen the Davidic line, alone, to rule over Israel, and there is no reason to doubt that such a decree would be conveyed through a prophetic proclamation. Whether such a proclamation was offered *immediately* after David's taking of Jerusalem or if it was pronounced at a later time during his reign is uncertain, but there are good reasons to accept the latter possibility. As we will see, threats to David's power surfaced well after the move to Jerusalem, including a major insurrection that accompanied a fragmenting of the royal Davidic family (see section 5.5 regarding 2 Samuel 9—20). In the wake of these events—with the nation reeling from internal crisis and the Davidic family injured during the suppression of the insurrection—a prophetic decree affirming YHWH's choice of David and his descendants would go a long way toward restoring some sense of monarchic stability and the hegemony of the Davidic house.

Some sort of royal doctrine leading to the Promise to David, then, likely surfaced during his reign (probably in oral form); the redactors of the book of Samuel have located it to the outset of his time in Jerusalem, perhaps as a way of identifying the city itself with the promise of monarchic durability—something that would certainly benefit subsequent Jerusalemite kings. The placement of 2 Samuel 8 immediately after the Promise follows the same editorial/redactional logic: the chapter spells out the grandeur of David's conquests (though the list cannot be seen as purely historically transparent) as "proof" that the oracle containing the Promise had begun to take effect as soon as it had been uttered, empowering David's conquests in the region as an expression of YHWH's favor.[38]

Second Samuel 8 forms the finale to a carefully crafted narrative detailing David's rise to power; it impresses upon the reader that the monarchy may have been hard-won, but the outcome was consonant with divine will. It is possible that an early version of a narrative regarding David ended at this point as part of an official doctrine regarding the ruling monarch, but as the book of Samuel continues, a narrative of royal propaganda gives way to a deeper and more troubled tale with a theology of kingship that goes beyond attempts to justify David's rise to power.

5.5. 2 Samuel 9–20: The "Succession Narrative"

With the brief exception of the miscellaneous materials in 2 Samuel 21–24, the remainder of the book of Samuel is concerned with the events and forces and figures regarding the potential successor to David. In particular, these chapters deal with threats to David's power in pursuit of the throne, and two different emphases emerge: first, the types of threats and the social groups supporting or prompting them, and second, the *cause* for these threats. Here we again encounter the distinction between the narrative as historical resource and as theological or ideological construct, for while the types of threats facing David speak to some genuine historical reality in early monarchic Israel, the cause for the events that unfold is presented as an example of YHWH guiding history for the sake of imparting lessons and instructing the audience in why things are the way they are.

First, a word on the term "Succession Narrative," a term which was coined by Leonhard Rost in his 1926 study of the book of Samuel.[39] While it is entirely likely that there are later flourishes, clarifications, and additions within these chapters (which has led some to question whether these chapters can be understood as a single narrative), most scholars still accept the view that they exhibit literary cohesion. In other words, an early Succession Narrative may have been updated and revised over time, but this was determined to some degree by the original text inherited by the revising scribe/scribes. Even if these chapters evolved in a piecemeal manner as some scholars have suggested, they nonetheless led to a masterful narrative in its current

---

38. Halpern 2001, 159.
39. Rost 1926.

form that is subtle, powerful, and useful in recovering what authors and audiences in antiquity would have found compelling. We will therefore use the term "Succession Narrative" to describe the turn of events the flesh out the remainder of the overarching narrative in the book of Samuel.

The Succession Narrative opens in a subtle but brilliant manner by returning the reader to the persistence of the Saulide line. As we have already seen, this chapter presents David as opening his home to Jonathan's son Mephibosheth, claiming that he will take care of him and safeguard his well-being. This, no doubt, is a veiled way of keeping tabs on him to ensure that should Mephibosheth make any attempt to reclaim the Saulide throne, David will know. This signifies that a large swathe of the population would have supported the return of a Saulide to power: one man could not overcome David's regime on his own, but with public support, a regime could be challenged and a new leader could be put in power. This is indeed the case in a few places in the book of Kings, where the **people of the land** install their preferred candidate on the throne (2 Kgs. 11:14; 21:24). For David to keep tabs on Mephibosheth clearly indicates that he was well aware that public support for the Saulides still existed. As such, the Succession Narrative begins with a clear statement that David's power was always on the verge of repudiation by his subjects. Internal dissolution was an ever-present possibility.

This difficult state of domestic affairs is compounded by what occurs in the following chapter, where David's emissaries, sent to Ammon to establish a diplomatic relationship, are abused and humiliated before being summarily sent back to David. The manner of their humiliation includes the forced shaving of their beards, a ritualized act reminiscent of mourning rites, implying that Hanun the king of Ammon wished death upon them and their sovereign David. In antiquity, this constituted not simply a grave insult but, when projected upon the sovereign of an entire kingdom, it was effectively a declaration of war.

It is notable that Hanun's motivation is the advice by his peers that David's delegation had designs on conquest; though this is possible, it is unlikely. A survey of David's foreign alliance show that his interests as a ruler were restricted to Judah and the northern Israelite tribes, with foreign allies recruited to reinforce the boundaries David created. Ammon would have been one such ally, and David therefore probably did not intend to survey Ammonite territory for military purposes.

Sidebar 4.28: Facial Hair and Shame in Ancient Near Eastern Culture

The forced shaving of the beards of David's emissaries—whether historically accurate or not—is a type of shaming ritual that ancient audiences would have recognized. Israelite men wore their beards as a cultural and even ethnic symbol, and the forced shaving of a beard would have been taken as an insult to the community to which an individual belonged. It was also reminiscent of mourning rituals, where individuals might shave their hair or beards to mourn dead family members. To forcibly shave someone's beard would therefore serve as a sort of "hex," wishing death upon the victim's family.

However, the reputation of David within Israel must have preceded him when his delegation went to Ammon—the Ammonites' suspicion was piqued no doubt due to the perception of David as a dangerous warlord by much of the population he ruled. The stakes are therefore raised: tenuous circumstances at home are exacerbated by the beginning of war between David and the Ammonites. Pressure from outside his borders invariably weakened David's administration within his borders.

All of this makes the opening line of 2 Samuel 11 especially pregnant with meaning: we are told that it was the time of year when kings went off to war (in this case, a war against the Ammonites), but David remained in Jerusalem. It is while remaining behind that David spots a woman bathing on her rooftop and decides that he must indulge his sexual desire for her. This woman, of course, is **Bathsheba**, the wife of **Uriah the Hittite**, a soldier in David's army. By the end of the chapter, Uriah is dead, and Bathsheba becomes David's wife. In many respects, this simply continues what we have encountered before: David manages to take what he wants (especially when it comes to accruing wives) and someone standing in his way ends up dead. But it is difficult to avoid seeing something else at work in 2 Samuel 11.

Sidebar 4.29: Uriah the Hittite

Uriah is a fascinating character: he is an important fighter in David's army, carries a good Hebrew first name, and resides in Jerusalem but is still identified as "the Hittite." Scholars have generally recognized that the likelihood of Uriah actually being an ethnic Hittite is very unlikely, since the Hittite Empire had collapsed centuries earlier. The memory of Hittite influence in Canaan was probably closely associated with urban centers like Jerusalem, and it is thus probably a comment upon Uriah's residence in Jerusalem from before the time that David claimed it for himself and his reign. Uriah was a non-Israelite but probably still of Semitic origin, grafted into the Israelite social world during David's reign; this is but one of the small but significant pieces of evidence that point to a still-forming sense of Israelite identity, with the boundaries still somewhat permeable.

5.6. The Bathsheba/Uriah Episode in Closer Perspective

Several commentators have drawn attention to the exoneration of David for virtually every death that occurs in the book of Samuel—why does the narrative overtly blame him for Uriah's death? Indeed, further to the point, why does David even seek to have Uriah killed at all? David's attempt to bring Uriah home from battle to have him sleep with his wife is conceived in order to cover his own tracks at impregnating her. When Uriah refuses to do so, it is clear that David's adultery will become known. Why add murder to the list of sins?

Perhaps some of this can be explained by the very first verse of the episode, since 2 Sam. 11:1 tells us that although it was the time when kings went out to war, David remained in Jerusalem. Some have suggested that this points to David's complacency as ruler and his willingness to let his soldiers fight his battles. However, if 2 Samuel 9 is an indication of a volatile domestic situation, then David remained in Jerusalem because internal affairs in his kingdom demanded his attention, i.e., there was a real possibility for revolt. This is suggestive of David's tactics in dealing with his subjects, many of whom were all too ready to return a Saulide to power. David may have been a powerful warrior and effective warlord, but the role of a monarch demands a different skill set and a sense of diplomacy over one's subjects that David did not seem to possess.

Another important question is how to understand the circumstances surrounding the character of Bathsheba. Earlier interpretations (some of which still persist in contemporary commentaries) suggested that Bathsheba bathed on her rooftop in order to seduce David, and that she manipulated her way into the royal court. But a careful reading suggests otherwise. Given David's ambitions, appetites, and ruthlessness, it is unlikely that Bathsheba could have refused the king's advances and his request that she come to his palace while her husband was away at war. Moreover, the narrative expresses only David's wishes and desires—we hear nothing from Bathsheba, and the silence is telling, perhaps symbolizing her own inability to voice dissent in the face of a powerful and volatile ruler such as David. While the narrative stops short of accusing David of rape or sexual assault, it strongly implies coercion and Bathsheba's powerlessness to resist David's advances and commands.

The Bathsheba/Uriah episode serves as a poignant metaphor for how David conducted business over his larger kingdom—through indulging his desire for what he wanted regardless of the cost. The author or authors of the Succession Narrative continue the trend in the book of Samuel to point to David's massive flaws: his selfishness, his brutality, his ruthlessness. Other episodes hint at this even as they exonerate David.

Figure 4.15: *King David and Bathsheba Bathing* (2014): Artist Corona Monroe depicts the king as obsessed with Bathsheba's beauty.

But 2 Samuel 11 pulls no punches and calls David out on his behavior, perhaps as a comment on his approach to his monarchic reign: what he does to the undeserving household of Uriah and Bathsheba he has done to the entirety of Israel in his climb to power.

Immediately following this event, David is rebuked by no less than YHWH. In 2 Samuel 12, Nathan the prophet—the same prophet who declared the Promise oracle in 2 Samuel 7—brings David a case for adjudication. The case is in fact the famous parable of the rich man, the poor man, and the lamb that the former stole from the latter. When David rules that the rich man is guilty, Nathan reveals that the parable has in fact been about him: "You are that man," says Nathan (2 Sam. 12:7). Because David has stolen the lamb (Bathsheba) from the poor man (Uriah), "the sword shall not depart" from his house (v.10): David's remaining years will see his own family engulfed in conflict and bloodshed. And worse, David will be betrayed by a "familiar" (Hebrew *re'eykha*), someone who is close to him but who will attempt to wrest David's kingdom and possessions away from him.

We have already noted that David's guilt in the Bathsheba/Uriah episode is unique insofar as no attempt is made to excuse his sins. We might address the same issue with regard to the prophetic rebuke in 2 Samuel 12. If we are correct that the larger book of Samuel only thinly veins David's ruthlessness, then he would appear to go unpunished for many, many deaths and related violent transgressions. The great punishment pronounced upon him in 2 Samuel 12 would seem disproportionate if it was really just a tit-for-tat response to his conduct in 2 Samuel 11 (one person's death [though innocent, of course] vs. violence visited upon David's entire family). Indeed, one could question the divine justice of a condemnation of individuals in David's lineage who have as of yet done nothing to warrant punishment, and one could also note the problem this causes with later ideologies in Deuteronomy and related texts that children could not be punished for the sins of their ancestors (Deut. 24:16).

If, however, the Bathsheba/Uriah episode is a microcosmic metaphor for David's general practices as a ruler, Nathan's condemnation makes much more sense within the expanse of the larger narrative in the book of Samuel as an early account of an even earlier culture of conflict. Second Samuel 12 may follow on the heels of the Bathsheba/Uriah episode, but it addresses everything that earlier episode represents about David's actions and attitudes. The pronouncement of punishment is an expression of divine justice for the personal avarice demonstrated by David in establishing his kingdom. This is by no means indicated in any overt manner. In fact, the entirety of 2 Samuel 11—12 may have originally served a different purpose. Many scholars see in these chapters propaganda for Solomon's later rise to power, clarifying on the one hand that he really was an acceptable option for the throne (1 Kgs. 1:10 implies that there was some doubt in this regard), and explaining on the other hand why all of David's other children were eventually killed or otherwise rendered unfit to claim it.

Nevertheless, in its current setting, the pronouncement in 2 Samuel 12 stretches back to earlier episodes where David's violent streak is in plain sight (even if excuses are offered) and provides what many early audiences must have recognized to be a long overdue condemnation. The pronouncement actually conforms well to the strategy throughout the book of Samuel where a single text or plot point carries multiple levels of meaning, but more significantly, the pronouncement in 2 Samuel 12 corresponds to other ancient Israelite narrative traditions where a protagonist facilitates YHWH's plan for the unfolding of history but receives a rebuke for doing so in a morally questionable manner.

One need only look as far as the Jacob story in the book of Genesis for an apt parallel (Genesis 28—36; 37). Jacob amasses his social and financial fortune through deception, but must spend his mature years subject to a heartbreaking deception himself (the deception that Joseph, his favorite son, has been killed). Just as justice must be applied to Jacob, so too must it be applied to David in the book of Samuel. His rise to power, while necessary as a basis for what would become a stable monarchy, must also be scrutinized and condemned when the hero is found wanting. In order for the kingdom to endure under the aegis of the divine, the king must be subject to the same divine justice as those he would rule.

5.7. The Fallout of the Bathsheba/Uriah Episode: Absalom's Revolt

The expanse of material in chapters 13—20 shows the divine pronouncement of punishment immediately beginning to take effect much in the same way that 2 Samuel 8 (the record of David's conquests) follows immediately upon the oracle of the divine Promise. And just as the sequence of 2 Samuel 7—8 is arranged thematically rather than by chronological accuracy, we should view the events of 2 Samuel 13—20 as a thematic, theological reflection upon the historical events they describe. There is little reason to doubt that beneath this complicated narrative is a well-known memory of strife between David's sons for the right to succeed their father, and there is also no reason to doubt that the dominant son, Absalom, did eventually lead a revolt against David for the sake of claiming his throne. But these historical memories, rooted in genuine events, have been developed into a profound statement on the divine guidance of history: whatever happens in this narrative happens because YHWH wills it.

As a literary character, David's awareness of this theological fact is what guides his decisions and what ultimately licenses his triumph over adversity. That is, David is wise and accepts that what he is experiencing is an expression of YHWH's judgment upon him, and enduring it will lead to redemption. How closely this relates to the attitude of the historical David is a questionable matter; these chapters are better understood as a theologically-oriented writer's attempt to make sense of David's survival and successful maintenance of his monarchy in spite of overwhelming challenges and threats.

The majority of the narrative spanning these chapters deals with the revolt of Absalom, a moment of tremendous trauma and consequence for monarchic Israel. However, the revolt is prefaced by an equally traumatic series of events that show precisely how "the sword" has begun to take its toll on David's family: David's son Amnon is plagued by sexual desire for David's daughter **Tamar**, his half-sister. Taking counsel from his friend, Amnon engineers a situation where her safety is compromised. He rapes her and then immediately discards her, leaving her traumatized. When word of this reaches her full-brother Absalom, he takes measures to exact revenge: he kills Amnon and then flees the kingdom in order to evade reprisal. In these few chapters (2 Samuel 13—14), Absalom takes center stage: he is the agent of violence that reclaims his family's honor (by killing his sister's abuser) and his flight from the royal court echoes David's own fugitive status during Saul's reign. There is every indication, then, that he will be the "familiar" one who will betray his father and lay claim to his kingdom, since he is now re-enacting his own father's actions.

Figure 4.16: Gaspare Traversi, *The Slaying of Amnon* (1751); Staatsgalerie Stuttgart; Commons.wikimedi.org.

Sidebar 4.30: "Tamar" in 2 Samuel and Elsewhere

In 2 Samuel 13, tragedy befalls David's daughter Tamar, who is raped by her half-brother Ammon. Her subsequent fate receives no mention in the book of Samuel beyond the haunting notice that she lived, desolate, in her brother Absalom's household (2 Sam. 13:20). It is clear, however, that the trauma she endures in the story initiates a sequence of catastrophic events leading to the near usurpation of David from the throne by his son Absalom. Absalom, too, has a daughter named Tamar (2 Sam. 14:7)—was his daughter named after his sister? This is a possibility, but there is another Tamar in the Hebrew Scriptures, namely, the Tamar of Genesis 38. In that chapter, Tamar is the daughter in law of Judah who endures injustice at the hands of her father in law and who takes matters into her own hands to secure her rights to progeny and her place in the family. The Judah-Tamar story has many points of contact with the Succession Narrative; both tales probably emerge in response to traditions and problems associated with the legacy of David and his family. Nevertheless, the two Tamars probably attest to the existence of a legendary or even mythic figure called Tamar, associated with the fruitful tree of the same name (Hebrew *tamar* = "date palm") and connected to the fertility of the landscape. The authors of the Succession Narrative and Genesis 38 would have had this in mind when writing about the Tamars of their respective tales, each character symbolizing the sanctity of the land and the security of the people living in it. The suffering of a Tamar character on the literary level carried larger social connotations.

In a subtle way, the narrator is admitting that in his younger years, David was also a "familiar" who betrayed his royal liege Saul. The apple, it seems, does not fall too far from the tree, and the threat Absalom will pose is poetic justice visited upon David. This continues even as David and Absalom reconcile and the latter is allowed back into Jerusalem; the narrative specifies that Absalom surreptitiously seeks to win the hearts and minds of the public by positioning himself as a better alternative to David (2 Sam. 15:2–6). One is reminded of the manner in which David is heralded by the public upon returning from war with Saul, as celebratory chants laud him as a champion greater than the king (1 Sam. 18:7). One might also see here an echo of the elders of the northern tribes choosing David rather than a Saulide as their king (2 Sam. 5:1–3); populism, or at least popular assent, is an important part of Israelite royal legitimacy within the book of Samuel.

Absalom is very much becoming a "second" David by culling popular favor (though David's alleged popularity in the book of Samuel is very likely not an accurate reflection of historical reality, as we have seen), thereby apparently building some claim to legitimacy in displacing his father. But he only does this after slaughtering Amnon and therefore eliminating his competition through violent means. The rape of Tamar in 2 Samuel 13 provides justification for this (the murder of Amnon as an "honor killing") but this, too, is a literary turn that echoes the justifications and excuses provided for David as his own competitors die en route to his claiming of the throne.

Absalom is revealed to be playing both sides against the middle, adopting a pose that values populism while simultaneously engaging in a more clandestine game of dirty politics. The implication of the narrative, then, is that if Israel supports him, they support someone as flawed as David in his younger years, one who will place his own ambitions over the welfare of the people. Yet the younger David, who more closely resembles Absalom, is different than the David we encounter at this point in the narrative. The fact that Nathan's oracle in 2 Samuel 12 has already revealed to David the error of his ways means that the older David has a deeper understanding of YHWH's workings in history and a better sense of the burden and responsibility that comes with kingship. He is a man forced to confront his sins and to reckon with his fate as a result of them.

In short, the David of the Succession Narrative is transformed from his earlier state of mind into a man of piety and wisdom. The author of the narrative has crafted an elegant dynamic where the despotism associated with David's reign does not dissipate but is symbolically transferred to Absalom, while David himself is recast as a figure finally worthy of the throne, but one who must go through an expiatory rite of exile and return before once again laying claim to it.[40]

The few chapters addressing the revolt itself are laden with intrigue and great detail relating how David was forced to flee Jerusalem with his supporters while Absalom and his circle managed to make it the base of operations for the revolt. There has certainly been a degree of embellishment brought to this material but many features seem rooted in fact. First, the emphasis on sage advice/wise counsel is probably quite an authentic detail: the great advisor to Absalom is a man by the name of **Ahitophel** (2 Sam. 15:12), whose advice and counsel is touted by the author as tantamount to YHWH's own **divine word** (2 Sam. 16:23). Yet David has managed to plant a "mole" in Absalom's circle—the wily Hushai—who provides information to help David eventually reclaim the city and overturn the revolt. The narrative implies that statecraft is a dangerous game requiring more than diplomacy; it requires a combination of ruthlessness and political wisdom. Yet for all this, the narrative is clear at one point that even the best wisdom cannot out-maneuver divine will: 2 Sam. 17:14 states that the great Ahitophel's "good counsel" was reversed and overturned by divine decision. True wisdom, then, rests in recognizing YHWH's intentions, submitting to them, and then taking whatever steps are necessary to implement them as an agent of the divine.

---

40. Hutton 2009: 371–76.

Sidebar 4.31: Wisdom and Sages in Ancient Israel

We have already seen that different traditions of wisdom surface in the Hebrew Scriptures and in the book of Samuel in particular. In the Succession Narrative, wisdom is strongly associated with political administration/statecraft. The figures Hushai and Ahitophel are presented as paragons of wisdom to whom political figures such as David and Absalom defer; the author of the Succession Narrative goes so far as to say that Ahitophel's wisdom rivaled revelation from the divine in its accuracy and power (2 Sam. 16:23). That such potent sage wisdom could be overturned (as the Succession Narrative relates) affirms that despite its apparent power, YHWH's divine intent remains the ultimate power in the unfurling of historical events, and that true wisdom rests in recognizing the nature of this divine intent.

Since the entire book of Samuel has emphasized the chosen-ness of David, the outcome of the revolt is not surprising: Absalom fails and meets his demise at the hands of David's chief officer Joab, and David himself reclaims the throne and his reign over Israel. However, this "triumphant" turn of events thinly masks a great social rupture, as the Succession Narrative makes clear that most of the Israelite population stood behind Absalom. David's return to power, then, can hardly be seen as something that his subjects would welcome. Rather, there is every indication that his reclaiming of the throne left the Israelite population fearful of what he might do in retaliation for their treachery.

An indication of this may be seen in 2 Samuel 20: following the defeat of Absalom, a Benjaminite named **Sheba the Bichrite** (a kinsman of Saul) attempted another revolt against David. The revolt is easily suppressed, with Sheba fleeing for safety to the northern city of Abel bet Maacah. Upon learning that David's forces had come to the walls of the city, the citizens kill Sheba and fling his body over the walls in order to avoid what they must have imagined to be a vicious attack awaiting them. Thus even a northern city sympathetic to the Saulide line (which explains why Sheba fled there) feared David enough to capitulate to his rule. By the end of the Succession Narrative, David sits upon a throne encircled by a fearful public, a broken family, and a kingdom reeling from injury.

5.8. 2 Samuel 21—24

The book of Samuel as it now stands ends with this strange collection of texts containing archival data, lists, poetry, and narrative. It constitutes a sharp break from the lean, linear narrative of the preceding chapters. This is especially the case when one looks to the first two chapters of the book of Kings, which seems to pick up, directly, on the storyline of the Succession Narrative. Chapters 21—24 are thus often viewed as a sort of secondary appendix, a pedestrian addition to the book, and are often sidelined when emphasis is placed on the narrative flow of the Succession Narrative to 1 Kings 1—2 (especially since many scholars view 1 Kings 1—2 as the original conclusion to the Succession Narrative).

Sidebar 4.32: Appendixes in the Book of Samuel and Deuteronomy

David and Moses are the two most important figures in the narrative traditions of the Hebrew Scriptures; the slight advantage or priority goes to Moses, as suggested by the relationship between Psalm 89 (which ends with a depiction of the fall of the Davidic monarchy) and Psalm 90 (which affirms that the traditions of Moses could rehabilitate the faithful). An example of the parallels forged between these two archetypal characters is the creation of appendixes in the books that respectively preserve the bulk of their deeds and impact (Deuteronomy for Moses; the book of Samuel for David). Both books contain an assortment of details regarding the final activity of each figure, and both books contain important and ancient poems that should be taught, studied and performed (Deuteronomy 32—33; 2 Samuel 22—23). The late redactors of these two distinct bodies of text probably sought to present one as consistent with the other, even though the major figures each text represents were rather different in terms of their role in the formation of Israelite social, ethnic, religious, and intellectual mythology.

This is unfortunate, for while 2 Samuel 21—24 may seem like an interruption and probably derives from a relatively late editorial or redactional hand,[41] these chapters possess important information regarding pivotal moments in the earlier narrative of David's reign

---

41. Leuchter 2010.

as well as key clues to how the narratives surrounding David were constructed to support his monarchic accomplishments.

The archival details in 2 Samuel 21 and 2 Samuel 23 do not carry the same carefully-crafted agenda or ideological design as the apologetic or propagandistic stories about David encountered earlier in the book of Samuel. They are therefore valuable in getting a sense of the events that the architects of the book eventually used to create the story of David's rise to power and to offer alternative accounts of events from his reign in need of defense or explanation. Second Samuel 24 also possesses important information on how, and why, the larger narrative of the book of Samuel took its shape. In 2 Samuel 24, David takes a census of his people, which leads to a great plague. The plague is abated with David's penitent behavior, which includes the purchase of space from a resident of Jerusalem named **Araunah** which comes to serve as the locus of an altar David builds.

In this episode, many scholars see an author engineering certain memories and facts related to David's desire to build a temple—something that 2 Samuel 7 outright denies him. The taking of a census (to estimate potential tax and workforce resources) and purchasing of altar space are important steps in orchestrating temple construction, but this appears to have been put on hold in the face of a plague which befell the population.[42] Second Samuel 24 possesses the type of information that suggests that the plague was interpreted by those who suffered through it as YHWH's angry response to David's attempt to build a temple; in the ancient world, a king denied the opportunity to be a temple builder is a king repudiated by the deity or deities he serves.

It may be that in the fact of this apparent repudiation from YHWH, scribes and propagandists working on David's behalf engineered not only the narrative of 2 Samuel 24 but the ideology resulting in the promise oracle of 2 Samuel 7—which explains how David's restriction from building a temple does not compromise his status as YHWH's chosen king for Israel. Indeed, most of the book of Samuel seems to revolve around the idea while YHWH chooses and then repudiates others (such as the Elides or Saul), he does not do so with David. To the end of the book, David remains central to YHWH's intentions for Israel, which strongly suggests that the book's early audiences were somewhat less confident about this king.

---

42. See again Meyers 1987.

Bibliography

Ackerman, Susan. 1993. "The Queen Mother and the Cult in Ancient Israel." JBL 112: 385–401.

Halpern, Baruch. 1991. "Jerusalem and the Lineages in the Seventh Century BCE: Kinship and the Rise of Individual Moral Liability." In *Law and Ideology in Monarchic Israel*, edited by Baruch Halpern and Deborah W. Hobson, 11–107. JSOTSup. Sheffield: Sheffield Academic Press.

_____. 2001. *David's Secret Demons: Messiah, Murderer, Traitor, King*. Grand Rapids: Eerdmans.

Hutton, Jeremy M. 2009. *The Transjordanian Palimpsest: The Overwritten Texts of Personal Exile and Return in the Deuteronomistic History*. BZAW. Berlin: De Gruyter.

Joseph, Alison. 2015. *Portrait of the Kings: The Davidic Prototype in Deuteronomistic Poetics*. Minneapolis: Fortress Press.

Kallai, Zechariah. 1999. "Biblical Historiography and Literary History: A Programmatic Survey." VT 49: 338–50.

Kreutzer, Siegfried. 2006. "Saul—not always—At War: A New Perspective on the Rise of Kingship in Israel." In *Saul in Story and Tradition*, edited by Carl S. Erlich and Marsha C. White, 39–58. FAT. Tübingen: Mohr-Siebeck.

Lehmann, Gunnar. 2003. "The United Monarchy in the Countryside: Jerusalem, Judah and the Shephelah in the Tenth Century BCE." In *Jerusalem in Bible and Archaeology*, edited by Andrew G. Vaughn and Anne E. Killebrew, 117–62. Atlanta: SBL.

Leuchter, Mark. 2008. *The Polemics of Exile in Jeremiah 26—45*. Cambridge: Cambridge University Press.

_____. 2010. "The Sociolinguistic and Rhetorical Implications of the Source Citations in the Book of Kings." In *Soundings in Kings*, edited by Klaus Peter Adam and Mark Leuchter, 119–34. Minneapolis: Fortress Press.

_____. 2013. *Samuel and the Shaping of Tradition*. New York/Oxford: Oxford University Press.

_____. 2015. "The Rhetoric of Convention: The Foundational Saul Narratives (1 Samuel 9—11) Reconsidered," in *Journal of Religious History* 39: n.p.

McCarter, P. Kyle. 1980a. "The Apology of David." *JBL* 99: 489–504.

_____. 1980b. *I Samuel*. AB. Garden City: Doubleday.

Meyers, Carol R. 1987. "David as Temple Builder." In *Ancient Israelite*

Religion, edited by Patrick D. Miller et al., 357–476. Philadelphia: Fortress Press.

Miller, Robert D. 2005. *Chieftains of the Highland Clans: A History of Israel in the 12th and 11th Centuries BC*. Grand Rapids: Eerdmans.

Na'aman, Nadav. 1996. "The Contribution of the Amarna Letters to the Debate on Jerusalem's Political Position in the Tenth Century BCE." *BASOR* 304: 17–27.

Pfoh, Emanuel (w. Keith Whitelam). 2013. *The Politics of Israel's Past*. Sheffield: Sheffield Phoenix Press.

Pioske, Daniel. 2015. "Memory and its Materiality: The Case of Early Iron Age Khirbet Qeiyafa and Jerusalem." *ZAW* 127: 78–95.

Polak, Frank. 2003. "Style is More than the Person: Sociolinguistics, Literary Culture, and the Distinction between Written and Oral Narrative." In *Studies in Biblical Hebrew: Chronology and Typology*, edited by Ian M. Young, 38–103. JSOTSup. New York: T & T Clark.

Rost, Leonhard. 1926. *Die Überlieferung von der Thronnachfolge Davids*. BWA(N)T 42. Stuttgart: Kohlhammer.

Schniedewind, William. 1999. *Society and the Promise to David*. New York/Oxford: Oxford University Press.

____. 1995. *The Word of God in Transition: From Prophet to Exegete in the Second Temple Period*. JSOTSup. Sheffield: Sheffield Academic Press.

Seow, Choon-Leong. 1989. *Myth, Politics and the Drama of David's Dance*. HSM. Atlanta: Scholars Press.

Van der Toorn, Karel. 2007. *Family Religion in Babylonia, Syria and Israel*. Leiden: Brill.

Wilson, Robert R. 1980. *Prophecy and Society in Ancient Israel*. Minneapolis: Fortress Press.

5

Kings (1—2 Kings)

1. Introduction

1.1. Name

Before talking about the more interesting features of the book, we need to establish that 1—2 Kings is more properly called just "Kings." The forty-seven chapters of 1—2 Kings were originally one book that was divided into two parts for the simple reason that it was too long to fit onto one scroll.[1]

A logical place to divide a story about the forty kings of Kings in half would be at the death of one of these monarchs, but 1 Kings ends by interrupting the reigns of Jehoshaphat of Judah and Ahaziah of Israel, and 2 Kings picks up the story in the midst of their reigns. So, while the reason for the division was valid at the time, since we no longer are limited by scroll-length there is no compelling reason to continue to speak of the books of 1—2 Kings, except when referring to a specific text. This chapter will therefore refer to the book (singular, not plural) of Kings.

---

1. The Jewish Talmud refers to Kings as a single book (*B. Bat.* 14b–15a).

1.2. Why Study Kings?

Now that we've established what to call the book, we can talk about why people avoid Kings and yet why it still profitable to study it. Kings is not nearly as popular as its neighbor in the canon, the book of Samuel (which also started out as one book). Many readers of the Old Testament avoid the book of Kings, thinking of it as tragic, confusing, or worse, boring. Terence Fretheim says, "Read 1 Kings 15—16 or 2 Kings 15 when you are having trouble getting to sleep!"[2] Even biblical scholars think of Kings as a cure for insomnia.

Kings *is tragic*. Solomon's sin leads to the division of the monarchy, and then persistent apostasy result in exile for both nations of the divided monarchy, first for Israel by Assyria, then for Judah by Babylon. The book ends with David's heir, King Jehoiachin imprisoned in Babylon.

But tragedy is part of life, and while some may try to avoid it, everyone will experience it. The book of Kings narrates a tragedy that is meant to be instructive. Readers who are willing to listen to its tragic story can benefit from its wisdom.

Kings *is confusing*. There are forty kings and many of them have similar, or even identical, names. To make matters worse, the names of rulers change randomly, or sometimes the text doesn't give the ruler a name, calling him simply the "king of Israel." The focus of the narrative frequently flips back and forth between the kingdoms of Israel and Judah.

But this chapter will help you make sense of the confusion, by explaining the historical background (who was Tiglath-pileser III?), illuminating the literary features (what is a regnal formula?) and discussing the theological message (why did both Israel and Judah end up in exile?). In addition, tables and charts will summarize vital information about rulers, dates, patterns, and features of the book.

Despite Fretheim's perspective on the book, Kings *is not boring*.[3] It includes not only important information about prophets, priests, and kings, but also engaging narratives of trash talking, battles and bloodshed, healings, deliverance, and supernatural provision. God speaks through his prophets, even using a deceptive divine messenger, and as a result rulers are both anointed and assassinated. The miracles

---

2. Fretheim 1999, 2.
3. I don't think Fretheim thinks the book as a whole is boring. He wrote an excellent commentary on Kings (1999).

of Kings involve lightning and leprosy, axes and arrows, bowls and jars, lions and bears, chariots and horses, death and resurrection. Your investment in reading the book of Kings will be rewarded.

1.3. Kings in the Canon

1.3.1. Canonical Breakdowns

Where does the book of Kings fit in the canon? It depends on your tradition. The Hebrew and Greek Bibles position Kings in different sections of Scripture, and the Jewish, Christian, and scholarly traditions each have a different name for the section of the canon where Kings is situated.

Kings is about kings, but it is also about prophets, with literally hundreds of prophetic individuals serving both as the heroes and as the villains of the narrative. This prophetic emphasis of the book is reflected in the traditional Jewish term for this section of Scripture, the **Former Prophets**. Curiously, the three other books that make up the Former Prophets (Joshua, Judges, and Samuel) feature only a few prophets (Samuel has more than the other two). Within this framework, the Latter Prophets are part of what are sometimes called the Major Prophets (Isaiah, Jeremiah, and Ezekiel) and the Minor Prophets (Hosea, Joel, Amos, Obadiah, Jonah, Micah, Nahum, Habakkuk, Zephaniah, Haggai, Zechariah, and Malachi). Combined, the Former and Latter Prophets make up the *Nevi'im* or the Prophets, which represents the second consonant (N) of the acronym for the Hebrew Bible, the Tanak (T-N-K), along with the first section, the *Torah* (the Law or Pentateuch), and the third section, the *Ketuvi'im* (the Writings). Although English Bibles position the book of Ruth in the middle of the four books of the Former Prophets, within the Hebrew breakdowns Ruth is considered part of the Writings.

Scholars have a different name for these four books, the **Deuteronomistic History**, since each of the books bear signs of editing or redaction that is reminiscent of the book of Deuteronomy. As the culmination of this history, Kings has been the focus of much research into how this Deuteronomistic redaction may have taken place (see "Composition" below).

In the Greek **Septuagint** (LXX), 1–2 Samuel and 1–2 Kings were combined into a four-part history of the monarchy entitled A, B, C, D *Basileiōn* or "Kingdoms." Within the Greek breakdowns, 1 and 2 Kings would be the third and fourth books of this series (also called, in Latin, *Regnorum* III and *Regnorum* IV). It is reasonable to link Samuel and Kings. Not only do the books of Samuel and Kings share a focus on the monarchy, but there is also a continuity of storyline connecting the books since the initial narrative of 1 Kings features many characters from 2 Samuel (e.g., David, Joab, Solomon, Bathsheba, Nathan).[4]

Yet another breakdown is often seen within the Christian tradition, where Kings is considered part of the **Historical Books** of the Old Testament, which is the breakdown used for this textbook. While these other three divisions are more clear-cut, this one is more ambiguous since it is difficult to define exactly what a "historical book" is. The books of 1 and 2 Chronicles (one book originally) and Ezra—Nehemiah (one book originally) are usually included among these Historical Books, but scholars are unsure where to include the books of Ruth and Esther. This confusion is even found in the textual traditions. In the LXX canon, Ruth and Esther are located next to other Historical Books (Ruth between Judges and Samuel; Esther after Ezra—Nehemiah), whereas in the HB they are located near non-historical books (Ruth, between Proverbs and Song of Songs; Esther, between Lamentations and Daniel). While uncertainty exists about some of these books, there is no debate that Kings should be considered among the Historical books.

1.3.2. Prophetic Parallel Texts

While many of the prophets with books named after them probably ministered during the 450 year period that the book of Kings covers (Jeremiah, Ezekiel, Amos, Hosea, Micah, Zephaniah, Nahum and Habakkuk), surprisingly only Jonah and Isaiah are mentioned explicitly in the book (2 Kgs. 14:25; 19:2, 5, 6, etc.).[5]

In addition to their common prophetic interest, another link between the Former and Latter Prophets is established by the extensive sections of 2 Kings that are virtually identical to sections of prophetic literature. Readers of the New Testament encounter a similar phenomenon in the Synoptic Gospels which repeat certain stories with little or no variation (e.g., Matt. 12:1–8; Mark 2:23–28; Luke 6:1–5). In Kings, the narrative of the reign of righteous King Hezekiah

---

4. I discuss the idea that Samuel and Kings were once part of a unified work in Lamb 2007, 260–61.
5. The book of Kings includes individuals named Jeremiah, Obadiah and Zechariah, but none of these are clearly the same as the prophet associated with the prophetic book.

is repeated almost verbatim in the book of Isaiah (2 Kgs. 18:13–20:19; Isa. 36–39). (While Chronicles follows Kings in English Bibles, Isaiah follows Kings in the Hebrew Bible.) Similarly, the books of Kings and Jeremiah conclude with an identical account of the fall of Jerusalem and final captivity of Judah (2 Kgs. 24:18–25:30; Jer. 52).

Since most scholars think the Kings versions of these accounts predated their prophetic parallel texts, Isaiah and Jeremiah will not be discussed as a possible source for Kings.[6] While it is impossible to be certain about which came first, these sections of Kings or their prophetic parallels, the fact that these sections were repeated suggests that the biblical authors wanted to emphasize the lessons of these stories: Hezekiah's righteousness led to deliverance from Assyria and Judah's unfaithfulness led to captivity in Babylon.

1.3.3. Relationship with Chronicles

The biblical book that overlaps most significantly with Kings is Chronicles, which includes numerous parallel passages. Most scholars agree that the books of Kings and Samuel were used as a source by the Chronicler and not the other way around.[7] Therefore, a discussion of the relationship between the book of Kings and the book of Chronicles will be delayed to chapter 7.

1.4. Confusion about Kings and Kingdoms

Not surprisingly, Kings is about kings. Which sounds simple until you start reading Kings, and then it is easy to get confused. This section will first explain four problems that make Kings difficult to understand, and then provide some solutions to help you work through the confusion.

First, Kings has too many kings to keep track of. While Samuel goes into depth describing the reigns of only two kings (Saul and David), the book of Kings chronicles the reigns of forty, two from the United Monarchy of Israel (David and Solomon) and nineteen each from the Northern Kingdom of Israel and the Southern Kingdom of Judah.[8] It is difficult to keep track of these forty names, so a family tree of the kings

---

6. See Wiseman 1993, 46.
7. See Williamson 1982, 19.
8. The books of Samuel and Kings record sections of David's reign.

of Israel and Judah is provided (**Figure 5.1**) so you see where Menahem of Israel and Manasseh of Judah fit in to the story (both are evil).

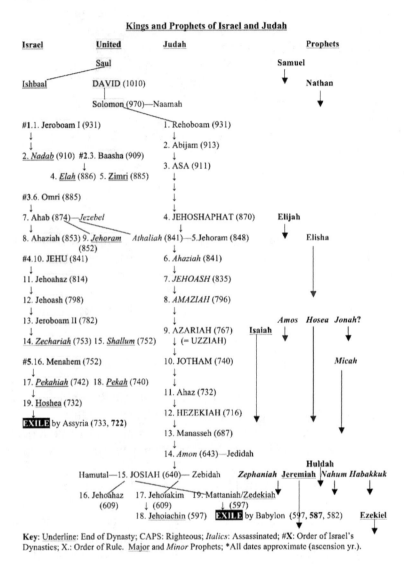

Kings and Prophets of Israel and Judah

Figure 5.1: Kings and Prophets of Israel and Judah

Second, kings' names are confusing in Kings. Five sets of rulers have identical names (Jeroboam, Ahaziah, Jehoram, Jehoash, and Jehoahaz) and, to make things more confusing, Jehoram of Judah came to power while Jehoram of Israel was already ruling (2 Kgs. 8:16). (What were their parents thinking?) Other rulers have similar names (Amaziah and Azariah; Zimri and Omri; Pekahiah and Pekah; Jehoiakim and Jehoiachin; Ahab, Ahaz and Ahaziah). For the first four pairs, the reign of the second immediately follows after that of the first. To add to the name confusion, several of the rulers' names are changed. Neco of Egypt changes Eliakim's name to Jehoiakim, and Nebuchadnezzar changes Mattaniah's name to Zedekiah (2 Kgs. 23:34; 24:17). Azariah is also called Uzziah (2 Kgs. 15:13, 30; see also Isa. 6:1).The names of several rulers are randomly shortened (Jehoash to Joash; Jehoahaz to Joahaz) with no explanation. Sometimes the text provides no name at all for a king. Within the prophetic cycles of Elijah and Elisha the text often simply refers to the current ruler as "the king of Israel" (e.g., 1 Kgs. 20:28, 31, 32; 2 Kgs. 5:5, 6, 7) making it difficult to be certain into which reign the narrative is meant to be set. Even to biblical scholars these royal names are confusing.

For all of these rulers, Figure 5.1 should reduce some of the name confusion, but a few other guidelines should provide further help to clarify the identity of a ruler. To distinguish between rulers with the same name in this chapter, the respective kingdom will always be given (e.g., Jehoram of Israel and Jehoram of Judah), which will solve most of these problems, except for Jeroboam, since two of them ruled Israel. To distinguish between these rulers, roman numerals will be given (Jeroboam I and Jeroboam II), even though these are not present in the text. For the two rulers whose names are shortened, the longer form will consistently be used (Jehoash, not Joash; Jehoahaz, not Joahaz). Rulers whose names change will consistently be referred to by the more popular primary name in Kings (Azariah, Jehoiakim, and Zedekiah; not Uzziah, Eliakim, and Mattaniah) even if the relevant text uses the alternative form. For rulers with similar sounding names, I can't help you. Some things you have to do for yourself.

Third, Kings' coverage of kings is inconsistent. The text slows down for six rulers, narrating their reigns in detail over several chapters (Solomon, Jeroboam I, Ahab, Jehu, Hezekiah, and Josiah), whereas for most kings the text speeds up, recording only the bare essentials of their reigns in a few verses (e.g., Abijam, Nadab, Elah, and Amon), leaving the reader wondering about the variation in depth of coverage. It is difficult to explain the disparity in depth among these rulers. Perhaps it is due to the level of detail included in the source material (see 2.1.2) available to the author.

But it is not surprising that Kings goes into greater depth for these six rulers, since they are particularly instructive examples to learn from, both positively and negatively. They include three who are unusually righteous (Jehu, Hezekiah, and Josiah), two who are usually evil (Jeroboam and Ahab), and one who starts out righteous but ends up evil (Solomon).

While the text goes into greater depth for these six, it still includes the basic information in a standard format, the regnal formulas, for all thirty-eight rulers of the divided monarchy. This information is summarized conveniently in two tables, one of which (Table 5.1) appears below in the discussion of regnal formulas (2.3), and the other (Table 5.2) appears at the end of this chapter.

Fourth, the kingdoms of Kings are confusing. The book of Kings begins and ends with a single monarchy, which doesn't sound too bad. The narrative focuses on the United Kingdom of Israel under Solomon at first, and then Judah in isolation after the exile of Israel at the end. But because of what happens in the middle, the terminology associated with kingdoms can be confusing: United Monarchy and Divided Monarchy; Israel and Judah; the Southern Kingdom and the Northern Kingdom. And to make it worse, "Israel" means different things along the way.

So, let us take a moment and define these terms. The **United Monarchy** encompasses all of the Israelite tribes, which were ruled over first by Saul and then David in Samuel.[9] The period of the United Monarchy continues into Kings as David's son Solomon manages to hold his father's empire together (1 Kings 1–11). But after Solomon dies, his son Rehoboam loses all the tribes except Judah to Jeroboam, which begins the era of the **Divided Monarchy** (1 Kings 12–2 Kings 17).[10] Rehoboam and his heirs rule over what is referred to as **Judah**, or the **Southern Kingdom**. Jeroboam and the kings after him rule over what is referred to as **Israel**, or the **Northern Kingdom**. While the text always refers to Solomon's kingdom as "Israel," it will be referred to here as the United Monarchy to avoid confusion between Solomon's realm and the Northern Kingdom of the Divided Monarchy. The period of the Divided Monarchy continued until the Northern Kingdom was exiled by Assyria (2 Kgs. 17:6).

---

9. Although, David's early years were characterized by civil war as he ruled over Judah initially before he was anointed ruler over Israel and Judah (2 Sam. 2:4; 5:3).

10. The text appears to be inconsistent whether the Southern Kingdom included just Judah, or Judah and Benjamin (1 Kgs. 12:20–23).

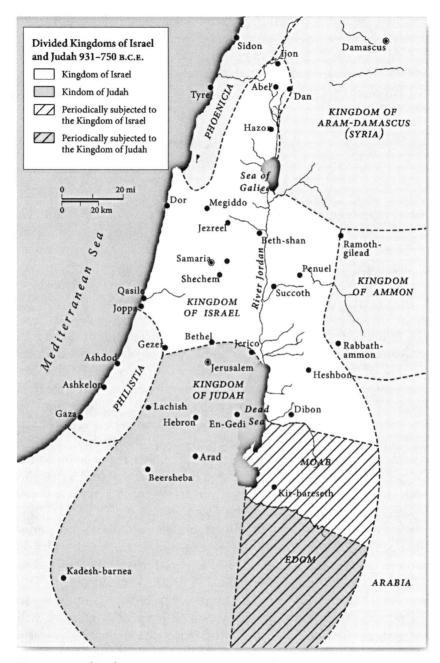

Figure 5.2: Two kingdoms.

This final period is sometimes called "Judah alone" (2 Kings 18—25) since Israel as a sovereign nation ceases to exist. In these final chapters of Kings, the name "Israel" can refer to the Northern Kingdom (e.g., 2 Kgs. 18:1; 21:3; 23:19), the United Monarchy of Solomon (2 Kgs. 24:13), or the people that God identifies himself with generally (2 Kgs. 19:15, 20; 21:12, 15).

2. Literary Concerns

2.1. Composition of Kings

Before examining the book of Kings as a historical or theological work, it is necessary to discuss it as a work of literature, specifically reflecting on how it was initially composed and later redacted, as well as its two distinctive literary features regnal formulas and prophetic narratives.

2.1.1. Who Wrote the Book of Kings?

The Talmud attributes the authorship of the book of Kings to **Jeremiah** (*B. Bat.* 14b–15a).[11] While this idea fits in well with contemporary notions of authorship as one individual who is responsible for composing a work, scholars do not generally follow this Talmudic conclusion. Stylistically, Kings shares more connections to Deuteronomy than Jeremiah (see 2.2), and since the book itself mentions no author, any conclusions about authorship must be considered speculative. As this section will discuss, the composition of Kings was probably more complicated than a single author writing in isolation, but could have involved multiple authors, scribes, editors, redactors, and perhaps even scribal communities.

What should we call the people responsible for the composition of the book of Kings? Scholars use a variety of terms for the various authors, editors, or Deuteronomistic redactors of the book (the Historian, Dtr, DtrH, DtrP, DtrN, Dtr1, Dtr2, etc. ; see 2.2 below). There are two problems with using this terminology. First, it is confusing to the non-specialist because it assumes high levels of familiarity with the various views on Deuteronomistic redaction. Second, as scholarly opinions shift, the standard conventions change; speaking simply of Dtr forty years ago was typical, but twenty years ago scholars more

---

11. See Cogan 2001, 84.

frequently used Dtr1 and Dtr2. Therefore, when speaking generally about the person or people responsible for the composition of the book of Kings, I will use the traditional term "author" (not authors).[12]

2.1.2. Royal Annals

Since the text repeatedly informs readers that the composition of Kings involved historical sources, we know that one of the earliest steps of the composition process must have involved scribes who initially recorded these **royal annals**.[13] The books of Kings and Chronicles are unique in the Hebrew Bible for including numerous references to sources.[14] Three distinct documents are referred to a total of thirty-three times in the book of Kings.

First, the *Annals of Solomon* are mentioned only once at the end of Solomon's narrative (1 Kgs. 11:41). Presumably, this Solomonic document must have included extensive details about the king's reign, since his narrative is far longer than any other ruler in the book of Kings. Also, this first royal source is unique in that it focuses exclusively on only one ruler, while the other two sources combine royal records for series of rulers.

Second, the *Annals of the Kings of Israel* are mentioned seventeen times in Kings, immediately after a Northern king's death notice (e.g., 1 Kgs. 14:19; 15:31; 16:5). Only two Northern rulers lack a reference to these Northern annals: Jehoram and Hoshea. Surprisingly, the three northern rulers with the shortest reigns (Zimri, Zechariah, and Shallum), each less than a year, still qualified to receive a notation in the northern annals despite their brief tenures, while the two rulers without a notation have moderately long reigns (Jehoram: twelve years; Hoshea: nine years).

Third, the *Annals of the kings of Judah* are mentioned fifteen times in Kings, again after death notices (e.g., 1 Kgs. 14:29; 15:23; 22:45). Only four Southern kings lack a reference to these Southern annals (Ahaziah, Jehoahaz, Jehoiachin, and Zedekiah).[15] As we compare the rulers with no source reference, the two from the North with the

---

12. Some scholars also speak simply of the "author." See, among others, Cogan 2001, 89; and Wiseman 1993, 53.

13. For an extended discussion of the sources used in Kings, see the commentary of Jones 1984, 47–77.

14. Another historical source, the book of Jasher, is mentioned twice in the Former Prophets (Josh. 10:13; 2 Sam. 1:18). The Book of the Wars of YHWH is mentioned in Num. 21:14.

15. The queen Athaliah also lacks one of these references, but the narrative of her rule includes none of the other formulaic information (see the discussion of Regnal Formulas).

three from the South, we see a pattern of fewer references during times of crisis or chaos. Rulers who lack references include the two killed during the insurrection of Jehu (Jehoram of Israel and Ahaziah of Judah; 2 Kgs. 9:24, 27), and most of the final rulers of their respective kingdoms (Hoshea of Israel and Jehoahaz, Jehoiachin, and Zedekiah of Judah).

Some English versions (e.g., ESV, NAS) translate the Hebrew expression for these royal documents, *sēper dibrê hayyāmîm*, as "book of the Chronicles," but, just to be clear, the Chronicles or Annals mentioned in Kings are not the book of 1–2 Chronicles that appears directly after 1–2 Kings in English Bibles. They are ancient royal records that no longer exist.

Some scholars speculate that these annals never actually existed but were merely invented to give greater credibility to the book; however, most scholars are not convinced by this theory.[16] Assuming these hypothetical documents actually existed, *who composed them?* It is impossible to say, but royal scribes are the most likely candidates, perhaps individuals like Shaphan the royal secretary who was involved in the finding of the book of the law during Josiah's reign (2 Kgs. 22:3–12). Within the book of Esther, the recording and recalling of the Persian royal annals play a significant role in thwarting the plans of Haman to assassinate Mordecai, Esther's uncle (Est. 2:23; 6:1–2).

2.1.3. How Were These Royal Annals Used?

How were these annalistic records used in the composition process? The fact that these annals are mentioned so frequently (over thirty times) suggests they were readily available, at least to the author, and that they were used frequently. While King Ahasuerus of Persia had his royal records read to him when he was having troubles sleeping (like a bedtime story? See Est. 6:1–2), presumably the author of Kings utilized royal records in a different manner.

Since the book of Kings covers a vast sweep of Israel's history, from the final days of David to the restoration of Jehoiachin, a period of four-and-a-half centuries, the author could have relied on these annals for much of the historical information included in the book (regnal years, synchronisms, names of parents, etc.), much of which appears in the regnal formulas (see 2.3 below).

---

16. See the discussion in Cogan 2001, 91n10.

Just as the royal annals of Ahasuerus recorded not just historical details, but narratives, such as the narrative of how Mordecai uncovered an assassination plot against the king, the royal annals of Israel and Judah could have recorded stories of other acts of these rulers. Some of these stories may have been included in the book of Kings.

According to Kings, these annals included additional information about the reigns of these rulers and their other accomplishments not included in the book. These references usually describe these royal deeds in a rather formulaic manner, but many of them also mention additional information: wars fought (1 Kgs. 14:19; 22:45; 2 Kgs. 13:12), conspiracies committed (1 Kgs. 16:20; 2 Kgs. 15:15), the might (gĕbûrâ) of the king (1 Kgs. 15:23; 16:5, 27; 22:45 [MT 22:46]; 2 Kgs. 10:34; 13:8, 12; 14:15, 28; 20:20), borders expanded (2 Kgs. 14:28), sins committed (2 Kgs. 21:17), cities built (1 Kgs. 15:23; 22:39), an ivory house built (1 Kgs. 22:39), a pool and conduit built to bring water into the city (2 Kgs. 20:20).

Typically these sources are mentioned in the context of a rhetorical question: "Now the rest of the acts of Solomon . . . are they not written in the Book of the Acts of Solomon?" (1 Kgs. 11:41). Thus, these questions imply that the initial readers of Kings could access these royal records to find out about additional information not included in Kings. While these records may not have been available to the average Israelite (assuming they could read), even if later readers could not access them, repeated references to these annals would give greater credibility to the book of Kings.

Unfortunately, readers of Kings can no longer refer to these records. So, we are left to wonder about what could have been learned about the history of Israel if more information from these documents had been included in the book of Kings, since it is unlikely that these annals will ever be discovered.

2.1.4. Other Possible Sources

Beyond these three books of royal records, scholars speculate about other possible sources which could have been used in the composition process. Since Kings begins with the end of David's life and the story of Solomon's rise to power, scholars often theorize that the first two chapters of 1 Kings and the end of 2 Samuel (chapters 9–20) were part of a **Succession Narrative**, which told the story of how Solomon's older brothers were unworthy to reign in place of their famous father, thus establishing why a younger son like Solomon was chosen to succeed David.[17]

However, the connections back to the book of Samuel (e.g., continuity of characters, see 1.4) are not nearly as strong as those going forward to the rest of 1 Kings. This undermines the theory of an early Succession Narrative source used by the Kings author for the first two chapters. Solomon himself is only mentioned once in Samuel as an infant (2 Sam. 12:24–25), while in the first eleven chapters of 1 Kings, he consistently dominates the narrative (mentioned over 150 times). Additionally, the special name given to Solomon at birth in 2 Samuel (Jedidiah, "beloved of YHWH"; 2 Sam. 12:25) never appears Kings.

Because of the primary role that prophets play in the book of Kings, many scholars perceive that the author of Kings used a prophetic narrative source, often divided into cycles focusing on Elijah, Elisha, and other prophets.[18] It is impossible to determine definitively whether any documents were actually used as sources for the prophetic narratives of Kings, but since these narratives are definitely a major element of the book, their distinguishing features and characteristics will be discussed in greater depth below, alongside other literary features of the book (see 2.4.6, "**Prophetic Narratives**").

2.2. Deuteronomistic Redaction

Who combined these various sources and edited, or as scholars say, "redacted," them into the form that we have now for Kings? Much of the scholarly work on the book of Kings and the other books comprising the Former Prophets focuses on this question, specifically discussing possible theories of **Deuteronomistic redaction**, which we discussed in more depth in the Introduction. In this section we will look at specific Deuteronomistic issues related to the book of Kings.

As the final book of the Deuteronomistic History, Kings receives a lot of scholarly attention. The various redactional theories focus on the portrayal in the book of Kings of specific rulers, Solomon, Hezekiah, or particularly, Josiah. In Frank Moore Cross's theory of a double redaction, a Deuteronomist with a favorable view of monarchy (Dtr1) redacted the history during the reign of Josiah, while a later anti-monarchical Deuteronomist (Dtr2) redacted the material during the

---

17. The classic work on the Succession Narrative is Rost 1926 (English translation 1982).
18. See Jones 1984, 64–76.

exile. Both scholars who agree and those who disagree with the Cross school therefore devote most of their attention to Kings, particularly the later chapters of 2 Kings. While this tendency is understandable, any theories that attempt to explain how the four books of the Former Prophets came to be redacted need to take seriously the other three books in order to understand how this diverse material somehow became a unified work.

Just as the **judge cycles** distinguish the book of Judges from other historical books, so the **regnal formulas** distinguish the book of Kings. The next section of this chapter examines in more depth the structure and components of the regnal formulas, so this section will discuss their Deuteronomistic features and terminology. Among the various components of a regnal formula, the two in the middle, the evaluation and the explanation are most frequently considered by scholars to be Deuteronomistic. Almost all rulers of Israel and Judah are evaluated as doing "good" (yāšār; e.g.,1 Kgs. 22:43; 2 Kgs. 14:3; 15:3; 15:34) or as "evil" (ra'; e.g., 1 Kgs. 15:26, 34; 22:52; 2 Kgs. 3:2; 8:18) in the eyes of YHWH. The description of someone doing good or evil in "the eyes of YHWH" is repeated throughout Deuteronomy (4:25; 12:25, 28; 17:2; 21:9; 24:4), as well as in Judges, particularly in cyclical contexts (Judg. 2:11; 3:7; 12; 4:1; 6:1; 10:6; 13:1). The explanations for the royal evaluation are also thought to be Deuteronomistic since they focus on idolatry (for evil rulers) or on exclusive devotion to YHWH (for good rulers), both of which are important themes of the book of Deuteronomy (4:15–25; 5:8; 7:5; 9:12–16; 12:3; 27:15; 29:17; 32:16–21). Another important feature, which may or may not appear in regnal formulas, that links Kings to Deuteronomy are the numerous descriptions of individuals who somehow pursue YHWH with "all their heart" (e.g., Deut. 4:29; 6:5; 10:12; 11:13; 13:3; 1 Kgs. 2:4; 8:48; 9:4; 14:8).

2.3. Kings and Regnal Formulas

2.3.1. Israelite Regnal Formulas

Readers of the highly entertaining narrative of Samuel may be disappointed when they encounter the so-called regnal formulas of Kings, which begin appearing in the text shortly after Solomon's death.[19]

---

19. Provan summarizes scholarly views on the regnal formulas of Kings, including the divergent opinions regarding their redactional history, concluding that none of the perspectives are

For each ruler, the book of Kings provides detailed information about his rule and reign in a formulaic manner, more typical of an encyclopedia article. The book includes thirty-eight of these regnal formulas for rulers of the divided monarchy; thus they constitute a distinguishing feature of Israel and Judah's royal record, dominating the narrative particularly at the beginning and the end of the divided monarchy.[20]

What about formulas for David and Solomon? While the regnal formulas of Israel and Judah are similar, each has distinctive elements, and since the Northern formulas are slightly simpler, we will begin there. Table 5.1 displays a sample Israelite regnal formula for Jehoahaz son of Jehu. Table 5.2 (see at the end of the present chapter) displays the pattern of these seven elements in the narratives of each of the nineteen rulers of the Northern Kingdom.

Table 5.1: An Israelite Regnal Formula Example (Jehoahaz)

#	Elements	Jehoahaz of Israel (2 Kings 13:1–2, 8–9)
1	Synchronism	In the twenty-third year of Joash the son of Ahaziah, king of Judah,
2	Father's name	Jehoahaz the son of Jehu,
3	Reign length	Reigned over Israel in Samaria seventeen years.
4	Evaluation	He did evil in the eyes of YHWH.
5	Explanation	He followed the sins of Jeroboam . . . he did not turn from them.
	Narrative material[21]	*Aram oppressed Israel, Jehoahaz cried out for help . . . (2 Kgs. 13:3–7)*
6	Annals reference	Now the rest of the acts of Jehoahaz . . . are they not written in the book of the annals of the kings of Israel?
7	Death notice	So Jehoahaz slept with his ancestors, and they buried him in Samaria and his son Joash succeeded him.

Typically there are seven elements in each regnal formula for a Northern ruler divided into two parts, an initial section and a concluding section. The first part usually appears at the beginning of a ruler's narrative and includes five elements.

---

entirely convincing (1988, 33–35). For a discussion of regnal formulas for the Northern Kingdom, see Lamb 2007, 17–22.

20. The two rulers that lack a regnal formula, Tibni of Israel (1 Kgs. 16:21–22) and Athaliah of Judah (2 Kgs. 11:1–20) both reign in unusual circumstances (1 Kgs. 16:21–22; 2 Kgs. 11:1–16). Therefore both of them are omitted from these tables below.

21. The narrative material is not generally part of the regnal formula, see explanation below.

First, the *Synchronism* dates the beginning of the Northern king's reign relative to the Southern ruler who is already on the throne at that time. Seventeen rulers receive a synchronism, all except Jeroboam I and Jehu.

Second, the *Father's name* is stated to clearly identify the king, serving in the same way as a last name or family name is used today, since several kings of Israel and Judah share the same name. The regnal formulas of only two rulers (Zimri and Omri) lack a reference to their father's name.

Third, the text states the *Reign length*, in years for sixteen rulers, in months for two rulers (Zechariah, Shallum) and in days for one ruler (Zimri). Reign length is given for all nineteen northern rulers, the only element that appears in all regnal formulas for both the North and the South.

Fourth, the *Evaluation* of each ruler is stated, either as evil or righteous in the eyes of YHWH. The evaluation is the theological focal point of the regnal formula. Tragically, from the perspective of the author of Kings, sixteen Northern rulers are evaluated as evil. Some scholars state that all northern rulers receive evil evaluations,[22] but this conclusion is inaccurate on two points, since two Northern rulers receive no evaluation (Elah, Shallum), and one ruler is actually described as righteous in the eyes of YHWH, Jehu.[23]

Fifth, the *Explanation* for each ruler's evaluation is then provided. Seventeen of the Northern rulers are described as continuing in the sins of the founder of the divided Israelite kingdom Jeroboam I, specifically the golden calves that he set up at Dan in the north and Bethel in the south (1 Kgs. 12:25–33). This condemnation takes two distinct forms, either positively by walking in the sins of Jeroboam (e.g., 1 Kgs. 15:26, 34; 16:19, 26, 31) or negatively by not departing from the sins of Jeroboam (e.g., 2 Kgs. 3:3; 10:31; 14:24; 15:9, 18). The positive form is more often associated with earlier northern rulers (e.g., Nadab, Baasha, Zimri, Omri, Ahab), while the negative form is associated with later northern rulers (e.g., Jehoram, Jehu, Jeroboam II, Zechariah, Menahem). The two rulers without evaluations also have no explanation (Elah, Shallum), but even righteous Jehu is connected with the sins of Jeroboam. Apparently, Jehu's purge of the house of Ahab and the idolatry of Baalism was deemed sufficient to warrant a righteous

---

22. E.g., Cross 1973, 283.
23. See Lamb 2007, 17–27.

evaluation, overcoming his association with Jeroboam's golden calves (2 Kgs. 10:28–31).

Between the first and second part of the regnal formula, the text typically includes *Narrative material* about the life and reign of the ruler, which is distinctively less formulaic in nature. The narrative of Jehoahaz speaks about how he cried out to YHWH in the midst of his Aramean oppression and YHWH sent him a deliverer (2 Kgs. 13:3–7). After the narrative material, the final two elements typically appear together in the second part of the regnal formula.

The sixth element, the *Annals* reference, implies that additional information about the ruler's reign could be obtained from the annals of the kings of Israel (see 2.1.2, 2.1.3). The seventh and final element of the regnal formula, the *Death notice*, appears at the end of the ruler's narrative describing his burial and his successor. All ten Northern rulers who successfully pass on the throne to an heir receive a death notice, but the nine rulers whose reigns are ended by exile or execution in a conspiracy lack a death notice.

2.3.2. Judean Regnal Formulas

Judean regnal formulas share the same basic format (an initial and concluding section, separated by narrative material) and many of the same elements as those of their northern neighbors. Table 5.3 provides an example of a Southern regnal formula (for Jehoash); Table 5.4 (see the end of this present chapter) displays the pattern of the nine elements for each of the nineteen Southern rulers.

Instead of seven elements for the Northern formulas, Southern formulas include nine elements. Six of the Northern elements appear in Southern formulas: synchronism, reign length, evaluation, explanation, royal annals and death notice. The *Synchronism* is obviously not from the Northern, but from the Southern perspective, so the beginning of the Judean ruler's reign is dated from the current Israelite ruler. So, for example, for Abijam of Judah, when it says, "18th Jeroboam" under Israelite Synchronism, that means "the eighteenth year of the reign of Jeroboam I." Synchronisms are not present for Rehoboam or any rulers after Hezekiah, but for all eleven who reigned during the period of the divided monarchy. Just as it was for Israelite rulers, *Reign length* is given for all nineteen Judean rulers. All nineteen Judean rulers also receive an *Evaluation*: eleven rulers are judged to be evil and eight are deemed righteous. However, of the righteous, only two are evaluated as totally righteous (Hezekiah and Josiah, reflected in the table with bold: "right"), the other six righteous evaluations are all qualified. The regnal formulas of fifteen Southern rulers conclude with both an *Annals reference* and a *Death notice*, the same group of four rulers are missing both elements (Ahaziah, Jehoahaz, Jehoiachin, and Zedekiah).

Table 5.3: A Judean Regnal Formula Example (Jehoash)

#	Elements	Jehoash of Judah (2 Kgs. 11:21—12:3, 19–21)
1	Synchronism	In the seventh year of Jehu of Israel, Jehoash began to reign.
2	Accession age	Jehoash was 7 years old when he began to reign.
3	Reign length	He reigned 40 years in Jerusalem.
4	Mother's name	His mother's name was Zibiah of Beer-sheba.
5	Evaluation	He did was right in the eyes of YHWH.
6	Explanation	Because the priest Jehoiada instructed him.
7	High places	Nevertheless the high places were not taken away.
	Narrative material	*He repaired the temple . . .*
8	Annals reference	Now the rest of the acts of Jehoash . . . are they not written in the book of the annals of the kings of Judah?
9	Death notice	He was buried with his ancestors in the city of David; his son Amaziah succeeded him.

Among these six elements common to the formulas of the North and the South, the one that is the most different is the *Explanation* for the ruler's *Evaluation*. While most of these Explanations involve a comparison to a previous ruler, similar to the Northern Explanations, the variety of comparisons for Southern rulers are a stark contrast to the consistent association with Jeroboam I for Northern rulers. Thirteen rulers are compared to their father, or fathers (Abijam, Asa, Jehoshaphat, Amaziah, Azariah, Jotham, Ahaz, Hezekiah, Amon, Josiah, Jehoahaz, Jehoiakim, and Jehoiachin), understood either as their literal father or perhaps as an earlier royal ancestor. Depending upon which father is being referenced, the association may carry either negative or positive associations. Six rulers are compared to David, three righteous rulers are like him (Asa, Hezekiah, Josiah), two evil rulers are not like him (Abijam, Ahaz), and one ruler who receives a righteous evaluation is not as righteous as David (Amaziah). Two rulers are described as being like a king of Israel (Jehoram and Ahaz) which here constitutes a condemnation since almost all Northern rulers were evil. Six other individuals are mentioned in these Explanations, three good kings (Asa, Amaziah, and Uzziah [= Azariah]) and three bad kings (Ahab, Manasseh, and Jehoiakim). Two unique explanations involve the reason why Jehoash is righteous (the priest Jehoida instructed him) and why Manasseh is evil (he was followed the example of the nations that were driven out of the land). Adding to the variety of these Southern formulas, the explanatory characteristics are often combined: Jehoram and Ahaziah are like the kings of Israel and like Ahab; Amaziah is like his righteous father Jehoash, but not like the totally righteous David.

Three unique elements are present in the Judean regnal formulas which do not appear in the Israelite versions. First, instead of the Father's name, the *Mother's name* is given, presumably since all Judean rulers are from the lineage of David, readers already know that the father was usually the previous ruler. In the Northern kingdom, however, there are almost as many usurpers (nine) who take the throne as heirs (ten) who succeed to the throne, so providing the father's name is a helpful clarification. Only two of the nineteen Southern kings mothers are omitted (Jehoram and Ahaz).

Second, the ruler's *Accession age* is given for when he took the throne. The text records this number for seventeen rulers and omits the number for only two rulers from the early period of the Divided Monarchy (Abijam, Asa). Presumably this number was obtained by the author of kings from the royal records and perhaps there was a gap in the record for these two.

Third, the text mentions in nine of the regnal formulas that the *High places* (bāmôt), idolatrous locations for unauthorized worship, were not removed by the king. These cultic shrines are viewed highly negatively in the book of Kings, just as Jeroboam's golden calves were for Israel. Three of these rulers are evil (Rehoboam, Ahaz, Manasseh), but surprisingly, six of them are righteous (Asa, Jehoshaphat, Jehoash, Amaziah, Azariah, and Jotham). For these six, the continuing presence of the High places is what qualifies their righteous evaluation. The high places were present during the reign of Solomon, but he added more, and his son Rehoboam continued their proliferation (1 Kgs. 3:3; 11:7; 14:23). They survived until Hezekiah tore them down (2 Kgs. 18:4), but his son Manasseh rebuilt them (2 Kgs. 21:3). After Manasseh's grandson Josiah tore them down as well as Jeroboam's altar at Bethel (2 Kgs. 23:8, 15), they were not rebuilt, which explains why no kings after Hezekiah is condemned for their presence.

Figure 5.3: The ruins of Jeroboam's "high place" at Dan. Photo: Bibleplaces.com.

2.3.3. The Purpose of Regnal Formulas

Assuming they are not included to merely disappoint readers looking for an enthralling narrative, what purpose do the regnal formulas serve? While it is impossible to know precisely what prompted the author to include them, a possible reason suggests itself.

They give structure to a narrative that can seem convoluted. The regnal formula framework allows the author to chronicle the reigns of forty kings (David, Solomon, nineteen Northern and nineteen Southern rulers) over the course of over four hundred years, which includes a two-hundred-year period of two separate kingdoms. The text records this essential royal information about all rulers, even the ones with brief reigns. While longer-reigning rulers tend to have more narrative material than their shorter-reigning peers, from the perspective of their formulas, the ruler with the longest reign (Manasseh: fifty-five years) and the shortest reign (Zimri: one week) have roughly equal status. Thus, the formulas allow the narrative to go into more depth for certain important rulers (e.g., Solomon, Jehu, and Hezekiah), without completely ignoring the minor ones (e.g., Abijam, Zimri, and Jotham).

2.4. Prophets and Prophetic Narratives

Kings is about Kings, but, not surprisingly, as the final book of the Former Prophets, Kings is also about Prophets. In the books of Joshua and Judges, prophets appear only rarely (Josh. 14:6; Judg. 4:4; 6:8; 13:6, 8), but, beginning with the book of Samuel, they become more prominent as Samuel and Nathan support and condemn Saul and David. This prophetic trend continues in Kings as the text gives greater prominence to the role of prophets. One could even argue that despite its title, prophets are the real heroes of the story of Kings. While most of the kings were doing evil in the eyes of YHWH, the prophets were speaking and acting for YHWH.

Not only is Kings the most prophetic book of the Former Prophets, but it is arguably the most prophetic book of the entire Old Testament, at least in terms of the quantity of prophetic individuals and groups.

2.4.1. Prophetic Terms

Among Old Testament books, Kings has the most occurrences of terms for prophetic figures.[24] Forms of the word "prophet" (*nābî'*) appear 317 times in the Hebrew Bible.[25] Of these references, Jeremiah has the most (ninety-five), and Kings comes in second (eighty-four), while Chronicles comes in a distant third (thirty). The other books of the Former Prophets have a total of sixteen references (Joshua: none; Judges: one; Samuel: fifteen), so 84% of all the references of "prophet" in these four books are concentrated in Kings.[26]

The other term used synonymously with *prophet* in the Hebrew Bible is "man of God" (*îš (hā)'ĕlōhîm*).[27] A prophet is often called a "man of God" (e.g., Samuel: 1 Sam. 9:10–14; Elijah: 1 Kgs. 17:24; Elisha: 2 Kgs. 5:8). Forms of the phrase "man of God" appear over seventy times in the Old Testament (76 times in the ESV OT). The vast majority of these appear in Kings (fifty-one), with only eight total in the three other Former Prophets (Joshua: one; Judges: two; Samuel: five) and the rest scattered among the other OT books (e.g., Chronicles: six; Jeremiah:

---

24. See also my discussion of prophetic terms in the Former Prophets (Lamb 2010a, 176–77).
25. Including all forms of the noun, singular and plural.
26. The verb "prophesy" (*nābā'*) appears 115 times in the HB, the vast majority of these are in Jeremiah (forty) and Ezekiel (thirty-seven), with only a few in Kings (five) and a few more in Samuel (twelve).
27. The definite article is sometimes present, sometimes absent making a search for this phrase in MT difficult.

one; Ezra–Nehemiah: three). Although the vast majority of prophetic individuals named in the Former Prophets are male, curiously the first prophet, Deborah, and the last, Huldah, are female (Judg. 4:4; 2 Kgs. 22:14); however, the text does not refer to either of them as a "woman of God."

The other term used for a prophet in Kings is "seer" (*hōzeh*), but this word only appears once in the book (2 Kgs. 17:13), once in Samuel (2 Sam. 24:11), and nowhere else in the Former Prophets.[28]

2.4.2. Prophetic Figures

The prophets of Kings include individuals, both anonymous and named, as well as groups, both righteous and evil (from the perspective on the author). Table 5.5 ("Prophetic Figures in the Former Prophets") lists the prophetic figures of the Former Prophets, including all individuals and groups connected to the terms "prophet," "man of God," or "seer." Textual references are given in the left column and the middle column lists the prophet terms used for the prophetic individuals and groups (groups are underlined), including personal names (in **bold**) when they are given in the text. The rulers who are associated with these prophetic figures are listed in the right column. Rulers with an asterisk (*) are often referred to within the text simply as "the king of Israel" but the name given in the right column is the one suggested by the context.

Table 5.5: Prophetic Figures in the Former Prophets

Textual Reference	Prophetic Individuals and Groups	Ruler
Josh. 14:6	**Moses**, man of God	
Judg. 4:4	**Deborah**, prophet	
Judg. 6:8	Anonymous prophet	
Judg. 13:6, 8	Anonymous man of God	
1 Sam. 2:27	Anonymous man of God	
1 Sam. 3:20; 9:6–10	**Samuel**, prophet, man of God, seer	Saul, David
1 Sam. 10:5, 10; 19:20	Prophetic band, company	Saul

---

28. Samuel is also called a "seer" (1 Sam. 9:9, 11, 18, 19), but a different term is used (*rō'eh*).

1 Sam. 10:11; 19:24	"**Saul** among the prophets?"	Saul
1 Sam. 22:5; 2 Sa. 24:11	**Gad**, prophet, seer	Saul, David
1 Sam. 28:6, 15	Prophets who don't answer Saul	Saul
2 Sam. 15:27	**Zadok**, seer (?)	David
2 Sam. 7:2; 12:25; 1 Kgs. 1:8,10, 22,32	**Nathan**, prophet	David
1 Kgs. 11:29; 14:2, 18	**Ahijah**, prophet	Solomon, Jeroboam
1 Kgs. 12:22	**Shemaiah**, man of God	Rehoboam
1 Kgs. 13:1, 4; 2 Kgs. 23:17, 18	Anonymous man of God from Judah	Jeroboam
1 Kgs. 13:11, 18	Anonymous prophet from Bethel	Jeroboam
1 Kgs. 16:1, 7, 12	**Jehu** b. Hanani, prophet	Baasha
1 Kgs. 17:18; 18:22; 19:16; 2 Kgs. 1:9	**Elijah**, prophet, man of God	Ahab, Ahaziah
1 Kgs. 18:4, 13; 19:10,14; 2 Kgs. 9:7	Prophets killed by Jezebel	Ahab
1 Kgs. 18:4, 13	100 prophets saved by Obadiah	Ahab
1 Kgs. 18:19, 20, 22, 40; 19:1	450 prophets of Baal	Ahab
1 Kgs. 18:19, 20	400 prophets of Asherah	Ahab
1 Kgs. 19:16; 2 Kgs. 2:13; 3:11; 4:9; 5:3, 8, 13; 6:12; 8:7; 9:1; 13:19	**Elisha**, prophet, man of God	Ahab*, Jehoshaphat, Jehu, Jehoash
1 Kgs. 20:13, 22	Anonymous prophet	Ahab
1 Kgs. 20:28	Anonymous man of God	Ahab*
1 Kgs. 20:35, 38, 41	Anonymous son of the prophets	Ahab*
1 Kgs. 22:6, 7, 8, 10, 12, 22	400 prophets of YHWH	Ahab*, Jehoshaphat
1 Kgs. 22:7, 8	**Micaiah**, prophet	Ahab*, Jehoshaphat
2 Kgs. 2:3,5,7; 4:1,38; 5:22; 6:1; 9:1	Sons of the prophets	
2 Kgs. 2:7	50 of the sons of the prophets	

2 Kgs. 3:13	Prophets of the king's parents	Jehoram*
2 Kgs. 9:1	Anonymous young prophet	Jehoram / Jehu
2 Kgs. 10:19	Baal prophets killed by Jehu	Jehu
2 Kgs. 14:25	**Jonah** b. Amittai	Jeroboam II
2 Kgs. 17:13, 23	Prophets, seers warned NK, SK	
2 Kgs. 19:2; 20:1, 11, 14	**Isaiah**	Hezekiah
2 Kgs. 21:10 (cf. 24:2)	Prophets, servants of YHWH	Manasseh
2 Kgs. 22:14	**Huldah**	Josiah
2 Kgs. 23:2	Prophets	Josiah
2 Kgs. 24:2 (cf. 21:10)	Prophets, servants of YHWH	Jehoiakim

Several observations can now be made about the prophetic individuals and groups displayed in this table. Among the Former Prophets, Kings is unique for its remarkable quantity of prophets. The text of Kings provides names for ten prophetic individuals (Nathan, Ahijah, Shimaiah, Jehu son of Hanani, Elijah, Elisha, Micaiah, Jonah, Isaiah, and Huldah), whereas the previous three books of the Former Prophets (Joshua, Judges, and Samuel) only mention a total of seven prophetic individuals (Moses, Deborah, Samuel, Saul, Gad, Zadok, and Nathan). Among these individuals, Elisha stands out with far more prophetic textual references than any other prophet, including his mentor, Elijah. In fact after Solomon, Elisha is the most significant character in the book of Kings as his narrative dominates long sections of the text and spans the reigns of six Northern rulers (Ahab, Ahaziah, Jehoram, Jehu, Jehoahaz, and Jehoash; 1 Kgs. 19:16–21; 2 Kgs. 2:1—8:15; 9:1–3; 13:14–21). Additionally, Kings mention six anonymous prophets (e.g., 1 Kgs. 13:1, 11, 20:13, 28, 35; 2 Kgs. 9:1), while the other three books of the Former Prophets only mention three (e.g., Judg. 6:8; 13:6; 1 Sam. 2:27).

Kings also describes large groups of prophets. The good ones are often associated with Elijah and Elisha, and the bad ones, with Ahab and Jezebel. Jezebel killed a sufficient quantity of YHWH's prophets so that when Obadiah finally rescued some, he could only save a hundred (1 Kgs. 18:4). Elijah confronted 450 prophets of Baal and 400 prophets of Asherah on Mount Carmel (1 Kgs. 18:19 and then slaughtered them as retribution for Jezebel's prophetic purge. Micaiah confronted 400 prophets of YHWH, who give false prophecies of military success before the battle with Aram when Ahab was killed just as Micaiah had predicted (1 Kgs. 22:6). A prophetic company (literally, "the sons of the prophets") interacts extensively with Elisha during his ministry (2 Kgs. 2:3, 5, 7; 4:1, 38; 5:22; 6:1; 9:1). Jehu slaughters another group of prophets of Baal in his cultic reformation purge (2 Kgs. 10:19, 25, 28). Generic prophets hear the book of the law read by Josiah (2 Kgs. 23:2) and speak words of judgment to Judah in its final days (2 Kgs. 21:10; 24:2).

While the numbers for these groups are probably meant to be estimates and may involve overlaps, if one merely adds up the numbers, the book of Kings refers to well over a thousand prophets (1,416 to be precise): sixteen individuals (six anonymous plus ten named) and 1,400 in numbered groups (= 100+450+400+400+50). This tally does not include other texts which speak of "prophets" generally (e.g., 2 Kgs. 21:10; 23:2; 24:2).

Despite this prophetic plethora, Kings mentions only two of the prophets (Jonah and Isaiah) with books named after them (i.e., the Latter Prophets), and curiously ignores seven others who may have ministered during this time frame (Jeremiah, Hosea, Amos, Micah, Zephaniah, Nahum, and Habakkuk).

Obviously, at the beginning and end of the period of the monarchy, all the prophets are associated with the only kingdom available (United at the beginning, Judah at the end). However, during the period of the Divided Monarchy as recorded in Kings, there is a shocking absence of prophetic activity in the South. Between the reigns of Rehoboam and Hezekiah, no prophets are described as ministering in Judah.[29] The only Southern ruler who associates with prophets during this period of approximately two hundred years is Jehoshaphat, and he only does so in conjunction with Northern Rulers. While the absence of Southern prophets could be explained during the Divided Monarchy by the Northern emphasis of the narrative during this period, a similar prophetic absence exists during the reign of Solomon. The longest section of Kings without a prophetic reference (almost ten chapters; 1 Kgs. 1:32–11:29) occurs between the reference to Nathan at the beginning of Solomon's narrative and the reference to Ahijah at the

29. See Lamb 2010a, 179.

end. While the book of Kings primarily records divine communication to rulers through prophetic mediators (e.g., 1 Kgs. 13:2; 16:1; 17:2), during this section YHWH speaks three times to Solomon without reference to prophetic mediation (1 Kgs. 3:11; 6:11; 9:3).

2.4.3. Prophetic Speech

The primary task of a prophet is to mediate divine messages to the rulers and the people of Israel and Judah. This role of serving as YHWH's representative is reflected in the frequent use of the term "man of God" for prophetic individuals. Two primary formulaic expressions are used when prophets serve as divine messengers.[30]

First, "thus says YHWH" (*kōh 'āmar yhwh*) appears 44 times in the Former Prophets (in MT), 11 in the other three books (twice in Joshua, once in Judges, and eight times in Samuel) and 33 times in Kings (e.g., 1 Kgs. 11:31; 12:24; 13:2). All of the Kings occurrences of this formulaic expression are used in the context of prophetic speech to make it explicit that the message is meant to be understood as divine words, and not merely as human. It is used with Ahijah (1 Kgs. 11:31), Shemaiah (1 Kgs. 12:24), Elijah (1 Kgs. 17:14), Elisha (2 Kgs. 3:16), Isaiah (2 Kgs. 19:6), Huldah (2 Kgs. 22:15), as well as other prophets.

Second, "word of the LORD" (*dĕbar yhwh*) appears 60 times in the Former Prophets (in English ESV), 12 times in the other three books (twice in Joshua, not at all in Judges, and ten times in Samuel) and 48 times in Kings (e.g., 1 Kgs. 2:27; 12:24; 13:1). The "word of the LORD" comes directly to non-prophetic individuals (e.g., Solomon: 1 Kgs. 6:11), but more frequently comes to prophets such as Jehu, Elijah, and Isaiah (1 Kgs. 16:1, 7; 17:2, 8; 2 Kgs. 20:4). The most frequent usage of this expression, however, comes in the context of a fulfillment of an earlier prophetic message (e.g., 1 Kgs. 2:27; 13:5; 14:8; 15:29; 16:12; 17:16; 2 Kgs. 4:44).

The recipients of prophetic messages in Kings are also diverse, including the altar at Bethel (1 Kgs. 13:2), two widows (1 Kgs. 17:14; 2 Kgs. 4:1-7), a foreign general and a foreign emperor (2 Kgs. 5:10; 19:20-21), other prophets (1 Kgs. 13:18, 21; 20:36), the people generally (1 Kgs. 18:21-22; 2 Kgs. 17:13), but by far the most common individuals receiving prophetic oracles are rulers (see below, 2.4.4).

While sometimes the content of prophetic messages is

---

30. For a more extended discussion of prophetic terminology in the Historical Books, see "Word of God" in DOTHB, 999–1003.

unexpected—involving deception of a prophet and a king (1 Kgs. 13:18; 22:22) or trash talking other prophets (1 Kgs. 18:27)[31]—generally these messages can be divided into three categories: counsel, predictions, and judgments.

Prophets provide *counsel* to rulers in times of warfare and crisis. Shemaiah advocates for peace between Judah and Israel at the beginning of the Divided Monarchy (1 Kgs. 12:24), and much later in the narrative Elisha does the same between Israel and Aram (2 Kgs. 6:8–23). The humble responses of Ahab and Hezekiah to dire messages from Elijah and Isaiah, prompted YHWH to inform his prophet to relay a message to these rulers that he had changed his mind and would reduce the severity of the consequences (1 Kgs. 21:28–29; 2 Kgs. 20:5–6).

Prophetic speech often includes *predictions* of both good and bad news, involving a variety of outcomes. Elijah predicts first drought (1 Kgs. 17:1), and later rain (1 Kgs. 18:41), and Elisha predicts abundant provisions at the end of a long siege (2 Kgs. 7:1). Elisha and Isaiah predict imminent death in several cases (2 Kgs. 1:16; 7:2–20; 20:1), while Elisha and Huldah predict longer life for both Hezekiah and Josiah (2 Kgs. 20:5–6; 22:18–20). YHWH speaks through his prophets of both future deliverance for the nation (2 Kgs. 19:6, 21–34) and of future destruction and exile for the nation (2 Kgs. 17:23; 20:16–18; 21:10–16; 22:15–17; 24:2). King Ahab receives predictions of both defeat (1 Kgs. 22:17) as well as victory (1 Kgs. 20:13, 28; 22:6). Elisha and Jonah proclaim military success for Jehoram of Israel (2 Kgs. 3:19), Jehoash of Israel (2 Kgs. 13:19), and Jeroboam II (2 Kgs. 14:25).

Most of the prophetic *judgments* in Kings target idolatry (1 Kgs. 11:33; 13:2; 14:9; 18:18; 2 Kgs. 1:16; 21:11; 23:17) and disobedience (1 Kgs. 11:33; 18:18; 2 Kgs. 17:13). Other minor themes receiving condemnation include injustice (1 Kgs. 21:19–24), greed (2 Kgs. 5:26–27) and the shedding of innocent blood (2 Kgs. 21:16; 24:4).

2.4.4. Prophetic Deeds

Making and breaking rulers. Often prophetic speech will include or lead to prophetic actions, and the people who are affected most directly by the words and deeds of prophets are rulers. In Kings, prophets make and break rulers, removing one from power and then installing a new one in his place, just as Samuel did for Saul and David in Samuel.

---

31. See Lamb 2014, "Trash Talking."

Nathan served as the catalyst first to quash the rebellion of Adonijah and then to establish Solomon as David's successor (1 Kgs. 1:11–45). Ahijah removes the Northern tribes from Solomon's son Rehoboam and gives them to Jeroboam; he also condemns Jeroboam's dynasty (1 Kgs. 11:31–35; 14:7–14). Jehu son of Hanani first replaces Nadab son of Jeroboam with Baasha, then replaces Baasha's son Elah with Zimri (1 Kgs. 16:1–4, 7). Elijah, with the assistance of Elisha and his prophetic apprentice, prophesies the destruction of the house of Ahab and the establishment of the house of Jehu (1 Kgs. 21:20–26; 2 Kgs. 9:7–10). Elijah and Elisha also work together to bring down the Aramean king Ben-hadad and replace him with Hazael (2 Kgs. 8:13).

Prophets support rulers in other ways by anointing them and delivering dynastic promises to them.[32] An early precedent for prophetic anointing of rulers was established when the first two rulers of Israel (Saul, David) were both anointed by Samuel (1 Sam. 10:1; 16:13). In order to help Solomon secure the throne in the midst of a succession struggle with his older brother Adonijah, Nathan the prophet and Zadok the priest anointed David's younger son (1 Kgs. 1:34–45). Elijah was commissioned by YHWH to anoint a prophet (Elisha), a Northern king (Jehu), and an Aramean king (Hazael) (1 Kgs. 19:15–16), but the text records Elijah performing none of these anointings. Elijah only throws his cloak over Elisha, Elisha informs Hazael that he will be king, and Elisha's apprentice finally anoints Jehu (1 Kgs. 19:19; 2 Kgs. 8:13; 9:6). The anointings of Solomon and Jehu are the only recorded royal anointings by prophets in Kings.

Several rulers receive dynastic promises in Kings (Solomon, Jeroboam I, and Jehu). However, the dynastic promises to Solomon and Jehu are given without an explicit prophetic mediator (1 Kgs. 2:4; 6:12; 8:25; 9:4–5; 2 Kgs. 10:30). Therefore, since only one of these promises comes via a prophetic mediator, from Ahijah to Jeroboam I (1 Kgs. 11:38), more will be said about dynastic promises below in the context of prophecy, promise, and fulfillment (4.3).

While YHWH is described as judging specific rulers, he also frequently judges their heirs or their entire dynasty. Unlike the dynastic promises in Kings, these dynastic judgments are typically delivered by a prophet. When Ahijah condemns Solomon the punishment is delayed so that it falls upon his heir, Rehoboam (1 Kgs. 11:31–35). The judgments pronounced against Jeroboam I, Baasha, and

32. See Lamb 2007, 48–54; 223–30.

Ahab of Israel (delivered by Ahijah, Jehu and Elijah respectively) all involve the death of their sons and the cutting off of their dynasty (1 Kgs. 14:7-14; 16:1-4, 7; 21:20-26). Even righteous King Hezekiah of Judah receives a dynastic judgment as his future heirs will be exiled and be made into eunuchs (2 Kgs. 20:16-18).

Figure 5.4: In the foreground, bears attack youths who had mocked the prophet Elisha; in the background, Elijah ascends to heaven in a flaming chariot. Medieval French manuscript, now in the Bodleian Library (MS Douce 336); Commons.wikimedia.org.

Other Prophetic Actions. Prophets did not only support and condemn rulers, but they affected other individuals, as well as rulers, in the area of health, provision and nature. Prophets brought healing and life, illness and death, often in tandem. An anonymous prophet first withered the hand of Jeroboam and then after the king's intercession, the prophet then healed the king's withered hand (1 Kgs. 13:4-6). Elisha first healed Naaman the Aramean general of leprosy, but when his servant Gehazi lied about the reward, the prophet cursed him with leprosy (2 Kgs. 5:10-14, 27). Later in the narrative, Elisha struck the Aramean army with blindness to lead them secretly into Samaria, only to heal them of their blindness before telling the Israelite king to feed them (2 Kgs. 6:18, 20). Both Elijah and Elisha raised people from the dead (1 Kgs. 17:17-24; 2 Kgs. 4:8-37) and both prophets also had large numbers of people killed (1 Kgs. 18:40; 2 Kgs. 1:10, 12).

Prophets miraculously provided water for soldiers (2 Kgs. 3:16-17), and food for starving widows as well as for groups of men (1 Kgs. 17:14-16; 2 Kgs. 4:3-7; 4:43). Elisha purified water for a city (2 Kgs. 2:21-22) and purified stew for a company of prophets (2 Kgs. 4:41).

Prophets also defied nature. They called down fire from heaven (1 Kgs. 18:36-38; 2 Kgs. 1:10, 12) and called out lions and bears from the wilderness to attack people (1 Kgs. 13:21-24; 20:36; 2 Kgs. 2:24). They parted the Jordan River (2 Kgs. 2:14), made an ax head float on water (2 Kgs. 6:6-7), and made the sun's shadow move backwards (2 Kgs. 20:11).

2.4.5. A Prophetic Office?

Several scholars have speculated that there was a permanent prophetic office in Israel passed on from one generation to the next in the same manner as priests and kings passed on their role to their successor.[33] Two observations seem to support the idea of a prophetic institution. First, Kings includes a lot of prophets; second, Elijah passed on his prophetic role to his mentor Elisha (1 Kgs. 19:16-21).

However, both the textual evidence of Kings specifically and the Former Prophets generally do not support the idea of a continual prophetic office. While there are many prophets in Kings, the relative absence of prophets in Joshua and Judges suggests no official prophet for long periods of Israel's history. Even in Kings there are long periods where no prophets are mentioned (e.g., Solomon's reign). Also, in Kings, the various prophets often have overlapping ministries, making it difficult to determine who would have been considered the official prophet. Additionally, the institutionalized prophets associated with Ahab and Jezebel are consistently portrayed in a negative light, while Elijah and Elisha, who ministered outside official circles, are portrayed positively. Thus, the idea of a prophetic office is not a compelling theory based on the evidence of only one example of prophet succession.

2.4.6. Prophetic Narratives

Three long sections of Kings distinguish themselves from the rest of

---

33. For an argument in favor of a prophetic office, see Carroll 1969, 401. For my argument against the idea of a permanent prophetic office, see Lamb 2010a, 172-73.

the book by emphasizing the roles of prophets and by de-emphasizing the history of rulers. Several unique features of these prophetic narratives make them more appealing to readers than other sections of the book, which explains why they are more popular and familiar. In short, they tell great stories about prophets.

Defining the sections. Each of the three sections is set during the reign of one primary Northern ruler (Jeroboam I, Ahab, and Jeroboam), who interacts with one primary prophet (Ahijah, Elijah, and Elisha) and several other prophets who are often anonymous. The first prophetic narrative takes place during the reign of Jeroboam I, as he is initially supported, but later condemned by Ahijah, and he is first cursed with a withered hand, then healed by the same unnamed man of God (in two parts: 1 Kgs. 11:26–39; 13:1—14:18). The second narrative focuses primarily on the ministry of Elijah, who repeatedly clashes with King Ahab, and secondarily on the other prophets who engage with Ahab and his son Ahaziah both negatively and positively (1 Kgs. 17:1—2 Kgs. 2:12). The third narrative is set primarily during the reign of Jehoram and records the story of Elisha's supernatural ministry and his interactions with the Northern king, two women, an Aramean general and a prophetic company (2 Kgs. 2:13—8:15).

Entertaining narratives. Two characteristics of the prophetic narratives of Kings make them more entertaining than other sections of the book. First, the stories are dramatic, as the prophets risk their lives to confront rulers and armies. They perform supernatural deeds, rivaled in the OT perhaps only by the stories of the Exodus. Prophets sic lions and bears on prophets and boys, they call down fire from heaven and they fill the mountain-side with visions of chariots of fire (1 Kgs. 13:20–24; 18:36–38; 2 Kgs. 2:24; 6:17). Instead of briefly recording the stories of a series of rulers, these narratives go into greater depth about prophetic struggles with depression (1 Kgs. 19:1–18), loss (1 Kgs. 17:20; 2 Kgs. 2:12), and betrayal (2 Kgs. 5:19–27).

The second feature that makes prophetic narratives more interesting is that they lack those boring regnal formulas. The first concentration of regnal formulas for ten rulers (Jeroboam, Rehoboam, Abijam, Asa, Nadab, Baasha, Elah, Zimri, Omri, and Ahab; 1 Kgs. 14:19—16:34) appears in the text immediately after the first prophetic narrative focused on Ahijah and Jeroboam I.

After this concentration, the regnal formulas disappear from the narrative, and during two extended formulaic gaps (1 Kgs. 16:29—22:38; 2 Kgs. 3:4—8:15), the text narrates the ministries of first

Elijah and then Elisha. The absence of regnal formulas in these narratives thus brings prophets to the foreground and moves rulers into the background.

Distinguishing features. Other distinguishing features of prophetic narratives set them apart from the rest of the book of Kings. These narratives uniquely focus on Israel, giving the Divided Monarchy section of the book a strongly Northern flavor. Elijah and Elisha, in particular, spend most of their time in the Northern Kingdom (e.g., Mount Carmel, Gilead, Jezreel, Gilgal, Samaria). Within the prophetic narratives of Kings, the only Southern ruler who is mentioned, Jehoshaphat, only appears in connection with a Northern ruler (Ahab, Jehoram).

Generic individuals. Another unusual feature of prophetic narratives is that they often speak generically about Northern rulers, not identifying them by name but simply as "the king of Israel" (e.g., 1 Kgs. 20:4, 7; 22:2, 3; 2 Kgs. 3:4, 9; 5:5, 6; 6:9, 10; 7:6).[34] The broader context of these passages often make it clear who the anonymous ruler is meant to be (e.g., 1 Kgs. 20:2; 22:20; 2 Kgs. 3:5), but this anonymous feature of these narratives again diminishes the role of rulers. While many prophets also remain anonymous in these sections (1 Kgs. 20:13, 22, 28, 35, 38, 41), the primary prophets (Ahijah, Elijah, and Elisha) are named.

Several scholars believe that the battles of the "king of Israel" against Aramean rulers (1 Kgs. 20; 22:1–38) are incompatible with the time of Ahab's reign as the text claims, but belong to a later period, specifically during the reigns of Jehoahaz (Miller) or Jehoash (Pitard).[35] Despite their arguments, it is more reasonable to situate these narratives in the context of the reign of Ahab for three reasons. First, the text places them in the context of Ahab's reign after his initial regnal formula and before his final regnal formula. Second, while the text often refers to him merely as "the king of Israel," in each section the text does mention Ahab by name (1 Kgs. 20:2; 22:20). Third, the text repeatedly refers to Jehoshaphat, the king of Judah, by name (1 Kgs. 22:2, 4, 5, 7, 8, 10, 18, 29, 30, 32), and he did not overlap with either of these later Northern rulers suggested by these scholars.

Prophetic Sources. Because of the distinctive nature of the prophetic narratives of Kings, scholars speculate that there were prophetic sources.[36] The author of Kings clearly used royal records to write about

---

34. Three times the book of Kings speaks of "the king of Judah" without providing his name (2 Kgs. 3:9; 22:16, 18).
35. See my discussion of the views of Miller and Pitard in Lamb 2007, 201–4.

the reigns of rulers (see 2.1 above), so it is reasonable to assume prophetic sources were used to write these narratives about Ahijah, Elijah, Elisha, and other prophets. However, unlike the numerous references to the royal annals, there are no references to any prophetic records, so discussions about the nature of these unknown documents must be considered speculative and conclusions must be considered tentative.

3. Historical Issues

3.1. Historiography and Book of Kings

How historical is the book of Kings? (See discussion of historiography in the Introduction.) The book of Kings is not strictly "historical" in the sense that we understand history today. My younger son is taking an Advanced Placement test in World History as I write this sentence, and I can guarantee you that none of the questions will ask about what God actually did in the history of the world. Questions will focus on religious beliefs, but not on divine behavior. For us history is an objective record of what happened in the past (art, battles, conquests, developments, explorations, facts, etc.). The focus is exclusively on what humans did, not God. Historians leave the discussion of God's deeds to ministers and theologians.

The book of Kings, however, makes God the focus of its history. YHWH is the only character who appears throughout the book of Kings, from the first chapter to the last, mentioned over five hundred times in the book (and "God," *elohim*, is mentioned over two hundred times). Sometimes YHWH is passive and only spoken about. He does nothing actively until the third chapter of 1 Kings (3:5) when he appears to Solomon in a dream and he is silent during the final chapter of 2 Kings as his city and temple are being destroyed. But throughout the rest of the narrative, YHWH is working and active, he speaks, empowers miracles, blesses with wisdom and riches, judges rulers, and controls nations and emperors. Much of his speech and actions are mediated through prophets, but according to the text these mediations do nothing to limit his role or significance in the narrative. The theological focus may therefore disqualify Kings as a historical book in

---

36. See Wiseman 1993, 44–46; Cogan 2001, 92–94; Jones 1984, 64–77.

the modern sense, but in many other aspects the book qualifies as a source for the history of ancient Israel.

3.2. Relationships with Three Surrounding Empires

Before looking at how Kings presents itself historically, one needs to understand the historical context, specifically to look at the relationships between Israel, Judah, and the nations that surround them. These relationships will be discussed under two categories, first relationships with the three major empires of Egypt, Assyria, and Babylon, and second, relationships with the smaller neighboring nations of Ammon, Aram, Edom, Moab, Philistia, and Phoenicia.

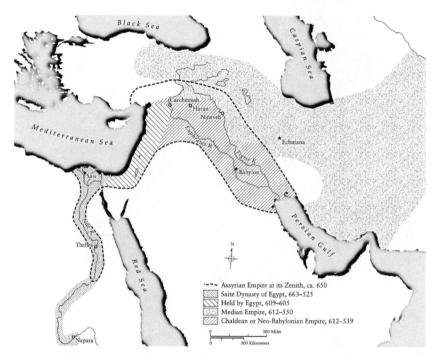

Figure 5.5: Three empires: The empires of Egypt, Assyria, and Egypt as they appeared in the seventh century BCE.

3.2.1. Egypt

Particularly during the beginning and the end of the book of Kings, the history of Israel and Judah was deeply affected by the empires of Egypt, Assyria, and Babylon. Early in Solomon's reign he established an alliance with Egypt by marrying the Pharaoh's daughter. When Pharaoh captured the Canaanite city of Gezar, he presented it as a dowry to Solomon's wife (1 Kgs. 9:16). Cogan concludes that the unnamed Pharaoh here is Siamun (c. 978–959).[37] Solomon's Egyptian alliance led to extensive trade as he imported many horses from Egypt (1 Kgs. 10:28, 29; see the prohibition against equine acquisitions in Deut. 17:16). However, the Judean-Egyptian alliance did not last long, as King Shishak (called Shoshenq I in Egyptian sources) of Egypt attacked Judah under Solomon's son Rehoboam (see the table of references to Egyptian rulers in 3.3 below).

Figure 5.6: Pharaoh Shoshenq I (the biblical Shishak) addresses his son, the high priest of Amun; relief from the Temple of Amon-Re at Karnak, 22nd Dynasty. Commons.wikimedia.org.

Interestingly, Rehoboam's northern rival, Jeroboam I, had fled from Solomon to Shishak in Egypt before coming to power (1 Kgs. 11:40), so it is reasonable to assume some type of alliance between the first Northern ruler and the Pharaoh. After Shishak, Egypt was ruled by a series of weaker rulers and consequently for the remainder of the

---

37. Cogan 2001, 301.

Divided Monarchy Egypt disappears as an active force in the narrative. Toward the end of this period, Hoshea sends a plea for help against the Assyrians to King So of Egypt (Osorkon IV?; 2 Kgs. 17:4), but Egypt continues to remain passive and no response is recorded in the text. Egypt finally reappears when King Neco of Egypt first defeats and kills Josiah of Judah at Megiddo, and then he deposes Jehoahaz of Judah and replaces him with his brother Eliakim, whom he renames Jehoiakim (2 Kgs. 23:29–35). Neco and his Assyrian allies were later defeated by the forces of Babylon under the control of Nebuchadnezzar at Carchemish in 605 BCE.

3.2.2. Assyria

Several ninth-century-Israelite rulers are mentioned in Assyrian inscriptions (Omri, Ahab, and Jehu; see 3.4 below); however, Assyria does not appear in the book of Kings until the text records the reigns of rulers from the mid-eighth century, beginning with Menahem (2 Kgs. 15:19).

The Neo-Assyria empire had two periods of dominance in the region, the first (883–783 BCE) near the beginning of the Divided Monarchy, and the second (744–612 BCE) which overlapped with the end of the Northern Kingdom, separated by a period of relative weakness.[38] During this first period of Assyrian strength, Shalmaneser III (858–824 BCE) campaigned to the west, where he encountered a coalition of rulers, including Ahab of Israel, at the battle of Qarqar. Shalmaneser claimed victory, but his continued campaign in the region would suggest that the outcome of the battle was not definitive. The Old Testament unfortunately never mentions this event, but an Assyrian inscription, the Kurkh Monolith (see 3.4 below) of Shalmaneser III, mentions Ahab and the other members of the alliance. Another interaction between Israel and Assyria is ignored by biblical sources; however, four Assyrian inscriptions record the tribute of Jehu of Israel to Shalmaneser III.[39] Underneath the inscription on the Black Obelisk is an image of Jehu presenting his tribute to Shalmaneser, which constitutes the oldest pictorial representation of a biblical character.

While the relationship between Egypt and Solomonic Israel involved intermarriages, treaties, trade, and gifts, the relationship between the late Northern Kingdom and Assyria involved tribute, conquest, exile,

---

38. See Grayson, "Assyria, Assyrians," in *DOTHB*, 100–101.
39. See Lamb 2007, 124–28.

and destruction. After Shalmaneser III, Assyria underwent a period of decline until its dominance in the region was reestablished by Tiglath-pileser III (745–727 BCE, also called "Pul"), who first required tribute of Menahem (738 BCE; recorded both in 2 Kgs. 15:19 and in Assyrian inscriptions, see 3.4 below). Then, under Pekah, he conquered most of the Northern Kingdom, taking captives back to Assyria (734–732 BCE; 2 Kgs. 15:29). This deportation was the first of five exiles mentioned in the biblical text (see Sidebar 5.1, "The Five Exiles of Israel and Judah," and Table 5.6).

Figure 5.7: King Jehu of Israel prostrates himself before Shalmaneser III; relief from the top panel of the Black Obelisk (ca. 827 BCE), from Nimrud; now in the British Museum. Commons.wikimedia.org.

The Judean king Ahaz voluntarily gave tribute to Tiglath-pileser III in exchange for help against Aram and Israel (734 BCE; 2 Kgs. 16:5–9; for Tiglath-pileser III's Summary 7 inscription, see below 3.4). Tiglath-pileser III's son, Shalmaneser V (726–722 BCE), originally made Hoshea a vassal, but when the northern king refused to continue to give tribute, the Assyrian king besieged the northern capital of Samaria (2 Kgs. 17:3–5). While it appears that Shalmaneser V captured the city, he died shortly afterwards so his predecessor, Sargon II, actually exiled the remainder of the nation (2 Kgs. 17:6), essentially ending the period of the Northern Monarchy in 722 BCE.

Assyrian's final major appearance in the book of Kings involves the son of Sargon II, Sennacherib (704–681), who invaded Judah (701 BCE). After capturing several major cities, he extracts a tribute from Hezekiah and besieges Jerusalem (2 Kgs. 18:13–18). His emissary, the

Rabshakeh proceeds to taunt Hezekiah, who refuses to surrender, instead the Judean ruler seeks out the prophet Isaiah and prays (2 Kgs. 19:1–19). According to the text, YHWH responded dramatically to the king's request by slaughtering 185,000 Assyrian soldiers, prompting Sennacherib and his forces to return to Nineveh, where the ruler was killed by his sons (2 Kgs. 19:35–37). Assyria essentially disappears from the narrative of Kings at this point.

Sidebar 5.1: The Five Exiles of Israel and Judah

While readers of the Hebrew Bible and even biblical scholars frequently speak of "*The* Exile" as if there were only one in Israel's history, the biblical text refers to five distinct exilic events. The first two deportations were committed by Assyria in the waning stages of the Northern Kingdom. The first of these two, by Tiglath-pileser III, in approximately 734 BCE was perhaps the largest of the five geographically, as the Assyrian ruler captured all of the Northern Kingdom except the tribe of Ephraim and took captives to Assyria. The campaign that resulted in the second Assyrian deportation was begun by Shalmaneser V, but Sargon II was the ruler who actually finished off the Northern Kingdom in 722 and deported much of the population. What is often referred to as the Babylonian exile included three separate exiles or deportations, all by Nebuchadnezzar. The first took place in 597 at the end of Jehoiachin's reign, the second when the temple was destroyed in 587 at the end of Zedekiah's reign, and the third in 582 while Jehoiachin was still in captivity. This final deportation is not recorded in the book of Kings, but in Jeremiah (52:30).

Table 5.6: The Five Exiles of Israel and Judah

Foreign Nation (Ruler)	Exiled Nation (Ruler)	Date (BCE)	Biblical Reference
Assyria (Tiglath-pileser III)	Israel (Pekah)	734	2 Kgs. 15:29
Assyria (Sargon II)	Israel (Hosea)	722	2 Kgs. 17:6
Babylon (Nebuchadnezzar)	Judah (Jehoiachin)	597	2 Kgs. 24:8–17
Babylon (Nebuchadnezzar)	Judah (Zedekiah)	587	2 Kgs. 25:1–21
Babylon (Nebuchadnezzar)	Judah	582	Jer. 52:30

3.2.3. Babylon

The empire replacing Assyria for dominance in the region was Babylon. People from Babylon are briefly mentioned in connection to the Northern Kingdom's exile (2 Kgs. 17:24, 30), but the first place the biblical text speaks of Babylon as an international force is when the Babylonian ruler, Merodach-baladan (see 3.3.6) sends an embassy to Hezekiah (2 Kgs. 20:12–13). After the Judean king welcomes this foreign delegation, the prophet Isaiah predicts that Babylon will carry off to exile Hezekiah's descendants (2 Kgs. 20:16–18). Shortly after his defeat of Egypt and Assyria at Carchemish, Nebuchadnezzar made Jehoiakim of Judah his vassal until the Southern ruler rebelled. After Jehoiakim's death, his son Jehoiachin came to power and ruled for only three months before Nebuchadnezzar first conquered Jerusalem in 597 BCE, deporting many of his citizens (2 Kgs. 24:10–16). Jehoiachin was exiled to Babylon; his uncle Zedekiah succeeded him, and when he rebelled against Babylon, Nebuchadnezzar came and captured Jerusalem a second time in 587 BCE, destroying the city and deporting more of its citizens (2 Kgs. 24:10—25:21). The book of Kings concludes with Jehoiachin still in Babylon, no longer in prison, but eating at the table of King Evil-merodach (2 Kgs. 25:27–30).

3.3. Relationships with Six Neighboring Nations

Thus, at the beginning and end of the book of Kings, the empires of Egypt, Assyria, and Babylon were the primary foreign influences on Israel and Judah, but sandwiched between this imperial inclusio, six smaller nations had a significant impact on the two kingdoms of the Divided Monarchy. Most of these nations were ruled by Israel during the reigns of David and Solomon (Edom, Moab, Ammon, and parts of Aram), but over the course of the Divided Monarchy most of them broke free. While David's method of maintaining control over these nations was militaristic, Solomon preferred intermarriage as he had wives from Ammon, Moab, Edom, and Phoenicia (1 Kgs. 11:1). Table 5.7 lists these six neighboring nations (with major cities in parentheses), including rulers mentioned in the text, their gods, and the relevant biblical references. See Figure 5.2, above.

Table 5.7: Six Neighboring Nations of Israel and Judah in Kings

Nation (cities)	Rulers	Gods	References in Kings
Ammon (Rabbath)	Baalis (Jer. 40:14)	Molech (or Milcom)	1 Kgs. 11:1, 5, 7, 33; 14:21, 31; 2 Kgs. 23:13; 24:2.
Aram (Damascus, Zobah)	Hadad-ezer, Hezion (Rezon), Tabrimmon, Ben-hadad I, II, III, Hazael, Rezin	Hadad	1 Kgs. 11:25; 15:18; 19:15; 20:1, 20, 22, 23; 22:1, 3, 31; 2 Kgs. 5:1, 5; 6:8, 11, 24; 8:7, 9, 13, 28, 29; 9:14, 15; 12:17, 18: 13:3, 4, 7, 17, 19, 22, 24; 15:37; 16:5, 6, 7.
Edom (Sela)	Hadad		1 Kgs. 9:26; 11:14, 15, 16; 22:47 [HB 22:48]; 2 Kgs. 3:8, 9, 12, 20, 26; 8:20, 21, 22; 14:7, 10.
Moab	Mesha	Chemosh	1 Kgs. 11:7, 33; 2 Kgs. 1:1, 3:4, 5, 7, 10, 13, 18, 21, 22, 23, 24, 26; 13:20; 23:13; 24:2.
Philistia (Gath, Gaza, Ekron)	Achish	Dagon, Ashtoreth, Baalzebub	1 Kgs. 2:39, 40, 41; 4:21, 24 [HB 5:1, 4]; 15:27; 16:15; 2 Kgs. 1:2, 3, 6, 16; 8:2, 3; 12:17; 18:8.
Phoenicia (Tyre, Sidon)	Hiram, Ethbaal	Baal, Astarte	1 Kgs. 5:1, 6 [HB 5:15, 20]; 7:13, 14; 9:11, 12; 11:5, 33; 16:31; 2 Kgs. 23:13.

3.3.1. Ammon

The first reference to Ammon (E of Israel, N of Moab) in Kings is in the context of Solomon's foreign wives who led him to apostasy (1 Kgs. 11:1–7), specifically Solomon's idolatrous worship of the Ammonite god Molech (or Milcom) is thrice condemned in the text (1 Kgs. 11:1, 5, 7). Solomon's successor, Rehoboam was one of the results of these foreign unions as his mother was Naamah the Ammonite (1 Kgs. 14:21, 31).

3.3.2. Phoenicia

Phoenicia (north-west of Israel) and Israel enjoyed a close relationship, as Hiram of Tyre supplied Solomon with cedar lumber for the temple (1 Kgs. 5:8 [HB 5:22]). According to the text, the relationship between Israel and Phoenicia was sometimes too close as Solomon's Sidonian wife led him into worship of the goddess Astarte and then Ahab's

Sidonian wife, Jezebel, daughter of King Ethbaal, led him into worship of the god Baal (1 Kgs. 11:5; 16:31–32).

3.3.3. Moab

Apart from Solomon's marriage with a Moabite woman, which of course led him into idolatrous worship of Chemosh (1 Kgs. 11:7, 33), Israel's relationship with Moab (east of Judah, south of Ammon) was adversarial. According to the Mesha Stela (see 3.4 below), Moab was a vassal of Israel under Omri and Ahab, but after Ahab's death Moab successfully rebelled (2 Kgs. 1:1). Jehoram of Israel allied with Jehoshaphat of Judah to attempt to recapture Moab (2 Kgs. 3:4–27). Moabite bands raided both Israel during the reign of Jehoash and Judah during the reign of Jehoiakim (2 Kgs. 13:20; 24:2).

3.3.4. Edom

To punish Solomon for his foreign marriages, including at least one to a woman of Edom (south-east of Judah, south of Moab), YHWH sent an adversary against Solomon, Hadad the Edomite (1 Kgs. 11:1, 14). Solomon also built a fleet of ships which he kept the Edomite port of Ezion-geber on the Red Sea, where ships constructed by Jehoshaphat were later wrecked by the forces of the Edomite deputy (1 Kgs. 9:26; 22:47–48). When the combined forces of Jehoram of Israel and Jehoshaphat of Judah attacked Moab, the king of Edom fought alongside them (2 Kgs. 3:8, 9, 12). Edom finally successfully rebelled against Judah under Jehoram (2 Kgs. 8:20–22), but they were later defeated severely by Amaziah of Judah (2 Kgs. 14:7).

3.3.5. Philistia

While the nation of Philistia (east of Judah along the Mediterranean Sea) was arguably Israel's primary rival in the book of Samuel (forms of the word "Philistine" are mentioned 183 times), they are relegated to a minor player in the book of Kings (mentioned only six times). Many of these Kings references appear in the context of Philistia simply as a geographical location (1 Kgs. 2:39, 40; 4:21; 15:27; 16:15; 2 Kgs. 1:2, 3; 8:2, 3). In a stark contrast to Samuel, there are only two instances in Kings where the Philistines are involved in warfare, and in both cases the

Philistine cities were being attacked, by Hazael of Aram against Gath, and by Hezekiah of Judah against Gaza (2 Kgs. 12:17; 18:8).

3.3.6. Aram

The nation that the Northern Kingdom had the most interaction with during the book of Kings was Aram (north-east of Israel; also called Syria); however, the status of the relationship was constantly changing. Since the text of Kings includes more information about Aram, Table 5.8 summarizes its rulers, the approximate dates of their reigns and references to them in both biblical and extra-biblical sources.

Table 5.8: Rulers of Aram in Kings[40]

Ruler	Dates (BCE)	References
Hadad-ezer		1 Kgs. 11:23; 2 Sam. 8:3–12; 10:16, 19; 1 Chr. 18:3–11
Hezion (= Rezon)	940–915	1 Kgs. 11:23; 15:18
Tabrimmon	915–900	1 Kgs. 15:18; *ANET* 655?; *COS* 2:152?
Ben-hadad I	900–860	1 Kgs. 15:18, 20; 2 Chron. 16:2, 4
Ben-hadad II	860–841	1 Kgs. 20:1–34; 2 Kgs. 6:24; 8:7, 9; *COS* 2:263, n. 23?
Hazael	841–806	1 Kgs. 19:15, 17; 2 Kgs. 8:8–29; 9:14,15; 10:32; 12:17, 18; 13:3, 22, 24, 25; 2 Chr. 22:5, 6; Amos 1:4; *COS* 2:155a; 162–63; 267c; 268b, c; 269d, 270b, 271a
Ben-hadad III	806–770	2 Kgs. 13:3, 24, 25; Jer. 49:27; Amos 1:4[41]; *COS* 2:155a ("Bar-hadad")
Rezin	750–732	2 Kgs. 15:37; 16:5, 6, 9; Isa. 7:1, 4, 8; 8:6; 9:11; *COS* 2:287a

The name Ben-hadad (or "Bar-hadad" in Aramaic) literally means "son of the god Hadad" in Hebrew and therefore may be a generic throne name for the ruler of Aram, analogous to "Pharaoh" as the ruler of Egypt.[42]

During the monarchy, Israel and Aram consistently alternated

---

40. See Walton 1994, 69.
41. See Hubbard 1989, 131.
42. See Jerome A. Lund, "Aram, Damascus and Syria" in *DOTHB*, 44.

between friendly and hostile relations.[43] Solomon traded with Aramean kings and yet the king of Damascus, a principal Aramean city, made raids into Israel throughout Solomon's reign (1 Kgs. 10:29; 11:23–25). During the early Divided Monarchy, Aram and Israel shift from being enemies, to allies and then back to enemies (1 Kgs. 15:19–20). Ahab and Ben-hadad II first engage in conflict, then make a treaty lasting three years, and eventually start fighting again (1 Kgs. 20:1–33, 34; 22:2–3). A similar pattern appears in the context of the ministry of Elisha as the king of Aram sends a gift to the king of Israel, then he attacks Israel, but in response, Elisha convinces the Northern king to prepare a feast for the Arameans which results in a temporary end to hostilities (2 Kgs. 5:5; 6:8–9, 22–23, 24–25). Sometime later, Ben-hadad II besieged Samaria, but when he became ill he sought out an Israelite prophet, Elisha (2 Kgs. 6:24–25; 8:7–8). Israel is at war with Aram under the reigns of Jehu, Jehoahaz, and Jehoash of Israel (2 Kgs. 10:32–33; 13:3–7, 17–24), but by the reign of Pekah, Israel is again united with Aram (2 Kgs. 15:37; 16:5).

Figure 5.8: An inscription partially covers a relief of Shalmaneser III of Assyria on the Kurkh Monolith (ninth century BCE), now in the British Museum. Photo: David Castor; Commons.wikimedia.org.

43. See Lamb 2007, 107–8.

Additionally, two extra-biblical sources appear to describe Aramean-Israelite alliances. The Kurkh Monolith of Shalmaneser III (see 3.2.2 above and 3.4 below) lists Ahab of Israel as an ally with Hadad-ezer of Damascus, alongside several other kings and nations at Qarqar (*COS* 2:263.d).[44] A variety of scholars believe that the Tel Dan Inscription (see Figure 4.9, above) suggests there was an alliance between Jehu of Israel and Hazael of Aram.[45] Neither of these alliances would have lasted long, since both of these Israelite rulers were frequently at war with Aram (1 Kgs. 20; 22; 2 Kgs. 10:32–33).

3.4. Kings: The Most "Historical" Book in the Bible

The book of Kings is arguably the most historically oriented book of the Bible. Three observations can be made to support this conclusion. *First,* Kings records far more historical information than any other biblical book. The regnal formulas of the book of Kings (see 2.3 above) contain detailed information, recorded in an organized, formulaic pattern that would not be out of place in more contemporary historical records. They include regnal years, royal synchronisms, genealogical information (fathers for both nations, mothers only for Judah), burial locations, and the name of each king's successor. For example, the regnal formula of Jehoshaphat, the fourth ruler of the Southern Kingdom, records that he came to power in the fourth year of Ahab of Israel's reign, when he was thirty-five years old, he reigned twenty-five years, and his parents were Asa and Azubah (1 Kgs. 22:41–42). When he died, he was buried in Jerusalem and was succeeded on the throne by his son Jehoram (1 Kgs. 22:5). The book of Kings contains forty of these regnal formulas.[46] Historians value this type of detail provided in these regnal formulas since they allow them to draw chronological, genealogical and geographic conclusions about ancient Israel.

Outside the context of regnal formulas, the chronological information in Kings becomes more detailed as specific months and even days of the month are recorded associated with three significant events in Israel's history: the construction of Solomon's Temple (1 Kgs. 6:2, 37, 38; 8:2), the dedication of Jeroboam's golden calves (1 Kgs. 12:32,

---

44. Hallo and Wiseman believe Hadad-ezer should be identified with Ben-hadad II; see *COS* 2:263, n. 23.
45. See Lamb 2007, 106–7.
46. Not all forty of these regnal formulas include all of the historical data, see 3.2.

33), and the fall of Jerusalem and destruction of the Temple (2 Kgs. 25:1, 3, 8, 27).

Why do other biblical books not typically include these chronological details? One can envision several reasons: they may not have had access to the relevant sources, and details can be boring.[47] For example, the book of Ruth begins, "in the time of the Judges" (Ruth 1:1), but a historian would ask while reading this introduction, "Which judge and how long had they been ruling?" It does not matter to the author of Ruth. And the book of Ruth tells a great story.

Second, Kings also includes more explicit references (over thirty) to historical sources than any other biblical book except perhaps Chronicles (see also 2.1.2 above).[48] While most other books of the Old Testament do not bother to mention sources, these references suggest that the author of Kings wanted to validate the story recorded in these pages. Even though we can no longer access these sources, the fact that they were apparently available to the initial readers suggests that the reliability of the information could have been confirmed or denied. Therefore, the constant repetition of references to these annals gives greater authority and legitimacy to the historical record of Kings. Cogan observes how these source notices "bear a certain similarity to the bibliographic footnotes one often finds in modern works."[49]

Third, Kings specifically provides the names of foreign emperors, more so than any other OT book. In most books of the Hebrew Bible the rulers of Egypt, Assyria, and Babylon are unnamed. Genesis and Exodus together mention the Pharaoh of Egypt 178 times (e.g., Gen. 12:15, 17, 18; Exod. 1:11, 19, 22), but never give him a name. If Exodus were to definitively confirm that Ramesses II was the Pharaoh at the beginning of Exodus, the debate over the early or late dating of the Exodus would be solved.[50] The pattern of the anonymous Pharaoh carries into most other books of the Hebrew Bible (e.g., Deut. 6:22; 1 Sam. 2:27; 1 Chr. 4:17; Neh. 9:10; Ps. 135:9; Isa. 19:2; Jer. 25:19; Ezek. 17:17). Similarly, most OT books do not provide names for the rulers of Assyria and Babylon (with the exception of Nebuchadnezzar). Jonah and Nahum, the two prophetic books that focus on Assyria and its capital Nineveh,

---

47. See the Fretheim quote in 1.2.
48. While Kings only refers to three sources (see 3.1), Chronicles mentions a greater variety, both royal records (e.g., 1 Chr. 9:1; 27:24) and prophetic records (e.g., 2 Chr. 9:29; 12:15).
49. Cogan 2001, 90.
50. Exodus does however mention that the Israelites were building a supply city named Ramesses (Exod. 1:11). See also the article by Brent A. Strawn, "Pharaoh" in DOTP, specifically sections 2.1 and 2.2, "Who is the Pharaoh of the Exodus?"

speak generally of the king "of Assyria" or "of Nineveh" (Jon. 3:6; Nah. 3:18) but mention no actual historical figure. Isaiah's extended prophetic oracles against Babylon (Isa. 13:1–14:23) leaves the identity of the ruler unknown (Isa. 14:3). For much of the book, Kings follows this generic practice (e.g., 1 Kgs. 3:1; 9:16), but interestingly for historians, among Kings' sixteen references to the Pharaoh of Egypt it mentions four specific rulers by name (see Table 5.9). The name of only one other Pharaoh appears outside of Kings in the Old Testament (Hophra/Apries).

Table 5.9: Rulers of Egypt in Kings

Egyptian Ruler	Dates (BCE)	Kings References (8 total)	Other OT References (10 total)
Shishak[51] (= Shoshenq I)	945–924	1 Kgs. 11:40; 14:25	2 Chr. 12:2, 5, 7, 9
So (= Osorkon IV?)[52]	?	2 Kgs. 17:4	
Tirhakah	690–664	2 Kgs. 19:9	Isa. 37:9
Neco	610–595	2 Kgs. 23:29, 33, 34, 35	2 Chr. 35:20, 22; 36:4; Jer. 46:2
Hophra (= Apries)	588–569		Jer. 44:30

Thus, the vast majority of Old Testament books leave the Pharaoh anonymous, only four provide names. Isaiah mentions one, Chronicles and Jeremiah two. Kings, however, mentions four Pharaohs by name.

This pattern of providing names for foreign emperors continues during the Assyrian and Babylonian periods of Israel's history. Kings speaks of four Assyrian rulers by name (see Table 5.10), so of the five Assyrian rulers mentioned by name in the Hebrew Bible, only one is not mentioned in Kings (Sargon).[53] Three **Babylonian** rulers are also mentioned specifically in Kings (see Table 5.11).

While the empires of Assyria and Babylon were not as enduring as that of Egypt, at least in terms of being actively involved in the history of Israel, the biblical pattern of anonymous rulers continues for these two nations from Mesopotamia. The nation of Assyria is mentioned in eight prophetic books (Isaiah, Jeremiah, Ezekiel, Hosea, Micah, Nahum,

---

51. L. Depuydt, in *DOTHB*, 243.
52. See Kitchen on the identification of So as Osorkon IV. Kitchen 2003, 15–16.
53. Wiseman argues that the unnamed "savior" for Jehoahaz of Israel was Adad-nirari II of Assyria (2 Kgs. 13:5; Wiseman 1993, 240).

Zephaniah, and Zechariah), but only one of these, Isaiah, mentions specific rulers by name. Additionally, four other biblical books mention Assyria without naming a ruler (Genesis, Numbers, Psalms, and Lamentations). Among books that mention Assyrian rulers, Ezra mentions one, Chronicles two, Isaiah three and Kings again mentions the most with four.

Table 5.10: Rulers of Assyria in Kings

Assyrian Ruler	Dates (BCE)	Kings References (12 total)	Other OT References (15 total)
Tiglath-pileser III (also "Pul")	745–727	2 Kgs. 15:19, 20, 29; 16:7, 10	1 Chr. 5:6, 26; 2 Chr. 28:20
Shalmaneser V	727–721	2 Kgs. 17:3; 18:9	
Sargon II	721–705		Isa. 20:1
Sennacherib	690–664	2 Kgs. 18:13; 19:16, 20, 36;	2 Chr. 32:1, 2, 9, 10, 22; Isa. 36:1, 17, 21, 37
Esarhaddon	610–595	2 Kgs. 19:37	Isa. 37:38; Ezra 4:2

Table 5.11: Rulers of Babylon in Kings

Babylonian Ruler	Dates (BCE)	Kings References (7 total)	Other OT References
Merodach-baladan (= Marduk-apla-iddina II)	721–710	2 Kgs. 20:12	Isa. 39:1
Nebuchadnezzar	605–562	2 Kgs. 24:1, 10, 11; 25:1, 8, 22	85 non-Kings ref's: Ezra 1:7; 2:1; Jer. 21:2, 7; Daniel 1—4.
Evil-merodach (= Amēl-Marduk)		2 Kgs. 25:27	Jer. 52:31

Among these foreign rulers, only Nebuchadnezzar of Babylon is mentioned specifically by name on a consistent basis (over ninety times in the HB, including six times in Kings). Only two other Babylonian rulers are named in the OT, and the pattern of greater specificity we have observed thus far with Egyptian and Assyrian rulers holds true, for these two as Isaiah and Jeremiah each mention one while Kings mentions both of them.

Additionally, many of the references for these rulers outside of the book of Kings appear in parallel texts from Chronicles, Isaiah, and Jeremiah (Shishak, Tirhakah, Neco, Tiglath-pileser III, Sennacherib,

Esarhaddon, Merodach-baladan, Evil-merodach) that may have used Kings as one of their sources.

Why is it significant that Kings gives the names of foreign rulers? By providing these imperial names, the text is displaying a heightened interest in historical information relative to other books of the OT. Whereas the book of Exodus' lack of Pharaonic specificity leaves biblical historians uncertain about issues of dating of the Exodus, Leo Depuydt observes that, uniquely in the case of Shoshenq, "Egyptian chronology has been derived from biblical chronology, not the other way around."[54] Thus, Kings (and Chronicles, for Shoshenq/Shishak) serves as a historical source for Egyptologists like Depuydt because it does not leave rulers anonymous. As we will soon see, several foreign rulers "return the favor."

3.5. Rulers of Israel and Judah in Non-Biblical Sources

Nineteen extra-biblical inscriptions mention rulers from Israel and Judah, providing significant external validation for the historicity of the book of Kings. Table 5.12 lists these inscriptions, their approximate date, the ancient Near-Eastern (ANE) ruler who commissioned the inscription (all rulers except Hazael, Mesha, and Nebuchadnezzar are from Assyria), the Israelite or Judean ruler mentioned, and finally the reference in either *ANET* or *COS*. While most of the identifications with biblical rulers are generally acknowledged by scholars, in the two instances where uncertainty exists, a question mark next to the ruler's name is included (Tel Dan Inscription and Tiglath-pileser III's Annals).

Table 5.12: External References to Rulers of Israel and Judah

Source (19 texts)	Date (BCE)	ANE Ruler	Ruler of Israel or Judah[55]	Reference
Kurkh Monolith	852	Shalmaneser III	Ahab	*COS* 2:263d
Tel Dan Inscription	820	Hazael of Aram[56]	David, [Jeho]ram? of Israel, [Ahaz]iah? of Judah[57]	*COS* 2:161–62a
Moabite Stone	835	Mesha of Moab[58]	Omri, Omri's son (=Ahab)	*COS* 2:137–38

54. See Depuydt, in *DOTHB*, 243. Chronicles mentions Shishak (2 Chron. 12:2, 5, 7, 9) and Neco (2 Chron. 35:20, 22; 36:4). Jeremiah mentions Neco (Jer. 46:2).

55. Additionally, Jehoiachin and Zedekiah are spoken about without a reference to them by name, see *ANET* 564a.

Calah Bulls	841	Shalmaneser III	Omri,[59] Jehu	COS 2:2267c
Kurba'il Statue	838	Shalmaneser III	Omri, Jehu	COS 2:268d
Marble Slab	838	Shalmaneser III	Omri, Jehu	COS 2:268d
Black Obelisk	827	Shalmaneser III	Omri, Jehu	COS 2:270a
Tell al-Rimah	797	Adad-nirari III	Joash of Israel	COS 2:276a
Calah Annal 13	738	Tiglath-pileser III	Menahem	COS 2:285c
Annals	734	Tiglath-pileser III	Azriau = Azariah?	ANET 282–83[60]
Iran Stele	733	Tiglath-pileser III	Menahem	COS 2:287a
Summary 4	730	Tiglath-pileser III	Pekah, Hoshea[61]	COS 2:288a
Summary 7	730	Tiglath-pileser III	Jehoahaz = Ahaz of Judah	COS 2:289c
Azekah Inscription	701	Sennacherib	Hezekiah	COS 2:304d
Taylor Prism Sennacherib Prism	701	Sennacherib	Hezekiah	COS 2:302–3
Prism B	674	Esarhaddon	Manasseh	ANET 291b
Cylinder C		Ashurbanipal	Manasseh	ANET 294b
Ration list	570	Nebuchadnezzar of Babylon	Jehoiachin	ANET 308c-d

Several relevant observations need to be made about these inscriptions. The vast majority of these sources, sixteen, are Assyrian inscriptions, while two are West Semitic (Mesha, Tel Dan), and one, Babylonian. These inscriptions belong to six Assyrian rulers (Shalmaneser III, Adad-nirari III, Tiglath-pileser III, Sennacherib, Esarhaddon, and Ashurbanipal), to two West Semitic rulers (Mesha of Moab and Hazael of Aram), and one Babylonian (Nebuchadnezzar).

56. While the Tel Dan Inscription does not clearly identify its author, most scholars believe it to be Hazael, see Lamb 2007, 102–10.

57. Kitchen (2003, 17) perceives Ahab of Israel and Jehoram of Judah to also appear in the Tel Dan Inscription.

58. Mesha is mentioned once in Kings (2 Kgs. 3:4).

59. Jehu is described literally as a "son" (*mār*) of Omri in the four inscriptions from Shalmaneser III, although some scholars believe *mār* should be understood to signify that Jehu was from the land of Omri (i.e., Israel). The "land" (*māt*) or the "house" (*Bīt*) of Omri is mentioned in inscriptions from Adad-nirari III, Tiglath-pileser III and Sargon II. See Lamb 2007, 29–40.

60. See also ZIBBC 3:168–69.

61. Hoshea and Pekah appear to be included in two additional inscriptions of Tiglath-pileser III, see COS 2:291a, 292d.

Three of the Assyrian rulers (Tiglath-pileser III, Sennacherib, and Esarhaddon) are named in Kings (2 Kgs. 15:29; 18:13; 19:37; see 3.2), as are Hazael, Mesha, and Nebuchadnezzar (1 Kgs. 19:15, 17; 2 Kgs. 3:4; 9:14, 15; 24:1).

Fifteen rulers from Israel and Judah appear in these nineteen inscriptions, including one United Monarchy ruler (David), eight rulers from Israel (Omri, Ahab, Jehoram, Jehu, Joash, Menahem, Pekah, and Hoshea), and six rulers from Judah (Ahaziah, Azariah, Ahaz, Hezekiah, Manasseh, and Jehoiachin). Thus, a significant percentage of the forty rulers mentioned in the book of Kings appear in external sources (15/40 = 37.5%). Many of these rulers and other biblical characters from Kings also appear in seals and seal impressions.

3.5.1. Rulers in Seals and Seal Impressions

Dozens of seals and seal impressions (*bullae*) have been found that bear the names of rulers and other individuals from the book of Kings.[62] Seals and signet rings were used by royals, nobility and officials to authorize official documents (Gen. 38:18; Exod. 28:26; Esth. 3:10; 8:2; Jer. 22:24; Hag. 2:23). When Jezebel was conspiring to frame Naboth so Ahab could acquire his vineyard, she used Ahab's royal seal to legitimate her correspondence (1 Kgs. 21:8).

Several problems make definitive connections between names on inscriptions and biblical characters difficult. Many seals were not found in official excavations where they could be more accurately dated, but in antiquities markets, which are often suspected of producing forgeries. Additionally, many people in biblical times shared the same name, and for some seals the brevity of these seal inscriptions do not provide adequate details for confident identification.

However, it is reasonable to assume many of these seal names could refer to actual rulers and biblical figures. While many people may share the same name, most ancient Israelites would not own a seal, but the royals and officials mentioned in Kings would be likely candidates for seal ownership as they would need to authorize official documents. Additionally, numerous seals provide sufficient information to make more confident identifications with biblical characters.

Seals usually include two personal names, but some may include only one, and others as many as three. Seal inscriptions typically begin

---

62. I do not claim Table 5.12 is exhaustive, but merely comprehensive. I have referred to two other lists of seals; see Lemaire 2004; and Kitchen 2003, 19–21.

with the Hebrew letter *lamed* prefixed to the first name signifying the owner of the seal (e.g., "belonging to Shema"; the phrase "belonging to" is omitted in the table). A second name is usually provided to distinguish the owner or to establish the owner's authority. The relationship between the first and second person is usually stated between the two names. Typically, the first person is a servant or son of the second. When the phrase "son of" is omitted, it is clearly implied. While a few of the first names are royal, more frequently the second is that of a ruler and sometimes the inscription will merely say the owner is a son of the king without providing a name. To make the lettering readable on the *bulla* impression (Hebrew is read right to left), on a seal the letters themselves as well as the order of the letters were inverted (left to right). For simplicity, I will not distinguish between seal inscriptions and *bulla* impressions, but speak merely of the former.

Table 5.13 lists both seal inscriptions in the left column with personal names that appear in the Hebrew Bible in bold. The middle column lists the biblical references for the bolded names from the left column. The right column lists publications for the seal references. The majority of the biblical references are from the book of Kings, but other relevant biblical texts are also included below.

Table 5.13: Seals Mentioning Names of Biblical Characters

Seal inscriptions	Biblical references	Seal references
Jezebel	1 Kgs. 16:31; 18:4, 13	*WSS* 740; *BAR* 34.2:32–37, 80
Shema, servant of Jeroboam (II)	2 Kgs. 14:23, 24, 27	*COS* 2:200; *WSS* 49–50
Abdi, servant of Hoshea	2 Kgs. 15:30; 17:1	*BAR* 21.6:48–52
Abiah, servant of Uzziah (=Azariah)	2 Kgs. 15:1, 6, 32	*COS* 2:200; *WSS* 50, 51n4
Shebaniah, servant of Uzziah (=Azariah)	2 Kgs. 15:1, 6, 32	*COS* 2:200; *WSS* 50, 51n3
Shebaniah, servant of the king	2 Kgs. 18:37; Isa. 22:15	*BAR* 35.3: 45–49, 67
Ahaz, (son of) Jehotham (=Jotham), king of Judah	2 Kgs. 15:38; 16:1	*BAR* 24.3:54–56, 62
Ushna, servant of Ahaz	2 Kgs. 16:1, 2	*COS* 2:200; *WSS* 51n5

Hezekiah, (son of) Ahaz, king of Judah	2 Kgs. 16:20; 18:1	*BAR* 25.2: 42–45, 60; 28.4: 43–51, 60
Ushna, servant of Hezekiah	2 Kgs. 18:1	Deutsch 2003[63]
Domla, servant of Hezekiah	2 Kgs. 18:1, 9	*BAR* 28.4: 43–51, 60
Amariah, (son of) Hananiah, servant of Hezekiah	2 Kgs. 18:1; 2 Chr. 31:15	*BAR* 28.4: 43–51, 60
Yehozarah, son of Hilkiah, servant of Hezekiah	2 Kgs. 18:37	*COS* 2:200; *WSS* 172–73n407
Manasseh, son of the king (= Hezekiah?)	2 Kgs. 21:1, 9	*IEJ* 13.2: 133–36; *WSS* 55n16
Azaliah, son of Meshullam	2 Kgs. 22:3	*WSS*: 237, 90; *BAR* 17.4:26–33
Ahikim, son of Shaphan	2 Kgs. 22:3, 12	*WSS*: 181–82n431
Gemariah, son of Shaphan	2 Kgs. 22:12; Jer. 36:10	*WSS* 191, n. 470; *BAR* 17.4:26–33
Azariah, son of Hilkiah	2 Kgs. 22:4; 1 Chr. 6:13	*WSS* 596; *BAR* 17.4:26–33
Hanan, son of Hilkiah the priest	2 Kgs. 22:4, 8, 10	*WSS*: 59–60, n. 28; *BAR* 17.4:26–33
Jehoahaz, son of the king (= Josiah?)	2 Kgs. 23:30, 31	*WSS* 54n13
Gedaliah, overseer of the (royal) house	2 Kgs. 25:22, 23	*COS* 2:198; *WSS* 172n405
Jaazaniah, servant of the king	2 Kgs. 25:23	*WSS* 52, 102, 103, 104, 202n8, 174, 175, 511; *BAR* 21.6:48–52
Elishama, son of the king	2 Kgs. 25:25; Jer. 41:1	*WSS* 53n11
Ishmael, son of the king	2 Kgs. 25:25; Jer. 41:1	*BASOR* 290–91: 109–14
Pedaiah, son of the king (= Jehoiachin?)	1 Chr. 3:16–18	*WSS* 56n19
Jerahmeel, son of the king (=Jehoiakim?)	Jer. 36:26	*WSS* 175, 414; *BAR* 17.4:26–33

Baruch, son of Neriah	Jer. 32:12	*WSS* 417; *BAR* 17.4:26–33
Seraiah, (son of) Neriah	Jer. 51:59	*WSS* 390; *BAR* 17.4:26–33
Baalis, king of Ammon	Jer. 40:14	*BAR* 25.3: 46–49, 66

Twenty-nine inscriptions are listed in the table; of these, twenty-four mention individuals with the same name as characters in the book of Kings. Ten royal names are mentioned on the seals, three from Israel (Jezebel, Jeroboam II, and Hoshea), six from Judah (Azariah, Jotham, Ahaz, Hezekiah, Manasseh, and Jehoahaz), and one from Ammon (Baalis). Five seals have owners with royal names (Jezebel, Ahaz, Hezekiah, Manasseh, and Jehoahaz), two of these seals identify the owner as a king of Judah (Ahaz and Hezekiah), while two others identify the owner as a son of the king (Manasseh and Jehoahaz).

Figure 5.9: Wax impression of the seal of Jaazaniah, featuring a fighting cock; ca. 6th century BCE. From A Manual Excavation in the Near East (University of California Press, 1934).

---

63. *Biblical Period Hebrew Bullae: The Josef Chaim Kaufman Collection* (Tel Aviv: Archaeological Center Publications): 13a–c.

The likelihood of identification between biblical figures and individuals on the seals increases dramatically when an inscription mentions multiple people in the proper relationship. For example, the seals of both Ahaz and Hezekiah mention their fathers (Jotham and Ahaz) and that they were each kings of Judah, making it highly probable (barring a forgery) that these seals actually belonged to these rulers.

Six seals mention that the owner is a "son of the king" without stating the ruler's name (Manasseh, Jehoahaz, Elishama, Ishmael, Pedaiah, and Jerahmeel). While some scholars think this phrase may not claiming the owner is a member of the royal family,[64] all six of these "sons" appear to be literally royal sons based on the biblical texts.

Based on information from three seals and two biblical verses (2 Kgs. 22:3, 12), the family tree of one non-royal scribal family involving five members can be constructed: Meshullam is the father of Azaliah, the father of Shaphan the scribe, the father of Ahikim and Gemariah.

3.6. Chronology

3.6.1. Problems

The numerous references to synchronisms, accession ages, regnal years, and other numerical data in the book of Kings give its historical interest a decidedly chronological flavor. While many readers of Kings do not bother to add up the numbers to see how well they cohere, the abundance of chronological information regarding years, months, and sometimes even days is apparently too large of a temptation for readers and scholars with a mathematical orientation. As one begins to manipulate the figures a variety of problems begin to arise.

Some of the chronological problems seem minor. The text states that the second ruler of Israel, Nadab, came to power in the second year of Asa of Judah and he died in the third year of Asa's rule, so his reign should have been one year, but according to his regnal formula he reigned for two (1 Kgs. 15:25, 28).

While a one-year discrepancy could perhaps be ignored, other problems are more significant. During the initial period of the divided monarchy a discrepancy of three years appears in the chronologies of the Northern and Southern kingdoms. Jeroboam I of Israel and

---

64. See Barkay 1993.

Rehoboam of Judah came to power at the same time as the Divided Monarchy began (1 Kgs. 12:1, 20). When he rebelled against Jehoram of Israel, Jehu killed both Jehoram and Ahaziah of Judah at the same time (2 Kgs. 9:24, 27). Therefore, the combined regnal years for Northern and Southern rulers during this period should be the same. From the beginning of the Divided Monarchy until the rebellion of Jehu there were nine Northern (Jeroboam I, Nadab, Baasha, Elah, Zimri, Omri, Ahab, Ahaziah, and Jehoram) and six Southern (Rehoboam, Abijam, Asa, Jehoshaphat, Jehoram, Ahaziah). However, the nine Northern rulers' total is 98 (= 22+2+24+2+0 [7 days rounded down] +12+22+2+12), while the six Southern rulers' total is only 95 (= 17+3+41+25+8+1).

The text gives two different dates for the accession of Jehoram of Israel, in the second year of Jehoram of Judah and in the eighteenth year of Jehoshaphat of Judah (2 Kgs. 1:17; 3:1). Since the text states that Jehoshaphat reigned for twenty-five years, this yields a nine-year discrepancy between Jehoshaphat's eighteenth year and Jehoram's second year.

Yet another problem appears when comparing the date for Sennacherib's invasion of Judah. Kings places the event in the fourteenth year of Hezekiah's reign (2 Kgs. 18:13; 714 BCE), while Assyrian records situate it thirteen years later, in 701 BCE.[65] These one-, three-, nine-, and thirteen-year discrepancies are just a sample of the chronological problems that the mathematically inclined reader may notice in the text.[66]

3.6.2. Responses

Scholars respond to the chronological problems of the book of Kings in three ways. First, some scholars point out that by ancient standards of historiography the chronology of the book of Kings was relatively accurate.[67] Second, other scholars have concluded that these chronological problems are irreconcilable and that attempts at harmonization are futile or misguided.[68] Third, others scholars such as Thiele, Galil, Tetley, Hayes and Hooker, and Kitchen have attempted to solve Kings' chronological Gordian knot.[69] As they attempt to make sense of these mysterious numbers they often refer to differences in

65. See Thiele 1965, 10; Cogan and Tadmor 1988, 228.
66. For other examples, see Thiele 1965, 7–11.
67. See Wiseman 1993, 27.
68. See Thiele's discussion of these perspectives (1965, 11–13).
69. See Thiele, Galil, and Kitchen.

dating conventions which may be used to explain some of the problems.

3.6.3. Solutions and Dating Conventions

Annual calendar. Unlike our Julian calendar, which begins in January, in the biblical world the new year began either in the spring, during the month of Nisan (March/April), or in the fall, during the month of Tishri (September/October). While it seems likely that Israel and Judah used different calendars, scholars disagree on which one was used by which nation, as Edwin Thiele thinks Israel used the Nisan calendar and Judah used the Tishri calendar, while Galil flips these two conclusions.

Accession year. Differences in the starting point for the calendar are often discussed alongside the different conventions that account for a ruler's accession year since rulers typically die inconveniently at random points in the year, not on New Years' Eve (whether in the month of Nisan or Tishri). In the ancient Near East, two conventions were used. In the **ante-dating system** (or "the nonaccession year system"), the period between a ruler's accession and the next New Years day was considered his first regnal year. The ante-dating system was used in Egypt and in the early period of Israel's monarchy, from Jeroboam I to Jehoahaz.

In the **post-dating system** (or "accession year system"), the ruler's first regnal year begin at the next New Years day. The post-dating system was used in Mesopotamia, in Judah and in the late period of Israel's monarchy, from Jehoash to Hoshea. While the Southern Kingdom consistently used the same system, the change in convention for the Northern Kingdom is reasonable. Jeroboam came to the throne after an extended time in Egypt (1 Kgs. 11:40) where ante-dating was used, and after the reign of Jehoash Israel was under the influence of Assyria where post-dating was used.

For example, if, over the course of ten years in early Israel, ruler A reigned for three full years, but then died six months into the year (serving three-and-a-half years total), and his son ruler B reigned the remaining six months of that year, plus six more full years before his death (six-and-a-half years total), then the transition year would be credited as a full year for B, with nothing for A, despite the fact that they each reigned six months of that year. In the ante-dating system of early Israel, A's regnal years would be recorded as three, while B's would be seven. However, if these rulers were Judean, then in the post-dating system, A would have reigned for four years and B for only six. Thus, the different accounting practices result in different numbers (7/3 versus 6/4) despite the same chronological data. Over the course of numerous kings the differing conventions of calendars and accession year reckoning could be blamed for some of the minor discrepancies, but to account for some of the more significant problems co-regencies are often used.

Co-Regencies. A co-regency occurs when there is an overlapping reign, so an heir would reign in conjunction with his father, and the period of overlap would be considered part of both the father and the son's reign. The text records several examples of this practice. Solomon came to power while his father David was still alive (1 Kgs. 1:32–39), and when Azariah was struck with leprosy, his son Jotham governed the land in his place (2 Kgs. 15:5). Co-regency was a practice common in Mesopotamia since it would increase dynastic stability by giving the heir greater legitimacy and responsibility while his father still lived, as the example of David and Solomon illustrates.[70]

If, for example, Jehoshaphat of Judah and his son Jehoram had an extended co-regency, as scholars like Thiele suggest, then the nine-year discrepancy mentioned above could be accounted for since the second year of Jehoram's reign and the eighteenth year of Jehoshaphat's reign could have been the same.

While Thiele's solution, first proposed in 1965, receives wide acceptance among conservative constituencies, no solution can claim a broad consensus and it is unlikely any other theory will fully resolve the chronological problems of the book of Kings.

3.7. Israel's Early Story

3.7.1. Genesis

A review of Israel's early history, specifically highlighting the points of connection between their past and their current monarchic situations, will provide essential background to better understand the historical context of the book of Kings. Israel's story in the book of Kings ends in the same place where it began back in the book of Genesis. The ruler Jehoiachin is living in Babylon, in southern Mesopotamia, where he was an exile (2 Kgs. 25:27–30); the patriarch Abraham (Abram, initially)

---

70. Wiseman 1993, 31.

was living in Ur of the Chaldeans in southern Mesopotamia when he started his journey toward Canaan (Gen. 11:31).

While they were primarily located in the land of Canaan, the wanderings of Abraham and his descendants (Isaac, Jacob, and Joseph) included multiple trips to the north-west, to Mesopotamia (Haran), and to the south-east, to Egypt. Genesis ends with the family of Jacob (who was renamed "Israel" during a divine mud-wrestling match; Gen. 32:22–32) extending their holiday on their final visit to Egypt. Shortly before his death, Jacob blesses each of his sons (Gen. 49). As part of his blessing, Jacob prophesies that the royal scepter and staff will never depart from Judah (Gen. 49:10), which foreshadows the Davidic Covenant pronounced by Nathan (2 Sam. 7) and leaves the diligent student of Scripture wondering why Kings ends with the Davidic heir from the tribe of Judah, Jehoiachin, without a royal scepter and staff, languishing as a Babylonian exile.

3.7.2. Exodus

The situation of the oppressed Israelites in Egypt at the beginning of Exodus (Exod. 1:11–14) provides another point of similarity with the Israelites in at the end of Kings, as much of the nation is being carried away into captivity in Babylon (2 Kgs. 24:14–16). Just as the Israelites plundered Egypt during their departure from Egypt after the ten plagues (Exod. 12:35–36), so the Babylonians plundered the treasury of the temple in the book of Kings after their initial conquest of Judah (2 Kgs. 24:13).

After the destruction of the Egyptian army at the Red Sea, YHWH delivers the Ten Commandments to Moses on Mount Sinai (Exod. 7—20). Immediately after committing to obey all these commands, several of which specifically target idolatry (Exod. 20:2–17; 24:3), Israel commits one of the most egregious sins in their history when Aaron constructs a golden calf and the nation worships it (Exod. 32:1–6). Therefore, Jeroboam I's decision at the beginning of his reign to follow Israel's idolatrous example is particularly shocking (1 Kgs. 12:25–33). Jeroboam constructed not one, but two golden calves, one each at the northern and southern borders of Israel (Dan, Bethel), even apparently using Aaron's own words at their public installation: "Here are your gods, O Israel, who brought you up out of the land of Egypt" (1 Kgs. 12:28; Exod. 32:4). While Aaron's calf is only mentioned in a few contexts outside of Exodus 32 (e.g., Deut. 9:16, 21; Neh. 9:18; Ps. 106:19),

Jeroboam's calves are mentioned in connection with almost every other northern ruler (e.g., 1 Kgs. 15:30; 16:2, 19, 26, 31).

Figure 5.10: "A man of God" confronts King Jeroboam as he offers sacrifice to a golden calf; *Jeroboam Offers Sacrifice to the Idol*, by Jean-Honoré Fragonard (1751). École nationale supérieure des Beaux-Arts.

The rest of Exodus is devoted to the planning and building of the various holy objects, including two representations of God's presence in the midst of his people, the Ark of the Covenant, and the Tabernacle. The Tabernacles served as an early precursor to the Temple built centuries later by Solomon (1 Kgs. 6), and the Ark was installed by Solomon into his newly constructed house of worship (1 Kgs. 8:1–9).

3.7.3. Deuteronomy

Two events from the reign of Josiah establish connections with the book of Deuteronomy. First, the "book of the law" is found (2 Kgs. 22:3–13), which many scholars think may have been a version of the book of Deuteronomy.[71] (See also Sidebar 5.2, "The Date of Deuteronomy"). Second, Josiah commanded that the Passover be celebrated (2 Kgs. 23:21–22). While YHWH commanded that the Passover be observed perpetually (Exod. 12:24–27; Deut. 16:1–8), the

71. See Cogan and Tadmor for an extended discussion of scholarly perspectives on the identification of this book (1988, 293–95).

only other recorded observance of the festival in the Former Prophets occurs in the beginning of the book of Joshua (Josh. 5:10–11).

Many of the laws of the Pentateuch do not have any particular connections to the period of the monarchy, but the so-called "Law of the King" provided guidance for Israel's rulers (Deut. 17:14–20), despite the fact that from the historical perspective of Deuteronomy, the monarchy was still several hundred years in the future. Many of the specific limitations on royal power in the Law of the King (horses, wives, and wealth) seem to specifically target the excesses of King Solomon (1 Kgs. 4:26; 10:23; 11:3), and therefore some scholars believe these laws were written after his reign as a critique of his behavior.

3.7.4. Joshua, Judges, Samuel

After the destruction of Jericho, Joshua utters a curse against anyone who would rebuild the city (Josh. 6:26), and the book of Kings records how Hiel of Bethel reaped the consequences of this prophetic word as his decision to rebuild Jericho cost him two sons (1 Kgs. 16:34). The cyclical formulations of the book of Judges share similarities with the regnal formulas of Kings (see 2.3 above). Both appear frequently throughout their respective book and include evaluations of deeds done "in the eyes of YHWH." The book of Judges ends with the refrain "but there was no king in Israel" (Judg. 17:6; 18:1; 19:1; 21:25), that appears to look forward longingly to the period of the monarchy.

As noted above (2.1.2), the primary point of continuity between the books of Samuel and Kings is the continuity of storyline and the monarchy, which under David grew to a empire that he passed on to his heir, Solomon. Although, after the reign of Solomon, the extensive United Monarchy of Samuel quickly becomes the fractured Divided Monarchy of Kings. But for the Southern Kingdom of Judah, the eternal dynastic promise given to David in 2 Samuel 7 appears to endure until the end of Kings, as his descendant King Jehoiachin survives in Babylon.

4. Theological Themes

4.1. Introduction

The book of Kings recorded history, but with a particular interest in theology, specifically in telling the story of YHWH and his people during the period of the monarchy. The theological interest is seen not only in the hundreds of textual references to YHWH, but also in the way the various characters in the narrative respond to YHWH and his commands, in obedience and worship, or rebellion and idolatry.

4.2. Disobedience and Judgment

Perhaps the most significant theological message emphasized by the book of Kings is that rulers who obey YHWH were blessed and those who disobey were judged. The textual concern for obedience is seen repeatedly in the regnal formulas which evaluate rulers as good or evil in the eyes of YHWH based their obedience to the law. Since the primary act of disobedience condemned in the text is idolatry, the following section (4.3) will be devoted to that topic, while this section will look at other forms of disobedience.

4.2.1. Greed

Deuteronomy's law of the king forbids rulers from acquiring great quantities of horses, gold, and silver (Deut. 17:16–17). Curiously, the ruler who could be accused of "breaking" (if one assume the law pre-dates the monarchy) this prohibition most blatantly, Solomon (1 Kgs. 10:14–29), is not condemned for it. From the perspective of the narrative, this absence of judgment may be attributable to his request of wisdom and not wealth during his interaction with YHWH as a young ruler (1 Kgs. 3:5–14). However, two other examples of greed are condemned in the text of Kings. When Ahab, with assistance from Jezebel, orchestrates the death of his neighbor Naboth in order to acquire a vineyard, the prophet Elijah pronounces a gruesome death involving blood-licking dogs (1 Kgs. 21:1–22). When Gehazi, the servant of Elisha, returns to accept the gift from Naaman the Aramean general that the prophet had refused, Elisha declared that the leprosy that left Naaman would cling to Gehazi for the rest of his days (2 Kgs. 5:19–27).

4.2.2. Prophetic Disrespect

Deuteronomy also commands the people to give heed to genuine prophets of YHWH (Deut. 18:15), so when prophetic individuals are disrespected the consequences are severe. When King Ahaziah of Israel sends two groups of fifty soldiers to get Elijah after he had pronounced judgment on the ruler, the prophet sends fire down from heaven to consume them (2 Kgs. 1:1–16; the third group of fifty soldiers groveled first, so they were spared). When a gang of teens taunted Elisha calling him "baldhead," the prophet called down two she-bears to attack the lads (2 Kgs. 2:23–25). When an Israelite captain doubted Elisha's optimistic prediction regarding falling food prices in the midst of a famine, Elisha delivered a pessimistic prediction for the captain, which was fulfilled as he was stampeded to death by starving Israelites at the city gate (2 Kgs. 7:1–3, 16–20).

4.2.3. Judgments Involving Lions

In Leviticus, YHWH declares that if his people do not obey him, he will send wild animals against them (Lev. 26:21) and this prediction appears to be fulfilled in Kings, specifically with lions, although in each of the three examples the punishment doesn't seem to fit the crime.

In the first case, after an unnamed Judean prophet delivers a message of judgment to Jeroboam I, he is convinced by another prophet to stay and eat and therefore to ignore an earlier divine command to return home immediately (1 Kgs. 13:1–32). While eating, the second prophet declares that for the act of disobedience (that he led his friend into!) the first prophet would be killed by a lion, which took place as soon as he headed home. The second beastly encounter involves a member of the prophetic guild, who in attempt to make a point to King Ahab, commanded another member to strike him, and when the second prophet refused, the first predicted a deadly lion attack, which took place immediately (1 Kgs. 20:35–36). (The next prophet didn't hesitate to deliver the blow.) The third example takes place after the Northern exile when the new residents of the land brought in by the Assyrians do not worship YHWH, so he sends lions to kill some of them until a priest can be brought to teach them about the law of YHWH (2 Kgs. 17:25–28).

While each of these examples seem a bit unfair as the "crimes" included listening to the wrong prophet, not hitting a prophet, and not worshipping an unfamiliar God, in each case these narratives in Kings make the point that YHWH wants his people to obey; otherwise the consequences will be severe.

4.2.4. Intermarriage

The Law of the King mentions nothing about foreign wives (see earlier comments about the dating of this law), although it does forbid a king from having many wives (Deut. 17:17), which would seem to apply to Solomon with his seven hundred wives and three hundred concubines (1 Kgs. 11:3). However, foreign intermarriage is condemned elsewhere in Deuteronomy (7:3–4), and this is what both Solomon and Ahab are condemned for by the text (1 Kgs. 11:4–8; 16:31–33) specifically because in both instances their wives reportedly led them into idolatry, which leads us to the next section.

4.3. Worship and Idolatry

4.3.1. Proper Location: the Temple

The kings that Kings praises most dramatically are the ones who worshipped properly (David, Jehu, Hezekiah, and Josiah) and the ones the book condemns most severely are the ones who didn't (Solomon, Jeroboam, Ahab, and Manasseh). Right worship is primarily concerned with right location, which mainly involves the temple in Jerusalem. When YHWH prevented David from building a temple, he granted that his son could do it (2 Sam. 7:13). The early chapters of 1 Kings narrate Solomon's fulfillment of this word, beginning with temple preparation (chapter 5), then construction (chapter 6), and finally dedication and prayer (chapter 8). Throughout this process, YHWH frequently speaks directly to Solomon to encourage and exhort him (1 Kgs. 3:5–14; 6:11–13; 9:3–9; 11:11–13). After the Solomon narrative, the temple is mentioned during Joash of Judah's renovation project (2 Kgs. 12) and when rulers plunder its treasures. Not only do foreign rulers (Shishak of Egypt, Jehoash of Israel, and Nebuchadnezzar of Babylon) take from the temple treasury (1 Kgs. 14:25–26; 2 Kgs. 14:13–14; 24:13), but also Judean rulers (Asa, Joash, Ahaz, and Hezekiah) make a habit of doing so in order to give tribute to foreign powers such as Aram and Assyria (1 Kgs. 15:18; 2 Kgs. 12:17–18; 16:8; 18:15). While the early chapters of 1 Kings narrate the rise of the temple, the final chapter of 2 Kings narrates its fall and destruction, forming a temple inclusio for the book.

4.3.2. Improper Practices

Kings targets two forms of improper worship practices. First, every northern ruler is condemned for not departing from the sins of Jeroboam I, which involved not removing the golden calves he had set up in Dan and Bethel (e.g., 1 Kgs. 15:26, 34; 16:19, 31). Second, rulers for both nations are judged for worshipping at high places (e.g., 1 Kgs. 3:2–3; 12:31–32; 15:14; 22:43; 2 Kgs. 12:3; 14:4; 15:4) since they contributed to idolatry and apostasy. Other minor practices condemned in the book include constructing an Asherah, or sacred pole (e.g., 1 Kgs. 15:13, 16:33; 18:19; see Deut. 16:21), divination and witchcraft (2 Kgs. 17:17; 21:6), and making children pass through fire (2 Kgs. 16:3; 17:17; 21:6; 23:10), which appears to be a euphemism for child sacrifice (Deut. 18:10).

4.3.3. Reforming Rulers

However, five rulers (Asa, Jehu, Joash, Hezekiah, and Josiah) were praised for their religious zeal as they instituted reforms such as tearing down altars, removing idols, punishing Baal worship, or repairing the temple (1 Kgs. 15:1–13; 2 Kgs. 10:18–27; 12:4–16; 18:3–6; 23:1–20). The most severe examples of reform movement involved slaughter of worshippers of foreigner gods. After the conflict on Mount Carmel, Elijah commands the slaughter of the prophets of Baal (1 Kgs. 18:40). As the final step in his violent rebellion to seize the Northern throne, Jehu arranges the massacre of the worshippers of Baal (2 Kgs. 10:18–27). The reformation of Josiah involved the slaughter of the priests of the high places, fulfilling a prophecy delivered to Jeroboam I (1 Kgs. 13:2–3; 2 Kgs. 23:15–20).

4.4. Dynastic Oracles

The prophetic discussion above focused on prophetic individuals, their deeds and their narratives (2.4), this section will examine the content of their message. Kings reveals how God's sovereignty can be seen in the words of his prophets, as they deliver prophecies and promises that were fulfilled in the book.

4.4.1. Dynastic Oracles from Samuel

Dynastic oracles are perhaps the most frequent type of prophecy in Kings, but before looking at examples from Kings, we need to go back to the book of Samuel. The prophet Nathan delivered a dynastic promise to David declaring that his descendants would rule "forever" and that his son would build YHWH a temple (2 Sam. 7:12–16). New Testament interpreters often comment that Jesus's Davidic royal lineage should be connected to this dynastic oracle.

However, Nathan delivered another dynastic oracle to David, not a promise, but a curse (2 Sam. 12:10–11), and while much has been written about the Davidic promise, the Davidic curse has been largely overlooked despite their similarities. Both are given by Nathan the prophet to David the shepherd/king, both focus on his dynasty, both are said to last forever ('ad 'ōlām). In the promise, mercy will never leave his house, and in the curse, the sword will never leave his house (2 Sam. 7:15; 12:10). The impact of Nathan's two dynastic oracles continues throughout the book of Kings.[72]

4.4.2. Dynastic Promises in Kings

As Nathan predicted, a son of David, Solomon, successfully constructed YHWH's temple, which incidentally endured until the end of the Davidic dynasty (1 Kgs. 6; 2 Kgs. 25:8–17). While David's grandson Rehoboam lost control over the Northern tribes, Davidides essentially kept control of the Judean throne for over four centuries (except for six years when Athaliah reigned; 2 Kgs. 11:1–16). Kings does not include explicit fulfillment notices regarding the Davidic promise, but three so-called "lamp" oracles seem to refer to it in contexts where one would expect a dynastic judgment.[73] In each instance, an evil ruler (Solomon, Abijam, and Jehoram), or his son, is allowed by YHWH to continue to reign over the throne of Judah so that David could have a "lamp" in Jerusalem (1 Kgs. 11:36; 15:4; 2 Kgs. 8:19).

Three rulers in Kings receive dynastic promises (Solomon, Jeroboam I, and Jehu). One might assume that as David's heir, Solomon would not require a dynastic promise since his royal lineage would be divinely guaranteed, but two features distinguish Solomon's promise from that of his father. First, unlike his father's, Solomon's promise was

---

72. See Lamb 2010b.
73. See Lamb 2007, 228–30.

conditional. Solomon's promise is repeated four times and in each instance it is conditioned on his obedience to YHWH's commands (1 Kgs. 2:4; 6:12; 8:25; 9:4–5). Second, the domain of Solomon's promise was Israel, while David's domain was unspecified. The context of David's promise would suggest the ruling domain was Israel (2 Sam. 7:6, 7, 8, 10, 11, 23, 24), but Israel is never explicitly mentioned in the crucial verses (2 Sam. 7:12–16). Although it was not repeated four times, Jeroboam I's dynastic promise was similar to Solomon's in other aspects, as conditional and with Israel as the domain to be ruled (1 Kgs. 11:38). To reward him for wiping out the royal house of Ahab, Jehu of Israel received a dynastic promise directly from YHWH (2 Kgs. 10:30). Like David's, Jehu's promise was unconditional; like Solomon and Jeroboam I's, the domain of his promise was Israel; but uniquely, his promise was for a specific number of generations, four.[74]

4.4.3. Dynastic Judgments in Kings

The rulers of Kings who received conditional dynastic promises (Solomon and Jeroboam) also receive dynastic judgments (1 Kgs. 11:11–13, 31–35; 14:7–14). For Solomon, the author of Kings need to reconcile the tension between the differing promises granted to David and Solomon and to answer the question of why Rehoboam lost the majority of the people early in his reign. Despite his father's apostasy and his own evil deeds, as a beneficiary of his grandfather's promise Rehoboam was allowed to continue to rule (the lamp oracle). However, his rule was limited to Judah since Solomon's promise granted rule over the entire nation of Israel only if he were obedient. When Solomon was led into idolatry by his many foreign wives, YHWH responded as he had threatened by removing the Israelite tribes from his son Rehoboam.

Just as Solomon's dynastic judgment was delayed to the reign of his son, Jeroboam's judgment for idolatry targeted his son Nadab, who only reigned two years (1 Kgs. 14:7–14; 15:27–28). The pattern continues as the consequences of the dynastic judgments against Baasha and Ahab of Israel are meted out during their sons' reigns when their dynasties are cut off (1 Kgs. 16:1–13; 21:20–26; 22:38; 2 Kgs. 9:7–10, 36). Both Northern rulers are condemned for idolatry and their family

---

74. See also Lamb 2010c.

members are cursed to be consumed by canines (1 Kgs. 16:4; 21:19, 23–24; 2 Kgs. 9:10, 36).

The final two rulers targeted by dynastic judgments are both Davidic kings over Judah. The descendants of both Hezekiah and Manasseh are condemned to be exiles (2 Kgs. 20:16–18; 21:10–15). Surprisingly, as many Davidic rulers (Solomon, Hezekiah, and Manasseh) are targets of dynastic judgments as are Northern rulers (Jeroboam, Baasha, and Ahab).

Ultimately, all of these prophetic fulfillments in Kings are meant to emphasize God's sovereignty. The book repeatedly reminds readers that in the past YHWH displayed his power by delivering his people from Egyptian enslavement (1 Kgs. 8:16, 21, 51, 53; 9:9; 2 Kgs. 17:7, 36). The book ends by tragically recording how the prophecy of exile during the reign of Manasseh is fulfilled by Nebuchadnezzar's destruction of Jerusalem and the temple (2 Kgs. 21:10–15; 25:1–26). According to Kings, God is sovereign over rulers, dynasties, his people, and the nations.

4.5. Spiritual Leadership

One of the primary theological concerns of Kings is the spiritual leadership of Israel and Judah. While earlier sections of this chapter have discussed the offices of king and prophet, this section will discuss the ways leaders, not only kings and prophets, but also priests and women, exercise their gifts to influence others in the spiritual realm by encouraging obedience to God and by speaking the words of God.

4.5.1. Kings

While the people looked to their political rulers to provide spiritual leadership (1 Kgs. 8:1; 2 Kgs. 23:21), the assessment of Kings is strongly negative toward the rulers of both kingdoms. Almost all northern rulers are condemned as evil (except Jehu, see 2 Kgs. 10:30), since they follow in the sins of Jeroboam I. While southern rulers fare better than their northern counterparts, only three Judean kings receive unqualified positive spiritual evaluations (David, Hezekiah, and Josiah), and Manasseh is blamed for the eventual destruction and exile of Judah (2 Kgs. 21:11–15; 24:3–4).

The book of Kings emphasizes the fact that the behavior of rulers affects the nation. Positively, two kings led national times of spiritual dedication and celebration. After he completed the temple, Solomon had the building dedicated before the nation, and then he led them in an extended prayer, before offering sacrifices (1 Kings 8). In the midst of these festivities, he also blessed and exhorted the assembled nation (1 Kgs. 9:54–61). In response to the finding of the book of the Law, Josiah commanded a national celebration of the Passover, which the text states was like no other (2 Kgs. 23:21–23).

Negatively, the idolatry of rulers often led the nation into sin. For Israel, the ruler who is blamed most frequently for leading the nation into sin is Jeroboam I, as his golden calf altars at Dan and Bethel survived beyond the Northern exile, and each time the sins of Jeroboam are mentioned the text makes it clear that he was responsible for leading the nation into sin (e.g., 1 Kgs. 14:16; 15:26, 30, 34; 16:2, 13, 26; 21:22; 22:52). For Judah, the ruler who is blamed for leading the nation into sin and ultimately into exile was Manasseh (2 Kgs. 21:11, 16; 24:3–4).

4.5.2. Prophets

Much was written about the role of the prophets above (2.4), but this section will merely point out that the real spiritual leaders of Israel and Judah in the book of Kings were the prophets. Prophets speak for YHWH, delivering oracles of both promise and judgment. They not only encourage rulers during times of political crisis (2 Kgs. 19:20–34; 20:4–6; 22:18–20), but also condemn rulers for disobedience and idolatry (1 Kgs. 14:7–16; 16:1–7; 21:17–19). Three prophets play major roles in the narrative over the course of several chapters (Elijah, Elisha, and Isaiah), other prophets have minor roles (Nathan, Ahijah, Shemaiah, Jehu, Micaiah, Jonah, and Huldah), while other prophetic individuals are briefly mentioned anonymously (1 Kgs. 13:1, 4, 11; 20:13, 22, 28, 35, 38, 41; 2 Kgs. 9:1).

4.5.3. Priests

Earlier in Israel's story, priests such as Aaron, Eli, or Ahimelech featured prominently in the narrative. However, in Kings, priests generally play minor roles. The priests Abiathar and Zadok supported opposing sides at the beginning of Kings as David's sons were competing to see who would succeed their father, with Abiathar on the losing side (Adonijah) and Zadok on the winning side (Solomon; 1

Kings 1–2), but neither contributed significantly to the final outcome. For the next thirty chapters of Kings, priests are largely ignored, mentioned only briefly (1 Kgs. 4:2, 4, 5), or as anonymous groups carrying the ark (1 Kgs. 8:3–11), or as attending to Jeroboam's two altars (1 Kgs. 12:31–32), until the priest Jehoiada finally plays a crucial role in bringing the boy prince Jehoash of Judah to his father's throne after Athaliah had ruled for six years (2 Kgs. 11:1–21).

The priest Uriah merely constructs a new altar based on the Assyrian model that King Ahaz had constructed. Two priests (Seraiah and Zephaniah) are mentioned briefly among the Babylonian exiles (2 Kgs. 25:18). While many of these other priests in Kings play insignificant roles, two other priests are mentioned as spiritual leaders in crucial contexts. After the Northern exile, while lions are terrorizing the imported residents of Samaria, the Assyrian ruler brings in an unnamed priest to effectively teach the people how to worship YHWH. During the reign of Josiah of Judah, the priest Hilkiah finds the book of the law which served as a catalyst for the Josianic reformation (2 Kgs. 22:3–20).

4.5.4. Women

While women did not have as much power as men in the biblical world, a consistent series of women serve as examples and leaders in the book of Kings. Most of these women function outside the realm of official positions of power, as they influenced and led the men who were around them.

The text of Kings mentions several negative examples of queens (Solomon's wives, Jezebel, and Athaliah), but it also includes two positive examples of queens and one of a princess. Bathsheba and the prophet Nathan effectively advocated for her son Solomon to become the next ruler after David (1 Kgs. 1:15–31). The mysterious queen of Sheba not only testifies to Solomon's wisdom, but also blesses and praises his God YHWH in the process (1 Kgs. 10:1–13). After the death of Ahaziah of Judah (by Jehu of Israel), his mother Athaliah seized the Judean throne by killing the rest of the royal family. The daughter of Jehoram (Ahaziah's father), Jehosheba, then risked her life to protect her nephew the infant prince Jehoash for six years until Jehoiada brought him to power (2 Kgs. 11:2–4). This little-known princess thus rescued not only her nephew, but also the Davidic line from extermination.

Several prophets ministered during the reign of Josiah, most notably Jeremiah (Jer. 1:2) and Zephaniah (Zeph. 1:1), and yet when the priest Hilkiah found the book of the law, Josiah's officials inquired of the prophetess Huldah to interpret what it meant (2 Kgs. 22:11–20). She predicted disaster for the nation because of their idolatry, but found words of comfort for the repentant ruler Josiah, involving a peaceful death, which create a prophetic tension with his recorded death in battle at Megiddo (2 Kgs. 23:29–30).

The stories of four anonymous women of little status are also recorded in the text as positive examples of faith, sacrifice, and obedience. While the primary point of the narrative of the two prostitutes is to reveal the extent of Solomon's wisdom, a secondary point, and perhaps more shocking, is that one of the women was willing to give up her son to the other in order to save the life of the infant (1 Kgs. 3:16–28). Thus, a prostitute is held up as an example of a parent willing to make sacrifices for sake of her child. During times when the nation and rulers were characterized by disobedience, two widows faithfully obey word of a prophet. The widow of Zarephath risks her own life and that of her son to first fed the prophet Elijah in the midst of a severe famine (1 Kgs. 17:8–15). In his first public address in Luke's gospel, Jesus recalls the widow of Zarephath's story (Luke 4:25–26). During the ministry of Elisha, a widow whose husband was a prophet faithfully filled up her oil jars to provide for herself and her family (2 Kgs. 4:1–7).

One of the most dramatic examples in Kings of faithfulness and compassion is found in a servant girl who ministered to the wife of Naaman the Aramean military commander (2 Kgs. 5:1–5). The girl was captured from Israel on a raid, probably led by her future master, Naaman. While she would have plenty of reasons to hate her masters, she informs her mistress that Naaman would be healed of leprosy if he were to go see Elisha the prophet in Israel. Her comment serves as the catalyst for the general's healing, which led to Naaman's bold declaration that "there is no God in all the earth except in Israel" (2 Kgs. 5:15). The servant girl thus not only displays confidence in God's ability to heal through his prophet, but also she shows profound compassion by loving her enemy.

Figure 5.11: *The Judgment of Solomon*, by Nicolas Poussin (1649);
the Louvre.

5. Commentary

5.1. The United Monarchy Under Solomon (1 Kings 1—11)

The narrative of Solomon, son of David, can be divided into four
sections, at the beginning, his rise (1 Kings 1—2), in the middle, his
wisdom (1 Kings 3—4) and his temple (1 Kings 5—9), and at the end, his
fall (1 Kings 10—11).

5.1.1. Solomon's Rise (1 Kings 1—2)

Since the book of Kings begins by telling the story of Solomon's
accession to the throne, scholars (specifically Rost and his followers)
have linked 1 Kings 1—2 with 2 Samuel 9—20 as part of the so-called
Succession Narrative. The title "Anti-Succession Narrative" may be
more appropriate, however, since none of David's sons appear
particularly worthy to be king.[75] They are rapists (Amnon and
Absalom), a murderer (Absalom), and usurpers of the throne (Absalom,
Adonijah). While Solomon may not have been as bad as his older
brothers, his blank pre-coronation CV does not make him a strong
candidate for the royal position, in contrast to his father, who made
a career of racking up impressive accomplishments prior to assuming
the office of king (killing Goliath, slaying tens of thousands, twice

---

75. See Lamb 2007, 249.

refusing to kill Saul, rescuing the city of Keilah while on the run from Saul).

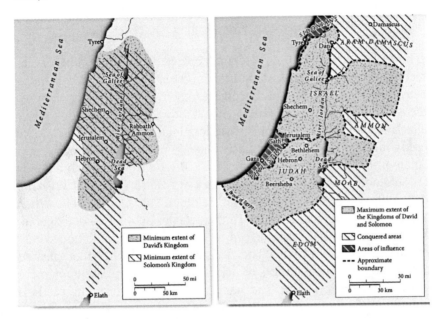

Figure 5.12: Solomon.

As the text introduces him in Kings, Solomon is totally passive, allowing others (the prophet Nathan, the priest Zadok, his mother Bathsheba, his father David) to advocate on his behalf and set him on the throne. David's final words to his successor include both a pious instruction to obey YHWH, and a vicious commission to take out David's enemies (Joab and Shimei), as Robert Alter states, "a last will and testament worthy of a dying mafia capo."[76] The passive Solomon of 1 Kings 1 morphs into the terminator of 1 Kings 2. To establish his throne, Solomon slowly begins to fulfill his father's request and gets rid of his own enemies as well. In each case a justification is given for the sentence. Adonijah, his brother, is killed for asking for David's bed-warming concubine Abishag. Abiathar, the priest who supported Adonijah, is replaced by Zadok, who supported Solomon. Joab, David's general, is struck down for supporting Adonijah. Shimei, David's enemy, is terminated when he goes outside the Jerusalem-sized

76. Alter 1999, 374.

enclosure set up for him. Thus, all of Solomon's enemies are vanquished, and his reign consolidated.

5.1.2. Solomon's Wisdom (1 Kings 3–4)

A hint of Solomon's later problems appears at the beginning of this section as we learn that Solomon established an alliance with Egypt by marrying Pharaoh's daughter. However, the rest of these two chapters focus on the wisdom of Solomon and how it enabled him to rule effectively and to establish his royal legitimacy. While Saul and David used military might to establish their reputation and legitimacy, Solomon had no military exploits. Thus the text provides an apology for Solomon's rule here, despite his lack of accomplishments. Wisdom, not military success, is what gives Solomon the right to rule. When YHWH appeared in a dream with the offer of an open-ended "genie-like" wish (he should have asked for more wishes!), Solomon wisely requested wisdom to rule. The decision of the young ruler pleased YHWH so that, in addition to wisdom, he was granted two more unspoken wishes, wealth, and honor. This first of three interactions between Solomon and YHWH without a prophetic mediator (1 Kgs. 3:5–14; 6:11–13; 9:3–9) is concluded with a dynastic promise conditioned upon obedience, exhorting the new ruler to walk faithfully before YHWH as his father David walked (except, one presumes, when he was committing adultery and murder). The text then narrates how Solomon displayed wisdom by offering to chop in half the remaining living child of the two arguing prostitutes, thus revealing not only the identity of the true mother, but also the legitimacy of Solomon's reign to the entire nation.

The tone of the text shifts from Solomon's exercise of wise judgments in 1 Kings 3, to his exercise of wise administration in 1 Kings 4, as first his cabinet are listed (recorder, military commander, palace manager, secretaries, and priests) and then his twelve food administrators and their respective domains are recorded. A brief note about how the entire nation was eating, drinking, and happy is included in the text, along with a comment that they were as numerous as the "sand of the sea," echoing the language of promises given to the Patriarchs (Gen. 22:17; 32:12).

After a record of Solomon's dietary provisions (his exotic tastes included gazelles and roebucks) and his massive quantity of horse stables, the chapter concludes by praising the extent and magnitude of

Solomon's wisdom, supposedly greater than the wise men of Egypt and Mesopotamia ("the east"), which included the writing of thousands of proverbs and songs. Solomon's unique status as an unparalleled sage is supported by the wisdom literature of the Old Testament which connects him to Proverbs (1:1; 10:1; 25:1) and the Song of Solomon (1:1; 3:7, 9, 11), Psalms (the headings of Psalms 72 and 127), as well as alluding to him in Ecclesiastes without mentioning his name (1:1, 12, 16). In the New Testament, Jesus claims to be associated with something even greater than the wisdom of Solomon (Matt. 12:42; Luke 11:31). Solomon would need all of his wisdom to construct his magnificent temple.

5.1.3. Solomon's Temple (1 Kings 5—9)

The next five chapters focus on Solomon's temple: preparation, construction, dedication, and prayer. For lumber, Solomon relied on his father's ally to the north, Hiram of Tyre, to provide cedar and cyprus from Lebanon (1 Kgs. 5:1–12). For stone, he used Israelite forced quarry stone (1 Kg. 5:13–17). Jeroboam I would later complain to Rehoboam, that his father Solomon's hand was heavy on the people for forced labor projects like the building of the temple and other projects (1 Kgs. 12:4).

The text dates the beginning of the temple to the 480th year after Israel left Egypt (1 Kgs. 6:1), which causes some readers to situate the Exodus to the mid-fifteenth century BCE, but this round number does not need be taken literally, since it involves the multiplication of two numbers with symbolic significance for Israel (twelve and forty). Here it may merely signify twelve generations of forty years. The detailed explanation of the temple plan and construction in 1 Kings 6 is reminiscent of similar descriptions for the tabernacle (Exodus 25—26; 35—36). Interrupting these descriptions is a brief account of YHWH's second direct word to Solomon, where he repeats the conditional dynastic promise to the ruler (1 Kgs. 6:11–13). The dimensions of the temple were roughly ninety feet long, thirty feet wide, and forty-five feet high (sixty cubits by twenty cubits by thirty cubits; a cubit was about eighteen inches). The materials included cypress, cedar, and olivewood, as well as stone and gold.

Before describing the bronze work furnishings, the text details the construction of Solomon's palace complex (1 Kgs. 7:1–12). While his temple took seven years to build, his palace took thirteen years (1

Kgs. 6:38; 7:1), and included the House of the Forest of the Lebanon, the Hall of Pillars, the Hall of the Throne, and a house for Pharaoh's daughter. Hiram of Tyre was brought in to fashion the bronze work (1 Kgs. 7:13–51), which included two columns, a bronze "sea" (picture an above ground swimming pool—fifteen feet in diameter and seven-and-a-half feet high—used for holy purposes), ten stands and other pots, shovels, and basins. The chapter concludes by listing gold articles made by Solomon (altar, table, ten lampstands, flowers, lamps, tongs, cups, snuffers, basins, dishes, fire pans, and doors).

To dedicate the new temple, Solomon brought the nation together, triumphantly bringing in the ark, carried on poles by priests, not on a cart like his father did initially, at the cost of the life of Uzziah (2 Sam. 6:6–7). The ark was empty, except for the two tablets with the Ten Commandments written on them (1 Kgs. 8:9; Deut. 10:1–5). These references to the ark (1 Kgs. 8:1, 3, 4, 5, 6, 7, 9, 21) are the last in the narrative of the Former Prophets, thus Israel's symbolic representation of YHWH's presence disappears (until found later by Indiana Jones). The remainder of this chapter, the longest by far verse-wise in the book of Kings (sixty-six verses), is dominated by the speech of Solomon, first as a relatively short inaugural address to the people reminding them of the deliverance from Egypt and the promise to David that his son would build a temple (8:14–21), then as an extended dedicatory prayer to YHWH (8:22–53). The prayer begins by recalling the Davidic dynastic promise, then repeatedly asks that God would hear the prayers of his people, forgive them, and help them in contexts of relationship with neighbors, in warfare, in famine, in exile, even listening to the prayers of foreigners who cry out for help. After his prayer, Solomon blesses the people, and prays they may know that YHWH is God since "there is no other" (ironically, in light of his apostasy in 1 Kings 11). Then he offers a massive sacrifice (often interpreted as hyperbolic), of 22,000 oxen and 120,000 sheep, over the course of seven days.

YHWH appears to Solomon for the third time in 1 Kings 9:1–9, repeating his conditional dynastic promise, emphasizing both the rewards for obedience (a secure dynasty; 9:3–5) and the severe consequences for disobedience (taunting, exile, and destruction). The text then records Solomon's other construction projects, built with forced labor, including his fleet of ships, anchored at the port city of Ezion-geber on the Red Sea (1 Kgs. 9:15–28).

5.1.4. Solomon's Fall (1 Kings 10–11)

After detailing the visit of the queen of Sheba and her gifts of gold, spices, and precious stones, the rest of 1 Kings 10 serves as a transition between Solomon the wise temple builder and Solomon the apostate. While the explicit critique of Solomon's apostasy is delayed to 1 Kings 11, his imminent downfall is suggested by many textual clues in 1 Kings 10.

It could appear that the chapter is merely revealing how YHWH has blessed Solomon and thus fulfilled his promise to the ruler because of his request for wisdom at the beginning of his reign. However, this interpretation is excluded by the preponderance of allusions here to Deuteronomy's Law of the King (Deut. 17:14–20), and in each instance Solomon appears to be "breaking" the law's prohibition in a blatant manner (see Sidebar 5.2, "The Date of Deuteronomy"). While we don't know when the Law of the King was written (did Solomon know about it?), the canonical order of the text makes it appear in 1 Kings 10 that Solomon wasn't merely divinely blessed, but that he's blatantly disobedient. Deuteronomy prohibits a king from acquiring many horses (Deut. 17:16), but Solomon had 1,400 chariots and 12,000 horses (1 Kgs. 10:26). Kings are not to import horses from Egypt (Deut. 17:16), but Solomon did exactly that (1 Kgs. 10:28). The amount of silver and gold a king owns is meant to be limited (Deut. 17:17), but Solomon made silver as common as stone in Jerusalem (1 Kgs. 10:27), and each year Solomon received an amount of gold that must be considered "beastly" (666 talents of gold; 1 Kgs. 10:14). The only prohibition from Deuteronomy 17 that Solomon does not break in 1 Kings 10 is the limitation on many wives (Deut. 17:17), but that of course is the subject of 1 Kings 11.

While Saul and David both had many wives, Solomon took polygamy to a new level as his wives included seven hundred princesses and three hundred concubines, which would seem to break Deuteronomy's quantitatively ambiguous restriction against "many wives." However, the condemnation in Kings does not focus on the quantity of his wives, but on their foreignness, which led him to worship other gods (e.g., Astarte of Sidon, Chemosh of Moab, Molech of Ammon).[77] Despite Solomon's wisdom, his extended previous interactions with YHWH, and his faithful construction of the temple, in YHWH's final address

---

77. See my discussion of polygamy in the Old Testament (Lamb 2015, 59–86).

to the ruler he is severely condemned. The negative condition of the dynastic promise is invoked as the kingdom is going to be torn away, but because of Solomon's father David, YHWH says he will diminish the punishment in two ways, by delaying it one generation and by allowing the tribe of Judah to remain under his son. Immediate consequences befall Solomon, however, as YHWH is said to raise up adversaries to harass his kingdom (Hadad the Edomite and Rezon the Aramean; 1 Kgs. 11:14–25).

Despite a lot of negative press later in the book of Kings, Jeroboam I makes a strong first impression as a competent and responsible leader. In the spirit of the dramatic sign acts of later prophets such as Isaiah (naked for three years; Isa. 20:2–3) and Ezekiel (lying on his side for 390 days; Ezek. 4:4–5), the prophet Ahijah first shreds his new garment into twelve pieces, then commands Jeroboam to keep ten pieces for himself, symbolizing the ten northern tribes that will be taken from the son of Solomon. Jeroboam receives a conditional dynastic promise that will be revoked later due to his construction of the altars at Dan and Bethel. Jeroboam has to flee to Egypt when Solomon finds out about his interaction with the prophet, and he remains there until the death of Solomon. Thus, the career of Jeroboam appears to mimic that of Solomon as both got off to a strong start, received dynastic promises from YHWH, but ended up finishing poorly.

Sidebar 5.2: The Date of Deuteronomy

The date of the composition of the book of Deuteronomy is a particularly important one for the book of Kings. While scholarly views for a date range from the time of Moses to the post-exilic period, many scholars believe that the book of Deuteronomy primarily took its shape during the seventh century BCE, perhaps during the reign of Josiah. But even scholars who accept the seventh-century date acknowledge that the book could include much older material. A lost "book of the law" is found early in Josiah's reign (2 Kgs. 22:3–13), which some scholars think could be an early version of Deuteronomy.

The issue of Deuteronomy's date comes to a head in Kings in the Solomon narrative, as the ruler appears to be described as "breaking" many of the restrictions placed on rulers in the "Law of the King" (Deut. 17:14–20; 1 Kings 10—11). But if Deuteronomy didn't exist yet is it even appropriate to speak of him breaking a Deuteronomic law?

While we don't ultimately know when Deuteronomy was written, some form of law is repeatedly mentioned in the book of Kings before the reign of Josiah, during the reigns of Solomon, Jehu, Amaziah, Hoshea, and Manasseh (1 Kgs. 2:3; 2 Kgs. 10:31; 14:6; 17:13, 26, 27, 34, 37; 21:8). The law book that was found in the temple during Josiah's reign may not have been lost for long. Regardless of when Deuteronomy was written, the text clearly holds the rulers of Israel and Judah accountable to obey whatever form of the law was available to them.

We should also note that scholarly opinion often changes over time. While there is currently general agreement about Deuteronomy's date, one still can't be certain as many of the arguments for a specific date are subjective, and it is possible, perhaps even likely, that consensus will shift on this subject.

Therefore, when Deuteronomy and Kings appear to intersect, like in the Solomon narrative, I will merely observe some of the points of connection without engaging each time in a speculative discussion of whether Deuteronomy was already written or not. From the perspective of the text as we have it in its present canonical form, these rulers appear to be subject to the law, even that of Deuteronomy.

5.2. The Divided Monarchy: The Early Years (1 Kgs. 12:1–16:28)

The next section of 1 Kings tells the story of the early years of the Divided Monarchy, including Jeroboam's rebellion against Rehoboam, his construction of the altars at Dan and Bethel, and prophetic condemnations against Jeroboam's altars and his dynasty. Then the tone shifts from prophetic narrative to recordings of regnal formulas for both Southern (Abijam and Asa) and Northern rulers (Nadab, Baasha, Elah, Zimri, Omri, and Ahab).

5.2.1. Israel: Jeroboam I (1 Kgs. 12:1-14:20)

Jeroboam I, who served as Solomon's project manager in charge of forced labor, is transformed into an ancient version of Cesar Chavez as he advocated for the rights of oppressed laborers who were forced into hard service during Solomon's many building projects (1 Kgs. 12:1-4). Rehoboam unfortunately did not inherit his father's wisdom so he ignored the wise advice of the elders and listened to the foolish advice of his young advisors. The youngsters respond with two trash-talking taunts.[78] One claimed that Solomon disciplined with whips, but Rehoboam will discipline with scorpions, and the other claimed that Rehoboam's "little finger" was thicker than his father's loins (some things never change). Rehoboam, in a rare wise move, only repeated the scorpion taunt, but his arrogant response prompts Jeroboam and his entourage to break away, and the Northern tribes went with him as Ahijah has prophesied. When Rehoboam began to pursue the rebels, yet another prophet, Shemaiah, forbade him from starting a civil war. The text then provides Jeroboam's rationale for committing one of the biggest sins in the history of Israel (1 Kgs. 12:25–33; see Sidebar 5.3, "What Was so Bad about Jeroboam's Altars?"

Figure 5.13: Rehoboam's taunt, that his "little finger" is thicker than his father's loins, depicted by Hans Holbein the Younger (ca. 1520s) in a wall painting in the Great Council Chamber of Basel Town Hall.

A mysterious prophet from Judah appears and curiously speaks directly to Jeroboam's altar at Bethel predicting that a future ruler, Josiah, will destroy the site and slaughter its priests (1 Kgs. 13:1–3). While Kings records the fulfillment of the prophecy approximately three centuries later (2 Kgs. 23:15–20), many commentators[79] observe that a prophecy as specific as this (naming the future ruler, Josiah) must have been added to the narrative after the "fulfillment" had already taken place.

78. For more on biblical trash talking, see Lamb 2014.
79. E.g., Jones 1984, 264; Cogan 2001, 375.

When Jeroboam invited him to a meal, the Judean prophet refused because he had apparently received a previous command from YHWH to leave immediately, but he was later persuaded to delay for a similar offer by a prophet from Bethel (1 Kgs. 11:7-19). However, during the meal, the Bethel prophet told the Judean prophet that because of his disobedience, into which he had tempted him, he would be killed by a lion. This bizarre story is presumably recorded at this point in the narrative to remind readers of the importance of obedience, even for people like Jeroboam or this prophet who have been called by YHWH for a leadership task.

Ahijah delivered Jeroboam's initial call to lead, as well as the final judgment against him and his house for his disobedience. Jeroboam's idolatrous behavior is contrasted with that of David, who according to the text at this point was totally obedient, his adultery and murder having been curiously omitted from the recollection of David. Jeroboam's dynastic judgment also includes the first of an extended series of canine consumption condemnations (dogs eating royal flesh and drinking royal blood) that target Northern rulers (1 Kgs. 14:11; 16:4; 21:19, 23, 24; 22:38; 2 Kgs. 9:10, 36).[80]

Sidebar 5.3: What Was so Bad about Jeroboam's Altars?

To prevent the people from returning to Solomon's temple in Jerusalem, Jeroboam decided to build two altars, one at Dan in the north and one at Bethel in the south, to give Northerners alternate sites for worship. While Jeroboam's logic would have made sense in his own context, most modern readers would presumably also find it reasonable today, since decisions regarding places of worship are often based on proximity. It is conceivable that Jeroboam meant them to be places for people to worship YHWH. What was so bad about these altars?

While the text does not clearly state why Jeroboam's altars were such a grave error, condemned literally dozens of times throughout the book (e.g., 1 Kgs. 15:30, 34; 16:2, 19, 26, 31), four of their aspects would be problematic for the biblical authors. First, Jeroboam's motivation, that if he does not build these altars he would lose the people, reveals a lack of trust in the word delivered by Ahijah the prophet (1 Kgs. 11:31). Second, Jeroboam's selection of two locations goes against the thrust of

---

80. See also Lamb 2014.

Deuteronomy's emphasis that YHWH will choose the place of his own worship (Deut. 12:5, 11, 14, 18, 21, 26). Third, the altars were associated with cultic innovations including non-Levitical priests, high places, and a new religious festival. Fourth, the construction of golden calves is the same crime their ancestors committed at Mount Sinai and shockingly, Jeroboam even uses the same language as Aaron to introduce them (Exod. 32:4).

5.2.2. Judah: Rehoboam, Abijam, Asa (1 Kgs. 14:21–15:24)

Rehoboam's final days are recorded along with the account of King Shishak of Egypt's plundering of the treasures of the temple and the royal palace. Thus, in the generation after Solomon, Rehoboam managed to lose some of the treasury to Shishak and most of the people to Jeroboam.

The reign of Rehoboam's son, Abijam, over Judah (1 Kgs. 15:1–8) is told briefly with reference to the Israel-Judean civil war in the context of Abijam's short three-year reign. Over the course of his forty-one year reign, Abijam's son Asa removed temple prostitutes and idols, and thereby this first Judean reformer earned praise within the text, despite the continued presence of the high places. Asa's solution to the Israelite civil war was to convince Aram to break their alliance with the Northern Kingdom and ally with him.

5.2.3. Israel: Nadab, Baasha, Elah, Zimri, and Omri (1 Kgs. 15:25–16:28)

The reigns of five Northern rulers, Nadab, Baasha, Elah, Zimri, and Omri, are recorded briefly without extensive narrative elaboration (1 Kgs. 15:25–16:28). Four are guilty of walking in the ways of Jeroboam because they did not remove the altars at Dan and Bethel. Curiously, Elah is not associated with the same crime and receives no regnal evaluation (2 Kgs. 16:8). Dynastic turmoil characterizes this period of Israel's history. Three of the five are unable to be succeeded by their own heir (Nadab, Elah, and Zimri) and each of these three also reign for two years or less. Two conspiracies remove rulers from power, Baasha against Nadab, and Zimri against Elah. The text explains that the evilness of the rulers led to the dynastic chaos that was predicted by the prophets (Ahijah the Shilonite and Jehu son of Hanani) as the refrain "the word of YHWH" is repeated four times in this section (2 Kgs. 15:29; 16:1, 7, 12).

5.3. The Divided Monarchy:
Elijah and the Northern Israel (1 Kgs. 16:29—2 Kgs. 2:12)

5.3.1. Ahab, Jezebel, and Elijah (1 Kgs. 16:29—19:21)

During the reigns of the houses of Omri and Jehu, the Northern Kingdom was more stable dynastically than it had been previously. The narrative focuses on prophets in the Northern Kingdom in this middle section of the book of Kings.[81] While Omri's son Ahab interacted with several prophets, he is most frequently associated with one of Israel's most famous prophets, Elijah. Ahab's other association, which defined his reign, is his marriage to Jezebel, daughter of King Ethbaal of Sidon, a union that is blamed, just as Solomon's was, for the king's idolatrous practices which included worship of Baal and Asherah (1 Kgs. 16:31–33).

One of the longest continuous narratives in the book of Kings recounts Elijah's ministry during the extended drought, his conflict with the prophets of Baal on Mount Carmel, then his flight from Jezebel and his depression (1 Kings 17–19). During the famine, YHWH provided for the prophet first with bread and meat delivered by ravens, then with cakes prepared by a widow (1 Kgs. 17:4–6; 8–15). Ironically, the widow who provided for Elijah during the famine was from Zarephath, which was ruled by Sidon, the land of Jezebel, the wife of Ahab. Thus, Sidonian women served both as Elijah's persecutor and as his provider. When the widow's son dies, she rebukes the prophet, and he responds with an emotional appeal to God as he stretches himself out three times over the corpse. The text records that YHWH heard his prayer and that the boy was revived (1 Kgs. 17:17–24).

---

81. Since the king of Israel is often unnamed in the context of the prophetic narratives (1 Kings 17—2 Kings 8), several scholars (e.g., Miller, Pitard) argue that specific incidents are not set in their proper chronological context, but should be moved into the context of earlier or later kings. I find their arguments unconvincing (see Lamb 2007, 201–4), and therefore in this chapter it will be assumed that incidents are set in the reign of the correct ruler.

Figure 5.14: Elijah competes with the prophets of Baal on Mount Carmel. Fresco from the third-century CE synagogue at Dura Europos.

While Elijah was hiding out in the land of Zarephath, Jezebel had been killing off the prophets of YHWH. One of Ahab's officials, Obadiah, hid a hundred prophets in caves, feeding them with bread and water (1 Kgs. 18:4). In the midst of a desperate search for animal fodder by Obadiah and Ahab, Elijah finally appears to an angry King Ahab, and calls for a competition between himself and the prophets of Baal and Asherah who belong to Jezebel. The god who sends fire down to consume the bull on the altar will be declared the winner. The Baal prophets go first and while they plead for a divine response, Elijah talks trash at them ("Perhaps [your god] is relieving himself?"). After Elijah douses his altar with twelve jars of precious water (in the midst of a drought!), his prayer is heard and fire comes down, consuming the bull, the altar, and even the water. Elijah then calls for the first of several religiously motivated slaughters in Kings (see also 2 Kgs. 10:18–27; 23:20) as the Baal prophets are terminated and the drought is ended.

Jezebel retaliates to the loss of her prophets by sending a messenger to Elijah promising that he would be dead in twenty-four hours (1 Kgs. 19:2), which surprisingly prompted the previously bold prophet to flee in fear. After journeying for a day, he sat under a broom tree and asked YHWH to let him die (1 Kgs. 19:4). While YHWH immediately responded to his previous request by torching the altar on Carmel, he refused to grant the request of his suicidal prophet. Instead he sends angels to fed Elijah, allowing him travel to Mount Horeb (Mount Sinai). There he is questioned by his God, who speaks not in earthquake, wind, or fire, but in the midst of silence (1 Kgs. 19:9–14). YHWH then gives Elijah a commission to anoint a new prophet in his place, Elisha, and two new rulers, Hazael over Aram, and Jehu over Israel (1 Kgs. 19:15–18). However, none of these anointings are performed by Elijah. Elijah merely throws his mantle over Elisha, Elisha informs Hazael he will be king of Aram, and Elisha's prophetic apprentice actually anoints Jehu (1 Kgs. 19:19; 2 Kgs. 8:13; 9:6).

5.3.2. Ahab's Battles with Aram (1 Kings 20–22)

Elijah disappears from the narrative for awhile, as the text records battles between Ahab of Israel and Ben-hadad of Aram (1 Kings 20). Ahab receives two prophetic victory predictions from unnamed prophets, but after Ahab proceeds to fulfill these prophesies, another prophet informs the king that he will die because he did not take the life of the Aramean ruler as YHWH had commanded.

Jezebel has no qualms, however, to take the life of their neighbor Naboth after her husband lusts after his vineyard (1 Kgs. 21:1-16), breaking at least three of the Ten Commandments in the process (false witness, coveting, and murder; Exod. 20:13, 16, 17). Elijah reappears to pronounce judgment on Ahab and Jezebel for their crime, declaring that dogs will lick their blood and eat their flesh (1 Kgs. 21:20-24). When Ahab responded with humility, however, YHWH relented, delaying his dynastic judgment to the next generation (1 Kgs. 21:27-29).

In the prophetic narratives of Elijah and Elisha, Southern rulers are essentially absent except when they engage in battle with their Northern allies. For Israel's next military engagement with Aram, before they go fight, Ahab and Jehoshaphat of Judah consult with a company of four hundred prophets, who reply in unison that they indeed will recapture Ramoth-gilead, which is currently held by Aram. The unanimous prophetic response seems too optimistic for Jehoshaphat ("Go up and triumph"; 1 Kgs. 22:6, 12). Ahab reluctantly mentions the other prophetic alternative, Micaiah son of Imlah, but he isn't Ahab's favorite seer since he only prophesies disaster for the ruler (although none of these oracles are recorded in the text). When Micaiah offers his first prophetic prediction, it sounds suspiciously similar to that of Ahab's court prophets ("Go up and triumph"), so much so that even Ahab rebukes him for not being honest (1 Kgs. 22:16). Micaiah's second oracle has the distinct air of authenticity as he foresees disaster as Israel is scattered like sheep with no shepherd, presumably because their shepherd/king is dead (1 Kgs. 22:17). He also explains the discrepancy between his word and that of Ahab's four hundred prophets is due to the fact that YHWH sent a deceptive spirit into their mouths (2 Kgs. 22:22–23), which elicited a cheek slap and a prison sentence from their leader, Zedekiah.

Ahab thinks he could outsmart Micaiah's dire prediction by wearing a disguise, while having Jehoshaphat wear his royal robes (and the Judean ruler naively agreed), unfortunately for the Northern ruler his disguise didn't fool an errant arrow which pierced his armor. Ahab's body was returned to the capital Samaria, and as they washed his chariot, dogs licked up his blood. While Ahab insisted that Micaiah be honest with him, the Israelite king still ironically chooses to essentially ignore the true prophet's message and fight Aram. Thus the text shows that, despite Ahab's clever plan, the prophecies of Elijah and Micaiah were still fulfilled as a random arrow was apparently divinely guided to take down a king (2 Kgs. 21:19; 22:17, 38).

5.3.3. Elijah's Final Days (2 Kgs. 1:1–2:12)

The first "half" of Kings ends at an unusual spot. After recording Jehoshaphat's regnal formula, 1 Kings 22 ends in the middle of Ahaziah of Israel's narrative as 2 Kings 1 tells about Ahaziah's conflict with Elijah. When Ahaziah is injured, he sends messengers to Baal-zebub to determine if he will recover. However, Elijah intercepts the king's messengers, telling them to inform the king that he will not recover. The king sends out a company of fifty soldiers to get Elijah, but the prophet calls down fire from heaven and the soldiers are consumed. After the same thing happens to a second company of fifty, the captain of the third company pleads for mercy, and their lives are spared, but Ahaziah's is not. He is succeeded by his brother Jehoram, one of only two fraternal successions in Kings (Jehoiakim of Judah succeeded his brother Jehoahaz; 2 Kgs. 23:31–34).

The story of Elijah's final departure is characterized by a formulaic dialogue. The prophet tells his apprentice Elisha to stay behind, but Elisha refuses (three times). The company of prophets inform Elisha that his master will be taken away, but Elisha tells them (twice) that he already knows that so they should shut up. Elisha's final request is a double portion of his master's spirit. Elisha witnesses Elijah being taken up into heaven with chariots and horses of fire which suggests that his final request of his master was granted (2 Kgs. 2:9–12).

5.4. The Divided Monarchy:
Elisha and the Northern Kings (2 Kgs. 2:13—8:29)

5.4.1. Elisha's Early Ministry (2 Kgs. 2:13—4:44)

After Elijah's departure, Elisha literally takes up his master's mantle and ministry, thus finally fulfilling in spirit YHWH's commission to Elijah at Horeb (1 Kgs. 19:16; 2 Kgs. 2:13). Elisha's first act is to purify a city's water supply and his second is to call down she-bears to attack a group of young lads for insulting him by calling him "baldhead" (2 Kgs. 2:19–25). While this latter story is troubling on several levels, the context suggests that the victims were more like a teenage gang than an unsupervised pre-school, which mitigates some of the scandalous nature of this story.[82] Some commentators speak of a complete slaughter, but this interpretation isn't required by the text, and logically doesn't make sense. For the attack to result in forty-two fatalities, all of them would have needed to hold still, waiting in line for their turn to be slaughtered by the two bears. Elsewhere in Kings, the text makes it explicit when wild animal attacks are fatal (1 Kgs. 13:24; 20:36; 2 Kgs. 17:25). While Elisha's she-bear attack may continue to trouble readers, his deeds in the following chapters are highly commendable as he repeatedly provides military assistance, food, water, and healing to people in need.

After a long absence, a Southern ruler reappears in the narrative, Jehoshaphat again, this time as an ally of Ahab's son, Jehoram, against King Mesha of Moab (2 Kings 3). Just as in 1 Kings 22, Jehoshaphat suggests seeking a prophet to help them, this time to locate desperately needed water. Elisha then informs the two kings he is only willing to help because he respects Jehoshaphat, so both water and victory over Moab will be divinely granted. The next day, the local stream fills up with water and the allied forces initially succeed against Moab until Mesha sacrifices his firstborn son. The text reports mysteriously that "wrath came upon Israel," stopping them short of complete victory.

The text then records Elisha performing miracles similar to those

---

82. See also my discussion of this incident in Lamb 2011, 95–99.

of Elijah, providing for a widow with supernaturally replenished jars of oil and raising from the dead the son of a Shunammite woman who had provided for him during his travels (2 Kgs. 4:1–37). Elisha then purifies contaminated stew for the company of prophets and he manages to make twenty loaves feed a hundred people with leftovers (2 Kgs. 4:38–44), a miracle performed more dramatically by Jesus in the gospels (Mark 6:30–44; 8:1–10).

5.4.2. Elisha and Aram (2 Kgs. 5:1–8:29)

During a period when Israel's primary enemy was Aram, a surprising story about "loving an enemy" is told involving the healing of Naaman, an Aramean commander with leprosy (2 Kings 5). When Naaman's captured Israelite servant-girl confidently declares he would be healed if he were to see the prophet Elisha, he contacts his king, who sends a letter and a gift to the Israelite king (the context suggests Jehoram). The Israelite ruler panics until Elisha tells him to send Naaman over to visit him. Naaman clearly expects that a person of his stature warrants a private consultation, but Elisha merely sends a message to tell him to wash in the Jordan River seven times to be healed. While Naaman is initially offended by the disrespect, he is willing to listen to the word of a servant, for the second time now, who says, basically, "what do you have to lose?" His Jordan bath does the trick and he returns, this time to an audience with the prophet, and makes a shockingly monotheistic announcement regarding YHWH's uniqueness (2 Kgs. 5:15).

Elisha refuses Naaman's gift, but his servant Gehazi thinks that a bad idea, so he pursues the commander, and informs him that his master has changed his mind. Gehazi then returns with Naaman's generous gifts of clothes and silver, which the servant promptly hid from his master. When interrogated about the matter, Gehazi lies to Elisha, who clearly had inside information, and therefore pronounced judgment; Naaman's leprosy will come upon Gehazi. The text clearly thinks that prophets aren't to be messed with. A few chapters later, the character Gehazi is redeemed as he advocates for the land rights of the Shunammite women whose son Elisha had raised from the dead earlier (2 Kgs. 4:18–37; 8:1–6).[83]

Elisha next manages to help the company of the prophets in their construction project by making a lost ax head float, prompting one to

---

83. Commentators argue whether the Gehazi land rights incident should be set before (Wiseman 1993, 213) or after (Hobbs, 101) the Naaman incident where the servant had acquired leprosy.

ask, "Why was this bizarre story included?" (2 Kgs. 6:1–7). While the story seems strange to modern readers, in the wild world of an Israelite prophet, floating ax heads are apparently just another typical day at work.

The next several Elisha stories come in the context of the ongoing conflict between Israel and their northern neighbor Aram. The king of Aram decides to hunt down Elisha after he realizes that the prophet is supernaturally revealing his secret troop movements to the king of Israel (the context again suggests Jehoram). The theme of prayers for the opening and closing of eyes permeates this narrative. When the Aramean forces surround the house, Elisha's servant panics, prompting a prayer from the prophet that he would see the horses and chariots of fire protecting them, an image similar to the one that Elisha witnessed as Elijah was swept up in the whirlwind (2 Kgs. 6:17; 2:11). Elisha then prays for blindness for the Arameans, allowing him to lead them into the Northern capital of Samaria, and once they have arrived he prays for the opening of their eyes. In response to the king of Israel's eager request to kill his Aramean enemies, the prophet commands instead that they feed them (2 Kgs. 6:21–22). After the feast, Aram and Israel are at peace for awhile.

As the narrative of Kings is laid out, it appears that the peace was short-lived. The text next records that Ben-hadad of Aram besieged Samaria, causing food prices to skyrocket and mothers to consume their own children (2 Kgs. 6:24–29), reminiscent of the cannibalistic horrors of the Deuteronomic curse for disobedience (Deut. 28:55–57). Finally, Elisha announces that within a day food prices would plummet, and when the king's captain responds cynically, the prophet utters a dire prediction for the captain (2 Kgs. 7:1–2).

The scene abruptly shifts to four lepers who live as outcasts outside the city gate (2 Kgs. 7:1–9). In desperation, the lepers decide to beg from the besieging Aramean army. However, when the lepers arrive, they are surprised to discover an empty camp site, abandoned in panic as the Arameans supernaturally heard the sound of Egyptian and Hittite forces, specifically chariots and horses. This theme is a re-occurring one in Elisha's narratives, this time without fire (2 Kgs. 2:11–12; 6:15–17). Ironically, the four lepers nobly decide to share their spoils of war with Samaria, the city that treated them as outcasts. As the starving residents of the city rush to plunder the Aramean camp, the cynical captain is of course crushed in the chaos, and the surplus of food causes prices to plummet as predicted.

After basically ignoring Judah for many chapters, the narrative finally shifts focus from the North to the South, as the reigns of two evil Judean rulers are recorded briefly. During his reign, Jehoram son of Jehoshaphat lost control over Edom, but more significantly for the history of the Divided Monarchy, he married Ahab's daughter Athaliah, and thus the cursed Israelite dynasty of Ahab and the blessed Judean dynasty of David are intertwined (2 Kgs. 8:16–24).[84] The two realms of the Divided Monarchy were united in other ways as Jehoram of Judah overlapped with Jehoram of Israel. To make matters more confusing, both rulers are also called "Joram" (2 Kgs. 8:16, 21, 24, 25).

The son of Jehoram and Athaliah, Ahaziah, next ascended to the Southern throne (he did not overlap with Ahaziah of Israel). He and his northern ally, Jehoram of Israel, went to fight against Aram at Ramoth-gilead, and when Jehoram was wounded, Ahaziah went with him back to Jezreel, where they would both soon met their demise at the hands of Jehu.

As Elisha's extended ministry begins to wind down, he plays the role of king-maker for two nations, finishing the task commissioned to Elijah on Mount Horeb (1 Kgs. 19:15–16). He first approached the Aramean capital, Damascus, where he informed King Ben-hadad's (II) messenger, Hazael, that the king would soon die, Hazael himself would succeed him, and he would commit atrocities against the people of Israel (2 Kgs. 8:7–13). Hazael then immediately fulfilled the prophecy by committing regicide (2 Kgs. 8:15).[85] Elisha's second act of king-making takes place in the next section.

5.5. The Divided Monarchy: The Final Years (2 Kings 9–17)

5.5.1. Israel: Righteous Jehu's Bloody Revolution (2 Kings 9–10)

To find the catalyst for Jehu's rebellion one needs to go back to Mount Horeb, when YHWH told Elijah to anoint Jehu as ruler over Israel (1 Kgs. 19:16–17). Elijah did not accomplish the feat, neither did his successor Elisha, but Elisha did delegate the task to a young unnamed prophet, who finally performed the deed, commissioning the new ruler to wipe out the entire house of Ahab in the process as Elijah had prophesied. Thus, Jehu's bloody revolution fulfilled several prophetic

---

84. See also Lamb 2010b.
85. Elisha's ministry continues past 2 Kings 8, as he delegates his apprentice to anoint Jehu and he prophesies victory for Jehoash over Aram (2 Kgs. 9:1; 13:14–19).

oracles, a theme repeated throughout the whole narrative (2 Kgs. 9:3, 6, 12, 26, 36; 10:10, 17, 30).

After a private prophetic anointing, Jehu initially appears reluctant to his officers, but once they hear about what happened they immediately declare him king (2 Kgs. 9:4–13). His reluctance now gone, Jehu travels to Jezreel, where Jehoram of Israel's sentinel recognizes him by his crazy chariot driving (2 Kgs. 9:17–20). On arriving, he trash-talks the king, insulting his mother, Jezebel, basically calling her a whore and witch (2 Kgs. 9:22), he kills Jehoram with an arrow and has his body thrown into the plot of Naboth. Then Jehu orders the killing of Ahaziah of Judah (2 Kgs. 9:23–29). Thus the biblical text attributes to Jehu the deaths of the two rulers who appear to be mentioned in the Tel Dan Inscription (see Sidebar 5.4, "Tel Dan Stele: The Death of Two Kings").

Figure 5.15: *The Death of Jezebel*. Engraving by Gustave Doré. Commons.wikimedia.org.

As Jehu approaches Jezreel, Jezebel curiously puts on makeup before insulting him by calling him "Zimri," the name of the shortest reigning Northern ruler who was killed by her own father-in-law, Omri (1 Kgs. 16:18). When Jehu calls up to her eunuchs to toss her from the window, they don't hesitate, presumably because they are happy to be rid of her. The text describes her death in graphic detail as her blood spatters the wall, horses trample her body, dogs eat her flesh, then deposit her remains on the field, and thus the final condemnation to consumption by canines is fulfilled (1 Kgs. 14:11; 16:4; 21:19, 23, 24; 22:38; 2 Kgs. 9:10, 36).

Jehu's reign of terror continues as he convinces the elders of Samaria to kill Ahab's seventy sons, the heads of which are presented to Jehu in decorative baskets (2 Kgs. 10:1–11). Jehu proceeds to slaughter the extended family of Ahaziah of Judah and the worshippers of Baal (2 Kgs. 10:12–27). The prophet Hosea, a contemporary of Jehu's great-grandson Jeroboam II, condemned the house of Jehu for the bloodshed of Jezreel (Hos. 1:4) which could reasonably be connected to Jehu's bloody rebellion since his triple-slaughter went beyond the original prophetic mandate.

YHWH rewards Jehu for his obedience to his commission with a four generational dynastic promise (2 Kgs. 10:30), and his dynasty is by far the longest in the history of the Northern Kingdom. Jehu is also the only Northern ruler to receive a righteous evaluation, uttered directly to him from YHWH (2 Kgs. 10:30). Despite his military background and his successful rebellion, over the course of his reign he lost significant territory to Hazael of Aram (2 Kgs. 10:32–33), the other ruler that YHWH had commissioned Elijah to anoint as king (1 Kgs. 19:15–16).

Sidebar 5.4: Tel Dan Stele: The Death of Two Kings

Not only does the Tel Dan Stele mention the "house of David" (see Figure 4.9 above), but it also appears to mention two rulers. Because of damage to the inscription—the stele was found in three pieces (called A, B1, B2)—it is impossible to be definitive about the identity of the two rulers. The two scholars (Biran and Naveh) who first published the inscription from the stele reconstruct the names as Jehoram of Israel and Ahaziah of Judah ("the house of David"), and many scholars follow these two scholars' reconstructed identifications. Most scholars think Hazael king of Aram (mentioned in 1 Kgs. 19:15; 2 Kgs. 8:15; 10:32) was the author of the inscription. If one follows Biran and Naveh's translation, then the inscription's author is claiming to have killed the same two rulers that the text claims were killed by Jehu in 2 Kings 9. So, who killed these two kings: Hazael or Jehu? A reasonable way to reconcile the apparent difference between the biblical text and Tel Dan inscription is to assume that Jehu and Hazael were in an alliance. The biblical text gives Jehu credit for the two deaths (2 Kgs. 10:4, 11), but he didn't actually slay Ahaziah; he only gave the command. If Hazael were the senior partner in the alliance, it would be reasonable for him to assume Jehu was following his orders.[86]

5.5.2. Judah: Righteous Jehoash's Temple Reparations (2 Kings 11–12)

When Athaliah, mother of Ahaziah, realizes her son the king is dead, she seizes the throne of Judah and kills the remaining members of the royal family, presumably not the ones related to her by blood (2 Kgs. 11:1). She manages to reign over Judah for six years, a problematic interruption to the Davidic line and to the dynastic promise of 2 Samuel 7. However, Ahaziah's sister, Jehosheba, manages to rescue one of Ahaziah's sons, her infant nephew Jehoash, from Athaliah's purge (2 Kgs. 11:2–3). Thus, the Davidic lineage is preserved, but by only a single thread.

Six years later, the priest Jehoiada orchestrates a coup with the military guards by declaring the seven year-old Jehoash king and by executing Queen Athaliah (2 Kgs. 11:4–16). Jehoiada begins a religious reformation by destroying Baal altars, and Jehoash continues the movement by restoring the temple which had fallen into disrepair (2 Kgs. 12:1–16). However, Hazael of Aram, who was initially promoted by Elisha and whose brutal reign was prophesied twice (1 Kgs. 19:17; 2 Kgs. 8:12), threatens Jehoash so that the Judean ruler plunders treasures from the newly repaired temple and presents them to the Aramean ruler, which successfully persuades him to withdraw (2 Kgs. 12:17–18). Jehoash is eventually killed in a conspiracy led by some of his own officials (2 Kgs. 12:20–21).

---

86. For a more extended discussion of this issue, see Lamb 2007, 102–10.

5.5.3. Israel: Jehu's Heirs—Jehoahaz, Jehoash, Jeroboam II, and Zechariah
(2 Kgs. 13:1–25; 14:8–16, 23–29, 15:8–12)

As YHWH promised, Jehu was succeeded by four heirs, Jehoahaz, Jehoash, Jeroboam II, and Zechariah, making his the longest dynasty in Israel's history. None of Jehu's descendants inherit the reforming zeal of their dynastic founder, and, presumably for this reason, they, like all other northern rulers except Jehu, receive an evil evaluation. Despite their negative evaluations, the text attributes various acts of piety to them (prayer and obedience to prophetic words), and records that they were more successful in warfare than Jehu the military commander. All of which begs the question, why are "evil" rulers are described in this positive manner? Presumably these descriptions of their piety and military success were present in the redactors' narrative sources, and therefore were allowed to remain in the text as it stands.

While Hazael of Aram had recently been successful against two righteous rulers, taking territory from Jehu of Israel and tribute from Jehoash of Judah, evil Jehoahaz was able to thwart Aram's attacks with prayer, as YHWH responded compassionately by sending a "deliverer" (2 Kgs. 13:3–4). Many scholars believe the deliverer was Adad-nirari III of Assyria since he campaigned against Aram during this period.[87]

Jehoahaz's son, Jehoash of Israel, overlapped briefly with Jehoash of Judah. To make things more confusing, just like Jehoram/Joram before them, both were also referred to as "Joash" (2 Kgs. 12:1; 13:10, 14). When Elisha was on his deathbed, Jehoash of Israel visited, wept, and cried out the same expression that Elisha had said as Elijah was swept into heaven ("My father, my father! The chariots of Israel and its horsemen"; 2 Kgs. 2:12; 13:14). In his final prophetic acts, Elisha first commanded the king to shoot an arrow, symbolizing victory over Aram Jehoahaz. Then Elisha commanded him to strike the ground with arrows. When Jehoash only struck the ground three times, Elisha rebuked his half-hearted response stating he would only defeat Aram three times, but not destroy them (2 Kgs. 13:14–19, 22–25). In one of the most bizarre incidents in Scripture, Elisha was associated with one final post-mortem miracle. When a dead body was thrown on a grave and randomly touched his bones, the dead man came back to life (2 Kgs. 13:20–21). Jehoash's victories were not limited to Aram, as he defeated

---

87. See Lamb 2007, 181–82n60.

righteous Amaziah of Judah, despite his best efforts to avoid conflict with his Southern neighbor, which he had warned would only hurt Judah (2 Kgs. 14:8–12). After the rout, Jehoash broke Jerusalem's wall and plundered its treasury and temple (2 Kings 14:13–14).

During his reign Jehoash's son, Jeroboam II, a relatively unknown ruler with a brief narrative, successfully re-established the northern borders from the Davidic monarchy, and thus fulfilled a prophecy from Jonah son of Amittai (2 Kgs. 14:25–28), the same prophet who famously was sent by YHWH to the Assyrian capital of Nineveh and was swallowed by a fish in the book of Jonah (Jonah 1—2). The final Jehuite, Zechariah, only reigned for six months before he was publicly assassinated by Shallum in a conspiracy (2 Kgs. 15:8–12).

5.5.4. Judah: Amaziah, Azariah, Jotham, and Ahaz (2 Kgs. 14:1–22; 15:1–7, 32–38; 16:1–20)

As soon as Amaziah, the son of Jehoash of Judah, came to power, he executed the royal servants responsible for his father's death (2 Kgs. 14:5–6). He then defeated Edom in battle, which Jehoash of Israel assumed caused him to be over-confident about his military might, leading to his challenge to the northern ruler (2 Kgs. 14:7–10). A conspiracy cut short Amaziah's reign, making him the third consecutive Judean ruler to be assassinated (2 Kgs. 9:27; 12:20; 14:19). After his father's death, Azariah came to power and he reigned for fifty-two years. Azariah was also called Uzziah (2 Kgs. 15:13, 30; Isa. 1:1; 6:1). Because he was struck with leprosy, he had to live in a separate house and his son Jotham appeared to serve as a co-regent while Azariah still lived (2 Kgs. 15:5–6). Jotham's record of his twenty-five year reign includes almost no information beyond his regnal formula (2 Kgs. 15:32–38).

Evil Ahaz broke the string of four (relatively) good Southern rulers (Jehoash, Amaziah, Azariah, and Jotham). Kings records his crimes, which included child sacrifice, sacrificing on the high places, and mimicking the religious practices of the Israelites to the North and the Assyrians (2 Kgs. 16:2–16). Ahaz is probably best known for his role in an encounter in the book of Isaiah in which he refused to ask a sign of the prophet, but Isaiah gave him one anyway, the birth of the child called Immanuel (Isa. 7:10–17). Matthew's Gospel connects this saying to Jesus as a prediction of his miraculous birth (Matt. 1:22–23). The book of Kings briefly mentions this incident in the context of explaining why Ahaz sought support from Tiglath-pileser III of Assyria against the threats from the coalition of Rezin of Aram and Pekah of Israel (2 Kgs. 16:5–9).

5.5.5. Israel: Shallum, Menahem, Pekahiah, Pekah, and Hoshea (2 Kgs. 15:13–31; 17:1–4)

The reigns of the five final Northern rulers were characterized by dynastic instability similar to those of the first Northern rulers (see 5.2.4). Two rulers had very short reigns (Shallum: 1 month; Pekahiah: 2 years); four rulers led conspiracies (Shallum against Zechariah; Menahem against Shallum; Pekah against Pekahiah; Hoshea against Pekah); and only one ruler was succeeded by an heir (Menahem followed by Pekahiah). Regnal formulas dominate the text in this section, with little narrative detail. But we do learn that Menahem was vicious toward the residents of Tiphsah, ripping open pregnant women, but conciliatory toward Assyria, presenting Tiglath-pileser III (also called Pul) with a generous tribute extracted by levying a fifty shekel tax on Israel's wealthy residents (2 Kgs. 15:16–20). Besides being a victim of Pekah's conspiracy, no additional details are provided for the two year reign of Menahem's son Pekahiah (2 Kgs. 15:23–26).

Pekah's rebellion against his predecessor appears to have motivated at least in part by political purposes. It was essentially a declaration of independence from Assyrian hegemony. Support for this idea can be seen in how Tiglath-pileser responded when the son of his Israelite vassal was removed from power: he conquered and exiled most of the Northern Kingdom (ca. 733–732 BCE; 2 Kgs. 15:29). While the second Assyrian exile was perhaps more important historically, this first exile was more significant geographically, dealing a death blow to the Northern Kingdom and leaving behind only what is referred to sometimes as the "rump state of Ephraim."[88] (See also Sidebar 5.1, "The Five Exiles of Israel and Judah" and Table 5.6.)

5.5.6. Israel Conquered and Exiled by Assyria (2 Kgs. 17:5–41)

The usurper Hoshea is infamous as the final ruler of the Northern Kingdom. When Shalmaneser V of Assyria discovered that Hoshea was seeking an alliance with Egypt, he besieged Samaria, and the Israelite

---

88. Jones 1984, 529.

ruler managed to survive for three years, but the city was eventually captured in 722 BCE (probably by Shalmaneser's successor, Sargon II).

While Israel's fall happened under his watch, Hoshea is not blamed for the tragedy. The text's homily reflecting on the reasons for the Assyrian captivity focuses the blame on the sins of the people, which included idolatry, worshipping at high places, making children pass through fire (a euphemism for child sacrifice), despising YHWH's covenant, rejecting his commandments and ignoring his prophets (2 Kgs. 17:7–18). The only king mentioned is, not surprisingly, the first king of divided Israel, Jeroboam I, since he led the nation into sin with his altars at Dan and Bethel (2 Kgs. 17:21–23). And thus the text focuses the blame for the tragedy of the northern exile onto the shoulders of their first king for the idolatrous precedent he established for his kingdom.

Before moving on to the story of Judah alone, the text reports what happened to the land of Israel. The Assyrians brought in exiles from other lands that they had conquered (2 Kgs. 17:24). When these foreigners worshipped other gods, YHWH sent lions to get their attention, so the king of Assyria arranged for priests to come and teach the new residents how to worship YHWH (2 Kgs. 17:25–28). Some followed these teachings, but many of the residents continued worshipping the gods of their own lands (2 Kgs. 17:29–41). The descendants of these people may be familiar to readers of the New Testament as the Samaritans, considered outcasts by most Jews, but not by Jesus (Luke 10:25–37; 17:16–18; John 4:1–42).

5.6. The Kingdom of Judah Alone (2 Kings 18—25)

5.6.1. Hezekiah and Sons Manasseh and Amon (2 Kings 18—21)

After focusing on the Northern Kingdom primarily throughout the history of the Divided Monarchy, the final eight chapters of 2 Kings shift to the Southern Kingdom, narrating the reigns of two good rulers (Hezekiah and Josiah) and six evil ones (Manasseh, Amon, Jehoahaz, Jehoiakim, Jehoiachin, and Zedekiah), concluding the book with the Babylonian exile.

Hezekiah is introduced as a religious reformer as he removed the high places, broke the sacred Asherah poles, and destroyed the Nehushtan (2 Kgs. 18:1–4), the bronze serpent crafted by Moses in the wilderness (Num. 21:4–9), which had survived to become an object of idolatrous worship and thus a target of his zealous reform. The text sings Hezekiah's praises as he was said to be more faithful than any king before or after him. He even rebelled against Assyrian rule, a stark contrast to his subservient father Ahaz (2 Kgs. 16:7–10); however, his rebellion was probably the catalyst for Sennacherib's invasion.

Before recording Hezekiah's extended conflict with Sennacherib of Assyria, the text retells the downfall of the Northern Kingdom (2 Kgs. 18:9–12; see also 17:5–8), which occurred in the fourth year of Hezekiah's reign. Thus, Hezekiah's resistance to Assyria can be contrasted with Hoshea's capitulation. However, righteous Hezekiah still offered a tribute to Sennacherib, which included plundering gold from the temple as Jehoash had done earlier (2 Kgs. 12:18; 18:16). At several points the text of 2 Kings 18—19 is confusing, causing some scholars to perceive multiple sources (A and B) or multiple Assyrian campaigns (701 and 688 BCE).[89]

The bulk of Hezekiah's narrative from 2 Kings (18:13—20:19), including Sennacherib's unsuccessful Judean campaign, is repeated in the book of Isaiah (36:1—39:8; see above 1.4.2). The supposed discrepancies between the biblical and Assyrian accounts of Sennacherib's invasion dominate academic discussions of this narrative.[90] The problem of the date of Sennacherib's invasion is discussed above (3.6.1).[91] For purposes of this discussion, it will be assumed to be 701 BCE. Both Kings (2 Kgs. 18:14) and the Taylor Prism (COS 2: 303d; see image) record that Hezekiah gave a tribute to Sennacherib that included thirty talents of gold. While these texts differ on the amount of silver (three hundred talents in Kings versus eight hundred talents in the Taylor Prism), this discrepancy must be considered slight in light of the agreement concerning the gift itself and the exact amount of gold.[92]

Perhaps the most significant discrepancy centers on the outcome of the campaign. Sennacherib claims victory, bragging that he locked up Hezekiah "like a bird in a cage" (COS 2:303c), but Kings eventually describes a slaughter of 185,000 Assyrian soldiers (2 Kgs. 19:35–37). However, these two accounts can be reconciled by assuming an element of hyperbole in each case.

---

89. For a summary of views, see the article on "History of Israel 5: Assyrian Period," by Brad E. Kelle and Brent A. Strawn in *DOTHB*, 472–73.
90. See the extended excursus in Cogan and Tadmor 1988, 246–51.
91. See also Cogan and Tadmor 1988, 228.
92. For explanations for the differing numbers see Cogan and Tadmor 1988, 229; Wiseman 1993, 274.

Figure 5.16: The Neo-Assyrian king Sennacherib's annals, inscribed on a stone cylinder called Taylor's Prism (after its discoverer); from Nineveh, ca. 691 BCE. The British Museum. Photo: David Castor; Commons.wikimedia.org.

Both the biblical and Assyrian sources state that Sennacherib was highly successful in Judah as he captured all the fortified cities of Judah (2 Kgs. 18:13; *COS* 2:303c). Both sources speak of Hezekiah submitting to Sennacherib in the form of a generous tribute. Both describe the Judean city of Lachish as one of Sennacherib's primary conquests: the biblical text states that Sennacherib set up temporary headquarters at

Lachish (2 Kgs. 18:13–14), and Sennacherib had reliefs commissioned for his palace at Nineveh that portray his victory over Lachish.[93] Neither source claims that Sennacherib actually defeated Jerusalem. If the Assyrian ruler had captured the Judean capital, it is likely that the successful siege of Jerusalem, not Lachish, would have adorned his palace walls in Nineveh.

Figure 5.17: A file of prisoners from besieged Lachish. Bronze wall panel from the Southwest Palace of Sennacherib, in Nineveh, ca. 700–692 BCE; British Museum. Commons.wikimedia.org.

While the Hezekiah narrative covers his reform and Sennacherib's conquest of the Judean fortified cities succinctly, the narrative slows down to include the extended trash-talking interaction between Sennacherib's Rabshakeh, a royal official serving as a spokesperson, and Hezekiah's officials. The Rabshakeh begins by asking a barrage of rhetorical questions suggesting that YHWH has abandoned the residents of Jerusalem. He concludes by stating that YHWH told him to attack Judah. When Hezekiah's officials ask him to speak Aramaic, so the people would not understand, he responds by suggesting that all of Jerusalem's citizens should know that they are all doomed "to eat their own dung and drink their own urine" (2 Kgs. 18:27). He then lists all the cities the Assyrians have destroyed and whose gods have deserted them, implying that Jerusalem and YHWH are next on the list (2 Kgs. 18:33–35). The Rabshakeh's last comment creates a tension with his earlier statement that he was actually sent by YHWH, suggesting

93. *ANEP* #371–74, pp. 129–32, 293–94.

that both of these remarks are merely propaganda meant to intimidate the Judeans in order to provoke them to capitulate.

In response to the Rabshakeh's diatribe, Hezekiah and his officials lament, tear their clothes, and then send a message to the prophet Isaiah with a report and a plea to pray (2 Kgs. 19:1-4). The prophet replies that YHWH will cause Sennacherib to return to Assyria, where he will be killed (2 Kgs. 19:6-7). Meanwhile, Sennacherib moved from Lachish to Libnah, apparently in an attempt to prevent King Tirhakah of Egypt/Cush from assisting Judah (2 Kgs. 19:8-9). The Assyrian ruler, however, found time to send a message similar to the one delivered by the Rabshakeh earlier (2 Kgs. 19:10-13).

When Hezekiah received the Assyrian letter, he went to the temple, opened it before his God, and prayed that YHWH would hear Sennacherib's taunts and respond to deliver his people. This sign would thus reveal to all nations that YHWH alone is God (2 Kgs. 19:14-19), a monotheistic refrain more typical of Deutero-Isaiah (Isa. 40–55).

The response of YHWH mediated by the prophet Isaiah is unusual in four aspects. First, the oracle is fourteen verses long (2 Kgs. 19:21-34), much longer than most of YHWH's speeches in the book of Kings. Second, the language of the first half of the oracle is poetic (2 Kgs. 19:21-28). While prophetic books like Isaiah are full of poetic oracles, this speech is the longest example of poetry in the book of Kings. Third, throughout the poetic first half, YHWH addresses Sennacherib directly. Fourth, just as Sennacherib spoke taunting words through Rabshakeh to Hezekiah, so YHWH reciprocates with trash-talking through his prophet Isaiah to Sennacherib. Sennacherib will be despised and scorned and will have a hook in his nose and a bit in his mouth (2 Kgs. 19:21, 28), which is what Assyria typically did to its captives (see an image of this practice in Figure 5.18, the image of Esarhaddon with two captives). The text then narrates a supernatural slaughter of 185,000 Assyrian soldiers by an angel of YHWH, reminiscent of the Passover in Egypt (2 Kgs. 19:35; Exod. 12:29). Sennacherib returned to Nineveh, where he was assassinated by two sons, and his younger son Esarhaddon succeeded him (2 Kgs. 19:36-37).

Figure 5.18: The Esarhaddon Stele from Zincirli, depicting King Esarhaddon of Assyria with two captive kings pleading for mercy; after 671 BCE. Pergamonmuseum, Berlin. Commons.wikimedia.org.

The story of Hezekiah's healing, which appears next in the text, seems to have been set before the Assyrian slaughter, since YHWH promises to deliver the king from Assyria (2 Kgs. 20:6). YHWH first sends a message via Isaiah to Hezekiah that he would soon die (2 Kgs. 20:1). However, when the king weeps and cries out, YHWH changes his mind, and tells Isaiah to return and inform Hezekiah that he will live fifteen more years (2 Kgs. 20:2–6).[94]

The final episode of Hezekiah's narrative is perhaps the one where he is portrayed in the most negative light, as both naïve and callous (2 Kgs. 20:12–19). When ambassadors from King Merodach-baladan of Babylon come to Jerusalem, Hezekiah gladly shows them all of his treasures (see also discussion on Babylon above, 3.2.3). After establishing the facts of what happened with questions, Isaiah pronounces judgment on Hezekiah's naiveté, that both his treasures and his descendants will be carried off to Babylon in the future. While some scholars attempt to justify the behavior of "righteous" Hezekiah here, it is difficult to get around the fact that his final words are shockingly callous. He doesn't seem to care about the tragic fate of his descendants, since he knows that he will be secure.

Hezekiah's son Manasseh was the longest reigning ruler of Israel or Judah, at fifty-five years, but according to his regnal formula he was also one of the worst as he engaged in "abominable practices" including child sacrifice, idolatry, and sorcery (2 Kgs. 21:1–9). Since Deuteronomy's law of the king connects righteousness with long reigns (Deut. 17:20), Manasseh's record longevity would be problematic for a Deuteronomistic redactor. But apparently the fact that he reigned longer that one might expect based on Deuteronomy didn't hinder the author here from condemning him in the harshest terms possible. The text records that YHWH sent anonymous prophets to condemn his deeds and declare that he would punish and exile the nation of Judah just as he had done to the nation of Israel (2 Kgs. 21:10–16). While nothing positive is said about Manasseh in Kings, in Chronicles he repents as a captive in Babylon (2 Chr. 33:11–13).

Manasseh's son Amon is a "chip off the old block" as he commits many of the same sins his father did (2 Kgs. 21:19–25). He was killed in a conspiracy by his own officials, but the people of the land retaliated against the conspirators by killing them and then installed his eight year-old son Josiah on the throne.

---

94. For a discussion of Hezekiah's healing in the context of a theological analysis of texts where God does or does not change, see Lamb 2011, 140–41.

Sidebar 5.5: Hezekiah's Tunnel

Hezekiah's final regnal formula mentions a tunnel or conduit that allowed water to be brought from the Gihon spring into the city, which would have been vital during a siege (2 Kgs. 20:20). It is either called either Hezekiah's Tunnel or the Siloam Tunnel (see image), and was discovered in 1880. Its dedication inscription is dated to the reign of Hezekiah.[95] In the spring of 2014, I was able to walk the length of the tunnel, which is about a third of a mile long, about two feet wide, and only five feet high for long sections. It was an amazing experience, but not a good idea if you're claustrophobic.

Figure 5.19: A portion of Hezekiah's tunnel.
Photo: Tamar   Hayardenu;
Commons.wikimedia.org.

95. *COS* 2:145–46; *ANEP* #275, pp. 85, 280; see image.

Figure 5.20: Replica of the Siloam Inscription, eighth century BCE, recording the construction of Hezekiah's Tunnel; Israel Antiquities Authority. Commons.wikimedia.org.

5.6.2. Josiah's Reformation (2 Kgs. 22:1—23:30)

Just like his great-grandfather Hezekiah, Josiah was praised for his righteousness and reforming zeal. Ironically, the text declares that both of them were unique; there were none like them either before or after them (2 Kgs. 18:5; 23:25). The catalyst for Josiah's reformation was the finding of the book of the law as the king's officials were repairing the temple (2 Kgs. 22:3–10). Some scholars think this book may have been an early version of the book of Deuteronomy (perhaps based on texts in Deuteronomy, see Deut. 28:61; 29:21; 30:10; 31:26), but since the narrative here only provides limited information about this law any guesses regarding its identity must be considered speculative. It is difficult to know how long this law book was missing, since just a few chapters earlier the text speaks of Amaziah being condemned for breaking "the book of law of Moses" (2 Kgs. 14:6). Some scholars think it may have just disappeared during the reign of Josiah's grandfather, Manasseh.[96]

Josiah responds to the news with torn clothes (like Hezekiah), and then directs his officials to seek out the divine guidance from the prophetess Huldah, not Jeremiah or Zephaniah, who were also both ministering during Josiah's reign (Jer. 1:2; Zeph. 1:1). Huldah predicts

96. See Wray Beal 2014, 501.

disaster for Judah, similar to the prophets of Manasseh's day, but she declares that because of his humility, Josiah himself would be die in peace (2 Kgs. 22:15–20). Huldah's prophetic statement creates a textual tension, as Josiah was killed in warfare by Pharaoh Neco of Egypt (2 Kgs. 23:29). Scholars explain the prophetic tension by typically making two points. First, Josiah did die in war, but he was still spared the horrors that later befell his country at the hands of Babylon. Second, his body was buried with his ancestors so he was spared a dishonorable exposure.[97]

Josiah's reforms were exhaustive. He had the book of the law read publicly and then made a covenant to obey it along with all the people (2 Kgs. 23:1–3). All the Baal and Asherah vessels in the temple were removed and burned, and their priests were deposed (2 Kgs. 23:4–6). He broke down the houses of the male prostitutes and defiled the high places (2 Kgs. 23:7–14). He destroyed the altar erected by Jeroboam I at Bethel, as was prophesied by the unnamed prophet (1 Kgs. 13:2–3). But, curiously, no mention is made of the destruction of the Dan altar, last mentioned during the time of Jehu (2 Kgs. 10:29). Similar to Elijah and Jehu, he slaughtered idolatrous worshipers, this time the priests of the high places (2 Kgs. 23:20). He commanded a nationwide celebration of the Passover, unique since the period of the Judges (2 Kgs. 23:21–22). Despite Josiah's extensive reforms, YHWH did not change his mind as he did for Hezekiah regarding the judgment he declared would befall Judah.

5.6.3. Josiah's Sons (Jehoahaz, Jehoiakim, Jehoiachin, Zedekiah) and the Babylonian Conquest (2 Kgs. 23:31—25:30)

Josiah's reforms, while significant, did not appear to be permanent, as each of his four ruling descendants, three sons (Jehoahaz, Jehoiakim, and Zedekiah) and a grandson (Jehoiachin), is condemned for following in the practices of his evil ancestors. The text does not elaborate, and the judgments are more formulaic than usual. While the destruction of Jerusalem and the temple in 587 BCE is perhaps the most important date in the history of the Judean monarchy, the final chapters of the book of Kings narrate a series of steps in the process of the city's gradual subjugation.

Under the short three-month reign of Jehoahaz (609 BCE), Judah

---

97. See Ibid., 505.

first lost their autonomy to Egypt, which was likely the result of the continuation of Neco's campaign, which ended the life of Josiah. In addition to establishing a tribute upon Judah of silver (one hundred talents) and gold (one talent), Neco removed Jehoahaz from power, exiled him to Egypt where he died, and replaced him on the throne with his brother Eliakim, whose name was changed to Jehoiakim (2 Kgs. 23:31–35).

During Jehoiakim's eleven-year reign (608–598 BCE), Egypt was replaced by Babylon as the imperial power of the region. In 605 BCE, the Babylonian crown prince Nebuchadnezzar decisively defeated Egypt at Carchemish, and shortly after this victory his father Nabopolassar died so he became king. For three years, Jehoiakim was a vassal of Babylon, but when he rebelled (probably in 601 BCE), Nebuchadnezzar was apparently unable to retaliate immediately, so he encouraged neighboring vassals (Aram, Ammon, Moab) to raid Judah, an action that the text interprets as divine punishment for the sins of Judah's rulers (2 Kgs. 24:1–4).

Like his uncle Jehoahaz, Jehoiachin reigned for only three months (597 BCE), but during his short rule, Nebuchadnezzar besieged and captured Jerusalem, an event that can be dated from Babylonian records to March 16, 597 BCE. As the oracle of Isaiah had predicted after the visit of the Babylonian embassy (2 Kgs. 20:16–18), Hezekiah's descendant Jehoiachin was exiled to Babylon and many of valuable items from the temple and the royal treasury were carried away to Babylon (2 Kgs. 24:11–13). Additional exiles included members of the royal family, royal officials, soldiers, and artisans (2 Kgs. 24:14–16).

Nebuchadnezzar then replaced Jehoiachin with his uncle, Mattaniah, and changed his name to Zedekiah (596–586 BCE). In two aspects he followed in his brother Jehoiakim's footsteps, reigning for eleven years and rebelling against Nebuchadnezzar (2 Kgs. 24:17–18). While the Babylonian ruler was unable to punish Jehoiakim's insubordination, he made Zedekiah pay severely for his. After an eighteen-month siege of Jerusalem, Zedekiah and his soldiers fled the city, but Nebuchadnezzar caught them, slaughtering his sons in his presence before blinding him so that his last image was that of his sons' death (2 Kgs. 25:1–7).

The destruction of Jerusalem and the temple by the Babylonian forces is recorded in detail, as the temple and other important buildings were burned, valuable temple vessels were broken and carried to Babylon, and more citizens were taken into captivity.

Gedaliah was appointed to be governor of the land, but an anti-Babylonian contingent assassinated him before fleeing to Egypt (2 Kgs. 25:22–26). Many scholars think the book of Kings originally ended here (2 Kgs. 25:21)[98] because of the perception of an abrupt shift from the tragedy of the residents of Jerusalem, to the more hopeful situation of Jehoiachin in Babylon, which might seem out of place for a book that has been spiraling downward (with the exception of Josiah) for many chapters.

Figure 5.21: "I built these walls out of pure blue stone," reads an insription of Nebuchadnezzar II on the walls of ancient Babylon. This is the Ishtar Gate of the city, reconstructed in the Pergamonmuseum, Berlin. Commons.wikimedia.org.

The book (as we have it) ends by noting that, after thirty-seven years of exile (562 BCE), Jehoiachin was released from his Babylonian cell and allowed to eat at King Evil-merodach's table (2 Kgs. 25:27–30). Interestingly, a Babylonian ration list from the reign of Nebuchadnezzar mentions Jehoiachin and his sons.[99] Some scholars find a note of hope in what is sometimes called "Jehoiachin's restoration," but the fact that his diet and wardrobe have improved cannot mask the truth that he remained essentially an exile in Babylon. Thus, the record of Jehoiachin's fate is an appropriate conclusion for the story of two nations that, through the idolatry and disobedience of their leaders, ends tragically in judgment and exile.

98. See Wiseman 1993, 315.
99. *ANET* 308d; see Figure 4.4 above.

Bibliography

Alter, Robert. 1999. *The David Story: A Translation with Commentary of 1 and 2 Samuel.* New York: Norton.

Arnold, Bill T. and Hugh G. M. Williamson, editors. 2005. *Dictionary of the Old Testament: Historical Books.* Downers Grove: InterVarsity Press.

Barkay, Gabriel. 1993. "A Bulla of Ishmael, the King's Son." *BASOR* vol. 290–91: 109–14.

Biran, Avraham and Joseph Naveh. 1993. "The Tel Dan Inscription: A New Fragment." *Israel Exploration Journal* 45(1): 1–18.

Carroll, Robert P. 1969. "The Elijah-Elisha Sagas: Some Remarks on Prophetic Succession in Ancient Israel." *VT* 19: 400–415.

Cogan, Mordechai. 2001. *I Kings.* New York: Doubleday.

_____, and Hayim Tadmor. 1988. *II Kings.* New York: Doubleday.

Cross, Frank M. 1973. *Canaanite Myth and Hebrew Epic: Essays in the History of the Religion of Israel.* Cambridge: Harvard University Press.

Dietrich, Walter. 1994. "Martin Noth and the Future of the Deuteronomistic History." In *The History of Israel's Traditions: The Heritage of Martin Noth,* edited by Steven L. McKenzie and M. Patrick Graham, 153–75. Sheffield: Sheffield Academic Press.

Fretheim, Terence. 1999. *First and Second Kings.* Louisville: Westminster John Knox.

Galil, Gershon. 1996. *The Chronology of the Kings of Israel and Judah.* Leiden: Brill.

Hubbard, David Allan. 1989. *Joel & Amos.* Downers Grove: InterVarsity.

Jones, Gwilym H. 1984. *1 and 2 Kings.* 2 volumes. New Century Bible Commentary. Grand Rapids: Eerdmans.

Kitchen, Kenneth A. 2003. *On the Reliability of the Old Testament.* Grand Rapids: Eerdmans.

Knoppers, Gary N. 1993–1994. *Two Nations under God: The Deuteronomistic History of Solomon and the Duel Monarchies.* Atlanta: Scholars Press.

Lamb, David T. 2007. *Righteous Jehu and His Evil Heirs.* Oxford: Oxford University Press.

_____. 2010(a). "'A Prophet Instead of You' (1 Kings 19.16): Elijah, Elisha and Prophetic Succession." In *Prophecy and the Prophets in Ancient Israel,* edited by John Day, 172–87. New York: T&T Clark.

_____. 2010(b). "The 'Eternal' Curse: Seven Deuteronomistic Judgment Oracles against the House of David." In *For and against David: Story and History in the Books of Samuel,* edited by A. Graeme Auld and Erik Eynikel, 315–25. Leuven: Peeters.

____. 2010(c). "The Non-Eternal Dynastic Promises of Jehu of Israel and Esarhaddon of Assyria." *VT* 40: 337–44.

____. 2011. *God Behaving Badly: Is the God of the Old Testament Angry, Sexist and Racist?* Downers Grove: InterVarsity Press.

____. 2014. "'I Will Strike You down and Cut off Your Head' (1 Samuel 17:46): Trash Talking, Derogatory Rhetoric, and Psychological Warfare in Ancient Israel." In *Warfare, Ritual, and Symbol in Biblical and Modern Contexts*, edited by Brad E. Kelle, Frank Ritchell Ames, and Jacob L. Wright, 111–30. Atlanta: Society of Biblical Literature.

____. 2015. *Prostitutes and Polygamists: A Look at Love, Old Testament Style.* Grand Rapids: Zondervan.

Lemaire, André. 2004. "Hebrew and West Semitic Inscriptions and Pre-exilic Israel." In *In Search of Pre-Exilic Israel*, edited by John Day, 366–85. New York, T&T Clark. K. A.

Nelson, Richard. 1981. *The Double Redaction of the Deuteronomistic History.* Sheffield: JSOT Press.

Noth, Martin. 1943. Translated in 1981 by Jane Doull et al. *The Deuteronomistic History.* Sheffield: Sheffield Academic Press.

Rost, Leonard. 1926. *Die Überlieferung von der Thronnachfolge Davids.* Stuttgart: Kohlhammer. Translated in 1982 by Michael Rutter and David Gunn. *The Succession to the Throne of David.* Sheffield: Almond.

Smend, Rudolf. 1971 (German original). "The Law and the Nations: A Contribution to Deuteronomistic Tradition History." In *Reconsidering Israel and Judah: Recent Studies on the Deuteronomistic History*, 95–110. Winona Lake: Eisenbrauns. English translation of German original (printed in 2000).

Thiele, Edwin R. 1965. *The Mysterious Numbers of the Hebrew Kings.* Grand Rapids: Eerdmans.

Veijola, Timo. 1975. *Die ewige Dynastie: David und die Entstehung seiner Dynastie nach der deuteronomistischen Darstellung.* Helsinki: Suomalainen Tiedeakatemia.

Walton, John H. 1994. *Chronological and Background Charts of the Old Testament.* Grand Rapids: Zondervan.

Weinfeld, Moshe. 1972. *Deuteronomy and the Deuteronomic School.* Oxford: Clarendon Press.

Williamson, Hugh G. M. 1982. *1 and 2 Chronicles.* Grand Rapids: Eerdmans.

Wiseman, Donald J. 1993. *1 & 2 Kings.* Downers Grove: InterVarsity Press.

Wray Beal, Lissa M. 2014. *1 & 2 Kings.* Downers Grove: InterVarsity Press.

Table 5.2: Israelite Regnal Formulas

#	Ruler	Reference[100]	Judean Synchronism	Father	Reign length
1.	Jeroboam I	1 Kgs. 14:20		F	22Yrs
2.	Nadab	1 Kgs. 15:25	2nd Asa	F	2 Yrs
3.	Baasha	1 Kgs. 15:33	3rd Asa	F	24 Yrs
4.	Elah	1 Kgs. 16:8	26th Asa	F	2 Yrs
5.	Zimri	1 Kgs. 16:15	27th Asa		7 Days
6.	Omri	1 Kgs. 16:23	31st Asa		12 Yrs
7.	Ahab	1 Kgs. 16:29	38th Asa	F	22 Yrs
8.	Ahaziah	1 Kgs. 22:51[101]	17th Jehoshaphat	F	2 Yrs
9.	Jehoram	2 Kgs. 3:1	18th Jehoshaphat	F	12 Yrs
10.	Jehu	2 Kgs. 10:36		F	28 Yrs
11.	Jehoahaz	2 Kgs. 13:1	23rd Jehoash	F	17 Yrs
12.	Jehoash	2 Kgs. 13:10	37th Jehoash	F	16 Yrs
13.	Jeroboam II	2 Kgs. 14:23	15th Amaziah	F	41 Yrs
14.	Zechariah	2 Kgs. 15:8	38th Azariah	F	6 Mon
15.	Shallum	2 Kgs. 15:13	39th Azariah[102]	F	1 Mon
16.	Menahem	2 Kgs. 15:17	39th Azariah	F	10 Yrs
17.	Pekahiah	2 Kgs. 15:23	50th Azariah	F	2 Yrs
18.	Pekah	2 Kgs. 15:27	52nd Azariah	F	20 Yrs
19.	Hoshea	2 Kgs. 17:1	12th Ahaz	F	9 Yrs
	Totals		**17/19**	**17/19**	**19/19**

---

100. The reference is to their regnal years, typically at the beginning of a king's narrative.
101. 1 Kings 22:52 in MT.
102. Here the text calls Azariah "Uzziah."

Evaluation	Explanation[103]	Annals Ref.	Death notice
Evil[104]	JSins[105]	AR	DN
Evil	JSins	AR	
Evil	JSins	AR	DN
		AR	
Evil	JSins	AR	
Evil	JSins	AR	DN
Evil	JSins	AR	DN
Evil	JSins	AR	DN
Evil	JSins		
Right	JSins	AR	DN
Evil	JSins	AR	DN
Evil	JSins	AR	DN
Evil	JSins	AR	DN
Evil	JSins	AR	
		AR	
Evil	JSins	AR	DN
Evil	JSins	AR	
Evil	JSins	AR	
Evil			
17/19	**16/19**	**17/19**	**10/19**

103. The text explains their evaluation in terms of how these Northern rulers continue in Jeroboam's sins (the golden calves that he set up at Dan in the north and Bethel in the south; 1 Kgs. 12:25-33) in two distinct ways, either positively by walking in the sins of Jeroboam (e.g., 1 Kgs. 15:26, 34; 16:19, 26, 31) or negatively by not departing from the sins of Jeroboam (e.g., 2 Kgs. 3:3; 10:31; 14:24; 15:9, 18). The positive form is more often associated with earlier northern rulers (e.g., Nadab, Baasha, Zimri, Omri, Ahab) while the negative form is associated with later northern rulers (e.g., Jehoram, Jehu, Jeroboam II, Zechariah, Menahem).
104. Unlike other northern kings, Jeroboam's evil is not said to be done in the eyes of YHWH (1 Kgs. 14:9).
105. Jeroboam's explanation is more typical of Southern rulers, not acting like David (1 Kgs. 14:8).

Table 5.4: Judean Regnal Formulas

#	Ruler	Reference	Israelite Synchronism	Age	Reign Length
1.	Rehoboam	1 Kgs. 14:21		41	17 Yrs
2.	Abijam	1 Kgs. 15:3	18th Jeroboam		3 Yrs
3.	Asa	1 Kgs. 15:10	20th Jeroboam		41 Yrs
4.	Jehoshaphat	1 Kgs. 22:42	4th Ahab	25	25 Yrs
5.	Jehoram	2 Kgs. 8:16	5th Joram	32	8 Yrs
6.	Ahaziah	2 Kgs. 8:26	12th Joram[106]	22	1 Yr
7.	Jehoash	2 Kgs. 12:1	7th Jehu	7[107]	40 Yrs
8.	Amaziah	2 Kgs. 14:2	2nd Joash	25	29 Yrs
9.	Azariah	2 Kgs. 15:2	27th Jeroboam	16	52 Yrs
10.	Jotham	2 Kgs. 15:33	2nd Pekah	25	16 Yrs
11.	Ahaz	2 Kgs. 16:2	17th Pekah	20	16 Yrs
12.	Hezekiah	2 Kgs. 18:2	3rd Hoshea[108]	25	29 Yrs
13.	Manasseh	2 Kgs. 21:1		12	55 Yrs
14.	Amon	2 Kgs. 21:19		22	2 Yrs
15.	Josiah	2 Kgs. 22:1		8	31 Yrs
16.	Jehoahaz	2 Kgs. 23:31		23	4 Mon
17.	Jehoiakim	2 Kgs. 23:36		25	11 Yrs
18.	Jehoiachin	2 Kgs. 24:8		18	4 Mon
19.	Zedekiah	2 Kgs. 24:18		21	11 Yrs
	Total		11/19	17/19	19/19

106. Ahaziah of Judah has two synchronisms and unfortunately they do not agree. In one he begins in the 12th year of Joram (2 Kgs. 8:25) and in the other he begins in the eleventh year of Joram (2 Kgs. 9:29).
107. Joash's age at accession is given before his formula (2 Kgs. 11:21 [12:1 MT]).
108. The southern synchronisms end after Hezekiah's since the northern kingdom is wiped out and exiled by Assyrian (2 Kgs. 17:6).

Mother[109]	Evaluation	Explanation/ Comparison	HP	Annals Ref.	Death Notice
M	Evil[110]		HP	AR	DN
M	Evil[111]	Not David		AR	DN
M	Right	David	HP	AR	DN
M	Right	Asa	HP	AR	DN
	Evil	Ahab		AR	DN
M	Evil	Ahab			
M	Right	Priest	HP	AR	DN
M	Right	Not David	HP	AR	DN
M	Right	Amaziah	HP	AR	DN
M	Right	Uzziah	HP	AR	DN
	Evil	Not David	HP	AR	DN
M	**Right**	David	[112]	AR	DN
M	Evil	Nations	HP	AR	DN
M	Evil	Manasseh		AR	DN
M	**Right**	David		AR	DN
M	Evil	Fathers			
M	Evil	Fathers		AR	DN
M	Evil	Father			
M	Evil	Jehoiakim			
17/19	19/19	19/19	9/19	15/19	15/19

109. Southern regnal formulas typically do not state the name of the father since the previous king's concluding regnal formula often has just stated that his son succeeded him. However, it does include the new ruler's mother, which is not include in northern formulas.
110. Although the text doesn't say Rehoboam did evil, Judah did evil in the eyes of YHWH during his reign (1 Kgs. 14:22).
111. The text doesn't describe Abijam as "evil" but instead says he committed all the sins of his father (1 Kgs. 15:3).
112. Hezekiah removed the high places (2 Kgs. 18:4), Manasseh rebuilt them (2 Kgs. 21:3) and then Josiah removed them again (2 Kgs. 23:19) and they were not rebuilt.

6

Ezra—Nehemiah

1. Introduction

How is a national or ethnic identity affected by the looming presence of a foreign empire? Who may lay claim to their sacred history, their rites and rituals, their land and resources? What measures can be taken by those whose memories of the past differ from others who believe themselves to have connections to common ancestry and experiences? These are the major questions that emerge from a reading of Ezra—Nehemiah (EN), a book that many scholars identify as an eye-witness to the extended moment when Israelite religion transitions into ancient Judaism by virtue of the deeds of the characters depicted in its pages. Later Jews such as **Ben Sira** and the author of **2 Maccabees** looked to Nehemiah as a paragon of Jewish virtue (Sir. 49:13; 2 Macc. 2:13–15), and the Rabbis would emulate Ezra as the archetype of the learned Torah scholar (Sanhedrin 21b—22a).[1] But EN is also about the way some factions in post-exilic Judaism attempted to identify

---

1. In this chapter, we will periodically use the terms "Torah" and "Pentateuch" interchangeably, though they carry different nuances. "The Torah" can refer to the Pentateuch, but the Hebrew term *Torah* can also refer more generally to sacred instruction rooted in text. This is fitting, as scholars do not agree on whether the historical Ezra would have had a fully formed Pentateuch during his period of activity. But it is clear that Jewish tradition remembers him as having access to such a document, and the overall picture of EN creates the impression, at least, that Ezra was somehow connected to the public promulgation of a fully formed Pentateuch.

themselves, and nobody else, as the bearers of earlier Israel's relationship with God, especially in light of how that deity had directed a powerful foreign empire (Persia) to conquer and dominate the known world.

EN holds a special place in the historiographic tradition of the Hebrew Scriptures, as it contains a trove of information regarding the formation of the early collection of Hebrew Scriptures, the personnel responsible for this, and the social groups for which it was originally intended. The authors who contributed to EN—a deeply composite work—shed light on these various ideologies and social groups by virtue of engaging earlier works of Scripture, especially biblical legal tradition and the works of various prophets. In this sense, EN is also a profoundly inter-textual work and provides readers with a clear window into early forms of exegesis that would persist for centuries, indeed, down into the Common Era in early rabbinic and Christian thought.

1.1. The Name of the Book

In the MT tradition, EN is two books in one: the first part titled "Ezra," the second "Nehemiah." Ancient rabbinic sources reckoned them as a single work compiled and shaped by Ezra himself (*Baba Bathra* 15a). This is reflected in the name of the book in the Septuagint Tradition, *Esdras*. However, the Septuagint tradition offers a further complication, because it preserves two different "Esdras" traditions: the one that stands closer to the MT version of EN is known as **Second Esdras**. But another collection, called **First Esdras**, contains very different contents that include part of the Book of Chronicles and that, for some reason, completely eliminates the Nehemiah material. Most scholars view the *First Esdras* tradition as a late reworking of the original EN material that was preserved in the MT and the *Second Esdras* text in the LXX, though others argue for the priority of *First Esdras* and see it as the basis for a more expansive *Second Esdras* composition. For the purposes of our discussion, we will focus only on the material preserved in *Second Esdras*, for that material has the closest affinities to the MT version of EN and therefore reflects the older and fuller literary tradition inherited by the authors/audiences of both the MT and the LXX.[2]

---

2. The Septuagint also preserves other works known as *Third* and *Fourth Esdras*, which are visionary/apocalyptic works and not genuinely connected to the material we will cover in this chapter.

1.2. Approaching the Study of EN

There was a time when historians looked to EN as a fairly clear historical resource, written around the time of the events they describe and thus providing a witness of sorts to the actual unfolding of history in the early and mid-Persian periods. Coming to EN from this perspective, they imagined that the end of the **Babylonian Exile** (587–538 BCE) saw a restoration of the exiled people of Judah to their homeland under the auspices of a supportive Persian government, which ushered in an era of peace, prosperity, and unity for the early Jewish world. A surface reading of EN would seem to support this case: the book begins with the statement that the Persian emperor **Cyrus the Great** freed the exiled Jews, continues with an account of how the Persian imperial system ultimately supported those who rebuilt the Jerusalem temple, goes on to highlight the role of Ezra as a galvanizing social-religious figure who promoted religious integrity and standards of faith, and concludes with a record of how both Ezra and his successor Nehemiah rebuilt communities and established the Pentateuch as the holy book of the Jewish people—all with the approval of the Persian imperial court.

Figure 6.1: Cyrus the Great of Persia. Image courtesy of Wikimedia Commons.

But more recent scholarship has highlighted the difficulty with accepting this narrative as a clear or accurate representation of what actually took place. The contents of EN construct both propagandistic and polemical tableaus regarding the return from exile, the establishment of family structures in the ancestral homeland (referred to as the Persian province of "Yehud"), indictments of leadership, and debates over how to interpret the past and what it means for the audiences of the authors' day. EN attempts to lay out a social vision for a specific community with a particular view of the past and a narrow, decisive understanding of tradition. A careful reading of the work demands an interrogation of its constituent parts, and reveals a fragmented Jewish world still recovering from the fall of the monarchy the conditions of exile.

One of the central and most persistent points that EN uses to mount its arguments is the relationship of the Jewish people to the Persian authorities who ruled over them. In particular, the question arises: who constitutes the Jewish people? For EN, the answer is simple: those who experienced exile and who returned in a succession of waves in the late-sixth through mid-fifth centuries BCE, a group that EN calls in Hebrew the *bene ha-gola* or "the descendants of the exile." Despite the variety in the blocks of material that have been redacted to create EN, all parts seem to agree that the **gola community** constitutes the sole heir to the legacy of pre-exilic Israel. In two places, Ezra 2 and Nehemiah 7, we encounter an extensive list of families who are counted as the legitimate community of return. The origins of the information contained in these lists are contested, and the overwhelming likelihood is that they do not reflect the actual names of people who returned from Mesopotamia in 538 BCE or 522 BCE (the years where major groups of Jews made the trek to Yehud). Yet they create and contribute to the view that those who rebuilt the temple, and those who were to accept the Torah as the basis of their relationship to God, counted the exilic experience as a fundamental qualification of communal viability.

Figure 6.2: Persian Yehud.

Sidebar 6.1: Judahite Life During the Era of the Babylonian Conquest (597–587 BCE) and Exile (587–539 BCE)

The remnants of monarchic era Judah during the Neo-Babylonian period lived in different corners of the ancient world following Babylon's conquest of Judah and the eventual displacement of its native population. Many of these surviving Judahites experienced exile to Mesopotamia, settled by their captors in major cities such as Babylon itself but also other locales such as Tel Abib somewhat further north along the Euphrates River (see, for example, Ezek. 3:15). Others took up residence within the boundaries of the Judahite homeland but away from their ancestral tracts of land. In either case, the Neo-Babylonian period saw immense disruption of a traditional way of life among former residents of monarchic Judah. Life for those who suffered captivity and resettlement in Mesopotamia has been illuminated in recent years by the publication of documents discovered at locales called Tel Al-Yahudu ("the city of the Judahites") and Našar, which contain the names of Judahites engaged in daily economic and social interaction during this period. These Judahites developed mechanisms for coping with the trauma of exile that allowed them to negotiate between functioning in their new environment and maintaining a connection to the cultural heritage left behind in the homeland.

Other places within EN echo this concept: Ezra 8, for example, depicts a delegation of religious leaders commissioned by the Persian emperor to govern Jewish affairs in Yehud and beyond. Similarly, the families who are party to the covenant-pact in Nehemiah 10 are those with ties to the lists in Ezra 2/Nehemiah 7, thus possessing connections to the eastern Diaspora that experienced the earlier exile. Nowhere is this qualification clearer than in the introduction to Ezra himself, who is called up from Babylon to serve as the leader of the Jewish world and to regulate life in Yehud (Ezra 7:6–10). The other Jewish communities that survived down to the mid-fifth century (which we will examine further below) are either categorized as foreign or passed over in silence within the chapters of EN. Indeed, it is with the conflicting claims of these other groups that the parameters of the *gola* community's social identity are most clearly defined, as earlier common traditions are claimed exclusively to belong to them. But EN is also characterized by the persistent question of who claims the right to lead the *gola* group itself. The opening chapters of EN point to the **Aaronide priests**; the closing chapters point to Levites working alongside the lay governor Nehemiah, and both Ezra 7–10 and Nehemiah 8 point to Ezra as a sort of **liminal** figure interfacing both ends of the spectrum. This has led to much scholarly disagreement regarding how to assess these different collections of material, how to date the events they depict, and even whether or not certain events or the main actors therein ever truly existed.

Sidebar 6.2: The Aaronide Priesthood

Many theories abound regarding the origins of the Aaronide priesthood who, during the Persian period and beyond, dominated Jewish cultic life in the Jerusalem temple. One of the most common is that their ancestry may be traced to pre-monarchic Israel and a priestly clan who claimed descent from a saintly figure named Aaron. One faction of this priestly clan, represented by the priest known as Zadok from the David and Solomon narratives in Samuel–Kings, came to hold an official place in the Jerusalem temple during the monarchic as the chief priests of the Davidic kings. Other priestly groups throughout the kingdom of Judah were eventually subordinated under their sphere of influence (and probably came to see themselves as part of an extended Aaronide clan network), with the Zadokites maintaining their place at the top of the sacral chain of power. This was severely compromised during the Babylonian Exile with the destruction of the Jerusalem temple, but the Persian authorities empowered the Aaronide priest Joshua to function as a leader of the restored Jerusalemite community in the final decades of the sixth century BCE. The Zadokite traditions from the monarchic period were now made part of a larger priestly structure that—together with the lay office of the provincial governor and his agents—regulated Jewish life in Yehud and very likely held a position of importance for Jews living in other places as well.

Central to all of this is Ezra himself, who is variously identified as the high priest of his day, a Levite-like teacher of religious doctrine, a Persian government official, or simply a literary invention of the authors of EN meant to facilitate the telling of a tale and legitimize the gubernatorial policies of Nehemiah. Though some dimensions of this last point may be worth considering, most scholars do not accept the view that Ezra is simply a fictional character but was, indeed, a genuine historical figure with priestly heritage and administrative rank. However, through teasing out the available details in EN regarding his activity, we may see how Ezra came to serve as a palimpsest, a conceptual figure drawn from authentic memory but repeatedly recast to promote a variety of values, traditions, and agendas. Looking to the disparate presentations of Ezra within EN sheds much light on the diversity of claims to leadership emanating from different corners of the *gola* community throughout several generations.

2. Literary Concerns

One of the most pressing issues in approaching EN is the relationship between the work's manifold sources, its major plot points, and its overarching literary structure. EN connects several different periods into one linear storyline: the return(s) from the Babylonian Exile (538 and 522 BCE) and rebuilding of the Jerusalem temple (515 BCE), the activity of Ezra under the charge of the **Artaxerxes I** (458 BCE; or, for some scholars, **Artaxerxes II** in 398 BCE)[3]; and the governorship of Nehemiah (ca. 445–430 BCE). At first glance, the literary arrangement of EN seems to set all of these into quite a coherent line of events, but a closer look reveals several episodes whose literary arrangement traverses both temporal and social rifts.

2.1. Was A "Book of Ezra" Ever Separate
from A "Book of Nehemiah"?

The biggest issue, literarily speaking, is the plot/structural divide created by the categorization of EN into a "book of Ezra" (Ezra 1—10) and a "book of Nehemiah" (Nehemiah 1—13). Though the aforementioned ancient witnesses viewed them as a single work, some commentators have made the case that these books developed independently and were only secondarily joined in the late stages of the formation of the Jewish canon.[4] One argument in supporting this position is that the later Second Temple Jewish sources seem to isolate Nehemiah from Ezra and favor him: the references to Nehemiah in 2 Maccabees and Ben Sira make no mention of Ezra. For scholars advocating the model of two independent works, this suggests that a "book of Nehemiah" may have been adopted by certain scribal-ideological circles as a symbol of their values, whereas different groups

---

3. See below under HISTORICAL ISSUES for more detailed discussion.
4. Kramer 1993; VanderKam 1992.

adopted a "book of Ezra" as the basis for their religious and social purviews—this might account for the *Esdras Alpha* tradition preserved in the Septuagint, as noted above.

The majority of scholars, however, see EN as a patchwork of redacted sources that demands both Ezra *and* Nehemiah as major characters in a single, cohesive work. This patchwork follows a thematic pattern found in other parts of the Hebrew Scriptures. Ezra provides a sacral basis (as a priest) for Nehemiah's lay leadership in a manner that draws from a similar model of successive leadership found with traditions regarding Moses/Joshua, Samuel/David, Jeremiah/Baruch, all the way down to the early chapters of Ezra 1—3 with the priest Joshua and the governor Zerubbabel. Ezra and Nehemiah form a similar binary pair, providing a blueprint for how the leadership of a layperson must be informed by the sacred dimensions of his predecessor's work.

There are other reasons, too, for viewing EN as a single work. First, both a proposed "book of Ezra" and "book of Nehemiah" possess stretches of material that are not about either character at all. As we will see, most of the book of Ezra takes place long before Ezra enters the scene, and the central unit in the book of Nehemiah (Nehemiah 8—10) virtually removes Nehemiah from the action altogether. Second, both parts of EN draw from similar sources and utilize them with a deliberately paralleling strategy. This is especially evident in the repeated "list of returnees" in Ezra 2/Nehemiah 7, where the parameters of communal legitimacy are delineated before a particular institution—the temple cult (in Ezra 3) and adherence to the written Torah of Moses (Nehemiah 8)—ratifies their status as the "true" Israel.[5] One might also look to the parallel prayers of Ezra 9 and Nehemiah 9: in these chapters, priestly figures (Ezra in the former, the Levites in the latter) engage in **penitential prayer** for similar purposes and via very close rhetorical patterns.

Finally, there are the figures of Ezra and Nehemiah themselves, both of whom originate in the **Eastern Diaspora** (the Jewish communities in Babylon and Persia); both of whom affirm their Jewish identity in Yehud by drawing from the same venerable earlier source traditions (notably, the Priestly and Deuteronomistic passages of the Pentateuch); and both of whom are close confidants of the Persian emperor and representatives of imperial powers in the western provinces, making the observance of these older source traditions a

---

5. Eskenazi 1988.

matter of good citizenship within the empire. There is much, then, to support the view that EN was conceived from the outset as a single work affirming a social and ideological vision for Jewish life in the Persian period (even if its latest compositional portions date from an early Hellenistic context). Its partitioning into two parts—one focusing on Ezra and the other focusing on Nehemiah—is complementary and constantly looks forward or backward to each part as the reader combs through its verses. We should therefore move ahead and evaluate EN as a single book.

2.2. Sources and Redaction in EN

Several distinct blocks emerge within EN, which scholars often identify with a variety of sources behind the current shape of the work:

1. Ezra 1—6: The return from exile and rebuilding of the temple.
2. Ezra 7—8: The selection of Ezra by the emperor Artaxerxes to oversee Jewish life in the province of Trans-Euphrates, and the account of Ezra's delegation to Jerusalem.
3. Ezra 9—10: The problem of intermarriage within the *gola* community of Yehud and Ezra's penitential prayer.
4. Nehemiah 1—3: Nehemiah's return to Yehud to rebuild the wall surrounding Jerusalem.
5. Nehemiah 4—6: Enemies both foreign and domestic contend against Nehemiah and his supporters in the rebuilding of the wall; the wall is completed against these odds.
6. Nehemiah 7: Nehemiah reads the "book of genealogies," a list of the Jewish families who had earlier returned from the Babylonian Exile.
7. Nehemiah 8—10: The sudden re-appearance of Ezra to read the *Torah* of Moses to the congregation outside the temple; the penitential prayer of the Levites, and the communal signing of a covenantal pact.
8. Nehemiah 11—13: The identification of lay and sacral leaders, Nehemiah's restoration of the faithful to their offices, and Nehemiah's cleansing of the temple and its staff from impurity and illegitimate marital unions.

Many of the documents within these structural units are authentic works drawn from archival states and redacted into the book.

However, it is also the case that a number of alleged sources in EN are probably either adaptations of once-independent source documents or original compositions in their entirety. But even the original compositions nonetheless allude to or reference documents, policies or practices that were widely known or recognized, and scholarly disagreement persists regarding the scope and nature of these texts. The following constitute some of the major units that hold together the larger narrative of Ezra—Nehemiah and, in places, propel it forward:

The Cyrus Edict (Ezra 1:1-4). This brief but important text, which initiates EN, is presented as the words of the Persian emperor Cyrus the Great, dated ostensibly to 538 BCE. For many years, scholars have recognized that the current shape of this edict is very unlikely to be an authentic Persian court document. The locution of these verses presents Cyrus as affirming the global sovereignty of YHWH, who consequently charges him as ruler of a huge international empire to empower the elite of Judah to return to Jerusalem and rebuild their temple. Moreover, according to these verses, Cyrus declares this to everyone in his empire, Jew and Gentile alike. Apart from the fact that there is no extra-biblical evidence for such a decree regarding the Jews and Jerusalem attested elsewhere in Persian court documentation, it seems highly unlikely that the fate of such a small group of people (the Jews of the Diaspora) would be of such high concern for Cyrus, whose conduct was, by all accounts, more fixated upon the major social and cultural forces of the day such as Egypt, Babylon, and Elam.

On the other hand, it is well known that Cyrus did indeed decree amnesty for those who had suffered exile and captivity under Babylon, and this obviously included Jews in various corners of his realm. Moreover, the restoration and reinforcement of temples throughout the Persian Empire was a practical matter for the royal court, since imperial administration on the regional level was conducted through temples and their priesthoods. Temples were places where law could be administered, taxes could be collected, and reports on local affairs could be collected and conveyed to the royal court. Finally, though Yehud was a very small province, its geographic location was strategically significant as a gateway to Egypt and the Mediterranean Sea. Support for a local population amenable to Persian authority and interests would have been worthwhile for Cyrus and his successors.

Sidebar 6.3: The Cyrus Cylinder

Upon taking power, Cyrus decreed amnesty for various peoples who had been taken captive and displaced by the kings of Babylon who had preceded him while simultaneously strengthening his own relationship with the priestly circles in Babylon. The famous Cyrus Cylinder, produced by Babylonian scribes in 538 BCE, contains a version of Cyrus' decree of amnesty, but also a declaration of his legitimacy as the new ruler of Babylon even though he was of foreign origin. The early Persian rulers understood very well the need for propaganda emerging from the hands of figures of local and traditional authority; the Cyrus cylinder represents a Babylonian pro-Cyrus circle, and sheds much light on the positive image granted to Cyrus in the Hebrew Scriptures and their socio-political contexts.

Figure 6.3: The Cyrus Cylinder, ca. 583 BCE; now in the British Museum. Photo: Mike Peel; Commons.wikimedia.org.

Considering these factors, the Cyrus edict in Ezra 1:1–4 is best viewed as a Jewish adaptation of a widely-promoted royal policy of restoration and temple support stemming from the early Persian period. The author of Ezra 1:1–4 sought to work the memory of this policy as it applied to Yehud into a larger narrative where the building of the temple and empowerment of the Aaronide priesthood was viewed both as a matter of prophetic fulfillment (Ezra 1:1) and good Persian civil responsibility. The author of the passage should be identified with the same scribal circle responsible for the shape of Ezra 1—6, which emphasizes the temple, the priesthood, and the essential nature of both to the survival of the Jewish people in the context of foreign imperialism and potentially hostile neighbors.

Several scholars have drawn attention to the points of contact between these opening chapters of EN and Book of Chronicles; the authors of Ezra 1—6 appear to have developed these chapters around the same time, and perhaps even in conversation with, the development of the Book of Chronicles, which most scholars would date to the late-fourth century BCE.[6] It is likely, then, that the author of the Cyrus edict in Ezra 1:1-4 lived toward the tail end of the Persian period or, perhaps, in the early years of the Hellenistic era, who sought to infuse a priestly reorientation to the entirety of the Ezra—Nehemiah corpus, at a time when the Aaronide priesthood in Jerusalem enjoyed political and social power over the Jewish world of Yehud.[7]

The List of Gola Returnees (Ezra 2:2-67/Neh. 7:5-72). This extensive list claims to present the full number of those who returned from exile under the leadership of Zerubbabel and Joshua in 522 BCE. It appears in both parts of the Ezra—Nehemiah corpus—once in Ezra 2 and again in Nehemiah 7—and the variations between both appearances are small enough that commentators view both chapters as containing the same essential roster of names. Questions abound, however, regarding whether both chapters have drawn from a common source or if one chapter has drawn from another. Since Ezra 2 appears in the context of a work that dates from a rather late point of compositional origin (Ezra 1—6), Nehemiah 7 was probably copied by the authors of Ezra 2. But other scholars point to the repetition of language from the last few verses of Ezra 2 that lay beyond the list, arguing that they appear in Nehemiah 7 because the author of that chapter utilized the material in Ezra 2 as a source.

Regardless of which chapter first incorporated this list, analyses of its contents in recent years have called into question its viability as a transparent window into who returned from the Diaspora in 522 BCE. The numbers of people reported in the list seem far too high to match what archaeology suggests about the population in and around Jerusalem in the late-sixth century BCE. The list more likely reflects information abstracted from an administrative census or other sort of accounting of population from a somewhat later period, probably the mid- to late-fifth century BCE when such population numbers would have been more likely.[8]

Nevertheless, given the purpose this list serves in both Ezra 2 and

---

6. See the next chapter for a more detailed discussion of Chronicles and its period of composition.
7. Williamson 1983.
8. Lipschits 2005, 160–68.

Nehemiah 7 in identifying the *gola* returnees, it is difficult to imagine that the names recorded in the list were anything but descendants of those who did in fact return from the eastern Diaspora. Since EN is so concerned with the special nature of the *gola* group, the families and clans detailed therein are probably those who maintained strong connections to relatives and peers who remained in Babylon and Persia, though the possibility remains that some of the homeland population managed to become part of this distinct group (Ezra 6:21). The large population represented in the list probably collapses people from various waves of return over an extended period of time, all symbolically associated with that of Zerubbabel and Joshua.

The double-appearance of the list is unique in EN; while the work contains many rosters of names, family affiliations, etc., this is the only one that occurs twice. One might argue that this is evidence that EN was once two separate books, and that the list in Ezra 2/Nehemiah 7 was part of a secondary redaction that linked them together. But formal parallels do not necessarily serve cosmetic purposes; they carry exegetical and hermeneutical significance. The appearance of the list immediately before the initial efforts to rebuild the temple (Ezra 3) and immediately before Ezra reads the Torah (Nehemiah 8) equates one with the other as a binary pair.[9] The parallel also suggests that the Torah extends the sanctity of the temple out to the entirety of the community—a concept that scholars have noted is characteristic of the **Holiness stratum** of the Book of Leviticus. The redactors of Ezra–Nehemiah may well have had affiliations with this Priestly ideology and sought to create their work as a literary embodiment of it.

Sidebar 6.4: The Priestly "Schools" Behind the Book of Leviticus

Leviticus currently occupies a central position in the Pentateuch and is presented as a collection of ritual instructions given by YHWH to Israel through Moses at Sinai. Upon closer inspection, however, the book of Leviticus evidence the worldview of two different priestly groups who contributed to its contents. Leviticus 1—16 is primarily concerned with detailed rituals where agency is restricted to the priestly descendants of

---

9. Eskenazi 1988.

Aaron. It is through them, and them alone, that Israel may experience a relationship with YHWH via the conduct of sacrifice, and much attention is paid to the variety of sacrifices that these priests much perform in order to maintain order and holiness (that is, intimacy with the divine in a manner full of mythic and cosmic potency). Leviticus 17—26, by contrast, seems to extend the idea of holiness beyond the realm of the sacrificial cult/ritual and contains an abundance of regulations for social and ethical interaction. It is in these chapters that we encounter a vision of society where the ordinary Israelite can attain and maintain holiness through ordinary action carried out according to divine will. As such, many scholars identify Leviticus 1—16 with the "Priestly" (P) stratum of composition running through the Pentateuch (found in texts such as the creation account in Gen. 1:1—2:4a and the account of Moses' transgression in Num. 20:2-13) while Leviticus 17—26 is credited to a "Holiness" (H) school more concerned with social institutions and ideas whose work is also found throughout the Pentateuch (e.g., Exod. 30:9; Num. 15; 29:1-2). Scholars generally view the P traditions as earlier than H, with the H authors developing P's language and ideas and often glossing or redacting P passages with H material, though it may be that writers more closely associated with P ideology continued to work well beyond the time of the H authors. Leviticus 27 appears to be a redactional summary of the entirety of the book's contents, incorporating elements of both P and H language and ideology—this may reflect an Aaronide scribe familiar with both schools of thought, capping the book of Leviticus in a way that allows for it to function within a Pentateuch that contained multiple sources.

The Aramaic Letters in Ezra 4—6. These chapters contain some of the most contested material within the whole of Ezra—Nehemiah. First, there are questions regarding how authentic the sources are, insofar as they present themselves as official correspondence between people beyond the Yehudite *gola* community and two different Persian emperors (namely, Artaxerxes I and **Darius**). These letters also contain a fair amount of detailed "insider" knowledge of Jewish religious tradition and even lexical formulae native to Jewish texts that would not have been readily known by gentile adversaries. Second, it is immediately evident that these letters are out of chronological sequence: a narrative set in the late-sixth century beginning with the Edict of Cyrus and describing the waves of return (Ezra 1—3) is suddenly interrupted by a letter dated to the middle of the fifth century BCE (the Artaxerxes correspondence in Ezra 4). This is followed by a brief introduction returning the reader to the late-sixth century and correspondence related to the reign of Darius and invoking the name of Cyrus once more (Ezra 5—6).

Because of the odd order of these letters, some commentators question their authenticity, reasoning that the author of this material did not even know the historical sequence of the Persian rulers, let alone the particulars of their policies and correspondence. Finally, critics of the authenticity of these letters point to the nature of the Aramaic language in which they are transmitted, noting that linguistic features suggest a much later period of compositional origin than the late-sixth to mid-fifth centuries BCE, as well as some lapses in conventional imperial language when these letters are compared with extra-biblical sources from the Persian court.[10]

Nevertheless, there are grounds for identifying these letters as authentic correspondences drawn at least in part from official archives. First, certain anti-Jewish defamatory language is included therein regarding the troubled past of Jerusalem—something that is difficult to see originating with a Jerusalem scribe in the Persian period, since Jerusalem was the only place where scribal authority was rooted. To draw attention to Jerusalem's past problems would be to impugn the viability of one's own work as a scribe, which suggests strongly that the text containing such a critical view originated in a non-Jewish scribal context. Second, the sequence of material in these chapters evidences the manner whereby archival search reports would have been committed to a single scroll: more recent material would have been found first (ergo the literary placement of the Artaxerxes correspondence), followed by older material from deeper within an archive added thereafter (ergo the literary placement of the Darius correspondence).

In other words, the sequence of correspondence does not show the author's ignorance of the history of Persia's rulers but, in fact, reveals that the letters were compiled and copied onto a single scroll during the time of Artaxerxes, and that this single scroll was the source that the author of Ezra 1—6 utilized.[11] The Aramaic letters in Ezra 4—6 are therefore best viewed as a combination of authentic archival material filtered through the scribal culture of the Jerusalemite scribes who preserved them and, finally, the religious agenda of the authors of Ezra

10. Grabbe 1994, 30—41.
11. Steiner 2006.

1—6, who certainly introduced some additional notices and changes in presentation intended to situate their work as the agenda-setter for the ensuing contents of the book.

The "Ezra Source" (Ezra 8—10, Nehemiah 8).[12] Much debate surrounds whether or not the materials in Ezra 8—10 may be credited to a discreet source deriving in part from Ezra himself. Certainly, the material in Ezra 8—9 are viable candidates insofar as they are written in the first person and feature the sort of language one might associated with someone of priestly pedigree such as Ezra who also held a high ranking imperial office. Ezra 8 contains a good deal of emphasis on matters relating to imperial provisions for the temple and its cult, as well as a thorough detailing of individuals of various priestly ranks who were part of Ezra's delegation to Jerusalem. And Ezra 9, concerned as it is with the intermarriage crisis, contains an account of Ezra positioned as intercessor between the public and the divine through his penitential prayer, one that draws from authoritative texts that would have been known to members of the priesthood. Ezra 10, by contrast, is a third-person account of events, and is therefore often viewed as a much later addition to an earlier corpus or tradition embedded in Ezra 8—9. For some scholars, then, Ezra 10 is a supplement to an older and more authentic record of events written by Ezra himself in Ezra 8—9, and constitutes an example of the reception history of those ostensibly earlier chapters.

While a strong case can indeed be made for Ezra 10 as the work of a later scribe, it is by no means assured that Ezra 8—9 should be credited to Ezra himself. Much in these chapters indicate a succession of redactional additions or blocks that reflect differing scribal perspectives. For example, Ezra 8:21–30 leans quite heavily toward a pro-priestly perspective with its emphasis on fasting, sacral separation and hierarchies, and the provisions for temple dedication; Ezra 8:15–20, by contrast, is interested especially in the recruiting of Levites as teachers, scribes and learned administrators to join Ezra's delegation, with nary a mention of funds or temple provisions. Indeed, vv. 15–20 appear to interrupt an otherwise coherent accounting of events, which suggests that a scribe has overwritten or supplemented an earlier tradition with a Levite-focused section.

Ezra 9 presents its own difficulties along similar lines. The prayer placed into Ezra's mouth within that chapter contains features that

---

12. See section 2.2 below for Ezra 7, which demands a special category of consideration.

are consistent with priestly ideology—the very idea of a penitential prayer, in fact, fits well with priestly concepts of confession and expiation—and draws heavily from passages from the **Priestly source** in the Pentateuch (especially in Leviticus, see Sidebar 6.4 above). However, the prayer draws equally as heavily from Deuteronomy, which possesses a very different socio-religious worldview than Priestly texts like Leviticus.[13] It is possible to credit this to a learned figure like Ezra who must have known both streams of tradition, but the equal measure given to both traditions in the prayer suggests that they had already been combined into a single authoritative scriptural work by the time the prayer was composed.

The penitential prayer form of Ezra 9 looks ahead to the prayer of the Levites in Nehemiah 9, a prayer that predates the era of both Ezra and Nehemiah and was therefore probably quite well known to the author of Ezra 9. A case can be made, then, that Ezra 9 was shaped in conscious awareness of major units of material in the book of Nehemiah, and was composed as part of a larger literary strategy attempting to support what we find in Nehemiah by establishing precedent in the days of Ezra. The later introduction of Ezra 10 interrupts this, but also manages to round out the event with additional details that more strongly associates Ezra's actions with earlier and authoritative tradition (compare Ezra 10:1 to Deut. 31:12).

Nehemiah 8 provides us with a different angle of view, detailing Ezra's reading of what may be a complete Pentateuch (see section 5). Its placement in the book of Nehemiah and its connection to the ensuing materials in Nehemiah 9–10 has led some scholars to view it as separate from the other Ezra texts and written specifically for its current location. And indeed, the narrative sequence of Nehemiah 8–10 coheres very well in a way that leaves the Levites with tremendous exegetical and scribal authority as Ezra's agents within the narrative (and, therefore, the trustees of Ezra's authority beyond it). It is notable, however, that if Nehemiah 8 provides a paradigm for Levite exegetical authority, it does so by utilizing a decidedly priestly text: Neh. 8:13–18 takes up legislation found in Leviticus 23, a central text for the Aaronide priests of Jerusalem. While one might make the case that this demonstrates that Priestly teachings must be subjected to Levite-scribal exegesis, it also makes those Priestly teachings the starting point for all subsequent discourse. If there was an authentic tradition

---

13. A discussion of the difference between the Priestly texts and Deuteronomy is that of Weinfeld 2004, 84–90.

involving Ezra and the standardization of authoritative texts, a Priestly unit such as Leviticus 23 would be consistent with Ezra's own Aaronide credentials.

So to what degree, then, can we ascribe anything in Ezra 8—10/ Nehemiah 8 to a putative "Ezra Source"? Rather than an "Ezra Source," it is perhaps better to speak of an Ezra *tradition*, that is, a memory from the mid-fifth century BCE regarding the religious policies and social orchestration enacted under the authority of Ezra, which included an account of a delegation returning from Babylon (Ezra 8), an episode involving Ezra's intervention into a crisis involving mixed marriage (Ezra 9—10), as well as a tradition involving the creation of an official collection of religious literature under Ezra's authority as a learned scribe and government official (Nehemiah 8; cf. Ezra 7:6, 10). It is impossible to reconstruct the specific nature of this tradition, but it is likely that the texts we currently possess used this memory and related external text sources as the basis for their own adaptations. Similar processes are found in the book of Kings, where the redactor or redactors relate events based on external textual sources. The authors of Kings, however, direct the reader to consult these sources, whereas the redactors of EN do not—perhaps because EN as a singular literary work attempted to "control" how those textual sources could be read or understood.

Ezra 7 and the Artaxerxes Rescript (Ezra 7:12-26). This source is without doubt the most important and most contested in EN research. Ezra 7 begins by introducing us to Ezra himself via a long genealogy (see section 5) and notices regarding his scribal credentials. This leads into the **Artaxerxes Rescript**, which is presented as an authentic document penned (or at least dictated) by the Persian Emperor Artaxerxes. (Whether this is Artaxerxes I or II remains a matter of debate.) We will cautiously accept Artaxerxes I as the emperor associated with Ezra's mission, which would thus be dated to 458 BCE (see section 3).

The Rescript certainly possesses an air of officialdom. It is transmitted in Aramaic, the official language of Persian administration and diplomacy, and highlights the relationship between Jewish law and imperial policy/decree, implying a connection between the two. Scholars debate how to interpret this relationship, but what is beyond debate is that the Persian emperors did support local legal and religious traditions as part of the imperial political order. For many, then, the Rescript is a testament to a genuine mission of Ezra, where the Persian emperor charged him with overseeing Jewish affairs in Jerusalem (and beyond) according to traditional Jewish law.

Figure 6.4: Artaxerxes II; relief from his tomb in Persepolis. Photo: Mardetana; Commons.wikimedia.org.

At the same time, there are elements within the Rescript that weigh against its authenticity. The style of Aramaic is, for one, somewhat later in form than extra-biblical documentary evidence from the same ostensible era. Second, the Rescript shows a familiarity with the intricacies of Jewish ritual life and religious thought that a Persian emperor would not have known or been able to address with such specificity. Finally, the style of Ezra's commission does not match the style of how Persian emperors commissioned other officials to take on major administrative duties in their empire. The Rescript shows enough knowledge of Persian conventions to support the view that its author knew of some official document that did license Ezra as a government official with authority over Jewish life in some way. In its current form, though, the Rescript is best seen as a later composition of a Jewish scribe who sought to construct a more particular memory of Ezra and his mission, and one that seems to interact with concepts spread throughout EN more generally.[14]

The Nehemiah Memoir (Nehemiah 1—6, 13). The first person narrative material identified by most scholars as the Nehemiah Memoir is also usually viewed as the most historically reliable material in EN, in large part drawn from Nehemiah's own official record of his duties as governor of Yehud from 445–432 BCE. This does not mean, of course, that the contents of these records are unbiased or historically accurate, but they appear to present at least an authentic view of events and society from the vantage point of a high Persian official of Jewish background with a particular social agenda. Still, the sections of the Memoir are arranged with an eye to theme; they tell a narrative from Nehemiah's perspective rather than relate the historical sequence of events which transpired under his tenure. Moreover, it is clear that whatever materials may be traced to Nehemiah directly were augmented over time as the Memoir developed. Redactional layers are evident throughout these chapters,[15] pointing to the re-composition of material to incorporate religious and political developments that emerged in the wake of Nehemiah's tenure as governor.

Sidebar 6.5: Persian Provincial Governors and Administration

The vastness of the Persian Empire demanded a great degree of administrative oversight. While the Persian emperors empowered local priesthoods to conduct religious affairs and oversee customary life among their attendant populations, economic and political affairs relating to the province's place in the empire was regulated by court-appointed governors and administrative agents who answered directly to the emperor. Ancient documents from the Persian period reveal a close association between the royal court at Persepolis and quotidian affairs in the provinces; provincial governors represented the voice of the emperor in these regions, and regular correspondence between the court and the provincial governors maintained a fairly continuous mutual awareness of circumstances between the center and peripheral territories. The Persian emperors also employed what is often understood as a sort of reconnaissance network, stationing agents throughout the empire as the ruler's "eyes and ears"—Zech. 4:10 seems to refer to this in its application of such agency to YHWH (rather than a human emperor).

---

14. Blenkinsopp 2009, 51–52.
15. Wright 2004, 340–41.

One candidate as a late addition to an overwritten Memoir is the list of builders of Nehemiah's wall in Nehemiah 3. Many of the people identified in the list are from the Aaronide priestly elite, which contrasts with other indications in the Memoir that the builders of the wall more broadly represented the various families of the *gola* community beyond the Aaronide priesthood. This also seems ideologically inconsistent with passages in the Memoir where the priests are a problematic group worthy of criticism and even sidelining. Nehemiah 5 and 13 contain accounts of Nehemiah enforcing traditional laws in a way that usurps Aaronide priestly authority, and Neh. 13:22 indicate Nehemiah's closer allegiance with Levite, not Aaronide, groups. Nehemiah 3 may therefore be a rather late development in EN, perhaps stemming from the same (Aaronide) Priestly authors who produced Ezra 1—6 and composed in order to make the case that Priestly influence should encompass space well beyond the precincts of the temple.[16]

Other parts of the Memoir, though, should certainly be traced either to Nehemiah himself or to records regarding Nehemiah's activity adapted into a first person narrative by the scribes who inherited Nehemiah's own writings. Different levels of text may be found in Nehemiah 1, for example, where a secondary layer of narrative has supplemented material stemming from Nehemiah, added in anticipation of events occurring later in the Memoir but built around Nehemiah's report regarding his interaction with Artaxerxes and his charge to return to Jerusalem. This includes the verses often entitled "Nehemiah's Prayer" (Neh. 1:5-11a), which may be a literary composition from a secondary hand, but one that remembers that Nehemiah did engage in penitential prayer—an idea consistent with a figure given to broadening sacred space beyond the temple and its priesthood, and a tradition attested by his day long practiced by Levites with whom he later partnered (Neh. 13:10, 22, 30). But even this material was appended to an earlier account that virtually all scholars accept as deriving from Nehemiah's interaction with Artaxerxes, setting it in conversation with texts throughout EN.

So, as with much of EN, Nehemiah's Memoir would appear to be a combination of original documents from Nehemiah and the interpretation that accompanied them as they were preserved and transmitted. Features in the Memoir are consistent with what is known

---

16. Wright 2004, 119.

of high ranking provincial officials and governors in mid-fifth-century Persia. Nehemiah's economic and religious initiatives are at home in an account at least beginning with his own retelling of the events of his day, and Nehemiah's own affiliation with the sectarian group whose views are reflected throughout EN finds reasonable and practical expression in his overturning of power structures that benefitted the Aaronide priesthood in the temple (who otherwise would have held the majority of political and social influence at the time).

The Levites' Prayer (Nehemiah 9). Virtually all scholars agree that the prayer in Nehemiah 9 is considerably older than the mid-fifth-century BCE narrative setting in which it appears. The major arguments situate its origins sometime in the mid- to late-sixth century BCE, and a careful consideration of its theology and social perspective reveals an agrarian worldview consistent with that of a population firmly entrenched in the land but lacking a centralized political and sacral establishment (i.e., a temple). For this reason, scholars usually assign the poem to a homeland community living under Babylonian rule during the exilic era or to the early returnees in the years before the re-building of the Jerusalem temple.[17] The redactors of Nehemiah 8–10 selected the poem to serve as the centerpiece of the unit precisely because it carried a relatively ancient pedigree predating the rebuilding of the temple.

A key to understanding the prayer's compositional origins rests in the fact that it is uttered by Levites of the *gola* community in its current literary context. Several commentators over the last few decades have argued that virtually no Levites endured exile; the assignment of the prayer to Levites in this context, then, is sometimes viewed as a memory or even subtle admission that the prayer originated with homeland Judahites and *their* Levitical priests.[18] While there is evidence to the contrary regarding Levites being taken into exile, there most certainly were Levites who remained in the homeland during the exilic period, and there are good reasons to view these Levites as the originators of the prayer. Levites such as the prophet **Jeremiah** had already been associated with the genre of penitential prayer by the late pre-exilic period, and Levites would have been the religious leaders of homeland groups responsible for producing such liturgical works during the time when older religious institutions such as the Jerusalem temple in the homeland lay in ruin.

---

17. Leuchter 2014.
18. Ibid.

Sidebar 6.6: Levitical Rifts in the Early Persian Period

While sources relating to the fifth and fourth centuries BCE point to the Levites as a generally unified sacral group, it is likely that this was not always the case in the Persian period. The period of the Babylon Exile saw communities fragmented in different ways, but the great dividing line appears to separate those in captivity over against those who remained behind in the land. Among both groups could be found Levites; the liturgical poem in Nehemiah 9 probably derives from homeland Levites during the Babylonian Exile, while Levites among those in foreign captivity developed texts and traditions more specific to the exilic experience. Upon the return to the homeland, Levites of the *gola* group would have carried a worldview rather different than those who had stayed in Judah, and clashes regarding the proper understanding of tradition, history, social organization and ritual expressions were inevitable. The emphasis on Levites in various parts of EN (Ezra 8:15–20; Nehemiah 8) may reflect memories of efforts enacted by the political leadership in Jerusalem to bridge gaps between these Levite factions and unify them in a common cause and purpose.

But ultimately three important features suggest that homeland Levites of the exilic period stand behind the prayer. First, the prayer's linguistic profile has a "northern" Israelite flavor to it, i.e., it seems to use a modality of expression associated with literary works originating in the northern kingdom of Israel before its fall in 721 BCE. Many scholars believe that a number of Levite refugees fled to Judah at the end of the eighth century BCE, and these Levites remained fixtures of the Judahite hinterland down to the end of the monarchic era. The northern linguistic features of the prayer would be explained if it originated with Levites whose own origins and traditions of expression derived from northern Israelite environments. Second, the prayer invokes major moments in Israel's national memory very similar to how they eventually appear in the Pentateuch; this suggests that the prayer's authors were highly literate and intimately familiar with the sources that underlie what became the major Pentateuchal narratives, and such literacy was to be found among Levites by the late pre-exilic period and beyond.

Third, the prayer's liturgical forms closely match those elsewhere identified with Levites. The second half of Neh. 9:17 uses the same language as a recurring cultic formula found throughout the Minor

Prophets (drawn from Exod. 34:6–7), inserted into those works by the Levite scribes of the late Persian period who edited them into a cohesive collection.[19] A comparison is instructive:

> But you are a God of forgiveness, *gracious* and *compassionate, slow to anger* and *abounding in loving kindness*; And You did not forsake them (Neh. 9:17)

> YHWH, YHWH, the *compassionate* and *gracious* God, *slow to anger, abounding in loving kindness* (Exod. 34:6)

If Levites redacted similar language into the oracles of the Minor Prophets, this supports the view that Levites stand behind Neh. 9:17 as well. What is more, Neh. 9:25 is highly reminiscent of the Song of Moses (Deuteronomy 32, especially vv. 14–15), a very ancient liturgical poem that formed the basis for Levite self-identity and mythology from the early monarchic era down to its redaction into the book of Deuteronomy (which was itself probably authored and redacted by Levites).[20] In many different ways, then, the prayer in Nehemiah 9 connects to Levite tradition; that the redactors of Nehemiah 8—10 credit Levites with uttering it affirms that it was widely regarded as such by the time they placed it in these chapters.

Sidebar 6.7: The Minor Prophets—a "Book of the Twelve"

The "Former Prophets" in the Hebrew Scriptures is composed of Joshua—Kings, i.e., the principle narrative units of the Deuteronomistic History. The "Latter Prophets" are the collection of prophetic texts taking the names of prophetic figures and containing collections of oracles; this is divided further into the "major" prophets (Isaiah, Jeremiah, Ezekiel—so named because of the length of these books) and the shorter books known as the "minor" prophets (Amos—Malachi). However, most scholars see these prophetic books as inter-related and redacted to form a single book of their own called in ancient Jewish sources the "Book of the Twelve." The redactors of the Book of the Twelve were Levite scribes of the late Persian (or possibly early Hellenistic) periods who copied the contents of these independent works onto a single scroll; rabbinic tradition explains this as an attempt to make sure that the individual books were not lost (*Baba Bathra* 13b),

---

19. Nogalski 2010, 40–46.
20. Leuchter 2007, 314–16.

but the cross-references from one book to another within each work suggests that this act of redaction onto a single scroll was conceived to create a unique body of teaching and wisdom. The Levite scribes responsible for this were perhaps attempting to create an intellectual and spiritual curriculum reflecting their own worldviews drawn from sources that would have already held significant authority as prophetic revelation.

The Communal Pact (Nehemiah 10). This is one of the many lists found throughout EN, but it holds a particularly special place in understanding the origins of the book and its ideology. While earlier scholars such as Morton Smith viewed this list as a very late addition to EN (Smith assumed it to be from the third century BCE),[21] this list delineates members of the community probably most closely associated with the historical Ezra and Nehemiah in its current form. Capping off the unit of Nehemiah 8—10, the individuals named in this list are most probably the **haredim** ("tremblers," see Ezra 9:4; 10:3 and the COMMENTARY below) who adhered to a specific ideology of separation and elevation over others within the *gola* community.[22] The list is not simply a register or population archive but a **pact**—that is, a fellowship bound to a sacral outlook. As with the Levites prayer, the inclusion of the list into a relatively late section of EN infuses the surrounding chapters with authenticity and rhetorical power.

The question, however, is whether this group called the *haredim* standing behind the pact derives from Ezra's period of activity or from the time of Nehemiah some fifteen years later. Two potential answers emerge as options based on the placement of the list in the current form of EN. The first option is that the list is indeed more closely connected with Ezra himself and derives from a group that formed under his leadership during his mission to Yehud in 458 BCE. In this case, the pact signatories formed a **support group** that challenged Aaronide priestly political leadership in Ezra's time and paved the way for Nehemiah's later policies. The formation of such a religious group matches well with the image of Ezra as both royal emissary and learned scholar/scribe of sacred law. The placement of the pact within a unit

---

21. Smith 1961, 355–59.
22. On the *haredim* as a sectarian group within the *gola* community, see Blenkinsopp 2009, 85n86.

dominated by the force of Ezra as a teacher of *Torah* may reflect an ancient awareness or perception that the community reflected by the pact was always closely connected to Ezra's mission.

A second option is just as possible, namely, that a group which formed under (or even after) Nehemiah's gubernatorial tenure was associated with Ezra through the redaction of the pact into Nehemiah 8–10. If this option is accepted, then the redactors of Nehemiah 8–10 are probably descendants of the pact's signatories, who sought to reify their religious and social position by aligning their ideology with the memory of a towering figure like Ezra. Ezra thereby became a "patron saint" of this group, paving the way for other Jewish groups to claim Ezra as their symbolic predecessor or founder.

A brief list here summarizes the sources in EN and where they stand within the book:

- Administrative lists (Ezra 2/Nehemiah 7; Nehemiah 10; 11–12)
- Official documents and correspondence (most of Ezra 4–6; early sources worked into Ezra 7)
- The Nehemiah Memoir (Nehemiah 1–6, 13)
- Ezra Traditions (oral and written sources; Ezra 7–10; Nehemiah 8)
- Traditional prayers (Neh. 1:5-11; Nehemiah 9)
- Adaptations from temple records (Ezra 1:1-4; Ezra 3; parts of Ezra 5–6; Nehemiah 3)

2.3. Charting the Composition History of EN

Given the extensive sources and different angles of vision embedded in EN, any theories regarding the shaping of the work must be tentative. However, a general picture does seem to emerge regarding the process of the book's formation, especially regarding two major sources from the mid-fifth century BCE. First, a memory or narrative regarding the influential authority of Ezra would have been either well-formed on the oral level or possibly even committed to writing (or, perhaps, preserved in different written sources). Second, and around the same time, a preliminary form of Nehemiah's Memoir would have been transcribed and kept in an official archive in Jerusalem. By the late-fifth to early-fourth centuries, Nehemiah's policies would have been well known (even if the leadership of the Aaronide priests limited their effectiveness), and ideological connections between him and Ezra would have been forged by those entrusted with the archival Nehemiah documents. The shaping of an early version of a combined EN narrative would have begun to form at this time, probably at the hands of the *haredim* which looked to these figures as their patrons, founders and role models.

Once a basic narrative connecting Ezra and Nehemiah was established, blocks of material were probably added over a fairly long period of time (i.e., Nehemiah's prayer, the Artaxerxes Rescript, the third-person narrative in Ezra 10), and the base narrative itself was probably adjusted as it was transmitted both textually and orally within the community of *haredim*. This same group eventually formed the important block of material in Nehemiah 8—10, where Ezra's *Torah*-reading ceremony took place beyond the temple, thereby forming an elect community beyond the reach of the Aaronide priests. Yet by the end of the Persian period or the outset of the Hellenistic era (mid- to late-fourth century BCE) this literary material had been taken over by the Aaronides, who exercised control over the archives of important texts in Jerusalem and who probably produced copies to be preserved in the **temple library**.

Sidebar 6.8: Temple Libraries in Antiquity

In the ancient world, temples were not simply places to sacrifice or engage in rituals/ceremonies but were also the repositories of sacred texts. Because the contents of texts were often understood as divine in origin, temple libraries became sacred spaces: access to these libraries were generally restricted to priests and/or priestly scribes, and they alone were privileged to consult, study and teach the contents of such text to larger audiences. An abundance of evidence from across the ancient Near East further indicates that many texts were never meant for public audiences but were the exclusive property of these elite learned figures, used to transmit secret knowledge and maintain a sense of power over populations who valued sacred writings but who themselves possessed limited literacy. Temple libraries were also places where these texts were re-copied and, in the process, reshaped and expanded with the words and ideas of successive generations of priestly-scribes who had access to them. In many ways, these literary activities were understood as a form of revelation-through-writing: the expansions and additions to earlier texts would themselves become

---

> part of what was re-copied and studied, and thus made part of the
> divine instructions and disclosures believed to reside in sacred
> documents.

At this time, the scribes working on behalf of the Aaronide priests added blocks of material that re-focused the traditions to resonate with the interests of the priesthood. This includes the narrative of Ezra 1—3 (which, it must be stressed, knows and draws from much earlier sources), the letters in Ezra 4—6, a reshaping of the Artaxerxes Rescript, and the wall-building episode in Nehemiah 3. By the late Persian or early Hellenistic period, then, EN probably existed in a form fairly similar to what we currently possess. It was eventually categorized with other temple-centered historiographies from the same period such as the Book of Chronicles (ca. 350 BCE) as part of the temple library, and later writers such as Ben Sira (ca. 180 BCE) or the author of First Esdras (ca. 100 BCE) could mine it as a source for re-conceptualizing the past for subsequent audiences.

3. Historical Issues

The events depicted in EN fit loosely into the following timeline:

Table 6.1

Approximate Year	Historical Setting	Episodes in EN
587–539 BCE	Babylonian Exile	Not narrated, but presupposed throughout EN
538 BCE	Cyrus's Decree of Amnesty	Ezra 1
522 BCE	Darius comes to the throne	Ezra 2—3
515 BCE	Darius remains on the throne	Ezra 4—6[23]
458–450 BCE	Reign of Artaxerxes I	Ezra 7—10, Nehemiah 8—10
445–432 BCE	Reign of Artaxerxes I	Nehemiah 1—6, Nehemiah 11—13

As the timeline above indicates, the setting of events in EN is twofold. The latter half of the book is set primarily in the reign of Artaxerxes I (465–424 BCE). The first part of the work, however, is set in the mid- to late-sixth century BCE, and despite its fairly late compositional origins (see section 2), it possesses some reliable information from that time. In the last few decades of the sixth century, the Persian government did indeed support the rebuilding of the Jerusalem temple, in no small part because it served a very practical economic and administrative purpose in the eyes of the Persian court.[24] Part of the support of local temples (such as that of Jerusalem) no doubt stems from the political ethic established during the reign of Persia's first emperor Cyrus the Great, who sought to reverse the more draconian policies of the Neo-Babylonian empire he inherited.

The circumstances behind this relatively easy transition of power relate to internal problems plaguing the upper echelons of Neo-Babylonian society: the last king of the empire, **Nabonidus**, had removed himself from the holy city of Babylon and took up residence in the Aramean/Syrian city of Harran, promoting the religious traditions of that city as central to his rule and consequently offending the priestly and political leadership in Babylon. The insulted elite of Babylon recognized the rising star of Cyrus via his successes in the east, and welcomed him as a replacement for their own apostate ruler. Upon entering the city of Babylon, Cyrus paid respect to the Babylonian deity **Marduk**, restoring the influence of the traditional Babylonian priesthood and earning their support. This was followed by Cyrus' policies of restoring captive people, including Jews, to their traditional homelands.

3.1. The Return to and "Restoration" of the Homeland

The notice in Ezra 3:8 that the rebuilding of the Jerusalem temple did not take place until ca. 520 BCE is confirmed by the oracles of **Haggai and Zechariah**, two Jewish prophets active during this period. But the rebuilding of local-level temples for repatriated populations would have been a sound strategy for an empire bent not only on

---

23. Much of the material in these chapters date from a period long post-dating Darius' reign, but they are set within a narrative depicting the building of the temple in Jerusalem, and thus are assigned here to the time of Darius.

24. Trotter 2001.

demonstrating discontinuity with neo-Babylonian policy but also on ensuring centers of regional support. The rebuilding of temples under imperial mandate would have played upon deeply-rooted mythological understandings among most of these populations, where native kings secured the favor of patron deities by building temples in their honor.

A Persian policy of supporting local elites (in many cases, the descendants of once-royal families) in rebuilding these temples would not only function as demonstrable and tangible propaganda in favor of the empire, it would insinuate the empire into the mythology of the repatriated population—their connection with their deity and their past would be mediated through Persian intervention. Such a policy would hold practical purposes as well: temple structures were effective centers for tax revenues, treasury storage, and strongholds from which Persian authorities could maintain a communication network to keep an eye out for strife or unrest in more distant territories.[25]

The latter point would have been especially important by ca. 520 BCE; conflict had characterized the reign of Cyrus' successor **Cambyses** (ruled 530–522) who was in turn succeeded by Darius in 522. The succession of Darius saw a degree of unrest and uncertainty throughout the empire due to the problematic reign of his predecessor and concerns that stability within the various satrapies and provinces would suffer with the change in leadership. To this end, Darius embarked on a propagandistic campaign with multiple fronts. The famous **Bisitun Inscription** "reset" the terms of Persian imperialism with a mythological emphasis, rooting the political status quo in the events of the heavens and the will of **Ahura Mazda**, Persia's deity.

Figure 6.5: The relief and inscription describing Darius I's conquests, on Mt. Behistun (Bisitun), Iran; in Old Persian, Elamite, and Babylonian. Commons.wikimedia.org.

25. On the temple as an administrative and tax center, see Schaper 1997.

Sidebar 6.9: The Bisitun Inscription

When Darius I came to the throne in 522 BCE, he commissioned a huge inscription detailing the circumstances of his rise to power to be placed on a cliff side in Bisitun (sometimes called "Behistun"), a strategic spot that saw much commercial and military traffic. The inscription equated his rise to power with the acts of the Persian high deity Ahura Mazda purging the landscape of "the Lie," i.e., the forces of chaotic evil represented by Darius' adversaries. The inscription repeats the account in three ancient languages using a common Cuneiform script (Elamite, Akkadian, and Old Persian) suggesting the cosmic and historical significance of the event and establishing a sort of origin myth empowering Darius' rule and the character of the empire under his control. The inscription also concludes with the notice that copies of its contents be transmitted throughout the empire so that every province and its population were woven into the myth itself—these copies of the inscription thus became the subject of cultural and even a sort of theological study by the learned classes of scribes and priests throughout the empire.

The importance of this inscription is attested by the fact that copies of it were spread throughout the empire—it became part of the curriculum of priests and scribes, including those in Jewish communities such as Elephantine in Egypt and, no doubt, in Jerusalem as well. But the support of local temples at this time would have bolstered Darius' political efforts as well, reinforcing imperial presence and reifying imperial ideology within local cultures. It is not surprising, then, that the oracles of Haggai and Zechariah appear to simultaneously prod the *gola* group in Yehud to step up their efforts in rebuilding the Jerusalem temple. At the very least, imperial policy seemed to favor Jewish religious interests; more likely, imperial policy provided an opportunity for local leadership to increase their prestige and power with the backing of the empire's massive economy, administrative technologies, and military resources. It is ultimately this historical context that the authors/redactors of Ezra 1—6 recall when shaping their account, redirecting the reader to a time when the temple and its priesthood were the primary representatives of imperial power.

3.2. Who Came First, Ezra or Nehemiah?

One of the most pressing questions among research into EN is whether Ezra indeed preceded Nehemiah, as the canonical sequence of EN would suggest. Ezra 7—10 and the Nehemiah Memoir (in its broadest sense) take place some sixty to seventy years later, though this remains more of a debated matter than a cursory reading of the text suggests. Most scholars accept that Nehemiah was active during this time, and thus support the traditional date of 445–432 BCE as the background to his tenure, during the reign of Artaxerxes I. The textual evidence within EN strongly supports this dating, as does external evidence from the **Elephantine Papyri**, which date from the same period.

Sidebar 6.10: Elephantine

In the early-twentieth century, a trove of ancient Aramaic documents were discovered at a site along the Nile river in Egypt called the isle of Elephantine. Many of these documents date back to the mid- to late-fifth century BCE, roughly contemporaneous with the activities reported in the book of Nehemiah and written by members of a Jewish community living at the site. According to these documents, the Jews at Elephantine held the priesthood in Jerusalem in high regard but also possessed their own local temple and priesthood, both of which served as social anchors for Jews living in the area. The version of Judaism practiced in this community is rather different than what the biblical record suggests about the Judaism of the time, with a concept of YHWH that preserved features of pre-Deuteronomic ideology and, notably, without any references to a Pentateuch or other major texts found in the Hebrew Scriptures. Jewish life at Elephantine suggests that while Jerusalem and its temple faculty were recognized as important symbols of identity among Jewish communities beyond Yehud, the religious practices and texts developing in Jerusalem had yet to find a place as "standard" sources for Jewish practice and belief across the Jewish social universe under Persian imperial control.

Figure 6.6: A letter from the Elephantine Papyri in which Yedoniah and other priests write Bagoas, governor of Judah, requesting authority to rebuild a Jewish temple at Elephantine; 407 BCE. Commons.wikimedia.org.

The question of Ezra's dating, however, is more complicated. As noted above, the sequence of material in EN places Ezra before Nehemiah, situating him also in the reign of Artaxerxes I (458 BCE, specifically). The majority of scholars accept this traditional dating, noting that the dispatching of high-ranking religious/administrative officials at this time would dovetail with attempts to maintain imperial order after a period of political turbulence in 460 BCE, which saw the surfacing of rebellion within the borders of the empire.[26] However, a growing number of scholars have accepted a different date for Ezra, assigning his mission to the year 398 BCE, which would be the seventh year of Artaxerxes II (405–359 BCE). This period, too, saw conflict within the borders of the empire related to the change in leadership at the royal court; thus the same argument for situating Ezra's mission as part of an attempt to establish order throughout the empire can be used to justify the later dating of Ezra's mission. In this case, Ezra's religious/ethnic policies followed upon those initiated by Nehemiah, lending

26. Blenkinsopp 1988, 114.

further support from a direct emissary of the emperor to practices and policies first promoted by a provincial governor.

A third position on the relative dating of Ezra and Nehemiah has emerged as well: that both figures worked at the same time, occupying different social, religious and political roles, and both during the reign of Artaxerxes I. This approach views the material associated with Ezra as governed by a cultic/priestly calendar, whereas the Nehemiah material is dated according to a civil/administrative calendar. Close readings of the various dated notices throughout EN lends support to the view that two different systems for dating were known to the redactors of the book and may well have been applied to records relating to one figure or the other. This is further supported, of course, by the fact that Ezra is remembered as an Aaronide and at various turns seems highly concerned with the role of the temple and its cult (contrasted to Nehemiah, who only turns attention to the temple in Nehemiah 13, and even then, subordinates it to his administrative power).[27]

The pivotal text in this suggestion is Nehemiah 8, and in particular, Neh. 8:9, which affirms that Nehemiah himself was present at Ezra's *Torah*-reading ceremony:

> And Nehemiah, who was the *tirshatha* [governor], and Ezra the priest the scribe, and the Levites that taught the people, said to all the people: "This day is holy to YHWH your God; mourn not, nor weep," for all the people wept when they heard the words of the Law.

It is from this verse that the remainder of the evidence is evaluated, but it is for this very reason that most scholars have been hesitant to accept the proposal. Nehemiah 8 shows signs of heavy redaction throughout; even if it was drawn from an old narrative tradition regarding Ezra, it has undergone development in successive stages of development, and this very easily accounts for the addition of Nehemiah's name to the account. A late redactor recognizing the chapter's placement within the section of the book dealing with Nehemiah must have added the latter's name to the chapter for purposes of narrative consistency, and it cannot be overlooked that apart from the brief mention of his name, Nehemiah serves no other purpose in the chapter. In essence, the addition appears cosmetic, and

---

27. Demsky 1994.

the views regarding separate periods of activity for both Ezra and Nehemiah thus appear more likely.

Though the dating of Ezra after Nehemiah remains a distinct possibility, a few reasons weigh in favor of accepting the traditional view that Ezra preceded him. The matter of **cultural memory** inherited by the redactors of EN factors into our evaluation, and this memory appears to consist of a picture of Ezra that initially aligned him with the priesthood. Though EN emphasizes Ezra's scribal role more than his priestly credentials, his scribal function regularly appears to qualify or even replace his priestly status. This suggests that an earlier version of the Ezra tradition has been secondarily shaped to curb a once-prominent priestly dimension of his character. Ezra's priesthood is attested and then curbed in various places; his ritual priorities are broached and then neglected in favor of a different emphasis that moves away from a temple-centered interest and highlights his administrative and scribal agency.

Sidebar 6.11: Cultural Memory and the Biblical Record

The biblical record is not disconnected from historical events, but it is not a reliable reflection of the details characterizing those events. It is, however, a powerful testimony to how different communities remembered those events and used them to construct a sense of connection to the past. The study of cultural memory is the study of how communities preserved details and re-used them to sustain (and just as often, to re-direct) traditions, social hierarchies, ethics, and boundaries. We encounter strong examples of this in the Pentateuch, where the memory of a break with Egyptian hegemony in the late-thirteenth century BCE ultimately led to the formation of the Exodus narrative as a telescopic allegory for genuine but varied experiences with Egyptian culture. The different features of the Exodus narrative reflect memories preserved in various parts of Israelite society: rural/agrarian, priestly, royal, military, prophetic, etc. The study of the Exodus narrative tells us little about the actual circumstances of the late-thirteenth century BCE, but much about how authors and audiences in the period of monarchic Israel understood those events and packaged them into durable discourses. The same approach may be taken to the study of the Persian period texts such as EN: events, individuals, and institutions are remembered in a way that carried ideological potency for the various groups that remembered them. The characterization of neighboring populations in Ezra 4—6, the

---

benevolence of Artaxerxes in Ezra 7 and Nehemiah 1–2, and even the deeds and accomplishments of Ezra in Ezra 7–10 and Nehemiah 8 reveal much about the scribes (or the communities/groups these scribes represented) who shaped the texts to resonate with the memory of these figures, or who revised earlier texts to countenance past events that they believed should be addressed therein.

Whoever shaped the Ezra material did so for the benefit of what follows, i.e., the Nehemiah Memoir, where similar issues emerge regarding scribal-administrative authority rivaling the priesthood. This suggests that an early and important figure named Ezra, a man tied to the Aaronide priesthood who represented the voice of the royal imperial court and who probably carried scribal qualifications, did in fact precede Nehemiah. But it was the memory of this man that was shaped for the benefit of a group closely connected to Nehemiah or who saw themselves as his successors or disciples. In a sense, then, Ezra followed Nehemiah, insofar as the literary character named Ezra was shaped and developed after Nehemiah's tenure as governor. The Ezra of history may have had only limited similarities to the Ezra who emerges as a character in EN.

3.3. Social Divisions in Fifth- to Fourth-Century BCE Judaism

Understanding the difference between Ezra the literary character and the historical Ezra upon which that character is based is important with regard to viewing EN in its actual historical and social context. EN presents a social vision that largely represents that of a small group of people, a proto-sect, within the *gola* community. From this perspective, sacral and political leadership vested in the Aaronide priesthood is constantly challenged, but this in and of itself points to the reality that this view attempted to challenge. Beyond EN (and even within it, as the addition of Ezra 1–6 attests), the Aaronides were the main power brokers between the Jewish world and the Persian Empire of which it was a part. As elsewhere in the Persian Empire, the priests in Jerusalem served as mediators of imperial interests to their local populations. The Elephantine papyri show deference to priestly leadership in Jerusalem, and the expansion of Aaronides into **Samaria** in the late-fifth century (leading to the production of the **Samaritan Pentateuch** probably in the fourth century) points to the recognition of Aaronide dominance among YHWH-worshippers in that territory as well.[28]

Thus the Aaronide priesthood was the dominant intellectual and cultural force of the time, forging connections to Jewish groups within and beyond Yehud that were at odds with the interests of other members of the *gola* community who ancestors were restored to the homeland toward the end of the sixth century BCE. The attitude of the sectarian group standing behind much of EN is understandable when viewing events from this angle, but it is also indicative of the "parent" community of this group, namely, those Jews still residing in the Eastern Diaspora, especially in/around Babylon.

Sidebar 6.12: The Samaritans

During the monarchic period, the northern kingdom of Israel outshined the southern kingdom of Judah in terms of population, agrarian resources, military power, wealth and international interaction. The Assyrian conquest of 734–721 BCE brought the northern kingdom to an end: much of the population was sent into exile, and refugees fled south to Judah for asylum. Yet a good number of the northern population remained in the land, now called the province of Samerina by the Assyrians, and living alongside foreign transplants settled there by the Assyrian military. Following the return from Babylonian Exile, members of the *gola* community appear to have had interactions with these northern populations, the latter of whom claimed to share in the cultural heritage of those who were attempting to rebuild Jerusalem (Ezra 4:2). Nevertheless, some members of the *gola* community sought to draw social boundaries between themselves and this northern population, viewing them as having little (or no) claim to a shared Israelite heritage. Within the biblical record, this attitude seems to have emerged as dominant, though it is clear that this was not always the case. The northern population in question—who came to be known as the Samaritans—continued to see themselves as strongly connected to ancient Israelite heritage and preserving their own temple sanctuary on Mount Gerizim flanking the ancient Israelite assembly site at Shechem. The fact that the Samaritans developed and preserved a version of the Pentateuch extremely similar to what developed in Jerusalem (though the differences are important) substantiates the

---

28. For a full study of the Samaritans and the connection between their cult and the Aaronide cult in Jerusalem, see Knoppers 2013.

view that at least some of the Aaronide priests viewed the Samaritans and the Gerizim temple as a legitimate community and sanctuary (respectively) where their newly-redacted document to be taught and used in ritual contexts. Nevertheless, the attitude toward the Samaritans (or their forebears) in EN became more widely adopted in later Second Temple Judaism, as evidenced in both the rabbinic tradition and in the episode involving Jesus and the Samaritan woman preserved in John 4.

EN repeatedly appeals to connections to this community as the basis for authority; the community is "recharged" when leadership from the east reaches Jerusalem.[29] This points to a view of sanctity and covenantal legitimacy that very likely was fostered by those situated in the Eastern Diaspora.

By contrast, the homeland communities in Yehud possessed a very different perspective on sacred geography, communal identity, and the meaning of history. Though the biblical tradition suggests (and periodically states in unqualified terms) that the population of Judah was almost entirely taken into exile (e.g., 2 Kgs. 25:21), archaeological evidence has revealed that as much as 80% of the Judahite population remained in the homeland during the Neo-Babylonian period.[30] Some scholars have concluded that for these people, life continued virtually unabated, but this is not the case: most of this homeland population suffered significant disruptions and dislocation from their ancestral territories, forced to flee mostly to the northern frontier of Judah and into the region of Benjamin. A degree of agrarian continuity was maintained in this geographic context (suggested by the decree of **Gedaliah ben Ahikam** in Jer. 42:9–10), but separation from the ancestral estates and the trauma of the Babylonian military conquest prompted the development of profound reflections on the relationship of the community to the land and, in particular, the tattered remnants of religious cultic and royal structures that tattered the landscape.

For this community, rebuilding a life in the land following the events that ravaged it was the foundational claim for continuity with the pre-exilic past. This is evident already in Neo-Babylonian period texts such

29. This position has been argued most convincingly by Bedford 2002.
30. Lipschits 2005, 160–68.

as the biblical book of Lamentations, where the engagement with the ruined city of Jerusalem stands at the center of religious expression; some scholars have also placed the oracles of **Deutero-Isaiah** (Isaiah 40—55) in this geographic context and indeed in conversation with Lamentations on the terms of mythic restoration of the people and their land. But Persian period texts like the Book of Ruth further highlight the purview of the homeland communities, where the intertwining with agrarian institutions and social structures is what sanctifies life and Israelite identity.[31] The rebuilding of the Jerusalem temple in the late-sixth century BCE constituted a restoration of agrarian culture, for the temple had served as a cosmic and economic anchor for that culture in earlier eras.

Sidebar 6.13: The Many Authors of the Book of Isaiah

Few prophetic works in the Hebrew Scriptures are more complicated to examine than the Book of Isaiah. Though the words of the original eighth-century BCE prophet may be identified in substantial portions of the book (Isaiah 1—12; 28—33), large expanses of text derive from later writers. Most scholars recognize that Isaiah 40—55 derive from an anonymous prophet of the mid- to late-sixth century BCE (usually called "Second" or "Deutero" Isaiah), and some portions of Isaiah 34—35 are often credited to this writer as well. The material in Isaiah 56—66 is also usually assigned to a later writer or group of writers (usually called "Third" or "Trito" Isaiah) and dated to the early Persian period (ca. 520–500 BCE). Still other material comes from other writers, such as the oracles against foreign nations in Isaiah 13—23 and the "Isaiah Apocalypse" in Isaiah 24—27 (usually dated to the mid-fifth century BCE). Finally, Isaiah 36—39 is essentially a copy of 2 Kings 18—20, creating a connection between the book of Isaiah and the late-eighth-century BCE events depicted in those Deuteronomistic chapters, but inserted into the book of Isaiah at a much later time. All of these literary sources, however, obtained the status of prophecy and function as extensions of the original Isaiah's prophetic ministry in Jerusalem, even though they represent approximate two hundred years of subsequent scribal development.

---

31. For an overview of scholarship on the dating of Ruth, with cautious support for origination in the early Persian period, see Schipper 2015, 22.

The notice in Ezra 4:1–2 that "adversaries" of the *gola* community approached them to participate in the rebuilding of the temple probably preserves a sense of the attempts by some homeland communal leaders to participate in the rebuilding efforts. This memory is transformed into a discourse on the illegitimacy of regional populations with foreign heritage, which carries an air of authenticity since foreign groups were indeed brought into the region during the Neo-Assyrian period (2 Kgs. 17:24). There is no reason to doubt that the elites of these groups attempted to build ties to the Jewish elites repatriated to Yehud. But participation in the rebuilding of the temple would have been of principle interest to the leaders of homeland Jewish groups.

The critical stance taken by EN against the Aaronides who intermarried with the homeland community suggests that some degree of support for the rebuilt temple may indeed have come from some corners of the homeland population (whose involvement in temple restoration may have been solidified through these marriages). The conclusion of the Book of Ruth—which concerns the ancestry of King David—provides some oblique evidence for this (Ruth 4:17–22). But it is also suggested by the oldest sections of **Trito-Isaiah** (ca. 520 BCE) which is critical of the exclusivity of the Aaronide priesthood and which allows for the incorporation of various groups into those permitted to participate in the temple cult (Isa. 60:3–10).

In any case, what is certain is that the Judaism of the Persian period was multi-faceted, contentious, and tense. Even within ostensible communities (such as the *gola* group), division and competition bubbled to the surface, with factions and oppositions forming across a variety of boundary markers. The community-within-a-community responsible for the strict *gola* ideology of most of EN represents one such faction, a forerunner to the Jewish sectarianism that emerged in the final centuries of the Second Temple period. What all of these groups shared, however, was a deep sense of anxiety that lingered from the memory of the Babylonian Exile, the axial point at which all mythic, cosmic and social norms were violently disrupted.

The commencement of the Persian period provided a backdrop for some reconnection with the past, but there could be no genuine continuity. Those of the *gola* mindset possessed a sense of identity hard-wired to Mesopotamia that had not been a part of Israelite self-concepts before the exile, and those of the homeland community who managed to build bridges with some members of the *gola* group were confronted with traditions that formed during the exilic period that had not characterized their own religious sensibilities. Different ways of accounting for these opposite poles of experience surfaced in various ways—the wholesale rejection of certain ideas and liturgies by some factions, or the claiming and standardization of texts by the Aaronides and the scribal establishment in the Jerusalem temple—but what endured throughout the Persian period was a fear that the balance of the cosmos was delicate and could be disrupted once again if the faithful did not maintain strict fidelity to authoritative teachings and maintain strict boundaries between their communities (however they defined them) and those who did not belong.

4. Major Themes

4.1. The Power of the Persian Empire

There is nothing more prominent in EN than its appeal to the standards, language, hierarchies, and mythologies associated with the Persian Empire. All legitimate leadership in the Jewish world is qualified by imperial mandate, and the most outstanding figures in the book (Ezra and Nehemiah themselves) are high-ranking imperial envoys. The organization of time and geography within the book is also contingent upon those determined by the Persian Empire: calendar events, provincial borders, and partitions of spaces both specific and general turn on the terms of imperial divisions and demands. Plainly put, Judaism in EN is a subset of Persian order, and it is for this reason that whenever strife or conflict arises, resolution is obtained only through appealing to imperial power. An oft-cited example is, suitably, the Artaxerxes Rescript (Ezra 7:12–26), where the resources of the Jerusalem temple (both in terms of finances and personnel) are to be regulated according to YHWH's command but only as declared by the emperor Artaxerxes himself. The opening chapters of the book similarly organize the history of the early Restoration to the homeland according to imperial decree, and Nehemiah's religious initiatives are essentially licensed by his imperial office. On every level, Persia is the vehicle through which Judaism is actualized and reinforced.

4.2. Insiders and Outsiders

Within the aforementioned imperial order, EN advocates for the partitioning of the Yehudite Jewish community into strict gradations of legitimacy. Homeland groups who did not endure exile are excluded; those who could trace their lineage to the exilic experience (the *gola* group), on the other hand, could participate in civic and religious life in and around Jerusalem. There are indications that within EN, this is more of an ideological construct than an historical reality: both Ezra and Nehemiah take the high-ranking priests to task for intermarriage beyond the ranks of the *gola* community, but this suggests that the religious elite in Yehud was divided over just how exclusive insider status could or should be. This perhaps relates to the emergence of the *haredim* who appear to revolve around the figure of Ezra, who in turn is presented as their leader. Members of this sect invariably saw even *gola* community members as outsiders if the latter did not share their ideology. Alternatives to identity formation saturate EN in a way that earlier literature of the pre-exilic period does not demonstrate.

4.3. The Jerusalem Temple

Sanctuary spaces had always anchored Israelite communities and communal identity throughout its history; by the end of the pre-exilic period, the Jerusalem temple was the sanctuary-par-excellence that served this purpose, and EN attempts to emulate that legacy in its treatment of the temple as a centralizing axis for the restored *gola* community. Most of EN's contents relate in either direct or oblique ways to the role that the temple plays in identity formation, politics, festival observance, and legal tradition, though this varies from unit to unit within the book. Ezra 1—6, for example, presents the temple as the very heart of the community; the very opening verses of this unit make the rebuilding of the temple not only the concern of the Persian emperor Cyrus but the fulfillment of earlier Israelite prophecies (Ezra 1:1–4).

The Nehemiah material moves in a somewhat different direction, insofar as the emphasis appears to be on the city of Jerusalem more than the unparalleled importance of the temple. This is especially the case in Nehemiah 3, the account of the rebuilding of Jerusalem's wall, but even here, priestly figures are emphasized (see section 5), which implies the essentialness of the temple and its resources to the project. The Ezra material occupies a medial position, identifying the temple as an important but not exclusive concern of Ezra's mission. Despite these shades of grey, it is the consistent and cumulative interest in the temple's role that affirms its importance as a motif within EN and the community that produced it.

4.4. Law/Torah and Its Interpretation

Perhaps more than anything else, though, it is the role and function of Law within EN that emerges as its major concern and indeed as its major contribution to the history of Judaism. Later rabbinic tradition assigns to Ezra a position equal to that of Moses in typological merit (Sanhedrin 21b; Sukkah 20a) due to his reading, teaching and explication of *Torah*, and Ezra is presented as the leader of a guild of exegetes that the Rabbis saw as their direct forebears.[32] This great legacy vis-à-vis the *Torah* tradition is no doubt due to the dual depiction of Ezra as a scribal exegete (Ezra 7:6, 10) and as the master of ceremonies in the public reading of the Law (Nehemiah 8). And it is indeed the idea of the Law that interacts most strongly with the initiatives taken by Ezra, Nehemiah, and even the imperial overlords who granted these figures the political powers they possess.

Sidebar 6.14: The Pentateuch and *Torah*

Since its initial redaction in the mid-fifth century BCE, the Pentateuch functioned as an ever-expanding foundational document for Jews in antiquity, and came to be known as "the Torah"; when speaking of "the Torah," Jews in antiquity and even more contemporary periods usually have the Pentateuch in mind. But the term *Torah* did not always relate to the Pentateuch; indeed, it pre-dates the redaction of the Pentateuch and carried a fairly loose definition. The term *Torah* is applied to the individual sets of ritual instructions in Leviticus 1—7 and priestly (oral) instruction in Jer. 18:18 and Ezek. 7:26, to the book of Deuteronomy (implicitly) in 2 Kgs. 22:8–11, and to parental wisdom in Psalm 78:5. In these texts, *Torah* does not relate to the Pentateuch but to sacred teaching; that the Pentateuch came to be identified as "the Torah" reveals that it either eclipsed all other forms of sacral instruction or, perhaps better, absorbed them symbolically to such a degree that it became the highest expression of those traditions. But even if this is the case, the Pentateuch could itself be subjected to the act of Torah-instruction. This seems to be the case in Nehemiah 8, where Ezra's

---

32. Megilla 15a; 17b; Targ. Mal 1.1. See further Leuchter 2012.

> reading from a document called "the Torah" is paralleled by the Levite scribes' teaching of its contents to the congregation. Similarly, it may be that the "Torah of God" in Ezra 7:10 refers to the Pentateuch as a document, while the reference to "the *Torah* of Moses" in Ezra 7:6 refers to a method of inquiry and the resulting understanding that arises from it (ascribed rhetorically to Mosaic origins).

Much of this has to do with the importance of Law as an ordering principle within ancient Persian culture itself, where the *data* ("imperial command") of the king was to be observed as though it were divine instruction. Indeed, Ezra 7:25–26 suggests a sort of equivalency between Jewish Law and imperial *data*; it remains debates as to whether or not the Pentateuch was understood as a manifestation of imperial data or if the idea of *data* simply informed how the Pentateuch was subsequently understood and applied. It is also likely that EN's exegesis of earlier laws and presentation of this exegesis at the hands of Ezra and his supporters (especially in Nehemiah 8) points to the development of interpretive methods that came to be seen as the keys that unlocked and actualized the divine power of traditional scripture as enduring sacred instruction for the Jewish social world. There can be no denying the fact that the Jewish Pentateuch/*Torah* and a tradition of its interpretation emerge from this historical period in history in substantial form, and EN's deep interest in the role of Law bears witness to the ideology accompanying that process.

5. Commentary

5.1. Ezra 1—6

These chapters describe in detail the impact of the rise of Cyrus the Great, the first emperor of the Persian empire, and his declaration of amnesty for Jews whose ancestors had been forcibly taken to Babylon generations earlier (Ezra 1:1-4). The narrative wastes no time in identifying how quickly the community mobilizes after this opportunity is presented to them: within the very same years that the declaration is offered (538 BCE), a group of dedicated, determined returnees comes together and embarks on a trek to rebuild Jewish life

411

in the homeland, i.e., the former kingdom of Judah now known as the province of Yehud (Ezra 1:5–10). The leader of this group identified as "the governor of Judah" is a figure known as **Sheshbazzar** (Ezra 1:8)—some scholars have identified him with the "Shenazzar" of 1 Chr. 3:18, a descendant of the Judahite royal line. This identification is uncertain but certainly possible, for the promotion of the native leaders of different cultures to positions within the imperial authorization was common practice in the Persian empire and indeed draws from a tradition of similar praxis employed by the Babylonians who preceded them.

Yet in the final analysis, it is not the return of Sheshbazzar that commands the reader's attention but the activities surrounding a later wave of return led by **Zerubbabel** and **Joshua** in 522 BCE (Ezra 2—3). Moreover, there is no question as to the pedigree of either leader: Zerubbabel is a descendant of the royal line, and Joshua is a descendant of the Jerusalemite high priestly line. It is under this diarchy of Aaronide priest and Davidic governor that the restoration to the homeland takes place in earnest. That this return is introduced immediately after the return of Sheshbazzar is narrated—and left unresolved—suggests that successful restoration could only occur as a team effort between different leadership circles bringing their respective social and political capital to the enterprise.

That both Zerubbabel and Joshua are chosen to work in tandem by the Persian administration most certainly led to tension between supporters of a priestly hierocracy on the one hand and supporters of the Davidic descendants on the other. But as the very opening verses of EN make clear (via the invocation of Jeremiah's famous seventy-year oracle, Jer. 25:11), prophecy is aligned with Persian political dominance as a vehicle for divine will. And indeed, as the restoration effort ensues, the narrative claims that this diarchy is supported by the divine sponsorship as well, for it is through the voice of prophets such as Haggai and Zechariah that YHWH gives his seal of approval to the efforts of the community under the leadership of Zerubbabel and Joshua.

The high point of the unit, beyond doubt, is the account of the foundation laid for what would become the second temple in Jerusalem (Ezra 3). Independent witnesses for the construction of the temple in the books of the prophets Haggai and Zechariah (chapters 1—8 in the latter),[33] where both prophets offer oracles speaking to the centrality of the institution and the need to rebuilt it. The perspectives of the

412

prophets differ, but both affirm that the survival of the *gola* community in the homeland depended on a functioning temple and cult—something that Ezra 3 narrates in very clear and detailed terms. The narrative is often used as a basis for reconstructing the actual event or the events surrounding it, but Ezra 3 is probably a composition long postdating the event, looking back upon it from the purview of a writer steeped in a successful temple that had become the centrifugal force in Jewish life.

It should not be surprising, then, that the chapter, and indeed the entirety of Ezra 1—3, culminates in the event of the temple's foundation ceremony, an event that is presented as the immediate product of the returned community's interests. It is also highly significant that the *people* are credited alongside the leadership with re-establishing the temple: in the ancient near east, the building of temples was a privilege of kings which cemented an eternal relationship between the king and the deity to whom the temple was dedicated. This relationship is extended to the entire restored community, and to the exclusion of others claiming an authentic connection to YHWH.

The rhetorical structure of these chapters reinforces how the reader is to understand the status—both socio-political and sacral—of the *gola* group. With the efforts of the people behind the re-founding of the temple, Ezra 1—3 shows that the *gola* community (Ezra 2) receives the favor not only of Persian court (Ezra 1) but also of the ancestral deity (Ezra 3). But the authors/redactors of these materials inherited an important ideological trait, namely, that the restored *gola* community was completely different and was to be completely separate from the nation surrounding them. This ideology, as we have already noted, is attested in a good deal of literature datable to the Persian period, and survived for a long time as a motif characterizing later literary shaping as well.

To this end, the authors/redactors of these chapters included a succession of official correspondence between the surrounding peoples and the Persian overlords who sponsored the *gola* community. This correspondence has occasioned a good deal of attention from scholars precisely because it bears a high degree of authenticity (though it most certainly reflects some deliberate revisions, additions, and adjustments by later Jewish scribes as well) and indicates that

---

33. It is generally recognized by researchers that Zechariah 9—14 stem from the hands of a different author than the oracles in chapters 1—8.

there was, indeed, tension between the restored *gola* group and the neighboring polities. The format and sequence of these chapters furthermore reveal that these tensions were not quickly resolved but persisted for a long time; the implication is that Jewish life could be sanctified under Persian political hegemony, but vigilance was required against long-standing threats that continued to endure. What follows in Ezra 4—6 demonstrates the nature of that threat: it is political. These chapters contain detailed correspondence allegedly stemming from official archives (probably maintained and reinforced during Nehemiah's tenure as governor) between hostile neighboring communities and the Persian emperors. The correspondence is overtly identified as drawn from an official source/archive, which consequently portrays the triumph over adversity as a political matter as well.

This confrontation leads to the extended campaign to disrupt the rebuilding of the Jerusalem temple, a problem that the ensuing official correspondence reveals is a persistent problem. The letters in Ezra 4—6, preserved in the **Aramaic language**, are probably generally reliable and substantially authentic, though they have been shaped by later hands to account for broader figures and religious currents/ traditions in Persian period Judaism. Reference to the prophets Haggai and Zechariah, for example, present the prophetic tradition as supportive of imperial edicts (Ezra 5:1-2; 6:14) to which these letters allude, though the oracles of these prophets do not attest to such agreement or support. The overall effect of these chapters, however, create a tableau that promotes a theology where a confluence of different and authoritative writings are used to support religious identity and agendas revolving around the temple and the community it supported.

Sidebar 6.15: Aramaic Language and Aramaic Culture

Aramaic was an alphabetic Semitic language, easily mastered and transmitted, that became the *lingua franca* of diplomats and administrators in the ancient Near East from the eighth century BCE onward. But during the Persian period, Aramaic was promoted to something more than just a governmental or diplomatic utility.

Aramaic was a language of elite and even cosmic discourse, adopted across the Persian empire as a way to superimpose imperial reality upon older local traditions and cultures. To translate a traditional document into Aramaic was to affirm its place in the Persian imperial world. Aramaic script (the actual calligraphic shape of individual alphabetic letters) also carried cosmic potency: a document could still be written in the Hebrew language, but the writing of the Hebrew words in Aramaic script interfaced the document with Persian imperial mythology such as that found in the Bisitun Inscription (also transmitted in Aramaic copies throughout the empire). Most scribes in the Persian Empire were bilingual with Aramaic fluency complementing their knowledge of their native language tradition. But in addition to this, Aramaic-trained scribes were also enculturated in a vast amount of mythological and esoteric knowledge (mostly drawn from very ancient Babylonian scholarly traditions) now also transmitted in Aramaic. Aramaic language was a herald of a profoundly impressive and ancient body of knowledge and wisdom, an elite intellectual culture projected over the cultures now subsumed within the Persian Empire.

5.2. Ezra 7–8

Finally, several chapters into the book of Ezra, the narrative introduces us to Ezra himself. The buildup to this moment is recognized and even admitted to by the narration, as Ezra 1:1 begins with the statement "after these things . . . ," i.e., after the turbulent events of the preceding six chapters. "After these things" is therefore quite a loaded statement, as it suggests that history had unfurled for the very purpose of leading the Jewish world of the time to a figure like Ezra, and that only he could reconcile the tensions that permeated nearly ever verse of the book's opening chapters. Here we encounter the distinction between history and historiography: the redactors of EN have drawn on genuine events, genuine individual accomplishments and powerful communal memories to reframe history to match their interests. In this case, the redactors have shaped the text so that the all-important episodes of the late-sixth century BCE are presented as unresolved until Ezra's introduction, which suggests that the redactors already inherited a tradition regarding Ezra's towering stature as a leader in the Jewish world of their era.

The historicity of Ezra is not in much doubt (with only a few exceptions), but the particulars of this evidence remains debated, ranging from Ezra's priestly credentials to his specific role in the Persian administration to even the date of his commission and period of activity. Let us consider first the question of his priestly credentials. Ezra 7:1–5 provides us with an extended genealogy for Ezra, by far the longest genealogy for an individual figure in the Hebrew Bible. This alone affirms the massive importance the redactors ascribe to him, especially since the genealogy is clear that Ezra is from an Aaronide priestly lineage tracing directly back to **Zadok** (the founder of the Jerusalem priesthood) and even to Aaron himself. The problem, however, is that the genealogy cannot be taken at face value. Ezra's father, for example, is identified as Seraiah, the last priest of monarchic-era Jerusalem (ca. 587 BCE), but this is an historical impossibility. If Ezra's commission is dated to 458 BCE (as we have argued), this would place his activity over a century after the fall of Jerusalem, so Ezra's father could not have been the Seraiah who served in the temple at the time of its destruction.

It is possible that the highlighting of Seraiah speaks to Ezra's more distant descent from the same person, skipping over a few generations for rhetorical effect. This, we might note, is consistent with the broader narrative context, which skips at least five decades between the last events mentioned in Ezra 6 and the situation at the outset of Ezra 7. If events are telescoped, then generations might be telescoped as well. But this brings us to the second problem with Ezra's genealogy, namely, that genealogies in antiquity were constructed for socio-political purposes, and this included the grafting of unrelated individuals into established priestly lineages. This does not mean that Ezra possessed no Aaronide heritage; in fact, the claims of Ezra 7:1–5 would only be acceptable to an ancient audience if that audience already believed Ezra was part of the priestly caste. However, it is impossible to assume that the lineage recounted in Ezra 7:1–5 is historically accurate based on our understanding of genealogical formation in the ancient world, not to mention the clear indications that the genealogy as it stands already plays with historical facts, as discussed above.

Sidebar 6.16: Biblical Genealogies

The Hebrew Scriptures are full of genealogies, a genre of text that the Gospel writers also use to great rhetorical effect. Genealogies establish groups relationships but also establish rank within them, and studies into the formation of genealogies in both ancient and modern societies reveal that they are fluid and malleable. That is, a genealogy can change to reflect changes in group dynamics. This is evident especially in the Levite genealogies in the book of Numbers and 1 Chronicles 6, where some Levite names appear in different order than others. For example, Num. 26:58 identifies the Mushite priestly clan as among a small (and very ancient) set of Levite groups, and many scholars view the Mushites as a lineage of genuine antiquity and significant power on the basis of other pieces of textual evidence. However, by the time the Mushites appear in 1 Chronicles 6 (as the ancestor "Mushi" in v. 4), they are but a common division of Levite clans in parallel with other and boasting no special status or antiquity. Genealogies may also be used for symbolic or hermeneutical purposes: genealogical structures can "write out" episodes or periods that authors wish to avoid discussing, or establish closer connections between individuals separated by many generations by skipping the names of figures from those intervening decades or even centuries.

The second issue pertains to Ezra's actual role, which carries both sacral and imperial dimensions. We are informed in Ezra 7:6–10 that even more important than Ezra's priestly background is his background as a scribe—he is a "trained **scribe** in the *Torah* of Moses," and had committed himself to its study, teaching and promulgation. It is possible that the redactors of EN are trying to amplify the social and religious credentials of scribes beyond their secondary status to Aaronide priests (certainly the "norm" during the Persian period and even beyond). Does Ezra 7:6–10 attempt to say that his scribal traits trump his priestly background? Or does it suggest the opposite, namely, that Ezra's scribal skill and commitment is a function of his venerable priestly heritage? While priests are regularly criticized throughout EN, the institution of the priesthood itself may be a separate issue, and it remains difficult to determine whether or not Ezra, as a "scribe," counters or augments the potential influence of priests in Persian period Judaism.

Sidebar 6.17: Scribes

As noted above, scribes in the Persian period were trained in Aramaic language and culture, were schooled in esoteric knowledge and enjoyed access to temple libraries where sacred texts were stored and studied. Scribes thus carried a sacral pedigree: to be a scribe meant that an individual had some sort of special knowledge of the cosmos and divine intention. But scribes were also active well beyond these restricted spheres. Scribes in antiquity were standard figures in the royal court, ministers of state and diplomats. Scribes also served the public, providing professional services for non-literate people in need of written services. The Mesad Hashavyahu text is an example of such a service, written by a scribe for an ordinary citizen in need of conveying a written petition but lacking the abilities to do so on his own. Though this text dates from the era of monarchic Israel, it reflects the type of function that scribes played down into the Persian period as well among the lay population of Yehud.

Figure 6.7: Replica of the Mesad Hashavyahu ostracon; Archaeological Museum Beit Miriam, Kibbutz Palmahim, Israel. Commons.wikimedia.org.

But in addition to being a scribe, Ezra is also identified, obliquely, by another term which occurs in his royal commissioning by Artaxerxes. According to Ezra 7:14, Artaxerxes empowers Ezra to "oversee" (Aramaic *le-baqrah*) Jewish concerns not just in the province of Yehud but throughout the entirety of the **satrapy** of Trans-Euphrates wherein it was located. In other words, Ezra is to govern as a sort of viceroy over Jews throughout the entire satrapy, a role that appears to be implied in other passages within Ezra 7 as well. While one may debate whether or not Ezra's scribal role is meant to trump his priestly credentials, it seems that his role as an imperial viceroy in Trans-Euphrates is indeed meant to convey a sense that the reach of the priesthood is subordinate to their place within a larger imperial whole, and one that has been entrusted to Ezra by no less than the emperor himself.

How much of this is a genuine memory of Ezra's historical function, however, cannot be determined with confidence. The source providing us with this information is the commissioning letter (ostensibly) stemming from the emperor Artaxerxes himself, the Artaxerxes Rescript (Ezra 7:12–26). The depiction of Ezra as imperial viceroy matches what is known of such administrators on the satrapal level, insofar as the Persian emperors established a complex network of reporters and even spies—the "eyes and ears" of the court—throughout their realm who were in need of oversight. But we have already seen that the Rescript's authenticity is not certain (see section 2). It seems safest, then, to view the Rescript as stemming from the redactors of EN who attempted to build an image of Ezra's imperial duties, based on actual memories regarding the role he played as a satrapal viceroy or perhaps simply attempting to portray him functioning in such a way due to the legacy of his accomplishments as an agent of the Persian court.

As suggested above, the redactors of EN have attempted to legitimize Nehemiah's later conduct and the legacy of his policies by recruiting the stature of a major figure like Ezra to establish precedents. Put differently, Nehemiah is presented as simply carrying out, in faithful and pious fashion, what his predecessor Ezra had established years earlier. Whoever the historical Ezra was, and whenever he lived and worked, a version of that man and his accomplishments becomes the cornerstone of the book of EN and Ezra 7 provides us with the prism through which the redactors refract their impressions of him. He is a liminal figure, standing between the Jewish world and the Persian court, between the priesthood in Jerusalem and exilic scribal groups, and pure rhetorical design and genuine history. In this sense, he is similar to Moses, who also stood between social, historical and cultural spaces in the Pentateuchal narratives, so it is not entirely surprising that as the unit continues with Ezra 8, Ezra's mission to Jerusalem is presented as a sort of second Exodus and Wilderness narrative. Though he is not a stranger in a strange land contending against a hostile foreign king, he nonetheless leads a group of Jews from a foreign land, through the wilderness, and ultimately to the land of their ancestors. And also like Moses, he leads this delegation with the law of YHWH firmly fixed in his hand as the vehicle through which authority is to be exercised under his watch.

With Ezra 8, Ezra recruits the right mixture of people to his delegation to ensure that upon his arrival in Jerusalem, he possesses enough supporters to ensure the success of his efforts and teachings. The various figures we are told that Ezra brings with him in his delegation serve these purposes, and the connection to Moses here may be made to the various sub-leaders Moses is said to have rallied during his time leading Israel through the wilderness, especially ranks of Levites recruited to serve as YHWH's priestly agents in varying capacities under Moses' guidance (Exod. 32:26–29; Deut. 33:8–11). Ezra 8:15–20 informs us that Ezra, too, recognizes the importance of Levites and sees to it that they are brought under his authority just as Moses had called the Levites to serve under him. In this episode, Ezra sends emissaries to recruit Levites from the city of **Casiphia**, a location that is depicted in cultic terms (Hebrew ha-maqom in v. 17, "the [sacred] place").

This has given rise to much scholarly speculation about what sort of "sacred place" Casiphia was. Some commentators have suggested that in Casiphia—a city in the heartland of Mesopotamia—stood some type of surrogate temple that the exilic population frequented and in which Levites were trained and served as ritual/cultic leaders. Others have posited that the Levites of Casiphia had established some type of proto-synagogue, a forerunner to the houses of sacred study and prayer that would emerge later in the Hellenistic period.[34] There is insufficient evidence to sustain either theory, but the latter proposal is probably somewhat closer to the reality. First, the very fact that Ezra was a resident of Babylon and a skilled, learned scribe reveals that such

---

34. For a more detailed discussion, see Leuchter 2009.

groups existed throughout the Jewish communities of Mesopotamia. Second, it is precisely during the Persian period that Jewish scribal groups were introduced to the tradition sacred scholarship of Mesopotamia, so it is likely that a group of Levites residing in Casiphia had developed some well-known facility as scribes and exegetes of native traditions subjected to these new norms. Ezra's recruiting of these Levites therefore served two simultaneous purposes: it cast his mission/delegation as conforming to authoritative and ancient traditions about Moses, but it also ensured that his supporters were intellectually current, sophisticated, and capable of setting Jewish affairs within a cosmopolitan Aramaic cultural context.

Sidebar 6.18: Sacred Space in Ancient Israel and Ancient Judaism

In most religious traditions, space plays an important role in the definition of social identity and worldview. Emergent Israel (i.e., the Israel of the pre-monarchic period) seem to have possessed a view of the highlands themselves as a sacred space, a special place sanctified by their deity where he planted his people to grow and flourish (Exod. 15:13, 17). This concept became associated with ancient sanctuary sites like Shechem, Shiloh and Beth El, connected to the traditions about the ancestors and serving as the meeting places of different lineages as well as the place of communion with the deity. This ideology was eventually transferred to Jerusalem and its temple, which by the Persian period was understood as the center of the Jewish cosmos and the place from which the holiness of YHWH could flow out to the rest of the world. Yet during the period of the Babylonian Exile, other concepts of sacred space emerged as a way to cope with the trauma of forced displacement and residence in foreign lands. Texts and literary traditions created and taught in these places came to serve as surrogates for the now-destroyed temple, and the production and study of text became a surrogate for rituals once conducted at the temple. By the mid-fifth century BCE, a temple cult was once again active in Jerusalem, but the textual/study traditions fostered at these other sites—sacred places in a rather different way—had become a fixed feature of traditional devotion.

Ezra 8 concludes with a report of Ezra's appropriation of monetary resources for the Jerusalem temple and his entrusting of those resources to the agents working underneath him. At first glance, this report appears to direct attention to the temple cult, and has led some scholars to view a priestly agenda underlying these verses (and, indeed, the entirety of Ezra 7—8). But one must make a distinction between a cultic concern or focus and a specifically priestly focus. Just as Ezra 7:1-5 conditions how we perceive the text's statements regarding his scribal skills, so too should the Levites of Casiphia episode in Ezra 8:15-20 shade the purpose of the cultic emphasis in these verses. It is, after all, the same figures that Ezra has recruited to his delegation who are entrusted with resources for the temple—not the priests of Jerusalem who are already ensconced therein, since there is no indication that the funds, vessels and other treasures mentioned in this closing report were ever handed over to the ruling priestly clan stationed in the temple on Ezra's arrival.

5.3. Ezra 9—10

The commissioning of Ezra and the account of his delegation immediately gives way to what is arguably the central event in the entirety of EN, namely, Ezra's separation of the community from "**the people of the land**" and his dissolution of mixed marriages. This remains one of the most troubling narratives for both literary analysis and the historical reconstruction of fifth-century BCE life in Yehud. On the literary level, Ezra 9—10 constitutes a single narrative, but switches from a first person account voiced by Ezra himself into a third person account in Ezra 10 voiced by an anonymous author. Scholars have puzzled over this shift, with most arguing that Ezra 10 must be a later addition to an existing Ezra narrative ending in Ezra 9; it is, therefore, viewed as a different source, perhaps drawing from older records or archival data but entering the book of EN at a fairly advanced stage in its growth.

This may be the case, but it is significant to note that the shift from first person to third person is an effective stylistic device. The various authors of EN were familiar already with earlier Israelite texts that exhibit similar shifts—the book of Jeremiah, in particular, moves back and forth between Jeremiah's first person oracles and different third person narrative units (see, e.g., Jeremiah 26—27; 33—34; etc.), and the book of Isaiah contains similar, though more limited, examples of this technique (Isaiah 36—39 as third person narratives within a sequence of largely first person oracles). Even if Ezra 9 and Ezra 10 derive from different sources, their pairing creates a sense of continuity between Ezra's activity and earlier prophetic pronouncement, lending the impression that the latter is finally fulfilled through Ezra's mission and actions.

Historically, the episode of Ezra 9—10 is problematic because its contents are extremely polemically charged, impugning what seems to be the entire high-ranking cast of the Jerusalem priesthood and many outstanding members of the community for "foreign" intermarriage. The real question here is whether these marriages were genuinely regarded as illegitimate ethnic intertwining or if it is only the authors of Ezra 9—10 who cast them in such a manner. Though ethnic boundaries are strongly emphasized throughout EN, we have seen that this is primarily a view developed and advanced by the *gola* community in relation to Jews of the homeland rather than in relation to nations who did not share in the pre-exilic heritage of monarchic period Judah. Marriages between members of the *gola* community and those of the homeland community could help establish land tenure, providing for greater prosperity in a region primarily devoted to agriculture for sustenance and profit.

The very fact that so many priests are indicted in Ezra 9—10 indicates that social and economic reconciliation between the *gola* and homeland groups *was* the norm, not the exception, by the mid-fifth century BCE, adopted by the religious leadership and lay population alike. For these people, the homeland groups were not necessarily beyond reach or redemption, theologically speaking, and were certainly not considered "foreign."

Sidebar 6.19: "Foreign" and "Native" in the Hebrew Scriptures

Ancient Israel possessed a mythology where YHWH their deity cleared the landscape and sanctified it for Israel's residence. From the vantage point of a contemporary reader, this appears as a fairly monolithic way of conceiving of Israelite ethnicity, but the closer one looks at the biblical record, the more complicated the matter becomes. Nationality as we understand it was not on the conceptual horizon of ancient Israelites. In early Israel, the term "native" could relate to membership within a tribe or clan residing in a particular tract of land; an Israelite from another tribe or territory could conceivably be a "foreigner" to those with deep attachments to ancestral land. With the rise of the monarchic states this changed somewhat, with degrees of kinship forged through participation in common state-based society but boundaries still maintained on familial levels. The fall of the northern kingdom (721 BCE) and the influx of northern refugees into Judah led to reformulations of what "Israelite" ethnicity might mean; by the late monarchic period, a foreigner was primarily someone who was not a resident of the land of Judah. By the Persian period, circumstances changed: populations living in Yehud who had no connection to the experience of exile into Babylon were viewed as "foreigners" by the *gola* community (who saw themselves as the true "natives"), even if they claimed to descend from common pre-exilic populations as those who had returned from exile. The irony, of course, is that the *gola* community could easily be viewed as the "foreign" group, since their residence in the land was relatively new. The idea of "native" vs. "foreign" became a potent polemical or propagandistic weapon, used to claim or deny tradition, space, and political power.

It is clear, though, that some members of the *gola* community viewed these marriages as dangerous. Children born from these marriages could lay claim to inheritance resources that might otherwise be retained or claimed by *gola* members, and this may have been viewed not simply as a financial problem but as a cosmic or theological one as well. Marginalization from the community might lead to marginalization from the temple cult and from social standing on the level of government, both of which were viewed as connections to YHWH's will as expressed through the Persian imperial world order. And, indeed, a recurring theme throughout EN is the tenuous social and cultic position of the communities of Yehud—a constant state of competition, replete with charges of sedition and religious corruption, characterizes interaction between the diverse groups addressed in the book.

What we encounter in Ezra 9—10 is a narrative that concentrates this tension into a single episode, one that makes a strong rhetorical case in a particular direction for the benefit of a particular faction—most probably, that of the *haredim* referred to in Ezra 9:4 and 10:3, who appear to have viewed Ezra as their leader or who later rallied behind his name and memory. Intermarriage between *gola* and homeland groups was in all probability a living issue throughout the Persian period, but it is impossible to determine if this highly charged narrative reflects an actual historical moment or if it is a symbolic narrative conceived to dramatize, and clarify, the exclusive *gola* ideology.

The centerpiece of the episode is certainly the prayer recited by Ezra in Ezra 9:6–15. The initial few verses of the chapter establish the mixed marriages as the reason for the prayer, especially with respect to the issue of the "holy seed" (Ezra 9:2) at risk of being compromised—carrying forward the concept of the *gola* being ethnically different and recruiting a term regarding progeny to characterize the group. The issue may be the possibility of the "holy seed" being tarnished or diluted, but it may also be the issue of the "holy seed" being extended to non-*gola* populations, thereby legitimizing them in an irrevocable manner. Whatever the case, Ezra's prayer is uttered in order to intensify the boundaries around the *gola* and their future progeny by confessing sin and appealing for divine mercy in the face of the alleged disregard for divine will (vis-à-vis the mixed marriages).

Here, the authors of the episode draw from a liturgical form that had gained increased currency by the mid-fifth century BCE, that of the **penitential prayer**. Already in the late monarchic period, this type of exhortation had emerged as part of the prophetic tradition, with the prophet standing at a distance from a cult under criticism, offering an alternative to the rites and rituals of expiation and purification conducted by the priests. The use of this form by Ezra is therefore especially appropriate given the criticism lodged at the priesthood in Ezra 9–10; it suggests that the priestly ritual was, on its own, insufficient at facilitating expiation and re-connection to YHWH. In this way, Ezra's prayer extends the theme we have already detected in Ezra 8, namely, that priestly spheres of conduct must be subordinated to Ezra's imperial and scribal authority.

The tenor of Ezra's prayer has garnered great scholarly attention also for its many allusions to earlier traditions already regarded as authoritative by the authors of Ezra 9–10. In Ezra's prayer, one finds many allusions to the book of Deuteronomy as well as the Priestly literature in the Pentateuch; this is important because the Deuteronomic and Priestly traditions are rather distinct in their understanding of the divine, law, sin/transgression, purity and holiness, and concepts of forgiveness and restoration (personal and communal). As noted above, most scholars see these works emerging from very different scribal groups with unique and often mutually exclusive views of Israelite identity, history, and theology. But the exegetical strategy of the prayer seems to harmonize these different sources. For the authors of the prayer, all of these traditions were fair game and were open to reuse for the sake of legitimizing their social and political preferences.

Alongside this combination of legal traditions, Ezra's prayer also invokes the prophets (Ezra 9:11–12), and presents these Deuteronomic and Priestly terms as emerging from prophetic teaching. The passage in question does not name these prophets, and most commentators see an attempt to connect Ezra's prayer to the prophetic tradition only in general. However, closer scrutiny suggests that the authors have the prophets Jeremiah and Ezekiel in mind. Ezekiel appears to have originated the ideology behind the *gola* community in general, as his oracles emphasize the uniqueness of those taken into exile and the accursed status of those who remained in the land. And the oracles of the prophet Jeremiah develop a discourse of the land being defiled by the corruption of the people—a theme very much at the heart of Ezra 9—10—as well as language regarding the giving of sons and daughters in marriage among those living in exile (Jer. 29:5–7). The authors of Ezra's prayer have taken this to another level, interpreting it to mean that marriage can only take place between families who earlier experienced exile. In addition, Jeremiah, and Ezekiel would have been recognized as the major prophets of the exilic period, and thus the channels for YHWH's voice to those in exile. For a *gola*-oriented set of authors and audiences, the invocation of these prophets (however subtle) sets Ezra as the trustee of their teachings and authority, fit to interpret and implement their words to suit an agenda presented as consistent with them.

The episode continues in the sudden switch to the third person narrative in Ezra 10—the opening verses of the chapter introduce the reader to a new character, Shechaniah the son of Jehiel, who implores Ezra to take charge of the matter and enforce the dissolution of mixed marriages within the *gola* community (vv. 1–4). Shechaniah remains somewhat elusive within EN, but most commentators agree that he must have been a ranking member of the faction of haredim that stood behind the move to separate entirely from the homeland groups. His words to Ezra here suggest that Ezra's leadership over this group involved a degree of power-sharing between himself as a sacral leader and other important members of the community.

Sidebar 6.20: Jeremiah's Letter to the Exiles

According to Jer. 29:1–3, a delegation of state officials traveled to Babylon in the year 593 BCE—four years after the captivity of leading citizens following Babylon's conquest of Jerusalem. With this delegation, the prophet Jeremiah apparently sent a letter advising those captives to settle in for the long haul. The letter reads:

> Thus says YHWH of hosts, the God of Israel, unto all the captivity, whom I have caused to be carried away captive from Jerusalem unto Babylon: Build houses, and dwell in them, and plant gardens, and eat the fruit of them; take wives, and beget sons and daughters; and take wives for your sons, and give your daughters to husbands, that they may bear sons and daughters; and multiply there, and be not diminished. And seek the peace of the city whither I have caused you to be carried away captive, and pray unto YHWH for it; for in the peace thereof shall you have peace. (Jer. 29:4–7)

In this letter, Jeremiah lays out a divine command from YHWH that the captives of 597 should look to their immediate surroundings as a space in which YHWH willed for them to reside. To attempt to rebel against their captors was, in fact, to resist divine intention. The remainder of Jeremiah 29 preserves the back-and-forth between those who disagreed with Jeremiah's words and the prophet's counter-arguments. In the end, Jeremiah's letter became the basis for a new sense of group identity for the captives of 597. Based on the letter, they came to see themselves as the special, elect group that YHWH had set aside from the corrupted citizens who still resided in Jerusalem and the land, and Jeremiah's letter became a sort of community charter for their own unique sense of sacred identity.

It is notable that Ezra 10 repeatedly refers to Ezra as "the priest" (vv. 10, 16), and his activity is focused on emphasizing communal transgression and leading public rites of expiation and confession over "the congregation" (vv. 12, 14). The two complement each other in some manner, as suggested by Shechanaiah's words: Ezra functions as a qualified master of ceremonies, but is characterized as the representative of ideas and values that Shechaniah and others must have espoused which challenged Aaronide priestly authority. Ezra 10 does not identify Ezra as the high priest or chief priest, but the emphasis on his priestly title and duties coupled with his interaction with Shechaniah and other members of the community positions the *haredim* as powerful rivals of the social order that had obtained under the Aaronide priesthood more generally.

Ezra 10 thus testifies to an attempt, or at least the desire, of the *haredim* to set the entire religious agenda for the *gola* community over against other points of view and systems of belief that had developed within that community down to the mid-fifth century BCE. Whether this attempt was successful or not is left unclear in the current form of EN; the narrative ends with the notice of who was subject to the forced dissolution of the "mixed" marriages, but there is no additional information provided regarding the efficacy of the policy or its duration. Indeed, the very next episode within EN is that of Nehemiah's mission to Yehud to serve as governor (Nehemiah 1), an event that takes place some thirteen years after Ezra's alleged activity in Jerusalem, and we are not informed about what occurred over this thirteen years gap. The tale of Ezra's activity—at least within the primary narrative spanning Ezra 7—10—ends on this ambiguous note, which begs the question as to what purpose the redactors of Ezra 7—10 thought this might serve.

If the memory of Ezra was rhetorically reshaped by the redactors, then one strong possibility is that these redactors end the primary account of his activity where they do because the issue of separation from the homeland groups was a theological argument in need of more practical political justification. That justification emerges from the redactional shaping of Ezra's mission, and Ezra 10 serves as the culmination of a narrative through-line that we may trace all the way back to Ezra 7, with its relativizing of earlier power structures in Yehud to the new standard represented by Ezra and his imperial commission. This continues in Ezra 8 with the assembly of a sacred delegation presented as a typological mirror of the earliest sacral caste formed by Moses himself in the mythic past but also qualified by the new potency of enculturation in Aramaic scribal scholarship—implying that the Jerusalem priests were subordinate to these new sacerdotal figures. This is followed in Ezra 9 by Ezra's prayer, which by drawing from variant traditions also rooted the agenda of the *haredim* in authoritative precedent.

Ezra 10 continues this by showing how the community actualizes Ezra's liturgical professions and, by extension, the will of YHWH as preserved in the earlier authoritative traditions upon which he relies. The dissolution of the marriages becomes the manifestation of this, revealing that for the *haredim* and the redactors of Ezra 7—10, the exclusive purity and piety of the *gola* community was the ultimate purpose of the restoration to Yehud under Persian auspices and an imperial agent such as Ezra. Ezra 10 makes the final case that YHWH valued the purview of the *haredim* because it is the agency of the Persian Empire, at every step of the way, which facilitated and justified their separation from all other groups claiming Jewish heritage in Yehud.

5.4. Nehemiah 1—3

Immediately following the account of the intermarriage crisis, the narrative moves to the introduction to Nehemiah and his commission as emissary of the royal court of Artaxerxes. The abrupt change leads some to see the Nehemiah narrative as the beginning of an entirely new literary work joined to the book of Ezra only at an extremely late date, and several good cases can be made for the original independence of the Ezra source material from that of the Nehemiah source material. However, EN possesses too many parallels to be viewed as primarily independent and distinct entities, and the quick shift from Ezra 10 to Nehemiah 1 may be read instead as an indication of continuity: that is, Nehemiah's gubernatorial tenure is a natural "next step" following the type-scene we encounter in the intermarriage crisis in Ezra 9—10. Read this way, the principles of communal uniqueness beginning with the purging of mixed marriages in Ezra 9—10 is carried out in a more thoroughgoing manner by Nehemiah's overall approach to governing the province of Yehud, and indeed the account of Nehemiah's activity repeatedly returns to this theme and the notion that the *gola* community's position in the land is both separate from the those of other groups and sponsored/favored by no less than Artaxerxes himself, the power standing behind Nehemiah's local authority in the province.

The emphasis on the privileged nature of *gola*-heritage is apparent from the outset of the Nehemiah account, which returns the reader to the Persian court in the eastern Diaspora (the capital city of **Susa**). This, we have already seen, is an essential feature of social and religious legitimacy in Ezra—Nehemiah, and thus the "returns" to this setting when introducing Nehemiah into the narrative. Though scholars generally do not doubt that Nehemiah himself originated in the eastern Diaspora before returning to the homeland as a royal emissary, the choice to begin the narrative in this context bestows upon him not only a degree of social prestige but also a brand of piety that ancient audiences would have associated specifically with residence in Mesopotamia. Throughout the period of the Babylonian Exile and indeed well into the fifth century BCE, Jewish theologians developed a sense that the cosmic center of the world was somehow tied to Babylon as much as Jerusalem. This is found especially in the book of Jeremiah, where the prophet's oracles repeatedly emphasize the favor of YHWH visited upon those taken to Babylon and aligns the record of revelation with the regnal history of Babylon's kings.

Figure 6.8: Pillar capital in the form of a bull, from Darius I's palace in Susa. Now in the Louvre; Commons.wikimedia.org.

By highlighting Nehemiah's origins in this same eastern geographical setting, his political goals are thus aligned with this religious-mythic ideology and positioned as an expression of divine will as much as Persian politics. But the narrative goes even one step further, as the Nehemiah narrative begins with a superscription nearly identical to the superscription to the book of Jeremiah (Neh. 1:1; Jer. 1:1), thus eliminating any doubt in the mind of the reader that no less than the record of Ezra's activity, Nehemiah's role is intimately tied to the fulfillment of prophecy.

It is significant that Nehemiah's first narrated act is a penitential prayer (Neh. 1:4–11) following word from his brother Hanani that Jerusalem laid in a compromised state. The prayer immediately recalls that of Ezra in Ezra 9 and similarly invokes various Pentateuchal traditions, but the outstanding feature of the prayer is its use of the term "servant." Virtually every verse of the prayer revolves around this term, identifying Moses, Israel, and finally Nehemiah himself as YHWH's servants. The hermeneutical strategy of this prayer is highly sophisticated, for the term "servant" also obviously carries political overtones in the context of an imperial system. In the ancient near east, the term "servant" indicated submission to a dominant political power—Israel's kings had, in the past, regularly identified themselves as the "servants" of foreign emperors. The use of this term in Nehemiah's prayer indicates that his piety as a Jew and thorough submission to YHWH is somehow at home in Persian statecraft; at the same time, the use of this term in such a pious prayer might be part of an argument that this emissary of the royal court was not simply an imperial bureaucrat but a man deeply committed to the religious heritage of his people. In both cases, the prayer manages to carry forward some of the impulses already encountered in the Ezra narrative, where the will of YHWH and the impetus of the imperial court are set in tandem with each other.

Nehemiah 2 continues with a surprisingly intimate account of Nehemiah's dialogue with the emperor Artaxerxes. Nehemiah, as the royal cup-bearer, informs the emperor of Jerusalem's dilapidation and requests a leave of absence to help restore it. Artaxerxes immediately consents and provides Nehemiah with resources and written assurances of safe travel to his destination. Nehemiah's choice of language and demeanor in the presence of Artaxerxes is a parade example of deference to the emperor's power and the protocol of the imperial court: requests are couched in formulaic language and recognition of the king's complete authority informs Nehemiah's first-person narration.

On the other hand, however, that same first-person narration makes clear that Nehemiah's motivation is at every turn informed by his piety and devotion to YHWH: the request to return to his ancestral homeland is made only after an apparently private/silent prayer to YHWH (vv. 4–5) and Artaxerxes' permission is granted due to "the good hand" of YHWH placed upon Nehemiah (v. 8). Finally, Nehemiah refers to himself once more as a "servant," but this time, it is as a servant of Artaxerxes (v. 5). The dialogue between Nehemiah and Artaxerxes thereby connects on several levels to the prayer in the preceding chapter, and royal prerogative and religious devotion are intertwined. When Nehemiah is on his way with letters of passage from Artaxerxes, the letters take on sacral dimensions to the ancient Jewish audience, establishing imperial policies and conduct not only as an expression of divine will but as a model of pious devotion.

The second half of Nehemiah 2 shifts into a more dramatic mode: Nehemiah reports that upon his return to Jerusalem, he took time to secretly survey the city's conditions before finally announcing that repairs to the city wall were in order. While we are informed that many of the local authorities displayed enthusiasm for the project, three notable figures voiced harsh dissent: Sanballat, Tobiah and, Geshem, all of whom are identified with foreign ethnicities (Horonite, Ammonite, and Arabian, respectively) and who are positioned within the Memoir as great adversaries to Jewish interests, and the chapter anticipates this earlier in v. 10 by identifying them as enemies of the "children of Israel." The phrase "children of Israel" is a potent rhetorical device, as its appearance is more common in pre-exilic sources. Its appearance here suggests that Sanballat, Tobiah, and Geshem are somehow avatars of older, even mythic enemies of the ancestors, and that Nehemiah's initiatives are thus essential to an ongoing struggle against such enemies (see above, section 2.2, regarding the implications of the letters in Ezra 4—6).

Scholars, however, have pointed to the fact that one of these "enemies," Tobiah, possesses a good Yahwistic name (Hebrew tovîyah—"YHWH is my goodness" or "YHWH is good to me"). Tobiah's identification as an Ammonite is most likely a reflection of his geographical residence and not his ethnicity; he was, in all likelihood, a Jew who was simply not a member of the *gola* community under Nehemiah's charge. But this only continues the persistent ideology within Ezra—Nehemiah that the *gola* community was the true, and exclusive, inheritor of Israelite status and its religious legacy; all others who claim such a connection are illegitimate.

Figure 6.9: *The Rebuilding of the Temple under Ezra and Nehemiah*, pen and ink over pencil tracing, by Julius Schnorr von Carolsfeld, ca. 1846. Commons.wikimedia.org.

The issue taken by Tobiah, Sanballat and Geshem with Nehemiah's mission was therefore probably strictly a matter of economic or political interest, not religious or ethnic. But the Memoir, as we have seen, equates politics with religion and has already presented Nehemiah's mission as equally a matter of Persian administration and divine will. The characterization of political adversaries as foreign religious enemies is thus an easy step, and establishes a pointed "us vs. them" rhetoric that looks ahead to one of the most important dimensions of the Memoir, namely, the rebuilding of the Jerusalem city wall in Nehemiah 3. Building projects elsewhere in the Hebrew Bible receive some attention but usually little more than a few verses, and even those are fairly sparse or general in tone. The exceptions to this are the accounts of the building of the Jerusalem temple in 1 Kings 6—8 and that of its rebuilding in Ezra 3. This is to be expected, as temples were perceived in the ancient world not only as centrifugal sites for community identity but as portals to the realm of the divine. It is highly significant, then, that similar attention is given to the building of Jerusalem's wall in Nehemiah 3, which goes into great detail regarding the corners of Yehudite society who participated in this enterprise.

The account of the wall project is the defining event in Nehemiah's career as it was remembered by the later shapers of the Memoir. It is not only a rebuilding of the wall but, as Wright puts it, a rebuilding of identity. Participation in the project is itself an affirmation of one's standing in the exclusive *gola* community under Nehemiah's charge, but as we have seen, this carries a double meaning: alignment with Nehemiah simultaneously secures one's place within the political structure of the Persian Empire and one's place within the community chosen by YHWH to be the bearers of his covenant. In a sense, this same concern informs the narrative of Ezra 3 in relation to the building of the temple, but the fact that it now pertains to the building of the Jerusalem city wall indicates that the special political-sacral status in question extends well beyond the temple precincts and its priestly faculty. The city of Jerusalem itself emerges here as the anchor of Jewish identity, and the temple is subordinated to it.

Sidebar 6.21: Nehemiah's Wall

Nehemiah 1—6 is mostly concerned with Nehemiah's efforts to rebuild the wall of Jerusalem. Though there is no archaeological evidence for this structure, there is no reason to believe that it was not built—only that it was a symbolic rather than utilitarian enterprise and not constructed in a manner that would endure for an extended period of time. The wall, however, becomes a vehicle for identifying and binding together different lineages of *gola* families and clans in Yehud, all of whom contribute to its construction within the narrative of Nehemiah's Memoir. The rebuilding of the wall by all of these families and clans becomes, as biblical scholar Jacob Wright has put it, a way of "rebuilding identity" as a cohesive community with strong ties to Jerusalem and its social/religious role in Jewish life.[35]

All the same, it is important to note that Nehemiah 3 recounts the building of the wall with a particular emphasis on priestly families. The event is punctuated at regular intervals with reminders that priests were prominent contributors to the rebuilding effort. How much of

35. Wright 2004.

this is historical is a matter of debate, since EN in general shows signs of development well into the Hellenistic era and at the hands of priestly editors/redactors. It may be that an original account of Nehemiah's activity was supplemented or even over-written by scribes with priestly interests and biases—in which case, the predominance of priests in Nehemiah 3 may be an attempt to steer a populist-oriented narrative in the direction of priestly authority. This would, in effect, make a case for priestly authority as nested well beyond the temple precincts, an idea that survived in later Jewish sectarian thought such as that of the Pharisees, who saw holiness as something that could take root in non-cultic contexts. But even this presupposes a circumstance where sanctity was extended beyond the traditional roost of priests under Nehemiah's leadership with which later priestly redactors had to contend. This attests to the durability of his policies that repositioned and redefined authority and identity as contingent upon imperial-civil activity and not only sacral or ritual conduct.

Yet despite the participation of disparate social castes within Nehemiah's community, the closing portion of Nehemiah 3 (vv. 33–37) reveal that all is not well—the enemies of the community already identified much earlier in the Memoir (Sanballat and Tobiah) appear to see the wall project as a threat upsetting the balance of power in the region. The motivation for this indignant attitude toward the wall project is presented here as yet another example of the "anti-Jewish" attitudes of these antagonists, building upon the earlier antagonism they exhibited at Nehemiah's mere attempt to better the circumstances of the *gola* community. But it is much more likely that their opposition to Nehemiah's wall project was rooted primarily in concern that the Yehudite community under Nehemiah was in fact engaging in a program aimed at disrupting stability in the region.

The rebuilding of the wall could certainly be viewed as a pre-emptive effort at fortification in the anticipation of battle, especially since the wall project was conducted while the specter of militant revolts elsewhere in the Persian Empire remained fresh in public memory. The broader characterization of Sanballat and Tobiah as enemies of the Yehudite community may constitute an attempt by the redactors of the Memoir (or possibly by Nehemiah himself) to disqualify concerns regarding the wall project as emerging from unjustified ethnic prejudices; by so doing, the texts collectively affirm that the rebuilding project was hardly conceived for illegitimate purposes. Rather, the threats from these enemies of Yehud take on greater force, justifying the creation of a wall for the protection of the community bound together by the symbolic importance of Jerusalem.

5.5. Nehemiah 4—6

The chapters immediately following the account of the rebuilt wall are intimately connected to the closing notice in Nehemiah 3, as we learn that while the wall was being rebuilt, Nehemiah and his community remained vigilant and armed themselves against possible violent threat. The nature of this threat is spelled out in the first few verses of the chapter: it is, not surprisingly, the same enemies mentioned in previous chapters, only now, the potential for conflict is amplified. The Memoir claims that Sanballat, Tobiah and a confederation of opponents were poised to disrupt (through violent means) the wall-rebuilding project; how much of this is historically accurate remains debatable, but it seems reasonable to conclude that these verses attest to regional dispute regarding centers of power. Until Nehemiah's time, Yehud had been overshadowed by the province of Samaria in the north, and the rebuilding of its wall (along with, no doubt, other forms of economic and military reinforcement) would obviously upset the balance of power not only for the elite of Samaria but also for surrounding territories. Whatever means were actually deployed by Nehemiah to maintain the integrity of his gubernatorial policies are represented in Nehemiah 4 as a matter of communal union and vigilance, coupled of course with piety. Nehemiah 4:3, 8 pair the preparations for battle with prayer to YHWH, which contributes, again, to the presentation of Nehemiah's political actions as bearing sacral overtones.

But it is also highly significant that this chapter emphasizes the manner in which the citizens of Yehud prepared themselves for battle. We are informed that the citizenry continued to build the wall with construction tools in one hand and a weapon in the other. Moreover, the weapons are described in vivid terms: swords, spears, and bows, i.e., the weapons of the professional military, not of an *ad hoc* civilian militia. This is reinforced by the subsequent comments that the building activity was buttressed by coordinated military deployment, with battalions set in strategic place to protect those who continued to build the wall (vv. 7, 15–17). All of this, however, is subsumed under the rubric of holy war, as Nehemiah declares that "our God will fight for us" (v. 14) should the adversaries launch any attack. Not only does this declaration tap into some of the oldest traditions regarding YHWH's relationship to his people in Israelite religion (cf. Exodus 15; Judges 5; Psalm 68), it identifies both the people's defensive measures and the construction of the wall itself as an invocation of YHWH as a warrior and the entire affair as a devotional act.

Figure 6.10: Detail from a frieze of archers and lancers in Darius I's palace in Susa; now in the Louvre. Commons.wikimedia.org.

Whatever the historical reality was behind Nehemiah's wall project, Nehemiah 4 characterizes it as an expression of religious piety and not strictly a matter of politics. Such an argument may well have formed in the wake of charges by surrounding Persian officials that Nehemiah's conduct in Jerusalem was somehow working against the interests of Persian politics in the region—which, we have seen, is repeatedly presented as virulent anti-Jewish in the rhetoric of the Memoir, providing the antagonistic foil for the presentation of Nehemiah as an early Jewish hero.

For many scholars, what follows in Nehemiah 5 presents somewhat of a conundrum, since the chapter contains a report of an economic crisis and Nehemiah's execution of policies to address and resolve it. At first glance to contemporary readers, this seems to break with the wall-building materials in Nehemiah 3—4, and is not uncommon for commentators to suggest that Nehemiah 5 is out of place or even the result of some textual corruption in the transmission of written traditions. However, Nehemiah 5 is entirely at home in its present setting when we realize that it carries forward the idea of Nehemiah as a Jewish hero by demonstrating that his actions to resolve the economic crisis are every bit as important in defining Jewish identity as the building of the wall and the defense of the population.

A closer look at Nehemiah 5 lays bare what is at stake: the terms of debt between poorer and wealthier members of the *gola* community threaten the integrity of the group. In the ancient world, debt was often repaid through forms of servitude, and the community thus stood on the precipice of several transgressions: Pentateuchal law prohibits an Israelite from subjecting a member of his own community to debt slavery (Lev. 25:39), and the pre-exilic prophets had declared YHWH's judgment against Israelite communities for engaging in these practices (Jer. 34:8–22). Nehemiah's quick action in compelling his wealthy peers to forgive the debts (Neh. 5:8–13) not only protected the poor but maintained the covenantal terms addressed in the earlier Pentateuchal and prophetic traditions. Not only, then, does Nehemiah 5 conform to the pattern within EN of binding together imperial and Jewish authority, but it also demonstrates that the reconstruction and supporting of social and religious values must accompany the reconstruction of Jerusalem's wall if the community involved in the latter was to remain strong and cohesive.

All of these motifs converge in the finale to a major structural unit of the Memoir, namely, Nehemiah 6. In this chapter, Nehemiah continues his first-person report of challenges and threats as he completes the work on Jerusalem's wall, and the familiar cast of adversarial characters (Sanballat, Tobiah, Geshem) receive their expected mention. Sanballat, for example, writes a letter where he charges Nehemiah with attempting to establish monarchic credentials through his building efforts, which squares with the earlier charges of rebellion and sedition lobbed against the *gola* group within Ezra—Nehemiah. However, Nehemiah 6 also introduces another dimension of threat—that of prophetic voices poised to upset the cohesion of the community and Nehemiah's leadership of it. Part of Sanballat's letter accuses Nehemiah of recruiting prophets to herald his would-be kingship (v. 7), which reveals that the status of prophets and the nature of prophecy was a live issue in the period.

The issue of prophecy is of particular importance. Nehemiah 6 makes mention of a few figures who are depicted in quasi- or full prophetic terms; in Neh. 6:10, we encounter one Shemaiah b. Delaiah b. Mehetabel, who offers an oracle to Nehemiah that he takes asylum within the temple for his own protection. Nehemiah informs the reader that he "discerned" that this oracle was false and that Shemaiah was in fact working in the interest of his adversaries, which highlights the view in EN that authoritative prophecy was a phenomenon of an earlier time enshrined in written records. It is for this reason that the study of written text becomes important in the ensuing chapters, but this idea also sets the terms for how other prophets are mentioned in the remainder of the chapter—Neh. 6:14 speaks of "Noadiah and the rest of the prophets," who apparently constituted a prophetic faction working against Nehemiah as well.

We do not learn much about Noadiah or these other prophets beyond their alleged adversity to Nehemiah's leadership. According to Nehemiah, they attempted to put him "in fear," which is not inconsistent with how the legitimate prophets in the biblical tradition function: they attempt to move their audiences to fear YHWH according to the terms of their oracles. But the Memoir does not preserve their oracles or any details regarding their political or sacral perspectives. Within the rhetorical parameters of Nehemiah 6, the implication is that Noadiah and her prophetic peers are false prophets who do not represent the will of YHWH but who, like Shemaiah, are commissioned by enemies of the community; they are regarded as "false prophets."

At the same time, this is never stated, and there are reasons to question whether this would have been a widely held belief in Nehemiah's time. It is significant that Noadiah is a female prophet: we are told virtually nothing about her beyond this fact, and thereafter, she is simply associated with a band of enemy prophets that Nehemiah condemns. We must bear in mind that within EN, women are often targets of the authors, and it may be that in order to justify the condemnation of this prophetic band, a female member of their ranks is highlighted and implied to be their leader. Like the women of the homeland in Ezra 9—10, Noadiah is presented as a religious threat to the *gola* group under Nehemiah's charge; Neh. 6:14 manages to imply that Noadiah and the other prophets present a similar threat. With the precedent of Shemaiah a few verses earlier, this threat is further qualified as bearing the stain of foreign influence.

5.6. Nehemiah 7

The careful construction of opposition in Nehemiah 6 chapter suggests that these prophetic voices were accepted by a good number of people in Nehemiah's time, and that his opposition to them (and the opposition of his followers) required significant justification. By presenting these prophetic figures as opponents to the wall-building project, Nehemiah 6 polarizes what was probably a very complex political reality and creates two camps: one that stood against Nehemiah's efforts to reconstitute the Jewish people through rebuilding Jerusalem, and one that stood against these efforts altogether. But since Nehemiah 6 also draws lines between the prophets of Nehemiah's day and the "true" prophets whose words were enshrined in text by that time, another important feature of EN resurfaces: the importance of authoritative text and the careful study of those texts as hallmarks of identity.

Nehemiah 7 initiates a succession of chapters where this theme receives increased and explicit attention. The chapter begins with Nehemiah's ordering his community following the completion of the wall project, and the first thing he does after this is turn to "the book of the genealogy of those who came up," that is, the register of names of the founding families of the *gola* community. We have already seen that this list, which appears also in Ezra 2 (with only very minor differences), was likely drawn from genuine archives and probably represents a population census of mid-fifth century BCE. In the context of both Ezra 2 and Nehemiah 7, however, this list obtains the symbolic role of delineating the legitimate inheritors of "Israelite" status due to their origination among families who endured the exile to Babylon in an earlier era. From this perspective, the list is not simply a list, but a witness to history in literary form—and thus an authentic vehicle for revelation.

In contrast to the prophets of Nehemiah 6, who are depicted as still delivering their prophecies as oral performances, EN consistently emphasizes prophetic revelation as a matter of written record, something that must be consulted and studied in order for its terms to be understood and applied. Part of the reason for this is that by the Persian period, prophetic texts were a part of the temple library and obtained a central position as part of the religious and intellectual curriculum of the elite. This, too, applied to other texts that were made part of the temple library, which included various forms of literature like communal lists such as what we encounter in Nehemiah 7. The deposition of such documents into the temple library rendered them more than mere lists: they became vehicles for revelation, repositories of information that, like prophecy, imparted divine will. Again and again, EN presents its contents as sacred discourses—indeed, EN appears to be a sort of parallel or corollary to the actual temple library fostered by the redactors of the work and the community they represent.

It is for this reason that Nehemiah turns to the list in Nehemiah 7 and studies it. The consultation of the list represents an act of devotion, declaring Nehemiah's faith in written revelation and sacred text over against contemporaneous religious posturing from the opposition groups mentioned in Nehemiah 6. In this way, Nehemiah is positioned as following in Ezra's footsteps, since Ezra is a scribe devoted to the study of sacred text (Ezra 7:6, 10). This sets the terms for Nehemiah's actions here, where the consultation of a sacred text (in this case, the list of *gola* returnees) reinforces his resolve in the face of opposition by making clear that his actions have heretofore conformed to social and religious ethics supported by authoritative written curriculum. But for the reader, Nehemiah's consultation of the archives further distances the oral discourses of the opposition factions from the hallmarks of religious authenticity. The *gola* group is enshrined in archival texts; the oracles of Noadiah and her prophetic peers are not (Nehemiah 6 alludes to them but does not record them). The redactors of EN have created a subtle but effective gauge for declaring continuity with the past—textualization heralds sacred legitimacy.

5.7. Nehemiah 8—10

In a dramatic shift from the *foci* of the Nehemiah Memoir, the narrative suddenly turns attention to Ezra, a figure who has not been seen, heard or mentioned since the end of Ezra 10. Gone are the discussions of the wall-building project, the strife with hostile neighbors, and even the first-person narrative form. Instead, Nehemiah 8 sets up a formal third-person narrative tableau: Ezra congregates the entirety of the *gola* community outside the temple (at the "water gate") and brings forward the "Torah of Moses" (v. 1) to read to the congregation. Beyond the redactional addition in Neh. 8:9, Nehemiah does not factor into the narrative; for the next few chapters, indeed, Nehemiah plays no real role. Rather, all attention is commanded by Ezra and his scribal/administrative agents. The likelihood is that an original and independent Ezra tradition has been redacted into its current location to serve some sort of rhetorical purpose—perhaps as a way of affirming that the events reported in the Nehemiah Memoir should be viewed in conversation with memories about Ezra, or as a way of indicating that Ezra and Nehemiah served different but complementary and consistent purposes in the rebuilding of early Jewish identity in the fifth century BCE.

In any case, one of the great questions regarding Nehemiah 8 has surrounded the identity of the "Torah of Moses" mentioned in v. 1—is it the same "Torah of Moses" mentioned in the introduction to Ezra in Ezra 7:6, or the "Torah of YHWH" from Ezra 7:10? Was it somehow connected with the law of the God-most-high mentioned in the Artaxerxes Rescript?

Sidebar 6.22: The Dura-Europos Synagogue

The Dura-Europos Synagogue in eastern Syria dates from fairly early in the Hellenistic period (ca. third century BCE) and contains a large number of expressive images reflecting the community's system of belief. Some of these images dovetail with narrative traditions in the Hebrew Scriptures. One image in particular shows a learned man of advanced age reading from a scroll; many have postulated that this represents Moses or Ezra, since these two figures are the outstanding scribe-teachers of *Torah* in Jewish antiquity.

Scholars remain divided on how best to identify this document. The emergence of Deuteronomy in the late-seventh century BCE already had utilized the term "Torah" to describe the contents of Moses' valedictory address, and there is no shortage of reliance upon the language of Deuteronomy throughout EN. So it may be that the phrase "Torah of Moses" in Nehemiah 8 is meant to invoke Deuteronomy, or at least a tradition or memory of how Deuteronomy was perceived and the role it played in earlier times. Alternately, the Priestly literature—especially the material in the book of Leviticus—also utilizes the term "Torah" repeatedly, and connects its contents with Moses as well. Moreover, since Ezra was himself a priest and since there is as much reliance on Leviticus as on Deuteronomy within EN, one might make the case that the "Torah of Moses" in Nehemiah 8 alludes to some form of the Priestly literature before it was worked into a larger context including Deuteronomy, the Exodus narratives, the Wilderness tradition, etc.

Figure 6.11: Ezra reads the scroll of the Torah; fresco from the third-century synagogue at Dura-Europos, Syria.

Most scholars have accepted the traditional Jewish view that Nehemiah 8 depicts the Pentateuch in its mature form, and that Ezra was the great mind responsible for compiling it and the first to teach its collective contents as a systematic, complete work. Part of the reason for this is that the book of Chronicles, written sometime ca. 350 BCE, knows and refers to a Pentateuch in essentially the same form as what has survived in the Canon.[36] Since Nehemiah 8 is set during Ezra's mission a century earlier, this would provide a comfortable amount of time from the premiere under Ezra of this Pentateuch to the point at which the Chronicler relied upon it as an authoritative source. Furthermore, a Pentateuch could build bridges between factions

36. Talshir 2001, 386–90.

within the *gola* community to reify its place and allegiance to the Persian imperial hierarchy. Indeed, Peter Frei's influential proposal regarding the Persian "authorization" of the Pentateuch has led many commentators to see its formation under Ezra as a sort of administrative and political enterprise (though many of these commentators take issue with some of Frei's assumptions and arguments about the degree of imperial authorization or influence involved).[37]

Sidebar 6.23: Ezra, the Torah, and Ancient Parallels

Scholars continue to disagree about how much historical information can be mined from Nehemiah 8, the chapter that presents Ezra as the trustee of the Pentateuch and its tradition of teaching. There are good reasons for seeing a the historical Ezra as somehow connected to the scribal enterprise that led to the redaction of the Pentateuch, not the least of which is the tale of Udjahorresnet, an Egyptian high official recruited by the Persian emperor Darius ca. 519 BCE to codify Egyptian law in a manner that benefitted Persian interests in the region. Researchers have frequently drawn parallels between the mission of Udjahorresnet and Ezra, seeing Ezra serving a similar purpose in Yehud with the codification of traditional Jewish laws (and related narratives) into the Pentateuch on behalf of the Persian authorities. But the theory that the Pentateuch was an imperially-sponsored enterprise has been strongly criticized over the last few decades of scholarly examination. It is more likely that the Pentateuch arose internally as a product of Jewish priest-scribes like Ezra who sought to coordinate Jewish traditions according to the prevailing elite intellectual customs of the time, but not necessarily as symbol of imperial power or authority over Jewish cultic/religious life. That the Aaronide priests of Jerusalem went on to use the Pentateuch as a basis for regulating Yehudite religious life and group identity contributed to the view that it benefitted Persian interest by maintaining social order, but this need not reflect direct imperial sponsorship of its production.

---

37. Frei 1984.

Figure 6.12: Statue of
the Egyptian scribe
Udjahorresnet; Museo
Gregoriano Egizio, the
Vatican. Photo: Sailko;
Commons.wikimedia.org.

There is every reason to accept the likelihood that Ezra contributed significantly to the eventual formation of the Pentateuch. His scribal training paired with his political influence could indeed stand behind the initiation of a project that sought to amalgamate earlier traditions into a single, authoritative national "constitution" for the *gola* community of Yehud. But whether a fully-formed Pentateuch should be credited to the historical Ezra of the mid-fifth century is a more difficult matter. Ancient narratives such as Nehemiah 8 serve ideological and symbolic rather than journalistic purposes; they are no transparent witnesses to events and are often composed decades or even centuries after the events they depict.

The consensus among most researchers is that while EN contains sources from the fifth century BCE, its primary formation extended well into the fourth century, i.e., around the same time as the formation of the book of Chronicles (which, we will see, holds a very different socio-political worldview), and there is good reason to see a core of the Pentateuch in the mid- to late-fifth century, at which point it reached a mature form. This likely took place at the hands of Levite scribes working in the Jerusalem temple; EN show strong associations between the Levites and the titular characters of each part of the book, so it is no wonder that the authors of Nehemiah 8 symbolically associated the work with Ezra himself. This would also explain the prominent role of Levites as Ezra's executive agents within Nehemiah 8, entrusted to teach and interpret the Pentateuch's contents—this reflects the reality of the late-Persian period to some degree, for the Levites of that time would have been responsible for teaching the Pentateuch to lay audiences who came to the precincts of the Jerusalem temple.

If the Chronicler used this same, newly formed Pentateuch, it is entirely possible that the authors of Nehemiah 8 lived and worked at the same time and sought to "claim" the Pentateuch for a different political or religious ideology. A memory of Ezra as a scribe, priest, and royal envoy who was well versed in much earlier Israelite tradition would be sufficient for the composition of a narrative that depicted him as the steward or trustee of the Pentateuch, employed for specific (and decidedly imperial) purposes. In this case, Nehemiah 8 represents how a group of late-Persian period writers conceived of Ezra, his authority, and the role of their own Pentateuch as a symbol of that authority. They highlighted the role of Levites in the account as a way of showing that even long ago, in the hoary day of the great Ezra himself, Levites had power. And they created a narrative that formed a model for how sacred texts produced and taught in the temple should be venerated, as well as the role they play in organizing and sanctifying the community.

Another important dimension of the Torah-reading ceremony in Nehemiah 8 are the somewhat obscure notices that as Ezra reads the text of the Torah, the Levite agents among the crowd "caused the people to understand the law" and "gave the sense" of what was being read (vv. 8, 12). One explanation is that the common language of the people was Aramaic rather than Hebrew, so the reading of ancient Hebrew texts required translation into Aramaic. This is certainly feasible given the cultural forces of the time, for Aramaic had become the *lingua franca* of the Persian Empire. But the notices might also suggest a tradition of teaching meant to accompany the reading of texts—especially sophisticated legal and covenant-treaty texts such as those in the Pentateuch that may have been hermetic or esoteric to the ears of a lay audience. Nehemiah 8 perhaps attempts to establish a liturgical standard where Levite instruction was to accompany and define the ways that older texts and teachings were to be understood and preserved for Hebrew speaking audiences, Aramaic speaking audiences, or both.

The foregoing suggestion is supported by the second half of Nehemiah 8, where we encounter a unique example of **inner-biblical exegesis** which perhaps preserves a particular teaching of the Levites with regard to older Pentateuchal legislation. Nehemiah 8:13–18 depicts Ezra convening a group of religious leaders to examine the Torah and in particular, the legislation regarding the observance of the feast of Tabernacles/Booths (Lev. 23:39–43). The narrative goes to specify in v. 15 that the people were to go out and collect various types of tree branches out of which they were to fashion their personal model Tabernacles/Booths, "as it is written," i.e., as commanded within the Torah. Yet Leviticus 23 does not contain this specific directive—it is not "written," in the textual sense, in the Pentateuchal law code subjected to analysis in Neh. 8:13–18.

Most commentators see this, then, as an example of an extra-biblical teaching or clarification derived from the general laws for the festival in Leviticus 23, and the phrase "as it is written" shows that this extra-biblical teaching is to be viewed as equally authoritative as the written text from which it was derived. Nehemiah 8, then, contains a parade example of how the Levites were to function in relation to the written Torah of Moses—like Ezra, they were charged with deriving new forms of instruction from the text, and these instructions were to be regarded as sacred outgrowths of the original written revelation. In short, Nehemiah 8 licenses authoritative teachings as well as authoritative texts, and communal identity is contingent upon both.

The prominence of the Levites in the previous chapter increases as they replace Ezra as the religious leaders of the *gola* community in Nehemiah 9. Ezra fades from view, but his interaction with the Levites in the Nehemiah 8 identifies them as authorized to lead in his absence as an old and persistent issue re-emerges, namely, the separation of the *gola* community from "all foreigners." As we have already seen, the status of "foreigner" is more of a polemical label than an accurate representation of a group's ethnicity within Ezra–Nehemiah: Tobiah the Ammonite is probably of Judahite descent, and the "foreign" women at the heart of the mixed-marriage episode in Ezra 9—10 were most likely homeland Judahites with ties to pre-exilic tradition. In

Nehemiah 9, however, the matter is approached in somewhat vague terms: the community seeks to fully separate from all foreigners, though no specific foreign "others" are named or mentioned. The community invokes what has already become a repeated trope throughout EN in a more general sense, which leads to the Levites' recitation of a penitential prayer in response.

The prayer is the centerpiece of Nehemiah 9 (vv. 4–37), which immediately follows upon the notice that the congregation sought to separate from foreigners (v. 2). A special sort of theological model is implied here: ethnic/national identity is attained not only by YHWH's sanctification of the group, but of the group's recognition of past infractions and declaration of repentance.[38] It was probably Levite groups who claimed this tradition on prayer, suggested also by the fact that Jeremiah—the prophet who is presented as engaging in similar penitential prayer (Jer. 14:1—15:4)—was also a Levite (Jer. 1:1; 32:6–15). While Aaronide priests commanded the privilege of serving at the sacrificial altar, Levites were strongly associated with liturgical poetry (e.g., the psalms of Asaph and Korah, both Levite groups), much of which eventually became the prayer curriculum in exilic and post-exilic Judaism, and which must have rivaled (or at least strongly complemented) the sacrificial system of the Aaronide priests.

The importance of the Levites and their prayer as a key to the community reconnecting with YHWH is part of a rhetorical strategy building on what we encounter in Nehemiah 8. In that chapter, community identity and theological orthodoxy is affirmed by the reading of the Torah, but this takes place outside of the Temple, not within it. This is actually counter to the standard practice throughout much of the Second Temple period and indeed throughout the ancient near east, where sacred texts were read in a temple complex. Nehemiah 8 moves the Torah beyond the temple, shifting the balance of power away from the temple priesthood and into a different sphere of influence. The same goal seems to undergird Nehemiah 9—Levites rather than Aaronide priests are the mediators between the people and their deity, with the latter making nary an appearance in the chapter. Moreover, the mediation intended to sanctify the community and facilitate their repentance takes place beyond the temple just like the reading of the Torah. In essence, the fate and future of the *gola* community is set not by priests officiating at YHWH's altar but by

---

38. A full study of Nehemiah 9 is that of Boda 1999.

scribes/administrators such as Ezra and the Levites who stand beyond the strictures of Aaronide power in the temple.

Much scholarly ink has been devoted to analyzing the contents of the prayer in Nehemiah 9 (see section 2.2 above). For our present purposes, we should note that the prayer is somewhat of a compendium of traditions one encounters elsewhere in the Hebrew Scriptures, especially the Pentateuch. The prayer knows the Exodus and Sinai/Wilderness tales well and these are cornerstones of the theology of the prayer's authors; whoever composed the prayer cannot imagine national existence without these pivotal foundation myths. But just as significant is the fact that national existence in the prayer is recognized to be a history of poor conduct and a disregard for those foundation myths—in particular, the apostasy involving the golden calf as we read about in Exodus 32 (Neh. 9:18). This act of flagrant disobedience set a standard of transgression that continued into the landed history of the people all the way down through the monarchic era and, as the prayer reveals, beyond (Neh. 9:36–37—most often regarded as a reference to Neo-Babylonian or Persian imperialism). Despite this recognition of apostasy, the authors of the poem begin with a powerful and definitive declaration that the land in which the live was promised by God to Abraham (Neh. 9:7–8); his descendants are thus poised to make good on that promise. The prayer's theology suggests that this can only finally occur once the petitioners uttering the prayer admit the nation's past guilt and consequently dissociate from it.

The prayer in Nehemiah 9 is thus a curious composition. It seems to know the traditions within the Pentateuch and the Deuteronomistic History in more or less their eventual canonical order/sequence (though this does not mean that the authors possessed written versions of these works in their canonical form), which would include Deuteronomy and the Priestly material and their concept of individual accountability to the covenant law. That is, the authors of the prayer make use of material derived from these works that do not hold individuals of a given generation accountable for the transgressions of past generations. This idea is also strongly attested in the prophetic tradition as well, which was certainly known to the redactors of Nehemiah 9.

Yet the entire purpose of the prayer hinges on the idea that the transgressions of the national past must be recognized and admitted before the community can look forward to divine favor and a secure future. By implication, other communities are excluded, their connection to pre-exilic heritage thereby severed and their positions within the Persian political/sacral order diminished (at least from the perspectives of the authors of Nehemiah 9). Whether or not this was ever actually the case is debatable, as there exists considerable evidence that these other non-*gola* communities maintained their claims on the past (and thus their identity as Jews in the present). But Nehemiah 9 fits squarely into the ideology permeating the entirety of EN which time and again attempts to limit covenantal and social legitimacy to the *gola* group alone.

The unit concludes in Nehemiah 10 with communal pact founded upon the preceding chapters, replete with an extensive list of signatories. Within EN, we have encountered various lists of names, but the list in Nehemiah 10 is especially poignant, identifying as it does the actual people (and, presumably, their family members) who self-identified as the *gola* community according to the exclusion of others. Given the fact that this list is included at the end of Nehemiah 8—10, the redactors of the unit seem to imply that these names constitute those who stood before Ezra during the *Torah*-reading ceremony in Nehemiah 8 and whose pious contrition was represented by the Levites who uttered the penitential prayer in the preceding chapter.

The list therefore becomes part of a narrative of sorts: the *Torah*-reading represents divine instruction, the Levitical prayer represents communal recognition of past wrongdoing, and the community itself emerges renewed and empowered as a result. For many scholars, the list in Nehemiah 10 is considerably older than the narrative context into which it has been redacted, and actually reflects the mid-fifth-century membership of a proto-sectarian group within the *gola* community.[39] This group perhaps serves as the first step toward what would emerge as full-blown Jewish sects such as the Sadducees and the Pharisees in later centuries. In both cases, groups within a larger recognized community establish distinct conditions of membership and identity upon which sacral and social authority are predicated.

---

39. See, *inter alia*, Sivertsev 2005.

5.8. Nehemiah 11—13

The final chapters of the book of Nehemiah return us to Nehemiah consulting archival sources. At first glance, they look primarily like random lists of names leading inexplicably back into a resumption of the Nehemiah Memoir in Nehemiah 13. However, given the thematic undercurrent in Nehemiah 7 and the progression of events in Nehemiah 8—10, it is clear by this point that the consultation of archival texts is not to be taken lightly. Rather, it provides a model of how a Jew should carefully consider the record of the past as an expression of divine will and utilize that record as a model for conduct in the present. Indeed, Nehemiah's own words and deeds are incorporated into this sacred curriculum: Nehemiah 12 brings the reader into the days of Nehemiah himself by mentioning the roster of clergy from his own time (v. 26), followed by records of Nehemiah's own words regarding actions taken during the wall-building efforts (vv. 31-46 [47]). The redactor of these chapters has thus engaged in a subtle meta-literary strategy: if Nehemiah's own words and deeds are part of the sacred curriculum he consults, then the writings of Nehemiah within EN are, by extension, also sacred curriculum one should consult to known divine will.

This leads us to the finale of the work, Nehemiah 13. In this final chapter, Nehemiah takes center stage once again, facilitating separation between the *gola* community and illegitimate outside groups, enforcing various laws regarding the observance of the Sabbath, cleaning out the Jerusalem temple and rededicating the Levites to temple service. In many ways, Nehemiah 13 presents Nehemiah finally harnessing the full range of his power set up many chapters earlier: it is difficult to imagine what it depicts without the background and credentials we encounter in Nehemiah 1—6. Nehemiah effectively wrests all power from the priesthood in Nehemiah 13, laying claim to teaching/enforcing religious law, extending his policies into the sacred precincts of the temple, and taking the initiative to empower the Levites (which contradicts the Pentateuchal texts subordinating the Levites to the Aaronide priests). But within the rhetoric of the book, Nehemiah is indeed able to do these things since the earlier chapters affirm on the one hand his own submission to religious orthodoxy and, on the other, his imperial/ administrative power. Nehemiah 13 positions his conduct not as personal initiative but as consistent with pious deference to authoritative traditions and an interest in carving out a tenable place for the *gola* community within the Persian imperial world. The lesson of Nehemiah 13 appears to be that good citizenship is tantamount to sacral behavior, and the precedents not only of Nehemiah 1–6 but the Ezra traditions both before and after that unit of material sets up Nehemiah 13 as a fitting ending pursuant to that civic ethic.

The empowerment of the Levites, in particular, has drawn a good amount of attention from commentators. The Pentateuch generally places Levites under the auspices of the Aaronide priests, and this was in all likelihood the normative hierarchical dynamic throughout the Persian (and, for that matter, early Hellenistic) period. But even many of those Pentateuchal traditions admit that the Levites occupied a medial position between the priesthood and the laity, with obligations and affiliations to both. There is thus probably an historical kernel to what we encounter in Nehemiah 13, insofar as a sacral but non-Aaronide caste could very well have aligned themselves with a rival authority such as the provincial governor, and it would certainly have been to Nehemiah's benefit as governor to have his political policies appear consistent with sacral interest represented by the Levites. But as we have seen, by this point in EN, the literary record of Nehemiah's policies has become a record of revelation. The *gola* community, its civil leaders, and the sacral cast empowered by those leaders are identified as an essential part of YHWH's plan for Israel—the reader of this material is thereby charged to accept the version of events it contains as a curriculum for structuring his or her own religious priorities and values.

Bibliography

Blenkinsopp, Joseph. 1988. *Ezra–Nehemiah*. Louisville: Westminster John Knox Press.

_____. 2009. *Judaism: The First Phase*. Grand Rapids: Eerdmans.

Bedford, Peter R. 2002. "Diaspora: Homeland Relations in Ezra–Nehemiah." *VT* 52: 147–65.

Boda, Mark J. 1999. *Praying the Tradition: The Origin and Use of Tradition in Nehemiah 9*. BZAW 277. Berlin: de Gruyter.

Demsky, Aaron. 1994. "Who Came First, Ezra or Nehemiah? The Synchronistic Question." *HUCA* 65: 1–19.

Eskenazi, Tamara C. 1988. "The Structure of Ezra–Nehemiah and the Integrity of the Book." *JBL* 107. 641–56.

Frei, Peter. 1984. "Zentralgewalt und Lokalautonomie in Achamenidenreich." In *Reichsidee und Reichsorganisation im Perserreich*. OBO, 55; Fribourg: Univesritätsverlag.

Grabbe, Lester L. 1994. *Judaism from Cyrus to Hadrian*. London: SCM Press.

Kraemer, David. 1993. "On the Relation of the Books of Ezra and Nehemiah." *JSOT* 59: 73–92.

Knoppers, Gary N. 2013. *Jews and Samaritans: The Origins and History of their Early Relations*. New York/Oxford: Oxford University Press.

Lipschits, Oded. 2005. *The Fall and Rise of Jerusalem*. Winona Lake: Eisenbrauns.

Leuchter, Mark. 2007. "Why is the Song of Moses in the Book of Deuteronomy?" *VT* 57: 295–317.

_____. 2009 "Ezra's Mission and the Levites of Casiphia." In *Community Identity and Judean Historiography*, edited by Gary N. Knoppers and Kenneth A. Ristau, 173–95. Winona Lake: Eisenbrauns.

_____. 2012 "The Book of the Twelve and the 'Great Assembly' in History and Tradition." In *Perspectives on the Formation of the Book of the Twelve*, edited by Rainer Albertz, James Nogalski, and Jakob Wöhrle, 337–52. BZAW. Berlin: De Gruyter.

_____. 2014. "Inter-Levitical Polemics in the Early Persian Period: The Evidence from Nehemiah 9." *Bib* 85: 269–79.

Nogalski, James D. 2010. "One Book and Twelve Books: The Nature of the Redactional Work and the Implications of Cultic Source Material in the Book of the Twelve." In *Two Sides of a Coin*, edited by Thomas Römer, 11–46. Piscataway: Gorgias Press.

Schaper, Joachim. 1997. "The Temple Treasury Committee in the Times of Nehemiah and Ezra." *VT* 47: 200–206.

Schipper, Jeremy D. 2015. *Ruth*. AB. New Haven: Yale University Press.

Sivertsev, Alexei. 2005. "Sects and Households: Social Structure of the Proto-Sectarian Movement of Nehemiah 10 and the Dead Sea Sect." *CBQ* 67: 59–78.

Smith, Morton. 1961. "The Dead Sea Sect in Relation to Ancient Judaism." *NTS* 7: 347–60.

Steiner, Richard C. 2006. "Bishlam's Archival Search Report in Nehemiah's Archive: Multiple Introductions and Reverse Chronological Order as Clues to the Origin of the Aramaic Letters in Ezra 4—6." *JBL* 125: 641–85.

Talshir, Zipora. 2001. "Several Canon-Related Concepts Originating in Chronicles." *ZAW* 113: 386–403.

Trotter, James. 2001."Was the Second Jerusalem Temple a Primarily Persian Period Project?" *SJOT* 14: 276–84.

VanderKam, James C. 1992. "Ezra—Nehemiah or Ezra and Nehemiah?" In *Priests, Prophets and Scribes*, edited by Eugene Ulrich, John Wright, Robert Carroll, and Philip Davies, 55–75. JSOTSup 192. Sheffield: Sheffield Academic Press.

Weinfeld, Moshe. 2004. *The Place of the Law in the Religion of Ancient Israel.* VTSup 100. Leiden: Brill.

Williamson, Hugh G. M. 1983. "The Composition of Ezra i–vi." *JTS* 34: 1–30.

Wright, Jacob L. 2004. *Rebuilding Identity: The Nehemiah Memoir and its Earliest Readers.* BZAW 348. Berlin: De Gruyter.

7

Chronicles (1—2 Chronicles)

1. Introduction

The Hebrew Scriptures are full of repetitions. Different versions of the same event appear frequently (think, for example, of the two accounts of the flood woven together into Genesis 6—9) legal stipulations recur in different contexts (the Ten Commandments appear in Exodus 20 and then again in Deuteronomy 5), prophetic texts use repeated and stereotyped phrases, etc. When biblical texts repeat themselves, however, it usually signals a shift in ideas or perceptions, or a new message or insight contained in the text under consideration. The book of Chronicles, which repeats so much of what we find in earlier texts (especially Samuel—Kings, but also the Pentateuch, Psalms, and various prophetic works) is a parade example of this, creating an entirely new landscape by repeating but also transforming earlier traditions. The Greek name for Chronicles, *Paraleipoménōn*, means "[the] things left aside," i.e., events that these earlier texts set aside from their range of discussion. But the Hebrew name for Chronicles is *divrei ha-yamim*, "the events of the days"—signaling that the details emerging from the repeated telling of these earlier events are indeed of great importance and worthy of serious consideration.

1.1. A Special Note on This Chapter

Though the book of Chronicles is an incredibly sophisticated and very carefully built narrative, it covers the same eras and events we see in earlier biblical compositions, including those treated elsewhere in this volume. Because of this, the present chapter will have far fewer sidebar discussions and images, as most of these additional pieces of information have already been applied to the events, institutions, and individuals addressed in earlier chapters of this book. As we will see, however, the material in Chronicles is anything but redundant; it covers many of the same issues and experiences, but sheds light on them in a way that tells us a great deal about how Jewish life, values, and memory had changed since the formation of the earlier texts wrought during the late-monarchic and exilic periods.

1.2. Approaching the Study of the Book of Chronicles

Because of its clearly derivative nature, Chronicles was long regarded as a somewhat less significant window into Israel's past by critical scholars. Chronicles of course received periodic attention, but never as much as the sources upon which it was so obviously founded. In part, this was a remnant of an unofficial bias (especially among North American scholars) that the pre-exilic period of Israel's history was worthy of more attention than that of the post-exilic era, the era in which Chronicles was written. Even among those who did devote attention to the formation of Chronicles, the tendency was to date it as early as possible. The classic perspective in North American biblical scholarship in this regard is represented by the work of Frank M. Cross and David Noel Freedman, both of whom argued that the author of the work was active during the restoration to the homeland in the early Persian period (ca. 520–515 BCE) and penned the work as a national history that incorporated the concerns of the restoration itself into its narrative of the past (Cross proposed several later additions to this base work).[1]

---

1. See Cross 1975; Freedman 1961.

Figure 7.1: The Tomb of Cyrus, Pasargadae, Iran. Photo: Alireza Shakirnea; Commons.wikimedia.org.

Contemporary scholarly views of Chronicles have changed, in large part due to a much wider recognition of the importance of the Persian period in which the work was produced. Scholars remain divided about how much of the Hebrew Scriptures originated during this period, but virtually all agree that the Persian period ultimately accounts for the penultimate (and in some cases, the ultimate) shaping of most of these biblical texts. Greater attention has been given to the diversity of Jewish life in this era and the very complex dynamic between these different groups as part of the Persian imperial superstructure. Advances in scholarly methods, too, have provided new ways to approach the matter, as biblical scholars have turned increasingly to social-scientific models, studies in cultural memory, and linguistic theory to fill the gaps in how Persian period Judaism was once understood.[2] Emerging from this is a much more intense emphasis on Chronicles: while its derivative nature is still widely recognized, this is no longer viewed as a strike against it but, rather, as a key for understanding the world that gave rise to it. It also allows researchers to identify the manner in which traditions were transmitted over generations in various contexts (oral, written, rural, official, native, imperial, etc.), all of which are attested in Chronicles.

Most scholars today view Chronicles as a product of the late Persian period (see section 3 below) and the work of an individual scribe (or group of scribes) strongly affiliated with the Jerusalem temple. This author or group of authors—termed "the Chronicler" for purposes of

2. See, e.g., Jonker 2010.

convenience—had ready access to a wide spectrum of texts and oral traditions, some quite ancient and others fairly contemporaneous with his own social world. The work of the Chronicler is especially significant for our understanding of this era, because there is precious little literature that directly addresses the events of this time.

Indeed, the late Persian and early Hellenistic eras have often been considered a "Dark Age" in the history of Judaism: following the fifth-century BCE events depicted in Ezra—Nehemiah, ancient Jewish texts are effectively silent about ensuing events until the **Maccabean period** in the mid-second century (found in 1—2 Maccabees). The great era which saw the struggle between Persia and Greece, and the shift of power from the former to the latter, receives almost no mention whatsoever in Jewish texts from that period. Here Chronicles is most helpful, because its transparent use of older sources allow us to see where, why, and how the Chronicler departs from those sources during this period (see below, section 3.9, for a proposal regarding a more specific date for the composition of Chronicles). This offers us great insights into the cultural, social, and intellectual trends of the very period for which we otherwise lack direct attestation in narrative form. The narrative of the past that we encounter in Chronicles tells us a great deal about the Chronicler's day, a pivotal period in Jewish history and, indeed, in world history as well.

2. Historical Setting

Unlike the roughly contemporaneous Ezra—Nehemiah, which deals with a limited set of historical periods, Chronicles is all over the temporal map. The work ends with a mention of the rise of the Persian Empire (in 539 BCE) but begins with the mention of Adam from the book of Genesis. In other words, Chronicles presents itself as a narrative spanning the history of humanity down to the Persian period. This is a potent rhetorical move, but it is not helpful for addressing a specific historical period from the view of critical scholarship, since the people and events in Genesis are best seen as examples of legend rather than history. There is certainly a degree of historical memory woven into the Genesis narratives, especially in the ancestral tales involving the Patriarchs and the children of Jacob.[3] But as most scholars agree, these

3. Hendel 2005.

narratives function as symbolic repositories of experience rather than as indications of actual events and social structures.

We shall restrict ourselves, then, to the bulk of the Chronicler's narrative, that is, Israel's monarchic era (ca. 1020–587 BCE). In this, our discussion will be somewhat briefer than in other sections of this book, for this period is addressed in the biblical books of Samuel and Kings, both of which have each received their own extensive treatment and discussion in the present volume. Nevertheless, some general remarks and observations are in order in relation to how the Chronicler would have remembered or read about this historical period. It is clear from various prophetic texts of the Persian period that the monarchic era was regarded as a particularly special, even sacred, historical epoch by Persian period Jews. The monarchy was remembered in different ways among differing populations in Yehud; it was also clearly remembered by the population that remained in the Eastern Diaspora during the Persian period, albeit in a manner quite distinct from those who were repatriated to the homeland. The Chronicler appears aware of these different traditions of memory regarding the past, so certain aspects of the monarchic era deserve mention here.

First and foremost, the institution of kingship during the early days of the monarchic period was very much a contested issue. Though the books of Samuel and Kings attempt to present a picture of a firmly fixed institution almost from its outset, these texts also preserve evidence that the majority of the Israelite population either resisted kingship altogether or were only nominally resigned to it. Kingship may have been a practical necessity by the late-eleventh century BCE for purposes of domestic order as well as defense against external threat, but it did not replace older tribal structures in a wholesale sense. Israel's first king, Saul, was unsuccessful in establishing a true monarchic state, and the extent of his kingdom was relatively limited to the central highlands of Manasseh, Ephraim, and Benjamin. It is quite likely that he was able to muster military allegiance from other Israelite clans and tribes, but this does not automatically equate to full monarchic sovereignty.

The accomplishments of David reached considerably further. The pro-David authors in 1–2 Samuel suggest that he united all the Israelite tribes and that his kingdom reached as far as the **Euphrates River**; what is more likely is that David forced some Israelite tribes into submission, and hedged his borders through alliances with neighboring powers. (See Figure 5.12, above in chapter 5.) Even if David did claim a larger kingdom that Saul, it was hardly a harmonious entity; much animosity against David seems to have characterized the entirety of his reign, and much bloodshed seems to have been the preferred vehicle for retaining its political integrity. Finally, Solomon's kingdom appears to have enjoyed larger borders, greater administrative infrastructure, and increased diplomatic relations, as well as the inauguration of the Jerusalem temple as the dominant symbol of "national" religious identity (though these features are certainly exaggerated in the Kings account). But the cost of these accomplishments was quite high: Solomon's administrative system challenged traditional tribal leadership, his building projects demanded forced labor from his population and heavy taxes, and his foreign policies were viewed as culturally questionable (especially his close connection to Egypt).

Sidebar 7.1: A United Monarchy?

Earlier generations of scholars assumed that the eras of David and Solomon saw a "United Monarchy" in earnest; that is, the biblical claims of a fully united league of tribes under the rule of both of these kings. As discussed in earlier chapters of this book, this is no longer generally accepted. The biblical authors of 1–2 Samuel and 1–2 Kings had an interest in presenting a past that spoke to their own reality, interests, and intentions, and it is likely that while a good deal of historical information can be mined from our extant sources, the sources have been arranged (and interpreted) by scribes of a later period to create a picture of the Davidic-Solomonic period that established ideals that they could actualize or advocate in their own day. While this was already the case in the Deuteronomistic redaction of the earlier sources, it is amplified in the Chronicler's own reading of these texts. It is very possible that the Chronicler included additional traditions of high antiquity into his re-presentation of the early monarchic period, but these have been positioned to support his own late Persian era interests.

In brief, Israel's early foray into monarchy was fraught with uncertainty, difficulty, violence, oppression, and certainly regret among some sectors of the population (if not most). It is no wonder that almost immediately after Solomon's death, the vast majority of Israel's population repudiated the entire idea of kingship under the

Davidic family (1 Kgs. 12:16) and seceded from the union, as it were. Furthermore, the formation of the northern monarchy under Jeroboam I and his successors appears to have yielded better results, appealing to more popular forms of religion and social organization and weaving them into the fabric of the state cult and political infrastructure. The northern monarchy was thus poised to better represent public interest than what had obtained under David and Solomon in the era of the "united monarchy," which the north seemed to regard as one of injustice and coercion. By the mid-eighth century BCE, this may not have been the case—the prophetic protests of **Amos** and **Hosea** indicate a serious social rift, with the urban elites abusing their power and privilege to the detriment of the rural village population, and this may have begun as much as a century earlier if the episode involving **Ahab** and **Naboth** in 1 Kings 21 is any indication.

The Assyrian destruction of the northern kingdom in the late-eighth century BCE was viewed in Judah as a punishment from YHWH (2 Kgs. 17:7–23), though the reason for this punishment was a matter of debate. It was alternately punishment for seceding from Davidic rule in Jerusalem, following the sacrificial cult of the northern state established by Jeroboam, disregarding the message of the prophets who criticized social and religious ills, or a combination of all of these. But the fall of the north did not mean the disappearance of the northern population, despite the statement in the book of Kings that all of Israel was exiled from its land (2 Kgs. 17:23). A good portion of the population remained, and a significant number of northern refugees fled into Judah (which was a vassal/supporter of Assyria) in the last decades of the eighth century. Many of these northern refugees settled in the major Judahite urban centers, especially Jerusalem; **northern Levites**, in particular, managed to integrate themselves into administrative and cultic positions in and around Jerusalem. Thus from the late-eighth century onward, Judah had a rather mixed population comprising urban elites, rural peasants (and, to be sure, rural elites as well), and northern refugees of diverse backgrounds.[4]

Up until this time, there had been major cultural and political distinctions between the northern and southern populations. Though interaction had always existed on smaller scales between northern and southern settlements and families, scholars have recognized that Israel saw itself as an entity rather distinct from Judah for centuries. That

---

4. For an overview, see Schniedewind 2004, 89–94.

is, Judah was not regarded as part of a **greater Israel**, and the idea of an Israelite tribal league into which Judah factored not something that characterized the early days of the monarchic period (the Song of Deborah in Judges 5, for example, makes no mention of Judah whatsoever).

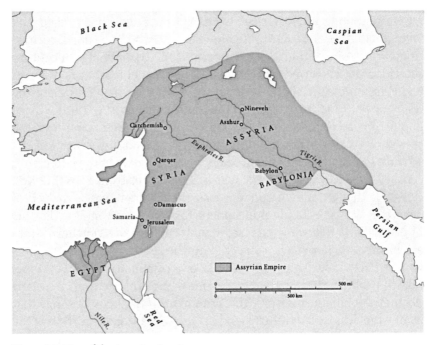

Figure 7.2. Map of the Assyrian Empire

Following the fall of the north and the flight of northern refugees into the south, however, the social and cultural divisions assigned to the terms "Israel" and "Judah" probably dissolved significantly. Judah emerged as the sole inheritor of the term "Israel" by virtue of its survival and its population now carrying a notable northern Israelite element.[5]

For many scholars, this is also the time when traditions about the past were likely reformulated to account for this new Judahite social reality: different traditions about the patriarchs were probably shaped at this time to reflect the merging of populations in need of a common history, as well as the formation of new and more expansive cultic traditions and practices (e.g., the incorporation of northern hymns and

5. Finkelstein 2011, 348–67.

prayers into the Jerusalemite cult) and, of course, the records both oral and written regarding kings and prophets from the north. All of this was filtered through the Jerusalem scribal establishment, mostly situated in the temple but certainly under royal auspices.

The reign of the Judahite king **Hezekiah** is especially important in this turn of events. The Assyrian king Sargon II died in 705 BCE, prompting Hezekiah to withhold his annual tribute to the Assyrian royal court. This was an act of rebellion, declaring that he and his kingdom were no longer subordinates to or supporters of the Assyrian empire. However, the new Assyrian king, Sennacherib, was a powerful ruler who did not tolerate such displays. Anticipating Sennacherib's retaliation, Hezekiah uprooted his urban population and placed them in the fortified urban centers, creating what some have called a **"hedgehog defense"** against the approaching Assyrian armies. In the process, Hezekiah also engaged in a sort of religious reform, decommissioning the traditional cult sites of the rural hinterland alongside his relocation of its population into the urban cities. On one level, this strategy proved less than effective, for virtually every major city in Judah was conquered by the Assyrians despite Hezekiah's best efforts to the contrary. Jerusalem withstood a multi-year siege and remained intact, but Hezekiah re-submitted as a vassal to Sennacherib and offered a massive payoff from the royal treasury to end the military threat against his kingdom.[6] Few who survived this crisis would have viewed Hezekiah's revolt against Assyria as a wise choice.

From another perspective, though, many enduring changes were accomplished during this period of crisis. The admixture of populations (northern refugees, urbanized rural peasants, the urban elites, etc.) could not deny that regardless of all events, Jerusalem and its temple remained intact. The importance of the Davidic line associated with this temple and this city was thus significantly amplified, even if this-or-that individual Davidic king engaged in questionable policies. In addition, prophetic materials from the eighth century BCE—the oracles of Amos, Hosea, Micah, and Isaiah—were probably redacted in the wake of the Assyrian crisis to reflect upon Jerusalem's miraculous survival,[7] and became core materials in the religious curriculum of Jerusalem's priestly and scribal establishment. Many scholars also see this era as the background to the formation of an early collection of psalms (especially those of northern origin)

6. Halpern 1991, 11–107.
7. Ibid.

as well as several wisdom sayings currently found in the **Book of Proverbs** (Prov. 25:1), part of an effort to examine and understand the role of Judah and its leadership in the confusing and traumatic events of the previous few decades.

Finally, the uneasy relationship between Judah and its Assyrian vassal became a matter of increasing speculation: to what degree, if any, was YHWH allowing Assyria to dominate Judah? Did this mean that the Assyrian deities dominated YHWH? Or was YHWH truly the dominant deity, orchestrating the players on the world's stage, as the prophet Isaiah seemed to affirm (Isa. 10:5)? However one chose to answer these questions, the fact remained that Assyria still dominated Judah for the next several decades, and thus Assyrian political culture continued to affect Judahite life on a daily basis in virtually every way. This period unfurled mostly during the reign of King **Manasseh** (reigned 687–642 BCE), who the biblical writers castigate in extreme terms but whose lengthy reign probably indicates cooperation with Assyria, resulting in calm and a degree of prosperity as well.

The last quarter of the seventh century BCE saw a change to the aforementioned state of affairs with the waning of Assyrian power. It was at this time that Judah's king **Josiah** (reigned 640–609 BCE) sponsored a cleansing of the temple (a symbolic act of independence from Assyrian hegemony), followed by a cultic purge of the territory he claimed as belonging to the Judahite throne. This purge (or reform) involved the clearing of foreign cult objects but also a clearing/demolition of traditional hinterland religious institutions and shrines, centralizing all cultic activity in Jerusalem and its temple. The goal of such a purge/reform was for Josiah to assert complete hegemony over territory that had previously been ultimately accountable to Assyria, but there were serious consequences to such a move. The purge included the decommissioning of local clergy, the curbing of **ancestor veneration**, and challenges to local traditions of jurisprudence, and it is all but certain that the majority of the population found Josiah's policies in this regard to be highly offensive and an affront to traditional religious values.[8]

Many scholars therefore see the composition of Deuteronomy around this time as an attempt to mediate between rural and royal sensibilities. Deuteronomy seems to account for many of the goals of Josiah's purge (the centralization of the cult, the sidelining of ancestral

---

8. Leuchter 2013, 19–22.

devotion, etc.) but sets those goals within the context of a covenant brokered between YHWH and his people, with the role of the king greatly reduced and limited to observing the law (Deut. 17:18–20). The book of Kings presents Josiah's purge/reform as a result of the discovery of this collection of covenant law (2 Kgs. 22:8—23:25), evidencing a later writer's attempt to cast Josiah in a positive light. But there can be little doubt that Deuteronomy's composition points to significant tension between the king and his subject given the severity of his cultic policies.

Josiah's untimely death at **Megiddo** in 609 BCE initiated a period of great insecurity as Judah's last kings wavered between Egyptian and Babylonian influence. It was during this time that Jeremiah (active ca. 620–580 BCE) emerged as the major prophetic voice of the era, counseling political submission to Babylon but religious fidelity to the principles of Deuteronomy (if not to the letter of its legislation). The prophet **Jeremiah**'s entanglements with the last kings of Judah—**Jehoiakim, Jehoiachin**, and **Zedekiah**—are not detailed in the book of Kings but receive extensive coverage in the narratives embedded within the book of Jeremiah, revealing the complex and even chaotic nature of Judah's last years. The prophet's words went largely unheeded, but once the Babylonian forces overran Judah and began to exile portions of its population (597 BCE), Jeremiah's oracles took on greater importance.

Sidebar 7.2: Judah's Twilight

The final decades of the Judahite monarchy saw much instability. Following Josiah's death in 609 BCE, his son Jehoahaz took the throne but was very soon deposed with the support of Egyptian forces; his brother Jehoiakim replaced him and remained in power until 598 BCE. Jehoiakim was succeeded by his son Jehoiachin in 597, but the Babylonian domination of Judah in the same year saw him taken captive (with many other leading figures of the day), and his brother Zedekiah was placed on the throne as a puppet of the Babylonian administration. Zedekiah ultimately rebelled against Babylon, which led to his deposition, the death of his family, the destruction of Jerusalem and its temple, the forced migration of a good number of its citizens to Babylon and the flight of Judahites from nearby towns and villages to the northern frontier of Judah, away from the melee.

Jeremiah's oracles were ultimately fully vindicated with the final destruction of Jerusalem and exile of its population in 587/586 BCE, proving to audiences in exile that his prophecies were indeed divinely mandated. The development of the book of Jeremiah during the exile, and the importance it obtained upon the repatriation of Jews to Yehud once the exile was over, points to a growing sense of self-consciousness in Israelite religion/early Judaism, with an intense focus on the literary record of the past as a means for discerning divine instruction and for ordering/orchestrating the present in accordance with YHWH's will. The final verses of Chronicles (2 Chr. 36:22–23) are suggestive of this new self-awareness, introducing as they do the rise of Persia at a time when history required examination through the lens of Israel's own religious traditions.

3. Literary Concerns

Chronicles tells a coherent, linear story at first glance. But when one looks more closely at the craft and method of the Chronicler in telling that story, the more complicated and sophisticated it becomes. By the Chronicler's day, scribes in the Jerusalem temple had been deeply enculturated in the expert skills of literary scholars from across the Persian Empire. They were privy to ways of reading, developing, and orchestrating existing texts that resulted in literary works that were greater than the sum of their parts in terms of symbolic complexity and cultural value. The Chronicler was no different, and applied his own formidable scribal skills to the sources available to him, which were vast and varied. What is unique is how the Chronicler deploys them, adapts them, departs from them, and in some cases, patently invents them. Whether genuine or contrived, the sources in Chronicles are points of departure for exegetical development and ideological/ theological speculation, serving as vehicles for the reader to revisit how those sources might be re-read in new historical and social contexts.[9]

---

9. For a discussion of the diversity of earlier biblical materials that served as the Chronicler's sources, see Talshir 2001.

Sidebar 7.3: Symbolic Source Citations

A good deal of literature from the Persian and Hellenistic periods see writers report about past events and cite sources—both oral and written—that they invented for the sake of their own historical works. Such a move would seem counter-intuitive by today's standards, where a clearly fictitious source would compromise the value of an historical retelling. However, historical works in antiquity were not always composed for the sake of journalistic or annalistic accuracy; they were creative and symbolic works, full of ideology and sometimes theology. They drew from mythic understandings of writing and texts, two phenomena that even in Persian and Hellenistic antiquity were viewed as mysterious and somehow connected to the realm of the divine. Written texts were, after all, attested in other parts of the Bible as heavenly documents (Ezek. 2:9–3:1; Zech. 5:2-3). For the Chronicler to invent similar sources, then, was to say something about the sacred and even mythic dimensions of the historical narratives in which these citations appeared as some sort of conduit to a larger and otherwise unreachable sacred reality.

It will be helpful to identify the major and recurring sources that the Chronicler uses as the backbone for his entire historiographic work or for major units therein:

3.1. The Pentateuch

As we have already noted, the Pentateuch factors significantly into the opening chapters of Chronicles; 1 Chronicles 1—9 provides extensive genealogies and annotations regarding the various families and figures it discusses, most of which are initially derived from information in the Pentateuch. This includes, first and foremost, the book of Genesis, as well as details from Exodus and Numbers. Yet the Chronicler also knows and utilizes materials well beyond genealogical details from the Pentateuch: laws from Exodus, Leviticus, and Numbers are presupposed in various places and inform the background of various episodes throughout the work. Deuteronomy, too, serves as a major cornerstone of the Chronicler's thought, especially with its theology of individual moral/legal liability (over against more corporate concepts of guilt and responsibility from other biblical traditions). The use of this material in Chronicles is different than its appearance in other texts of roughly the same era (such as Ezra—Nehemiah); the Pentateuch is utilized and conceived of as a complete, cohesive work, which indicates that the Chronicler worked in the wake of the final redaction of the Pentateuch into its current and mature form.

3.2. Samuel—Kings

Though the Pentateuch stands as a theological backbone in the Chronicler's work, it is Samuel—Kings that serves as the structural and narrative basis for the majority of Chronicles. Virtually all of 1 Chronicles 10—2 Chronicles 26 is based upon Samuel—Kings; in years past, most researchers accepted that the Chronicler simply had this material in front of him in a substantially complete form. Many scholars still advocate this position (which we may term the "consensus model"), but variations on this position have arisen, as well as some challenges. One of the more recent and intriguing challenges to the consensus model is that of Raymond Person, who sees Chronicles and Samuel—Kings (as part of the larger Deuteronomistic History) produced in essentially the same or overlapping historical periods by two different scribal groups, drawing from similar sources.[10] In this scenario, the scribe or scribes who produced Chronicles did not rely on Samuel—Kings in a linear fashion but shared the same material that led to the *production* of Samuel—Kings among the other scribal group. Major departures between the two arise from the predilections and choices of the individual scribes responsible for either work.

There is much in this approach that demands serious attention, especially regarding its accounting for scribal methodology. The Chronicler indeed exhibits signs of just this type of choice and predilection, something that we now know typified the manner in which scribes created or transmitted documents. But this understanding can apply to the Chronicler's use Samuel—Kings as a source, with the narrative and plot turns selectively reproduced by the Chronicler in conversation with other sources and doctrines, yielding a deliberate and hermeneutically resonant companion piece that could be read alongside of Samuel—Kings.

It should be noted that while Samuel—Kings was part of the Deuteronomistic History, Chronicles does not utilize the other Deuteronomistic texts such as Joshua or Judges in the same manner as

---

10. Person 2010.

Samuel–Kings. The Chronicler certainly knew these texts, but chose to circumvent their contents; the tales of violent conquest and pre-monarchic society were not directly relevant to his own project, one that addressed the legacy of Israel's monarchy for a post-monarchic social world. Chronicles resembles Ezra–Nehemiah in this way: it compartmentalizes history into discreet epochs, skipping over periods that detract from the overall rhetorical message.

3.3. Psalms

Chronicles relies periodically on various prayers and hymns currently found in the Psalter (the Book of Psalms). In most cases, these psalms are placed in the mouths of important characters who serve as bridges between the ancient setting of the narrative and the historical presuppositions of the words they speak. So, for example, King David arranges prayers from psalms that were conceived during the Babylonian exile (1 Chr. 16:8–36), which both establishes continuity between different eras of the past and which presents him as a prophet who envisions the future and expresses it through liturgical recitation. This use of various psalms also positions the reading and chanting of these prayers as a form of prophecy for those who do so in the Chronicler's day as well, namely, the Levites of the Jerusalem temple who are elsewhere equated with prophecy in Chronicles (see section 5). What this suggests about the Chronicler himself remains a matter of debate, but many scholars see a strong Levitical bent running throughout Chronicles, which may account for the interaction with the contents of the book of Psalms. The Chronicler assigns to the Jerusalem temple the central function in the formation of cultural, social and religious identity for late Persian era Jews, but also highlights the diversity of roles within that institution. Sacrifice as conducted by the **Aaronide priests** is important, but the recitation of prayer and *Torah*-instruction of the Levites is of equal importance. If various psalms were understood as both prayers to be recited and examples of sacred instruction, then Chronicles provides a narrative context where the latter concepts are demonstrated and rooted in authoritative precedent.

3.4. Prophetic Material

The Chronicler's usage of psalms is paralleled by his reliance on

469

prophetic materials as well. Many of the prophets mentioned in Chronicles are directly drawn from Samuel—Kings: Samuel, Nathan, Ahijah, Micaiah, Huldah, etc. In many of these cases, though, Chronicles suggests a much broader (though otherwise unattested) literary tradition associated with them—this is, as noted above, part of the Chronicler's rhetorical strategy in "inventing" prophetic sources and marrying them to the material he recruits from Samuel—Kings. But this may also be part of an attempt to envision prophecy as an expressly literary enterprise from its outset, since the Chronicler also clearly knows the written oracles of the Latter Prophets, especially those of Isaiah and Jeremiah. Furthermore, and in close dialogue with his use of material from the Psalter, the Chronicler identifies major Levite figures such as Asaph, Heman, and Jeduthun as prophets (see section 5), and these are also figures to whom various collections of psalms are credited within the Psalter. These prophetic Levites are thus presented as prophets like Isaiah, Jeremiah, Samuel, Ahijah, etc., i.e., they are the authors of sacred texts that possess oracular power when recited, consulted, or studied.

Sidebar 7.4: Iconic Texts

Scholars have come to recognize that literacy was quite limited in ancient Israel. Only a few figures in monarchic-era Israel were really capable of anything beyond the most rudimentary levels of literary education: priests, scribes, kings, high ranking military and administrative officials, and perhaps a few of the very wealthiest of laypeople. This is par for the course with ancient cultures more broadly, and persisted well into the Persian period. Although, while literacy was generally a restricted skill, texts themselves became more commonplace. Persian culture placed a high premium on the important iconic role of texts—inscriptions, decrees, letters, lists, etc. all became important symbols of status among those who handled and had access to them. They also projected and reinforced a sense of power across the vast reaches of the empire, and even people of limited literacy or no literacy at all must have recognized the importance that written works had to the brokers of imperial authority.

It is intriguing, then, that with the emphasis on written prophetic sources, Chronicles does not engage the oracles of other "writing" prophets such as Hosea, Amos, Micah, etc. And while Isaiah and Jeremiah receive coverage, the Chronicler seems to ignore **Ezekiel** entirely. The silence regarding Ezekiel is fairly easy to explain: Ezekiel advocates a separatist, exclusive ideology for his community and sought to maintain distinctions between them and other Judahites (see, e.g., Ezek. 14:22–23). This worked counter to the inclusive ideology in Chronicles, where diverse populations are brought into the fold of a "greater Israel." The issue regarding the other prophets is more complicated. It may be that some prophetic texts were simply less important or relevant to the Chronicler's enterprise, but additional considerations may have factored into his use/non-use of prophetic texts. For example, the **Book of the Twelve** (i.e., the "Minor Prophets") was redacted to make a case fairly similar to that of Chronicles, namely, that Levites entrusted with prophetic texts were an essential part of the temple cult and that their chanting and teaching of this material was a form of prophecy itself.[11] If this is so, then the Chronicler may have felt that his historiographic work could complement the Book of the Twelve and work in tandem with it without having to invoke its contents. (A similar relationship obtains between the book of Jeremiah and the Deuteronomistic History, which never mentions Jeremiah but which has much in common with its ideology and social vision). In any case, Chronicles relies on prophetic materials in a manner consistent with its reliance on the Deuteronomistic History and the Pentateuch—it is particular about what it invokes and how the sources are applied.

3.5. Priestly Lists and Registers

One of the most prominent of the Chronicler's sources are the copiously detailed lists of priests, Levites and other officials punctuating his narrative. It is here where the most noticeable departures from his historiographic sources are evident, as these lists are inserted strategically into otherwise concise accounts drawn from Samuel–Kings. Most scholars view these lists as derived from administrative sources in the library of the Jerusalem temple, which matches what we know of the function of temples elsewhere throughout the Persian Empire, especially in Mesopotamia and Egypt. Priestly lists and rosters were kept/deposited in the Elephantine

---

11. Leuchter 2014.

temple in Egypt both to affirm various priestly ranks and groups as part of the official clergy of that sanctuary and also to function as part of the religious curriculum therein. Priests, scribes and other literati read and studied those lists even as they read and studied other, more "obvious" religious texts, which resulted in an ideological-theological matrix where doctrine and agency were intimately intertwined. This was also a feature of Mesopotamian temples, where the duty roster of different priestly orders was made part of the official doctrine and ritual rhythm of the temple in question. In antiquity, the deposition of a duty roster of clergy list into a temple library effectively turned those documents into holy books, earthly parallels of **heavenly books**, which was also a priestly convention in the Jerusalem temple during the Persian period.

The Chronicler's use of material regarding the priestly and Levitical lists ensconced within his narrative infuses that narrative with the numinous and now-revelatory qualities of these temple texts. Here, again, Chronicles exhibits some similarities with Ezra—Nehemiah, where lists and registers are incorporated into the narrative to legitimize various factions (ostensibly) living in fifth-century BCE Yehud and to reinforce sacred instruction. For the Chronicler, however, the lists of priests, Levites, and other officials are retrojected back much earlier into the days of David and Solomon, hermeneutically presenting them as fundamental to the foundations of the Jerusalem temple planned by the former and built by the latter.

How early, then, are these lists? Could they actually date in part to the monarchic era? This is difficult to answer with certainty, because Chronicles does periodically preserve historically useful information that sheds important light on rather early events, especially with regard to the priesthood. And it is among priestly groups that official lists, registers, and rankings would have been preserved from the monarchic era, since such groups were always affiliated with administrative responsibilities and benefitted from higher rates of literacy than the larger Israelite population.

However, it is more than likely that whatever early details did survive from the monarchic era have been combined with priestly lists and registers from the Persian period, and probably from the Chronicler's own time. Genealogies are social constructs and fluid: old details and memories are sometimes passed over, sometimes telescoped, and often transposed onto later rosters of named figures to create connections between living priestly groups and ancient figures they wished to claim as ancestors.[12] It seems best to view the priestly and Levite lists as a combination of relatively late group details well known in the Chronicler's time and older details regarding important figures that were probably widely sustained and adopted across a spectrum of priestly groups throughout the Persian period.

3.6. Oral Genealogies

Related to the priestly lists and registers is the Chronicler's use of oral genealogies. The first nine chapters of Chronicles detail the extensive family structures of Israel's tribes, some of which rely on details from the Pentateuch and other authoritative texts. However, it is also very likely that the Chronicler utilized oral genealogies as preserved among the clans and tribes in/around Yehud in his own day. How these genealogies are deployed within Chronicles remains somewhat unclear, insofar as some details are obvious literary constructs while others possess more authentic features that suggest genuine relations between families and clans. It is also difficult to determine just how far back into the past these genealogies may be traced—as noted above, genealogical details can telescope ancestors, skip generations, or artificially link one family line to another.

What is more useful for our purposes is to observe that the way in which the Chronicler constructed his genealogies shows active awareness of the convention of oral genealogies preserved among his audience. The genealogies in Chronicles, while certainly literary works, utilize the oral formulations of **segmentary societies** such as that of the Chronicler's audience (i.e., the larger population of late Persian period Yehud).[13] The shape and function of the Chronicler's genealogies show influence from the function of oral genealogies in that larger social universe, and most likely incorporate material from those oral genealogies in the construction of a theology of kinship throughout his work.

3.7. Priestly *Halakha* (Authoritative Custom) and Temple Practice

Since the Jerusalem temple is so central an icon and theme in Chronicles, and since the Chronicler is almost certainly part of the priestly-scribal faculty of that temple, it is beyond doubt that the

12. Wilson 1977.
13. Levin 2004a; 2003.

customary ritual and legal practices preserved by the priests therein—known as *halakha*—informs the manner in which Chronicles narrates the past. In some places, this seems to create an ostensible tension. For example, the Chronicler maintains strong fidelity to the terms of ritual law found in the Pentateuch, where sacrifices are to be conducted in silence. This observation, made first by Israel Knohl, is evident upon reading the ritual instruction in the book of Leviticus.[14] Yet Chronicles also makes clear that prayers and hymns are to be sung alongside the offering of sacrifices within the temple, which was certainly a real feature of Second Temple ritual in the Persian period and beyond (attested also by several rabbinic texts concerning temple worship). Leviticus does not prohibit prayer or hymns, it simply does not mention them; this allowed the Chronicler to make room for the hymnic traditions he knew in his own day to complement the legislation for sacrificial rites. The Chronicler has thus woven two "sources" into each other, the legislation of Leviticus and the conventions of temple practice, even though the former makes no mention of these conventions.

Chronicles also features extensive speeches/sermons at various points in its narrative, often times in episodes relating to warfare, and credits those speeches/sermons to prophetic-Levite figures. This actually led earlier scholars to attempt to reconstruct a pre-exilic practice known as the **Levitical sermon**, but it is more likely that the Chronicler here adapts traditions of teaching from much later for his relating of important events in the past requiring sanctification. Levites had long been associated with traditions of sacral violence and holy war in Israelite religion;[15] their function within the faculty of the Jerusalem temple of the Persian period probably saw the fusion of this early tradition with their role as scribes and teachers of priestly doctrine. It would not be too great a conceptual leap for the Chronicler to draw from this Levitical custom in his own day and interpolate it into moments dealing with warfare within his narrative. Though these sermons are his own compositions, the form he utilizes is probably strongly influenced by the convention of sacral instruction taught in the temple during the Persian period.

14. Knohl 1995.
15. Baden 2011, 103–16.

3.8. Ezra–Nehemiah (?)

Earlier eras of scholarship assumed that the Chronicler was the author of Ezra–Nehemiah: both are Persian period compositions, both place great emphasis on the Jerusalem temple, and the linguistic character of both reflect a late stage in the development of biblical Hebrew. Though a few scholars today still see the Chronicler as somehow involved in the development of Ezra–Nehemiah, the aforementioned view has largely been abandoned as the differences between the works outweigh their similarities. It is possible, though, that the Ezra–Nehemiah corpus served as one of the Chronicler's sources. Supporting this possibility are a few textual units that these works share that seem to originate in Ezra–Nehemiah, such as the "Jeremiah doublet" in both 2 Chr. 36:22–23 and Ezra 1:1–4:

> Now in the first year of Cyrus king of Persia, that the word of YHWH by the mouth of Jeremiah might be accomplished, YHWH stirred up the spirit of Cyrus king of Persia, that he made a proclamation throughout all his kingdom, and put it also in writing, saying: "Thus saith Cyrus king of Persia: All the kingdoms of the earth has YHWH, the God of heaven, given me; and He has charged me to build Him a house in Jerusalem, which is in Judah. Whosoever there is among you of all His people—his God be with him—let him go up to Jerusalem, which is in Judah, and build the house of YHWH, the God of Israel, He is the God who is in Jerusalem. And whosoever is left, in any place where he sojourns, let the men of his place help him with silver, and with gold, and with goods, and with beasts, beside the freewill-offering for the house of God which is in Jerusalem." (Ezra 1:1–4)

> Now in the first year of Cyrus king of Persia, that the word of YHWH by the mouth of Jeremiah might be accomplished, YHWH stirred up the spirit of Cyrus king of Persia, that he made a proclamation throughout all his kingdom, and put it also in writing, saying: Thus says Cyrus king of Persia: All the kingdoms of the earth has YHWH, the God of heaven, given me; and He has charged me to build Him a house in Jerusalem, which is in Judah. Whosoever there is among you of all His people—YHWH his God be with him—let him go up. (2 Chr. 36:22–23)

Apart from some very minor differences in the shared material, it is clear that the Ezra version of this passage is longer and more complete; the Chronicles version is truncated, cutting off the final few words. We also encounter doublets in Neh. 11:7–9 and 1 Chr. 9:7–9; though both texts may simply have drawn from a common source, it is nonetheless possible that the Chronicler mined an extant version of Ezra—Nehemiah for this material. Additionally, one must note the role of Levites in Ezra—Nehemiah as teachers of *Torah* and as administrators, a role that is expanded in Chroniclers and projected back into the past (perhaps as a way of "trumping" the claims of Ezra—Nehemiah regarding the social location of Levites in the Persian period).

We must be cautious, however, in viewing Chronicles as drawing from a mature version of Ezra—Nehemiah: though the compositional origins of Ezra—Nehemiah pre-date the Chronicler's day, this does not mean that the Chronicler knew Ezra—Nehemiah in a form it currently resembles. Ezra—Nehemiah was very likely given its definitive shape during the same period that Chronicles was redacted (mid- to late-fourth century BCE), and portions of it probably continued to develop later than that. It seems likely that the Chronicler knew much of what is currently found in Ezra 7—10 and portions of the Nehemiah Memoir, as well as additional lists or registers that were in the possession of the scribes who shaped Ezra—Nehemiah. But other points of contact are perhaps better seen as part of a current of thought common in the period, including well known texts, oral traditions, social conventions, etc.

3.9. Charting the Composition History of Chronicles

As indicated above, most contemporary research into the formation of Chronicles sees it as arising in the mid- to late-fourth century BCE, i.e., the late Persian period down to the early Hellenistic era, with most favoring a Persian context for its composition. Unlike Ezra—Nehemiah, which seems to have grown in blocks over an extended period of time, most of Chronicles would have been constructed in a concentrated historical setting as part of a single scribal enterprise. The major sources utilized by the Chronicler certainly possessed their own complex redaction history (especially the Pentateuch, Samuel—Kings, and the Psalter), but Chronicles is a sort of meeting place for these diverse sources and draws from them with equal facility and fluency throughout its chapters.

This favors the view that the Chronicler produced his work largely at once, though there are some indications that this work received a few small additions after its primary composition/redaction. Much of this has to do with issues of dating; some scholars identify various passages as deriving from a subsequent redaction of an earlier corpus; this would include the **priestly courses** of 1 Chronicles 24–27 (see section 5). According to this theory, if the primary composition/ redaction is dated to the mid-fourth century, then this unit would have entered the corpus in the late-fourth century; if the primary document is dated to the late-fourth century, then this unit is even later. But an increasing number of researchers tend to see virtually the entirety of the work, including the aforementioned unit, as part of a singular and concerted compositional effort. A date of ca. 350–330 BCE appears to be the most popular approximation of when this might have taken place.

In this model, the only major unit that stands out as distinctively secondary might be 2 Chr. 36:22-23: these verses bring the narrative in Chronicles down to the Persian period, relating how the "word of Jeremiah" was fulfilled through the rise of the Persian empire under Cyrus and his decree of amnesty for the dispersed Jews. Though Jeremiah is mentioned in previous verses throughout the closing chapters of Chronicles, the locution in these final two verses differs from that which comes before, suggesting a later addition. Moreover (and as noted above), 2 Chr. 36:22-23 seems to be borrowed from Ezra 1:1-4, which might indicate an attempt the reframe the conclusion of Chronicles to look back specifically to an extant version of Ezra–Nehemiah. This would be a relatively late move in the development of Chronicles, datable probably to the late-fourth century BCE.

The question arises, though, as to why Chronicles would have been redacted around this time. Some scholars simply view Chronicles as part of the extended narrative currently spanning Chronicles–Ezra–Nehemiah, resulting in a single historiography to reframe how works like the Deuteronomistic History (which ends with the Babylonian exile) should be read in light of later developments that led to the rise of the Aaronide priesthood. If this was the case, it might explain why 2 Chr. 36:22-23 was added to the corpus, namely, to establish continuity with the narrative in Ezra–Nehemiah that begins with a virtually identical statement (Ezra 1:1-4). But even this begs a question: why would the priestly scribes ostensibly behind this work need to engage in such an extensive literary project, especially since they dictated what counted as scripture and authoritative teaching in Persian period Yehud? Moreover, why is Chronicles so focused on the Levites as the teachers of *Torah* and trustees of prophecy if Chronicles was conceived to be part of an Aaronide historiography?

Another possibility emerges, and that is that Chronicles advocates a view that supported the Aaronide priestly hierarchy but sought to factor it into a different way of thinking about history. By all indication, the Aaronide priests derived their political (and to a degree their sacral) power from the Persian authorities with whom these priests mediated on behalf of the Jewish world. Yet throughout the Persian period, Persia became increasingly threatened by Greece and had fought several battles against powerful Greek armies; this no doubt led to a certain destabilization within the Persian Empire. By the latter half of the fourth century BCE, the certainty of Persian political hegemony was no longer taken for granted as Greece continued to present a serious threat, especially in the figure of **Alexander the Great** (r. 332–322 BCE).

Sidebar 7.5: Major Battles Between Greece and Persia

Marathon	490 BCE
Thermopylae	480 BCE
Salamis	480 BCE
Plataea	478 BCE
Eurymedon	466 BCE

The composition/redaction of Chronicles may be related to the growing recognition that imperial fortunes could turn. The Chronicler created an historiography that accounted for the rising and falling of kingdoms (including that of Judah) but emphasized the perseverance of native institutions in the face of these shifting political tides: the Pentateuch, the prophetic texts, the agrarian clan system, the Jerusalem temple, its priesthood; all of these things are heralded in Chronicles as the basis for an enduring Jewish identity, not the role of those institutions within an imperial culture that may very well be swept away by the next foreign nation that YHWH saw fit to empower. Dating the redaction of Chronicles to ca. 350 BCE makes the Chronicler into a keen observer of Jewish national history and international politics; dating it later (to 330–300 BCE, for example) makes the

Chronicler an advocate for the endurance of Jewish social and religious institutions even with the new Greek regime under Alexander the Great and his successors. In either case, the Chronicler's work attempts to define the parameters of Jewish identity during a period of upheaval and change, suggesting the potential for cultural and religious continuity despite the waning of Persia or the rise of Greece under Alexander.

Figure 7.3: *Alexander at the Battle of Issus*; mosaic from the late second century BCE, in Pompeii. Museo Archeologico de Napoli; Commons.wikimedia.org.

4. Major Themes

4.1. The Torah of Moses

The idea of the Torah/Pentateuch is one of the dominant motifs throughout Chronicles. The Chronicler begins his work according to the narratives and genealogies found in the Torah, implying that this work is the key to the natural order of the world, relationships between social groups, and the unfolding of events. Law, of course, remains at the center of the Torah, and thus remains central to the Chronicler's

479

view of the past. When one transgresses divine law in the Torah, punishment ensues; when one upholds it, they are rewarded and judged well in the historiography. This latter point should not be underestimated. In ancient Israelite religion and early Judaism, a person's memory was considered sacred, and their descendants were charged with remembering their names and deeds. For the Chronicler to reward a ruler or major figure with a positive report of their lives and deeds constituted assurance that their memory would be sanctified, and this sanctification is predicated upon the adherence to YHWH's Torah.

4.2. The Authority of Levites, Priests, and Prophets

As we have seen, Levites are of tremendous importance to the Chronicler, and Chronicles repeatedly concerns itself with the details of their genealogies and responsibilities during Israel's monarchic history. Much of this has to do with the populist connection between Levites and the agrarian social world of the Chronicler's day: though Chronicles relays the events of kings and other elites, it was written at a time when most of the potential audience lived and worked in agrarian contexts in and around Jerusalem, and each population group likely had its tradition circles of Levites. The emphasis on Levites, then, was a strategy to connect the contents of Chronicles to the histories and fates of these communities, as the variety of Levite factions discussed in Chronicles must relate to the religious traditions and personnel that interacted with these communities. The sanctity of Levites in Chronicles spoke to the importance of these groups to the Chronicler's vision of history and hopes for a strong and secure national future.

But the Chronicler's interest in the Aaronide priesthood cannot be discounted. Though Levites receive more attention, Chronicles spends plenty of time discussing the priests who descend from Aaron and, most importantly, the temple sanctuary where they held high rank. The very fact that the Torah is so important to the Chronicler, in fact, is a testament to his high esteem for the Aaronide priests, since the Torah was largely a result of their literary initiatives and was the central document of their theology and sacred instruction. The many references to the Priestly laws in the Torah invariably legitimize the Aaronide priests in the historiography of Chronicles, and the

Chronicler's own language often presupposes the vitality of the legal and ritual discourses central to Aaronide teaching and theology.

In the end, though, it is prophecy that holds highest theological rank in the Chronicler's view of the past. Many of the prophets identified in Chronicles are of Levite/priestly background, evidencing the Chronicler's recognition that these offices were by no means mutually exclusive (indeed, the connection between Levites and prophets in Chronicles is especially strong). But other figures, some even foreign, bear the prophetic word of YHWH, and are thus portents of divine will as communicated not only to characters in Chronicles but to the audience of the text as well. Prophecy is the guiding force by which Torah, temple, kingship, and history are facilitated and in many cases evaluated and judged, and prophets are presented as important literary contributors to the Chronicler's own record of the past (since many of the ostensible sources cited by the Chronicler are characterized as prophetic writings).

Sidebar 7.6: Varieties of Prophecy

Prophecy is a phenomenon that anthropologists and religious scholars see in virtually all societies in antiquity (and, not infrequently, in the modern world as well). Prophecy in ancient Israel was similar in many ways to prophecy in Egypt, Greece, Syria, and Mesopotamia, where individuals were believed to serve as intermediaries between the divine and humanity. This manifested in many forms: trance states, spoken oracles, symbolic acts, dreams and, most significantly for the study of biblical literature, the writing of texts. Israel's prophetic tradition surely included non-textual practices and expressions, but the dominant form of prophecy in the Judaism of the Persian period appears to have been the written prophetic word in scrolls associated with the memory of once-living prophetic figures (Isaiah, Jeremiah, etc.). The non-textual forms of prophecy are attested in brief flourishes throughout the biblical record, but even these have been transmitted in the form of a written accounts and thus rendered a matter of textuality.

Figure 7.4: An aerial view of the site of the Temple Mount today, with the Haram as-Sharif (the Noble Sanctuary) at the center. Commons.wikimedia.org.

4.3. The Centrality of the Temple

As mentioned above, the Jerusalem temple is the central institution in the Chronicler's understanding of Israelite society in the past, which is a thinly-veiled way of advocating for its centrality in his own day. The arrangement of Israel's tribes anticipate the building of the temple, and the account of the temple's planning and building occupy the longest stretch of material in the core of Chronicles (1 Chronicles 12—2 Chronicles 9). The building itself is understood as a symbol not only of community unity but of YHWH's power as divine king and even divine warrior (see section 5 for commentary on 1 Chronicles 21). The festivals, rituals, personnel, texts, and cosmic significance of the temple permeates virtually all levels of the Chronicler's work and governs his view of world history as well—the final note in Chronicles relates to the rise of the Persian empire, whose sole purpose is to facilitate the return of Jews to Jerusalem, presumably to build and worship at the temple (2 Chr. 36:22–23; cf. Ezra 1:1–4).

4.4. The Merits and Problems of Kingship

Like his source material in Samuel—Kings, the Chronicler has mixed feelings toward the institution of kingship. However, he has almost completely positive perceptions of the founder of the Davidic monarchy, David himself. The Chronicler's presentation of David is one of a faithful servant of YHWH, a respectful follower of prophetic authority, and an adherent to the Torah of Moses. David's kingdom and his primary achievement (the planning of the temple) are fulfillments of divine intention of the highest order, and constitute the greatest good in Israel's landed history. Moreover, the negative episodes in the book of Samuel that leave a somewhat darker picture of David are completely silenced; for the Chronicler, David is a symbolic figure and a standard-bearer for his audience—and certainly for the kings who follow in his wake.

But inasmuch as the Chronicler favors David, he is clearly critical of later kings. Virtually all of the kings he discusses are problematic; many begin their reigns virtuously but end in chaos and transgression, while others waver between these polarities throughout their tenures on the throne. Even favorite kings such as Jehoshaphat, Hezekiah, and Josiah have moments of straying from divine will and, notably, the instructions of priests and prophets. The Chronicler views the accomplishments of David (and to a somewhat lesser degree, Solomon) in a different category than most of these other kings, and thereby reveals a skepticism regarding the very institution of kingship. While this raises questions regarding the nature of YHWH's covenant with Israel (since the Davidic covenant as voiced in 2 Samuel 7 was of longstanding importance), it also points to the Chronicler's ambivalence toward the ruling powers of his own day—the emperors of Persia who were but the last in a succession of foreign emperors to rule over Israel for a span of several centuries. Kingship for the Chronicler is secondary in importance to YHWH's will expressed through native institutions such as the temple and prophets/priests, which constitutes a subtle lack of confidence in the viability of foreign kings now controlling Jewish political fortunes.

Figure 7.5: Implements of Temple worship—menorot, incense shovels, shofars—surround the Ark in this floor mosaic from a fifth-century synagogue in Scythopolis. Israel Museum; Commons.wikimedia.org.

5. Commentary

5.1. 1 Chronicles 1—9

The first nine chapters of Chronicles consist of elaborate genealogies. Those reading Chronicles with an interest in plot or characterization often see little of compelling value in these genealogical lists, since genealogies are by definition devoid of plot devices, drama, or much characterization (if any) and appear to strictly serve as repositories of data; indeed, a common approach to biblical genealogies is simply to "fill the gaps" in biblical narrative or provide some contextual background regarding the individuals at the center of these narratives. But this represents a reading strategy that would not have necessarily characterized the ancient audiences for these genealogies. The Chronicler's genealogies provide potent statements on the relationship not only between his audience and the larger Israelite tribal network, but between Israel as a corporate nation and the entire scope of humanity as created by YHWH. The genealogies move from the ancient to the contemporaneous, the general to the particular, and tell a story of national and theological diversity along the way.

The Chronicler's genealogies are therefore very carefully wrought and highly designed works of literature, and disinterested readers who "skip" over them in order to arrive at the narrative proper (beginning in 1 Chronicles 10) miss crucial information regarding the social organization of Israel and indeed the structure of the cosmos reflected in Israel's social organization. Over the last few decades, scholars have identified intricate patterns in these genealogies that carry subtle but important messages regarding rank, holiness, the history of family/clan interaction and politics, and other vitally important sociological features that inform how the ensuing narratives must be understood. By beginning his work with these genealogies, the Chronicler provides the first and arguably the most forceful ideological statement in Chronicles: that all Israel, and all humanity, constitutes a single extended family. As a family, they are accountable to each other, and the apparent superiority of one lineage over another (royal, priestly, or otherwise) is ultimately nullified by the common heritage shared by all.

By the same token, the transgressions of one individual or another cannot be held against the larger lineage or group to whom that individual is connected—the full implications of such logic would be to impugn all humanity. The interconnectedness of human families in the Chronicler's genealogies is the first implied theological message of the work: honor, shame, sin, reward, grievance, and grudge: all of the well-entrenched sociological presuppositions of the audience regarding these common tropes of separation and hierarchy must be rethought or, at the very least, re-examined in light of Israel's place among the nations and the individual's place within Israel.

A major cultural and theological feature in the Chronicler's genealogies is certainly the relationship between the families/clans he discusses and the locations wherein he places them. Most of the toponyms mentioned in 1 Chronicles 1—9 are long-duration sites; that is, they are locales that were inhabited throughout most of Israel's landed history in the pre-exilic period, which seems to be of paramount significance for the Chronicler despite his own late Persian compositional context. It is also important to note that archaeological evidence indicates that many of these sites were not heavily settled or occupied in the Persian period, and only saw notable populations later in the Hellenistic era. While this has led some to the conclusion that the genealogies were therefore the product of the late Hellenistic era (and thus secondarily added to an extant version of Chronicles),[16] it is just as likely that the Chronicler and his audience carried deep and meaningful memories of these locations and possessed different traditions—religious, political, mythological, cultural, historical, etc.—regarding their significance. Cultural memory is an important dimension of the Chronicler's work and permeates virtually every major unit of Chronicles and its vision of the past, and few cultural memories are more meaningful to group identity formation that those associated with space and place.

Throughout most of Israel's pre-exilic history and indeed even beyond this period, kinship and ethnicity were strongly bound to land tenure. This dynamic is already attested in the **Song of the Sea** in Exodus 15, arguably the oldest text in the Hebrew Bible, and one where Israel's ethnogenesis is a matter of YHWH planting his people in the sacred highlands, charging them with tending to it.[17] Communities preserving this land indeed preserve themselves; communities in geographic proximity, sharing agrarian resources and worshipping in shared sacred spaces, grew into tribal networks over time. And this, of course, eventually led to the formation of a monarchic state—the principle era of interest for the Chronicler—through which land could be protected, allocated, and administered.

The period of the Babylonian exile saw the growth of new geo-mythologies and different communal structures arising from forced migration both beyond and within the ancestral homeland, and these communal structures countenanced each other during the first half of the Persian period (in periodically hostile ways, as suggested by Ezra—Nehemiah). In all such cases, the occupation of and residence in specific territories matters, but just as importantly, so does the *memory* of occupation or residence. Geographic space determined insider-vs.-outsider communal status on both ethnic and religious grounds and provided insight into the proper political/cosmic order.

All of this affects how we might view the invocation of space/place by the Chronicler. The situation of various clans in areas that were once densely populated but which in the Persian period were not may be profitably viewed as the Chronicler's attempt to cultivate or invoke old associations between the toponyms he mentions and the communal networks he constructs in his genealogies. Chronicles may

16. Finkelstein 2012.
17. Leuchter 2011.

486

have been composed for a late Persian period audience, but it is a narrative about the past, and, what is more, about a shared past in a shared land, one that could not be restricted to one partisan group over another, or that could be claimed by one privileged community.

Given the expansive-inclusive tendency in these genealogies (i.e., the Chronicler's interest in connecting Persian period Yehud to a larger human "clan" with common ancestry), the combination of toponyms with clans/families/tribes should not be viewed as a one-to-one indication of actual residence patterns but, rather, a rhetorical and even hermeneutical literary device regarding cultural memory of land common to a wide spectrum of the Chronicler's intended audience. The land was a common heritage for all Israel, and the weaving of remembered toponyms into the genealogies provides a bridge between the land of the past and the audience's common share in it. In this way, the Chronicler utilizes the toponyms the way he utilizes the fictitious prophetic "sources" later in his work: they are rhetorical devices meant to cultivate a way of remembering and even reading the landscape (just as the prophetic "sources" are meant to cultivate a way of reading earlier texts).

The obvious foci of the Chronicler's genealogies are the groups whose ancestors are represented therein and their assignment to the different tribes of Israel. Not all of the tribes of Israel are mentioned with equal attention; several tribes have very limited details provided for them, and the tribe of Zebulon is not included at all. Many scholars have attempted to account for this somewhat lopsided approach to the genealogies, and the majority have generally agreed that though the Chronicler is interested in appealing to Jewish groups in peripheral social and geographic locations, his work focuses on the major population centers and groups of highest social and religious significance in the Persian period—namely, Benjamin, Judah, and Levi. A comparison reveals that a disproportionate amount of attention is paid to these three tribes, signaling the political complexity involving each tribe/region.

This is by no means surprising when one considers the politics of the exilic and early Persian periods. Though a good number of Judahites were uprooted and taken captive to Mesopotamia in the early-sixth century BCE, most of the Judahite population remained in the ancestral homeland.[18] However, this population suffered much internal

---

18. Lipschits 2003.

displacement; archaeological (and some textual) evidence reveals that most of the remaining population had to flee from their traditional ancestral landholdings and take up refugee residency in the northern frontier of Judah and in the region of Benjamin. The biblical tradition in both the book of Kings and Jeremiah that presents the Benjaminite city of **Mizpah** as a new administrative center following the destruction of Jerusalem (2 Kgs. 25:22; Jeremiah 40—41) dovetails with the archaeological evidence, confirming that Judahites were settling in and around the Benjaminite highlands during this transitional period.

The early Persian period saw severe conflict between repatriates to Jerusalem/Judah from exile and those in Benjamin who were able to migrate southward to their traditional family lands. As attested in Ezra 1—6, the repatriates advocated almost total separation from those who identified with the homeland population (though Ezra 6:21 is suggestive of some "defection" from the latter to the former). Land tenure was most certainly at the heart of the issue, with the repatriates claiming authentic ownership of the land on religious grounds and appealing to imperial authority to support those claims. In time, repatriate and homeland groups intermarried, which facilitated the resolution of some conflicts involving land tenure, but this too was viewed by some repatriates as unacceptable.[19] The partisans supporting both Ezra and Nehemiah seem to have been the most vocal about these marriages, arguing that the marital unions were illegitimate because the homelanders were not Jews but foreigners (Ezra 9—10; Nehemiah 13). Residence within Judah was thus contested when it came to those who had returned south from Benjamin.

The emphasis on Judah and Benjamin is therefore very much at home in a late-Persian era composition that inherited a strong legacy of polemics, aggression, and conflict between groups connected to Benjamin (which would have included not only the Judahite refugees who fled there during the exilic era but longstanding Benjaminite clans as well) and those who settled in Judah, claiming it as their proper ancestral terrain. In the late Persian period, both Judah and Benjamin would have been subject to the same political authorities, both imperial (e.g., Persian-appointed governors) and priestly (the Aaronides in the Jerusalem temple). Though Judah receives greater textual space, Benjamin is the only tribe that actually receives two genealogical units (1 Chr. 7:6–12; 8). The first is situated among the

---

19. A full study of the Homeland/Repatriate conflict is that of Rom-Shiloni 2013.

northern tribal lists, the second it closer in textual space to the genealogy of the tribe of Judah. The Chronicler seems to be aware of the dual nature of Benjamin as both a northern refuge for Judahites during the exilic era and the geographic home (however temporary) of many residents of Yehud in his own time.

Sidebar 7.7: Yehud as a Persian Province

The Persian province of Yehud—part of the large Satrapy of Trans-Euphrates (Aramaic *ebar-nahara*)—was a small tract of land which comprised little more than the boundaries of the former kingdom of Judah and the former tribal territory of Benjamin. (See Figure 6.2, above.) Excavations at Ramat Rahel, a Persian period administrative site only a few kilometers outside of Jerusalem, contribute to our understanding of just how depleted a region this was throughout much of the fifth and fourth centuries BCE. As the provincial capital city, Jerusalem occupied a fairly limited sphere of influence, with other sites such as Ramat Rahel and probably Mizpah to the north serving as outpost of imperial governance to nearby territories. Yet while some scholars see Yehud's small size and population as an indication of its "backwater" status in the Persian Empire (coupled with its satellite geographical position in relation to the imperial heartland), it held an important place as a gateway to Egypt. Many of the Persian rulers attempted to maintain control over the valuable Egyptian lands, and it is therefore quite likely that Yehud received a fair amount of attention that would otherwise have left it an afterthought in the politics of the Persian royal court.

But this complex social/geographic function for Benjamin may even recall much earlier circumstances, for the region of Benjamin was claimed by both the kingdom of Judah and the northern kingdom of Israel during the monarchic era. Geographically speaking, Benjamin was literally situated between both polities throughout most of the monarchic era, and constituted a special prize on both religious and economic grounds. Its agrarian resources and strategic value was recognized by both kingdoms, and tales such as the Joseph story (in its pre-exilic form) attest to this by pitting Judah against Joseph as the protector of Benjamin.[20] There is a good case to be made, in fact, for the pre-eminent position of Benjamin and its population even before

20. Levin 2004b.

the monarchic era; royal control of such a territory, then, would carry much political prestige.[21] But just as important is the fact that Israel's first king, Saul, was a Benjaminite, and the Saulide royal family maintained a strong presence throughout the monarchic period as a potential alternative not only to the royal dynasties of the north but to the Davidic dynasty in Judah.

The eclipse of the Saulides by the House of David left a deep impact upon Israelite political discourse and identity, and many scholars have argued that during the decline of the Davidic dynasty in Jerusalem in the late-seventh and early-sixth centuries BCE, attention turned once again to the Saulides as potential political leaders. There is little doubt, too, that the Saulide family was an important political dynasty in the early Persian period as well;[22] the special attention given to the Benjaminite genealogies may be a tip of the hat to the influence of the Saulide legacy in the social world and memory of Persian Yehud. Nevertheless, the association of at least part of this genealogy with the northern (and thus more socially and geographically peripheral) tribes also declares that while those affiliated with the House of Saul are still fundamentally and essentially part of Israel's past, they do not occupy the central role in its present and future—that honor goes to Judah and Levi, the tribes who receive the lion's share of the Chronicler's attention not only in the genealogies but throughout the entire book of Chronicles.

Of these two central tribal entities, Judah receives the most attention. This is not surprising when we turn our eye both to the Chronicler's geographic and cultural setting (Judah/Yehud) as well as to the Chronicler's principal source, Samuel—Kings, which is a work that reflects a largely Judahite worldview. The Davidic line (1 Chronicles 3) is the subject of great detail in the Chronicler's genealogy of Judah, which is also not surprising. By the Persian period, the figure of David had become much more than just a political symbol. The late Persian era redaction of the Book of the Twelve (Hosea—Malachi), for example, routinely returns to David as a symbol of divine blessing mediated through prophetic teaching, and the Chronicler focuses on David in a similar manner in his ensuing narrative—the divine promise to David from 2 Samuel 7 is transferred to the community through the institution of the Jerusalem temple. It is worth noting, then, the special

21. Fleming 2003.
22. For example, the late-Persian or early-Hellenistic Scroll of Esther emphasizes Mordechai's Saulide heritage (Esth. 2:5).

mention of Nahshon b. Aminadab as "the chieftain of Judah" (1 Chr. 2:10). The Judahite genealogy contains many luminaries (including Peretz, the eponymous ancestor of David's clan), but only Nahshon is called Judah's "chieftain."

While this may speak to a particular memory of forms of social leadership/organization from the monarchic era (or earlier), it more likely represents the Chronicler's desire to emphasize the Pentateuchal source where the Nahshon is implied to be the broker of the marital relationship between his sister and Aaron (Exod. 6:7). For the Chronicler, this warrants special attention, foreshadowing—or, better, foregrounding—the relationship between the Judahite royal line and the priesthood who dominated the Jerusalem temple before and throughout the Persian period.

The Judahite genealogy also seems to have drawn from a broader and more well-preserved trove of sources than the other genealogies. The material in 1 Chronicles 2—4 knows and utilizes sources from the early monarchy through the late monarchic period regarding the various clans of Judah in a way that is more detailed than most of the other tribal genealogies. Beyond abstracting information from Samuel—Kings, the Chronicler seems to have had access to details that were probably long preserved among royal circles in Jerusalem regarding the citizenry of Judah and which were no doubt reconstructed (or even kept in textual form to a certain degree) during and after the Babylonian exile. The structuring of these sources into the carefully designed Judahite genealogy is suggestive of rank and influence among various Judahite clans in the late Persian period. We may cautiously assume that the more detailed the list of older ancestors and their relations, the more important each family may have been in antiquity; the Chronicler may then have woven the details of important families in his own day into these genealogies (with the Davidic line sitting squarely in the center and, of course, possessing the greatest degree of detail).

This leaves us with the last of the genealogical lists, namely, that of the Levites. Though Pentateuchal tradition identifies the Levites as a tribe with an eponymous ancestor named Levi, most scholars recognize that the Levites of the pre-state and monarchic periods were a sacerdotal caste rather than an actual "tribe." In Hebrew, the word *lewi* means "connected [one]," i.e., an individual who is separated from his biological family and is connected to the priesthood at a regional shrine and devoted to priestly service. The narrative in 1 Samuel 1—3 presupposes this process: Samuel's parents devote their son to priestly service at the Shiloh sanctuary, where he is effectively assimilated into the priestly family of Eli and eventually becomes a priest in his own right (which also explains why the Chronicler identifies Samuel as a Levite in 1 Chr. 6:18–23). By the eighth century BCE, Levites seem to have become "tribalized"; that is, narrative traditions from that period speak of Levites as a tribe like the other Israelite tribes (e.g., Exod. 2:1), and the Levite genealogies in the Pentateuch construct lineage networks which assume that Levites were viewed in such a light more broadly (e.g., Numbers 3–4, etc.).

Part of this must be viewed as the result of Levites as part of a monarchic society, where a priests at any given sanctuary (and the Levites under their charge) would have been woven into a larger official priestly network and hierarchy answering to the priesthood at the central sanctuary patronized by the king. This appears to be the case in monarchic Judah, where various priestly families at local sanctuaries were eventually understood as being offshoots of the Aaronide family whose chief representatives were stationed in the state's highest-order sanctuary, the Jerusalem temple.

The Levite genealogies in Chronicles work within this paradigm, signaling that the Chronicler was familiar with the history of the priesthood during the monarchic period. Indeed, the initial unit of the Levite genealogies focuses on the Aaronide priests and trace their lineage throughout the era of the monarchy (1 Chr. 6:1-3) before moving on to different Levite lineages (vv. 4ff). These verses point to the paramount role of the Aaronides within the temple establishment; no late Persian period author or audience would have ever imagined another priesthood holding that position, and all other priestly lines clearly functioned as a support to the Aaronide superstructure. The Aaronides are positioned in the temple, focused on altar duties while the Levites are situated around them, ministering to the needs of the sanctuary at large. But this is not a sign of lower rank so much as a reflex of social reality in conversation with the cultural memory of earlier Levite function. Sanctuaries were, after all, not simply places to offer sacrifices but social anchors where different lineages could affirm their allegiances and solidify a sense of kinship between each other.

The Levites seem to facilitate this in 1 Chronicles 6, serving at the sanctuary where different Israelite groups interacted and mediating between those groups and the Aaronide priests. While the Aaronides held the responsibility for the sacrificial cult and atoning for communal transgression (Leviticus 1–7; 16), the Levites would have been the all-important ombudsmen connecting the priesthood to the populations from outside the temple. To do this, Levites would have been required to maintain administrative records, engage in educational enterprises, manage different groups of devotees or pilgrims to the temple, and other duties where the needs of the agrarian population and the sacrificial cult of the Aaronides countenanced each other.

Finally, 1 Chr. 6:46–66 details the various cities throughout the tribal territories where the Levite clans were stationed (when not in service at the temple; see section 5.5), creating a social bridge between the spatial center and periphery. All of this is strongly implied through the structure of the genealogical details regarding the Aaronides and Levites, but they are simply a prelude to the role that Levites will play in more detail throughout the narrative of Chronicles and are an indication of how concerned the Chronicler is with the affirming the fundamental need of Levite activity and authority throughout the nation's past.

The genealogies in Chronicles end with an account of the lineages who settled in Jerusalem, drawing heavily from Nehemiah 11, which covers much of the same material.[23] Yet 1 Chronicles 9 departs from Nehemiah 11 in some important ways, chief of which is that in Nehemiah 11, the material is set within a narrative of a people's return from exile. In Chronicles, the names of Jerusalem's residents are abstracted from this historical backdrop altogether. They are set within a narrative that involves David's ordering of the community under the prophetic direction of Samuel (1 Chr. 9:22). The important groups covered in this chapter are still held in high esteem by virtue of their residence and function in sacred Jerusalem, but the text does not assign any privilege to them based on their association with a repatriated community possessing roots in Mesopotamia. Rather, like the other genealogical groups, they are of the land, reinforcing the Chronicler's rhetoric of inclusion and extended kinship (over against the separatist inclinations evident throughout Ezra–Nehemiah).

It should also be noted that Jerusalem here is portrayed as a wholly Israelite city, and this too stands at odds with earlier tradition. In Ezra–Nehemiah, Jerusalem is the center of Israelite/Jewish life, but only after it was restored under the auspices of Persia. And of course

---

23. Alternately, Nehemiah 11 and 1 Chronicles 9 may both rely upon a common source.

in the book of Samuel, Jerusalem only becomes an Israelite city once David claims it as his own personal property. Before this time it was a Canaanite town, and its Canaanite legacy was remembered as late as the days of Ezekiel (Ezek. 16:3). None of this surfaces in the Chronicler's treatment of Jerusalem and its population: the city is, like other sites alluded to in Chronicles, a fundamentally and exclusively Israelite site, and indeed a common space where Israelites from different tribal backgrounds could equally reside and call home. This dovetails with the utopian/rhetorical interest of the Chronicler. His vision of Jerusalem is shaped to present that city as the inheritance of all Israel and vital to their union as a cohesive nation.

5.2. 1 Chronicles 10–12

The Chronicler's narrative now turns to the primary theme of the work, namely, the history and organization of Israel's monarchy, with special emphasis on the foundation of the Jerusalem cult and the assignments of the temple priesthood. This issue is largely absent, though, in these transitional chapters, which collapse a much more extensive bounty of narrative material from 1–2 Samuel into a fairly condensed account of how the monarchy passed from Saul to David. The opening tableau in these chapters is very close to the source content, so much so that the reader might not notice any significant difference. But this makes the departure from the source material all the more impressive and notable: Saul dies on the battlefield of Gilboa as he does in the source narrative in Samuel, but the long stretches of inter-family violence between the Saulide and Davidic houses is completely eliminated from the account in Chronicles.

One might be tempted to see the Chronicler attempting to whitewash the events in his sources or suggest that they be forgotten or overlooked, but this is not the case—1 Chr. 10:13–14 makes clear that Saul dies for a number of "sins," presupposing that the reader not only knows the Samuel source but will consult it for additional detail. By extension, this means that the non-mention of the turbulence accompanying David's rise to the throne should similarly be read with (not against!) the Samuel material. Chronicles here leaves room for the reader to consider not an alternative history but which aspects of a collective history (and, perhaps, which aspects of a collective literary history) require attention or apply to Jewish life in the late Persian period. Chronicles functions as a hermeneutical lens, deliberately drawing attention to its sources while simultaneously raising questions about the degree to which perceptions or traditional understandings of those sources should be accepted or sustained.

Figure 7.6: *The Battle of Gilboa* by Jean Fouquet (15th century); Bibliotheque Nationale de France. Commons.wikimedia.org.

One such understanding may be the anti-Saulide polemic which stretched all the way back to the early days of the monarchy and which seems to have lasted down to the late-fourth century BCE. The early composition of narratives in Samuel in the tenth to eighth centuries went to great lengths to castigate Saul personally and impugn the viability of his royal dynasty, and this ethos was sustained in the Deuteronomistic History as well throughout the late monarchic and exilic periods. The hope of Davidic restoration in the early Persian period would have likewise stirred up anti-Saul sentiments among pro-Davidic partisans; the scroll of Esther seems to interface with this to a certain degree by making a descendant of Saul (Mordechai) rather than a descendant of David into the savior of the Jews. The presentation of Saul and the Saulides in Chronicles should be viewed in light of this larger social issue: the Chronicler abides by his sources, which could not be ignored or nullified.

Yet the Chronicler's narrative strategy makes Saul's downfall a matter of personal transgression, at which point YHWH himself transfers power to David. There is no demonization of his family or lineage, and no struggle between the Saulide or Davidic partisans is highlighted. Kingship here is not a political matter but entirely a theological one, and corporate guilt that might otherwise justify a condemnation of the Saulide line is removed from the panoply of theological possibility. Descendants of Saul are not to be condemned or punished for whatever led to Saul's own demise. This supports the theological and sociological implications of the genealogies in the opening chapters of Chronicles, where the tribe of Benjamin (Saul's own tribe) receives attention and an honorable place in the Israelite tribal assembly that will eventually support and be supported by the temple establishment.

But these chapters in Chronicles also set up a dynamic where kingship, from the outset, is somewhat diminished as a sacral institution—and that this applies directly to the institution of Davidic kingship. The Chronicler clearly picks and chooses what material he wishes to include in his narrative, and could easily have started the narrative not with the account of Saul's demise but with the material in chapter 11 where David rises in profile. Instead, the tale of Saul's demise makes clear that rank and privilege is a matter of fidelity to YHWH rather than political prestige or power. And this affects how we perceive what follows; 1 Chronicles 11 is primarily concerned with David's move to Jerusalem and the rank and reputation of his elite guard (the "mighty men" in vv. 22–47), which is prefaced by the brief tale of idealized servile behavior in vv. 18–21. In this chapter, David is presented as a role model for his elite guard, who obtain different ranks of honor based on the king's own standard of behavior. The narrative clearly draws from sources (much of which can be found in the closing chapters of 2 Samuel) but arranges them in such a way as to build upon the lesson of Saul's demise in the previous chapter. David's success as king is in his ability to effectively structure different orders and ranks of royal officials, whereas no such skill is ascribed to Saul.

Chapter 12 goes on to demonstrate that David's influence is recognized broadly throughout Israel: the various tribes align themselves with him willingly, with no indication whatsoever that tension between David and those once loyal to Saul remained. Chronicles presents a picture of Israel as a collectively-minded group who agree to participate in David's reign, recognizing his divinely-mandated royal authority. This will have serious implications for the Chronicler's picture of Israel throughout the work, one that is inclined toward integration and inclusivity (over against the separatist impulses in Ezra—Nehemiah). But this also indicates that whatever authority is vested in David is accepted and supported by the people, and this sets the stage for the ensuing chapters where David begins to orchestrate the Jerusalem cult around which the Chronicler sought to draw a picture of his idealized Israel. David's skill set in these chapters look ahead the role that he will play in defining that idealized Israel: after setting his own "house" in order, he demonstrates his readiness to set YHWH's house in order as well.

5.3.1 Chronicles 13—16

In these chapters, the Chronicler goes into detail regarding David's coronation as king of Israel and the strong connection between the royal office and the organization of the Jerusalem cult. This is by no means a subject of the Chronicler's own invention: kings throughout antiquity were viewed as the patrons of their national religions and the primary cultic agents in the sanctuaries they commissioned or restored. This was no different throughout most of Israel's history as well, as detailed passages such as 1 Kings 6—8 and brief glimpses like Amos 7:12 suggest. Yet the Chronicler's primary sources—the Deuteronomistic History and the Pentateuch—go to some length to qualify the degree to which kings could helm the cult; good kings do not take upon themselves the role of cult patron but instead follow the law (including laws about the cult), and the Pentateuch removes kingship from the equation altogether, rendering the priests the sole agents of sacral mediation.[24]

The Chronicler defers to his sources in many respects but also reckons here with historical memory and conventional ancient culture, and in so doing comes up with a sort of middle path. David is the chief *executor* of divine instruction regarding the cult; he does not helm the cult, but appoints Levite agents to populate and regulate the cult throughout these and later chapters. Thus David is presented as the cult's most avid supporter, but his orchestration of its internal features is not a matter of royal fiat but divine command.

Central to these chapters is the Ark of the Covenant, the most sacred

---

24. The only Pentateuchal text to mention Israelite kingship, Deut. 17:14—20, limits the king's activity to the study of the law (notably administered by Levite priests).

and ancient icon associated with the worship of YHWH. Most scholars would agree that in the Chronicler's day, the Ark was no longer actually in the Jerusalem temple (it was very probably plundered and destroyed by the Babylonians centuries earlier), but the memory of the Ark was kept alive by the earlier sources available to the Chronicler, in this case, 2 Samuel 6. First Chronicles 13 begins with a notice not found in earlier sources that the decision to bring the Ark to Jerusalem was not David's alone but one with which the public agreed; as with the larger picture of Israel in Chronicles, fidelity to cultic orthodoxy is the national default and the province of all Israelites (not just those who were responsible for rebuilding the temple in the late-sixth century BCE).

As in the source material in 2 Samuel 6, the transfer of the Ark does not go smoothly; it is interrupted by a first failed attempt resulting in the death of Uzzah (1 Chr. 13:9–14). That the Chronicler decided to include this detail from his source rather than exclude or gloss over it simply highlights the reality that the Ark, which symbolized and contained the power of YHWH, was no common item but one that required great care from the right agents. This reading is reinforced by the verses that follow (1 Chr. 14:1–17), for the Chronicler informs us that David has not been punished by YHWH but indeed flourishes politically even in the wake of Uzzah's death. The issue is not one of impious or immoral transgression but one that highlights the high stakes of holy objects. This paves the way for what we encounter in 1 Chronicles 15—16, namely, the highly detailed account of the successful transfer of the Ark conducted by the hands of the Levites. As we have already seen, the Levites receive great attention in the genealogical lists at the outset of Chronicles, but it is here where we find them finally taking up their roles as the primary agents of the cult, capable of handling the awesome power of the Ark and working together with David to ensure that it finds its way to Jerusalem without failure.

Figure 7.7: The Ark of the Covenant, relief on a pillar capital from the synagogue at Capernaum. Photo: Berthold Werner; Commons.wikimedia.org.

The relationship between David and the Levites in Chronicles is unparalleled. Second Samuel 15:24 points to an actual close association between the king and Levites during his reign, one that anthropological evidence suggests is very much at home in a society like that of Israel in the early-tenth century BCE.[25] But 1 Chronicles 15–16 provides unique details regarding the specific Levite orders who organized under David's direction; many of these details are recognized by scholars as deriving from the Chronicler's own time, with the Chronicler writing Levite circles of his own day into the story of Jerusalem's cultic foundations. The implication of these details is that the Jerusalem temple of the Second Temple period is in no way a lesser institution than that which stood in Jerusalem during the monarchic era, for the Levites of the late-fourth century are direct descendants of those who built its sacral foundations. This also implies a sort of partnership with David that could allow for the messianic "promise to David" (2 Sam. 7) to remain in place even in the absence of a Davidic king: *the Levites themselves* are the bearers of this promise.

The specifics regarding the Levites provided in 1 Chronicles 15 (especially vv. 4–10) has been the focus of great attention. The families

25. Hutton 2011.

499

of the Levites depicted in these verses are probably traditional families by and large; Kohath, Merari, and Gershom (or Gershon)[26] are names well known from the Pentateuchal narratives and elsewhere, and very likely have roots in monarchic-era Israel. But the Chronicler also provides additional names (Elizaphan, Hebron, Uzziel) and identifies many other smaller units of Levites on a subsidiary level. The construction of these associations is probably more a matter of the Chronicler's own composition than real social or kinship relationships. Genealogies, as we have seen, are fluid entities that serve social and political purposes more often than they preserve authentic historical details.[27] This is not to say that the names included here are fictitious: it is very likely that the named figures in this chapter (and others) were actual priestly or Levitical figures known to the Chronicler and his audience. But their genealogical connection to the more well-known Levite families creates rhetorical associations regarding all such figures (at a time, it should be noted, when priestly or Levite status appears to have been up for debate). In creating an image of an inclusive Jerusalem cult, Chronicles creates an image of an inclusive Levite caste. All have a role to play in the fate of Jerusalem.

These aforementioned roles are delineated clearly in the remainder of the chapter. The Levites are organized into different classes of singers (1 Chr. 15:16–25), with a wide variety of Levite names assigned specific types of songs, musical instruments, or positions as choral leaders. Whereas the book of Leviticus discusses the Israelite cult with nary a mention of prayer or hymn, 1 Chronicles 15 highlights the paramount significance of prayers, hymns, songs, and music to be conducted by the Levites, equating this dimension of the cult with security (the "gatekeeping" of vv. 24–25) and clarifying that only through proper Levitical praise could the Ark be successfully borne and transferred to Jerusalem (vv. 26–29). It is also notable that the Chronicler claims that the Levites—not the Aaronide priests—were responsible for conducting sacrifices upon the Ark's transfer (v. 26). Here we encounter one of several places where the Chronicler seems to challenge the temple's priestly hierarchy, suggesting that the great importance of the Aaronides (who throughout the Persian period dominated the temple) was rivaled by that of the Levites.

This foregoing point is significant, for other Persian period texts provide indications that the Aaronide priests were primed to eclipse

26. On the relationship between Gershon and Gershom, see Leuchter 2012, 494–97.
27. Levin 2003; 2004a.

the legacy of the Davidic kings. The Chronicler seems to contest this through his characterization of the Levites as close partners of David. This is further attested by 1 Chronicles 16, the majority of which is David commissioning the singing of a thanksgiving hymn, and one that draws from material in the book of Psalms (especially Psalms 96, 105, and 106).[28] The locution here is intriguing, as it implies that David was somehow involved in the creation or composition of the hymn, though it is sung by Levites of the Asaphite order. Two things demand our attention. First, David's use of the Psalmic material links him to the role just delineated for the Levites as **cultic singers**; by implication, it is the Levites charged from this point onward with singing such praises that connects back to kingship. Their duties in this regard keep the "lamp of David" continuously lit in the temple, not the claims of the Aaronide priests or their sacrificial/ritual responsibilities.

Second, the sources for this hymn are widely recognized to have been Judahite-composed psalms of rather late period (Psalms 105 and 106 are generally considered exilic in origin), but they are sung by "Asaph and his guild" (v. 7). The "Psalms of Asaph" in the book of Psalms are strongly northern in concern, expression, mythology, and language, which has led many researchers to identify the Asaphite Levites as a northern group.[29] In 1 Chronicles 16, then, the Chronicler has David working closely with a northern group that is credited with singing southern praises. This is not meant to be taken literally by any means, but is instead a symbolic discourse: old categories and divisions, be they north/south, Levite/Aaronide, early/late, are immaterial insofar as David is concerned. The king could give thanks for the Ark's safe transfer to Jerusalem in partnership with Levites of many different varieties, all of whom have an equal share in partnering with the king. Indeed, the only attention that the Aaronides receive in this chapter is a footnote at the end that their representative Zadok went with his kin to conduct sacrifices at Gibeah at the (temporary) tabernacle sanctuary there.[30] Even so, Zadok and his kin were accompanied by the Levites Heman and Jeduthun whose duties as cult singers overshadow the sacrificial rites of the Zadokite group (vv. 39–42).

28. Ben Zvi 2007.
29. Cook 2004, 61; 126–27.
30. See section 5 above in the discussion on the book of Samuel for additional details regarding Zadok.

Sidebar 7.8: The Levites in Chronicles

The origin of the Levites is remarkably complicated, but they seem to have developed throughout the monarchic era as a caste of priests that occupied a social space between family-based religious cultures and state-based religious institutions, especially in the northern kingdom of Israel. Some Levites were probably once associated with sanctuary sites that transitioned into royally-sponsored shrines and sanctuaries, leading to tensions between the religion of the state practiced at these sites and the values of the Levites who were disenfranchised from them. The Asaphite Levites (taking their name from some founding saint figure named Asaph) are probably one such group; many units in the book of Psalms are credited to them (Psalms 50; 73—83) and possess both ideological and linguistic features that strongly suggest northern origins. As such, the Psalms of Asaph provide a window into the traditions of these early northern Levite groups who eventually migrated south to Judah and whose descendants found a place in the cult of the Jerusalem temple. It is the legacy of the Asaphite Levites that the Chronicler has in mind when discussing the place of these same Levites in the formative days of the temple and the sacral traditions of Jerusalem.

5.4. 1 Chronicles 17—22

This unit begins with what is arguably the most important instance of prophecy in Chronicles, namely, the oracle containing YHWH's "Promise to David," where an eternal covenant is established between the deity and the Davidic line (1 Chr. 17:1–15). This version of this oracle in Chronicles closely follows the source material in 2 Samuel 7, and for good reason: 2 Samuel 7 was among the most well-known texts to literate audiences in early Judaism, and was certainly also known to less- or non-literate audiences in a substantial oral form. Second Samuel 7 is also among one of the most overwritten and exegetically revisited texts in the history of the Hebrew Bible, revised repeatedly to reflect changing circumstances and subjected to new interpretations over the centuries of its growth.[31]

The Chronicler's version of this oracle shows that the source material in 2 Samuel 7 had become quite fixed by his day, and the

---

31. Schniedewind 1999.

Chronicler regarded it as a work from which he could not significantly depart. To do so, in fact, would have worked against his own interests in promoting a vision for the temple's role in Jewish life, because the temple remained the most visible and enduring symbol of the Davidic covenant. The Promise to David could be utilized to promote the Chronicler's vision for a temple-based Jewish world, but it was in some ways quite sacrosanct. Any deviation from the source would call into question the legitimacy of the Chronicler's narrative regarding the ordering of the temple's priestly and Levite faculty. The same applies to the account of David's pious response to the oracle he has received (1 Chr. 17:16–27): the response is essentially identical in content to its source material in 2 Samuel 7. Despite the strong hermeneutical and transformative ethos running throughout Chronicles, some traditions could not be altered.

The chapters that follow (1 Chronicles 18–20) effectively summarize the record of David's wars from 2 Samuel. Though these chapters contain few embellishments or changes, the sequence of material spanning 1 Chronicles 17–20 in sum creates a particular theology that is implicit but not overt in the source material in the book of Samuel. The account of David's wars offers prooftexts, in a way, for the Promise to David and David's pious reply in 1 Chronicles 17. That is, 1 Chronicles 18–20 depict David's successes and triumphs as a sign of divine blessing.

This is intriguing, because while 2 Samuel 8 seems to function in this way in relation to 2 Samuel 7, the remainder of David's battles in the book of Samuel are presented not as signs of blessing but as punishment for the Bathsheba affair (2 Samuel 11–12). It is unlikely that the Chronicler imagined that his audience was unfamiliar with this tradition, or would not know/read the textual source behind his own composition. Rather, the presenting of David's wars as proof of divine favor served two purposes. First, it promoted a method of reading the sources, suggesting that divine favor could and did include justice for transgression; punishment was not always a sign of divine chastisement and could in fact function as a testament to the active nature of the covenant relationship between YHWH and his subjects. Second, it affirms that even if David's battles involved personal trauma and difficulty, the battles were nonetheless won. This affirmed YHWH as a divine warrior who triumphs over adversity through the unfolding of history as much as through miraculous interventions (such as the parting of the Red Sea in Exodus 14–15).

Figure 7.8: David's soldiers slay his rebellious son Absalom (upper panel); David awaits news (lower panel), scenes narrated in 2 Samuel but not Chronicles; illumination from the Morgan Leaf Picture Bible, ca. 1250; now in the J. Paul Getty Museum. Commons.wikimedia.org.

The concept of YHWH as a **divine warrior** permeates a good deal of the Hebrew Bible. The earliest poetic materials conceive of YHWH in this way (Exodus 15; Habakkuk 3; Psalm 68) and a variety of narrative traditions are similarly informed by this theology, where the human agents engage in a ritualized form of behavior mirroring YHWH fighting against cosmic and earthly foes, including Levites (Exod. 32:20). The motif remained quite powerful down into the Persian period, surfacing both in oracles within the late prophetic literature (e.g., Zechariah 9; 14) and in the construction of the book of Psalms (Psalms 2; 29; 97; 98; 124; etc.). Both the redaction of the Psalms and the redaction of the prophetic literature took place in roughly the same era

504

as the composition of Chronicles, and (as observed above) both of those other works similarly seem to emphasize Levites interests.

Since the Chronicler similar cares deeply about promoting the importance of the Levites, the similar emphasis (albeit in a somewhat veiled form) on the divine warrior motif is appropriate. Indeed, the eventual planning and construction of the temple following the account of David's military exploits connects strongly to very ancient mythic patterns where the divine warrior builds his heavenly sanctuary after defeating his cosmic enemies.[32] The Chronicler's narrative may therefore have been part of a literary movement involving the Psalms and the redaction of prophetic texts that sought to highlight how the temple was not just a place for sacrifice or an economic hub but was a potent icon of YHWH's warrior dimensions, symbolizing his dominion over the entire universe.

First Chronicles 21 fleshes out the implications of the previous few chapters, introducing into the narrative a decidedly cosmic character—the **Satan**—who is presented as the force that moved David to engage in a wrongful census taking (v. 1). The account of David's census is based on the source material in 2 Samuel 24 where David's census leads to a terrible plague which befalls all of Israel; the place of this episode in the book of Samuel is probably the result of Deuteronomistic editing, displacing it from an earlier position in the story of David's reign. Some scholars have viewed 2 Samuel 24 in relation to David's inability to build the temple—the argument is that David had indeed actually intended to build a temple, the plans for which were subverted by a plague that was somehow connected to his taking of a census (probably for taxation revenues).[33] This may well have led to the earliest form of the Promise to David, conceived as prophetic propaganda to provide David with ongoing legitimacy even in the face of the plague and the absence of a temple project.

The book of Samuel dissociates the Promise to David from the account of the census and plague, but the Chronicler's reworking of this material re-connects them. This may simply have followed oral lore current in the Chronicler's day regarding the "real" reason why David did not build the temple (a reason that the book of Samuel denies), yet the Chronicler engages in a brilliant exegetical strategy here by following the flow of events in the book of Samuel (i.e., having the Promise to David come first) and at the same time, amplifying

32. See Hanson 1973, 54.
33. Meyers 1987.

the cosmic/mythic dimensions of 1 Chronicles 17—20 by crediting the census and its fallout to the Satan as YHWH's cosmic enemy.

Sidebar 7.9: "Satan" as a Cosmic Figure

The "satan" of longstanding Jewish and Christian traditions has origins in the figure named *satan* ("adversity") or *ha-satan* ("the adversary") in the Hebrew Scriptures, but this figure is not the embodiment of evil that we encounter in the much later writings of the New Testament and beyond. The figure called *satan* appears three times in the Hebrew Scriptures: once in Zech. 3:2, again in chapters 1—2 in the book of Job, and finally the brief notice in 1 Chr. 21:1. In none of these cases is the figure identified as a representative of evil or the chief enemy of the divine. Indeed, the *satan* of Job 1—2 is a welcome member of the divine council in heaven, and the *satan* of 1 Chr. 21:1 is best understood as a symbol of disorder that constantly threatens the social and religious world anchored by the Jerusalem cult of the Chronicler's day. It would only be after the development of alternate mythologies by different Jewish groups in the Hellenistic period (evidenced in the book of Enoch and in the Dead Sea Scrolls) that the New Testament writers would equate the *satan* of the Hebrew Scriptures with demonic entities found in the writings of these other groups.

The material in the chapter that contains YHWH inflicting pestilence and a destructive angel upon the people (vv. 14–15) suddenly become part of the cosmic drama that follows the much older mythic patterns. Furthermore, the penitence displayed by David and the Israelite elders who followed him (vv. 16–17) restore balance and order, revealing an important aspect of the cosmic drama in the Chronicler's imagination: prayer and theological fidelity are not simply acts of deference to YHWH, but constitute powerful weapons in nullifying the effects of cosmic chaos.

It is after this display of penitent confession that David is able to forge ahead with his plans (he secures the space for the temple from Ornan in vv. 18–29). From the mythological perspective, 1 Chronicles 21 is the high note in a crescendo of events, raising the mythological tone of David's earthly battles in the previous chapters to a point where a final, cosmic conflict plays out. In the end, David triumphs because of his pious confession, and this is YHWH's triumph as well. In the final chapter of the unit (1 Chronicles 22), David's instruction for building the temple thus take on a role similar to that of Moses' instructions to Israel in the Pentateuch: both figures have heralded the divine warrior and shepherded Israel through ritual conflicts or trials, and their oral instructions for orchestrating a sacred society (Deuteronomy for Moses, the plans for the temple for David) are enshrined in a lasting text.

5.5. 1 Chronicles 23–27 (The Priestly Courses)

This unit is usually regarded as somehow special within the narrative flow of Chronicles. It contains an extensive amount of information regarding the temple faculty, especially the roles, schedules and duties of the Levites therein. The priestly faculty in these chapters are arranged into twenty-four divisions (or "courses"), and later Jewish literature such as the Mishnah (ca. 200 CE) contains oblique indications that these divisions were not idealized constructs but actually did characterize the organization of the sacerdotal staff in the Jerusalem temple. For this reason, some scholars have identified these chapters as secondary additions to the base narrative of Chronicles, i.e., an attempt to "update" the work to reflect the reality of Judaism in the Hellenistic period.[34]

Contemporary researchers, however, are more inclined to assign these chapters to the Chronicler and view them as an essential part of his narrative and vision for the temple. While there can be little doubt that much of what we encounter regarding the temple, its faculty, and its social role in Chronicles is somewhat utopian in nature, this does not preclude the possibility that historically authentic details or sources have been woven into that utopian vision. Like the genealogies at the outset of the work, the information embedded within 1 Chronicles 23–27 may well reflect the social topography of late Persian Yehud and its cultic culture.[35]

Most of 1 Chronicles 23 deals exclusively with the Levites *en masse*: their families/clans, the number of those of proper age for sacerdotal service, and those specifically assigned to temple-based duties. The chapter contains an extremely high number of Levites counted by David—thirty-eight thousand—which suggests that the Chronicler has inflated the numbers from the genuine sources he possessed (especially since most archaeologists estimate that the total number

34. Williamson 1979.
35. Kim 2014.

of residents in Jerusalem in the Persian period was approximately five thousand). This and other details are obviously attempts by the Chronicler to say something about the need for Levites and their responsibilities rather than relate an uninflected account of personnel.

The following chapter, 1 Chronicles 24, is divided into two parts, the first of which deals with the Aaronide priesthood and its social divisions. While the Chronicler places greater emphasis on the Levites than on the Aaronide priests throughout his work, he nonetheless recognizes their authority and importance; this was an inescapable realization, actually, since all evidence shows that the Aaronides held the majority of political and religious power throughout the Persian and Hellenistic periods.[36] Even if the Chronicler sought to make a case for Levites as an anchor-institution in Israel, due credit had to be given to the Aaronides, and in all likelihood, the Chronicler himself constructed his work under their auspices and influence.

The material in 1 Chronicles 25 details the musical duties of the Levites in the temple cult. The specific role each group of Levites is to play is determined by the casting of sacred lots (vv. 8–31). In other words, YHWH himself is conducting the "Levitical orchestra," as it were, which only highlights the importance of this aspect of their function. We must recall that earlier, the successful transfer of the Ark to Jerusalem was due to the involvement of the Levites, including the musicians/singers among them. Sacred music is presented there, and in 1 Chronicles 25, as a powerful vehicle for mediating and perhaps even containing/restraining the power of the deity.

It is no accident that some of the Levite singers are identified as "prophets" (vv. 3–5), suggesting that their liturgical chanting channels YHWH's presence and actualizes his will. The view that texts actually contained the living voice of the gods was a common belief in the second half of the first millennium BCE and characterizes the way that some Israelite scribal groups conceived of their own compositions.[37] If this is so, then the Levitical chanting of these texts must have been viewed as a form of prophetic behavior, justifying the Chronicler's equation of Levitical singing with prophecy.

A list of gatekeepers and guards follows in 1 Chronicles 26. It has been noted that the list of gatekeepers (vv. 1–19) closely matches the duty rosters of late Babylonian temple personnel.[38] But the role of

---

36. Watts 2007, 161–72.
37. Van der Toorn 2007, 206–13.
38. Wright 1990.

gatekeeper is by no means a common task or perfunctory duty; the Levite gatekeepers are not simply security guards for the temple. When we bear in mind the events of the Census Crisis in 1 Chronicles 21, it becomes clear that the Levite gatekeepers serve as guardians or mediators of the destructive angel whose presence still resides in the temple. The chapter also contains information regarding Levites who oversee financial/treasury matters for the temple as well as Levites who serve as administrators beyond its precincts (vv. 20–32), but even these duties are charged with a degree of cosmic potency, maintaining the day-to-day business of an institution that served as the portal to heaven and a safeguard against cosmic threat.

Sidebar 7.10: The Levites and Music in the Jerusalem Temple

The Persian period sources such as Chronicles and Ezra–Nehemiah are deeply interested in the Levites as performers of texts. In Ezra–Nehemiah, this stands out prominently as readers/teachers of *Torah*, but Nehemiah 9 does include the performance of a Levitical prayer as a song, and the concept of Levites as cultic singers and musicians permeates much of Chronicles as well. The singing of music occurs in ritual settings often in Chronicles, and strongly suggests that in the Persian period, Levite singing and musicianship was somehow understood as a way to invoke the presence (or attention) of the divine. Many scholars also see the performance of this music as a prelude to subsequent explanation of its meaning, accompanied by the study of the very textual compositions that had been performed.

The unit ends with 1 Chronicles 27, which is not about Levites at all but, rather, civilian officers. We encounter a roster of army officers, tribal leaders, and royal attendants, all of which might seem unrelated to the material in the previous chapters. There are, however, two reasons to see this chapter as strongly connected to the preceding details. First, the sequence of material is suggestive of the relationship between the temple and the surrounding society: the order established in the temple leads to an ordered Israelite social world, strengthening the central position of the temple within that world. Second, 1 Chr. 27:24 contains a brief but crucial reference to the census crisis in 1 Chronicles 21, indicating that the ordering of the civilian officers in this chapter is contingent upon the resolution of the violent cosmic drama of that earlier episode. The numbering of the people must be done in concert with the organization of the temple faculty and resources, rendering Israelite society a macro-reflection of the temple itself.

5.6. 1 Chronicles 28–2 Chronicles 9

This long expanse of chapters is bound together by the role of Solomon in the realization and construction of the Jerusalem temple, and in these chapters the Chronicler once again demonstrates how far from his source material he is prepared to go. Solomon's ascent to the throne is portrayed in 1 Chronicles 28 as a peaceful, public event, with David claiming in a coronation ceremony that YHWH chose Solomon out of all of his sons to inherit the kingdom and construct the temple (1 Chr. 28:4-6), leaving out any mention of the more turbulent and violent events we encounter in the "Succession Narrative" in 2 Samuel or the battle for the throne in 1 Kings 1–2. Solomon's place as David's successor is but part of the larger plan to build the temple, a reversal of the earlier material in Samuel–Kings where the temple is constructed as a function of royal fiat. Immediately following this, David conveys to Solomon the divinely-inspired blueprints for the temple and its contents. The cryptic note in 1 Chr. 28:19 ("All this do I give you in writing, as YHWH has made me wise by his hand upon me, regarding all the details of this plan") suggests that the verses containing the temple blueprints in the previous verses were taken from a document written by David and given to Solomon.

This fits with the larger trend in Chronicles for written revelation to eclipse oral prophetic performances. David is presented here as a sort of prophet, the temple blueprints become a form of prophetic text, and Solomon is designated the recipient and trustee of this written revelation. The implication is that the temple he constructs will also be the repository of these sorts of prophetic/revelatory textual records—which actually describes quite accurately how the Jerusalem temple *did* function in the Chronicler's day. The narration containing David's final adjuration to the public to willingly bring forth their sacrifices to the temple and uphold divine law, along with his prayer for Solomon to serve as a fit leader, recalls Samuel's farewell speech in 1 Samuel 12 or even Moses' farewell address in the closing chapters of Deuteronomy. In all cases, we find a prophetic figure offering his last words for the benefit of the community he has shaped and that he is leaving behind. First Chronicles 29 ends with the note that David carried out this duty successfully, summarizing his reign as one characterized by faith and honor (1 Chr. 29:30).

The opening chapters of 2 Chronicles are primarily concerned with establishing Solomon's wealth and wisdom (2 Chronicles 1) as preludes to his construction of the temple (2 Chronicles 2–7). In establishing these credentials, the Chronicler is sure to emphasize the unity of all Israel in supporting Solomon's reign; again, there is a deliberate break from any of the indications in the book of Kings that Solomon came to the throne under disputed conditions or that some corners of the population rejected his legitimacy. Some wisps, however, resonate in the background, such as the repeated emphasis on Solomon using foreign labor rather than forced Israelite labor to build the temple structure (2 Chr. 2:16–17 [English vv. 17–18]). This expands upon the brief notice in 1 Kgs. 9:22 that no Israelites were forced into labor—a statement that most scholars see as an attempt to counter what must have been a public perception that Solomon indeed did force Israelites into labor.

The fact that the Chronicler chooses not only to include this theme but to repeatedly address it suggests that at least some circles in the late Persian period believed the old tradition that Solomon built the temple against the will of his own people and exploited them in the process. The account of Solomon's construction of the temple ends with his speech-prayer in 2 Chronicles 6 and YHWH's answer to the prayer in 2 Chronicles 7 in the form of a public **theophany** (vv. 1–10) and dream revelation (vv. 12–22). Both "answers" follow precedents in the sources in the book of Kings, but the Chronicler draws from a broader palette of history, memory and theology in the dream revelation, presupposing events such as the Babylonian exile in a manner that extends the divine revelation from Solomon's dream to the late Persian period audience of his own day.

The final two chapters of this unit both follow and clearly contradict the tradition found in the book of Kings. Solomon's accomplishments are delineated in 2 Chronicles 8, which include the notice that he engaged in ambitious building projects; this matches what we find in the Kings account and must draw from a well-known tradition beyond textual records that Solomon engaged in significant royal construction efforts (this is, in fact, the reason cited for why the northern tribes eventually seceded; see 1 Kgs. 11:27).

Solomon Dedicates the Temple, by James Tissot (ca. 1896–902); in the Jewish Museum, New York.

However, the Chronicler's account contradicts Kings in stating that the Phoenician king of Tyre gave Solomon several cities in the north—when in Kings, it is Solomon who gives up Israelite cities to the Phoenician king as payment for resources used in his royal building efforts (including the temple and palace in Jerusalem).

While this contradiction may be the result of a different oral tradition regarding the legacy of Solomon, it more likely represents the Chronicler's interest in establishing a type of ideal standard for Solomon's reign, diminishing memories or literary features in earlier sources that call into question the political fitness of the man who constructed the temple. By contradicting the story of Solomon's giving over of the northern cities to a foreign king, the Chronicler paints a more palatable picture of a dedicated Israelite leader who followed sacral instruction from David and the prophets.

By contrast, 2 Chronicles 9 is rather consistent with the earlier tradition in Kings regarding Solomon's interaction with the **Queen of Sheba**. This famous tale emphasizes Solomon's wealth and wisdom as it does in the book of Kings (1 Kings 10), which is useful for the Chronicler's purpose: wealth, which was certainly concentrated at the

Jerusalem temple in terms of tax revenues, gifts and donations, is presented as a parallel to wisdom, i.e., wealth signifies wisdom. By the Chronicler's day, Jewish wisdom traditions had been cultivated at the Jerusalem temple and were taught and studied by its priestly-scribal faculty as part of a sacred curriculum. The highlighting of Solomon's great wealth, paired with its international scope (via the visitation of the foreign Queen of Sheba), has implications for the temple he constructed. It, too, is to be seen as a central space that demands the attention and awe of foreign audiences, as well as the allegiance of Jews living in foreign lands. The Chronicler was writing at a time when Jews lived in Yehud, Egypt, Syria, Babylon, etc., and the temple was to be venerated as a space that anchored their identities irrespective of their geographic locations.

Sidebar 7.11: Solomon in the Books of Kings and Chronicles

While Solomon is presented as the primary force behind the building of the temple in the Book of Kings, his role in Chronicles shows a shift in how the temple was understood by the Chronicler and, possibly, his audience. Building a temple in the ancient world was the act of a sovereign ruler; its construction affirmed that the king in question stood atop society as the chief representative of the gods worshipped in these spaces. The book of Kings seems closer to this model that Chronicles, but this is likely because such a model could no longer work for a story dealing with ancestors of Persian period Jews such as David and Solomon: by the Chronicler's day, the Jerusalem temple was no longer a symbol of a native Jewish ruler's autonomy but, rather, supported the authority of the Persian emperors who used the temple as an administrative center for Jewish life in Yehud. For the Solomon of Chronicles, then, the building of a temple could only be a symbol of the faithful execution of the will of an absentee ruler (i.e., David, who dies before the temple is constructed). This created a model for how devotion to the Jerusalem temple was not a step toward autonomy from Persia but was a way to support the will of an emperor living far away from Jerusalem and Yehud.

5.7. 2 Chronicles 10—16

The next several chapters in Chronicles are primarily concerned with the effects of the schism between the northern tribes and the south which led to the period of the divided monarchy (ca. 922–721 BCE). In the book of Kings, this schism is a central event, and the northern monarchy receives a tremendous amount of attention. But in Chronicles, virtually all attention is directed to the kingdom of Judah. This cannot be the result of a lack of interest in the northern tribes, as the Chronicler devotes a good deal of attention to these tribes in the introductory genealogies in 1 Chronicles 1—9 and returns his attention to them at later points in his historiography. What this does signal, however, is an attempt to portray Judah as the sole *legitimate* kingdom, due mostly to the fact that Jerusalem and its temple remained the official sanctuary of that kingdom. Given the importance of the temple in the Chronicler's day, it is not surprising that he emphasizes the kingdom of Judah, making its monarchic history the only monarchic history that his broad audience should collectively adopt.

To a degree, the opening chapters of this unit follow what we encounter in the book of Kings, with Rehoboam alienating the audience at Shechem (the oracle of Ahijah in 1 Kgs. 11:30–39 is omitted), though the Chronicler notes that both Judah and Benjamin remained loyal to Rehoboam in 2 Chr. 11:1 (whereas he retained influence over Judah alone in the Kings account). This matches the principle populations and regions that fell under the jurisdiction of the Jerusalem temple of the Chronicler's day. But the chapter is also a mixture of details that may be drawn from older accounts or records, such as the list of building sites and administrative policies that Rehoboam put into practice (2 Chr. 11:5–12), as well as a notice that Levites defected from the north and found a home for their religious and cultic duties in Rehoboam's realm (vv. 13–17). This, too, plays upon earlier sources or traditions, insofar as northern Levites did likely descend into Judah, but only after the fall of the north to Assyria (ca. 722 BCE).

The Chronicler may subtly be suggesting here that the schism between the north and south was as devastating an event as the Assyrian crisis, or at least as much of an affront to "authentic" Jewish tradition as the incursion of Assyria into Israel's affairs. The chapter ends with the notice that Rehoboam "dealt wisely" (v. 23), a full turnaround from his folly at the outset of his reign. By implication, his affiliation with the Jerusalem establishment and the Levites who gravitated to him during the course of his reign transformed him into a wise ruler. Nevertheless, Rehoboam goes on to spurn YHWH's laws (2 Chr. 12:1) after obtaining a position of strength and security, which leads to calamity via the incursion of the Egyptian Pharaoh Shishak into his kingdom, compromising Rehoboam's power and prestige (vv. 2–12). The end of his reign follows the account in Kings, with Rehoboam judged poorly and the kingdom maintained through divine will rather than adept leadership.

Immediately following the account of Rehoboam's reign, however, is the tale of a battle between Jeroboam and Rehoboam's son and successor, Abijah, where Abijah delivers a lengthy and theologically-loaded speech before claiming a great victory over Jeroboam's forces (2 Chronicles 13). There is no evidence elsewhere in the Hebrew Bible for such a confrontation, and the huge number of Israelite casualties reported (five hundred thousand) is a sign that the account cannot be taken as historically realistic. But the Chronicler uses this opportunity to demonstrate how some of the kings of Judah were wise, just, and religiously sound, to the degree that Abijah's speech constitutes a form of prophetic declaration that ensures a victory for his forces. Since the Chronicler pays little attention to the north, the fact that Jeroboam and his forces are key players in this event is important, as it shows that wayward political leadership cannot withstand a confrontation with that of Judah. In the Chronicler's day, this would invariably apply to the religious leadership in Yehud, who perhaps sought to direct religious ideology and a sense of community identity away from competing options more closely aligned with foreign political sensibilities.

Sidebar 7.12: Prophetic Variety in Chronicles

The Chronicler wrote at a time when many earlier traditions regarding prophecy had already formed. His composition attests to these different prophetic types, from visionaries to preachers to scribes/writers to randomly inspired individuals moved to ecstatic states or possessed by the divine spirit (some of whom were not even necessarily Israelites; see section 5.11).

Much of what follows deals with Abijah's son Asa, who receives high marks as a king by following prophetic instruction, supporting temple ritual, and defending his nation's borders—though the latter is mostly a function of the preceding two issues. The outstanding aspects of his regnal account are the particulars of the prophetic oracle offered by

Azariah (2 Chr. 15:1–7) and the account of his cultic reform (vv. 8–19). As to the former, Azariah's oracle qualifies as what earlier scholars termed a Levitical Sermon (as noted above), a form of address that may have characterized how Levites taught religious ideas in the Chronicler's day. Azariah's oracle-sermon draws from a variety of texts that Levites in the late Persian period would have known and used in their own teaching and liturgical duties. Likewise, the account of the reform and the public pledge of religious allegiance resonates with older traditions where the people, en masse, accepted the terms of YHWH's patronage.

It is telling, though, that the second part of Asa's reign shows the king "slipping" in terms of his allegiance. When faced with military threat, Asa capitulates and devotes temple resources to a foreign king (the Aramean Ben-hadad in 2 Chr. 16:2) rather than relying on YHWH's protection. When approached and chastised by the prophet Hanani (vv. 7–10), Asa does not repent but strikes out against the prophet and, by extension, against the divine message itself. This ultimately results in Asa falling ill and dying; the Chronicler is clear here that reward and punishment is a result of a person's choice to defer to YHWH's will and his prophetic messengers. But it also points to a pattern evidenced in previous episodes where a king's reign begins well and eventually dissolves due to that king's poor theological choices.

5.8.2 Chronicles 17–20

The aforementioned pattern perhaps serves the purpose of leading up to the reign of Jehoshaphat, one of the "hero" kings in the book of Chronicles who stands in stark contrast to his immediate predecessors. The book of Kings also looks kindly upon Jehoshaphat, which probably served as the point of departure for the Chronicler. Yet the Chronicler goes into much greater detail regarding Jehoshaphat's reign and credits him with accomplishments that the author of Kings does not. Chief among these is the notice that upon fortifying cities throughout his realm, Jehoshaphat deployed Levites, priests and other officials as scribal teachers of the "book of the law" (2 Chr. 17:7–9). Though the text does not specify which book this is, there is every reason to believe that the Chronicler intends for this notice to refer to the Pentateuch; the Chronicler generally equally accepts legal principles from different sources in the Pentateuch, suggesting their position within a single work, and one that had obtained a paramount place in the temple cult by the late Persian period. Jehoshaphat's political success is thus not simply a matter of his personal piety but of his promotion of the Pentateuch and the importance of its teachers.

Yet Jehoshaphat is not perfect; 2 Chr. 18:1–19:3 depicts his alliance with the northern King Ahab as a misguided venture, and recounts the story known from the book of Kings where the prophet Micaiah declares his vision of a military failure; Jehoshaphat goes out to do battle nonetheless. The Chronicles account presents Jehoshaphat as praying to YHWH for assistance in the face of threat (2 Chr. 18:31), showing the king's return to piety, but upon his return to Jerusalem he is castigated by the prophet Jehu ben Hanani for straying from the path of righteousness (2 Chr. 19:3). Perhaps in response, Jehoshaphat engages in a juridical reform, empowering both priests and Levites along with other responsible agents to see to it that life in Judah abides by the rule of divine law. In spite of all this, Jehoshaphat's reign is once more somewhat tarnished: 2 Chronicles 20 is concerned with conflict between Judah and the Semitic kingdoms east of the Jordan, and reports that Jehoshaphat engaged in an alliance with another northern Israelite king, Ahaziah (v. 35). Their joint endeavors to launch a navy are met with failure, showing once more that Davidic descent does not guarantee divine favor—only deference to the law, to prophecy, and to YHWH does.

5.9.2 Chronicles 21–28

This series of chapters largely follows the material we encounter in the book of Kings, depicting the reigns—mostly problematic—of various rulers in Judah from the late-ninth to the late-eighth centuries BCE. Periodically, however, the Chronicler does intervene into his source material to rearrange it or introduce new items into it, and always for the purpose of clarifying a theological point. In most cases, that point is that calamity befalls those who veer from fidelity to YHWH through his priestly and prophetic agents. Many of the rulers in this expanse of material waver between adhering to proper religious principles when under the influence of righteous counselors and descending into apostasy when led astray.

A clear example is that of Joash, the son of Ahaziah (2 Chr. 24:1–17). Following the religious reform of the priest Jehoiada, Joash is placed in power and follows Jehoiada's instruction. His resulting actions are judged to be righteous: he takes measures to support the temple and the positions of the Levites therein. However, following Jehoiada's death, Joash appears to be corrupted by political agendas (vv.17–18), and pays no heed to prophetic warnings (vv. 19), including that of Jehoiada's own son Zechariah, who Joash puts to death (vv. 20–22). For his sins, Joash himself is killed (v. 25). The example of Joash is indicative of the Chronicler's general regard for monarchic leadership—it is ultimately a misguided office, held by rulers who possess little ability to make proper choices despite earlier associations with pious role models, and whose descent into viciousness poses a genuine threat to YHWH's true servants.

It is also worth observing that the forces which trigger this response in Judah's kings are quite literally all around them. In the case of Joash, it is Judahite high ranking officers; in the case of his grandfather Jehoram, it is his own wife, a daughter of the northern king Ahab who influences him to "walk in all the ways of the kings of Israel, as the house of Ahab did" (2 Chr. 21:6). The line between Davidic king and northern-apostate king is very easily blurred or eradicated, which calls into question what, exactly, is special about the Davidic line. The Chronicler emphasizes the enduring nature of YHWH's fidelity to the Davidic house, but it becomes clear that most of the kings who reign after David are poor partners in that relationship. And yet it is around this house that more certain and dependable groups—Levites, priests, and prophets—continually revolve. An example of this is the "letter of Elijah" found in 2 Chr. 21:12–15, wherein the great northern prophet Elijah condemns Jehoram for his sins. The appearance of this letter is unparalleled in the book of Kings, where Elijah interacts exclusively with the northern kings and makes no reference to David, Jerusalem, or the kings ruling therein.

Sidebar 7.13: Text as Prophecy

By the late-fourth century BCE, most of Israel's authoritative prophetic traditions could only be accessed through the texts that preserved them; prophecy was literally a textual phenomenon. Even the sort of Levitical singing that was understood as carrying a prophetic quality was still a matter of singing hymns that were preserved in textual form (e.g., the Book of Psalms, but probably other books or written collections as well). Finally, the Chronicler also lived in an era where the writing, arranging and study of text was understood as a vehicle for revelation from the gods, in some ways replacing the older forms of prophecy where an individual arose and gave an oral performance of divine revelation. In such an environment, it is fitting that the Chronicler presented so many of the prophets of the past as writers and their oracles as textual compositions. The written word was the divine word to the Chronicler—which obviously carries implications for how his own historiographic composition would be understood.

Though the Chronicler pays scant attention to the northern kings, he could not ignore the tales regarding **Elijah** who had by the late-fourth century BCE become a sort of patron-saint of the prophetic tradition (see, e.g., Mal. 3:23–24). Moreover, he could not imagine that such an important prophetic figure did not have a message that pertained to the Davidic kings. The introduction of Elijah's letter solves this problem—the prophet could remain firmly fixed in the north (as per the older tradition and sources) but the Davidic monarchy falls under his prophetic gaze through the testimony of the letter which, of course, serves as a vehicle for the Chronicler's own view of the Davidic king Jehoram and the line he represents. It may be that YHWH's enduring fidelity to the Davidic house is conceived by the Chronicler to be less about the viability of David's descendants and more about how that royal dynasty managed to be the center of attention that resulted in the accumulation of sacred literature (symbolized by Elijah's letter) containing YHWH's words for later audiences to be able to access.

A reframing of what fidelity to the Davidic house might have meant to the Chronicler is suggested by his account of the reign of Ahaz (2 Chronicles 28), who is portrayed as impious, idolatrous, and likened to the northern kings (v. 2). According to the Chronicler, Jerusalem itself is overrun during Ahaz's reign—a massive departure from the material in Kings—as part of the hostilities associated with the **Syro-Ephraimite War**, with its population taken captive into the northern kingdom. It is only through the efforts of the prophet Oded (v. 9) that they are restored, and there is no indication that this restoration to Jerusalem has anything to do with Ahaz or his Davidic pedigree. Thus once again, prophetic authority becomes increasingly identified with the relationship between YHWH and Jerusalem. The "House of

David" thereby also increasingly becomes abstracted from individual Davidides, evolving into a trope for the sanctity of a place and the priestly-prophetic tradition surrounding it. It is an individual Davidide's choice to defer to the tradition which might allow him to find a place in that "house," and as the Chronicler tells it, most of those Davidides ultimately choose poorly.

5.10.2 Chronicles 29–32

This unit of material deals with Hezekiah, a king that the Chronicler celebrates as a hero of Davidic and Solomonic proportions. In fact, many scholars have observed that with the account of Hezekiah's reign, the Chronicler attempts to present him as a "second" Solomon,[39] one who perfectly actualizes the theological charges and needs of Israel by restoring proper temple service, cultivating civic religious values, and defending the safety of his subjects against foreign threat. All of this is achieved because Hezekiah demonstrates perfect faith in YHWH (2 Chr. 31:20–21) and, unlike many of his predecessors, did not falter and relapse into illegitimate alliances or religious practices. In making the case for Hezekiah's superiority, the Chronicler dips deeply into a wide array of traditions, relying on legislation regarding sanctuary service from Priestly literature of the books of Leviticus and Numbers, but also aligning the king's reform measures throughout the boundaries of the realm with the legislation and ethics of the book of Deuteronomy. This is not the first time that the Chronicler brings these diverse traditions together (and it will not be the last, either), but it demonstrates that an ideal ruler is one who defers to authoritative tradition *en masse* rather than favoring this or that text which may benefit a special royal interest of agenda.

The opening canto of the Hezekiah account is strongly informed by the king's speech to the Levites (2 Chr. 29:5–11), which not only charges them to carry out their duties in purifying and ordering the temple cult but invokes the terms of history as the basis/motivation for the proper execution of these duties. In Hezekiah's words, the errors of the past led to chaos and exile; the proper ordering of the temple and its sancta could counter any such threats. This carries important implications regarding how history itself is understood in Chronicles: it is not a mere sequence of events but a series of theological lessons,

---

39. Williamson 1977: 119–25.

and investigating the past yields revelation regarding divine will for the present.

The remainder of the chapter focuses primarily on the Levites's carrying out of Hezekiah's instructions: they prove to be diligent adherents of the terms of the speech, and thus model how holiness can be attained through a proper understanding of history and its theological lessons. But two additional and subtle features of the chapter point to the Levites playing such an exemplary role for the implied audience of the Chronicler's work. First, the chapter notes that while (Aaronide) priests went about their duties in line with Hezekiah's instructions, the Levites did so with greater zeal and skill: "the Levites were more upright in heart to sanctify themselves than the priests" (2 Chr. 29:35). This suggests somewhat of a challenge to the Aaronide priests; the Chronicler does not here criticize the theology or routine of the Aaronide priests, but seems to point to the fitness of the Levites to conduct those duties as well. This is not a usurpation of the Aaronides's power, but rather an argument that Levite responsibilities in the Chronicler's day should be expanded, and that such an expansion could be of benefit to the important sacral routine of the temple.

The second feature of the chapter is that upon addressing the Levites, Hezekiah refers to them as "my sons" (2 Chr. 29:11). In what way should this phrase be understood? Though there are indications that members of the royal household in monarchic Judah did periodically serve in priestly capacities (2 Sam. 8:18), it seems unlikely that Hezekiah's locution here is meant to imply actual biological kinship between himself and the Levites. Indeed, given the tremendously detailed genealogies at the outset of the work, it is quite improbable that the Chronicler here ignores the clear distinctions between the Levitical genealogies and those of Judah to which the royal family belonged.

The phrase "my sons" more likely relates to the role that Hezekiah played in the official temple hierarchy as envisioned by the Chronicler. The kinship language of "father" and "son" is applied elsewhere to master and pupil in scribal contexts, and inscriptional evidence from the monarchic period in Jerusalem identifies royal stewards as the "sons" of the king. This same patron-client relationship is implied in Hezekiah's language here, which serves as somewhat of a complement to our earlier observation that the Promise to David and the Davidic "house" is becoming less about the biological lineage of David and more about the inner workings of the temple that the eponymous ancestor of that royal line planned and empowered his successors to execute and build. The Levites, as "sons" of Hezekiah, continue to actualize the Promise to David by keeping the "house" in order and maintaining its suitability for cultic service and divine visitation.

Figure 7.10: Seal and impression (left) of "Yehoahaz, son of the king." Late-seventh or early-sixth century BCE. Israel Museum.

The next major moment in Hezekiah's reign is the account of his keeping of the Passover (2 Chronicles 30). This is a departure from the source material in Kings, where no such ceremony is observed; it may be that the Chronicler here combines the Kings account of Josiah's Passover (2 Kgs. 23:21–23) with the records or memories of Hezekiah's reign. This is not entirely surprising, since scholars have long observed that the authors of Kings established strong connections between Josiah and Hezekiah, presenting the activities of the latter as a prefiguration of the policies of the former (centralization, cult reform, etc.). The book of Kings had earlier forged comparisons between these two kings, so the Chronicler's assignment of a **Passover** celebration to Hezekiah would not have surprised the ancient audience of the late Persian period. However, what is rather surprising is the emphasis that the chapter places on the role of letters sent throughout the realm to decree and mandate the observance of the Passover—this is clearly the Chronicler's literary invention, assigning to the late-eighth century BCE day of Hezekiah literary norms that were much more at home in his own period.

Even more important, though, is the notice that these letters were circulated throughout the tribes of the north. In Hezekiah's day, the northern kingdom had been conquered by Assyria, and for centuries there existed among Judahites an ideology that the northern population had either been exiled from the land or corrupted through the influx of foreign peoples resettled there by the Assyrians. The tradition in Ezra–Nehemiah is quite vocal about this: in that work, northerners are considered cultural and religious outsiders, barred from participation in the rebuilding of the temple (Ezra 4:1–4). This makes all the more remarkable the Chronicler's choice to *include* this same population in the national Passover festival, a holiday of covenantal renewal and communal religious/historical affirmation. As with the attention given to the northern tribes in the introductory genealogies and the notice of the northern Levites leaving Jeroboam's regime, the Chronicler advocates an inclusive attitude where populations with disparate ties to Israel's past can be included in the community—provided they align themselves with the cult of the Jerusalem temple and the teachings emanating from that institution.

The account of Hezekiah's reform in 2 Chronicles 31 follows suit by including northern and southern populations in policies that reaffirmed the special nature of Jerusalem, its temple and its priestly faculty. Like the authors of Kings, the Chronicler notes that Hezekiah shattered illegitimate cult icons and shut down the "high places," i.e., rural sites of sacrifice throughout the hinterland. It is notable that the Chronicler leaves out the notice in Kings that Hezekiah destroyed the bronze serpent "that Moses had made" (2 Kgs. 18:4). This omission may reflect the Chronicler's view that Moses could never have ever fabricated an icon that a good king should destroy. The Chronicler is content to speak in generalities about the icons that Hezekiah destroys without drawing attention to an example that could create a theological complication. Perhaps to counter this or to draw attention away from it, the Chronicler's account of the reform goes on to focus on Hezekiah's arrangement of the Levite faculty in the temple, positioning him once again as a sort of second David or Solomon, and thus the executor of earlier prophetic instruction.

Sidebar 7.14: Hezekiah and the Nehushtan

Second Kings 18:4 reports that Hezekiah engaged in a sort of religious reform that included the destruction of an item called the Nehushtan, a bronze serpent that was constructed by Moses according to tradition (Num. 21:5–9). The destruction of this Mosaic icon probably has something to do with Hezekiah's urbanization of the countryside that required the abandonment of long-standing rural cult icons, though the Chronicler omits this notice. Two good reasons may stand behind this omission: first, Hezekiah is presented in quite positive terms in the Chronicler's narrative, and the standard for such an evaluation usually requires a king's adherence to the principles of the Torah of Moses. A notice that pits Hezekiah against the Moses tradition (such as 2 Kgs. 18:4) would work against the Chronicler's rhetorical interests. But it may also be that the Chronicler wished to downplay the possibility of Moses as the creator of a cult icon that the Book of Kings presents in highly critical terms. In either case, the Chronicler's decision to omit this detail from 2 Kgs. 18:4 shed much light on his desire to create a consistent (if theoretical) history of faith and tradition from sources that periodically contained conflicting information.

The final episode in the Hezekiah account details the king's defensive measures against the forces of the Assyrian king Sennacherib; Chronicles condenses much of what is encountered in Kings, but it also goes into some detail that the Kings account leaves out. The Chronicler narrates how Hezekiah went about fortifying and defending Judah, especially regarding a project to restrict water access to the invading Assyrians (2 Chr. 32:2–4). These verses may have points of contact with memories regarding an actual water-related project undertaken by Hezekiah in anticipation of Sennacherib's invasion, namely, the creation of the **Siloam tunnel** that allowed for water to enter Jerusalem during the subsequent Assyrian siege of the city. The Chronicles account does not focus extensively upon this project, but instead continues on to emphasize *why* Hezekiah's measures were legitimate: because they allowed him to gather in a diverse group of Israelites and remind them that as powerful as the Assyrian forces might be, YHWH their God is more powerful (vv. 6–8).

The depiction of the Assyrian siege is especially intriguing when describing the rhetoric of the Assyrian officers (his "servants," as opposed to Hezekiah as YHWH's "servant"). In addition to presumably oral proclamations, we are informed that "he"—probably Sennacherib himself—writes a letter meant to "taunt" YHWH, proclaiming that no god could withstand Assyrian power, and YHWH will not be able to either. This letter is not attested in the episode preserved in the book of Kings (or the parallel account in Isaiah 36–39); it is the invention of the Chronicler, similar to the invention of Elijah's letter several chapters earlier. The Chronicler presents Assyria as recruiting the sacred technology of textuality to promote a particular religious ideology, one that challenged the orthodoxy championed by Hezekiah. But the fact that the chapter ends with Hezekiah emerging triumphant and ending his reign with distinction and blessing signifies that textuality is not easily made sacred. The words of an Assyrian king cannot carry the same history-affecting power as the written word of YHWH.[40]

5.11.2 Chronicles 33–36

The final chapters of Chronicles are a literary and hermeneutical tour-de-force. They follow their source materials very closely while managing to spin exegetical discourses of great complexity out of them. The first canto in this unit, 2 Chronicles 33, switches gears from the entirely positive account of Hezekiah to a more complicated depiction of his son and successor Manasseh. Manasseh is remembered in the book of Kings as the worst of the Judahite monarchs and is blamed for the Babylonian Exile (2 Kgs. 21:10–15; 23:26–27), and the Chronicler retains much of this tradition by depicting the beginning of his reign as riddled with wickedness. But the Chronicler also presents Manasseh as penitent and repentant; faith and righteousness is possible, even for someone who is surrounded by condemnation in other sources.

Intriguing is how the Chronicler accounts for this departure from Kings: Manasseh's wickedness is recorded in "the acts of the Kings of Israel" (v. 18), but his contrition and redemption is preserved in a prophetic source called "the history of the seers" (v. 19). Is this "history of the seers" a reference to the Chronicler's own work? The Chronicler's affinity for prophecy-as-literature may suggest that his own historiographic composition is a prophetic work, that is, "a history of the seers." This is a tempting possibility, but must remain

---

40. The Chronicler here may be developing an idea already evident in the source material in the Book of Kings, where the speech of the Assyrian officer Rabshakeh takes on the rhetorical form of prophetic speech; see Rudman 2000.

speculative. The chapter ends with a brief retelling of the Amon narrative, which contains no substantial differences from the parallel account in Kings. Amon is murdered, the murderers are dispatched, and the people of the land place Amon's son Josiah on the throne (v. 25).

This brings us to the account of King Josiah's reign, which is perhaps the most pivotal moment in the book of Kings and which holds a position of high importance for the Chronicler as well. There are very strong overlaps between the two accounts, but the Chronicler's version contains unique features and important differences. Whereas the record of Josiah's famous cult reform in Kings follows the discovery of the "scroll of law" (probably a version of the book of Deuteronomy), Josiah's reform activity in Chronicles begins *before* the discovery of that scroll (2 Chr. 34:3-7). This is due to the notice that Josiah, under the tutelage of the priesthood, developed a sense of personal piety and theological orthodoxy (v. 3). For the Chronicler, the discovery of YHWH's written law is not what inspires belief, but serves as a reward for one's own decision to pursue religious righteousness.

The Levites are once again important players in this episode. True to form, the Chronicler presents Josiah as organizing and empowering Levites during his reform of national religion, and even suggests that when the book of Kings refers to Josiah's interaction with prophets (2 Kgs. 23:2), these prophets were actually Levites (2 Chr. 34:30).[41] Certainly by the Chronicler's day, prophecy had been "claimed" by Levites: Levites scribes saw their activity as a form of prophetic responsibility.[42] In a tradition so concerned with the authority of sacred text (such as the scroll discovered in the temple) and its impact on society, the proper agents of text—the written will of YHWH—are identified as Levites, reaffirming this same view of Levites that exists in earlier episodes within the Chronicler's historiography.

The Chronicler also adds some intriguing flourishes to his source material in describing the circumstances leading to Josiah's death. In Kings, we are informed that Josiah encountered the Pharaoh **Neco**, who killed him at Megiddo. In Chronicles, however, Neco is presented as a prophet who speaks an oracle or warning to Josiah, which Josiah ignores—and the ignoring of this prophetic word is what does him in. Furthermore, Josiah is only mortally wounded by Neco in Chronicles,

---

41. Leuchter 2009.
42. See Nogalski 2010 for this concept active within the redaction of the Book of the Twelve (Amos—Malachi).

and actually dies in Jerusalem, where we are informed that the prophet Jeremiah led the people in ritual mourning and laments for Josiah's death (a detail not found in Kings).

Figure 7.11: City gate of Iron-Age Megiddo, Israel. Photo: Martin Boesch. Commons.wikimedia.org.

The Chronicler here makes several important points: revelation can be derived from non-Israelite sources (e.g., Neco as a prophet), and earlier accounts of history are deliberately characterized as telling only part of the story (e.g., the lack of details regarding Jeremiah, who makes no appearance in the book of Kings). The Chronicles account points to an intellectual culture that is expansive, with more to learn and glean than the extant sources might otherwise imply.

The appearance of the prophet Jeremiah at the end of the Josiah account begins a series of references to that prophet which continue to the very end of the Book of Chronicles. It seems that the Chronicler looked to the book of Jeremiah as a source not simply to "fill in the gaps" of the narrative in Kings but as a primary trove of theological insight and historical detail. Throughout the historiography of Chronicles, we encounter references to prophetic literary sources that the Chronicler claims to have drawn from; most scholars view these as theoretical or symbolic sources rather than actual ones, but they pave the way for the Chronicler's reliance upon the book of Jeremiah.

Yet it is also clear that the references to Jeremiah are invoked to work alongside the constant attention to the Levites throughout Chronicles. In the final two chapters of Chronicles (2 Chronicles 35–36) especially, the name of Jeremiah seems to be invoked in places where Levites would otherwise appear. Jeremiah is the ostensible teacher of kings (2 Chr. 36:12), the conductor of liturgy (2 Chr. 35:25) and the speaker/writer of oracles regarding the direction of history and the rise/fall of political powers (2 Chr. 36:21). The appeal to the Jeremiah tradition here is obviously deliberate: that tradition had seen Israel through the rise and fall of Babylon (Jeremiah 25; 50–51), and is utilized at the very end of Chronicles to address the rise of Persia (2 Chr. 36:22-23). The implication is that this same tradition could be invoked at a time when Persia, too, might see its end at the hands of yet another empire (Greece) rising in power over the ancient world and, consequently, over the Jews of late Persian Yehud as well. The book of Chronicles ends on this ambiguous note, but infuses into it a sense of hope: prophecy is alive and well—though now in literary form—and thus YHWH continues to speak to his people through works like Chronicles itself. And Jerusalem, despite the ebb and flow of history, still stands, serving as a symbol of the Jewish people's solidarity and survival throughout time.

Bibliography

Baden, Joel S. 2011. "The Violent Origin of the Levites." In *Levites and Priests in History and Tradition*, edited by Jeremy M. Hutton and Mark Leuchter, 103–16. Atlanta: SBL.

Ben Zvi, Ehud. 2007. "Who Knew What? The Construction of the Monarchic Past in Chronicles and its Implications for the Intellectual Setting of Chronicles." In *Judah and the Judeans in the Fourth Century BCE*, edited by Gary Knoppers, Oded Lipschits, and Rainer Albertz, 349–60. Winona Lake: Eisenbrauns.

Cook, Sephen L. 2004. *The Social Roots of Biblical Yahwism*. Atlanta: SBL.

Cross, Frank M. 1975. "A Reconstruction of the Judean Restoration." *JBL* 94: 4–18.

Finkelstein, Israel. 2011. "Saul, Benjamin, and the Emergence of 'Biblical Israel': An Alternative View." *ZAW* 123: 348–67.

_____. 2012. "The Historical Reality behind the Genealogical Lists in 1 Chronicles." *JBL* 131: 65–83.

Freedman, David Noel. 1961. "The Chronicler's Purpose," CBQ 23, 436–42.

Fleming, Daniel. 2003. "History in Genesis." *Westminster Journal of Theology* 65: 251–62.

Halpern, Baruch. 1991. "Jerusalem and the Lineages in the Seventh Century BCE: Kinship and the Rise of Individual Moral Liability." In *Law and Ideology in Monarchic Israel*, edited by Baruch Halpern and Deborah D. Hobson, 11–107. JSOTSup 124. Sheffield: Sheffield Academic Press.

Hanson, Paul D. 1973. "Zechariah 9 and the Recapitulation of an Ancient Ritual Pattern." *JBL* 92: 37–59.

Hendel, Ronald S., ed. 2010. *Reading Genesis: Ten Methods.* Cambridge: Cambridge University Press, 28–46.

Hutton, Jeremy M. 2011. "All the King's Men: The Families of the Priests in Cross Cultural Perspective." In *Seitenblicke: Literarische und historische Studien zu Nebenfiguren im Zweiten Samuelbuch*, edited by Walter Dietrich, 121–51. OBO 249. Fribourg/Göttingen: Academic Press/Vandenhoeck & Ruprecht.

Jonker, Louis C. 2008. "Who Constitutes Society? Yehud's Self-Understanding in the Late Persian Era as Reflected in the Books of Chronicles." *JBL* 127: 707–28.

Kim, Yeong Seon. 2014. *The Temple Administration and the Levites in Chronicles.* CBQMS. Washington: CBA.

Knohl, Israel. 1995. *The Sanctuary of Silence.* Minneapolis: Fortress Press.

Levin, Yigal. 2003. "Who Was the Chronicler's Audience? A Hint from His Genealogies." *JBL* 122: 229–45.

____. 2004a. "From Lists to History: Chronological Aspects of the Chronicler's Genealogies." *JBL* 123: 601–36.

____. 2004b. "Joseph, Judah and the Benjamin Conundrum." *ZAW* 116: 223–41.

Leuchter, Mark. 2009. "The 'Prophets' and the 'Levites' in Josiah's Covenant Ceremony." *ZAW* 121: 31–47.

____. 2011. "Eisodus as Exodus: The Song of the Sea (Exod. 15) Reconsidered." *Bib* 93: 321–46.

____. 2012. "The Fightin' Mushites." *VT* 62: 479–500.

____. 2013. *Samuel and the Shaping of Tradition.* Oxford: Oxford University Press.

____. 2014. "Another Look at the Hosea/Malachi Framework in the Twelve." *VT* 64: 249–65.

Lipschits, Oded. 2003. "Demographic Changes in Judah between the

Seventh and the Fifth Centuries BCE." In *Judah and the Judeans in the Neo-Babylonian Period*, edited by Oded Lipschits and Joseph Blenkinsopp, 323–76. Winona Lake: Eisenbrauns.

Meyers, Carol R. 1987. "David as Temple Builder." In *Ancient Israelite Religion*, edited by Patrick D. Miller, Paul Hanson, and S. Dean McBride, 357–76. Philadelphia: Fortress Press.

Person, Raymond R. 2010. *The Deuteronomistic History and the Book of Chronicles*. Atlanta: SBL.

Rom-Shiloni, Dalit. 2013. *Exclusive Inclusivity: Identity Conflicts between the Exiles and the People who Remained (6th–5th Centuries BCE)*. New York: Bloomsbury.

Rudman, Dominic. 2000. "Is the Rabshakeh Also Among the Prophets? A Rhetorical Study of 2 Kings XVIII 17–35." *VT* 60: 100–110.

Schniedewind, William. 2004. *How the Bible Became a Book*. Cambridge: Cambridge University Press.

_____. 1999. *Society and the Promise to David*. New York/Oxford: Oxford University Press.

Talshir, Zipora. 2001. "Several Canon Related Concepts Originating in Chronicles." *ZAW* 113: 386–403.

Van der Toorn, Karel. 2007. *Scribal Culture and the Making of the Hebrew Bible*. Cambridge, MA: Harvard University Press.

Watts, James W. 2007. *Ritual and Rhetoric in Leviticus: From Sacrifice to Scripture*. Cambridge: Cambridge University Press.

Williamson, Hugh G. M. 1977. *Israel in the Book of Chronicles*. Cambridge: Cambridge University Press.

_____. 1979. "The Origins of the Twenty-Four Priestly Courses: A Study of I Chronicles XXIII–XXVII." In *Studies in the Historical Books of the Old Testament*, edited by J. A. Emerton, 251–68. VTSup 30. Leiden: Brill.

Wilson, Robert R. 1977. *Genealogy and History in the Biblical World*. New Haven: Yale University Press.

Wright, John W. 1990. "Guarding the Gates: 1 Chronicles 26.1–19 and the Roles of Gatekeepers in Chronicles." *JSOT* 48: 69–81.

Glossary

Aaronide priests: the ruling priesthood in Jerusalem during the Persian period (and beyond), who traced their ancestry to the priestly family of Aaron.

Accession year: differences in how to account for a ruler's year of accession (ante-dating system or post-dating system) could explain some of the chronological discrepancies in 1, 2 Kings.

Agrarian: a form of communal lifestyle characterized by farming, herding, and a connection to rural landscapes.

Ahab: one of the major kings of the northern kingdom of Israel (whose reign is detailed in 1 Kings 17–2 Kings 9) known to have clashes with prophets such as Elijah and Micaiah ben Imlah.

Ahitophel: a well-known sage and political figure in Jerusalem; one of the organizers of the revolt against David carried out by Absalom, David's son.

Ahura Mazda: the chief deity of Zoroastrian religion and the imperial deity of Persia.

Alexander the Great: the Macedonian warrior king who conquered the Persian Empire and expanded its boundaries. It is under Alexander that Hellenistic thought began spreading throughout the ancient world.

Amalekites: a nomadic people who generally lived in the Negev and were at war with Israel during the time of the Judges and the early monarchy.

Amarna Letters: letters from petty Canaanite rulers to the Egyptian Pharaoh dating from the fourteenth century BCE that provide cultural context for Israel's history and mention many cities and locations that appear in the Historical Books.

Ammonites: a people to the east of Israel and north of Moab who allied with other peoples against Israel during the time of the Judges and fought with Israel during the monarchy.

Amos and Hosea: important prophets from the mid-eighth century BCE whose oracles were directed against the northern kingdom of Israel.

Ancestor veneration: rites and ceremonies associated with the dead, usually conducted by their living descendants.

Ante-dating system: a convention for calculating regnal years where the first partial year of a ruler's reign is counted as the first year, used in Egypt and in the early period of Israel's monarchy (see also Post-dating system).

'apiru or Ḫabiru: a group of people living in Canaan and mentioned in the Amarna Letters (and other texts) that some scholars think may be linked to the word Hebrew, and thus to the Israelites.

Aramaic language: an alphabetic Semitic language related to Hebrew, adopted by Mesopotamian empires and, later, the Persian empire as the official language of diplomacy. Under Persia, Aramaic also became a sacred language, utilized by scribes and religious scholars for the study of holy texts.

Aram: nation to the north-east of Israel (also called Syria) that had extensive interactions (both war and peace) with the Northern Kingdom during the book of Kings.

Araunah: a leading resident of Jerusalem pre-dating David's arrival there; often considered by scholars to have been the king of the city before David claimed it as his own.

Ark of the Covenant: a sacred portable chest that was housed in the tabernacle during the wilderness wanderings, the time of the judges, and the early monarchy. It was carried into warfare by Israel, most notably around Jericho (Joshua 6). Eventually it was moved into the temple by Solomon (1 Kings 8).

Artaxerxes I: Persian emperor from 464–424 BCE.

Artaxerxes II: Persian emperor from 404–358 BCE.

Artaxerxes Rescript: a source found in Ezra 7:12–26 that purports to be a letter from the emperor Artaxerxes officially commissioning Ezra to oversee Jewish affairs in Yehud.

Babylon: Mesopotamian empire that replaced Assyria in the region and conquered Jerusalem in a series of conquests and deportations.

Babylonian Exile: the captivity and forced migration of major populations from Jerusalem and its environs in the early-sixth century BCE, spanning roughly 50 years (587–538 BCE).

Babylonian Talmud: rabbinical documents dating from the third to fifth centuries recording commentary and interpretation on, among other things, biblical texts including theories of authorship.

Barak: general of Israel's forces during the judgeship of Deborah who defeated Jabin king of Canaan.

Bathsheba: one of David's wives, the mother of David's successor Solomon, and a central figure in one of the major controversies of David's reign.

Battle of Carchemish: a battle of international significance where Babylon emerged as the major power in the ancient Near East.

Ben Sira: an important Jewish sage in Jerusalem, active ca. 190 BCE.

Ben-hadad: a Syrian (Aramean) ruler of the ninth century BCE based in Damascus.

Bisitun Inscription: a major, multilingual public inscription carved into a cliffside in western Iran, detailing how the emperor Darius followed the will of the god Ahura Mazda in purging corruption from the empire.

Book of Proverbs: a collection of wisdom texts drawing from diverse sources claiming legitimacy through the invocation of King Solomon's name as an authorizing patron.

Book of the Twelve: a literary work that wove together the smaller prophetic books of the Bible (Hosea–Malachi), probably redacted during the late Persian period.

Call Narratives: stories where a biblical character (e.g., Joshua, Gideon, Samuel) receive a divine call to ministry typically with formulaic elements (e.g., commission, objection, sign).

Cambyses: Persian emperor from 530–522 BCE.

Canaanites: initial residents of the land of Canaan that the Israelites gradually drove out to take possession of the land.

Casiphia: a city in central Mesopotamia that served as a hub for a group of Levites living in exile.

Cities of refuge: designated cities where a person who unintentionally killed another person could flee to avoid retribution from those who may want to exact vengeance (see Numbers 35; Joshua 21).

Conquest: the Israelite occupation of the Promised Land of Canaan as described in the book of Joshua.

Co-regency: an overlapping reign, typically of a king and his son the crown prince (see 1 Kings 1; David and Solomon). Since overlapping years may be credited to both rulers, this practice could explain some chronological discrepancies of the book of Kings.

Cultic singers: musicians in the Jerusalem temple cult, mostly composed of Levites trained in the recitation and chanting of sacred poetry and song.

Cultural memory: the manner in which the memory of ideas, events, institutions and individuals is preserved and utilized within multiple generations of social groups.

Cyrus the Great: the founder of the Persian Empire in 539 BCE, who assumed control of the Babylonian empire and who decreed amnesty for all captured people, including former citizens of Judah.

Darius (I): Persian emperor from 522–486 BCE.

Dead Sea Scrolls (DSS): a collection of manuscripts found near the Dead Sea which originated from the ancient community at Khirbet Qumran. Their discovery (between 1946–1956), was a source of great excitement to scholars and others because the scrolls contained not only many works providing invaluable information about religious life in the late Second Temple period, but also the earliest copies of sections of the Hebrew Bible. Unfortunately, many of the scrolls are badly damaged.

Deborah: judge and prophetess of Israel who called Barak to lead the army and who composed a victory song afterwards.

Deutero–Isaiah: an anonymous prophet whose oracles have been worked into the book of Isaiah, usually identified with Isaiah 40–55 and dated to ca. 540 BCE. Other passages in the book of Isaiah, however, are periodically credited to Deutero-Isaiah as well.

Deuteronomistic History: a term used by scholars for the books of Joshua, Judges, Samuel and Kings, since they contain language reminiscent of the book of Deuteronomy.

Deuteronomistic redaction: editing performed by redactors with a strong interest in theological values that stem from the book of Deuteronomy.

Divided Monarchy: period in Israel's history after the nation was split into separate kingdoms, the northern kingdom of Israel (ruled over by Jeroboam I and his predecessors) and the southern kingdom of Judah (ruled over by Rehoboam and his predecessors; see United Monarchy).

Divine warrior: a concept of the divine in the ancient world where a deity is envisioned engaging in battle against cosmic enemies. In ancient Israel, this was an important aspect of YHWH, evident in a number of psalms and narratives.

Divine word: a concept relating to YHWH's intentions for Israel's history, often conveyed through prophetic proclamation but also revealed through the unfolding of historical events.

Doublet: a verse or brief story that has a close parallel elsewhere in a biblical text.

Dream theophany: pertaining to the belief in antiquity that divine forces could reveal themselves of their will to humans during a sleeping/dream state.

Duplicates of heavenly books: holy texts, usually produced by priestly-scribes within temple structures, reflecting or paralleling divine writs produced in the heavens by divine forces.

Dynastic oracles: a message delivered by a prophet to a ruler promising an extended reign for the ruler's heirs, the most famous of which is Nathan's oracle to David (2 Samuel 7).

Eastern diaspora: the community of Jews residing in Babylon and Persia during the Persian period.

Ecstatic Prophets: figures who experience trance-like states, entering an altered state of consciousness often believed to be evidence of possession by a divine spirit.

Elders: traditional tribal leaders in agrarian social groups holding juridical and often ritual authority.

Elephantine papyri: a collection of Aramaic documents found in an archive at the site of Elephantine, an ancient Jewish colony on the Nile river in Egypt.

Elijah: one of the major prophets in the biblical tradition and a legendary figure of northern Israelite religious lore. Elijah is presented as the leader of a guild of prophets in the ninth century BCE, who later biblical writers associated with a final day of divine judgment (Mal. 3:23).

Ephraim: Joseph's younger son, also the tribe of his descendants and the land that they took possession of in the middle of Canaan.

Ephraimite highlands: the hill country in the northern/central region of ancient Canaan.

Epic-Bardic: one of three "voices" discerned by Niditch in the book of Judges that told tales of heroic exploits of charismatic deliverers (see also Humanist, Theologian).

Euphrates river: one of the major rivers bounding the region of Mesopotamia. The Euphrates is a well-known boundary marker in a number of biblical texts, and was used by the Persians as a boundary for the organization of adjacent satrapies.

Evil Spirit: a type of minor divinity believed to be able to influence or afflict an individual in antiquity.

Exile: while Israel and Judah underwent at least five deportations, the term "Exile" usually refers to the period when many of the residents of the southern kingdom of Judah were forced to live Babylonian captivity (roughly, 587–515 BCE).

Ezekiel: a major prophet active in Mesopotamia during the Babylonian exile, Ezekiel carried Zadokite/Aaronide priestly heritage and his oracles are steeped in priestly ideas and language.

Former Prophets: the books of Joshua, Judges, Samuel and Kings, according to the Hebrew divisions of the Old Testament. The Latter Prophets include the Major and Minor Prophets.

Gedaliah ben Ahikam: the governor of Judah following the fall of Jerusalem, with an administration based in the Benjaminite city of Mizpah. Gedaliah was assassinated in ca. 582 BCE by partisans with allegiance to the Davidic royal house (Jeremiah 41).

Gola community: a group of Judahites repatriated to their homeland from Babylon, who fostered a sense of exclusive communal identity and a sense of religious elitism based on their exilic experience.

Greater Israel: a term referring to the broadest spectrum of tribes, clans, and related groups that counted themselves as part of Israelite society.

Haggai and Zechariah: two biblical prophets active ca. 520 BCE in Jerusalem.

Halakha: laws and customs emanating from priestly teaching, often but not always rooted in biblical sources or laws.

Haredim: a sect active in the mid-fifth century BCE with a sense of group identity grounded in a particular type of religious observance; this groups appears to have looked to Ezra as their leader.

Harvest/wine festival: religious/cultural events celebrating the seasonal fertility of the land.

Heads: see above, "Elders."

Hedgehog defense: a method of defense against an invading army where rural populations are urbanized and city walls and resources are reinforced.

Hezekiah: Judean king who was evaluated as righteous, initiated numerous reforms, and withstood the siege of Sennacherib of Assyria.

High places: places of worship on hills and mountains that are often associated in the Hebrew Bible with idolatry and were therefore condemned (e.g., 1 Kgs. 3:2–3).

Holiness stratum: a compositional source in the Pentateuch deriving from a priestly group concerned with the holiness of the community beyond the confines of the sanctuary and its cult.

Honor/shame culture: a system often characterizing tribal societies where rank and authority are based on a group's maintenance of honor (usually at the family or clan level).

Humanist: one of three "voices" discerned by Niditch in the book of Judges that told tales with little or no assessment about the behavior of the characters (see also Epic Bardic, Theologian).

Inheritance: materials and resources usually maintained within family structures that are passed on to successive generations.

Inner-biblical exegesis: a phenomenon where the author of a specific biblical text utilizes material from an earlier biblical text, often for purposes of ideological legitimacy or to advance or transform earlier traditions.

Ishbosheth: Saul's son and royal successor, whose authority was short lived and eclipsed by David.

Israel: alternative name for Jacob the son of Isaac, also for the people of the land of Israel, the United Monarchy of Israel, and the Northern Kingdom of Israel.

Jebusite: pertaining to the people of Jebus, a Canaanite clan pre-dating Israel's emergence in the land and claiming Jerusalem as one of their major cities before David claimed it.

Jehoiachin: one of the last kings of Judah, who was taken captive to Babylon in 597 BCE and remained an important royal figurehead down to roughly 560 BCE even while living in exile.

Jehoiakim: son of Josiah, one of the final rulers of Judah, who paid tribute to Pharaoh Neco of Egypt.

Jeremiah: a major prophet from the late seventh to early sixth centuries BCE whose oracles and teachings became foundational for Jews living in exile and those who returned to rebuild Yehud.

Joshua: an Aaronide priest selected by Persian authorities to co-lead a wave of returnees to Jerusalem in 522 BCE and to serve as chief priest, sharing leadership duties with the Davidide Zerubbabel.

Judah: the fourth son of Jacob, also refers to the tribe of his descendants, as well as the Southern Kingdom of Judah.

Judge cycles: the middle section of the book of Judges that narrate cyclical stories of the heroic judge-deliverers of Israel who rescue Israel from the oppression of their enemies.

Judges: Israelite leaders who listen to cases and make decisions (Deut. 16:18–20; Judg. 4:4–5), or rule over the nation of Israel and deliver them from their enemies in battle (the book of Judges).

Kings: heads of a monarchic society, often holding sacral responsibilities over the religion of the realm as well.

Kiriath Yearim: a city in Judah housing a multi-clan religious sanctuary, where icons and shrines venerated by different lineage groups in the region were maintained.

Levite scribes: a collection of writers, editors, redactors, and sages who emerged from the Levite priesthood, often viewed as active in the late monarchic period (ca. 700–587 BCE) through the Persian period (538–332 BCE).

Levitical sermon: a form of address found in the Book of Chronicles where a Levite-prophet delivers a divinely inspired speech or lecture.

Liminal: a term relating to a position—often a social position—that is between more defined group identity boundaries, "betwixt and between."

Lot: a method used in the book of Joshua to allocate the tribal land territories.

Maccabean period: also known as the Hasmonean period, describing the rule of the Hasmonean priest-kings in Jerusalem spanning roughly 163–160 BCE.

Man of God: a type of prophet in ancient Israel capable of mediating between lay populations and the deity or deities they worshipped.

Manasseh: the older son of Joseph and the tribe of his descendants, and the land that they possessed both on the east and the west side of the Jordan River. Also refers to the evil son of Hezekiah who ruled after his father.

Marduk: the traditional high god of the Babylonian pantheon.

Masebah: a stone pillar used in ancient worship practices to represent devotion to a deity at a sacred location.

Masoretic Text (MT): a collection of manuscripts of the Hebrew Bible written in Hebrew which is the primary source for most modern translations of the Old Testament. The Hebrew texts were originally written without consonants (as evidenced in the DSS), but during the seventh to tenth centuries, a Jewish group called the Masoretes added vowels.

Megiddo: an important city in northern Israel that played a role as an administrative center for most of the monarchic period.

Mephibosheth: the son of Jonathan and youngest grandson of King Saul.

Merneptah Stele: an Egyptian stele dated to the reign of the Egyptian pharaoh Merneptah, son of Ramesses the Great, which contains the oldest (and the only Egyptian) reference to Israel, currently housed in the Egyptian Museum in Cairo.

Messianic ideology: a concept originally expressing the special status of David and his lineage as YHWH's "anointed" ones (the word "messiah" comes from the Hebrew mashiach, "anointed").

Midian: people south of Moab who allied with other peoples against Israel during the time of the Judges.

Mizpah: an ancient city in the central highlands of Canaan and the site of a sanctuary where kingship was first ratified in the days of Samuel and Saul. Mizpah became an important administrative site under the Babylonians in the early-sixth century BCE.

Moab: nation to the south-east of Judah that was at war with Israel throughout the period of the judges and the monarchy.

Nabonidus: the last king of the Neo-Babylonian empire (556–539 BCE) who broke with traditional religious practice and established the center of his empire in the Syrian city of Haran. Nabonidus also promoted the god Sin to the primary position in the imperial pantheon, which further angered the priests of Babylon.

Naboth: a landowner in northern Israel unfairly charged with treason and executed in order for Ahab to be able to claim his land (1 Kings 21).

Neco: a Pharaoh of the 26th dynasty who ruled Egypt from 610–595 BCE. This Pharaoh is credited with the killing of Josiah at Megiddo in 609 BCE.

Necromancer: a religious specialist capable of consulting the dead or raising the spirits of the underworld.

Neo-Assyrian Imperialism: the expansion of political authority over the western Semitic states (including Israel and Judah) by the Assyrians from roughly 840–627 BCE.

Nob: a sanctuary city in the region of Benjamin where an early group of Levite priests resided during the reign of King Saul.

Northern Kingdom: during the period of the Divided Monarchy the ten northern tribes (also called Israel) which rebelled and separated from the Southern Kingdom (also called Judah).

Northern Levites: a class of priests in northern Israel with strong connections to the Moses traditions; many of these Levites eventually fled south following the fall of the northern kingdom in 721 BCE.

Officer: either a royal administrative or military figure heralding the authority of a monarch.

Pact: a social bond or agreement to which various parties pledge allegiance or affiliation.

Penitential Prayer: a form of prayer, both communal and individual, invoking historical traditions for the purpose of securing forgiveness from past transgression.

Pentapolis: the five Philistine cities (Gaza, Ashdod, Askelon, Gath, and Ekron) that bordered Israel and Judah to the south-west, along the Mediterranean Sea.

Pentateuch: the first five books of the Hebrew Bible—Genesis, Exodus, Leviticus, Numbers, and Deuteronomy—which immediately precede the Former Prophets.

People of the land: in the monarchic period, this phrase related to a powerful agrarian political group. In the Persian period, however, the phrase is used derisively, to identify agrarian communities as non-elite and unfit to participate in temple-based activity.

Philistines: a people to the west of Judah that waged war with Israel during the period of the judges and the United Monarchy.

Post-dating system: a convention for calculating regnal years where the first partial year of a reign is not counted, but regnal years begin at the next New Year's day, used in Mesopotamia, Judah, and the later period of Israel's monarchy (see also Ante-dating system).

Priestly courses: the organization of various priestly clans into rounds of service-duty in the Jerusalem cult.

Priestly source: a compositional source in the Pentateuch deriving from a priestly group concerned with the dependence of Israelite society upon the exclusive holiness of the sanctuary and its cult.

Priests: individuals who represent a bridge between the realm of humanity and the realm of the divine, often charged with specific and exclusive ritual responsibilities and authority.

Primary History: a scholarly model for viewing the books of Genesis–Kings as a single storyline setting the history of Israel within a larger history of the world.

Promise to David: an oracle from YHWH, given through the prophet Nathan in 2 Samuel 7, ensuring David an enduring dynasty over Israel and based in Jerusalem.

Prophetic Narratives: extended narrative sections of Kings that record the saga and miraculous deeds of prophets such as Elijah and Elisha.

Prophets: a broad-ranging term that is best defined as humans empowered to speak on behalf of the divine to a given audience or community.

Queen of Sheba: a queen, perhaps from Southern Arabia who, after hearing of Solomon's wisdom, came to visit and gave a generous gift to the king.

Queen Mother: an office in the kingdom of Judah held by the mother of the ruling king, characterized by holding the authority to impart political advice and probably carrying religious/cultic duties as well.

Redaction: an editorial process where multiple sources are modified to create a unified document. Many scholars believe the books of Joshua–Kings underwent a process of redaction by Deuteronomistic editors.

Redactors: editors who perform redaction, combining and modifying multiple documents to create one document. Many scholars think the final authors of the Former Prophets were Deuteronomistic redactors.

Regnal formulas: chronological notices embedded in the royal narratives that record not only basic information about kings (length of reign, parents, death notice), but also an evaluation as evil or righteous.

Royal annals: written documents that recorded information about the reigns of various rulers of Israel and Judah that the authors of Kings repeatedly refer to.

Royal Apology: a genre of ancient literature, where a text was composed on behalf of a king to justify his rise to power.

Samaria: a Persian province north of Yehud, named after the once-capital city of the northern kingdom of Israel.

Samaritan Pentateuch: the version of the Pentateuch preserved among the Samaritan community that still persists today and serves as the sole scriptural work for that community. Most scholars view it is deriving from an ancient variant of the Pentateuch that developed in Jerusalem.

Satan: in the Hebrew scriptures, the term *satan* can simply mean "adversity," but is periodically a reference to an agent of cosmic chaos. The *satan* of Job 1–2, for example, is not an enemy of YHWH but part of the divine council whose discussion with YHWH leads to the disruptions endured by Job.

Satrapy: a geographic subdivision of the Persian empire, encompassing a number of smaller provinces.

Scribe: a social type carrying great power and responsibility with regard to the production of important (and often sacred) texts. Scribes also often carried political and religious authority due to their literary skills.

Second Maccabees: A late-second-century BCE historiographic work relating to the Maccabean revolt against the Seleucid Greeks and the political activity of the Maccabean/Hasmonean family.

Segmentary societies: populations organized by lineages that are understood to be loosely related to each other, each led by an elder/chieftain or groups of elders/chieftains.

Septuagint: a translation of the Hebrew Bible into Greek by supposedly seventy (hence the abbreviation, LXX) Jewish scholars in Egypt during the third and second centuries BCE While largely in agreement with the Masoretic Text, there are several significant differences between these two textual traditions. New Testament references to the Old Testament are often based on the LXX.

Shaphanide(s): the scribal group connected to the family of Shaphan, one of the major scribal officers of Josiah's reign mentioned in 2 Kgs. 22:8–11.

Sheba the Bichrite: a dissident from the tribe of Benjamin and partisan of the Saulide royal family, who attempted to lead a rebellion against David.

Sheshbazzar: an early leader of the *gola* community, selected by Persian authorities to lead a return of Jews from Babylon to the homeland in the province of Yehud in 538 BCE.

Siloam tunnel: a major engineering feat enacted during the reign of king Hezekiah, where a tunnel was dug from within the walled city of Jerusalem to the Gihon spring, enabling the city to have a fresh water supply during the campaign of Sennacherib in 701 and the siege of Jerusalem that same year.

Song of the Sea: the poem in Exod. 15:1–18, often regarded by scholars as the oldest biblical composition with origins in the pre-monarchic period.

Southern Kingdom: during the period of the Divided Monarchy the remaining tribe of Judah that stayed under the rule of the Davidides (also called Judah).

Succession Narrative: a unit of chapters in the book of Samuel (2 Samuel 9–20) identified by most scholars as a single story detailing revolts against David and attempts to claim his throne.

Support group: a small but cohesive community that galvanizes around prophets, priests, or other religious figures.

Susa: one of the capital cities of the Persian Empire.

Syro-Ephraimite War: a conflict in 735–734 BCE involving a coalition between the northern kingdom of Israel and the Aramean populations of Syria against the threat of the Assyrian forces under Tiglath-pileser III.

Tamar: a personal name (meaning "date palm" in Hebrew), pertaining to a character in Genesis 38 or to the daughter of David in 2 Samuel 13. There is also reference to another Tamar—the daughter of David's son Absalom—in 2 Sam. 14:27.

Tel Dan Inscription: an important text found in 1993 during an archaeological dig in northern Israel, which contains the only reference to David outside of the Hebrew Scriptures.

Temple library: the archive of sacred texts preserved in the Jerusalem temple, to which priests and scribes had mostly exclusive access.

Temple Sermon: a prophetic speech given by the prophet Jeremiah in 609 BCE in the courtyard of the Jerusalem temple. The content of the sermon is usually identified with Jeremiah 7:3–15; a narrative depicting the event is found in Jeremiah 26.

Theologian: one of three "voices" discerned by Niditch in the book of Judges that was concerned with covenant loyalty and obedience (see also Epic Bardic, Humanist).

Theophany: a moment where a deity reveals his/her nature and will to an individual or community.

Transjordan: the land east of the Jordan River that was originally occupied by the tribes of Reuben, Gad, and Eastern Manasseh.

Tribal allotments: after the Israelites conquered the Promised Land it was divided up by lots among the tribes into definitively bounded allotments.

Trito-Isaiah: an anonymous prophet who composed chapters 56–66 in the book of Isaiah, dated usually to ca. 520 BCE.

United Monarchy: period in Israel's history when the nation was united under one king (Saul, David, and Solomon) before the division into Israel and Judah (see Divided Monarchy).

Uriah the Hittite: the first husband of Bathsheba and one of David's soldiers. Uriah was probably not an ethnic Hittite, but the term relates to his longtime residence in Jerusalem, which was once part of the Egyptian/Hittite administrative system in Canaan.

Valedictory Speech: a type of address given by a political or religious leader before their departure from public view or office.

Wilderness: a mythic space in ancient Near Eastern thought—often but not exclusively identified with desert regions—where threatening cosmic forces lurked.

Wisdom: an intellectual tradition throughout the ancient Near East where social and personal well-being could be secured through study, awareness, and understanding.

Zadok: one of David's priests in Jerusalem, promoted to chief priest of Solomon's kingdom and founder of a priestly dynasty that retained power over the Jerusalem cult for the remainder of the monarchic period.

Zedekiah: a son of Josiah, one of the final evil rulers of Judah, who witnessed the death of his sons immediately before being blinded and taken into captivity in Babylon.

Zerubbabel: a Davidic descendant selected by Persian authorities to co-lead a wave of returnees to Jerusalem in 522 BCE and to serve as governor, sharing leadership duties with the Aaronide priest Joshua.

Author Index

Scripture Index

Psalms (*continued*)
106......19, 501
106:19......309
106:34......25
114......174
124......504
127......325
135:9......296
136......19

Proverbs
1:1......325
10:1......325
25:1......325, 464
31:11–31......202

Ecclesiastes
1:1......325
1:12......325
1:16......325

Song of Solomon
1:1......325
3:7......325
3:9......325
3:11......325

Isaiah
1–12......406
1:1......345
6:1......257, 345
6:1–13......60
7:1......293
7:1–9......119
7:4......293
7:7......90
7:8......293
7:10–17......345
8:6......293
9:11......293
10:5......464
10:22......74
13–23......406
13:1–14:23......297
14:3......297

19:2......296
20:1......298
20:2–3......197, 328
22:15......302
24–27......406
28–33......406
34–35......406
36–39......19, 255, 406, 422, 525
36:1......298
36:1–39:8......348
36:17......298
36:21......298
36:37......298
37:9......297
37:21......90
37:22–29......100
37:38......298
39:1......298
40–55......351, 406, 535
56–66......406, 547
60:3–10......407

Jeremiah
1:1......430, 448
1:2......321, 355
1:4–10......60
2:6......25
7:3–15......546
7:12......209
7:12–15......4
11:3......90
13:1–11......197
13:12......90
14:1–15:4......448
18:18......410
21:2......298
21:7......298
22:24......301
25......528
25:11......412
25:19......296
26......546
26–27......422
26:1–3......209
29......427